LATTER LEAVES
IN THE LIFE OF

LORENZO SNOW

Lorenzo Snow (USHS)

LATTER LEAVES
IN THE LIFE OF

LORENZO SNOW

5TH PRESIDENT OF THE CHURCH OF JESUS CHRIST OF LATTER-DAY SAINTS

DENNIS B. HORNE

WITH MATERIAL PREPARED IN 1890 BY

ORSON F. WHITNEY

CFI
AN IMPRINT OF CEDAR FORT, INC.
SPRINGVILLE, UTAH

ISBN 13: 978-1-4621-1075-9 (hardback)
ISBN 13: 978-1-4621-1192-3 (leatherbound)

Published by CFI, an imprint of Cedar Fort, Inc.
2373 W. 700 S., Springville, UT 84663
Distributed by Cedar Fort, Inc., www.cedarfort.com

The Library of Congress has cataloged the hardback edition as follows:

Horne, Dennis B., author.
Latter leaves in the life of Lorenzo Snow / Dennis B. Horne.
pages cm
Includes bibliographical references and index.
ISBN 978-1-4621-1075-9 (alk. paper)
1. Snow, Lorenzo, 1814-1901. 2. Church of Jesus Christ of Latter-day Saints--Presidents--Biography. 3. Mormon Church--Presidents--Biography. 4. Mormons--United States--Biography. I. Title.

BX8695.S75H67 2012
289.3092--dc23

[B]

2012032783

Cover design by Angela D. Olsen
Cover design © 2012 by Lyle Mortimer
Edited and typeset by Melissa J. Caldwell

Printed in the United States of America

10 9 8 7 6 5 4 3 2

To Celia & Chelsey

and also

Lorenzo & Orson

CONTENTS

Foreword

by Cynthia Snow Banner,
Great-granddaughter of President Lorenzo Snow
and President of the Lorenzo Snow Family Association

Without a doubt, the Lord prepared Lorenzo Snow to fulfill a vital mission at a critical time in the history of the Church. Yet, even more important, Lorenzo was called by the Lord to be a husband and father in Israel, an eternal patriarch like unto his Heavenly Father. He, like the Prophet Joseph Smith, had the heavens open to him.

Joseph taught: "God Himself was once as we are now, and is an exalted man, and sits enthroned in yonder heavens! That is the great secret. If the veil were rent today, and the great God who holds this world in its orbit, and who upholds all worlds and all things by His power, was to make Himself visible,—I say, if you were to see Him today, you would see Him like a man in form—like yourselves in all the person, image, and very form as a man; for Adam was created in the very fashion, image and likeness of God, and received instruction from, and walked, talked and conversed with Him, as one man talks and communes with another."[1]

At the meeting in which Lorenzo Snow was sustained by the Twelve Apostles as the President of the Church, he expressed the same thought: "I had one revelation or manifestation in my early career which became my star, so to speak, and which I have always had before my mind. I put the meaning of it into couplet form, as follows: 'As man now is, God once was; As God now is, man may be.' That was revealed to me with power; the Holy Ghost was upon me for a long time, and I knew it was my privilege to be like Him whom I afterwards knew was my Father and God."

In 1884, at his seventieth birthday celebration, Lorenzo told his gathered posterity that when he first gained a testimony of the gospel, "he was unmarried and would have remained so, had he not received an understanding of the law of celestial marriage." He further said: "My heart and soul—all the energies and ambition were enlisted in the service of God, and I thought I could not better please or serve Him than by employing my entire time, unburdened by family cares, in the great field of missionary labor." But such was not meant to be. In a private interview with the Prophet Joseph Smith in Nauvoo, a full explanation of the principles of celestial and plural marriage showed him his clear duty and privileges by conformity to that law.

Lorenzo's divine destiny was to become a husband and a father. His sister Eliza R. Snow expressed her conviction of his call as a father in her biography of him: "When the head of this family, having gained his exaltation, and holding the keys of eternal lives and endless increase, will gather around him all that belongs to his house; saved, redeemed, resurrected, and glorified, to reign over them as king and priest unto God for ever, when there will be no trial, no weakness, no pain, and no death, and where perfect union and unfading affection will bind all together in the perfection of bliss and the majesty of the glorified sons and daughters of the Eternal Father."

With this future potential in mind, Lorenzo expressed his most tender thoughts to his family: "Language is powerless to express the deep feelings of my heart for this holy and sacred opportunity . . . of standing here and beholding this glorious and heavenly inspiring spectacle." Of his wives, he said, "God has called them to be associated with [me] through time and eternity, to assist in [my] duties and responsibilities and share [my] glory and dominion."

It is appropriate that President Snow is honored and revered throughout Zion for having been its fifth Prophet, Seer, and Revelator, but there is a deeper and more personal love that rests in the hearts and flows in the blood of his descendants.

One devoted descendant of Lorenzo (and his wife Harriet) told me that, as a child, her father knew Lorenzo in Brigham City, Utah. Grandfather Lorenzo was a very kind man, her father recalled, and the people of Brigham City loved and respected him. It was a great honor when Lorenzo would visit. Her father remembered Lorenzo holding him on his knee and how tender he was. Once, Lorenzo gave him a five-dollar gold piece, and he treasured it for many years. He felt Lorenzo's eyes were one of his most striking features. When his grandfather looked at him, he felt Lorenzo could see right into his heart, know what kind of a person he was, and whether or not he had done something wrong.

This relative mentioned that she is honored to be Lorenzo's descendant and looks forward to meeting her great-grandfather in the spirit world.

Sarah Minnie Ephramina Jensen Snow, Lorenzo's ninth and last wife, was my great-grandmother. She was only seventeen when she quietly married Lorenzo, on June 12, 1871, in the Endowment House in Salt Lake City—on the same occasion that one of Lorenzo's older daughters married. Minnie and Lorenzo's marriage was known only to a few and remained secret for a time, owing to the strong negative attitude toward polygamy prevailing in non-Latter-day Saint circles. It was not until November 1871, after President Snow returned from a trip to Palestine (Israel) that Minnie lived with him openly as his wife. Of this marriage, she said: "Had I traveled the world over or devoted a lifetime in the search of an ideal [suitor], I could not have found a more congenial companion—a better husband and father. In twenty years of our married life I have proven him to be a man of superior intellect, taste and culture, of a highly appreciative nature, pure and chaste in all his habits, in a word, a thorough gentleman, and an unkind word has never passed between us."[2]

Lorenzo and Minnie had five children: three daughters and two sons. My grandfather LeRoi C. Snow, born in 1876, was their eldest child. Rhea Lucille, their last child, was born in 1896 when Lorenzo was 82 and serving as President of the Salt Lake Temple.

I was able to visit Lorenzo's home in Mantua, Ohio, as a young mother. I walked where Lorenzo and his siblings worked and played and entered the home where he and his sister Eliza and others were taught by good Christian parents. I felt a sense of belonging and closeness to him that I had not known before. This experience helped me recognize how important his life was to me, and I needed to remember and appreciate him. Coming to know him in this more personal way caused me to want to live better—to strive to live the same principles of righteousness he did—and become worthy to someday stand with him as a member of his eternal posterity.

In 1997, Noryln Snow Torres (then one of his last living grandchildren) and I felt impressed to plan a special family reunion to honor Lorenzo on the one hundredth anniversary of his becoming the President of the Church. For a year we collected descendant information on Lorenzo's wives. We established the Lorenzo Snow Family Organization and asked seven family members to act as presidents of their matriarchal lines. On August 8, 1998, over two hundred descendants met in the Bountiful Utah Tabernacle. As I stood before that group, meeting to honor Lorenzo as Prophet and Patriarch, I became aware that it was not only Lorenzo's life that we were commemorating, but his wives' lives as well. We were celebrating their many sacrifices and their love for him. I felt their joy to see their children once again gathered as a family. I felt their desire for us, as their posterity, to do the research and gather the records of their descendants and make sure their vicarious temple work was completed so none would be left out. I feel I have a responsibility to carry on the work of our family.

I know great-grandfather Lorenzo Snow as a prophet of God. He was foreordained before he came to earth to serve a special mission to build up the kingdom of God on earth. He was called as a patriarch to stand at the head of a great posterity. He lived and taught doctrines and principles of righteousness. He filled the measure of his creation, has gone on to Eternal Reward, and has set an example for us to follow.

April 2011

Acknowledgments

I express appreciation to the following individuals for their assistance, kindness, knowledge, and advice, unselfishly rendered to me during the research and preparation of this work: Cynthia Snow Banner, a properly proud great-granddaughter of President Snow; and Cheryl McClellan, an unrivaled authority on Lorenzo's early years in Ohio. Also Lee Donaldson, Edward J. Brandt, Bill Slaughter, Alan Morrell, Christopher R. Greenwood, Bryan Weston, and Roger Fluhman. Todd Christenson and Brandon Richins kindly offered me their perspectives. Other family and friends lent encouragement and showed interest, spurring my efforts.

Brian C. Hales and Gregory L. Smith shared information and educated opinion regarding the difficult and elusive issues surrounding plural marriage during President Snow's comparatively short administration.

Karin Chelsey Nelson Horne, who thankfully became my wife (after I lost my first to cancer), and thereafter a mother, shortly before I began this project, tirelessly retyped Orson F. Whitney's *Latter Leaves* manuscript from LeRoi C. Snow's typewritten, microfilmed, and scanned copy; proofread a late draft; typed a number of other necessary sources; and made many helpful suggestions while serving as a sounding board. She thoughtfully assisted with keeping my writing focused on the reading audience this work is mainly directed toward—regular Latter-day Saints that desire to know more about their beloved former prophet Lorenzo Snow.

I appreciate and honor my children Renae and Annette, who have watched their father write several books and have consequently lost time that could have otherwise been spent with them. I trust the sacrifice will prove worth it; Helen is yet too young to know the difference.

I express appreciation for the fine work of Cedar Fort, Inc., editors, especially Melissa Caldwell, Heather Holm, and Jennifer Fielding.

I also thank Orson F. Whitney, a past Assistant Church Historian (1900–1906) and member of the Quorum of the Twelve Apostles (1906–1931)—the assembler and author of a long-unpublished biographical manuscript (covering about five years of President Snow's life), of which I have used substantial portions herein. Whitney was a truly gifted man with whom I have come to feel an affinity and deep respect and admiration. Of him, my own grandfather once wrote: "I was set apart [for my mission] by Elder Orson F. Whitney of the Council of the Twelve, who lived in our . . . ward and who had once been bishop there. I was thrilled and inspired to have him bless me, for he was not only one of the greatest apostles, but had had the privilege of seeing the Savior. . . . I loved this man, too, because he was the poet among the General Authorities." So thought one Walter M. Horne who met, though but briefly, this giant among men, and had the sense and humility to recognize and appreciate the honor.

This privilege of seeing the Savior and counseling with Him was also given to President Snow. His and Elder Whitney's witness herein combine, as do that of Nephi and his brother Jacob in the Book of Mormon, to set forth sure and unimpeachable apostolic testimony of the living reality of Jesus the Christ, the Son of God, resurrected and occasionally ministering among His mortal servants and friends today.

Despite the assistance I received in preparation of this biographical history, I alone am responsible for its contents, opinions, conclusions, and inevitable errors.

INTRODUCTION

Lorenzo Snow—a prophet unfortunately much too little known today—was the last President of The Church of Jesus Christ of Latter-day Saints to have known and had the confidence of the Prophet Joseph Smith as an adult, yet he lived to see the twentieth century. A close associate of apostles and prophets for most of his life, he rose to become one of the greatest, yet humblest, of their number. As he often said, the "star" by which he lived his life was the almost indescribable testimony that came upon him by the power of the Holy Ghost soon after his baptism and confirmation. From that point onward, there was no turning back; he had obtained the witness necessary to his life's work.

As a missionary and apostle of mighty faith and sure conviction, Lorenzo Snow preached the gospel, wrote and published gospel tracts (pamphlets), administered the affairs of the Church, prophesied, healed the sick, raised the dead (and was brought back to life himself), sat in council among holy beings, saw visions, and stood in the presence of the resurrected, glorified Savior, Jesus the Christ in the holy temple, and spoke with Him face-to-face, as one man speaks with another.

President Snow instigated or advanced several worthy initiatives that have powerfully influenced the Church. He helped establish the beginnings of visitor and missionary training centers and the expansion of worldwide missionary work. He encouraged faithful and full tithe payment and regular professional audits of Church finances, holding solemn assemblies in temples, the writing of institutional Church history, reorganizing the First Presidency soon after the former President's passing, and quarterly testimony meetings of the Quorum of the Twelve.

Yet with all this, perhaps some of the greatest works he performed in the latter years of his lengthy ministry were of a less lofty nature. Lorenzo Snow was first a persevering and successful intermediary and diplomat among his brethren during a time when such was sorely needed. "He was a great peacemaker, often settling difficulties between men of strong and positive character that other men would not think of undertaking, and was successful," remembered an associate.[1] Second, after receiving divine direction, he steadfastly put in motion the necessary measures to resolve the massive debt problems the Church faced in his day. Indeed, as the leaves of his latter life unfolded, it became apparent that Lorenzo Snow's greatest work as President of the Quorum of the Twelve Apostles was to bring unity to that Quorum, and then as President of the Church, to bring temporal salvation to the Church.

Such a life deserves a thorough biographical recounting and the evidence indicates President Snow himself realized this fact and acted on it. His almost equally prominent sister, Eliza Roxy Snow Smith, produced the now nearly forgotten tome, *Biography and Family Record of Lorenzo Snow*, covering his life from birth to about 1884. Furthermore, Lorenzo asked Orson F. Whitney to update that record with a sequel carrying the story through 1889.

This development is a fortunate incident in itself, as remembered by Bishop Whitney:

> It was March, 1888, when Lorenzo Snow was sent to the Utah Penitentiary, convicted upon three separate indictments for one offense [cohabitation in plural marriage], and sentenced by [anti-Mormon] Associate Justice Orlando W. Powers to the aggregate term of eighteen months imprisonment. On July 4th, at the close of the prison [Sunday] service, at which I was the speaker, I had an interview with the venerable Apostle, and in the course of it predicted that he would not serve out his full term. "Well, I came prepared for it," said he resignedly. I then repeated the prediction.
>
> He had spent eleven of the eighteen months behind bolts and bars, when a decision from the Supreme Court of the United States shattered the illegal doctrine of "segregation" under which he had been convicted, and he went forth a free man. Meeting him at the Tabernacle shortly afterwards, I said: "I told you you wouldn't serve out your full term." "That's so, you did," was his smiling answer. "You are a prophet—you are a prophet."
>
> That little incident was the beginning of a close friendship between Brother Snow and myself. I spent many happy hours in his society,

> mainly at his home in Brigham City. We interchanged confidences, and he employed my pen in the production of a biographical sketch covering the period of his trial and imprisonment. While setting me apart for this task, he prophesied that I would "be lifted up and occupy places high and glorious in this life."[2]

From the foregoing quotation it is apparent that President Snow desired the preparation of *Latter Leaves* enough to employ Orson to write it (literally with a pen), to formally bless his efforts, and that President Snow either conceived the title himself or approved Orson's proposed designation. Lorenzo's son LeRoi C. Snow, as a teenager, "copied Orson F. Whitney's *Latter Leaves in the Life of Lorenzo Snow*," with a typewriter at his father's request.[3] The scanned file of *Latter Leaves*, constituting a major contribution to the present work, is believed to have been taken from LeRoi's typed copy (as microfilmed), located in the LDS Church History Library in Salt Lake City, Utah.[4]

President Snow's Personality and Character

Evidently President Snow's persona was enigmatic to many observers, even friends. He had been closely associated with all the previous prophets of the Church from Joseph Smith to Wilford Woodruff but did not resemble them in temperament or leadership style. He was more refined and educated than they had been and equally spiritually attuned.

One observer seemed at a loss to describe him: "He was . . . not only well educated, but a very refined and cultured gentleman. In his peculiarities he was altogether a different type of man to any of his predecessors who presided over the Church. It would be hard for me to exactly describe his personal traits in comparison with those of other great and good men who were his associates. Those who knew them all can appreciate what I mean by a statement of that kind. . . . As I said he was a peculiar man, different to any of his predecessors."[5]

A non–Latter-day Saint observer wrote:

> I had expected to find intellect, intellectuality, benevolence, dignity, composure and strength depicted upon the face of the President of the Church of Jesus Christ of Latter-day Saints; but when I was introduced to Pres. Lorenzo Snow for a second I was startled to see the holiest face but one I had ever been privileged to look upon. His face was a poem of peace, his presence a benediction of peace. In the tranquil depths of his eyes were the 'home of silent prayer' and the abode of spiritual strength. As he talked of the more sure word of prophecy and the certainty of the

> hope which was his, and the abiding faith which had conquered the trials and difficulties of a tragic life . . . I watched the play of emotions and studied with fascinated attention, the subtle shades of expression which spoke to plainly the working of his soul; and the strangest feeling stole over me; that I stood on holy ground; that this man did not act from the commonplace motives of policy, interest, or expediency, but he acted from a far off center.[6]

At his passing, a *Deseret News* editorial reviewed his personality profile:

> President Snow's mentality was a rare and varied combination. He was a natural financier, and at the same time a spiritually minded man, of literary tastes and poetic temperament. He was not sanctimonious: he could not be a fanatic or a bigot if he wished. He was too well-balanced for that—too broad-minded and charitable. He would never persecute a man for his opinions, nor interfere with his religious worship, however much he might disapprove of them. At the same time he was a pattern of piety, an exemplary Christian gentleman, zealous in and devoted to the cause that he deemed divine. No tyrant, but a man of firm will, prompt in scolding, fearless and thorough in executing his purposes. No politician, yet wisely politic, regardful of propensities and of all men's rights. No one ever imposed upon him without his knowing it, and few cared to impose upon him twice. Bland and soft-spoken, as a rule, he could be stern, and was plain and straightforward in expressing his opinions. Once convinced of the correctness of an idea, a doctrine, principle, policy or course of conduct, he adhered to it with inflexible resolution. In his public discourses he spoke straight to the point, and his manner and diction was entirely without ostentation. While spirited and independent, he was not combative in his disposition, but was essentially a man of peace, a humanitarian. . . . Placidity of mind, even in the midst of trouble and danger, was characteristic of President Snow. He made the best of every situation and readily adapted himself to his surroundings, however uncomfortable and oppressive they might be.[7]

Becoming an increasingly prominent Utahn, legislator, and Church leader, especially in his later years, Lorenzo Snow became the subject of continual press reports, having his movements and messages tracked and reported in the three local Salt Lake City newspapers—the *Salt Lake Tribune* (anti-Mormon), the *Deseret News* (Church-owned), and the *Salt Lake Herald*. Referring to President Snow, the *Herald* editorialized that "no newspaper interviewer ever received anything but a direct answer of unmistakable meaning from him. Oftentimes he believed it advisable to withhold information, but he never quibbled or attempted the least evasion. When he made a statement it was the truth, and had but one meaning."[8] This conclusion was fairly accurate, but perhaps slightly exaggerated. A *Tribune* correspondent reported the following attempt to obtain an interview: "President Lorenzo Snow, who returned from Bear River City yesterday, was seen during the afternoon and asked if he would express himself respecting the arrest of President Angus M. Cannon [then Salt Lake Stake president], on the charge of unlawful cohabitation [polygamy]. 'Not one word' was the President's reply, 'I am always willing to discuss matters with the newspapers when I deem such discussion proper,' President Snow continued, 'but in this case I have nothing whatever to say.'"[9]

About two years before his death, a famous (Presbyterian) writer interviewed President Snow for a newspaper story. The interview covered several subjects, with plural marriage, or polygamy, a prominent theme. For those with no knowledge of revelation and LDS doctrine, polygamy was the main subject that captured reader interest and increased circulation. Most of what was reported on the subject throughout the world was fiction, but on occasion some articles were fair:

> I had an hour's chat here with the venerable Lorenzo Snow, the President of the Church of Jesus Christ of Latter-day Saints, and the leader of the three hundred odd thousand Mormons who are scattered over the United States. Mr. Snow is now eighty-six years of age, . . .
>
> President Snow does not weigh more than 165 pounds, but he is very active. He had just returned from a Church meeting at Ogden, thirty-six miles away, and he told me that it was his custom to take long walks every day. . . .
>
> President Snow told me there was no doubt in his mind that the Father and Jesus Christ really appeared in person to Joseph Smith while he was upon earth, and that Joseph Smith had frequent and full directions for all things connected with the Church from on high. He said such revelations were manifested today, and I thereupon asked him point blank if he himself had ever had a revelation or direct manifestation from God.
>
> "I know that I have, and that several times," replied the President of the Mormons. "The first one was when I was a boy. My parents were very well to do. They sent me to college at Oberlin, Ohio, but I found the professors, they were Congregationalists, insisted I should believe as they did, and I left and went to Kirtland. There I met Joseph Smith and the Mormons. I attended their meetings and saw the brethren and sisters prophesying, speaking strange tongues, and giving forth

> the revelations they received from God. I was converted by them. I believed they had the true religion, and I joined the Church. So far my conversion was merely a matter of reason. I had had no manifestation, but I expected one.
>
> "It was about two weeks later, when I went out in the woods one day to pray, that it came. I was on my knees when I heard a rustling like that of a silk dress, and something came down upon me and enveloped me. I can't describe it, but I knew it was from the Lord. I was filled with ecstasy, and my sins seemed to have passed away. I was immersed in the presence, which stayed with me for perhaps an hour. It came again at night when I was in my bed. After that I had the power of conversion, and of healing by the laying on of my hands, and parties have told me that when my hands were placed upon them they experienced the same feelings I had in the woods. That was many, many years ago. I have been a Mormon ever since."
>
> Later on in the conversation I . . . asked the President whether polygamous marriages were still contracted in Utah. He replied: "I answer emphatically that they are not. There has not been one such, so far as I know, since I have been President of the Church."
>
> "Will there be more of such marriages in the future?" I asked.
>
> "No, I think not. We believe that plural marriages are in accordance with the will of God, and that if the rest of the world saw things in their true light they would be encouraged and approved by all. But they are contrary to the laws of the land, and it is sometimes best to omit the exercise of your belief for the greater good in other ways, trusting in the Lord to make all things right in the end."[10]

An examination of photographs indicates that Lorenzo seemed to evolve in his features over the decades from that of a rough frontier farmer and pioneer to the saintly and dignified countenance of a prophet in his last years.

President Snow had an oft-used gift for de-escalating conflict or deflecting heated argument with a gentle reproof mixed with humor.[11] He employed this gift time and again with a group of strong-willed, stubborn apostles that he led in one capacity or another for over eleven years. With a gentle redirect of conversation accompanied by a clever remark, he could quickly settle a rising temper or divert contrary thought. When he needed to "put his foot down," even with one of his counselors, he could do it with resolute firmness.

As he traveled throughout the Church, he occasionally encountered atypical situations that he met with humility and grace. One source related that "President Lorenzo Snow and [Elder] Francis M. Lyman were present at a stake conference at Richfield. After the opening song the stake president asked Brother Lyman whom he should call upon to offer the opening prayer. Brother Lyman said: 'Ask President Snow,' meaning to ask President Snow who should offer the prayer. Instead, however, the stake president asked President Snow to offer the prayer. President Snow graciously responded and before beginning the prayer expressed his pleasure in being called upon and said it had been a long time since he had been given this pleasure."[12]

As President of the Church, Lorenzo Snow's life was not one of constant excitement and drama, although he experienced his fair share of the full spectrum of human emotions—from deep sorrow and grief, to the sweetest elation and infusion of spiritual power. The burdens of leadership were heavy and lonely at times—especially the financial burdens of his last three years. Yet at this point of presidency (1898–1901) in Church administrative history, much mundane, menial office work, especially related to finances, was still performed by the First Presidency themselves. The following entry in the Journal History of the Church (a daily record of events) is indicative of many, though not most, days: "April 14, 1900: Presidents Snow and Smith were at the office. No business of particular interest was transacted, but there was considerable of routine affairs to which the brethren applied their attention."[13]

His life was a rich and varied mixture—one day he was exercising mighty faith in calling back the dead, and the next he was paying the bills. As Trustee-in-trust for the Church (the chief executive officer or president of a company or corporation), President Snow spent much of his time approving or denying various monetary amounts (called appropriations) sought or designated for a multitude of reasons, with many going unfulfilled. With final decision-making authority, he found himself functioning as a businessman, a loan originator and approver, an accountant, a real estate agent, a stockbroker, a negotiator, a final arbitrator of disputes, and sometimes even the petty complaint department. Many duties during his administration carried with them the trappings of adulation (when he traveled among the people he was often the most famous and beloved person they would ever meet), but much of his daily labor was also mundane and tedious.

It soon becomes obvious that President Snow loved people of all kinds and classes, but especially the poor and those who lived the gospel, kept the commandments, and strove to repent, improve themselves, and endure to the end. He had the highest hopes and desires for those of his own apostolic quorum and often expressed deep and tender feelings for them. One of those occasions was his birthday: "We now sang a hymn . . . after doing which President Franklin D. Richards presented in a very pleasing way to President Snow, he being today eighty years old, a beautiful basket of flowers, a gold pencil, and a gold pen and pencil combined. President Snow replied in a very nice way, expressing the hope that we would each live to be over a hundred years old, and then be translated and live eternally. 'These gifts may fade and decay, but the feeling which prompted their bestowal I will never forget in time or eternity,' he said."[14]

Plural Marriage during President Snow's Administration

Although it is a major theme herein, this biography is not meant to substantially contribute to the ongoing historical discussion of polygamy before or after the issuance of the Manifesto by President Wilford Woodruff in 1890 (see Doctrine and Covenants Official Declaration 1). Informed Latter-day Saints know that some plural marriages were quietly authorized after the Manifesto, although relatively few compared to previously, and that all sanction was completely withdrawn in 1904 with the so-called Second Manifesto of President Joseph F. Smith.[15] The question has arisen of whether President Snow knew about the very few authorized plural marriages that were evidently performed during his administration—he most likely did not. This extremely complex historical area holds much ambiguity and conjecture, with little certainty and a scant historical record to draw upon.

In a private interview with Elder Brigham Young Jr., of the Twelve, President Snow emphatically stated:

> There cannot be a plural marriage solemnized in this church without my consent and I have never given consent for this to be done since I became President of the Church. God has removed this privilege from the people and until He restores it, I shall not consent to any man taking a plural wife. . . . There is no such thing as men taking plural wives and keeping it secret. It cannot be done. Has any one of the apostles a right to seal plural wives to men by reason of former concessions made to them by the Presidency? No sir. Such right must come from me and no man shall be authorized by me to break the law of the land.[16]

President Snow made other like strong statements and declarations, as found in the pages of this biography. Yet some evidence suggests that his counselors, evidently without his knowledge or permission, still authorized some plural marriages during his administration.[17] Under such circumstances as these, we leave it to God, from whom all priesthood sealing authority is delegated, to judge and determine whether such unions will be honored by Him or not in the eternal realms ahead.

Personal Doctrinal Views and Perspective

When associating in close circles of trusted brethren, or while having private conversations with intimate friends, Lorenzo felt a measure of freedom to express personal views and speculation regarding various subjects. These personal and speculative notions were never taught publicly or in an official capacity and certainly did not represent settled Church doctrine. Yet it's sad to say, because they were expressed and recorded, enemies of the Church have sought to exploit them in anti-Mormon writings, using them to justify or promulgate false conclusions about Church teachings or the conduct of its past leaders.

One such example comes from the personal journal of an apostolic associate, Elder Abraham H. Cannon: "In the evening [we] had a conversation with Bro. Lorenzo Snow about various doctrines. Bro. Snow said I would live to see the time when brothers and sisters would marry each other in the church. All our horror at such a union was due entirely to prejudice, and the offspring of such unions would be as healthy and pure as any others. These were the decided views of Pres. Young, when alive, for Bro. Snow talked to him freely on this matter."[18]

These notions were never put in practice nor was such thought continued among succeeding leaders; yet critics still use them for deceitful propaganda purposes. Another example is Lorenzo's personal feelings about the use of meat when interpreting some provisions found in the Word of Wisdom (see Doctrine and Covenants 89). In a private meeting of the First Presidency and the Twelve, "President Lorenzo Snow introduced the subject of the Word of Wisdom, expressing the opinion that it was violated as much or more in the improper use of meat as in other things, and thought the time was near at hand when the Latter-day Saints should be taught to refrain from meat eating and the shedding of animal blood."[19]

President Snow, as well as any of the Brethren, then or now, was free to express his personal views in private conversation or council, but only when any such views were sustained by those councils acting officially were they then taught to the Church as doctrine.[20]

President Snow's close friends and associates understood this principle, as demonstrated by one of them:

October 10, 1898. Left to right: Marriner W. Merrill, John W. Taylor, Francis M. Lyman, Rudger Clawson, Heber J. Grant, M. H. Cowley, George Teasdale, A. Owen Woodruff, John Henry Smith. Front row: Anthony H. Lund, Brigham Young Jr., George Q. Cannon, President Lorenzo Snow, Joseph F. Smith, and Franklin D. Richards. (USHS)

> I will relate what he said to me in answer to a question, but would not like anyone to take it as doctrine for he did not so intend it, but rather to broaden my ideas in regard to the probabilities of God's mercy in the great eternal ages yet to come. I once went with a team and buggy from Preston, Idaho, to Malad, to convey Bro. Snow to the former named place where he was to assist the Presidency of the Stake in deciding where to build an academy [high school] for the Onieda Stake of Zion. On the way over I had a lovely visit with him and learned much regarding some of the prominent men of the Church in the days of the Prophet Joseph Smith.

Further:

> During our conversation he told me of the terrible dark days of Apostasy in Kirtland, Ohio, and that in the Kirtland Temple he saw the face of one of the disaffected Apostles, turn black. . . . The Apostle later repented of his bitterness toward the Prophet Joseph Smith, and died a faithful Latter-day Saint and active Apostle of the Lord.
>
> [I then asked him] my question concerning the Negro race: were they neutral?
>
> Bro. Snow told me during our ride through the canyon that he did not believe that the Negroes were born into black bodies because of neutrality in their pre-existent state, but he believed that they were born in the Negro Race because of a Pre-existent arrangement that Cain should be their progenitor in the flesh and that order or condition was not changed, notwithstanding the awful crime of which Cain was guilty in shedding the blood of his brother Abel.[21]

Lorenzo evidently formed his views on this matter from those expressed to him (privately and unofficially) by President Brigham Young, and at a later time and situation, related them in greater detail.[22]

The reader should remember that it is grossly unfair to impose contemporary societal norms and modern political correctness on good and inspired but imperfect people who lived in a different time and culture, and thereby impute shame or sin to them.[23] Such is a tactic of the modern extremist, activist, or anti-Mormon searching for ways to discredit past Church leaders. This particular issue was settled by revelation to President Spencer W. Kimball in 1978 (See Doctrine and Covenants Official Declaration 2).

The First Presidency and Council of the Twelve, 1890–1901

Most of President Snow's closest associates during the period covered by this biography, outside of family, were his fellow members of the Twelve and counselors in the First Presidency. When he became the President of the Twelve, the two leading quorums consisted of Wilford Woodruff, Lorenzo Snow, Franklin D. Richards, George Q. Cannon, Brigham Young Jr., Joseph F. Smith, Moses Thatcher, Francis M. Lyman, John Henry Smith, George Teasdale, Heber J. Grant, and John W. Taylor. As the 1890s passed and the Brethren died or were dropped from the quorum, Marriner W. Merrill, Anthon H. Lund, Abraham H. Cannon, Matthias F. Cowley, Abraham Owen Woodruff, Rudger Clawson, and Reed Smoot were added. Through some of these men's diaries, we are able to learn much about President Snow. These men worked with him on a daily basis; they fasted and prayed and broke bread with him; they sat in sweet council with him; they thrilled when they heard him bear testimony; they heard him preach in public and private; they knew his innermost thoughts and the greatness of his soul; they went to prison with him; and they spoke tenderly, reverently, and respectfully over his body after his death. Their names and accounts from records they left are copiously spread throughout this work, and readers may gain some passing familiarity with them also as they learn about President Snow. Church leaders such as Joseph Smith, Brigham Young, John Taylor, Erastus Snow (a distant relative), George A. Smith, Daniel H. Wells, Albert Carrington, James E. Talmage, J. Golden Kimball, B. H. Roberts, William B. Preston, and Charles W. Penrose are also mentioned.

Previous Works about President Snow

Given the fact that Lorenzo Snow was the fifth president of the Church of Jesus Christ, there is yet a seeming dearth of information readily available about him, at least in comparison to most of his contemporaries, predecessors, and successors. Having noted this, it is true that three full-length biographical treatments have been written (two being long out-of-print and one occasionally becoming available), as well as a few shorter works.

Eliza R. Snow Smith's book, already referenced, was published in 1884 and was largely meant for family and friends (to whom President Snow gave it with relish). After remaining out of print and languishing on the shelves of libraries, book collectors, and historians, the book was photomechanically reprinted in 1975 and many times since.[24] It contains superb information on Lorenzo Snow, his sister, their family, and Church history in general, but it is limited by a less-accessible writing style and does not cover the latter years of President Snow's life—the years covered by this "sequel" volume—that are the most important in many respects. (Most of chapters one and two herein are highly condensed and summarized from Eliza's book.)

Thomas C. Romney issued his *Life of Lorenzo Snow* in 1955 at the request of LeRoi C. Snow and with the approval of President George Albert Smith. This scarce publication enjoys a respectable reputation and has been appreciated because it reviews, in a limited measure, the latter periods of President Snow's life that Eliza's book predated.

Francis M. Gibbons saw his effort, *Lorenzo Snow: Spiritual Giant, Prophet of God*, published in 1982 and reprinted in paperback on occasion. A shorter piece and lacking in detail for modern readers and students of history, it presents the perplexing drawback of not containing a single note or reference for any sources, nor a bibliography.

More recently (in 2010) a prison diary or record book containing poetic letters written by President Snow while serving a sentence for plural marriage convictions was edited by two religious educators at Brigham Young University. This contains an excellent review of President Snow's legal battles and prison term, but it is insufficient for biographical matter outside its stated purpose of documenting the history surrounding his prison poetry.[25] (Beyond acknowledging his affinity for such verse, the present volume does not explore that facet of President Snow's literary endeavors.) The Church itself has also prepared and distributed materials on President Snow's life and teachings, including the regular curriculum manual *Teachings of Presidents of the Church: Lorenzo Snow*.[26]

Little of what Lorenzo Snow himself wrote has been published or studied widely. Making this point in a brief article exploring Lorenzo Snow's missionary work in England and publishing letters he wrote then, editors of a *BYU Studies* article state that their contribution "constitute[s] a significant addition to the small collection of published personal writings of the fifth President of the Church." Further, they state, "Aside from these few items, none of his personal writings have been published."[27]

The present work—properly using Orson F. Whitney's manuscript's title *Latter Leaves in the Life of Lorenzo Snow*—examines much more of President Snow's years as President of the Quorum of the Twelve and President of the Church than any other previous treatment. It is focused more on President Snow's latter missions, travels, arrest, legal struggles, prison term, church service, spiritual experiences, leadership of the Twelve, and, above all, prophetic administration, rather than his familial life.[28] It

Orson F. Whitney (USHS)

also enlarges on the small corpus of his published personal writings (mostly in the form of letters).

Orson Whitney's manuscript contribution—written from late 1889 to early 1890 in his occasionally verbose and poetically expressive style, and filled with the text of letters, court documents, witness transcriptions, legal speeches, and other such materials—has herein been trimmed to around a third of its original size, omitting much material originating with others but keeping most of the text by Whitney himself or President Snow. Whitney, who died in 1931, could have had no inkling that so much of his manuscript would one hundred and twenty years later become part of this larger biographical work, let alone retain its title.[29] In the present volume, most of chapters three through eleven, and part of twelve, constitute Whitney's work, with some light copyediting and inclusion of additional material. Further, Whitney's dictated "Journal History of the Church" entries are scattered throughout the remainder of the book (see below for explanation).[30]

Explanation of Sources

Snow family tradition holds that one of President Snow's descendants took a trunk-load of his papers, diaries, and correspondence to California at some point and burned it all, and that President Snow's son Oliver arrived on the scene too late to stop the desecration.[31] If true in some variation, as seems likely, this incident constitutes an irretrievable historical loss. It is thought that there is less original source documentation about President Snow than about any other modern prophet. Because no journal and little correspondence is known to exist for firsthand accounts relating President Snow's thoughts and movements in his later years, for research and writing purposes it became necessary to rely on what others observed and recorded for the main source material, at least from 1890 to 1901.[32] This lack of primary sources inevitably hinders narration and amplification of those intimate elements desired in a quality biography, but, thankfully, other strong sources still allow for a respectable and often superb and moving portrayal. In this case, the sources that provide the best information about Lorenzo Snow are the journals of his close associates, the Journal History of the Church, and newspaper reports. These valuable firsthand observations made by others, regarding President Snow's actions, feelings, and teachings, provide the best and possibly only recountings available for later portions of his life.[33] (See the Key to Source Abbreviations and the Bibliography for further information.)

LeRoi C. Snow as a Source

Much of what is commonly understood today about Lorenzo Snow's last three years has long been gleaned through the writings of LeRoi Clarence Snow, a favored son by President Snow's last wife Minnie. LeRoi (also spelled "LeRoy" or "Le Roie") wrote several articles, mostly published in the *Improvement Era* (precursor to the *Ensign*) or the *LDS Church News*, about his father.[34] He also assembled some rough notes for the beginnings of a biography he hoped to write but that never materialized.[35]

LeRoi C. Snow (1876–1963) (USHS)

Some of LeRoi's later-life recollections and reminiscences of his father's sayings and doings have been found to be inaccurate, embellished, or almost fictionalized. Other reports, however, are reliable and well corroborated.

Among the best substantiated accounts written (and quoted) by LeRoi was the appearance of the Savior to his father in the Salt Lake Temple. Others, such as his recollections of his father's spoken expressions in relation to a supposed prophecy about tithing payment and consequent rainfall during a severe drought in St. George, Utah, in the late spring and summer of 1899, are much less trustworthy. In the present volume, great care has been employed when using sources originating with LeRoi. Other historians have likewise wrestled with LeRoi's reliability as a source.[36]

Other Primary Sources

We are indebted to some peculiar parties for valuable information about President Snow. Arthur Winter, for instance, was hired as a clerk and sermon reporter in the Office of the President by President John Taylor. Although young at the time for such work, he was an excellent shorthand stenographer and wrote the official church reports for general conferences, many stake conferences, and other meetings such as funerals, special occasions, and temple meetings. He occasionally substituted as Secretary to the First Presidency (for example, "August 7, 1897: I have been acting as Secretary to the First Presidency during this week, in the absence of Brother George F. Gibbs").[37]

For the purposes of this biography, Arthur's contribution was to travel with President Snow, report his sermons to the Saints, and record his movements in his journal. This was especially important for the St. George tithing revelation trip, where Arthur's reports are probably the only extant records of some of President Snow's comments on tithing to various congregations. Also on that trip, Bishop Orson F. Whitney's son Horace (Race) reported sermons as a young and green reporter for the *Salt Lake Herald*. In addition, Lorenzo Snow's son LeRoi reported them as a special correspondent for the *Deseret News*. Then, as mentioned, Arthur Winter reported them officially for the Church itself—but these young men didn't report all of them or even the same ones. Arthur Winter's perspective as an employee in the President's Office also made his occasional comments regarding Lorenzo Snow especially interesting.

The "Journal History of the Church" is a daily catalog, scrapbook, and index of the history of the Church from 1830 to the present. It was inaugurated and created under the direction of Assistant Church Historian Andrew Jenson and is largely the result of his labors. It is very limited in some ways in that it is not comprehensive or interpretive, and most of it consists simply of newspaper clippings related to all things "Mormon" in the world. However, for the years that Lorenzo Snow was President of the Church, it steps forward as perhaps the single most valuable source used herein. During this time, the Journal History contains many references to the activities of the First Presidency in their office—who they talked to, what they did, and decisions they made. This collection of information is filled with references to President Snow's regular labors and is a treasure trove that has granted this book a richness in detail otherwise not possible.

With this fortunate "Journal" of LDS history in mind, it becomes especially significant to realize that Orson F. Whitney was hired by President Snow to work as an Assistant Church Historian under Church Historian Franklin D. Richards and one of his main duties was to update the Journal History and keep it current during the very years President Snow was the President of the Church. The following entry from Whitney's diary describes his duties:

> Assumed my new office of Assistant Church Historian. Spent the day at the Historian's Office getting hold of the reigns of my labors.
>
> I have taken Bro. Charles W. Penrose's place, he having gone back to his place as editor-in-chief [of the *Deseret News*] with my brother Horace G. Whitney as Business Manager, and I have as an assistant Bro. Dan Collett, as typewriter, and a good fellow in general, . . .
>
> My duties at the Historian's Office are the keeping up of the daily journal of the Church, a record of all events affecting its interests in any part of the world. The current history of the Church in fact. The work is behind some months. I began with the data of May 18, 1898.
>
> I have to correct [edit] the minutes of meetings [taken by secretary George F. Gibbs] held in the President's Office; the records of Missionary appointments and returns; the daily [news]papers, etc., and dictate a condensed account of affairs to the typewriter, Bro. Collett.[38]

It becomes clear that Orson Whitney has unwittingly but deeply influenced the content of this biography of his beloved friend and mentor.

To walk with a prophet through the foremost scenes of his life, figuratively speaking, is an overwhelming and humbling experience. Although but a mortal man, a prophet is called, authorized, and empowered to speak to mankind for God, imparting to them His will. This means the prophet has been tutored by spiritual experiences with the inhabitants of the Heavens. This also means the author of a book about such a prophet is enabled to partake in a slight measure of the adventure, drama, and sacred experience of an extraordinary life that God has influenced so impressively.

Lorenzo Snow seemed to have sensed that his own life and works, intertwined with those of his associates, would become known to future generations—in fact, in a way he predicted it:

> I will prophesy of them [the Twelve Apostles of his day], no, excuse me, I am not in the habit of prophesying; I will predict; I will say here, that

> in generations to come, the doings of these men [including himself] will be read, the account of their works in preaching the gospel to the nations of the earth, what they have suffered for the cause of God . . . and how they have passed through all this and everything by way of suffering that can be imagined, and have still adhered to and borne their testimony to the truth; their works will be read and in generations to come people will have just as much confidence in these men as they now have the Twelve Apostles whose doings are recorded in the New Testament. They are just as good men I have every reason to believe.[39]

Something akin to a prophecy is also found in the editorials published in the Church-owned newspaper the day President Snow died: "All the pages of his history cannot be published in print. They are in the archives on high and will be unfolded in due time, and when every man shall be judged according to his works will disclose a most remarkable career."[40] I had no access to the unimaginable archives kept On High, nor to some of them kept on earth, but was still able to shine a light on some latter leaves of this remarkable prophet's life.

Editorial note: Many primary source quotations have received minor silent editing for readability, such as expanding abbreviations, capitalization, modernization of spelling, and re-paragraphing. Also, because of the sheer volume of sources used, and their non-critical nature (as used herein) in original typescript or holograph form, these typed sources have not been proofread against the original documents, and therefore the possibility of some few textual errors in these quotations exists. Only the author carries responsibility for such mistakes. Otherwise, care has been taken to preserve source accuracy, context, and reliability. Further, the entire work has been copyedited and proofread.

Orson F. Whitney (USHS)

Introducing Orson F. Whitney—Biographical Contributor

As explained in the introduction, at President Snow's request, Orson F. Whitney prepared the first draft of a manuscript (covering Snow's life from 1884 to 1889) titled *Latter Leaves from the Life of Lorenzo Snow*, about a third of which is reproduced herein as most of chapters three through eleven. Since Whitney's long unpublished work contributes so richly to the present volume, this biographical sketch of his life is included to assist readers in gaining a fuller appreciation of his prowess with the pen, as well as his intimate association with President Snow, and his service as an Assistant Church Historian and Apostle of the Lord.

From the 1880s to the 1930s, "Bishop" Orson (Ort for short) Ferguson Whitney needed no introduction, becoming one of the most prominent citizens and churchmen of Utah. Yet by the second decade of the twenty-first century, he has largely been forgotten; even his remarkable literary legacy has failed to keep his memory alive. This dim collective recollection becomes a loss to the modern Church. Orson Whitney rubbed shoulders with some of the most prominent men of his time, leaders and thinkers both in the Church and those of the world. A man of deep spirituality, he saw visions; conversed with the Spirit; entertained translated beings; healed the sick; prophesied; cast out devils; rebuked the elements; endured sickness, trial, and hardship; and sat in collegial council with prophets and fellow apostles—and all this without reference to his best-known talents: powerful and persuasive oratorical ability and superb literary expression.

Orson Whitney served as a bishop for nearly three decades—becoming perhaps the most prominent ward bishop the Church has had—and then as a member of the Quorum of the Twelve Apostles for a similar period, though he preferred the title "Bishop" even to that of "Apostle" or "Elder." "Once a Bishop, always a Bishop," he once wrote, explaining: "The proverb has proved true in my case; for I am just as much a bishop today [1930], after many years of service in another position, as when I became the spiritual shepherd of the little flock residing in the Eighteenth Ward of Salt Lake City. 'Bishop,' my old-time friends and associates still call me, and I would not have it otherwise. I remain a bishop for another reason, though no longer acting as such. The Apostleship includes the Bishopric, and no office in the Priesthood is taken away by any subsequent ordination" (102).

Orson's literary productions and church service are little known today, except among LDS historians (and poets), gospel scholars, and bibliophiles that remember and recognize his voluminous contributions. Whitney's *History of Utah* (four large volumes), his *Life of Heber C. Kimball*, and his books of poetry, along with his autobiography, *Through Memory's Halls*, remain his most important and lasting works, though original editions have become scarce and are now considered collector's items. Along with his remarkable power of expression when speaking and writing, he also displayed penetrating intellectual and spiritual gifts, and he continues to be quoted on occasion by modern Church leaders in conferences and by authors of doctrinal and historical works. Yet his influence has not enjoyed the same staying power in LDS collective memory as such contemporaries as B. H. Roberts, John A. Widstoe, and James E. Talmage—although his strengths surely equaled theirs.

This sketch of Orson's life is principally drawn from two sources: the autobiography, published shortly before his passing (page numbers in parentheses after a quotation indicate use of this source); and his journals (recognized by dates in parentheses).[1] Other sources are found in the notes as usual. Although he could not have foreseen it while he lived, Orson F. Whitney has figuratively stepped out of the past to contribute much to this history of President Lorenzo Snow.

The unusual circumstances of Whitney and President Snow's first meeting and subsequent friendship are related in the introduction. They remained close from 1887 until President Snow's death in late 1901. They were kindred spirits with a love of poetry and gospel doctrine and principles. "You have a revealing mind—the power to grasp sacred mysteries, said President Lorenzo Snow, during one of our confidential talks" (411). Orson felt the loss keenly when President Snow died. "I attended the obsequies in the Tabernacle, and went with the funeral party by special train to Brigham City, the place of interment. At a meeting in the Eighteenth Ward Chapel that evening, I pronounced a eulogy on the life and character of my departed leader and friend" (240).

Whitney was born July 1, 1855, in Salt Lake City, to Newell K. Whitney and Helen Mar Kimball (daughter of Heber C. Kimball, a counselor in the First Presidency to Brigham Young) (21).

He showed exceptional ability and potential as a child, scholastically, dramatically, and musically. His near-photographic memory served him well throughout his life.

As he neared the transitional stage between youth and young adulthood, he found himself pondering how to earn a living and how best to employ his talents. This question became a major turning point in his life. He remembered:

> I had made up my mind to embrace the dramatic [acting] profession, and as the Salt Lake Theatre was not running regularly, I decided to go to New York, that Mecca of theatrical aspirants, and there begin my career. The winter past, I severed my relations with [my employer] and came home, resolved upon seizing the first opportunity to carry out my ambitious design. My parents were much opposed to it, but I was determined to do something, to be somebody, and the drama seemed the only opening for me at that time.
>
> In the intervals of odd jobs I kept up my practice of elocution, mastered Bacon's "Manual of Gesture," and in every way possible strove to fit myself for the stage. The time and effort were not wasted. What was done in that direction helped to prepare me for my subsequent and real career. I was all the more capable as a preacher, for having had some experience as an actor. . . .
>
> Meanwhile, my mother, finding that she could not dissuade me from my purpose, said resignedly: "Well, Orson, since you are determined to go, I shall not oppose you; and if I can sell a piece of land (she had inherited several lots from her father's [Heber C. Kimball] estate) I'll give you two hundred dollars to take you to New York."
>
> Overjoyed, I sought earnestly to bring about the realization of that promise. But alas! There was no sale for the land. July—August—September—went by, spent in an ineffectual struggle against fate. Something was in the way—the Hand of Providence, though I did not see it then. More than once a sale seemed imminent; then some question would arise and the whole thing fell through, carrying with it my fondest hope. I believe now—what I suspected then—that my mother's prayers were largely responsible for the situation and what grew out of it.

> October came. The General Conference of the Church convened, and I was called on a mission to the United States. There was no previous notice—such was not the custom in those days. It fell like a bolt from the blue. And mark what followed! No sooner had I signified my willingness to accept the call, than my mother sold her land without any difficulty, and gave me two hundred dollars to take me—not to the City of New York to begin a dramatic career, but to the State of Pennsylvania, my first field of labor as a missionary. (66–67)

Reflecting upon his early decisions in later years, he wrote:

> I think it was pride more than piety that induced me to go upon that mission. I felt that it would be a disgrace not to go, and would sadden the hearts of those who loved me whom I loved. Therefore I sacrificed my most cherished wish, laid my darling ambition on the altar, and took the will of the Lord, instead of my own will, for a guide.
>
> I have never done a wiser or better thing. If there is anything in my life that looks like success, it is because I decided as I did at that time, and because I have striven ever since to act upon the same principle.
>
> I know now that I had a testimony, a deep conviction of the Truth; but it was latent, undeveloped, like a gold mine in the depths of the earth. Something had to occur to bring it out. That something was my mission. (68)

Orson's mission changed him from a boy with some indifference to a man of spiritual maturity. His later reflections on his early experiences are of some interest: "Love of God, the very essence of religion, was always with me. I never doubted the Lord's existence, his goodness or his power. When in trouble my first thought was to pray to Him. I did not share the notion, expressed by some of my fellows, that 'the Lord doesn't want us to bother him about every little thing.' I have never believed that we trouble our Heavenly Father by craving blessings at his hand." (70). Having so stated, Elder Whitney related an early formative incident:

> A rather remarkable experience befell me when a child. I had lost my pocket knife—the first I ever owned. Grieving bitterly over the misfortune, I almost questioned Providence for permitting it to happen. Yes, I was just that unreasonable, not knowing any better, and being so constituted that it nearly tore my heart out to lose anything upon which I had set my affections. While sorrowing over my loss, I suddenly felt an influence of peace, and as I looked up to heaven through my tears, a ray of light seemed resting down upon me. All at once those splendid lines of Cowper's flashed into my mind:

> Judge not the Lord by feeble sense,
> But trust Him for His grace:
> Behind a frowning Providence
> He hides a smiling face.
>
> Never to my knowledge had I seen or heard that verse before. But be that as it may, it had the effect of drying my tears and giving me the assurance that I should find my lost knife. A few minutes later I walked down the path to my mother's gate, and there, half hidden in the dust, lay my precious treasure. How eagerly I pounced upon it, and how grateful I was for its recovery, I need not say. (71)

Orson's preparation for his mission included a brief visit with the Lord's Prophet—a mentor prized by Whitney all his life. "Shortly before leaving for the east," he wrote, "I met President Brigham Young, on the sidewalk near his office gate. It was my last sight of the great leader, who died while I was away. Smiling benignantly upon me he said: 'You are going on your mission?' 'Yes, sir,' I replied. [He said] 'That's right' (grasping my hand warmly). 'May the Lord bless you!' And the Lord did bless me, in a most remarkable manner" (72).

Elder Whitney filled an honorable and productive mission but had a slow and uncertain start. As he traveled east and tried new challenges, he discovered a talent for writing begin to blossom, with a ready readership of the newspapers that published his letters in Salt Lake City. This situation led him to perhaps the most profound and impressive spiritual experience of his life, one that forever after affected his perspective and focus. He explained in sobering detail how he was taught to keep his mind on his errand:

> I began a correspondence with the *Salt Lake Herald*—first, however, writing to the editor, Byron Groo, and asking him if that paper would publish what I might send. He promptly replied, "thanking me in advance" and encouraging me to proceed. . . .
>
> My communications to the *Herald*, the first one dated March 14, 1877, leaped at once into popular favor. This gratified me, of course, but I became so absorbed in the correspondence that it encroached upon hours that should have been given to religious study. Elder Musser chided me for it. "You ought to be studying the books of the Church," said he. "You were sent out to preach the Gospel, not to write for the newspapers." I knew he was right, but still kept on, fascinated by the discovery that I could wield a pen, and preferring that to any other pursuit except the drama, my ambition for which had been laid aside.

Then came a marvelous manifestation, an admonition from a higher Source, one impossible to ignore. It was a dream, or a vision in a dream, as I lay upon my bed in the little town of Columbia, Lancaster County, Pennsylvania. I seemed to be in the Garden of Gethsemane, a witness of the Savior's agony. I saw Him as plainly as ever I have seen anyone. Standing behind a tree in the foreground, I beheld Jesus, with Peter, James and John, as they came through a little wicket gate at my right. Leaving the three Apostles there, after telling them to kneel and pray, the Son of God passed over to the other side, where He also knelt and prayed. It was the same prayer with which all Bible readers are familiar: "Oh my Father, if it be possible, let this cup pass from me; nevertheless not as I will, but as thou wilt." As He prayed the tears streamed down his face, which was toward me. I was so moved at the sight that I also wept, out of pure sympathy. My whole heart went out to him; I loved him with all my soul, and longed to be with him as I longed for nothing else.

Presently He arose and walked to where those Apostles were kneeling—fast asleep! He shook them gently, awoke them, and in a tone of tender reproach, untinctured by the least show of anger or impatience, asked them plaintively if they could not watch with him one hour. There He was, with the awful weight of the world's sin upon his shoulders, with the pangs of every man, woman and child shooting through his sensitive soul—and they could not watch with him one poor hour!

Returning to his place, He offered up the same prayer as before; then went back and again found them sleeping. Again He awoke them, re-admonished them, and once more returned and prayed. Three times this occurred, until I was perfectly familiar with his appearance—face, form and movements. He was of noble stature and majestic mien—not at all the weak, effeminate being that some painters have portrayed; but the very God that he was and is, as meek and humble as a little child.

All at once the circumstances seemed to change, the scene remaining just the same. Instead of before, it was after the crucifixion, and the Savior, with the three Apostles, now stood together in a group at my left. They were about to depart and ascend into Heaven. I could endure it no longer. I ran from behind the tree, fell at his feet, clasped Him around the knees, and begged him to take me with him.

I shall never forget the kind and gentle manner in which He stooped, raised me up, and embraced me. It was so vivid, so real. I felt the very warmth of his body, as He held me in his arms and said in tenderest tones: "No, my son; these have finished their work; they can go with me; but you must stay and finish yours." Still I clung to Him. Gazing up into his face—for he was taller than I—I besought

> him fervently: "Well, promise me that I will come to you at the last." Smiling sweetly, He said: "That will depend entirely upon yourself." I awoke with a sob in my throat, and it was morning.
>
> "That's from God," said Elder Musser, when I related to him what I had seen and heard. "I do not need to be told that," was my reply. I saw the moral clearly. I had never thought of being an Apostle, nor of holding any other office in the Church, and it did not occur to me even then. Yet I knew that those sleeping Apostles meant me. I was asleep at my post—as any man is who, having been divinely appointed to do one thing, does another.
>
> But from that hour all was changed. I was never the same man again. I did not give up writing; for President Young, having noticed some of my contributions to the home papers, advised me to cultivate what he called my "gift for writing." "So that you can use it," said he, "for the establishment of truth and righteousness." I therefore continued to write, but not to the neglect of the Lord's Work. I held that first and foremost; all else was secondary. (81–83)

After absorbing such an impressive revelation of remonstration, Elder Whitney moved forward in his ministry with zeal and faith:

> I studied hard, wrote much, preached where opportunity offered, and lived in an atmosphere of prayer and meditation. I read and re-read the books of the Church; subjected myself to every requirement of its discipline, and became rooted and grounded in the faith. My life, my whole character, underwent a complete change. I became as zealous as I had been indifferent, and so necessary was the Gospel to my peace and happiness, that I marveled how I ever had done without it.
>
> A continuous chain of miraculous incidents accompanied my ministry. My testimony broadened and deepened, and more and more the spiritual side of my nature developed. In my mind's vision the past and future of all Time seemed open to my gaze. I saw my place in the eternal scheme of things; realized whence I came, why I am here, and what awaits me in the Great Hereafter. Life was no longer a mystery: its meaning was clear. Came to me in full effulgence that divine illumination which is greater than dreams, visions and all other manifestations combined. By the light of God's Candle—the Gift of the Holy Ghost—I saw what till then I had never seen, learned what till then I had never known. My soul was satisfied; my joy was full; for I had a testimony of the Truth, and it has remained with me to this day. (90–91)

When the time for his honorable release arrived, Elder Whitney set his mind once again to the critical question that had before so perplexed him, and which would soon face him again: what he should do in temporal pursuits; how to earn a living and begin life as a spiritually mature adult. He wrote:

> Before leaving the mission field, I had prayed that I might not go back into the old rut from which the Gospel had lifted me. I feared that I might do as other returned missionaries had done—throw off the harness of activity in the Priesthood and become indifferent to the things of God. Passages from my private letters, breathing a zealous spirit, had found their way into print, and I learned that some of my former friends had said, rather scoffingly: 'Oh, he'll get over that; they all do.' And I feared that it might be so. I therefore asked the Lord to give me something to do that would keep me in his service, too busy to lose interest in or zeal for the Cause. He certainly granted my petition and gave me the desire of my heart. (102)

But hindsight is clearer than foresight, especially where temporal concerns are involved. Whitney had a struggle to find his place and position once at home again. He had done some writing on his mission for the Church-owned *Deseret News*, so that was the first place he sought work:

> But there was no opening on the *News*, and after an ineffectual application at the office of the business manager, I went home a little crestfallen. As was my custom, I laid the matter before the Lord. Retiring to my room and kneeling with a closed Bible in my hands, I prayed for a message of comfort from its pages, having previously determined to take as an answer to prayer any passage of Scripture that I might turn to haphazardly. Opening the Good Book and without glancing at the page, I set my finger down on the third chapter of Proverbs, the first verses reading as follows:
>
> > My son, forget not my law; but let thine heart keep my commandments:
> >
> > For length of days, and long life, and peace shall they add to thee.
> >
> > Let not mercy and truth forsake thee; bind them about thy neck; write them upon the table of thine heart;
> >
> > So shalt thou find favor and good understanding in the sight of God and man.
>
> My prayer was answered; for though I read on to the end of the chapter—one rich with precious instruction—the substance of the matter then on my mind was in those first four verses. The promise that I should "find favor in the sight of God and Man," gave me new hope and confidence.

> It was the sixteenth of April, and I had been home from the States a little more than two weeks. Walking down Main Street as far as the Wells Corner, I met Angus M. Cannon, President of Salt Lake Stake, which then comprised all of Salt Lake County. To him I told my story, and he at once espoused my cause. "Go right over to the *News* Office," said he, "and tell Thomas Edward Taylor to give you something to do—and say I sent you. You have filled a good mission, and ought to have a place there."
>
> But I knew that Thomas Edward Taylor had a mind of his own—he and I had been schoolmates in boyhood; and I felt the need of a little more "church influence" before I again tackled him.
>
> Just at that moment I saw Brigham Young, Jr., standing at the front gate of the Gardo House—a structure since superseded by the Federal Reserve Bank Building. Knowing that his name, with that of George Q. Cannon, headed the editorial columns of the Church organ, I walked briskly in his direction and engaged him in conversation.
>
> "Come with me," he said, after I had stated my case; and forthwith we proceeded to the business office of the *Deseret News*.
>
> "Brother Taylor, can't you give Brother Whitney something to do?" inquired the Apostle.
>
> "I would like to, Brother Young," was the amiable reply, "but every place here is filled."
>
> "Give him some bills to collect."
>
> "Oh, the last man we sent out didn't earn his salt."
>
> "But you haven't tried Brother Whitney," urged my advocate, and so insistently that Thomas Edward finally gave way.
>
> He first put me to work adding up columns of figures (which of course was a great delight!) and then (more addition) sent me out collecting. I presented a bill to one of the Presiding Bishopric, and he nearly took my head off. "I don't need any dunning," said he, "I pay my bills." I didn't like the job, but kept on, hopeful of better days to come. And they came. (103–5)

Whitney worked for the *Deseret News* on and off for several years after his mission, soon becoming city editor. He didn't care for certain aspects of the job, including the hours and demands on his time, so when opportunity presented itself, he moved on to better things. In the meantime, the ecclesiastical church service in which he was to be engaged for over twenty-seven years was but a few weeks from realization. He described the call with style:

> My installation as Bishop came about in this manner. On my way to church that Sabbath evening I pursued an indirect course, lengthening

> my walk from the parental home on City Creek to the Deseret Bank corner, where, as I turned to go east, I was accosted by Laron Cummings, who had a room on an upper floor of the Bank building.
>
> "Come up to my room," said Laron. "Thank you," said I, "but I must go to meeting. They are going to put me in as Bishop tonight."
>
> He laughed, and I laughed and passed on, little dreaming that I had uttered in jest a prediction that was about to be fulfilled. I had been told that a new Bishopric would be installed that night, but as to the proposed personnel I knew nothing.
>
> When the President of the Stake said to the congregation: "It has been moved and seconded that Orson F. Whitney be the Bishop of the Eighteenth Ward," I was astonished. If the earth had opened and swallowed me, I could scarcely have been more surprised. . . .
>
> Called upon to express my feelings, I tremblingly took the stand and tremulously addressed the large congregation. I told them—what they already knew—that I was young and inexperienced; but that time would cure those defects; and I accepted my call to the mission field, trusting in the Lord to qualify me for my duties. . . .
>
> Apostle George Q. Cannon then addressed the meeting. "Bishop Whitney," he remarked, "said a good thing when he told us that time would remedy in him the defects of youth and inexperience. And I will add this: If the people of this ward will rally round him and hold up his hands, the time will come when they will think they have the best bishop in the Church."
>
> He did not say that I would *be* the best bishop—and of course I never was; but he said the people would think so; and that prophecy was abundantly fulfilled. During the well-nigh twenty-eight years of my bishopric, I had the love and loyal support of the good people of the Eighteenth Ward. They thought me the best bishop, just as children in a family think their father the best of men. It does not have to be a fact. It is a sentiment, and a wholesome one. (105–7)

Bishop Whitney's work as a reporter for the *Deseret News* took him around the state, adding subscribers, gathering news, meeting prominent people, and other duties as needed. During one such tour, he received an important blessing related to his future life:

> At the town of Hyrum I became acquainted with Father O. N. Liljenquist, the bishop of that ward, who was also a patriarch. From him I received my first patriarchal blessing, and it was a great comfort to me. I had been very downhearted over the unpromising state of my health, and the patriarch's words, fraught with the spirit of his holy calling, lifted

> me from the slough of despondency. He told me that while his hands were on my head my life passed before him like a panorama. He predicted to certain friends of mine, and subsequently to me, that I would yet be an Apostle. The date of the repeated prediction was April 6, 1886, twenty years before I was called to the Apostleship. Whenever I met this good man he had something to say about my future. "You will go upon many missions,' said he, 'and will pass through some narrow places, but will come out just about as successfully as a man ever did." (113)

Whitney continued with the *Deseret News*, served as bishop, and found himself elected to the city council (without having campaigned for the office), and time passed. Then,

> One evening in September, 1881, while seated in the City Council chamber—east main upper room of the old City Hall—I was handed a note from President Joseph F. Smith, who was a member of the Council, informing me that the Church Authorities had decided to send me to Liverpool. Like my friend Nicholson (who was home again) I was to do editorial work on the *Millennial Star*, the organ of the European Mission. I announced myself ready to go, and President Smith—then second counselor to President John Taylor—gave me his blessing. It was left for me to set the day of departure, and I fixed upon November first as the date of sailing from New York. Forthwith, I severed my relations with the *Deseret News*, and at the General Conference in October was formally called on a mission to Europe. Three of the Apostles—Wilford Woodruff, Franklin D. Richards and Moses Thatcher—set me apart, the first-named voicing the blessing. (123)

Whitney was asked to edit the *Star* and write editorials, as well as many other duties. This responsibility weighed heavily on him, and he entered one of several periods of depression that he experienced throughout his life:

> In November of that year I found myself in an over-worked, run-down condition, manifesting a decided lack of physical and mental vigor. I continued my labors, however, with unabated zeal. One morning I was endeavoring to write the usual editorial, but could make no headway, and wore out the whole day in a vain attempt to produce something worth reading. At last I threw down my pen and burst into tears of vexation.
>
> Just then the Good Spirit whispered: "Why don't you pray?"
>
> As if a voice had addressed me audibly, I answered, "I do pray." I was praying five times a day—secret prayers, morning, noon and

> night; and vocal prayers, with the rest of the household, at breakfast and dinner time. "I do pray—why can't I get some help," I asked almost petulantly, for I was heartsick and half discouraged.
>
> "Pray now," said the Spirit, "and ask for what you want." I saw the point. It was a special not a general prayer that was needed. I knelt and sobbed out a few simple words. I did not pray for the return of the Ten Tribes nor for the building of the New Jerusalem. I asked the Lord in the name of Jesus Christ to help me write that article. I then arose, seated myself, and began to write. My mind was now perfectly clear, and my pen fairly flew over the paper. All I needed came as fast as I could set it down—every thought, every word in place. In a short time the article was completed to my entire satisfaction. I read it to the President, and he approved it without the change of a syllable.
>
> This taught me a lesson; or rather, it reminded me of one I already knew, but needed to have emphasized. Prayer is not a matter of mere words, not a strip of stereotyped phrases. It is "the soul's sincere desire," and it was of such a prayer, and no other, that the Lord said: "Ask and ye shall receive." (151–52)

Not long after this incident, as part of an effort to improve his health, Elder Whitney was reassigned as a proselytizing missionary to get him out of the mission office and into fresh air.[2] He traveled throughout England without purse or scrip, having many inspiring adventures. About this time, he learned of the death of an infant son he had never seen, wounding his heart. He was granted permission to go home, and after a quick trip through Scotland and France, he did so. Upon returning, his first care was to obtain employment, which he did, landing his former job at the *Deseret News*, which he did not care for but needed nonetheless (173–75). He also continued to write poetry and received the accolades of his peers and associates (including Church leaders such as Presidents Taylor and Woodruff) for his verse. "President Taylor was always kind to me," he wrote. "A poet himself, he took an interest in my verses, and encouraged me to write. He also commended my public discourses. To the *Young Men's* magazine I contributed a poem dedicated to President Taylor. Set to music by Evan Stephens, 'The Overthrow of Gog and Magog' was sung with splendid effect by the Tabernacle Choir. My tongue as well as my pen was much in demand, and I was preaching, lecturing, and speaking at funerals almost constantly. This service was free, and I was more than willing to give it [free]" (176). Yet not all of life was rosy; personal sorrow came to Whitney when his younger brother Charles committed suicide in August 1886.[3]

Orson Whitney was undeniably headed for great things. Along with the prophecy contained in his patriarchal blessing, others also felt he would one day become one of the Twelve Apostles:

> During January and July, 1887, I preached in all the principal wards of Bear Lake Stake and in many of the towns of Central and Southern Utah, both trips being planned by Elder John W. Taylor, of the Council of the Twelve, who invited me to accompany him. Finding that he could not go north, he requested me to represent him and take someone along to assist me. Elder Charles W. Stayner consented to share the honor. In the south, Brother Taylor and I, with my son Race, went as far as Woolley's Ranch near Kanab—my first visit to that section. Not long afterward, while the Apostle and I were traveling together, he prophesied that I would yet be one of the Twelve. He little knew nor did I, that my call and ordination to the Apostleship, twenty years later, would fill a vacancy caused by his own retirement [resignation]. (182)

It was at about this time that Orson produced his first major historical work. While certain modern scholars have questioned some of his sources, or at least his interpretation of the sources, his ability to tell a powerful and dramatic life story was unquestioned.

> June 14, 1887, witnessed a large gathering of the Kimball Clan at Fuller's Hill Gardens, Salt Lake City; an affair commemorative of the eighty-sixth anniversary of the birth of President Heber C. Kimball. By request, I prepared and read to the assembly a sketch of Grandfather's life, and the impression it made was strong enough to unite the family upon the project of publishing the *Life of Heber C. Kimball.* The honor of writing it fell to me. Such was the origin of my first book. Completed in August, 1888, and published in the autumn of that year, it awakened widespread interest, and the entire edition was soon exhausted. For many years this *Life* has been out of print, but the demand for it continues. (185)

The reason for not reissuing the book in subsequent editions for many years reportedly had to do with Whitney's inclusion of many sacred spiritual experiences that some felt were not soundly documented or attested, and also because of its rousing defense of plural marriage—which in two short years was to be officially discontinued by the Church in the United States. Whitney himself had temporarily been barred by President John Taylor from entering plural marriage and taking a second wife, but this ban was lifted and he subsequently married a second wife.[4]

The 1880s proved to be a particularly difficult decade for the Church, especially its leaders. The United States Congress was trying its best to cede to fabricated public opinion and prejudice to stop the Mormons from practicing plural marriage, passing a succession of laws against the Latter-day Saint religion in an effort to destroy polygamy or the Church or both. Since its leaders were the most visible, they were hunted the most vigorously. This period of time became known as the "Crusade," an unforeseen side-effect of which was to increase Whitney's local fame:

> Many men of prominence were convicted, fined and imprisoned for refusing to put away their plural wives, married to them in good faith according to a principle of their religion, and who with their children were dependent upon these men for support.
>
> So many of the leading brethren were in prison or "on the underground"—as their enforced retirement was called—that I was brought to the front more and more, especially as a public speaker, and for a time was the most frequent occupant of the Tabernacle pulpit. "Unduly prominent," some said, and seemed to hold me personally responsible for the many calls that came to me. The logic of it was of course unanswerable!
>
> At the General Conferences, where epistles from the absent First Presidency were read to the assembled Saints, almost invariably I was chosen to do the reading. This, I suppose, was because I had a voice and knew how to use it—thanks to my early training in elocution and my subsequent experience upon the stage and in the mission field. (189)

It was at this time (March 1886) that President Lorenzo Snow was sent to the Utah Penitentiary, as explained later in this biography; and therefore it was also at about this time that Orson met President Snow after speaking to the prison Sunday School at the "Pen." Their destined friendship blossomed. As mentioned in the introduction, after his release from prison, President Snow commissioned Whitney to write *Latter Leaves*. Then, "In December 1887, President Snow's sister Eliza R. Snow Smith, poet and woman of prominence, passed away. Once more he had use for my pen, this time to compile and prepare for publication the proceedings at her funeral, where I had been one of the speakers" (193).[5]

On July 24, 1888, Whitney, with his first wife's gracious consent, married his only plural wife, May Wells, daughter of Apostle Daniel H. Wells (194). Then Orson endured one of several severe encounters with ill-health:

> August, 1888, found me prostrate with typhoid, which wasted me away almost to a shadow. My faithful [wife] Zina was with me through it all, waiting upon me tenderly, watching over me night and day. After the fever had run its course, I built up thirty pounds heavier than before, and felt much better for the change. My former weight (145 lbs) was too slight for my all but six feet of stature, and I had often prayed for a stronger physique and more vigorous health. It looked as if the Lord had taken this method of answering my prayer. At all events I was healthier and stronger from that hour. (195)

Whitney's life was full and useful; he had found his stride:

> My pen and tongue continued busy. It was about all I could do to respond to the frequent calls made upon me outside of my regular duties [as bishop]. One day in January, 1889, I was sent for by President Wilford Woodruff, then the senior of the Twelve Apostles. He wanted me to speak at the funeral of his brother Azmon, in Farmer's Ward. I responded to the President's request, and next day he said to me: "Brother Whitney, you are doing a great deal of good. You are preaching sound doctrine and comforting the hearts of the Saints, and the Lord is blessing you in your labors." Evidently he did not think me 'unduly prominent. (195–96)

Whitney seemed to go out of his way in his autobiography to mention these incidents of trust shown him by the General Authorities, for he experienced an occasional struggle and setback, and made some mistakes as well. Thus, he wrote: "At the General Conference in April, when Wilford Woodruff, George Q. Cannon and Joseph F. Smith were sustained as the First Presidency, I was one of the speakers. I mention these items to show that I possessed the confidence of the Church leaders during that perilous period" (196).

In 1889, Whitney was working as Salt Lake City Treasurer, an office to which he had been appointed to serve out the term of his suddenly deceased predecessor; but with the elections, a new party took office and assumed control, and by February of 1890, he was left without employment again. As good as things had been, he was faced with another time of temporal trial:

> Out of office and employment, with a large and increasing family dependent upon me, I well remember the feeling of dejection that came over me as I reflected upon my unpromising situation. From an upstairs window in my study, one day, I stood gazing out upon a snowstorm

> that was filling the air with feather flakes and covering the earth like a shroud. Watching one little flake as it descended and was blown hither and thither, I fell to moralizing: "A symbol, that, of my changeful life—blown about by the winds of fortune, with no fixed and permanent place"—meaning no steadfast occupation.
>
> Just at that moment the door bell rang, and a letter was brought in—a letter from President Lorenzo Snow. He was then the senior Apostle in the Council of the Twelve. Only a few days before I had been conversing with him and complaining a little of my lot. The letter was written at Brigham City and bore the date of March 25, 1890. Among other things it said:
>
> "Dear Brother: I shall look for a visit from you after Conference, when we will take the opportunity to sit down by ourselves and exchange thoughts and views confidentially.
>
> "You must not lose heart nor suffer yourself to be discouraged because of financial pressure. There is not an Elder in all Israel, endowed with ordinary sense and ambition, though he were a millionaire, if he lacked what you possess, but would gladly give his entire wealth, could he thereby secure the gifts of oratory and argument, the talent and ability that the Lord our God has so abundantly bestowed upon my admired and beloved friend, Bishop O. F. Whitney; and a moderate exercise of gratitude on the part of my aforesaid friend, I trust will ever fortify him against discouragement or despondency."
>
> Such a letter at such a time from almost anyone, would have had a comforting effect. But what shall I say of such a letter from such a man? It was positively overwhelming. I did not feel worthy of it, but was deeply moved by the kind, generous, fatherly spirit in which it had been written. It cheered my soul like a burst of sunshine. It was almost like a message from heaven.
>
> The writer of the epistle had said to me only a few days before: "Don't worry about income. Means will flow into your hands as fast as you have need of it." And he was right. It has always been so. I have never been rich, nor have I cared to be; but neither did I ever lack for the necessaries of life. And most of my blessings have come without my seeking, almost invariably as a surprise. (200–201)

During late 1889 to early 1890 Orson prepared the rough draft of *Latter Leaves*. However, in September President Woodruff issued a document that probably led to the shelving of the manuscript: "The autumn of 1890 saw the issuance of the famous 'Manifesto' stopping plural marriage. In the General Conference I was called upon to read it to the congregation. I also read, by request, the Articles of Faith, to remind the people of the Church's attitude in honoring, obeying and sustaining the law. The vote was then taken and the Manifesto accepted" (203). Because Whitney's original complete draft of *Latter Leaves* contains so much rhetoric in defense of plural marriage, it is not a stretch to conclude that with the Manifesto's issuance President Snow may have felt its release was no longer appropriate; publication expense may have been another reason.

In 1890, Whitney also began work on what would be his most voluminous writing project:

> I was told that a project was on foot for the production of a *History of Utah*, and that I had been mentioned as the prospective historian. My informant was Franklin S. Richards, one of the Church attorneys. A day or two later I was sent for by President Woodruff, and as soon as I entered his office . . . he said to a well-dressed man with whom he and President Joseph F. Smith had been conversing: "Dr. Williams, this is the man we have chosen to write the History." Dr. John O. Williams, who had been connected in a business way with Bancroft's *History of the Pacific States* and with Hall's *History of Colorado*, proposed to publish a *History of Utah*; the Church to select the historian and sanction the enterprise, he (Williams) to furnish the means of publication, put the work through the press, and distribute it. The desired sanction being given, I received my appointment, and was vouched for by leading men and women of the community. Thus the work began. (201–2)

> Dr. Williams paid me a salary of two hundred dollars a month, and part of the time my wife drew fifty dollars a month as my secretary. That was all I ever had out of it, though I was entitled by contract to twenty-five per cent of the net proceeds, minus the amount advanced to me in salary. Had the business prospered as anticipated, I might have pressed my claim; but as it did not, I forbore adding to the financial perplexities of the situation. (202)

> It was in May 1890, that I began this, the most voluminous of my literary works. To complete it required several years, during which I had many other duties to perform, and responded, as usual, to numerous calls for extra service in various directions. I was in love with my task—which lightened it greatly—but still it was strenuous and exacting, as anyone must know who has ever brought out a work of that character and magnitude. (203)

The project ran into many troubles, both financial and from misunderstanding:

> My duties were purely literary. At no time did I have anything to do with the business management; yet my name was used, without my consent, as if I had been the very head and front of the enterprise. Certain agents employed by Dr. Williams were reprimanded by him and discarded [dismissed] for this and other irregularities. But so much prejudice had been engendered that Williams, in June 1891, sold out the business, or the main part of it, to George Q. Cannon and Sons, whose purchase rescued it from impending disaster. . . . For my historical labors I was given the use of a desk in the west wing of the President's Office, and was promised all the help that the Historian's Office could render. But the scattered condition of the Church records, owing to the operations of the 'Crusade,' greatly interfered with the realization of that promise. My work, however, was read in manuscript to a committee of which the Church Historian, Franklin D. Richards, was chairman. (202–3)

This business arrangement and extensive historical writing project was much more complex than these summaries portray or space herein allows for review. It is one of few works that have received public endorsement from the First Presidency:

> Dear Brethren: You have doubtless learned that Bishop Orson F. Whitney, of this city, is engaged in preparing the *History of Utah*, and have probably received the Author's prospectus with accompanying testimonials from ourselves and other citizens. We wish it understood that we are heartily in sympathy with the project, and that it has our entire support. The author of the proposed work is a native of Utah, one in whom we have great confidence as an able writer and a conscientious historian. We believe his history, which is to be published in three large volumes [actually four], will be complete and reliable, and should be in the possession of every family; and can recommend it to the general public who desire to know the truth about our Territory and its people. We trust that the Latter-day Saints will give it their support and encouragement.
>
> Wilford Woodruff, George Q. Cannon, Joseph F. Smith.
>
> First Presidency of the Church of Jesus Christ of Latter-day Saints[6]

Then, wrote Orson:

> In April 1893, at the dedication of the Salt Lake Temple, I was invited to sit with the Presiding Bishopric on the west side of the great hall in which the proceedings took place, and by request, I offered one of the prayers from that stand. This, no doubt, was in honor of my grandfather, Presiding Bishop Newel K. Whitney. It was not the first

> Temple dedication that I had witnessed. Years before I had attended one at Manti, and on that occasion something very remarkable occurred. While sitting with my wife Zina in the midst of the congregation, I distinctly heard strains of music in the air about our heads. I supposed it to be from a band playing in the town; but was afterwards told by President Anthon H. Lund and others that no band was out that day. The conclusion was irresistible that the music had a heavenly source. (206–7)

In September 1898, Whitney asked his friend J. Golden Kimball to nominate him to become a state senator, which Kimball readily agreed to do. Elder Kimball records that "I nominated Bishop Orson F. Whitney, as State Senator. . . . R. K. Thomas and Orson F. Whitney were elected on first ballot. I was very much pleased as Bishop Whitney is a man of honor, intelligence, a rising young man, and a faithful Latter-day Saint and is loyal and patriotic. He has been kept back, and I felt very pleased indeed with his nomination."[7]

The years 1899 and 1900 were some of the most decisive and productive to that point in Whitney's life. Along with his election to the Utah State Senate, he became employed with the Church Historian's Office. He wrote:

> Two days after my election to the State Senate [in early January 1899], I sought an interview with President Lorenzo Snow, who was then at the head of the Church, President Woodruff having passed on. My object was to ask for the office of Assistant Church Historian, succeeding Elder Charles W. Penrose, who had been called to another position [managing editor of the *Deseret News*]. The President welcomed me with a beaming smile, saying: "Just the man I wanted to see." He told me that President Franklin D. Richards, the Church Historian, wanted me as an assistant in his office—the very thing I was seeking. At President Snow's suggestion I at once had an interview with President Richards, and got some understanding of the duties that would be required of me and upon which I was expected to enter at the beginning of the New Year. (225)

Whitney learned quickly: "My duties were to keep a journal of all important events pertaining to or in any way affecting the Lord's Work in any part of the world; also to prepare for President Richards, or help him prepare, any historical document that might be needed from time to time. Dan Collett was my capable assistant as typist" (226–27; these events in Whitney's life are also reviewed in the introduction).

Along with his work in the Historian's Office, Whitney eventually (in late August 1899) resumed his labors on the final installment of his four-volume *History of Utah*. It is not known whether this project was incorporated into his regular official duties or not, although it is known that he had previously received some help with the project. For instance, Andrew Jenson, of the Historian's Office staff, wrote (in August of 1893): "At the President's Office I was informed that I would be required to assist Bishop Orson F. Whitney with the third volume of his *History of Utah*"—showing that he received some data collection help at that time.[8] Orson himself wrote of the work in such a way as to imply there was intermingling of duties at some point, though not at first: "Meanwhile I continued working on the final volume of my *History of Utah*—the biographical book. A number of prominent citizens, whom I had invited to take their places, therein, solicited my services in the preparation of their biographies. While pursuing this task, along with other duties, I was suddenly stricken with a severe illness and suffered the most excruciating pain I have ever experienced. It was a case of renal colic. Two or three similar attacks followed, but after that there was no recurrence of the trouble" (225–26).

Lorenzo Snow (USHS)

Although busy at the office writing and researching, and also ministering to his ward flock, Whitney continued his occasional visits with President Snow: "This afternoon I had a very pleasant visit with President Lorenzo Snow at his house on Canyon Road, this city. We talked of many things. He assured me again of his friendship and confidence; he could talk to me as to but few men and the memories of our first conversations were among the most precious of his life, too. He told me he had a photograph of himself for me if I would call at his office for it" (April 23, 1899). With such a close relationship with President Snow, Whitney joined the ranks of others such as Rudger Clawson and Franklin D. Richards in Lorenzo Snow's high esteem. It was a bond that Orson Whitney cherished all his life, though President Snow lived for only two more years.

That May (1899), President Snow took his famous trip to St. George in Southern Utah, where he received the revelation reaffirming that all faithful Latter-day Saints should pay a full and honest tithe. The trip took two weeks, with the party returning late in the month. Orson wrote of his son's participation (as a special correspondent for the *Salt Lake Herald*) in his journal:

> Saturday, May 27, 1899, President Snow and party returned from the South today; my son Horace included. Apostle Francis M. Lyman and President Richards both told me that he was asked to speak at Scipio, and made a nice little address of five minutes which very much pleased the whole party and the congregation. Bro. Lyman says Race was "white as a sheet" but every word was in place. He patted him on the back for it. Race says Bro. Lyman said to the congregation: "This is a son of Bishop Orson F. Whitney, and he is the worthy son of a worthy father." President Smith spoke next and said it was remarkable that a young boy who had never spoken in public before could evince so much composure and speak so fluently. "Just that kind of young man we want to defend the truth," he added. Orson was proud of his son and became prouder after talking with the prophet the next day: "After meeting I met President Snow and wife Minnie and son LeRoy. They were enthusiastic over Horace, and his speech at Scipio. Sister Snow said: "He has taken his first step in the footsteps of his fathers." Pres. Snow said: "I don't believe anybody else ever spoke that well the first time. We were quite proud of him. I see you in him at every word, and that is saying a good deal." (May 28, 1899)

Later in June, Whitney wrote: "President Lorenzo Snow presented me with a fine large photograph of him; taken recently by Fox and Ingram" (June 9, 1899). By August, he recorded that, "A few days ago I resumed work on Vol. 4 of my *History of Utah*—the biographical volume—suspended since last fall. I have completed Willard Richards' biography; revised A. W. McCune and submitted it to him, and am now on Wm Budge" (Aug. 30, 1899). Whitney came to know a number of prominent Utahns through his project.

As an Assistant Church Historian, he began writing rebuttals to anti-Mormon articles (Sept. 15, 1899). Meanwhile, the year 1900 began well for Orson Whitney:

> I find myself in good health, firm in the faith of the Gospel, the Bishop of the 18th ward and employed in the Church Historian's Office. For the past three months I have been engaged upon the 4th volume of my *History of Utah*. I have just completed a sketch of the life and character of Pres. Lorenzo Snow to be published in the New Year number of the *Juvenile Instructor* and afterwards in his [entry in the] *History* [*of Utah*], and have been asked to prepare an address on the life and character of the late Pres. Franklin D. Richards, to be delivered before the State Historical Society and afterwards published in the *History*. Spent most of today in my office. (Jan. 1, 1900)

Later that March, Orson invited a few guests over for a social occasion at his home: "Last evening we had a little party at our home—45 E. 1st North—and had the place dedicated. The guests present were Presidents Lorenzo Snow, George Q. Cannon and Joseph F. Smith with his wives, [Presiding] Bishop William B. Preston, . . . [and] my counselors, . . . and we had a very happy time. After supper at 6:30 we all assembled in the parlor and after I had made a brief address, to which President Snow responded, President George Q. Cannon, at President Snow's request, offered [the dedicatory] prayer. It was very feeling and very comforting. The rest of the evening was spent sociably" (March 1, 1900). Later that Spring, with Orson continuing work on his fourth volume, he enjoyed some humor with one of the chief critics of the Church: "Judge Goodwin, of the [*Salt Lake*] *Tribune*, sent me back the biographical sketch I had prepared for the *History of Utah*—his sketch, which I had submitted to him and which was rather complimentary to him, with this line upon the margin, 'Bishop, is there any forgiveness for lying in your religion?' To which I answered by postal card: 'Judge: Yes, there is, Come along,' [signed] Bishop" (May 5, 1900). In July, he wrote in his journal, "I am forty-five today, in good health, still working at the Church Historian's Office and still upon Vol. 4 of the *History of Utah*." (July 1, 1900).

Other than his decision to go on his first mission, this was perhaps the most critical period yet in Orson Whitney's life. He took a step in an unforeseen direction—an effort to obtain another plural wife—this after the issuance of the Manifesto some ten years earlier; a Manifesto that he himself had read to the assembled tabernacle audience. On July 11, he ran into a member of the Quorum of the Twelve that had ties to the Mexican Latter-day Saint colonies where, unbeknownst to President Snow, a few plural marriages were still being authorized by his counselors and solemnized by the local stake president. "Apostle George Teasdale . . . this evening, made a certain suggestion to me upon which I may act [to obtain another plural wife]" (July 11, 1900). Orson's first (non-plural) wife, Zina Beal Smoot, had recently died, leaving him with only his one (plural) wife May Wells (m. July 24, 1888), and he now seriously considered the suggestion from Elder Teasdale. He thought about it and selected a candidate, named in his journal as "Georgiana." That Saturday he noted: "I got a buggy in the evening, about 6, and took the twins for a drive, May my wife [went] with me. We drove up to Fort Douglas and beyond to the mouth of Emigration Canyon and returned home, a fine drive. Later in the evening [I] took Georgiana for a drive, and made her a proposal, based upon Apostle Teasdale's suggestion and my wife May's remarks . . . at the lake last evening" (July 14, 1900).

A week later, with a grieving heart, he wrote: "Spent the forenoon in my office. Finished a poem entitled 'Zina' upon which I have been working for some days. Also continued working over old letters, mine and Zina's. A very tender task" (July 22, 1900). That August his attempt to obtain another wife ended abruptly:

> This evening I took probably my last drive with Georgiana. She sent for me asking me to come. I was not prepared for what she told me. It seems like a tragic dream. She is married; married and miserable; married and does not love her husband! It was a secret marriage. No one knows of it but myself, outside those immediately concerned. It took place only a short time ago. She shed bitter tears, the first I ever saw her weep, as she told me how mistaken she was, how she regretted this step she had taken, and how gladly she would retract it if it were possible. "I love you more than I ever did," said she, "and I have done nothing but weep since I took this step. I regretted it the moment I had taken it, and told him so; I don't know why I did it; except that I did not want to go back to work. I have lost the best and sweetest man that ever lived." This and much more she said. Her last words at parting were: "I love you with all my heart." (Aug. 11, 1900)

It is probably a good thing for Whitney that this attempt at another marriage never materialized—rumors of post-Manifesto plural marriages were creating great trouble for the Church and some of those involved were eventually officially disciplined.[9]

The death of his first wife, Zina, with its accompanying intense grief and heartache, and the foiled attempt to obtain a second, sent Orson into a deep depression, serious enough for him to almost wish he were dead. As a means of getting out of it, he decided to write an "epic" poem; an idea that had been suggested to him years before by historian Edward W. Tullidge:

So I waited, pondered, experienced and developed, until I felt myself a more fitting instrument for the Muse in the production of what I determined should be a work worthy of the mighty [gospel] theme. It was long after Friend Tullidge fell asleep [died], when the inspiration rested upon me that resulted in the creation of "Elias—an Epic of the Ages," generally regarded as the crowning feature of my literary career.

This poem was begun in the spring of 1900, not long after the death of my wife Zina, and while I was prostrate upon a bed of pain [grief]. The inspiration was timely. I needed something of the kind to occupy my thoughts and dispel my gloomy feelings. While pondering upon the situation, and wondering whether my life's work was drawing to a close, I heard or seemed to hear a Voice—inaudible to the outward ear, yet plain to the inward understanding—the same Voice that had spoken to me on former occasions in hours of distress or deep anxiety. It now said:

"Do you really wish to go?"

"No," I replied; "I must not go until I have finished my work."

"What would you like to do?"

"Something that would live when I am dead, and go on teaching the Truth after my mortal tongue is still."

"And what might that be?"

I reflected, and my thoughts took this form: I would like to write a poem embodying all that I have learned, thought or felt respecting the divine plan known as "The Everlasting Gospel." I would love to tell in heroic verse the sublime Story of God. "Mormonism," historically, doctrinally, prophetically—be that my theme, my task, with whatsoever else the Lord has for me to do.

No sooner had I come to this conclusion, than the first lines of the poem formed in my mind, and weak as I was, I sat up and wrote them down. Thus the work began.

It took years to complete it, for I could not, of course, give all my time to poetry. I was still a Ward Bishop and an Assistant Church Historian. But I worked upon the great theme whenever I could, and found much delight in so doing. It burned like fire in my brain, and I felt that I must get it out or it would consume me. Day after day—sometimes twelve hours or more at a stretch—month after month, and year after year, I toiled on in the intervals of office work and outside engagements, till the poem, if not finished, was ready for a trial reading. This was toward the close of 1902. (243–44)

Meanwhile, in August 1900, he printed the poem he had written in honor of his late wife, Zina, and gave it to his friends and family. Writing helped him to dispel the dark clouds of depression, so he wrote another poem that he titled "The Mormon" and also an article about Brigham Young for an eastern magazine (Sept. 1, 1900). Then later that September, Orson Whitney enjoyed another sweet and sacred visit with his beloved mentor and prophet: "President Snow sent for me today and at 3 pm I had a very pleasant interview with him in his office (Presidents Cannon and Smith were absent in Canada). The President . . . told me that my poem 'Zina' a copy of which I sent him, had moved him deeply. He shed tears while reading it. He thought it very fine" (Sept. 17, 1900).

Some weeks later, Orson Whitney wrote: "This day I remarried at the Salt Lake Temple, my wife May Minerva Wells, whom I first married as a second and plural wife July 24, 1888, at Diaz, Mexico. She is now my legal wife. Bishop John R. Winder [a councilor in the Presiding Bishopric and President Snow's main assistant in the temple] performed the ceremony, which took place about noon. Present, as witnesses: John Nicholson, Duncan McAllister, also May's mother, Lydia Ann Wells and Aunt Emmiline Wells" (Oct. 11, 1900). Orson Whitney had endured well his trials and tribulations of mortality so far and had been richly rewarded.

The next year, at the end of March 1901, Orson went on vacation, taking a route that happened to place him near a dying President George Q. Cannon in California:

> The drive ended for me at Monterey, where President George Q. Cannon was spending his last days. I found him in a comfortable little cottage on a hill overlooking the ocean. His wife Caroline and two or three children were with him; also his faithful friend Charles H. Wilcken, and a Doctor Clift of St. George, Utah, one of the California missionaries. Propped up with pillows, President Cannon, though very weak, took cognizance of all that was going on around, and conversed with comparative freedom. He expressed pleasure at my coming, as did all the rest, and greeted me with a cordial handclasp.
>
> I had arrived just as the brethren were about administering to him, and was invited to take part. "President Cannon, who shall use the oil and who shall bless you?" asked Elder Wilcken. "Let Brother Orson do both," was the reply. Thereupon I anointed him, blessed him, and bade him goodbye.
>
> Rejoining my son, who came by the next train from Pacific Grove, I returned to San Francisco, and on the second of April left for home. Ten days later I learned of the death of President Cannon at Monterey.
>
> I was glad of that interview with him. Always an admirer of Brother

> Cannon for his great talents, I had still other reasons for holding him in high esteem. During my early boyhood, whenever we chanced to meet, he would notice me, call me by name and speak kindly to me—he an Apostle, I a nobody. My heart went out to him, and my regard increased with the passing years. I felt thankful for the privilege of blessing him in his last hours. The date of the final interview was March 30, 1901. (238–39)

Orson's star continued to rise, and he was officially recognized for his appointed work in the Historian's Office:

> At the General Conference of the Church, in April, 1902, I was sustained as an assistant to the Church Historian, President Anthon H. Lund. I had held this position for over three years, without bearing the title. Andrew Jensen, A. Milton Musser, and Brigham H. Roberts were likewise sustained as Assistant Church Historians.
>
> In the preceding January the State Historical Society had elected me its president, and I held that office for the ensuing five years. The first President of the Society was Franklin D. Richards, at whose death, in December, 1899, I delivered the memorial address.
>
> Busy as ever, I wrote for various publications in and out of the Church, often preparing articles for others to sign, whose names were more widely known, more influential, and consequently more potent for good. Occasionally, articles to be signed by myself were solicited for histories, magazines and other publications. (240)[10]

In 1929 Elder B. H. Roberts described one such occasion from the past: "Sometime ago Elder Orson F. Whitney and myself were called into the office of the First Presidency and informed that the publishers of the *Encyclopedia Britannica* had applied to [Senator/Apostle Reed Smoot] for a revised article on the 'Mormon Church' and its 'Doctrine,' to take the place of its then present unsatisfactory article. While the new article would be accredited to [Smoot] as author, it was their desire that we jointly should prepare the manuscript for it. This, of course, we were both willing to do for the sake of the Church and furthering its interests."[11]

Of the various articles or statements ghost-written over the years by Whitney, perhaps the most famous was composed in October 1909, entitled, "The Origin of Man," that was signed by the First Presidency of Joseph F. Smith, John R. Winder, and Anthon H. Lund, and issued in November of that year. President Lund commented: "The [First] Presidency read the article on the origin of Man written by Orson F. Whitney. It was much improved from the original [draft]. As it will go out under our names the

Presidency made a few changes."[12] This official document authoritatively clarified for the Church that God Himself created mankind (Adam and Eve) in his image, both spirit and physical body, not using scientifically theorized evolutionary processes. Elder Whitney's scintillating phraseology is therein fully evident:

> It is held by some that Adam was not the first man upon this earth, and that the original human being was a development from lower orders of the animal creation. These, however, are the theories of men. The word of the Lord declares that Adam was "the first man of all men" (Moses 1:34), and we are therefore in duty bound to regard him as the primal parent of our race. It was shown to the brother of Jared that all men were created in the beginning after the image of God; and whether we take this to mean the spirit or the body, or both, it commits us to the same conclusion: Man began life as a human being, in the likeness of our heavenly Father.
>
> True it is that the body of man enters upon its career as a tiny germ or embryo, which becomes an infant, quickened at a certain stage by the spirit whose tabernacle it is, and the child, after being born, develops into a man. There is nothing in this, however, to indicate that the original man, the first of our race, began life as anything less than a man, or less than the human germ or embryo that becomes a man.
>
> Man, by searching, cannot find out God. Never, unaided, will he discover the truth about the beginning of human life. The Lord must reveal Himself, or remain unrevealed; and the same is true of the facts relating to the origin of Adam's race—God alone can reveal them. Some of these facts, however, are already known, and what has been made known it is our duty to receive and retain.[13]

In 1902, Whitney ran for the elective office of Salt Lake County Clerk, but lost, and therefore continued his work in the Historian's Office until 1906.[14] Orson also continued work on his poetry, and read "Elias, an Epic of the Ages" to packed houses, sometimes consisting of members of the First Presidency and other prominent people of Utah. One reading came in the Beehive house, the official residence of the President of the Church at that time. The poem was a matter of great personal importance to Whitney, and the honorary committee that took responsibility for its publication included the governor.

On December 23, 1905, Orson Whitney, recognized by then as one of the two greatest orators in the Church (B. H. Roberts was the other), spoke to a packed audience in the Salt Lake Tabernacle on the one hundredth birthday of the Prophet Joseph Smith. Roberts had been invited, but due to illness, all the time fell to Whitney (258). He continued to fill numerous speaking engagements and serve as bishop.

No date is given for the following narration from Whitney's autobiography, and he was evidently not at home when the episode occurred, but he still felt it to be a precious incident connected with his immediate family:

> Among the many interesting incidents connected with our little home on the hillside, there is one that should always be cherished by the members of my family. It will be better understood after reading what the Book of Mormon has to say upon the subject of the Three Nephites. My wife thus relates the incident:
>
> It happened many years ago. My husband was away, and the only members of the family in the house besides myself, were three of our little boys. It was early spring, and I was busy house-cleaning. Hearing the doorbell ring, I opened the door, and there stood an elderly man, with white hair and beard, clean, neatly dressed, straight as an arrow, and altogether respectable in appearance and respectful in manner. He carried a cane and held his hat in hand. He asked me if I could help him. I told him that I had no money, but if he needed food I would gladly give him some. Said he: "I would be very grateful."
>
> The unusual answer somewhat surprised me, but being much occupied, I paid slight attention. Showing him down into the dining room on the basement floor, I spread before him what food I had, and left him sitting at the table. The little boys were playing there at the time, and I told them to stay with the stranger and wait on him, while I returned to my work on the floor above.
>
> After a while I heard the patter of feet running up the stairs, and here came the boys, all breathless and excited, the oldest (Murray) exclaiming: "Mama, I bet that was one of the Three Nephites!"
>
> "What makes you think so?" I inquired.
>
> Here spoke up the second boy (Bert), who had a toothache when the stranger arrived: "I was holding my hand to my face, and he said, 'Son, what is troubling you?' 'My tooth aches,' I said. 'It will trouble you no more,' said he. And it stopped right then and hasn't ached since."
>
> The boys told me that the visitor, when departing by a back door, spoke these words: "Peace be unto you and your house." They likewise related how they rushed out after him, not seeing him pass the windows, and looked up and down the street and through the back yard, but could catch no glimpse of him.
>
> I do not think that I am over-credulous regarding such matters. But the impression made upon my mind by that venerable stranger and

> his pleasing address, coupled with the excitement of the boys and their expressed conviction as to who he was, caused me to marvel. I have never been able to entirely banish the thought that possibly the boys were right. (260–61)

Orson had lived a vibrantly useful life, despite certain errors in judgment that he eventually overcame and put behind him. He had served well and faithfully for the most part. His friend Joseph F. Smith knew his heart and mind as did his God. Under these circumstances, Orson Whitney's life was changed forever:

> The greatest honor that my life has known came to me in the month of April, 1906, when I was ordained an Apostle and called into the Council of the Twelve. This advancement, though a complete surprise to me and mine, fulfilled more than one prediction made concerning me during the previous quarter of a century.
>
> Three vacancies had existed in the Council, caused by the death of Marriner W. Merrill, and the retirement [resignation] of two other of the Twelve, John W. Taylor and Matthias F. Cowley, who had found themselves out of harmony with the changed attitude of the Church relative to the further practice of plural marriage. Those vacancies were filled when George F. Richards, Orson F. Whitney and David O. McKay became Apostles.
>
> Called at the General Conference in the Tabernacle, on Sunday the eighth of April, we were ordained by President Joseph F. Smith in the Temple, on the day following. Others taking part in the ordinations were Presidents John R. Winder and Anthon H. Lund; Elders Francis M. Lyman, John Henry Smith, Rudger Clawson, Hyrum M. Smith, George Albert Smith and Charles W. Penrose, of the Council of the Twelve; and Patriarch John Smith. The remaining members of the Council—George Teasdale, Heber J. Grant and Reed Smoot—were absent on duty elsewhere. (262)

His call to the apostleship was a truly special and valued experience for him, and he took pains to be observant of an issue related to his ordination and was humbled by the honor thus conferred upon him:

> Except in one particular, my ordination blessing, stenographically reported by Secretary George F. Gibbs, did not differ materially from the blessings pronounced upon Brothers Richards and McKay. And that exceptional item was left out of the Secretary's report, through a misunderstanding. The President had said that I would represent the Prophet Joseph Smith in the Council of the Twelve; but Brother Gibbs

The Council of the Twelve outside the Salt Lake Temple, 1930. Rear, left to right: Joseph Fielding Smith, James E. Talmage, Stephen L. Richards, Richard R. Lyman, Melvin J. Ballard, John A. Widtsoe. Front: Rudger Clawson, Reed Smoot, George Albert Smith, George F. Richards, Orson F. Whitney, and David O. McKay. Elder Whitney died one year later. (USHS)

> omitted this promise, so precious to me, thinking, as he subsequently explained, that those words were uttered after the President had taken his hands from off my head—which was not the case. I was right under his hands when the words were spoken, while the Secretary was writing at a table on the other side of the room.
>
> I forbore to mention the matter upon first reading the written blessing, supposing the President had seen fit to eliminate that part; and it was not until after his death and then upon the suggestion of his successor, that I inquired of Brother Gibbs and learned from him that he alone was responsible in the premises. Of course, the mere omission of words from a sheet of paper would not invalidate an act done by divine authority. But it would have been gratifying to me to have had the blessing just as it was delivered, as a matter of record.
>
> In the afternoon of April 9, the day of my ordination, the General Authorities, with their wives, met by invitation at the home of President John R. Winder, where we had dinner and spent a very happy evening. Our host, in greeting his guests, expressed the conviction that the right men had been chosen to fill the vacancies in the Council of the Twelve, adding that the impression made upon him to that effect was as vivid as the sudden turning on of a light.
>
> President Smith voiced a similar sentiment, and while still upon his feet, said: "I have wanted Orson in this Council for years." He had previously referred to me as "one of the staunchest and most faithful men in the Church," one who had "rendered valiant service as bishop, poet, orator and historian;" and he added: "I have long thought that he should stand among the leaders of this people." He mentioned my mother's relationship to the Prophet, also my kinship to President Heber C. Kimball, and said that I would represent both in the councils of the Priesthood. (262–63)

Elder Whitney did not leave much of a record in print regarding his apostolic service, feeling that an overview of the weekly routine was all that was necessary:

> During most of the time since my ordination, my duties have consisted of weekly visits to the Stakes, with occasional tours of missions, and such other service as the presiding authorities have required of me. Once a week, at a regular council meeting, the Apostles report their labors to the First Presidency and to one another, and join in prayer and the transaction of important Church business. There we receive our appointments from the President of the Twelve, sanctioned by the First Presidency, with general directions to govern us in the discharge of

> our sacred duties. On certain days we set apart and instruct missionaries, and on any and every day do whatever needs doing for the good of the Cause. Every three months the Twelve, or as many of them as can assemble, come together in a quarterly meeting, and every six months they convene in joint session with the First Council of the Seventy and such of the mission presidents as are able to attend; the latter reporting conditions and prospects in their fields of labor and receiving such advice and instruction as the Apostles see fit to impart. (265–66)

Miracles followed Elder Whitney's ministry. He wrote of one incident "which had passed out of my mind until recalled by one of the chief actors therein. A Sister Hanks, wife of one of the bishops, had become blind. She craved from me a blessing, which I gave. While my hands were on her head her sight came back, restored by faith and the power of God. Strange to say, I had forgotten this until Sister Hanks reminded me of it in after years" (269).

He reflected deeply upon such experiences as this and others like it scattered throughout his productive and faith-filled life.

> They are quite frequent in the experience of the Elders of the Church. I had been for some time an Apostle when the following incident took place. I was summoned with other brethren, one evening, to the bedside of a woman possessed of an evil spirit, which cursed us all the while we were blessing her. Tied down to the bedstead where she lay, the poor creature writhed and struggled violently. When, as voice in the administration, I mentioned the authority of the Priesthood, the obsessing spirit cried out, "You haven't any." I then rebuked the demon in the name of Jesus Christ, and commanded it to "come out of her." Instantly she collapsed, limp as a rag, and that was the end of the trouble. She recovered, but had no recollection of what had occurred while she was under the evil spell. (269–70)

Elder Whitney continued in demand as one of the finest public speakers in the Church. His phenomenal memory enabled him to call up text and verse and recite at will; his knowledge of the gospel allowed him to preach with powerful insight. Others appreciated his remarkable oratorical gifts, likely excelled by no one in the Church. "No man among the Church Authorities has commanded my love and reverence more than President Joseph F. Smith," he wrote. "He was no flatterer, but was always genuinely appreciative of anything commendable done by another. How well I remember one occasion in the Tabernacle, when he leaned over from the President's stand, after I had spoken, to whisper in my ear: 'Oh, Orson, I did so enjoy your discourse. I could have listened for another hour. It was altogether too short'" (278).

Whitney's literary skills and doctrinal acumen were put to use on formal church reading committees: "I served on various important committees—one to revise [correct minor errors in] the Book of Mormon prior to the bringing out of a new edition; and another, to pass upon the *Doctrine and Covenants Commentary*, a work compiled by Hyrum M. Smith and J. M. Sjodahl. All along since becoming prominent in my native community, I have had work of that kind to do. Robert C. Webb's 'The Real Mormonism,' and B. H. Roberts's splendid *History of the Church*, both were read, before publication, to a committee of which I was a member" (293).

Many years passed in the routine and constant grind of apostolic service. Being at the call of the First Presidency to come and go as requested meant further adventures were in store for Elder Whitney, although this assignment was to bring with it the greatest health-related trial of his life:

> In the Spring of 1921 I received an appointment to preside over the European Mission. It did not surprise me, nor was it at all unwelcome. I had long anticipated such a call, and was glad of a change in the scene and routine of my labors, being somewhat worn down, not so much by regular work, as by months of extra toil resulting in the production of a new book, "Saturday Night Thoughts," completed just before I left for Europe.
>
> My first intimation of the appointment came from President Heber J. Grant, while I was sitting one evening with my wife at a dramatic performance in the Social Hall. The President, coming from the other side of the house and taking a seat just behind us, asked me how I would like to go to Europe to preside. I answered that I would regard it as a high honor and a great opportunity; but mentioned the fact that I had an ailment which might require an operation, and would like time enough to make up my mind whether to have it done on this or the other side of "the water." He said I could have all the time I wanted, and there the matter rested. Subsequently I decided to postpone the operation and start upon my mission as soon as I could shape affairs to that end.
>
> I was set apart by President Grant on the 19th of May, and left Salt Lake City on the evening of the 24th. My wife went with me, also as a missionary, set apart to supervise the Relief Societies in European lands. (306)

In England, Elder Whitney was operated on for his "ailment" the nature of which he did not disclose in his life story though it is hinted to be heart-related. His recounting of his slow recovery after the operation is heart-wrenching and poignant (341–49). Something resembling a severe extended nervous breakdown blasted him while convalescing after the operation and necessitated a release from his mission and a long, traumatizing recovery period.

Finally home and in the hands of loved ones caring for him, Elder Whitney's trial was not over:

> Very soon President Grant and members of the Council of the Twelve, with other Elders, came to call on us. They blessed me repeatedly, promising complete restoration and continued usefulness in my sacred calling.
>
> At that time I could neither read nor write, nor even think clearly. There was a weight on my brain like an iron clamp, and I felt when walking as if I were lifting great chunks of lead. I doubt if any of the brethren, or even the members of my family fully understood my case or realized what I was passing through. How could they without a like experience? . . .
>
> The sympathetic reader can well imagine, therefore, the amount of privation that my long illness entailed. It was the loneliest, and in some respects the saddest period of my life. (348)

As time passed, he found things that he could do. "Early in December, at the solicitation of Hon. Franklin S. Richards, I undertook the revision [editing] of a manuscript of twenty-two chapters covering the life of his father, President Franklin D. Richards. This manuscript, prepared by a grandson [Franklin L. West] of President Richards, I carefully revised, added some parts, and engineered the book through the press, receiving for that service the sum of five hundred dollars. Though working hard, I felt the benefit of the literary exercise. It was virtually the beginning of my mental rejuvenation" (351).

Elder Whitney completely recovered his health and resumed his apostolic service. Choice experiences continued to be his. At some unnamed point in his life, he told of a special dream that came to him: "Many years later I had a dream of President Young which much impressed me. I seemed to be in a meeting where he had charge, and as I entered he came toward me, took my hand, and greeted me with affectionate warmth. His face beamed with smiles. He looked the embodiment of spiritual power. He spoke no word, but his whole manner seemed to

Orson F. Whitney (USHS)

say: 'God bless you! You are doing well, and I am watching over you with interest and satisfaction.' The impression made by the dream was most happifying" (94–95). When Whitney bore his special witness of the Savior, he could do it with sure knowledge—"During the M.I.A. Jubilee in June, I spoke at the Sunday evening service in the Tabernacle. My discourse was on the slogan: 'We stand for an individual testimony of the divinity of Jesus Christ.' In the course of my address I related my dream-vision of the Savior." (355–56)

In his patriarchal blessing, he was told he would command the elements by priesthood power. He recorded one such instance, though he noted there had been others: "At Wasatch, in Little Cottonwood Canyon [east of Salt Lake City], a fierce mountain storm was beating upon the tent where lay my sick wife, trying to sleep. The thunder and lightning were terrific, and nearly drove her wild. Offering up a silent prayer, I rebuked the tempest in the name of the Lord, commanding it to depart. Not another flash, not another bolt was seen or heard, where we were. But far down the canyon muttered the faint remnant of the retreating storm" (413).

He had also been promised communion with those loved departed souls who now reside beyond the veil. Again, this pronouncement was fulfilled:

> Early on the morning of April 24, 1918 . . . while I lay on my pillow, half asleep, half awake, a pair of hands were laid upon my head. My first thought was that someone was in the house who ought not to be, and that I must lie perfectly still in order to be safe. But the touch was so soft and gentle that all fear soon left me, and with my own hands I took hold of those resting upon my head. They were a woman's hands. Presently I saw my wife Zina, who had been dead for eighteen years. She was hovering over me. I held out my arms to her, and she came into them. It was all so real. I could not doubt that she was actually there, a guardian angel, watching over her children and me. (413).

In May 1930, Elder Whitney arranged to have his autobiography published, one of the last major acts of his life. He died of influenza on May 16, 1931, in Salt Lake City. Such was the extraordinary life of Orson F. Whitney, a major contributor from the past to *Latter Leaves from the Life of Lorenzo Snow.*[15]

Eliza R. Snow (USHS)

Chapter 1

A Review: From Birth to the Apostleship

Orson F. Whitney wrote *Latter Leaves in the Life of Lorenzo Snow* as a sequel to Eliza R. Snow Smith's *Biography and Family Record of Lorenzo Snow,* first published in 1884. As the title wording "latter" suggests, this means the present volume primarily covers the latter years of President Snow's life, from 1884 to 1901. Because most readers will not have read and will not possess *Biography and Family Record,* even in one of the public domain reprint or online editions, this chapter and the next comprise a highly condensed and summarized version of Eliza's production, with supplementary material added.[1] This overview is designed to aid the reader with a fuller perspective of Lorenzo Snow's first seventy years, at which point the story is pursued in much greater detail.[2]

Lorenzo Snow, son of Oliver and Rosetta L. Pettibone Snow, was born April 3, 1814, in Mantua, Portage County, Ohio. His father was a native of Massachusetts, his mother of Connecticut, and they were descendants of the genuine Puritan stock—those who fled from religious persecution in the Old World and landed on Plymouth Rock.

Early in the settlement of that portion of country, his parents (with their family, consisting of two daughters, Leonora Abigail and Eliza Roxcy) left the home of their youth and moved to what was at that period considered the extreme West, or, as it was sometimes styled, "the jumping off place," and settled in Mantua, Portage County, Ohio, making the eleventh family in the township. There, two daughters and three sons were added to the family: Amanda Percy, Melissa, Lorenzo, Lucius Augustus, and Samuel Pearce.

Although a farmer by occupation, his father was much abroad on public business, and Lorenzo, being the eldest of the three brothers,

Lorenzo Snow was raised but not born in this home in Mantua, Portage County, Ohio. (Photo used courtesy of Cheryl McClellan.)

was left in charge and, early in life, became accustomed to responsibilities, which he discharged with scrupulous punctuality and that inflexibility of purpose which ensures success. From early childhood, Lorenzo exhibited the energy and decision of character, which have marked his progress in subsequent life. Ever a student, at home as well as in school (most of his schooling after his twelfth year was during the winter terms), a book was his constant companion when disengaged from filial duties. With the exception of one term in a high school in Ravenna, Ohio, also a special term of tuition under a Hebrew professor, he completed his scholastic training in Oberlin College. Through the solicitation of an intimate friend connected with the college, he was induced to enter, and through whose influence, as a special favor, he was admitted.

Although religiously trained from infancy, up to this time Lorenzo had devoted little or no attention to the subject of religion, at least not sufficiently to decide in preference of any particular sect. In the progress of his development, his ambition strongly led in the direction of military distinction, though this ambition was not to be fulfilled. Instead he decided to attend Oberlin College. On his way to Oberlin, he accidentally fell in company with David W. Patten, an incident to which he frequently refers as one of those seemingly trivial occurrences in human life that leave an indelible trace. Lorenzo remembered:

> We traveled together on horseback from my father's home, at Mantua, Ohio, to Kirtland, a distance of perhaps twenty-five miles, he on his return from some missionary labor, I to commence a course of studies at Oberlin College.
>
> On the way our conversation fell upon religion and philosophy, and being young and having enjoyed some scholastic advantages, I was at first disposed to treat his opinions lightly, especially so as they were not always clothed in grammatical language; but as he proceeded in his

> earnest and humble way to open up before my mind the plan of salvation, I seemed unable to resist the knowledge that he was a man of God and that his testimony was true. I felt pricked in my heart.
>
> This he evidently perceived, for almost the last thing he said to me, after hearing his testimony, was that I should go to the Lord before retiring at night and ask him for myself. This I did with the result that from the day I met this great Apostle, all my aspirations have been enlarged and heightened immeasurably. This was the turning point in my life.[3]

Lorenzo became thoroughly acquainted with the profession and the practice of the Methodists, by which that popular institution was controlled; and, although he cherished friendly regards for the people, he was unfavorably impressed with their system of religion. A short time before leaving Oberlin, he wrote, asking me many questions concerning revealed religion, at the same time saying, "*If there is nothing better than is to be found here in Oberlin College, good bye to all religions.*" I answered his questions, and knowing he intended crowning his studies with a thorough knowledge of Hebrew, invited him to come to Kirtland at the close of his term in Oberlin.

There is some question at this point as to how much Lorenzo really knew about Mormonism. His sister Eliza had spoken to him of it, and as mentioned he had visited at some length with Elder David Patten, but exactly when he met Joseph Smith is uncertain.[4] His own account states:

> I saw for the first time Joseph Smith, the Prophet of the Lord. He was holding a meeting in the town of Hiram. He was about three miles from where I was born and brought up. He was standing by a door and talking to an audience of about 250 persons under a bowery. I was about eighteen years of age. I had heard something about the Mormon Prophet, I felt some anxiety to see him and judge for myself, as he was generally believed to be a false prophet. My mother and my two sisters (one of whom was Eliza R. Snow) received the principles of Mormonism and were baptized. At the time I refer to, Joseph Smith was not what would be called a fluent speaker. He simply bore his testimony to what the Lord had manifested to him, to the dispensations of the Gospel which had been committed to him, and to the authority that he possessed. As I looked upon him and listened, I thought to myself that a man bearing such a wonderful testimony as he did, and having such a countenance as he possessed, could hardly be a false prophet. He certainly could not have been deceived, it seemed to me, and if he was a deceiver he was deceiving the people knowingly; for when he testified

that he had had a conversation with Jesus, the Son of God, and had talked with Him personally, as Moses is said to have talked with God upon Mount Sinai and that he had also heard the voice of the Father, he was telling something that he either knew to be false or positively true. I was not at that time what might be called a religious boy, but I was interested in what I saw and heard there. However, being busy in other directions, it passed measurably out of my mind. Some two years and a half later, business called me to Kirtland. My two sisters had been there for some time, and I made my home with them. There I became perfectly acquainted with Joseph Smith, the Prophet. I sat at his table and had a number of conversations with him. . . .

Talking with President Joseph Smith, and being with him and with his father, I could not help but believe that there was something more than common in what was called Mormonism.[5]

Further:

It was Sunday, June 5, [1836], about a week after I arrived in Kirtland, that I first saw Father Smith [Joseph Smith Sr]. He was holding a patriarchal blessing meeting, in the Kirtland Temple, at which there were twelve or fifteen persons present. I was then searching to know whether there was any truth in Mormonism. I had never experienced anything supernatural, with one slight exception, and I did not know that anything supernatural had ever occurred among the children of men. I had heard Methodists, Presbyterians, and others relate their experiences, but I thought I could attribute all they said to natural causes. It was hard for me to be convinced that there could be such extraordinary manifestations as I saw exhibited in visiting the temple and listening to the testimonies of persons and hearing the extraordinary accounts of what the Lord had manifested to them.

It was at my sister's invitation that I attended this meeting conducted by Father Smith. I listened with astonishment to him telling the brethren and sisters their parentage, their lineage, and other things which I could not help but believe he knew nothing about, save as the Spirit manifested them unto him. After listening to several patriarchal blessings pronounced upon the heads of different individuals with whose history I was acquainted, and of whom I knew the Patriarch was entirely ignorant, I was struck with astonishment to hear the peculiarities of those persons positively and plainly referred to in their blessings. I was convinced that an influence, superior to human prescience, dictated his words. . . .

After this meeting, my sister introduced me to him, and in the course of the conversation he remarked: "Why, Brother Snow (he called me Brother Snow, although I had not been baptized, and did not know that I ever would be), do not worry," he said, "I discover that you are trying to understand the principles of Mormonism." "Yes," I replied, "that was the object I had in view." "Well," said he, "do not worry, but pray to the Lord and satisfy yourself; study the matter over, compare the scriptures with what we are teaching; talk with the brethren that you are acquainted with, and after a time you will be convinced that Mormonism is of God, and you will be baptized."...

He surprised me when he said, "Don't worry, take it calmly and the Lord will show you the truth of this great latter-day work, and you will *want* to be baptized." . . . I studied the principles. . . . I heard the Prophet discourse upon the grandest of subjects. At times he was filled with the Holy Ghost, speaking as with the voice of an archangel and filled with the power of God, his whole person shone and his face was lightened until it appeared as the whiteness of the driven snow. . . . Finally my prayers were answered and I was convinced of the truth sufficiently to want to be baptized to get a knowledge for myself of the testimony that Joseph Smith had seen God. . . .

In my investigations, [Lorenzo Snow writes in his journal], of the principles taught by the Latter-day Saints, which I proved, by comparison, to be the same as those mentioned in the New Testament taught by Christ and His Apostles, I was thoroughly convinced that obedience to those principles would impart miraculous powers, manifestations and revelations.

On Sunday, June 19, 1836, in the Kirtland Temple, Joseph arose in the pulpit just before the meeting closed and said: "A young man by the name of Lorenzo Snow wishes to be baptized, and Brother John Boynton [who was then one of the Twelve Apostles] will baptize him." After the meeting I was baptized in the stream that ran through Kirtland, and I was confirmed by Hyrum Smith who, with some others, laid hands upon me.

I received no special manifestation at that time, but I was perfectly satisfied that I had done what was wisdom for me to do under the circumstances. I had studied the scriptures and was convinced that the Gospel as preached by the Latter-day Saints was in accordance with that taught by the Son of God and by His Apostles in former days.

A peaceful, good spirit came upon me that I had never experienced before, and I felt satisfied at the sacrifice I had made.[6]

Lorenzo narrated further comments made by Father Smith, at the conclusion of the blessing meeting: "I remember an incident which occurred in Kirtland when I received my first patriarchal blessing from Father Smith. A better man never existed, nor was there a man better loved than he. I was introduced by my sister Eliza R., though at that time I was not a Latter-day Saint and had no idea of becoming one. He said to me: Don't worry, take it calmly and the Lord will show you, and you will want to be baptized. He told me another thing that greatly surprised me. He said, you will be great, and as great as you want to be, as great as God Himself, and you will not wish to be greater."[7] (The last comment from the Prophet's father would perplex Lorenzo for some years until he received a vision that explained it to him in great clarity.)

Meanwhile, Lorenzo continued to learn the doctrines of the Latter-day Saints. In Lorenzo's journal we find the following incidents recorded by himself:

> I was baptized by Elder John Boynton, then one of the Twelve Apostles, June, 1836, in Kirtland, Ohio. Previous to accepting the ordinance of baptism, in my investigations of the principles taught by the Latter-day Saints, which I proved, by comparison, to be the same as those mentioned in the New Testament taught by Christ and His Apostles, I was thoroughly convinced that obedience to those principles would impart miraculous powers, manifestations and revelations. With sanguine expectation of this result, I received baptism and the ordinance of laying on of hands by one who professed to have divine authority; and, having thus yielded obedience to these ordinances, I was in constant expectation of the fulfillment of the promise of the reception of the Holy Ghost.
>
> The manifestation did not immediately follow my baptism, as I had expected, but, although the time was deferred, when I did receive it, its realization was more perfect, tangible and miraculous than even my strongest hopes had led me to anticipate.
>
> Some two or three weeks after I was baptized, one day while engaged in my studies, I began to reflect upon the fact that I had not obtained a *knowledge* of the truth of the work—that I had not realized the fulfillment of the promise "he that doeth my will shall know of the doctrine," and I began to feel very uneasy. I laid aside my books, left the house, and wandered around through the fields under the oppressive influence of a gloomy, disconsolate spirit, while an indescribable cloud of darkness seemed to envelop me. I had been accustomed, at the close of the day, to retire for secret prayer, to a grove a short distance from my lodgings, but at this time I felt no inclination to do so. The spirit of prayer had departed and the heavens seemed like brass over my head.

> At length, realizing that the usual time had come for secret prayer, I concluded I would not forego my evening service, and, as a matter of formality, knelt as I was in the habit of doing, and in my accustomed retired place, but not feeling as I was wont to feel.
>
> I had no sooner opened my lips in an effort to pray, than I heard a sound, just above my head, like the rustling of silken robes, and immediately the Spirit of God descended upon me, completely enveloping my whole person, filling me, from the crown of my head to the soles of my feet, and Oh, the joy and happiness I felt! No language can describe the almost instantaneous transition from a dense cloud of mental and spiritual darkness into a refulgence of light and knowledge, as it was at that time imparted to my understanding. I then received a perfect knowledge that God lives, that Jesus Christ is the Son of God, and of the restoration of the holy Priesthood, and the fulness of the Gospel. It was a complete baptism—a tangible immersion in the heavenly principle or element, the Holy Ghost; and even more real and physical in its effects upon every part of my system than the immersion by water; dispelling forever, so long as reason and memory last, all possibility of doubt or fear in relation to the fact handed down to us historically, that the Babe of Bethlehem is truly the Son of God; also the fact that He is now being revealed to the children of men, and communicating knowledge, the same as in the Apostolic times. I was perfectly satisfied, as well I might be, for my expectations were more than realized, I think I may safely say in an infinite degree.
>
> I cannot tell how long I remained in the full flow of the blissful enjoyment and divine enlightenment, but it was several minutes before the celestial element which filled and surrounded me began gradually to withdraw. On arising from my kneeling posture, with my heart swelling with gratitude to God, beyond the power of expression, I felt I *knew* that He had conferred on me what only an omnipotent being can confer that which is of greater value than all the wealth and honors worlds can bestow. That night, as I retired to rest, the same wonderful manifestations were repeated, and continued to be for several successive nights.[8]

After receiving this testimony and witness of the actual living reality of the Father and the Son and their latter-day prophet, Lorenzo had much to consider.

> I received these truths with an open heart, and I was determined not to rest there. I was then attending a high school in the temple at Kirtland, and preparing myself for some eastern college or university. A professor by the name of Haws was teaching us, and President Woodruff and

other brethren attended this school. I began to be a little worried in my mind whether, after having received this wonderful knowledge, it was proper for me to remain without testifying in reference to it. Young men who had been sent out upon missions were returning and testifying of the blessings that had attended them in their traveling without purse and scrip in Ohio and other places, and I began to think that, instead of preparing myself for an eastern college or university, I ought to start out and bear testimony to what the Lord had so fully given me a knowledge of. At the same time I did not like to give up my prospects of an education, because I had had it in mind for a long time, and I then had the opportunity and the means to accomplish it. I concluded to go for advice to President Joseph Smith's first counselor [Sidney Rigdon], and with whom I had been acquainted before he joined the Mormons, when he was a Campbellite and used to preach in my father's neighborhood. I told him what I wanted, and he said, "Brother Snow, I would not give anyone else such counsel as I feel to give you, under the circumstances. If I were in your place, I would go on with my intentions and get an education." That was just the very thing I wanted him to say, and it pleased me, I was contented for a time; but in the winter season, hearing these young Elders testify of their success in preaching the Gospel, I began to think about it still more. The Lord had given me a knowledge that He was coming upon the earth, and that there was a preparation necessary to be made; He had given me all that I had asked for, and more; for the baptism which I received, of the Holy Ghost and the perfect knowledge then given to me was more real and convincing than my immersion in the cold water; and I felt that there was a responsibility resting upon me. So I shut up my books, laid my Latin and Greek aside, and I have never seen them since. I started out without purse and scrip, and under the circumstances that was about as great a sacrifice as I have ever made. I had not been accustomed to depend upon anybody for food or shelter. If I were going off any distance, my father would make sure that I started out with plenty of money for my expenses. And now, to go out and ask for something to eat and for a place to lay my head, was very trying to me, it being so different to my training.

I remember my experience the first night after I started out. About twenty miles from Kirtland I stopped at my aunt's. She was a Presbyterian, a very wealthy woman, and a woman of considerable experience. I was telling her that I expected to be treated like other Elders, turned out of doors, etc. and she said, "Lorenzo, I don't believe a word of that. They will know you are an honest man, and you will not be turned out." "Well," I replied, "I do not expect to be treated any better than my brethren,"—and I was not. After leaving my aunt that night, I walked

> several miles, and as the sun was going down I thought it was about time to make an experiment and ask for some place in which to stop. I did so, and I never shall forget the house—where it stood, its distance from the road, the picket fence, and the gate that I went through. I walked up to the house, knocked, and was bidden to come in. A gentleman and his wife were there, and I told them I was a "Mormon" Elder, traveling without purse or scrip, and would be very much obliged if I could get a night's lodging. They made some kind of an excuse. I told them I was not particular; the privilege to lie down on the floor with a blanket would suit me. But no, they did not want to keep me. Well, I had a little more courage when I came to the next house, but was met with the same objection. So it went on until I got to the ninth house, where I got a night's lodging, but had to leave without breakfast. The next day or two I arrived at one of my aunt's and preached there for the first time in my life. I was quite bashful then, and, not having spoken in public before, it was a very difficult thing for me to get up there and preach to my kindred and the neighbors who were called in. I remember that I prayed nearly all day preceding the night I was to speak. I went out by myself and asked the Lord to give me something to say. My aunt told me afterwards that she almost trembled when she saw me getting up to speak; but I opened my mouth and what I said I never did know, but my aunt said I spoke fine for about three quarters of an hour. I held another meeting the next night, and the night after that I was invited to speak in the Medina court house by the party who had it in charge. After I got through speaking there a gentleman came to me and said, "Now, Elder Snow, I am a much older man than you. You are a young man, just starting out, I see, to be a minister. I want to give you a little counsel. If you continue to talk as loud as you talked tonight, in six months you will be taken to the cemetery." I thanked him very much and told him I would try and benefit by his counsel. Then I thought I owed a duty to my uncles and aunts and my schoolmates, and they let me have the school house in which to preach to them. The house was nearly filled by my grandfather, my uncles and aunts, and a numerous lot of cousins. I thought I was going to convert them all, but after I got through talking and bearing testimony, all I could get from them was, "Well, Lorenzo is an honest boy, but he is deceived." Then I got the town house in the place where I was born and preached there, as well as in a Presbyterian meeting house. The result of it all was, I baptized a few, very few, of my classmates.[9]

Lorenzo received his patriarchal blessing from Father Joseph Smith (Sr.) in December 1836. This remarkable blessing became a source of spiritual strength to the new convert, as he pondered his future in the new life that had come to him as a Latter-day Saint. It included expressions almost unimaginable to those present, including the man who recorded it. "He [Father Smith] told me many extraordinary things. When the written blessing was shown to the Patriarch [for approval], he said that this brother [who wrote it down when spoken] has not written it all, as it was impossible for him, reared as he was in the sectarian traditions [of Protestant Christianity], to grasp it all, but I felt that it was enough. . . . He told me many extraordinary things that have occurred to me since in my past history, from 1836 to this hour."[10] (See Appendix 4 for the text of Lorenzo's patriarchal blessings.)

By 1838, Lorenzo's father Oliver left Kirtland and its persecution behind and moved to Adam-Ondi-Ahman.[11] (Sadly, most of Lorenzo's extended family and relatives rejected his efforts to teach them the restored gospel and became antagonistic toward the Mormon members of their widespread family.) On the journey, Lorenzo was placed in charge of a team and wagon, but became sick in Far West and had to remain at Sidney Rigdon's home, where he was nursed by Eliza for a few weeks until recovering. He then decided to continue his missionary service, traveling around Far West, where he was blessed for his labors by Father Smith and met Elder Thomas B. Marsh, then President of the Twelve Apostles. He found President Marsh sinking into apostasy and quickly left. During his travels in the area of Kentucky, he was saved from mob violence when one member of the mob mistook a Bible in Lorenzo's pocket for a pistol.

His travels and missionary work so weakened Lorenzo that he took some time off to work as a school teacher, during 1839 and early 1840. By May of that year, he moved on to Nauvoo, where the main body of Latter-day Saints were then beginning to settle and build a prosperous city and temple. While living in Nauvoo, Lorenzo received one of the great spiritual experiences and communications of his life:

> Early in the spring of 1840, I was appointed to a mission in England, and I started on or about the twentieth of May. I here record a circumstance which occurred a short time previous—one which has been riveted on my memory, never to be erased, so extraordinary was the manifestation. At the time, I was at the house of Elder H. G. Sherwood; he was endeavoring to explain the parable of our Savior, when speaking of the husbandman who hired servants and sent them forth at different hours of the day to labor in his vineyard.
>
> While attentively listening to his explanation, the Spirit of the Lord

rested mightily upon me—the eyes of my understanding were opened, and I saw as clear as the sun at noonday, with wonder and astonishment, the pathway of God and man. I formed the following couplet which expresses the revelation, as it was shown me, and explains Father Smith's dark saying to me at a blessing meeting in the Kirtland Temple, prior to my baptism, as previously mentioned in my first interview with the Patriarch.

As man now is, God once was:
As God now is, man may be.

I felt this to be a sacred communication, which I related to no one except my sister Eliza, until I reached England, when in a confidential private conversation with President Brigham Young, in Manchester, I related to him this extraordinary manifestation. (See Appendix 1 for further discussion of this experience.)

Lorenzo's trip to England was miserable for him, especially the ocean voyage with "deck passage," where he spent forty-two days enduring filth and privation. Once in England he served under the direction of Elder Brigham Young and others of the Twelve. He labored first in Manchester and then was called to preside over the branch and conference in London. He was successful in his work and baptized a number of English converts. Among other adventures, he found himself needing to cast evil spirits out of his living quarters, where they had come to trouble his slumber once too often.

As the presiding elder in London, Lorenzo was responsible for all the local affairs of the Church and was kept very busy. Letters to his parents and sister touch on some of his work:

I have sent you a tract [titled "The Only Way to be Saved"] which I have written and got published. I have published four thousand copies. It is expected that another edition will be wanted. Tho' they have been out of the press only a week or two, yet they have been mostly spoken for. Those of our publications which are cheap and the subject explained in easy and simple language is best liked in England and do the most good. . . . I have no time to idle but am constantly engaged, writing, publishing, preaching, meeting with the officers of the Church, prayer meetings, visiting the Saints as much as are seeking the Kingdom. I shall truly rejoice when I get thru' my labors in this country and [am] privileged to return home in peace realizing that I have faithfully discharged my duties to my Heavenly Father and cleaned my garments of the blood of this generation.[12]

Lorenzo found himself performing duties both joyous and sorrowful as he worked to build up the inner vessel and keep it free from corruption:

> So long as I remain on earth I wish to have grace sufficient to do right in all things. But as it seems to be the common lot of all Saints to err in some things I pray God that wherein I do err I may have meekness and humility sufficient to be set right.
>
> The work of the Lord is still prospering in the city. We have had one Kirtland[-type apostasy] scene in trimming up the Church, latterly lopping off some corrupt limbs and overgrown branches. . . . I can truly say that since I have been in London the Lord God of Israel has been my helper; otherwise I never could have stood and prospered.
>
> The Church is now firmly established, we have knocked out one rotten pillar of the Church, and one or two small braces, and have put in their places of the blood of Ephraim, firm as the eternal hills. We are now rejoicing in one mind and all pull on one and the same string. The Saints are many of them in London blessed with spiritual dreams, speaking in tongues, seeing visions, etc. . . . I have written letters to America quite latterly, some to our family, some to the Twelve, and to others. I baptized four last week, and some others have given in their names to be baptized this week. The Church is in a very prosperous condition. We have cut off five [members] latterly making eight we have expelled since I took charge of the Church. I have learned one thing if no more since I commenced teaching this generation; that is, to take a straightforward course in the name of the Lord, independent of sacrifice or consequences. . . . Remember me to Presidents Joseph and Sidney. I want they should not forget me in their prayers.[13]

Elder Parley P. Pratt, President of the European Mission, designated Elder Snow as the first counselor to the new mission president before leaving the mission field himself. One of his duties in this capacity put him in unusual company—Elder Lorenzo Snow presented to Her Majesty, Queen Victoria, and His Royal Highness, Prince Albert, through the politeness of Sir Henry Wheatley, two neatly bound copies of the Book of Mormon, which had been donated by President Brigham Young and left in the care of Elder Snow for that purpose.[14]

Soon thereafter, Elder Snow was released and assigned to assist 250 immigrants from England to Nauvoo. The return journey was more pleasant and accommodating than the former, although Elder Snow was surprised to be called upon to give a priesthood blessing to a sick ship's steward, who though on the verge of death, was healed.

The arrival of Elder Snow and his group at Nauvoo was a celebration, attended by a large crowd, among whom was the Prophet Joseph Smith. While Lorenzo was absent on this his first mission to Europe, changes had taken place with Eliza of eternal import, of which she supposed Lorenzo to be entirely ignorant. The Prophet Joseph had taught her the principle of plural marriage, and she was married to him for time and eternity. In consequence of the ignorance of most of the Saints as well as people of the world, on this subject, it was not mentioned only privately between the few whose minds were enlightened on the subject.

Not knowing how Lorenzo would receive it, Eliza did not feel at liberty and did not wish to assume the responsibility of instructing him in the principle of plural marriage, and either maintained silence or, to his indirect questioning, gave evasive answers. But she could not endure this—and something must be done. She informed her husband Joseph of the situation and requested him to open the subject to her brother. A favorable opportunity was soon presented, and, seated together on the lone bank of the Mississippi River, Joseph and Lorenzo had a most interesting conversation. The Prophet afterward told Eliza that he found that Lorenzo's mind had been previously enlightened on the subject in question and was ready to receive whatever the spirit of revelation from God should impart and while in England had given him an intimation of what at that time was, to many, a secret. This was the result of living near the Lord and holding communion with Him.

Lorenzo explained:

> There is no man that lives that had a more perfect knowledge of the principle of plural marriage, its holiness and divinity, than I had. It was revealed to me before the Prophet Joseph Smith explained it to me. I had been on a mission to England between two and three years, and before I left England I was perfectly satisfied in regard to something connected with plural marriage. When I returned to Nauvoo with my company of about 250, it was made manifest to me in reference to the truth of this principle. I was at Joseph Smith's one afternoon on a visit, and after conversing upon different subjects he asked me to walk out with him, as he wished to speak to me privately. We went down to the banks of the Mississippi river and sat down on a log that lay there in the sand. Then and there he explained to me the principle of plural marriage most perfectly and clearly; he told me in regard to the angel coming to him and making this principle known to him, and what would follow if he did not practice it. He informed me that my sister Eliza R. Snow

> had been sealed to him, and also mentioned the names of others. In that conversation, which lasted about half an hour, he told me all about it.[15]

At this private interview referred to above, the Prophet Joseph unbosomed his heart and described the trying mental ordeal he experienced in overcoming the repugnance of his feelings, the natural result of the force of education and social custom, relative to the introduction of plural marriage. He knew the voice of God—he knew the commandment of the Almighty to him was to go forward—to set the example and establish Celestial plural marriage. He knew that he had not only his own prejudices and prepossessions to combat and to overcome, but those of the whole Christian world stared him in the face; but God, who is above all, had given the commandment, and He must be obeyed. Yet the Prophet hesitated and deferred from time to time, until an angel of God stood by him with a drawn sword and told him that, unless he moved forward and established plural marriage, his priesthood would be taken from him and he should be destroyed! This testimony he not only bore to Lorenzo, but also to others—a testimony that cannot be gainsayed.[16] Lorenzo would later embrace this principle as authorized and taught to him.

He spent the next few years living in the vicinity of Nauvoo and its surroundings, teaching school at times and meeting with the Saints and Church leaders. He received a second patriarchal blessing in December 1843 (see Appendix 4). When persecution intensified, he was called to serve on a committee tasked with exploring possibilities for removal of the body of the Saints from Nauvoo to California or the Rocky Mountains. He was also called on a short-term mission to push for the candidacy of Joseph Smith for president of the United States. This work did not progress far when Joseph and Hyrum Smith were martyred in June 1844. Lorenzo thereby lost a true friend, counselor, and prophet.

Up to this time, Lorenzo lived as a bachelor. The great work in which he was engaged as a missionary of the gospel of salvation to the nations of the earth had so engrossed his mind and engaged the energies of his soul that virtually he had ignored the first commandment to multiply and replenish the earth. To devote his time, his talents to the ministry was his all-absorbing desire; and in consonance with this desire, he had cherished the idea that domestic responsibility would lessen his usefulness; and, until the law of celestial marriage was fully explained to him by the Prophet Joseph Smith, in a prolonged interview while the two were seated alone on the bank of the Mississippi river, as before related, he had not conceived the idea that marriage was one of the duties of the great mission of mortal life.

With him, marriage, as well as every other practical doctrine, was not only to be understood but also to be obeyed. It was one of his peculiarities to do nothing by halves; and when convinced of the duty of marriage, that it was a privilege accorded him in connection with his ministerial calling, he entered into it on an enlarged scale, by having two wives sealed to him in the holy bonds of matrimony, for time and eternity, at the same time; and not long after, another was added to the number, and then another. Thus, all at once, as it were, from the lone bachelor he was transformed into a husband invested with many domestic responsibilities. Probably a realizing sense of the fact that he had arrived at the mature age of thirty-one years in celibacy suggested to him the propriety of making up for lost time by more than ordinary effort.

Previous to the administration of those sacred sealing ordinances, he explained to each of the chosen ones the law, obligations, and object of celestial marriage, and that he might be expected to take others—that the ceremony being precisely the same for each wife, they would all occupy the same equal position, no one having a higher claim than another.

It was distinctly understood and agreed among them that their marriage relations should not, for the time being, be divulged to the world, but if circumstances should be such that he would wish to acknowledge as wife before the world either one of them, he should be permitted to do so. The first four wives were Charlotte Squires, Mary Adaline Goddard, Sarah Ann Prichard, and Harriett Amelia Squires (sister of the first).[17]

Early in the winter of 1845–46, the Nauvoo Temple was so far completed that the administration of the sacred ordinances of the holy priesthood was commenced and continued until about the first of February—thousands of the Saints receiving endowments and sealings. Lorenzo and his wives, among the number, had their washings, anointings, and endowments and were sealed at a holy altar, a privilege and blessing which they estimated above all earthly honors. When Lorenzo walked across the inner court of the temple proceeding to the altar, accompanied by his four wives, all stately appearing ladies, one of the temple officiates exclaimed, "And his train filled the Temple!"[18]

Sources suggest that some ambiguity exists for the exact dates of Lorenzo's marriages. Snow family sources list the following:

1) Charlotte Squires, married 1845; sealed January 17, 1846, in the Nauvoo Temple; born November 19, 1825; died December 23, 1849.
2) Mary Adaline Goddard, married December 19, 1845; sealed January 17, 1846, in the Nauvoo Temple; born March 8, 1812, died December 28, 1898.
3) Sarah Ann Prichard, married April 21, 1845; sealed January 17, 1846 in the Nauvoo Temple; born November 29, 1826; died December 1900.
4) Harriet Amelia Squires (sister of Charlotte), married June 17, 1845; sealed January 17, 1846 in the Nauvoo Temple; born September 13, 1819; died May 12, 1890.
5) Elenor Houtz, sealed June 1, 1848 in the Salt Lake Endowment House; born August 14, 1831; died September 14, 1896.
6) Caroline Horton, married and sealed October 9, 1853 in the Salt Lake Endowment House; born December 25, 1824; died February 21, 1857.
7) Mary Elizabeth Houtz, married and sealed March 5, 1857 in the Salt Lake Endowment House (another source says 1859); born May 19, 1840; died March 31, 1906.
8) Phoebe Amelia Woodruff (the daughter of President Wilford Woodruff), married and sealed April 4, 1859 in the Salt Lake Endowment House; born March 4, 1842; died February 15, 1919.
9) Sarah Minnie Jensen, married and sealed June 12, 1871, in the Salt Lake Endowment House; born October 6, 1855; died January 2, 1908.[19]

Another published source gives some alternate marriage dates and commentary.[20] Reason for the uncertainty can be found in the fact that at the time Lorenzo married his wives, polygamous unions were being kept from public knowledge, and such secrecy hinders the processes of historical inquiry. The lives of Lorenzo's wives await further historical attention. In addition, a tenth wife, Hannah Goddard, a sister of Mary Goddard, married Lorenzo on January 19, 1845, but soon thereafter deserted him for another man. While serving as President of the Council of the Twelve in the mid-1890s, Lorenzo spoke guardedly to his Brethren of this marriage: "President Snow . . . told of an experience of his youth, when one of his wives, 16 years old, was seduced by a man in this Church who was an editor, and this girl was afterwards sealed to her seducer without

Lorenzo Snow. Photo taken sometime after his call to the Twelve. (CA)

Lorenzo Snow (USHS)

Bro. Snow's knowledge. This man afterwards wanted to go to the temple, but he was not allowed to do so until he had obtained the permission of Bro. Snow. This editor afterwards raised several children by the woman he seduced."[21] In later years, critics and the uninformed have taken issue with the thought that some of Lorenzo's wives were as young as sixteen when they married him, but although unusual this was still acceptable for the culture of the time.

Not long after his first marriages, the Latter-day Saints were forced by increasing persecution and mob threats to leave Nauvoo and their beloved newly completed temple behind. The journey to Winter Quarters was miserable for most of the travelers. Lorenzo experienced a raging fever for several weeks and almost expired but survived to become the president of the branch of the Church in a small community nearby called Mt. Pisgah.[22] This assignment did not last long.

Early in the spring of 1848, Lorenzo was counseled by President Young to join him and his company and proceed to the valleys of the mountains—what would become Great Salt Lake City. Prompt to the instructions, he organized a company comprising about twenty-five families and started westward. On arrival at the "Horn," he was appointed captain over one of the "hundreds," embracing one hundred wagons. He selected Elder Leman Hyde captain over one "fifty," and Elder John Stoker captain of the other "fifty."[23]

Lorenzo, in an effort to better provide for the companies traveling to Salt Lake City, sent messengers to his extended Snow relatives, seeking donations of money, food, or other supplies. These messengers were rejected with the explanation that no one was going to help the Mormons. Lorenzo's own father, Oliver Snow, was unable to endure the persecution, loss of his farm, and new social status of association with the Mormons, so he had become embittered and turned against Joseph Smith.[24]

On the day his company left their encampment at the "Horn," Elenor Houtz was sealed to him by President Brigham Young. Lorenzo had met Elenor (often spelled Eleanor) years earlier. A family record relates:

> While the Houtz family were still living in Nauvoo, on a Sunday, Elenor and her parents were leaving church when Lorenzo Snow joined them. As they walked along, Lorenzo asked Elenor if she would promise to one day become his wife. Though at the time she was only fourteen she did make him that promise. It has been erroneously written that she married at fourteen, but church records and a letter written by Elenor to her uncle Jacob Houtz, states her marriage date as 19 January 1848. She was

> married [to Lorenzo] at Mt. Pisgah by President Brigham Young. In her letter she said, "Married at the Horn today and soon will start for the Salt Lake Valley. . . . I am now a Snow and darling Sister Eliza told me she is proud to be my sister."[25]

Lorenzo's journal reported: "I managed to discharge my obligations as captain of my 'hundred' very satisfactorily, for which I felt truly grateful to the Lord."

He arrived in the Salt Lake valley with his family without serious accident—all in good health and rejoicing in the blessings of prospective peace.[26] Soon after arrival, he was successful in obtaining what at that time was considered a fashionable log house.

On February 12, 1849, he was asked to put in an appearance at a meeting of the Quorum of the Twelve, then in session. Why or wherefore he could not imagine; but, with his characteristic promptitude, he went forthwith, ruminating in his mind whether he was called to answer some unsuspected charge or other; but a consciousness of faithful integrity to the duties assigned him predominated over every apprehension. To his great surprise, on arrival he was informed of his appointment to the Quorum of the Twelve and was then ordained a member of that quorum (age thirty-four). Elders Charles C. Rich, Erastus Snow, and Franklin D. Richards were also ordained into the quorum at the same time, under the hands of Brigham Young, Heber C. Kimball, Willard Richards, Parley P. Pratt, and John Taylor.

Elder Snow later recalled this sacred occasion:

> When I received the Apostleship, I well remember saying to my brethren, who were present, that very possibly the same sacrifices would be required of the modern Apostles as were experienced by the Apostles anciently, including their persecutions and martyrdoms. I said, in receiving this sacred calling, I felt as though it were ascending an altar where, perhaps, life itself would be offered. The Lord has said: "I have decreed in my heart that I will prove you in all things, whether you will abide in my Covenant even unto death; for, if ye will not abide in my Covenant, ye are not worthy of me." Seriously considering all this, I asked myself: Am I willing to accept these conditions—to so deny myself and suffer for the glory of God, and to honor and magnify this Apostleship?[27]

In the spring and summer he built a log house on his lot in Salt Lake City, which, although a little more ample in dimensions and a little improved in appearance, bore a striking resemblance to those he occupied in Pisgah.

Chapter 2

Life in the Apostolic Ministry—Founding Brigham City and Preaching the Gospel

Once established in the Salt Lake Valley, in 1849, Brigham Young placed Lorenzo Snow in charge of a community celebration of July 24 (the anniversary of the date the first company of pioneers entered the valley). Elder Snow carried out his assignment with a fair proportion of fanfare and pageantry. On this occasion there was singing, speeches, and the reading of the Declaration of Independence.

Elder Snow's next assignment was to travel among the Latter-day Saints to solicit donations meant to help the poor to cross the plains from eastern locations to Great Salt Lake City and the territory of Deseret (later Utah). This effort was the beginning of what became known as the Perpetual Emigration Fund. President Young recorded: "September 9, 1849: I presented the subject of a perpetual fund to gather the poor. The congregation voted that such a fund be instituted; that Willard Snow, John D. Lee, Lorenzo Snow, Franklin D. Richards, and John S. Fullmer, be a committee to collect and preserve said fund; and that Jedediah M. Grant take charge of the means [money] in the eastern country, under the direction of the First Presidency."[1]

Soon thereafter, at the October general conference, President Young called Elder Snow to establish a mission in Italy. He and others, forming a large missionary company, set out to meet adventures unknown. Lorenzo's journal reported some of these dramatic episodes:

> Recalling the scenes of the past, my mind reverts to the nineteenth of October, 1849, when, in solemn silence, I left what, next to God, was dearest to my heart—my friends, my loving wives and my dear little children. As I pursued my journey, in company with my brethren,

many conflicting feelings occupied my bosom. The gardens and fields in and around our new-born city, just emerging from nature's barrenness, through the faith, energy and the necessities of the exiled Saints, now struggling for subsistence, in a wild recess in the Rocky Mountains, were exchanged for the vast unbroken wilderness which lay spread out before us for a thousand miles.

If my mind still glanced onward, there was the stormy main, and, in the far distant perspective, a land of strangers—the field of my mission. We were hastening farther and still farther from the mighty magnet—Home. But we knew that the work in which we were engaged was to carry light to those who sat in darkness and in the Valley of the Shadow of Death, and our bosoms glowed with love and compassion toward them.

Some persons feared our horses were too enfeebled to bear us over the mighty plain; but when the snows began to fall, winds swept our pathway, and enabled us to pass without difficulty, while on our right and left the country was deeply covered for hundreds of miles.

One day, as we were taking our noontide meal, and our horses were quietly grazing on the prairie; the following thrilling scene occurred. A startling call resounded through our little camp, "*To arms! to arms! the Indians are upon us!*" All eyes were turned in the direction, and we beheld a spectacle, grand, imposing and frightful. Two hundred warriors, upon their furious steeds, painted, armed and clothed with all the horrors of war, rushing towards us like a mighty torrent. In a moment we placed ourselves in attitude of defense. But could we expect, with thirty men, to withstand this powerful host? Onward rushed the savage band with accelerated speed as a huge rock, loosened from the mountain's brow, dashes impetuously downward, sweeping, overturning, and burying everything in its course!

We saw it was their intention to crush us beneath the feet of their foaming chargers. They approached within a few paces, and in another moment we should be overwhelmed, when lo! an alarm like an electric shock struck through their ranks and stayed their career, as an avalanche, sweeping down the mountain side, stops in the midst of its course by the power of a hand unseen. The Lord had said, "*Touch not mine anointed, and do my prophets no harm.*

Many incidents occurred which called forth the remark that in our past experience the hand of the Lord had never been more visibly manifested. When we arrived on the banks of the great Missouri, her waters immediately congealed for the first time during the season, thus forming a bridge over which we passed to the other side; this was no sooner accomplished than the torrent ran as before.

On arriving at Kanesville, we were saluted with shoutings, firing of cannon, songs of rejoicing, and other demonstrations of welcome. During the few days of our stay, we experienced universal kindness from the Saints." The missionaries spent some time in the vicinity of Nauvoo and then traveled on to the east coast, then to England, and then to Italy. Lorenzo saw little success there, until he felt directed to work among the Protestant Waldenses in Piedmont. He wrote:

I am now in a Roman Catholic country. Its inhabitants are before my eyes continually. My heart is pained to see their follies and wickedness—their gross darkness and superstition. I weep that the day of the Son of Man has come upon them unawares, so little are they prepared to receive the voice from on high: 'Behold! the Bridegroom cometh; go ye out to meet Him!'

They are clothed with darkness as with a garment, and, figuratively speaking, they know not their right hand from their left. . . .

After I wrote the foregoing, I received a letter from Elders Stenhouse and Toronto. I have felt an intense desire to know the state of that province to which I had given them an appointment, as I felt assured it would be the field of my mission. Now, with a heart full of gratitude, I find an opening is presented in the valleys of Piedmont, when all other parts of Italy are closed against our efforts. I believe that the Lord has there hidden up a people amid the Alpine mountains, and it is the voice of the Spirit that I shall commence something of importance in that part of this dark nation.

Elder Snow and his companions had more success among the Protestants than the Catholics. The way was opened:

Soon after my arrival here, I considered it necessary to issue a publication in French; accordingly I wrote and compiled a work entitled, 'The Voice of Joseph,' containing Visions of Joseph Smith; discovery of the gold plates filled with Egyptian characters and hieroglyphics; their translation into the English language by the aid of the Urim and Thummim; the sacred history of ancient America, now clearly revealed from the earliest ages after the flood to the beginning of the fifth century of the Christian era; organization of the Church of Jesus Christ of Latter-day Saints; their persecutions; expulsion from the States of Missouri and Illinois; martyrdom of Joseph and Hyrum Smith; banishment of many thousand Saints; their travels in the western wilderness; their present location in Upper California [Utah]; their organization of the "State of Deseret;" the missionary labors of their Elders; sketch of their faith and doctrine.

After fruitless endeavors to find a proper person to translate this work, I found it necessary to send to England, where, through the kindness of Elder Orson Pratt, it was translated by a professor from the University of Paris.

I felt assured that the Lord had directed us to a branch, of the house of Israel, and I was rejoiced to behold many circumstances that reminded me of those with whom I had been associated in the valleys of the west. We endeavored to lay a foundation for future usefulness in silently preparing the minds of the people for the reception of the Gospel, by cultivating friendly feelings in the bosoms of those by whom we were surrounded. Yet it seemed very singular, and it was no small tax on my patience, to be weeks and even months in the midst of an interesting people without being actively and publicly engaged in communicating the great principles which I had been sent to promulgate. But, as I felt it was the mind of the Spirit that we should proceed at first with slow and cautious steps, I submitted to the will of heaven.

It was at this time that Elder Snow participated in one of the great miracles of his life:

September 6th.—This morning, my attention was directed to Joseph Grey, a boy of three years of age—the youngest child of our host. Many friends had been to see the child, as to all human appearances his end was near. I went to see him in the afternoon; death was preying upon his body—his former healthy frame was now reduced to a skeleton, and it was only by close observation we could discern that he was alive. As I reflected upon the peculiarity of our situation, my mind was fully awakened to a sense of our position. For some hours before I retired to rest, I called upon the Lord to assist us at this time. My feelings on this occasion will not easily be erased from my memory.

September 7th.—This morning I proposed to Elder Stenhouse we should fast and retire to the mountains and pray. As we departed, we called and saw the child—his eyeballs turned upwards—his eyelids fell and closed—his face and ears were thin, and wore the pale marble hue, indicative of approaching dissolution. The cold perspiration of death covered his body as the principle of life was nearly exhausted. Madam Grey and other females were sobbing, while Monsieur Grey hung his head and whispered to us, *"Il meurt! il meurt!"* (He dies! he dies!)

After a little rest upon the mountain, aside from any likelihood of interruption, we called upon the Lord in solemn, earnest prayer, to spare the life of the child. As I reflected on the course we wished to pursue, the claims that we should soon advance to the world, I regarded this

> circumstance as one of vast importance. I know not of any sacrifice which I can possibly make, that I am not willing to offer, that the Lord might grant our requests.
>
> We returned about three o'clock in the afternoon, and having consecrated some oil, I anointed my hand and laid it upon the head of the child, while we silently offered up the desires of our hearts for his restoration. A few hours afterward we called, and his father, with a smile of thankfulness, said, *"Mieux beaucoup! beaucoup!"* (Better, much, much!)
>
> September 8th.—The child had been so well during the past night the parents had been enabled to take their rest, which they had not done for some time before; and to-day they could leave him and attend to the business of the house. As I called to see him, Madam Grey expressed her joy in his restoration. I, in turn, remarked, *"Il Dio di cielo ha fatto questa per voi."* (The God of heaven has done this for you.)

Whether this was an incident of healing the sick or of raising the dead, is not fully settled; yet this mighty miracle softened the hearts of those among whom Elder Snow labored, and he began teaching and baptizing and organizing a branch of the Church. Elder Snow's letters mention being directed by the spirit in his ministry, in his guiding the work of others, and of miracles among the newly baptized people.[2]

After an absence of nearly three years, starting from Malta, and, after stopping a few days in Gibraltar, Lorenzo returned home by way of Portsmouth, London, Liverpool, New York, and St. Louis, arriving in Salt Lake City on July 30, 1852. His homecoming was of mixed feelings—great joy and deep sorrow. His daughter wrote: "Apostle Snow, husband and father, returned from his Italian mission on 30 July, 1852. He walked into his home during a very heavy rain; the roof was leaking, there was almost no food in the house, and Mary Adeline, Sarah Ann, and Sylvia were ill. Charlotte, his first wife, had died in 1850, while he was in Italy. He turned to his sister, Eliza, who was busy with the sick, and said that never, never, would they be neglected like that again, and he kept his promise."[3]

Again, quoting Lorenzo's journal:

> Arriving at my home in Salt Lake City, the long anticipated oasis of this portion of my life-journey, the beacon light which succeeded my arduous missionary labors, and shone with a brighter beam than all other earthly luminaries, the happiness of once again meeting my loved and loving family would have been full, but alas! there was a sad vacancy. A lovely one was not; one who ever met me with a smiling face and a

> loving heart, was not there to respond to love's sacred call; Charlotte, my dear wife, had been stricken down by death, and her beautiful form lay moldering in the silent tomb. Yet there was consolation in the thought that her pure spirit was mingling with holy beings above. A short time after Charlotte's decease, while I was in Italy, a sister in London, a very faithful Saint, the wife of Elder Jabez Woodard, had an open vision, in which she saw a beautiful woman, the most lovely being she ever beheld, clothed in white robes and crowned with glory. This personage told Mrs. Woodard that she was a wife of Lorenzo Snow.

Eliza believed that the Lord had taken Lorenzo at his word when he prayed and said he would sacrifice anything if He would restore the life of the young boy in Italy—that the sacrifice laid on the altar was his own dear wife Charlotte—in order to open the door to establish the Church in Italy.

The following autumn Lorenzo was elected to the Utah Legislature, and he continued a member until disfranchised in 1882 by the decision of the "Commissioners" appointed by the President of the United States, to execute the notorious Edmunds Law in Utah; and served, during ten years, as President of the Legislative Council.

He also went to work building a new home without a leaky roof: "Through the blessing of God upon my efforts with great economy and perseverance I succeeded far beyond my most sanguine expectations. I erected a large two-story adobe house, with nine rooms finished off several of them and moved into it with all my family, feeling truly thankful to the Giver of all good for the blessing of a comfortable and respectable habitation."

When his house was in course of erection, when no eye but that of God could see him, he frequently knelt within its foundation and prayed that the small means he could command might be blessed and multiplied in its use. Thus by economy, labor, effort, faith, and prayer, he succeeded.

Being an educated man with a refined character that enjoyed poetry and literature, Elder Snow organized at about this time what he called the Polysophical Society, a continuously enlarging group that studied fine art, literature, drama, recitation, music, and other improvements of society. This organization was the seed that eventually grew to become the Young Men's and Young Women's Mutual Improvement Associations (now known as the Young Men and Young Women Organizations):

Lorenzo Snow, age 53 (CA)

The most successful organization was the "Polysophical Society," under the patronage and in the mansion of President Lorenzo Snow, in the winter of 1852; this was the first nucleus of a varied intellectual character in the Church, and drew the lion's share of the latent talent in Salt Lake City. Its programs included productions in many modern languages. The Presidency and Twelve, honorary members, were generally there. A large orchestra furnished part of the music. Essays, poems, recitations, music, song, anecdote, experience and comment made a veritable feast for the soul. Public interest and enjoyment crowded weekly the spacious hall and adjoining rooms. President Snow, himself a collegian, enjoyed this success. A veritable boom followed, and similar organizations sprang up in the wards until dancing, which had been the leading recreation, became nearly obsolete. This was the basis upon which all the Mutual Improvement Associations have been built, providing recreation for both sexes, and the study of art, literature, science, religion, politics and amusement, refining, purifying, enlarging, under the control of the Priesthood all mental and intellectual forces.[4]

The interval that succeeded Lorenzo's Italian mission was occupied in the Polysophical Society, in school teaching, and in domestic and legislative labors, and occasionally accompanying President Young in his visits to the settlements and stakes of Zion, preaching, administering to the sick, and so forth.

The next mission to which he was called, in October 1853, was to locate fifty families in Box Elder County, sixty miles north of Salt Lake City. There a small settlement had been formed, which, for want of the right master spirit, had lost every vestige of enterprise and was without every aim in the direction of advancement. To diffuse active energies and a spirit of progress into this stereotyped condition of people was not unlike raising the dead, and a man of less strength of purpose would have faltered. Not so with the one in question. Prompt to the call, he went to work, laid out a city, naming it Brigham [City] in honor of the President of the Church, moved his family to the new city, and thus laid the foundation for the great financial cooperative enterprise, which subsequently he there built up.

When the county was organized by the authority of the Legislature, he was appointed to preside over it, as a stake of Zion. He was elected a member (and also president) of the Legislative Council, to represent the district composed of the counties of Box Elder and Weber.[5]

Here follows Lorenzo's own version of the situation:

> When I arrived in Box Elder County, I found the location where Brigham City now flourishes in a very unprosperous condition. Whether its change from a primitive state should be called improvement, i.e., whether it was better or worse for what had been done on the premises, would puzzle an antiquarian. Even the log meeting house, with its ground floor and earth roof, was more extensively patronized as a receptacle for bed bugs than for the assemblage of Saints.
>
> At first, in locating there, I only took a portion of my family, as a small and incommodious adobe hut was the only tenement attainable. During the summer and fall I succeeded in erecting a house, one story and half in height, thirty feet by forty. It being impossible to obtain shingles, I covered the building with slabs, and for two winters the rattling of those slabs, put in motion by the canyon breezes, supplied us with music in the absence of organs and pianos. I had thus covered the roof of my house, but before my front door was in, and all my floors laid, and before any plastering was done, our house was the stopping place and the home of President Brigham Young and his company of tourists, whenever they visited these northern settlements. We sometimes entertained as many as forty at once. As soon as my house was up and partly finished, I had all of my family with me; and on the occasion of these visits of the Presidency, my family all united to make our visitors as comfortable as possible.

Along with building the new settlement of Brigham City, Elder Snow continued to perform his apostolic duties and exercise the priesthood. At the time he received his patriarchal blessing under the hands of the patriarch, Joseph Smith Sr., father of the Prophet, he was told that the sick should even send handkerchiefs to him for his blessing, by which they should be made whole.

A striking instance in fulfillment of this prediction occurred in the winter of 1866. Brother William Smith, of Kaysville, Davis County, Utah, was taken very sick; his faith centered in God and in the ordinances of His house, instead of human medical skill; and he and his wife had, from experience, great faith in Brother Snow as an administrator, but he was forty miles away. It was winter, the weather cold and stormy, and the roads almost impassable, and they thought it preposterous to send for him and tried to content themselves with the services of those present.

But with all the faith that was exercised, with all that patient, skillful, and careful nursing all that love and affection could do for him he continued to grow worse, and gradually sank until his life was despaired of and his case considered hopeless by all but his heart-stricken, loving wife. She was hoping and praying with all the fervor affection inspires, when, by the promptings of the Spirit which brings "all things to remembrance," she recollected that when Brother Snow was at her home in Wiberson, England, in reading a copy of his patriarchal blessing, she was struck with the prediction that the sick should send handkerchiefs to him. Her heart took courage, and the light of eternity seemed to spread a halo around, and the thought was immediately suggested to her that, as her husband, now almost unconscious, was too far gone to act for himself, she might act for him, and forthwith she started to carry the suggestion into effect.

No time was lost in commissioning a messenger to go with all possible dispatch and take to Brother Snow a new silk handkerchief, with a note from Sister Smith containing her request, also instructions relative to and descriptive of her husband's condition. The messenger accomplished the trip, to and from, as expeditiously as the state of the roads would possibly admit.

When Brother Snow was made acquainted with the situation, his sympathies were much aroused. From long acquaintance, he had full confidence in their faithfulness and integrity. They had befriended him when on a mission in a foreign land, and from first acquaintance, with him and them, confidence was mutual.

We now copy from Brother Snow's journal:

> I took the handkerchief and a bottle of perfumery, and on retiring to my closet, I prayed, and then I consecrated the perfumery and sprinkled it on the handkerchief. I then again bowed before the Lord, and

> in earnest supplication besought Him to remember the promises He made through His servant, the Patriarch, whom He had now taken to Himself, and let the healing and life-inspiring virtues of His Holy Spirit be imparted to this handkerchief, and from thence to Brother Smith when it shall be placed upon him, speedily restoring him to life, health and vigor.
>
> As soon as the messenger returned, with the handkerchief neatly folded in an envelope, it was unfolded and spread over the head and face of Brother Smith, the apparently dying man, with almost instantaneous effect. His immediate recovery was observed with surprise and astonishment by all around, and well might they exclaim: "It is the Lord's doings, and it is marvelous in our eyes."

While in Brigham City, Elder Snow began putting in place and actively promoting the beginnings of a cooperative movement resembling the United Order, where the people contributed their labor and received in return what they needed to live on. This cooperative movement continued with great success for about twenty years, but as outside economic pressure, misfortunes, anti-Mormon persecution, and other factors took their toll, and as Elder Snow was absent fulfilling his call to travel as an apostle of the Lord, the cooperative effort eventually discontinued. During most of the time it was in operation, it was the temporal jewel of the Church, perhaps the finest success story approaching the United Order in the Church.

Space herein does not allow for a lengthy review of Lorenzo's efforts in the Brigham City cooperative movement or its eventual demise, but such information is available elsewhere.[6] Not surprisingly, during these years Elder Snow took the opportunity to preach the law of consecration and the United Order at most general conferences and at many other gatherings. His discourses during those times are filled with doctrine and exhortation relating to the effort.

Elder Snow continued to serve at the behest of the president of the Church. In 1864, President Young learned that a certain missionary named Walter M. Gibson had apostatized, and by various schemes and tactics had taken over the Church in Hawaii, where the natives followed his beguiling lead. He had instituted "priestcraft," meaning he charged the natives money to hold the priesthood and receive various blessings. A few that were not convinced wrote their missionary friends in Salt Lake City, detailing what Gibson had done and asking for advice.

In response, the First Presidency decided that Apostles Ezra T. Benson (grandfather of President Ezra Taft Benson) and Lorenzo Snow should visit the islands, and that Elders Joseph F. Smith, Alma Smith, and William W. Cluff should accompany them. Joseph F. Smith had previously served a lengthy mission in Hawaii and was by far the most familiar with the islands and surrounding waters. They left March 1, undergoing a series of adventures in their travels, including a stagecoach driver who would alternately sing as he drove, with the most beautiful voice the passengers had ever heard, and swear, using the most profane language they had ever heard.

But the worst stage of travel came after they boarded their sailing vessel and neared the islands. Eliza quoted from Elder W. W. Cluff's account of Elder Snow's drowning and subsequent restoration:

> We arrived at Honolulu, the capital of the islands, about the 27th of March. On the 29th we sailed for Lahaina, on the schooner *Nettie Merrill*, for the island of Maui, a distance of about ninety miles from Honolulu. On the morning of the 31st of March, we came to anchor about one mile from the mouth of the little harbor of Lahaina.
>
> Apostles Ezra T. Benson, Lorenzo Snow, Brother Alma L. Smith, and myself, got into the small boat to go on shore. Brother Joseph F. Smith, as he afterwards stated, had some misgivings about going in that boat, but the manifestation was not sufficiently strong to indicate any general accident. He preferred to remain on board the vessel until the boat returned. The boat started for the shore. It contained some barrels and boxes, the captain, a white man, two or three native passengers, and the boat's crew, who were also natives.
>
> The entrance to the harbor is a very narrow passage between coral reefs, and when the sea is rough, it is very dangerous on account of the breakers. Where the vessel lay the sea was not rough, but only presented the appearance of heavy swells rolling to the shore.
>
> As we approached the reef it was evident to me that the surf was running higher than we anticipated. I called the captain's attention to the fact. We were running quartering to the waves, and I suggested that we change our course so as to run at right angles with them. He replied that he did not think there was any danger, and our course was not changed. We went but little farther, when a heavy swell struck the boat and carried us before it about fifty yards. When the swell passed it left us in a trough between two huge waves. It was too late to retrieve our error, and we must run our chances. When the second swell struck the boat, it raised the stern so high that the steersman's oar was out of the water, and he lost control of the boat. It rode on the swell a short distance and swung around just as the

wave began to break up. We were almost instantly capsized into the dashing, foaming sea.

I felt no concern for myself about drowning, for while on my former mission I had learned to swim and sport in the surf of those shores. The last I remember of Brother Snow, as the boat was going over, I saw him seize the upper edge of it with both hands. Fearing that the upper edge of the boat, or the barrels, might hit and injure me as the boat was going over, I plunged head foremost into the water. After swimming a short distance, I came to the surface without being strangled or injured.

The boat was bottom upwards, and barrels, hats and umbrellas were floating in every direction. I swam to the boat and as there was nothing to cling to on the bottom, I reached under and seized the edge of it.

About the same time Brother Benson came up near me and readily got hold of the boat. Brother Alma L. Smith came up on the opposite side of the boat from Brother Benson and myself. He was considerably strangled, but succeeded in securing a hold on the boat.

A short time afterwards the captain was discovered, about fifty yards from us. Two sailors, one on each side, succeeded in keeping him on the surface, although life was apparently extinct.

Nothing yet had been seen of Brother Snow, although the natives had been swimming and diving in every direction in search of him. We were only about one-fourth of a mile from shore. The people, as soon as they discovered our circumstances, manned a life boat and hurried to the rescue. We were taken into the boat, when the crew wanted to row for the shore, and pick up the captain by the way. We told them that one of our friends was yet missing, and we did not want to leave. We discovered that a second boat had left the shore and could reach the captain as soon as the one we were in. Seeing this, the crew of our boat consented to remain and assist us.

The captain was taken ashore, and by working over him sometime was brought to life. Probably his life would not have been much endangered but for a sack of four or five hundred silver dollars which he held in his hand, the weight of which took him at once to the bottom. The natives dove and brought him up, still clinging to the sack. When his vitality was restored, the first thing he inquired about was the money; intimating to the natives, with peculiar emphasis, that it would not have been healthy for them to have lost it.

Brother Snow had not yet been discovered, and the anxiety was intense. The natives were doing all in their power to find him. Finally one of them, in edging himself around the capsized boat, must have felt Brother Snow with his feet and pulled him, at least partly from under it, as the first I saw of Brother Snow was his hair floating upon the water around one end of the capsized boat. As soon as we got him into our boat, we told the boatmen to pull for the shore with all possible speed. His body was stiff, and life apparently extinct.

Brother A. L. Smith and I were sitting side by side. We laid Brother Snow across our laps, and on the way to shore, we quietly administered to him and asked the Lord to spare his life, that he might return to his family and home. On reaching the shore, we carried him a little way to some large empty barrels that were lying on the sandy beach. We laid him face downwards on one of them, and rolled him back and forth until we succeeded in getting the water he had swallowed out of him.

During this time a number of persons came down from the town; among them was Mr. E. P. Adams, a merchant. All were willing to do what they could. We washed Brother Snow's face with camphor, furnished by Mr. Adams. We did not only what was customary in such cases, but also what the Spirit seemed to whisper to us. After working over him for some time, without any indications of returning life, the by-standers said that nothing more could be done for him. But we did not feel like giving him up, and still prayed and worked over him, with an assurance that the Lord would hear and answer our prayers.

Finally we were impressed to place our mouth over his and make an effort to inflate his lungs, alternately blowing in and drawing out the air, imitating as far as possible, the natural process of breathing. This we persevered in until we succeeded in inflating his lungs. After a little, we perceived very faint indications of returning life. A slight wink of the eye, which, until then, had been open and death-like, and a very faint rattle in the throat, were the first symptoms of returning vitality. These grew more and more distinct, until consciousness was fully restored.

When this result was reached, it must have been fully one hour after the upsetting of the boat. A Portuguese man, living in Lahaina, who from the first, rendered us much assistance, invited us to take Brother Snow to his house. There being no Saints in the place, we gladly accepted his kind offer. Every possible attention was given for Brother Snow's comfort.

Eliza also included Elder Snow's own account of this experience:

As we were moving along, probably more than a quarter of a mile from where we expected to land, my attention was suddenly arrested by Captain Fisher calling to the oarsmen in a voice which denoted some alarm, "Hurry up, hurry up!" I immediately discovered the cause of alarm. A short distance behind us, I saw an immense surf, thirty or forty feet high, rushing towards us swifter than a race horse. We had

> scarcely a moment for reflection before the huge mass was upon us. In an instant our boat, with its contents, as though it were a feather, was hurled into a gulf of briny waters, and all was under this rolling, seething mountain wave. It took me by surprise. I think, however, that I comprehended the situation in the midst of turbulent waves a quarter of a mile from the shore, without much probability of human aid.
>
> I felt confident, however, that there would be some way of escape; that the Lord would provide the means, for it was not possible that my life and mission were thus to terminate. This reliance on the Lord banished fear, and inspired me up to the last moment of consciousness. In such extreme cases of excitement, we seem to live hours in a minute, and a volume of thoughts crowd themselves into one single moment. It was so with me in that perilous scene.
>
> Having been somewhat subject to faint, I think that after a few moments in the water I must have fainted, as I did not suffer the pain common in the experience of drowning persons. I had been in the water only a few moments until I lost consciousness. The first I knew afterwards I was on shore, receiving the kind and tender attentions of my brethren. The first recollection I have of returning consciousness, was that of a very small light, the smallest imaginable. This soon disappeared, and I was again in total darkness. Again it appeared much larger than before, then sank away and left me, as before, in forgetfulness. Thus it continued to come and go, until finally I recognized, as I thought, persons whispering, and soon after, I asked in a feeble whisper, "What is the matter?" I immediately recognized the voice of Elder Cluff, as he replied, "You have been drowned; the boat upset in the surf." Quick as lightning the scene of our disaster flashed upon my mind. I immediately asked, "Are you brethren all safe?" The emotion that was awakened in my bosom by the answer of Elder Cluff, will remain with me as long as life continues: "Brother Snow, we are all safe." I rapidly recovered and very soon was able to walk and accompany the brethren to our lodgings.

Some years later Elder Heber J. Grant shared further insight into President Snow's drowning experience: "Lorenzo Snow was drowned, and it took some hours to bring him to life again. At that particular time the Lord revealed to him the fact that the young man, Joseph F. Smith, would someday be the Prophet of God. . . . It was revealed to him then and there, that the boy, with the courage of his convictions, who stayed on that vessel, would yet be the Prophet of God. Lorenzo Snow told me this upon more than one occasion long years before Joseph F. Smith came to the presidency of the Church."[7] President Snow also reflected on some of his life experiences during a meeting with close associates, commenting: "I never expected to go to the bottom of the Pacific ocean, but I did so once and the Lord preserved me and I got out."[8] He also told another congregation that "he was under sixty feet of water. He said he had previously always been subject to headaches, but drowning cured him."[9]

Soon thereafter the elders dealt with Walter Gibson. Their efforts were not immediately successful and they received a great deal of resistance from Gibson and many native Latter-day Saints that had aligned themselves with him, enjoying the illusionary prestige and priesthood offices he pretended to give them for their money. During one of the meetings in which the elders were endeavoring to convince the native Saints of Gibson's errors, Brother Snow arose and in his remarks prophesied that Mr. Gibson would see the time that not one of the Saints would remain with him.

The Apostles informed Mr. Gibson and the Saints that, when they departed for home, Elder Joseph F. Smith would be left in charge of the mission. They added that all those who wished to be considered in good standing in the Church should leave Lanai and return to their homes on the other islands, where the branches would be reorganized and set in order by the Brethren who would be left for that purpose. The next day, they returned to Lahaina, where they held a council and cut Mr. Gibson off from the Church (excommunicated him). They then returned to Honolulu, and about eight days after, Apostles Snow and Benson took passage on the bark (ship) *Onward*, for San Francisco.

Brother Snow's prophecy was literally fulfilled. The native Saints all left Mr. Gibson and returned to their former homes, as counseled. On landing in San Francisco, Elder Snow, while eating in a restaurant, experienced his first earthquake. Not knowing what was happening at first, he wondered why all the other diners ran outside into the streets. He was not injured, but the establishment he was in was, as were many other buildings around him.

He then returned to Brigham City and spent his time improving the flourishing cooperative businesses, ministering among the people as their stake president, and preaching the gospel. It was during his years directing the cooperatives that Elder Snow developed the financial acumen that would serve him so well in his administration as president of the Church in later years.

In May 1867, Elder Snow joined with his Quorum in the sad duty of convening a disciplinary court (council) on Elder Amasa Lyman, one of their number. He had been preaching that the Atonement of Jesus

Christ was not necessary for the forgiveness of sins and was therefore excommunicated.[10]

In August 1868, President Brigham Young visited throughout Northern Utah, stopping in Logan and Brigham City. On the twenty-fourth, while in his namesake city, he organized a School of the Prophets. This branch organization, with Lorenzo Snow as its leader, was a school in which the leading elders, Church leaders, and other worthy men of the community would meet to hear the gospel preached, discuss and seek to solve local economic and social problems, and improve their minds.[11] Because of the close-knit nature of this early Latter-day Saint community, as well as Elder Snow's apostolic influence, he was able to build great unity and spirituality in the membership of this school. Later, while President of the Church, Lorenzo reminisced about one special experience from those early days: "He referred to the time when, while presiding over the Box Elder Stake of Zion, he was given permission to carry on a School of the Prophets, and he improved the opportunity by calling together fifty or sixty men and partaking of the sacrament with them, as the Savior did with his Apostles in former times. The spirit of the Lord was poured out upon them."[12] Elder Snow had a gift for building brotherhood and lifting others.

In September 1869, Lorenzo entertained Elder Benson at his home, furnishing him a fine lunch. Elder Benson (and some friends) then drove in his team from Brigham City to Ogden, put his buggy in a barn, and as he walked toward the main house, he fell dead. Elder Snow attended the funeral two days later.[13]

Then a month later, as the story goes, at the October general conference Elder Snow gave his talk in the morning session. After that meeting, messengers came from Farmington, Utah, to President Brigham Young, informing him that for three days a fierce east wind had been blowing there; a train had been blown from the tracks and roofs from homes. LeRoi Snow wrote: "No afternoon meeting was held, and it is said that it was during this [time] that Pres. Young and party, including Lorenzo Snow, went to Farmington." Then, "It is said that it was on this day that Pres. Brigham Young rebuked a terrible East wind" which "soon abated."[14]

On October 10, 1870, Elder Snow had five deceased women sealed to him in the Salt Lake Endowment House, with his wife Phebe (Woodruff) acting as proxy. Then on April 10th, 1871, Elenor Houtz was sealed to Elder Snow in the Endowment House by Daniel H. Wells. This was likely a formal sealing of the previous civil ceremony.[15]

Minnie J. Snow (1854–1908), last wife of Lorenzo Snow; died from complications of an infected eye (USHS)

In 1871, Lorenzo added a final (ninth) wife to his large polygamous family—Minnie Jensen. When he began courting her, she was sixteen and he was fifty-eight, so convincing her to marry him was not easy. Minnie recorded: "Apostle Lorenzo Snow, after an extended acquaintance and to whom I was indebted for many pleasant visits, drives, etc., now proffered marriage. I was completely overwhelmed with the honor of the proposal. . . . I was a young, trusting, impulsive little wildflower when he sought me out; in his honest, manly, earnest way he wooed me. Unable to decide, I sought the Lord for guidance, and, at length, received a perfect assurance of my duty. My resolve was made and I accepted."

Despite the assurance, Minnie yet struggled with the idea of becoming a plural wife and giving up her youthful romantic dreams; however, she finally consented. She and Lorenzo were married on June 12, 1871, in the Endowment House in Salt Lake City, by President Young. The marriage was kept secret at the time because of persecution directed toward polygamists. This meant that the wedding reception for Minnie was also the wedding reception for one of President Snow's daughters that married at the same time. Minnie had to stand aside while her new niece received the congratulations from well-wishers instead of her. She later acknowledged that this made her heartsick and lonely.[16]

Lorenzo Snow (CA)

Minnie was evidently impressive

to her peers. One of them said that, "he [President Snow] married a rather fine, charming young lady whom I know had quite an appeal to at least one of my intimate friends; she was a vivacious, vigorous, and intelligent schoolmate of mine, and she had a promising but very young son, LeRoi, upon whom the father doted."[17] (Lorenzo did give his son LeRoi every advantage he could and employed him as a private secretary while he was President of the Church.)

In January 1872, Elder Snow preached one of the most powerful sermons to that point in his apostolic career. After reviewing the possibilities for the progression of men to become like their Heavenly Father, and the doctrine that the posterity of Adam are the offspring of God, he bore strong testimony, stating: "I testify before this assembly [in the Salt Lake Tabernacle], as I have testified before the people throughout the different States of the Union, and throughout [Europe], that God Almighty, through my obedience to the gospel of Jesus, has revealed to me, tangibly, that this is the work of God, that this is his gospel, that this is his kingdom." Further, "I would not be here today; I would not have traveled over the face of the earth as I have for the last thirty-five years unless God had revealed this unto me. . . . But I received a dispensation from the Almighty, and I could say and do say now, as the Apostle Paul said: 'I received not this gospel from man, but I received it by revelation from the Almighty.'"[18]

On the 26th of October, 1872, Elder Snow left home on a lengthy trip to Palestine (Israel). The main purpose for this trip was to rededicate the land to the Lord and for the return of the Jews as prophesied in scripture.[19] Another was to report to President Young the possibilities for expansion of missionary work around the world.

While on this tour, Lorenzo wrote a series of descriptive letters that were forwarded from time to time and published in the *Deseret News*. After returning, these letters were compiled, with those of other members of the party and published in a neat volume of nearly four hundred pages, entitled "Correspondence of Palestine Tourists." The group of tourists was gone for an extended period and visited many lands. November saw them in London, England; December in Belgium and France; Italy in late December and January, 1873. By February they had reached Egypt, and later that month and into March, they explored Palestine and Jerusalem and then moved on to Syria. April saw them in Greece; May, in Austria and Prussia, and then by July they had returned by the long road home, having spent nearly ten months abroad.[20]

While traveling, Elder Snow learned "through the press" that he had been called as a counselor to the First Presidency, along with four other men (Brigham Young Jr., Albert Carrington, John W. Young, and George Q. Cannon), at the April 1873 general conference. President Young explained that "He had now two counselors to aid him as Presidents of the Church, and he purposed selecting five more. According to the order of the Church, he had the privilege of having seven brethren to act in this capacity."[21] That August, Lorenzo wrote President Young a long letter reporting his "stewardship" or activities as president of the Box Elder Stake. At the April 1874 general conference, President Young used the wording of "Assistant Counselors" to the First Presidency, when these men were sustained. Elder Snow served in this capacity until President Young died. This assignment was in addition to his duties as a member of the Twelve, not in place of them. It is not known how much time Lorenzo and the other men devoted to this assignment counseling with the First Presidency, or how such duties may have differed from their regular apostolic service. John Taylor did not renew the calling when he became President of the Church.[22]

In August 1877, President Brigham Young visited Brigham City. This was the last time Elder Snow saw him, as he died shortly thereafter. While there, President Young installed President Snow's son Oliver as the new stake president. Also at about this time, President Young released all apostles from their duties as stake presidents and asked them to begin acting more in a unified Quorum capacity.

Elder Snow always felt the highest regard and esteem for President Brigham Young. He gave the prophet a very fine and expensive gold watch that he had received many years earlier from admiring friends. In return, some years after the above presentation of the gift, Lorenzo being in Salt Lake City on a visit, President Young sent a note requesting him to call at the office of the latter; he did so, and was invited by the President to accompany him to his carriage house, which was occupied by a number of carriages. By this time Lorenzo was in a quandary, silently wondering "what was up," when, to his great surprise and astonishment, President Young, pointing to a substantial and beautiful one, said, "Brother Lorenzo, that carriage is for you; I shall send it on your return to Brigham City." The carriage was nearly new and had been purchased at the factory at a cost of five hundred dollars. Feeling almost bewildered with surprise, Lorenzo protested against its acceptance, but on his arrival in Brigham City, he received a message that the carriage had been shipped. (Lorenzo Snow

Jr., one of Elder Snow's many sons, remembered that one reason President Young gave Elder Snow the new carriage was because he was getting so fat he could not get in and out of it himself, and therefore no longer needed it.)[23] Giving it to Lorenzo was a fine way for him to show his fondness for his younger associate. Such was their reciprocal relationship.

Over the years, President Young invited Elder Snow to accompany him and his party on various long excursions to the settlements throughout northern and southern Utah and Idaho. They spent many days traveling together, preaching, and counseling among the Latter-day Saints. President Young told the people in Manti, Utah, that Lorenzo Snow was responsible for beginning the traditions of the official town receptions when the prophet came to visit.[24] Whenever President Young visited Brigham City, he stayed at Elder Snow's home.

In 1879 Lorenzo turned sixty-five and an impressive birthday party was given him by his ever enlarging family. His thoughts turned in appreciation to his nine wives. In his journal, Lorenzo wrote:

> After years of companionship, I can truly say I have been perfectly satisfied, and have never, for one moment, felt that I had the least reason or occasion for regret. In making choice of wives—in view of continuing the relationship, not only through time, but through endless eternity, realizing my own lack of wisdom and incompetency of judging in this important matter, it has been my invariable practice to seek in humble, earnest prayer, the mind and will of God; and I acknowledge His guiding wisdom in this respect, and realize it impossible for me to feel sufficiently thankful for the good, noble-minded women He has given me, which applies to each without one exception.
>
> Previous to marriage, I explained my position as a public servant, a minute man—one to whom was committed a dispensation of the Gospel of the Son of God; and gave them to understand definitely that so far as this world's goods were concerned, my prospects were not very flattering, and to their praise be it written, their minds were elevated, and the desires of their hearts lifted far above the gross yearnings of frail humanity after perishable objects, and they have proven themselves superior to the hardships, privations, poverty, and even perils which the Saints, in the earlier periods of the history of the Church, experienced.
>
> Possessing, as they did, that rare gift—the gift of sound common sense, my wives all acted in concert, mutually assisting each other; and with all the inconveniences, hard work, and privations, to which, while raising our children, they have experienced through my frequent, and, at times, long absence and never have they, at any time, sought to detain

> me, or prevent my fulfillment of public duties; but on the other hand, have been and are co-laborers with me in the great work of the last days.

In 1883 Elder Snow and a few companions went to the Fort Hall Indian Reservation by Malad, Idaho, and attempted to obtain permission for Church missionaries to work and preach among the American Indians living there. They were unsuccessful, soon finding that while initially friendly, the local "Indian Agent," a Mr. Cook, was anti-Mormon in sentiment. He would not even let Lorenzo station a Mormon on the reservation to teach the people how to farm and raise better crops, so that the federal government would not have to support them. They visited among the American Indians on the reservation as much as they could and developed the best relations they could but were soon forced to leave.

Early May 1884 saw a large and well-attended family reunion in Brigham City, held to commemorate Elder Snow's seventieth birthday. Then on May 17, Elder Snow attended the dedication of the Logan Temple, having served as a member of a committee appointed by President Young to oversee its building and completion.[25]

Chapter 3

Forced into Hiding by Persecution for Plural Marriage

On March 22, 1882, the President of the United States, Chester A. Arthur, affixed his signature to the act passed by Congress that has since become famous, or infamous, as the Edmunds Law. It was so named from the fact that its author, framer, and principal supporter: Senator George F. Edmunds, of Vermont.

The Edmunds Law was supplemental to, and amendatory of, an act of Congress approved July 1st, 1862, entitled "an act to punish and prevent the practice of polygamy in the Territories of the United States and other places, and disapproving and annulling certain acts of the Legislative Assembly of the Territory of Utah." The purpose of the law of 1862 was to make the practice of plural marriage—a tenet at the time of The Church of Jesus Christ of Latter-day Saints—equivalent to the crime of bigamy, and to punish it as such by "a fine not exceeding five hundred dollars, and by imprisonment for a term not exceeding five years." It also annulled the ordinance of the provisional government of the State of Deseret, passed February 8th, 1851, incorporating The Church of Jesus Christ of Latter-day Saints and limited the amount of real estate to be owned by religious corporations in the Territories, to fifty thousand dollars. A proviso in the action disincorporating the Church stated that the act should "be so limited and constructed as not to affect or interfere with the right of property legally acquired under the ordinance named, nor with the right to worship God according to the dictates of conscience."

The first gun of the campaign thus opened, in the warfare waged by the United States government against The Church of Jesus Christ of Latter-day Saints, was fired in October 1884, two years and seven months after the passage of the Edmunds Law. Elder Rudger Clawson, who, under the law of God, had married two wives—the second one in the year 1883—and had thus failed to honor this law of man "forbidding to marry," was the victim.[1] He was tried before Chief Justice Charles S. Zane, in the Third District Court of Utah Territory, held at Salt Lake City; Mesrs. W. H. Dickson and C. S. Varian prosecuting; and by a jury from which every vestige of sympathy for Mormonism or Mormons had carefully been purged. Despite this precaution, however, and through the failure of the prosecution to produce, as a witness against the defendant, of his plural wife, the evidence was not found sufficient to convict. So thought four of the jurors who tried the case, non-Mormons though they were, and who for this exhibition of fairness toward one of the hated faith—which caused the jury to disagree and the defendant to be discharged—they were soundly berated by the *Salt Lake Tribune.*

Owing to the inflammatory and abusive articles of that newspaper in question, all during the first trial of Elder Clawson—where in some writings the witnesses whose testimony seemed favorable to the defendant were stigmatized as "liars" and "perjurers," while those whose evidence was regarded as damaging to his cause were lauded as "heroes"—an effort was made at his second trial, which followed within a few days, to obtain a change of venue to some other district. This request for this, however, was denied, and the defendant was again arraigned in the Third District Court, this time before a jury selected on the *open venire* plan. At this trial, Elder Clawson's second wife was produced and compelled to testify against him. At first the brave woman refused and was imprisoned by order of the court for declining to give evidence that would convict the man she loved, her husband in the sight of God and her people, and the father of the unborn child. After a night in the Penitentiary, in her delicate condition, she was brought before the court the next morning and, at the request of her husband, gave the required evidence. The result was his conviction. On the first count of the indictment, for polygamy, he was fined five hundred dollars and sentenced to a term of three years and six months in the Penitentiary; and on the second count, unlawful cohabitation, he was fined three hundred dollars and sentenced to six months imprisonment, the maximum penalty.

On Sunday, February 1, 1885, in the Tabernacle at Salt lake City, President John Taylor, who was destined to die in exile as a martyr during this persecution, made his last appearance in public. On that occasion, he addressed the vast assembly long and earnestly. He declared his determination to stand by the principles of truth which God had revealed, and be loyal to the covenants he had made with Him in sacred and holy places. As to casting off and forsaking his wives and children, bound to him eternally by the law of God, and trampling under foot the most sacred obligations, the effects of which reached into eternity, at the behest of man, said he, "I won't do it, so help me God!" At the same time he said he desired to honor the government and obey the laws of the land; he had done so to the best of his ability in relation to the Edmunds Law, by putting his wives in separate houses from that in which he himself dwelt, and his sister was now superintending the affairs of his household. Such was the gist of his impressive farewell discourse.

The course taken by President Taylor's decision to conform his domestic affairs to the requirements of the Edmunds Law, was similar to that pursued by other leading men of the community, who hoped they were thus placing themselves in positions of security. Alas, that hope was vain. The raid continued with unabated rigor, and the spirit of persecution rode rampant over the rights and liberties of the long-suffering people.

Realizing this fact as persecution in the guise of prosecution waxed hotter and hotter, the First Presidency, most of the Apostles, and many other leading or prominent elders of the Church went into voluntary exile, separating from their families, and either hiding in secret places near to home, or wandering abroad, or performing missions in various parts of the world.

This brings us to the personal experience of Apostle Lorenzo Snow, from the spring of 1885, to that of 1889—four years of heroic and eventful history.

In the early part of May 1885, Apostle Lorenzo Snow, at his quiet and peaceful home in Brigham City, northern Utah, received intimations from friendly and reliable sources that a plan was being laid for his capture. The warning message came from Ogden, the county seat of Weber County, about twenty miles south of Brigham City, and one of the centers of the First Judicial District.[2]

Knowing well the character and conduct of the officials entrusted with the administration of the Edmunds Law, and feeling assured, from events that had already occurred, and from threats openly made by the "crusaders" of what they still intended doing, that an Apostle of the Church, one of its leading spirits, to whom the people looked for guidance and instruction, would stand little chance of receiving fair treatment if he fell into their power, Brother Snow wisely determined not to be taken. He had broken no law; not even the unrighteous and oppressive measure that had laid its cruel hand with iron clutch upon so many bleeding hearts throughout Utah; for, following the example and counsel of his President and chief, now in exile with many others, he had, upon hearing of the passage of the act, conformed as far as possible to its requirements.

But now he knew that this would not avail. Nothing but flight or concealment would preserve his liberty, and, though naturally averse to taking any course that looked like fear or lack of faith in God, he felt no disgrace, whatever the thoughtless might think or say, to follow in the footsteps of his Brethren, the brave prophets of ancient and modern times—and even the Savior himself—and evade his enemies, inasmuch as "his time had not yet come." Accordingly, he retired from public view, first "hiding up" at home for about a fortnight, and finally, as danger drew nearer, bidding family and friends farewell and journeying to distant parts.

His inclination led him to the Pacific Coast. There among the groves and flower gardens, fanned by ocean breezes and lulled by the music of splashing waves and murmuring fountains of the lovely Californian paradise, he sought respite and repose for a brief season from his cares and toils.

His letters home contain some beautiful bits of sentiment and description that fell from his pen during those days of exile and lonely meditation. In one, he thus describes the locality in which he was then tarrying. The letter was written from San Francisco and bore the date of June 21, 1885:

> I am located near a beautiful cemetery, and every hour of the day women, young and old, and frequently even men pass my quarters bearing flowers and bouquets to place on the tombs and graves of those whom in life were objects of their love and affection; especially on the Sabbath, visitors are numerous, some to strew the grave of the dead with tributes of love and sweet remembrance, others, to gratify curiosity and to admire the beauty and loveliness of the surroundings. Magnificent tombs built of costly material, lofty marble columns surrounded by beautiful marble statues are seen all around these extensive grounds.
>
> Beautiful shrubbery also, and a variety of ornamental trees, together with the charming cypresses with their pretty conical forms, waving their boughs in the ocean breeze, add their attractiveness to the lovely scene; grottos with their cooling shades, fountains with gold-fish sporting in their waters, grass plats here and there, ornaments with fragrant shrubs, the graves and tombs adorned with floral wreaths or covered with bright, red roses like burning stars festooned with graceful vines, and a thousand other fair flowers filling the air with their sweet and exhilarating perfumery. You will say Oh, what a charming locality

for a busying place. Very well, my Dear, your language will thus express exactly what it is. One can almost feel that in the midst of all this beauty and loveliness the grave loses its gloom and sadness, and in the midst of such charming scenery one could lie down and die pleasantly. Skulls and cross-bones to create fear and terror in suggesting a yawning tomb and cold, cruel grave, are not allowed in these precincts, nor anything that is unsightly or inharmonious.

One thing I noticed I thought remarkable: in reading many hundred inscriptions on the tombs and marble columns I met with but one that gave an age as advanced as my own, but were chiefly under 40 and 45 years. I often visit this spot to meditate and to admire the tranquil beauty to be enjoyed here.

I am quite secluded and only 10 minutes walk from the cemeteries. One in particular on Laurel-Hill is more extensive, magnificent and grand than the one I have been attempting to describe; In nearly the same distance lies Golden Gate Park of over one thousand acres, the whole tastefully and artistically laid out in carriage ways, gravel walks, adorned on either side with green plants, fragrant shrubs formed and trimmed into beautiful shapes and cultivated strips of ground supporting roses and flowers of all varieties, I believe, under Heaven, gathered from every clime and country.

Under date of June 22nd, he related the following pathetic incident:

On the 18th of June a sad accident occurred in which a German gentleman 35 years of age and his two sons aged 11 and 13 years were drowned together in the Sacramento River. They were buried in the Masonic Cemetery. As I was strolling through these grounds, breathing the inspiring breeze, filled with the perfumes of ten thousand flowers, and admiring the beauty and loveliness of the surrounding scenery, my attention was arrested by an approaching funeral procession bearing the remains of the deceased above mentioned.

The procession was lengthy and displayed considerable pageantry; some fifty carriages in fashionable style drawn by horses of high mettle, driven by coachmen appropriately caparisoned—the whole preceded by a band of music with instruments of silver, clad in elaborate uniforms. The band was followed by a military company elegantly equipped. After these came the hearses—one black, decorated with black plumes—the other two with white. The hearses were very elegant and elaborate. Tall flag staffs with their flags folded around them covered with black crepe, carried by the members of the band and military, added much to the appearance of the grand cortege.

I selected an elevated point which commanded a view of the procession and the adjacent surroundings, from which to gaze upon the moving, mournful train, as it passed slowly along through the broad avenues and over the meandering carriage ways, bearing in the stillness of death—in sleep that does not waken, the father and his two sons—the widow in tears; and weeping, fatherless children, a scene that seemed sufficient to arouse even in a heart of adamant the warmest feelings of sympathy.

The procession stopped when within about 10 yards of the place of interment. Planks were stretched across the graves on which a coffin was placed, as it arrived, being borne at intervals from the hearses by the pallbearers while the band continued its solemn dirge. Then followed the closing scene which was too impressively mournful to be forgotten. The grave diggers, five in number, were leaning upon their shovels, twelve men in uniform with carbines stood motionless apparently as marble statues ready to discharge their pieces at the word; the flags and banners shrouded in black, friends of the mourners and the dead, ready with beautiful flowers and bouquets in token of sympathy, to adorn the graves; the widow, overcome with grief being supported on either side; the clergyman of noble, manly, dignified mien standing upon a grassy knoll beneath a shady cypress, deeply moved by the sorrow and affliction, spoke in the German language words of deep affectionate sympathy and consolation, in a voice sad and mournful.

Happening a few days later to visit the same cemetery, I witnessed ceremonies at a grave which were of a very different character. The officiating Clergyman was, in appearance, altogether unlike the fine dignified, sympathetic German. His whole demeanor being clearly suggestive of the religious hypocrite. His discourse, delivered without expression of feeling or sympathy, consisted chiefly of repetitions of borrowed expressions, sentences committed to memory, rehearsed in a dry, drawling monotonous voice like a simple, half-witted schoolboy. This was followed by the Lord's prayer, read in a low, moaning, guttural voice, as if coming from the deepest recess of the tombs: "Give us this day our daily bread," which struck me as the climax of the ridiculous.

The dullest imagination could readily fancy from a moment's gaze at the speaker who was richly and fashionably dressed, flourishing a gold-headed cane in person strikingly corpulent with flushed rubicund countenance, that he had no occasion to call for bread, that he had not only enough bread but plenty of wine and beer, the two latter superfluities especially.

Another letter, written twelve days earlier than the foregoing epistle, contains the following:

> I imagine that bogus justice at Ogden will now begin in a few days its fanatical and malicious operations set and spring its traps upon us unfortunate victims. Very well, if my presence is desirable and I am thought of sufficient importance let them ascertain my whereabouts, send me a suitable escort, pay expenses, and I shall be pleased to afford them the accommodation of my presence and submit to injustice.
>
> My health is wonderfully improved since I arrived in this locality; appetite good, plenty to eat, mush and milk for breakfast, roast lamb for dinner and mush and milk for supper; could have greater variety but do not want it.
>
> You ask how I employ myself? Well, I read the news, study authors, write articles for publication, correspond with a few worthy choice spirits, like yourself for instance, and look after my daily journal. For exercise and amusement I walk over dreary wastes, over tiny green hills, through lovely vales clothed in rich verdure, saunter through beautiful parks adorned with trees and shrubbery of delightful foliage in all their various hues and shades peculiar to their nature; or strolling through charming cypress groves enlivened by enchanting songsters sitting in the branches. Or perhaps climbing some lofty mountain and looking far away upon the great blue ocean; or down beneath where its serf is lashed into fury as it dashes upon the rocky shore foaming and leaping into a thousand irregular fantastic forms, producing sounds like the thunders of heaven, inspiring a deep sense of the power and majesty of nature.
>
> When wearied of these scenes of wonder and sublimity, I descend and promenade through the pretty walks of some beautiful garden appropriated for the benefit and enjoyment of the public and there sit by some fountain watching the lively sports of the gold fish; or in the cooling shades of a grotto reclining on a bed of a thousand flowers thinking or dreaming of home, sweet home, of dear wives and children that God has given me, and I love supremely and would rather die than abandon.
>
> I thank you for kindly offering me an asylum but think it would hardly be proper. I cannot flatter myself that the war [raid] is yet over, but possibly will be prosecuted with more vigor and sharpness and, quite likely, if the war-fiends fix their minds on arresting me at whatever expense, they can trace me to my whereabouts. Leaving the country would be my only security. In fact, were it not for the counsel given me,

> I might perhaps feel somewhat uneasy regarding my probable arrest, and the operation of the courts.
>
> I notice in several instances, that when persons have been at the trouble and expense of hiding several long and weary months, on the first day of their return have been arrested and dragged into court. I shall follow counsel fearless of consequences. I feel well and no discouragement, and that the end, though perhaps distant, will prove satisfactory, profitable and glorious.

On 9th of July President Snow wrote a family epistle from which the following is taken:

> The other day while strolling along in the Masonic Cemetery enjoying and admiring its beauties and various attractions, I was suddenly aroused from my contemplations and struck with a sense of approaching danger by a strange sound or voice in earthly mutterings, low moanings as in deep distress as though issuing from the tombs. I stood a moment gazing about to discover, if possible, the cause of the alarm. At last in peering through the shrubbery and tall rosebushes, I saw something in human form, enfolded, apparently in a long white sheet. The idea struck me at once it was an escaped maniac [mental patient] who had taken the funny notion of practicing his voice in singular style which he fancied would be most in keeping with the surrounding solemnities. Aware of the dangers and ferocious nature of maniacs, I felt it wise and prudent to exercise caution. Yet anxious to see and know more, I started in the direction of the object in white, stealthily working my way along where the underbrush appeared the thickest, when suddenly emerging from a clump of sweet briers there stood out in bold relief, veiled in white, the fearful object of my alarm. A Catholic Priest, clothed in his white surplice, reading over the dead body of someone ready to be interred. I hastily withdrew, retired to my lodging, went immediately to bed, ashamed and disgusted with the part I had played.

But these solitary rambles and pensive reveries, so dear to poetic minds, were destined soon to end. The call of duty, to which no man ever turned a more willing ear than Lorenzo Snow, no matter what sacrifice it entailed, now came to change his lot.

At San Francisco, in the latter part of July, he received a communication from the First Presidency, forwarded to him from his Utah address, and calling him to missionary work among the Indians, or Lamanites (American Indians):

Salt Lake City, July 2, 1885.
Pres. Lorenzo Snow,
Brigham City,

Dear Bro. Lorenzo:

Our attention has been called to the condition of the Indians and the necessity of laboring among them in teaching them the principles of the Gospel. You doubtless remember that in the fall of 1882 I was greatly moved upon by the spirit of the Lord to lay upon the Twelve the duty of opening the Gospel to the Lamanites and furnishing them with teachers to enable them to progress in the knowledge of its principles.[3]

I laid before the council with great plainness the necessity for this, showing to them that when we raised up branches among the whites [European converts] we did not neglect them and leave them to themselves, but considered it our duty to furnish them with Elders and other officers to instruct them in their religion and to maintain the organization established among them.

I felt greatly moved upon at that time to impress upon the Apostles the importance of this labor and that they should take the matter in hand and see that, under their direction, the Lamanites who had been baptized were properly instructed. . . .

I have felt greatly impressed to have you, Brother Lorenzo, while you are keeping out of the way of your enemies, visit the various tribes to which you can get access in accordance with the appointment which was made for yourself, Bro. F. D. Richards and Bro. Moses Thatcher at the time of which I speak, November, 1882.

You may select such a company to accompany you as you think will be safe. I think that you will find Bro. Amos Wright an excellent aid as one of your company. He has shown a zeal in this direction that is very commendable and his familiarity with the Shoshones and their language will make him a useful laborer in the field.

The Indians desire our counsel. The Lord is visiting them. He gives unto them visions and dreams. They are preparing for the truth, and we should as His Ministers, do our part in lifting them up from their degraded condition. . . .

With kind regards,
In the Gospel
John Taylor
Geo. Q. Cannon.

To this interesting epistle Apostle Snow responded as follows:

San Francisco
July 20th, 1885.
Presidents Taylor and Cannon,

Dear Brethren:

Your letter of instructions just received, has been delayed through misunderstanding regarding my address. Here in my lonely retreat hearing from you and learning of your health and safety created a feeling of thankfulness and inspiration of rejoicing. I have been in San Francisco and vicinity over a month, with two objects in view, health and safety.

I hid up two weeks in Brigham City, but finding that through inability to communicate freely with family and friends without exposure, and my health failing I took a sudden notion of coming west, and watch and wait for further developments in our judicial District.

Before leaving, however, I assisted the Brethren off who were most exposed, some on missions, others to places of safety and erasing the footprints to their discovery, &c. During this time I received a number of notes of warning, from sources supposed to be reliable, that a plan was being laid for my arrest. A few days before I left the public gaze, a messenger was sent, at night, post-haste from Ogden, warning me of approaching danger. The morning of the day I left Bro. —'s son dispatched a messenger with a note stating he had reasons for believing that U.S. Marshals, in a few hours, would be in Brigham City.

When I last saw you, your parting words were: "Keep out of the hands of the enemy." In Pres. Woodruff's last letter to me, he said: "If you never hear from me again, and I never see your face remember these, my last words, don't fall into the hands of the enemy." I wish to say so much by way of explaining the cause of my absence from home. My health has much improved while here and I am quite able, physically, and willing and anxious to enter, at once, upon your plans, and, with heart and soul, endeavor to carry out your instructions. . . .

May God continue to bless you and preserve you, is ever the prayer of

Your Brother in the Gospel
Lorenzo Snow

This humble and whole-souled response, so characteristic of its author in accepting the important mission placed upon him by his official superiors, in due time, brought the following letter of instructions:

Salt Lake City,
July 27, 1885.
Elder Lorenzo Snow,
San Francisco, Cal.

Dear Brother:

Your esteemed favor of the 20th inst. has been received and perused with pleasure. We are glad to hear from you, to learn of your good health and that you are free to move around according to your pleasure.

The events which are taking place in our Territory give great force to the words of the Prophet respecting the time when everyone shall "sit under his own vine and fig tree without any to molest or make afraid."

We are glad that you have been successful in keeping out of the clutches of your enemies, which is far better than being in their hands. It was gratifying to learn that before getting out of the way yourself you counseled and helped the other Brethren who were in danger to place themselves in positions of security.

Having thus discharged your duty you could enjoy your own freedom and security with feelings of satisfaction. . . .

With kind regards, and praying the Lord to bless you with health of body and strength of mind, and return you with peace and safety.

We remain your Brethren in the New and Everlasting Covenant

John Taylor
Geo. Q. Cannon.

On Saturday, the 8th of August, several days subsequent to the receipt of the foregoing letter, Apostle Snow left San Francisco by steamer, bound for Portland, Oregon. The distance between the two cities is seven hundred miles. He arrived at the latter port on the following Monday.

From Portland, our Apostle went by train, 240 miles to Pendleton, Umatilla County, a town of about 1,500 in population, situated in the immediate vicinity of the Umatilla Indian Reservation. This reservation is in north-eastern Oregon and embraces an area of 326,000 acres, about one-fourth of which land is mountainous and covered with timber. The remainder is prairie-rolling hills, generally well watered and adapted to grazing and agricultural purposes. It is considered by many to be the finest portion of the state.

To say that he fully appreciated the situation and prospect before him, realizing the wisdom and discretion necessary to the successful performance of his mission among these Indians, is only to credit him with that intelligence, diplomacy, and sound judgment that have ever characterized his apostolic labors, at home or abroad. Elder Snow then wrote of his proselytizing plans to the First Presidency. On receiving an answer to his letter containing suggestions that made up his report to the Presidency, Apostle Snow at once prepared to journey homeward. The views of the Presidency were that, for the present, in lieu of establishing a mission among the tribes named, it would be better to carry out more in detail the work already commenced at the Fort Hall and Wind River reservations, according to instructions previously given.

Chapter 4

Missionary Work in Exile and Arrest

On September 10, 1885, Elder Snow set out for home, where he arrived on the night of the sixteenth. His coming was of course kept secret; only the members of his family and a few friends being made aware of his presence in their midst.

The main object of his return was to organize a company for a missionary expedition to the Wind River or Shoshone Reservation in Wyoming, which expedition he organized, completed, and reported to the First Presidency.[1]

With the Apostle Lorenzo's interesting report of his mission to the Wyoming Indians and the successful issue of the undertaking, the Presidency was highly pleased. It was doubtless a source of great satisfaction to the leaders of Israel, upon whom rested the burden of general authority, pent up and prevented as they were from appearing in public and verbally delivering their instructions relating to the Lord's work, or circulating freely among the people, to feel that they had live and capable Elders as their assistants, who, so far as power in them lay, would not suffer the interests of Zion to languish.

The letter of the Presidency to Apostle Snow, apprising him of these appointments, was written immediately on receipt of his report. Their epistle concluded as follows:

> Since we last wrote you we have been steadily employed, as usual, in attending to the business devolving upon us. Our enemies have been very active in their efforts to entrap us, but, thanks to the Lord for His preserving care, we have thus far been delivered. We enjoy today a degree of freedom, which, if not so large as we have had, and as we hope to have again is still much greater than our enemies would permit

> us to have if they had us in their power. We rejoice in the enjoyment of good health and a goodly share of the spirit of God. Besides these precious blessings, we have kind friends, plenty of food and raiment, and are well sheltered, so that, on the whole, we feel that we have abundant cause for thanksgiving. We do the best we can under the circumstances, and with the help of the Lord, shall continue to do so, and wait with patience the good pleasure of our Father respecting the future.
>
> One thing is more and more apparent, that the Lord has not permitted this condition of affairs to prevail without a cause or an object. The people are being tried in many respects, as never before. The true character of many professed Saints is being brought to light, and the wrong-doer and the faithless are being discovered and the fruits of their lives are being brought to light.
>
> We suppose you have access to the papers, and in this way keep yourself informed respecting passing events. The vindictiveness of our enemies does not abate; in fact, they appear to grow worse and worse.
>
> With kind regards, and praying the Lord to bless you and preserve you from the hands of all your enemies, we are your brethren in the new and everlasting covenant.

This letter like all the others from the First Presidency from which we have quoted, was signed by John Taylor and George Q. Cannon. Their associate in the quorum, Elder Joseph F. Smith, was then in exile in a foreign land.

Meanwhile, another head to the hideous hydra of judicial persecution had shown itself, inconsistent, unconstitutional, and oppressive as was the Edmunds Law itself. With the strained and conflicting interpretations of the federal courts up to the latter part of the year 1885, the climax of infamy and cruelty was yet to be reached. We refer to the origin of the iniquitous "segregation scheme," concocted by the public prosecutor and adapted by the federal courts for the punishment of Mormon polygamists.

It will be remembered that Judge Zane in the Pratt case before sentencing the defendant expressed his regret that the law did not provide a heavier penalty for unlawful cohabitation, which he considered almost if not quite as criminal as polygamy. In subsequent cases, the Chief Justice expressed a similar sentiment. Mr. Dickson, taking the hint, forthwith began weaving out of his inventive brain a web of sophistry and legality with which to meet the contingency.

His theory was this: that, while the Edmunds Law provided, as the maximum penalty for unlawful cohabitation, six months imprisonment and a fine of three hundred dollars, there was nothing to prevent the segregating of the offense named into any number of indictments against that same person and the including of any desired number of counts in the same indictment. Thus, making it possible by this multiplication of penalties, to send a man to prison for periods ranging from six months to the full term of his natural life, and to fine him in any sum from three hundred dollars to as many millions.

This astounding theory was introduced into court on the 16th of September, 1885. On that day, the grand jury of the Third District came before Chief Justice Zane and stated by their foreman that they desire further instructions on a certain point that they suggested Mr. Dickson lay before the court. Accordingly he made the following statement: A case had come up for investigation by the grand jury, in which a man was charged with unlawful cohabitation, and the evidence tended to show that since February 1883, he had lived a portion of each week with each wife. Mr. Dickson had informed the grand jurors that they might, under those circumstances, if they believed the evidence, present a separate indictment for each month and each week during that period and had suggested the propriety of finding at least one indictment for each one of the three years. Some of the jurors were in doubt as to the legality of such a proceeding, and they had come into court for instructions.

Thereupon, the court instructed the jury that an indictment might be found for any portion of time, within the three years past, in which the offence was proved to have been committed, whether it be for a year, a month, or a week.

Thus was the infamous "segregation" mill set in motion. Thus was it made possible, by this wicked perversion of law and maladministration of justice, for a Mormon accused of a simple misdemeanor, the maximum penalty for which was a fine of three hundred dollars and six months imprisonment, to be mulcted [cheated] in any sum, even millions of dollars, and be imprisoned for the remainder of his natural life.

Men serving for unlawful cohabitation, could be re-indicted, for the same offense they were then suffering, before leaving their prison cells,[2] and be kept there for as long a period as their vindictive persecutors might desire. The offense being but a misdemeanor, from judgment upon which there was no appeal, these high-minded representatives for Christian morality and the majesty of American law could then revel in injustice to their hearts content, out Herod in their cruelties, and none might say to them "nay." But their triumph was destined to be of short duration.

Friday, November 20, 1885, will long be remembered by the family and friends of Apostle Lorenzo Snow, as an eventful day in history. At daybreak on that memorable morning, Apostle Snow was arrested by United States deputy marshals. The following graphic account of the capture is from the pen of Sister Minnie J. Snow, an eyewitness of the event, at whose house he was apprehended. Says she:

> I was aroused on the morning of November 20th, 1885, just as day was dawning, by a knock on my chamber-door. Maria, the servant-girl, had come to tell me that a man was at the kitchen door, asking for admittance. Upon hearing his knock she had gone to the door, but when about to slip the bolt it occurred to her that the hour was much too early for Olsen, the hired man, to waken her, as was his custom, to get the key to the barn: She also remembered my warning not to admit any strange person without my knowledge. She therefore demanded "Who's there?" Without replying, the stranger asked, "Is Bro. Snow at home?" and also requesting her to open the door. Upon learning this, I directed her to keep quiet and admit no one. I sprang from my bed; hastily surveying the situation, I discovered the house to be surrounded by men whose dark forms were just discernible in the gray dawn of day, and two carriages with steaming horses fastened near the gate in front.
>
> Hastily repairing to my husband's chamber, I found him sleeping quietly, to be awakened by the unwelcome and startling intelligence that the U.S. Marshals were present, come to arrest him. He quickly but coolly prepared to evade them, while I answered the call-bell; this and the Office bell were kept loudly clanging by impatient hands, while at every door and window loud knocking and excited voices clamored for admittance producing the most discordant tumult and confusion outside.
>
> I inquired, "Who is there?" "Open the door please," came the response. "Excuse me but I cannot admit strangers when alone," I answered. "We are officers of the law—my name is Vandercook, we have come to search for Mr. Snow," was the response. "Oh," said I, "Very well, if you will wait a moment for me to dress, I will admit you." "All right. Be as quick as you can, please," was the reply.
>
> My husband by that time was dressed; helping to conceal him in a very ingeniously planned retreat, previously arranged, I now made his bed and carefully removed all evidence of his presence. In leaving the room I stumbled over his hat, which had been dropped in his haste, and hid it in a drawer. Now, hastily donning a wrapper, slippers, etc. I opened the door and confronted Marshals Vandercook and Greenman, and asked them politely if they had a warrant to search the house, if so I should like to examine it.

Mr. Vandercook (the Marshal), drawing a paper from his pocket, assured me that it authorized the search and proffered to read it to me.

Thanking him, I expressed a preference to read it myself, but upon glancing at it I found this impossible, as it was yet too dark; so I invited them into the parlor while I endeavored to decipher the scrawling characters by the light of a lamp. While thus engaged, Mr. Vandercook employed himself in kicking under the sofa, peeking behind the piano, chairs, &c.

They lit a candle and searched the cellar and second story, thoroughly the ground floor, passing the place of concealment. Oh how my heart beat with joy and gratitude, as I supposed they were now through and their search fruitless. On descending the stairs they paused in the hall, and Mr. Vandercook said to Marshal Greenman: "Well Captain, I guess our man isn't here; are you satisfied?" Greenman slowly replied, as a puzzled look rested on his face, "No; there must be some other place." They then relit the candle and began as before going through the parlor, dining room, office, my chamber, patting down the beds (in one lay my little babe but 3 months old) then entered my husband's room, gliding stealthily about patting the bed, drawing out the dressing case drawers, &c. until at last they discovered the secret door. After succeeding in opening it I could stay no longer, but ran into the parlor and closing the door, fell upon my knees and fervently besought the Lord that they might overlook the inner door, if possible in his purpose. I cannot describe the agony of those moments and hope I may never again have to endure it. In coming into the dining room, I met Maria with Rois [LeRoi] and Mable, my children who burst into tears when they saw my face, so pale and anxious, saying, "Mama they won't take *you* will they, why do you look so?" I could only say, "Pray, pray hard, for Papa." Turning, I met Vandercook who said they were puzzled over a place they had discovered and wished me to explain. I followed, and found they had explored the first apartment and Capt. Greenman was just rising and coming out when Vandercook espied a splinter raised by the end of a screw which had just pierced through the wood, from the other side; this he investigated and became satisfied that it led to an opening, which he directed me to explain, or he must get an ax and force it open. I saw now there was no hope, and so said he must do so then if he could find one. He left a moment and procured a hatchet. I knew Mr. Snow could hear all that was going on, and how terrible to feel there was no chance now for escape, and I so powerless to help him. I took my babe and closed the door to hide my anxious agitation, as I heard them demand Mr. Snow to come out, or they would cut down the partition. To which he replied, emerging from his concealment, "Well

> gentlemen, I have endeavored to avoid you but it seems without success; you will have no further trouble."[3]
>
> They then read the warrant, requiring him to be in Ogden forthwith. I now appeared and as the children saw their Papa for the first time since May, and now in the hands of the marshals they ran, and clinging to him wept bitterly. What a meeting for them; a scene that affected even Captain Greenman, who had been left in charge while the others went in search of witnesses in the case.
>
> We hastily prepared breakfast and invited Greenman to join us, but he declined saying that they would take breakfast at the Warm Springs, halfway to Ogden.
>
> Friends now flocked in to proffer any possible assistance. On his way to the carriage which was to take him to Ogden a crowd of young men gathered around Bro. Snow saying, "Give us the word and they shall never take you from town." But he replied, "It's all right; Providence has so ordered this matter." He left directions for all the family who had been subpoenaed to follow on the first train, which we did, full of hope that the testimony would be insufficient to indict him.

Thus it was that Apostle Snow fell into the hands of the enemy he had so long and successfully evaded. It appears that the posse of marshals who effected his arrest, had left Ogden in vehicles about an hour after midnight on the 19th, stealthily in the stillness making their way northward, and arriving at Brigham City, surrounded the house in which their venerable victim was sleeping, just at daybreak. Deputy Marshal Vandercook was the leader of the party, which also included Deputies Greenman, Perkins, and four others. Who the informer was upon whose information the midnight raid was planned and executed, though suspected, may never be definitely known until the day of judgment dawns, and the doom of the traitor—the "betrayer of the brethren"—overtakes him as a nemesis from which he flies in vain.

The peaceful town of Brigham was thrown into a fever of excitement when it became known what was taking place at the residence of Apostle Snow. Without doubt the inhabitants of the city would have risen almost *en masse* and rescued their beloved leader from the hands of his captors had he permitted such a thing to be done. But to this he would never have consented. Wise and forbearing, strong in sense of right, and brave in conscious innocence and rectitude, such men as Lorenzo Snow prefer to "suffer wrong rather than do wrong," and so, in calm dignity, quelling every thought of violence or resistance to the officers of the law, he submitted quietly to their demands and advised his friends and would-be rescuers to do likewise.

Ogden was reached by the marshals and their distinguished prisoner before two o'clock in the afternoon. He was immediately taken before U.S. Commissioner F. T. Black, where he gave bonds in the sum of $1,500. For his appearance before that functionary at 7:00 p.m. Hon. David H. Peery and Hyrum S. Young Esq. were the Apostle's sureties. Elder Snow accepted Brother Peery's invitation to become his guest while in Ogden.

Seven o'clock came and the Federal Court room, where the Commissioner sat, was thronged with eager auditors, anxious to drink in the details of the "Mormon Apostle's" examination. But in this they were disappointed; no examination was held. but after some time consumed in waiting, it was announced that the defendant would be required to execute a new bond in the sum of $1,800, for his appearance at ten o'clock the next morning. This was accordingly done, the former sureties continuing on the new obligation. Eight witnesses being placed under bonds to appear at the hour named, the court adjourned. In these proceedings, the Government was represented by Assistant Prosecuting Attorney V. Bierbower, and the defense by C. C. Richards Esq.

An eyewitness of the scene, writing to the *Deseret News* under the *nom de plume* of "Weber," paid the following high tribute to the calm dignity of demeanor worn by the defendant:

> It was gratifying to observe that Brother Snow appeared as calm and dignified in his demeanor as he does on ordinary occasions. The tenor of his disposition was unruffled, and he exhibited no trace of excitement whatever.
>
> There was no twitching of the mouth, no feeble shaking of the knees and no averting of the eyes. He looked his friends and foes not with a bold impertinence, but with the calm dignity and placid smile of a man who is cognizant that he is being persecuted or prosecuted for daring to obey the high behests of heaven, as they have been revealed, and as he has embraced them, with the full conviction that they are principles which are pure, holy, and elevating, physically and morally, and for the redemption of fallen, debased human nature."

Saturday morning, November 21st, Apostle Snow waived preliminary examination before the Commissioner and was held in bonds to answer any indictment that the Grand Jury might return against him.

Leaving his affairs at Ogden in the hands of the able counsel employed to defend him, and trusting in Providence for the outcome, Elder Snow returned to Brigham City to resume his labors in behalf of the Indian Missions in Idaho and Wyoming, at the point where operations were suspended by his arrest. His desire to see these missions firmly established and in thorough working order was greatly intensified by what had lately befallen, and more zealously than ever, if possible, he now pushed forward the projects he had formed.

The arrest of Brother Snow had created a widespread sensation. Being the first one of the Apostles to fall into the power of the persecuting officials, and withal an aged man, now in his seventy-second year, and one whose classic mind and refined nature made him anything but a fit companion for criminals, to whose society, behind bolts and bars, his unfeeling captors hoped to consign him, the news of his capture spread like a wave of evil tidings. Throughout the community and wherever the facts were known, he at once became a cynosure of friendly thought and sympathy.

On the 5th of December, Apostle Snow received word from C. C. Richards Esq. his attorney in Ogden, that on that morning the Grand Jury of the First District had returned eight indictments, and the court had ordered warrants to be issued for the parties. Mr. Richards further stated that he had been informed that the Grand Jury had had but two cases before them for consideration— those of Lorenzo Snow and David M. Stuart—and he inferred from this and other things, that at least four of the bills were against the former.

Soon after receiving this intelligence, Elder Snow repaired to Ogden, where he was detained for several days answering to indictments, and so forth, three bills (not four) having been found against him by the Grand Jury. During his stay in Ogden, a demurrer to each indictment was interposed and argued by Judge R. K. Williams, one of his counsel.

The demurrers being overruled, the defendant entered pleas of not guilty.

On the same day, he returned home. Three days later he received the following telegram:

Ogden, Utah
Dec. 19, 1885

President Lorenzo Snow:
This afternoon your three cases were set for trial Monday, December 28th, the indictment for this year to be tried first.

C. C. Richards

Another telegram, subsequently received, reads as follows:

Salt Lake, Utah
Dec. 22, 1885

Hon. Lorenzo Snow:
We are trying for a continuance—will advise you as soon as we know.
F. D. Richards

But the continuance asked for was not granted, and the trial day remained as set upon the calendar of the court.

On that day—December 28th—the following letter was written to Apostle Snow by the First Presidency.

Salt Lake City, Utah
December 28th, 1885
Elder Lorenzo Snow,
Brigham City,

Dear Brother:
Your esteemed favor of the 21st, in which you inform us of the arrangements which you have made to have the labor connected with the North Indian Mission attended to by Brother F. D. Richards and M. Thatcher, has been received.

We are greatly pleased with the spirit which your letter breathes and feel thankful that you enjoy the spirit of the Lord to so goodly an extent that you feel to accept His providences, whatever they may be, without murmuring. We exercise all the faith we can in your behalf, and while we know our God is able to deliver His Servants and people, shall it seem to be His providence at the present to permit the wicked to exhibit the spirit they are of, and by their wicked acts help to fill up the cup of their and the Nations iniquity, we sincerely hope you will escape the snares which they have spread for your feet; but the past conduct of these men who have your case in charge, does not warrant us in feeling very sanguine that justice will be shown. If you are convicted however, it will be one of the greatest outrages and mockeries of justice ever perpetrated or witnessed in this land.

Accept our love, and we pray God to be with you by His Spirit and power, and give His angels charge concerning you.

We are your Brethren

John Taylor
Geo. Q. Cannon

Chapter 5

Trials and Convictions under Segregation Law

The case of the United States versus Lorenzo Snow, on the docket of the First District Court, was finally reached on Wednesday, December 30. As stated, three indictments had been found against the defendant in pursuance of the "segregating" process—born several months before in the Third District Court at Salt Lake City, but here practically inaugurated—by means of which the time of his alleged offense (unlawful cohabitation)—was divided into three periods, namely, the years 1883, 1884, and 1885, each year being covered by a separate indictment.

A brief discussion ensued as to the evidence to be admitted in the trial. Counsel for the defendant claimed that only such evidence as referred to the time charged in the indictment could be admitted in this case. It was understood that there were two other indictments against the defendant, and it would manifestly be unfair to use the same evidence in two or more cases. They could only consider the conduct of the defendant during the period of time between January 1, 1885 and December 1885, for this case.

The Court stated that the conduct of the defendant toward the ladies alleged to be his wives prior to the time named in the indictment could be admitted, according to the rulings of the Supreme Court of Utah and the Supreme Court of the United States. He should, therefore, hold that any testimony tending to show that the defendant held out to the world, or said that these ladies were his wives, or claimed them as such during the time of the indictment, was material and admissible. The defense was given the benefit of an exception. The calling of witnesses came next in order. Lorenzo's wives were examined on the witness stand, as were others.

The last day of the dying year of 1885—a year fraught with so much sorrow and suffering to the prosecuted people of Utah, and a day destined to witness one of the most flagrant outrages upon justice ever perpetrated in a civilized community—had dawned. By ten o'clock, the federal courtroom, the scene presented the same crowded appearance that had characterized it on the preceding day.

Some minutes elapsed during which Apostle Snow, who was promptly on hand at the hour set for the continuation of his trial, was engaged in earnest conversation with his attorneys—and then the bailiff, rapping sharply with a pocketknife—an improvised gavel—on the clerk's desk brought the assembly to order, and judge and jury being in their places, the court was duly opened for the day. A little extraneous business having disposed of, the case of the *United States vs. Lorenzo Snow* was called, and proceedings resumed at the point reached when the court adjourned the evening before.

The vast throng which had assembled not only filled every available seat in the courtroom, but also crowded every aisle, passage, and hallway, within or leading to the chamber of justice, while hundreds of eager souls, unable to secure even standing room within hearing distance of the intensely interesting proceedings, reluctantly retired from the vicinity, or remained in the street in groups, discussing the probable outcome of the trial.[1]

Inside, at the bailiff's call to order, an almost breathless silence settled upon the scene. It was broken by the court, who inquired as to the order of the addresses of counsel, instructed the officers to maintain perfect order during the proceedings, and reminding the vast concourse of spectators that the continued courtesy of the court, permitting them to be present in crowds, depended on their observing strict decorum, directed the arguments to begin [arguments herein omitted].

It may have been wondered why the government was represented in so important a trial by but one man, and that one lawyer of such limited ability as Mr. Bierbower proved himself to be. The reason? The conviction of Lorenzo Snow was a foregone conclusion, a result predetermined and prearranged, and no more vigorous a prosecution was deemed necessary. The anti-Mormon conspirators, who, with iron heel, were grinding justice and liberty into the dust in their mad efforts to destroy the Church of God. No defense, however able and convincing, would avail. Judge and jury were arrayed against him. Lorenzo's real offense, as shown by the specious argument of his prosecutor, was in being an Apostle, and his conviction and punishment were assured. It therefore needed no more able a champion than the one chosen, to bolster up the weak and tottering fabric of the prosecution. One man was enough; more would have been superfluous, a mere waste of ammunition.

Judge Powers then gave his charge to the jury. The jury filed out of the courtroom in charge of Deputy Marshal Steel, and it being late in the afternoon, the court took a recess until 7:30 p.m.

Some time before the hour set for reassembling, a messenger from the jury room waited upon Judge Powers at his hotel, with the intelligence that the jury had agreed upon a verdict. The officer was told to go back and inform the jury that a recess had been taken until half past seven until which time it would be useless for them to return to the courtroom. Meantime, speculation was rife as to the result: the friends of the defendant, though not without gloomy forebodings, being sanguine that justice demanded a verdict of acquittal, and his political and religious opponents, knowing whereof they spoke, as freely predicting a verdict of guilty.

But the hour at length arrived, and back streamed the great crowd to the courtroom. Deputy Marshal Hansen threw open the doors and admitted the eager multitude. Judge, jury, counsel, officers, and the accused were all in their places. Presently several members of the defendant's family came in and seated themselves near his side.

Amid a deep hush, the foreman of the jury, at the call of the clerk asking for the delivery of the verdict, arose and responded: "Guilty."

All eyes were at once turned toward the defendant. Not the movement of a muscle was manifest, in form or feature. With the same calm look, full of gentleness and dignity, which had characterized him throughout these proceedings, he sat there unmoved amid the sympathetic gaze of friends and the gloating glances of his enemies. There was something Christlike, the look of meekness and resignation, mingled with compassion for his persecutors, which rested like a halo of peace upon that benign and placid countenance.

The silence which prevailed for some moments after the rendering of the verdict was broken by F. S. Richards, of the defendant's counsel, who arose and gave notice of a motion for a new trial and asked for indulgence in the preparation of papers. The request was granted.

Apostle Snow, still on bail in this case and two others, which were set for hearing early in January, at the earliest opportunity set out for home.

The second trial of Lorenzo Snow, which took place on Monday and Tuesday, the 4th and 5th days of January, 1886, was in many respects a duplication or abridgment of the first. It had, however, some peculiar features. Speeches were given and witnesses examined, but with similar results to the first.

The court charged the jury in much the same language as it had formerly used but added: "That if the jury found beyond a reasonable doubt that the defendant had during the year 1884 a legal wife living at Brigham City, Box Elder County, Utah Territory, from whom he was not divorced; that he recognized as his wife, held her out as such, contributed towards her support, and that during the year he lived in the same house with the woman Minnie and recognized her as his wife, associated with her as such, holding her as his wife, then the offense of unlawful cohabitation is complete, and you will find the defendant guilty."

Of course this paved the way for a verdict of "guilty," which was accordingly rendered by the jury, through their foreman, after an absence from the courtroom of a very few moments.

Fast following on the heels of the second trial, came the third and last in the celebrated case of the *United States vs. Lorenzo Snow*. It occurred the same afternoon that witnessed the close of the second trial.

Haste and hurry characterized the subsequent proceedings. The defendant was arraigned on the indictment charging him with unlawful cohabitation during the year 1883. His plea of former conviction in bar of further prosecution for the same offense was entered, demurred to, and the demurrer sustained. A jury was empaneled, and after being examined by the prosecution as to statutory qualifications, was accepted by the defense without examination or challenge. The result of the trial was already known. The only object being to dispose of the indictment and complete the record for the purpose of a new trial or an appeal, any action that would delay proceeding was undesirable.

No arguments were made by the attorneys, and the court charged the jury in substantially the same language as at the second trial. Conviction was thus rendered certain, and a verdict of acquittal was not hoped for. The jury went through the form of retiring but speedily returned with the verdict: "guilty as charged in the indictment."

Thereupon the court fixed as the time for passing sentence in all three cases and for hearing arguments on the motions made for new trials: Saturday, January 16th.

The defendant was held in bonds of \$15,000–\$5,000 in each case—pending further proceedings. His alleged offenses, be it remembered, were mere misdemeanors, punishable at most, in the aggregate, by a fine of \$900 and eighteen months imprisonment.

Apostle Lorenzo was stoic in the tribulations which had now beset him. Who can read without admiring the following effusions of his pen and tongue? The first a letter to the Presidency written soon after his last trial:

> Brigham City, January 8, 1886
> Pres. John Taylor and Geo. Q. Cannon,
>
> Dear Brethren:
>
> Next Saturday the 16th inst., I am to receive my triple sentence, comprising three indictments, for living and cohabitating with my wives; having been convicted without a shadow of evidence.
>
> The fine, costs and imprisonment will, of course, be strained to the utmost. It is even surmised that I may be sent to the States [prison outside Utah Territory]. I am very thankful to the Giver of all good for the bodily health and buoyancy of spirit which He so confers on me, that I feel perfectly resigned with calm submission to the inevitable, and am enabled fully to acknowledge the hand of God and His overruling providences in whatever has or may occur.
>
> And yet it requires an effort to suppress regrets that I am under the necessity of so abruptly closing my missionary enterprises, but if I can serve the holy cause which is dearer to me than life and promote the glory of God by passing through the ordeal of incarceration in a Penitentiary, I am perfectly willing.
>
> I am glad and it affords me great consolation that I was arrested while in the discharge of public duties endeavoring to perform them as a faithful servant of God.
>
> Please accept my grateful acknowledgments of your kindness and wise counsels. The approval of God and your approbation shall be as ever objects of my highest aspirations.
>
> Hoping that for Zion's sake, you might sufficiently retain your freedom so as to counsel, direct and comfort her faithful sons and daughters.
>
> I am your friend and Brother in the
> New and Everlasting Covenant
> Lorenzo Snow

Two days later, he gave a farewell address to a congregation in the Brigham City Tabernacle, of which the following are excerpts:

> I am thankful for the opportunity of addressing this large audience, most of whom I recognize as my intimate friends and associates, for whose spiritual, moral and intellectual advancement, and temporal prosperity, I have labored diligently through a period of over thirty

years, ever since the establishment of its first dwelling or hamlet.

This, I presume, will prove my last opportunity, for some length of time of addressing you, being now under bonds of six thousand dollars, to appear next Saturday, the 16th inst., at Ogden, to receive sentence for cohabiting with my wives, having been pronounced guilty for the same offense, under three indictments. Undoubtedly my sentence will embrace the extreme limit the law allows—eighteen months imprisonment, nine hundred dollars fine, with costs of prosecution added.

I do not now propose to enter into details respecting the three trials under those indictments, resulting in verdicts of guilty without one particle of evidence by which to justify such verdicts. . . .

To "multiply," was the first commandment given to our first parents. Purity in matrimonial intercourse, I always believed, should accompany that command, and I have always endeavored to observe faithfully its practice. I married because it was commanded of God, and commenced in plural marriage, I contracted marriage with four women about the same time, and with a mutual understanding with each that they were to be equal—neither was to take or assume the status of a first or legal wife. Two of them were united to me in the sacred bonds of matrimony at one and the same time, by the same ceremony. The other two shortly after, also at one and the same time, and in like manner. . . .

I go to prison with the full assurance that I can serve God and His purposes—magnify my calling, and prove to the world, my faith and sincerity in the principles I have taught, during fifty years among many nations—that Jesus is the Son of God—that He has revealed His Priesthood, and the fullness of the ancient Gospel, and established His Church by revelation.

When I received the Apostleship, I well remember saying to my brethren, who were present, that very possibly the same sacrifices would be required of the modern Apostles as were experienced by the Apostles anciently, including their persecutions and martyrdoms. I said, in receiving this sacred calling, I felt as though it were ascending an altar where, perhaps, life itself would be offered. . . .

If we succeed in passing through the approaching fiery ordeals with our fidelity and integrity unimpeached, we may expect at the close of our trials, a great and mighty outpouring of the Spirit and power of God—a great endowment upon all who shall have remained true to their covenants. We must be more eager to cultivate friendly relations with our neighbors, together with love and affection for our wives and children that peace may dwell in our households, and confidence in the midst of the people.

"Fifty millions of people" are said to be calling loudly for the extermination of the "Mormons." If it be a fact that our religion is divine, established of God, there is no cause for alarm, nor even anxiety or uneasiness. Tens of thousands, through the teachings of the sacred Gospel know it to be true—a fact, by immediate revelation to themselves. Therefore, these "fifty millions of people," are not fighting the "Mormons," or their religion, but they are fighting God and His purposes. . . .

The Church, no doubt, needs purifying—we have hypocrites among us—milk and water Saints—those professing to be Saints but doing nothing to render themselves worthy of membership; and too many of us have been pursuing worldly gains, rather than spiritual improvements—have not sought the things of God with that earnestness which becomes our profession. Trials and afflictions will cause our hearts to turn to our Father who has so marvelously wrought out our redemption and deliverance from Babylon. . . .

While thus living we may look forward far away into the spirit land, with full assurance that, when reaching that happy clime, we shall be crowned with the sons and daughters of God, and possess the wealth and glory of a Celestial kingdom.

The Apostle Paul in his time taught the Saints to have the same mind in them as was in Christ Jesus, who, finding himself in the form of God, thought it not robbery to be equal with God. The Apostle John, on the same subject says; "When Jesus appears we shall be like Him." "Every one that hath this hope in him purifieth himself even as God is pure."

As man now is, God once was. This was shown to me, many years ago, as clearly as the noon-day sun. We advance from babyhood to childhood—thence to boyhood, manhood, then to the Godhead [Godhood]. This then is the "mark of the prize of man's high calling in Christ Jesus."

We are the offspring of God, begotten by Him in the spirit world, where we partook of his nature as children here partake of the likeness of their parents. Our trials and sufferings give us experience, and establish within us principles of Godliness.

Jesus has, in our day, visited this world, and been seen of men on different occasions. He appeared on the 3rd day of April, 1836, to the Prophet Joseph Smith and Oliver Cowdery, in the Temple at Kirtland, Ohio. . . .

I now will bring my remarks to a close. In a few days I must leave family, kind friends and associates with whom I have spent so many pleasant hours in "The city I love so well"—proceed to Ogden—receive my sentence, then retire to private life within my prison walls, for "The word of God and testimony of Jesus."

> I hope to address you again, many times in this life though this may be my last—however I shall expect to meet you in yonder world, clothed in robes of celestial beauty, amid the glory of the Sons of God, where grief and suffering shall have ceased—when tears no longer will moisten your cheeks, and sighs and moans no more be heard, but where peace and joy forever reign, in those realms of glory, honor and immortality.

Lorenzo Snow was one of the first in this dispensation to grasp the glorious and astounding truth—for astounding it was when first enunciated—that God is man made perfect, and that man is God in embryo. Nor did he receive this from man, nor from any earthly source. His own mind conceived it while kindled into divine activity by the fire of the Holy Ghost.

"As man now is, God once was;
As God now is, man may be."

Thus was whispered in faultless rhythm by the Spirit of Truth, that sublime idea to the poetic soul of this favored son of God. But he kept his own counsel, lest persecution should ensue, and in due time was rewarded by hearing from the lips of the Prophet of God, the President of the Church—whose sole right it is to receive revelation for the Church—that the doctrine of the manhood of God and the Godhood of man, was as true as it was daring and sublime.

Is it marvelous that men, so believing and blessed with the Spirit of that belief, should be capable of enduring with patience for the Truth's sake—knowing, as they do, that even in the midst of the deepest tribulations they are but climbing the steep and prickly path by which God their Father and Jesus, their elder Brother, once mortal like themselves, were made perfect through suffering?

Again was Elder Snow brought before Judge Powers. The sixteenth of January had arrived, the day set for passing sentence upon the defendant and for previously going through the form of a hearing upon his motions for new trials.

The judge, the attorneys, the defendant, and the spectators—a vast throng—being all in their places, order was called, and the proceedings began.

The three cases against the defendant were taken up at once, the Judge remarking that he could decide the questions raised in all of them by a single ruling.

No one familiar with his record doubted his ability to do this, nor to make short work, in that ruling, of any plea that might be put forth in favor of the Mormon Apostle.

The grounds upon which the defense had moved the court to set aside the verdicts and order new trials in these cases were as follows:

1st – The court erred in the decision of questions of law arising during the course of the trial.

2nd – The court misdirected the jury in matters of law.

3rd – The verdict is contrary to evidence.

4th – The verdict is contrary to law.

The arguments having been made upon the motions, and the same submitted to the court for decision and determination, it was ordered that said motions be overruled and denied. An objection to this ruling was duly taken by the defense.

Nothing now remained for the court but to pronounce judgment and sentence upon the prisoner.

"Lorenzo Snow, you will stand up," spoke the judge.

The Apostle arose and looked the court straightly and steadily in the eye. The vast throng which crowded the courtroom leaned forward, listening with breathless anticipation.

The judge reminded the prisoner of the various steps already taken in his case since the finding of the three indictments by the grand jury, and that the next thing in order was the passing of sentence upon him.

"Have you anything to say why sentence should not be pronounced?" asked the court.

The Apostle Lorenzo, like the Apostle Paul, then answered for himself; a few of his expressions follow:

> Your Honor, I wish to address this court kindly, respectfully, and especially without giving offense. . . .
>
> In reference to the prosecuting attorney, Mr. Bierbower, I pardon him for his ungenerous expressions, his apparent false coloring and seeming abuse. The entire lack of evidence in the case against me on which to argue, made that line of speech his only alternative in which to display his eloquence; yet, in all his endeavors, he failed to cast more obloquy [disgrace] on me than was heaped on our Savior. . . .
>
> Inasmuch as frequent reference has been made to my Apostleship, by the prosecution, it becomes proper for me to explain some essential qualifications of an Apostle. First, an Apostle must possess a Divine knowledge by revelation from God, that Jesus lives—that he is the Son of the living God.
>
> Secondly, he must be divinely authorized to promise the Holy Ghost; a Divine principle that reveals the things of God, making known

> His will and purposes, leading into all truth, and showing things to come, as declared by the Savior.
>
> Thirdly, he is commissioned by the power of God, to administer the sacred ordinances of the Gospel, which are confirmed to each individual, by a Divine testimony. Thousands of people now dwelling in these mountain vales, who received these ordinances through my administrations, are living witnesses of the truth of my statement.
>
> As an Apostle, I have visited many nations and kingdoms, bearing this testimony to all classes of people—to men in the highest official stations among whom may be mentioned a President of the French Republic. I have also presented works embracing our faith and doctrine to Queen Victoria and the late Prince Albert of England.
>
> Respecting the doctrine of plural or celestial marriage, to which the prosecution so often referred, it was revealed to me and, afterwards in 1843, fully explained to me by Joseph Smith, the Prophet.
>
> I married my wives because God commanded it. The ceremony which united us for time and eternity was performed by a servant of God, having authority. God being my helper, I would prefer to die a thousand deaths than renounce my wives and violate these sacred obligations. . . .
>
> In conclusion, I solemnly testify, in the name of Jesus, that the so-called Mormon Church is the Church of the living God, established on the rock of revelation, against which the gates of hell cannot prevail.
>
> Thanking your Honor for your indulgence, I am now ready to receive my sentence.[2]

The heroic address of the convicted apostle was listened to by the vast throng with rapt and respectful attention. At the close of the apostle's address, Judge Powers said: "Mr. Snow, the Court desires to ask you, for its own information, what course you propose to pursue in the future concerning the laws of your country?"

Apostle Snow: "Your Honor, in regard to that question; I came into this court—the prosecution had, perhaps, sixteen witnesses. By the evidence of those witnesses I was proved guiltless of the charge contained in the indictments. I had three witnesses. Only two of them were able to testify anything in relation to my case. There was not, your Honor, one scintilla of evidence showing that I had cohabitated during the last three years, or since the passage of the Edmunds Law, with more than one woman. This your Honor, I believe, would readily concede. Well, I have obeyed that law, I have obeyed the Edmunds Law. Your Honor, I am guiltless, I am innocent. Well, now, your Honor, asked me what I am going to do in reference to the future. Having been condemned here and found guilty after having obeyed that law, I am sorry—I regret that your Honor should ask me that question, and, if your Honor please, I should prefer not to answer it."

Then said the judge: "The Court, Mr. Snow, from its own knowledge of you and from your reputation, which came to the Court before you were ever arraigned here, became and is aware that you are a man of more than ordinary ability. The Court is aware that you are a scholar. The Court is aware that you are naturally a leader of men; that you have a mind well adapted to controlling others and for influencing and swaying others, and for guiding others. No matter in what land you might have lived, or in what position you might have been placed, you have those attributes which would naturally have caused people to turn toward you for advice and counsel. You are a man well advanced in years, and you have been favored by time, because it seems to have touched you but lightly with its finger [Lorenzo was seventy-two years old at this time]. The Court feels, that in view of your past life, of the teachings that you have given the people, of the advice and counsel that you desire to stand as an example of one who advocates, and the jury has found also, practices in violation of the law, the Court must pass sentence in these cases in a way and manner that will indicate to this people that the laws of the land cannot be violated with impunity, even by one as aged, as learned and as influential as yourself.

"The sentence of the Court, therefore, is: That on the indictment No. 741 you will be confined in the Penitentiary for the period of six months, that you pay a fine of $300 and the costs of prosecution, and that you stand committed until the fine and costs are paid; and that at the expiration of your sentence in that case, that you must be given—believe as you state to me you do believe—concerning the laws of your country; and recognizing, further, that you are among the very leaders—a leader of leaders among those who advocate that it is right that the law of the land should be violated, it cannot exercise the leniency and the mercy that it would be glad to extend to a man of your age[3] if it were not for your great influence and your great power for good or for evil. I sincerely believe that Lorenzo Snow could cause this people to obey the laws of the Union, and put an end to the trouble and discord in this Territory, if he chose so to do. Believing that, and being fully aware that you will not do that as to indictment No. 742—you will be confined in the Penitentiary of Utah for the period of six months and pay a fine of $300 and the costs of prosecution, and that the expiration of your sentence in that case, that in indictment No. 743 you will be confined in the Penitentiary for the period of six months, and that you pay a fine of $300 and the costs of prosecution, and that you stand committed until the fine and costs are paid. You will be remanded into the custody of the United States Marshal."

An appeal was taken to the Supreme Court of the Territory, from the order overruling the motions for new trials, and from the final judgment thus rendered. Pending further proceedings, the defendant was permitted to continue on bail in the sum of fifteen thousand dollars.

Chapter 6

The Utah Territorial Penitentiary

The Supreme Court of Utah, at the time of which we are writing, consisted of Chief Justice Zane, who sat in the Third District Court at Salt Lake City; Associate Justice Boreman, of the Second District, at Beaver; and Judge Powers, of the First District (all anti-Mormon bigots), the court which was held alternately at Ogden and Provo.

The time had not come for the assignment of a fourth judge to the Utah bench; hence the injustice and absurdity of allowing a District Judge to assist in revising his own decisions was still in vogue.

The Snow cases, on appeal from the First District, came up for argument in the supreme court, at Salt Lake City, on Thursday, the 28th of January, eight days after the appeal to that tribunal had been taken. The proceedings occupied nearly the entire day. Judge Harkness and F. S. Richards Esq. appeared for the appellant, and Attorney W. H. Dickson in behalf of the government. The Supreme Court of Utah upheld the verdicts: "After careful examination of this record we find no grounds sufficient to reverse the judgment of the district court, and it is therefore affirmed."

Associate Justices Powers and Boreman both concurred in the decision.

On application of the counsel for the defendant, it was ordered that the remittitur be stayed for thirty days. It was the afternoon of Saturday, February 13th, just one week from the day of the Supreme Court's decision in the Snow case for 1885. That tribunal was again in session prepared to render opinions in the two remaining cases.

By a majority of the court, the decision of the district court was affirmed. Thus did the Supreme Court of Utah Territory put the seal of its approval upon this flagrant wrong. Thus did a majority of that court practically agree that a man proven innocent of the offense of which he was accused should still be punished for that offense, and that the maximum penalty meted out for it by law should be multiplied by three.

The questions involved in the Snow cases, which the Utah Courts, to the extent of their jurisdiction, had now disposed of, were deemed of sufficient public import to warrant and even demand an appeal to the Supreme Court of the nation. The question of "segregation" alone was one of vital moment, affecting as it did, presently and prospectively, the liberties of hundreds of unfortunate victims of the "crusade." A test case was needed. Lorenzo Snow's was that case; and in his person the suffering people of trampled Utah made one more appeal for justice at the bar of the highest tribunal in the land.

On the 24th of February, eleven days after the last decision of the Utah judges in these cases, Attorney F. S. Richards wrote to his friend and client that he had appealed his cases and that the appeal would be heard sooner than expected.

This intelligence was highly gratifying, not only to Apostle Snow, who had scarcely hoped for so favorable an issue, but likewise to his friends and family. The citations were issued with a view to having the cases before the Supreme Court on the second Monday of the ensuing October. An additional bond of $250 in each case was required of the appellant. Earnest efforts were now made to have the Snow cases advanced on the calendar of the Court at Washington; for though the citations had issued for October, it was hoped in view of the weighty question involved, that the Supreme Court could be induced to set the trial for sometime in April.

But this hope was born to be blighted. All efforts toward the desired end proved abortive. It soon became evident that a further sacrifice on the part of the venerable Apostle—the sacrifice of his personal liberty—would be necessary before the end sought could be attained.

There was something suggestive of this deed of heroism in the noble act of self-sacrifice now determined on by Apostle Lorenzo Snow. Weary of the delay, worn with suspense, and while not courting martyrdom, willing to serve his people and the cause of God in the emergency that had arisen, on the 13th day of March 13, 1886, he voluntarily surrendered himself to the United States Marshal and requested to be taken to the Penitentiary. So Lorenzo Snow passed behind bolts and bars, there to join his brethren, immured as living martyrs within those gloomy walls, this faithful and devoted servant of the Lord.[1]

The Utah Penitentiary, where Apostle Snow and the Brethren were confined was a primitive structure of forbidding aspect occupying a prominent site on the elevated bench-land, a few miles south and east of Salt Lake City [now the Sugarhouse area]. The Penitentiary faced west. The walls of the enclosure, which covered an area of about one acre, were four feet thick and twenty feet high.

The following description of the interior of the Penitentiary, its officers, prison fare, and discipline at the time of which we are writing—some months before the improvements since made were inaugurated—is from the graphic pen of John Nicholson, who also served a term therein and was liberated just after the imprisonment of Apostle Snow:

> All the buildings within the enclosure are constructed of wood. With the exception of the eating room and bathhouse, they are built of pine—mostly two inches thick by eight inches wide. The walls are formed by laying those boards flat, one upon the other and fastening them together with large iron spikes, with the four corners being jointed. The ceiling is made similarly, the edges of the plank forming the surface. The floor is constructed after the same pattern as the ceiling, the entire structure, both on the exterior and on the inside, having a decidedly ribby aspect. The whole is covered by an ordinary shingle roof.
>
> Near the northwest corner stands an insignificant and squatty structure, as will be judged by its interior dimensions, its width being about ten and its length about twelve feet. The height is proportionate. Inside is a strong iron cage which monopolizes most of the space, as it is about seven feet long and six wide, the height being probably six feet six inches. This sad-looking edifice is used for a variety of purposes, the meager facilitics of this whole institution renders this extensive utilization absolutely necessary. Occasionally it does duty as a hospital for the sick, the number of patients being necessarily limited to one, and of attendants the same.

Utah Territorial Prison in 1855, located in what is now Salt Lake City's Sugar House Park area. (USHS)

It has occasionally also been utilized as a place of solitary confinement for refractory convicts, who have gone beyond prescribed rules of the prison.

Another capacity in which it has figured has been that of an insane asylum on a small scale. A law passed by the Legislature provides for the placing of insane convicts in the Territorial Lunatic Asylum, so that the prison will in future be happily free from that class of unfortunates.

Near the other corner—the southwest—to the right of the entrance to the yard, is another structure of the same character. Indeed it is almost the counterpart of the one just described, including the iron cage interior attachment.

Facing the gate in a line are the two most pretentious buildings of the interior. They are the bunkhouses or cells, where the prisoners are locked up at night. The first incorporates bunkhouses Numbers One and Two, the former being the first reached as we advance eastward. Attached to its front is a small room used as a guard house, for the use of the officers on duty inside the enclosure.

The dimensions of the interior are: thirty feet long by twenty feet wide, the height from floor to ceiling being twelve feet. The visitor is instantly impressed with the comfortless appearance of the room, and the rigid economy that has been used in the utilization of a limited space. The manner in which the sleeping accommodations are arranged reminds one forcibly of the passenger steerage of a large ship. The sleeping bunks extend entirely around three walls, that which contains the entrance being the only one exempt from those peculiar sleepers. They are in three tiers, being one over another, the space between being about three feet. Each bunk is six feet six inches long, by four feet six inches wide, and parallel with the wall lengthwise. The number of bunks in

Pencil sketch of the Utah Territorial Prison at about the time Lorenzo Snow served his sentence. (USHS)

Number One is thirty-two, and as each is intended for two inmates, there is sleeping accommodation in that particular cell for sixty-four convicts, and it has been of late generally almost, if not quite full.

Around the room, in front of the lower tier of bunks, is a rough board, placed on uprights which does duty as a seat.

There is but one entrance to the cell—a strong door made of iron bars, crossing each other at intervals of four inches, and fastened together with rivets, or, considering their size, they might as appropriately be called bolts.

Bunkhouse Number Two is in the same building, and is in general features similar to that just described. It is considerably smaller, however, being twenty by twenty feet, and has only two, in the place of three, tiers of bunks; consequently its sleeping accommodations are but one half that of the other.

Number Three is detached from the other bunkhouses, being situated a few feet further eastward. It is a recent addition to the premises, having been erected in the summer of 1885. It is similar to the others. It is twenty-six feet long and twenty feet wide. There are, as in Number One, three tiers of bunks, of which there are twenty six, the room thus affording sleeping conveniences for fifty-two convicts. There are five small windows, protected by iron gratings, of the same size as those heretofore described. Thus far the sole occupants—varying from forty to fifty in number—have been men convicted of unlawful cohabitation, and prisoners who are employed in various capacities on the outside of the Penitentiary proper. They are called "trusties," the title being derived from the fact that their occupations give them opportunities to escape, which it is not presumed they will take advantage of, besides their being necessarily trusted in other respects.

In warm weather these cells are infested with vermin in the shape of bed bugs. The interstices between the planks give them ample breeding facilities, which they do not hesitate to take advantage of. The consequence is, that they make incursions in "shoals and nations," subjecting the hapless convicts to annoyance that falls but little, if anything, short of torture. Different remedies have been employed upon the plague of the prison, but thus far they have only mitigated the evil without approaching its abatement.

The officers of the prison consist of the Warden, Turnkey, and eight Guards. The will of the first named official is supreme under the law and the United States Marshal, the supervisor oversight of the Penitentiary devolving upon the latter.

As stated, Apostle Snow was driven out to the Penitentiary on the evening of March 12th, 1886. Among the many marks of kindness shown him in the interim between his conviction and imprisonment was the following, received from two prominent physicians of Ogden (one of them a non-Mormon), and which he was now in a position to fully appreciate.

> Ogden, Utah, Jan. 16th, 1886
> To the Warden, Utah Penitentiary:
>
> Dear Sir:-
>
> In consideration of the advanced age (72 years) of the bearer, Lorenzo Snow, and also of his usually delicate condition, we the undersigned, take the liberty of stating that we fear his health would be seriously jeopardized by depriving him of his hair and beard, as he has worn the latter 16 years on this account.
>
> Could you, consistently, with your duty, depart from your usual rule, in this instance, you would, in all probability avoid the risk of serious consequence to Mr. Snow and confer a favor on.
>
> Yours Respectfully
> Jno. D. Carnahan M.D.
> J.P. Allen M.D.

Agreeable to this polite request, Warden Dow kindly permitted his venerable prisoner to wear his hair and beard as usual, during the entire term of his imprisonment.[2] In various other ways, so far as consistent with the prison rules, Apostle Snow was treated by his guards and keepers with marked consideration and respect.[3]

Chapter 7

Serving Time in the "Pen"

Apostle Snow had been in prison not quite two months when he addressed the first of a series of letters to his family, giving them in interesting style the results of his experiences and observations in his new place of abode:

> Utah Penitentiary, May 4, 1886
>
> To My Family:-
>
> In every position of life whenever we find that few, or many, of its features, are somewhat of a disagreeable character, our thoughts should seek out and contemplate those of a pleasant nature, the bright and sunny side, discarding in our reflections whatever breeds unpleasantness or tends to that which is unprofitable. In my present situation and surroundings, and in describing them, I trust I may be credited with aiming to carry out the above sentiment.
>
> You doubtless remember that this is a United States Institution, ostensibly designed in the interest of the public, to correct the habits, improve the manners, cultivate the morals and educate in a general way those who become members of the Establishment.
>
> In a general sense we are here as the invited guests of the Nation, boarded and lodged all at Government expense, a remarkable instance illustrating in a striking manner that spirit of philanthropy pervading the bosom of our Mighty Republic.
>
> The Institution comprises about one hundred and fifty students under the immediate supervision of President [Warden] G. M. Dow, a gentleman of ability, genial, kind and generous, admirably qualified for the responsible position he occupies. Thus far, he has proven very fortunate, not only in maintaining good order, discipline, and a healthy feeling throughout the various departments of the Establishment, but

also of securing the respect and esteem of nearly, if not quite, all the members and officers of the Institution.[1]

This establishment embraces a number of separate edifices, each appropriated to some special important purpose, the whole surrounded by lofty embattlements including also a dry park of rather small dimension; which serves for promenading and various kinds of amusements. The enclosure contains a little rising of one acre—"*Multo im parvo.*" The most promising of those structures is occupied by President Dow, his wife and children. Not having enjoyed the pleasure of an introduction, I cannot speak from personal observation, but Mrs. Dow is spoken of as being a lady of fine appearance, intelligent, talented, of a lively disposition, kind, polite, and affable.

The evening I arrived, while waiting in the drawing room for the honor of admission into the interior of the Premises, I was very pleasantly entertained in a chit-chat with their Eldest Son, a sprightly little fellow of some ten years, much above the average of his age in general intelligence and conversational abilities; he is now under the able tutorship of the distinguished Prof. Rudger Clawson of Salt Lake City.

This U.S. Institution is provided with a drawing room for the reception and entertainment of visitors, under such regulations that are not troubled by lengthened visits trespassing upon our patience and valuable time for which ingenious precaution we feel very grateful, as it preserves us from committing the gross blunder in etiquette, by showing, at any time, impatience and uneasiness so as to become apparent that we wish him to go. Thirty minutes is the time allotted to begin and end these interviews. No one is admitted to this drawing room without proper credentials, showing his character and worthiness to interview such of us as he signifies, and his card must bear the endorsement of a person of distinction, one in high esteem and confidence with the present reigning Administration of our National Government. This also is an admirable measure as it aims to protect us from being annoyed by people of low habits and doubtful character.

We have a dining hall of sufficient dimensions to seat, at once, all the gentlemen of the Establishment; also a nice cozy apartment devoted to bathing purposes. Likewise another pretty little apartment used for washing the hands and face, mornings prior to breakfasting.

We lodge in three separate buildings distinguished by the numbers 1-2-3. Number three is 20½ feet by 26½ feet, embracing sleeping apartments, arranged to accommodate two gentlemen each. Those sleeping rooms jut out except at one end of the building from the inside walls all around the Hall in three consecutive rows, one above the other presenting from an inside view an appearance highly picturesque, and rather amusing when occupied by the sleepers, and illuminated by the glaring light of a magnificent chandelier, suspended directly from the center of the ceiling.

The space left between those three rows of dormitories is about twelve by twenty-two feet. From 6 p.m. until 9 p.m. generally about fifty persons occupy this space together with chairs and three tables. Those three hours of association show how large bodies can be crowded successfully into minor spaces, without destroying their components which suggests even to a dull and ordinary imagination that the occupants are not naturally belligerent.

The wishes of the officers are seldom if ever expressed in harsh and domineering terms, but kindly and respectfully as become gentlemen in their intercourse with one another. This inspires and promotes good feeling between ourselves and those guardians of our interests.

At 6 p.m. we form into a close column, single file, the hour being marked by three sonorous strokes of the bell used on such occasions. Two officials quickly approach, gaze a moment, doubtless in admiration of our military aspect, and picturesque attire, then intimate their pleasure that we retire, one by one, to our sleeping apartments.

To protect us during our repose from outside intrusion, a metal door is then closed after us and secured by two locks of curious construction. We entertain the most grateful feelings for this delicate consideration and appropriate arrangement on the part of our executors. Of course being here as the invited guests of the Nation we have reason to expect from a great and magnanimous government this kind and respectful attention, and furnished with such polite and affable gentlemen to watch our interests and provide so carefully for our safety.

From 6 to 9 our time is variously employed, depending perhaps though not invariably upon our past habits and customs, some to improve their minds, increasing their stock of scientific knowledge by the study of history, language, bookkeeping, mathematics; others engage in amusements such as novel reading, consulting foreign papers, desultory conversation, dominoes, cards, checkers &c. &c.;[2] others are satisfied in doing little or nothing except gathering ideas by looking on, and taking in the situations; while a limited few indulge occasionally in light talk, not confining themselves strictly to language the most pure or refined.

On the admission of new members and the retirement of those, whose term as guests of the Institution has elapsed it is the invariable custom to honor them with an ovation consisting of speeches, songs, recitations, instrumental music on the cornet, clarinet, banjo; also, jig, clog dances and other enlivening recreations.[3] Precisely at nine o'clock, the time being intimated by gentle taps on our metal door, we immediately withdraw to our chambers of repose (4 feet in width by 6 in length and 3 in height) conversation ceases and silence reigns supreme. Amid profound stillness and deep slumbers of the midnight hour, the spirit often asserting its independence, leaving its earthly tenement soars aloft, and swift as light wings its way to our far off homes, holds pleasing converse with our loved inmates, and then as we awake at early morn, we feel possessed of a sweet and refreshing spirit permeating our bosoms.

Lorenzo Snow

(To be continued.)

A second letter of a later date, continued the story as follows:

Utah Penitentiary, May 13, 1886

To My Family:-

Having washed and arranged our toilets according to our taste and ability, we wait breakfast, our anxiety tempered by the relative demand of our appetites. The event watched for at length is announced, when, as though by magic, one hundred and fifty occupants, young and old, of various nationalities pour from their sleeping tenements, marshal instantly into two columns, converging at a point adjoining the dining hall.

We describe the scene as it probably would appear to an observer. It will be noticed this picture possesses many phases oddly made up of strange mixtures, quite opposite in the natures, which viewed as a whole are singularly striking, and on account of its peculiarities has attracted the attention of many persons in quest of ariguralities or whatever may minister to a lively imagination, or to supply material for philosophical, moral or religious contemplation. Therefore it is not uncommon on these occasions to notice crowds of enthusiasts posted upon the top of the walls surrounding our establishment, gazing down upon our dual ranks, displaying in their changing countenances a curious combination of emotion and sentiment such as astonishment, sympathy, admiration, sorrow, profound respect, risibility, etc. etc.

The first aspect which strikes the beholder is our imperfect struggle to assume a correct military attitude, the failure of which unfortunately shows that the maneuver has resulted in the formation of but an awkward squad, doubtless awakening feelings of the ludicrous. Many, for the greater number of these files, are seen to possess intelligent and attractive countenances indicating a high state of intellectual, moral and religious culture, impressing the observer with feelings of interest and sentiments of profound respect. Another curious feature in the Exhibit appears in the grotesque colors and arrangement of our construes, consisting of two broad rings artistically arranged so that they run horizontally around pants, vest and sack coat equidistant from one another. The one ring a coal, glossy black, the other a pure, snowy white, following each other alternately as before described.

When the eye of a visitor catches this grotesque point in the scene, and we note its effect, having long cultivated feelings of forgiveness, we pardon his ill-breeding and wretched lack of etiquette when discovering him in convulsions of laughter.

Another distinguished feature (this I feel a pride in mentioning) is the peculiar air of dignity, stately, noble bearing, and majestic mien of the greater portion of this body of men, evidently born to lead and control.

Well, having said so much, we are now prepared to march our serpentine columns, not to the gory field of conflict, to cut the enemy in pieces, but, into a dining hall to attack and consume the refreshments gratuitously furnished.

The tables are primitive in their construction, seemingly very antique, and the benches for seats may be described in the same words. Tin plates, tin cups and spoons constitute the table appointments apparently of ancient manufacture, as though they might have been employed, perhaps, in the service of the Antediluvians. Knives and forks do not appear in this quarter, except in a few solitary instances where they are found combined in the reduced form of pocket knives.

Coffee, meat, potatoes and bread, all in generous quantities, grace the table at our morning repast meal. At noonday, meat and bread, with, occasionally a light soup. Supper is made up of tea and bread.

Strange though it may appear, yet facts show that many of our Gentlemen positively fatten, and some even achieve a state of corpulence, on this simple and primitive diet. Of course to be successful in such attainments of our physical condition and generous proportions, as a rule, one must possess a healthy constitution with a naturally aggressive appetite, combined with a clear conscience. Speaking of myself, as I aspire but to the maintenance of the latter quality, therefore, when I emerge hence, my present figure, I fancy, will not have assumed those physical distinctions.

Every Sabbath religious service is held in the dining hall, by Clergymen of various Sects in Salt Lake City, each in their turn. We have a magnificent choir made up of convicts who assist at the services except at the "Mormon" meetings, these are served with invited singers. The chorister is a "Mormon" convicted of cohabitation; the organist serving sentence for burglary—breaking open a safe at Ogden; another member, for effecting an abortion; another a Negro convicted of rape, &c. Notwithstanding this seeming drawback of respectability, it's a splendid choir, discoursing charming and splendid music, all too in an artistic style, nearly above criticism.

It is curious though, and highly amusing to observe this prison choir, their heads and faces clean shaven, their grotesque costumes—attired as performers at a circus, or actors in a comic scene, earnestly engaged as important factors in these solemn and reverential ceremonies.

At first thought, on taking in this scene, one is liable to be led to the ridiculous notion that the Stage and Pulpit had, at last, harmonized their differences, had met and embraced, each in its own way and style, the one in its habiliments of mournfulness and deepest feelings of piety and solemnity; the other in the fanciful, burlesque costume, frolicsome and frisky mood. The mistake however is a bad one, but easily corrected by observing the appearance and character of the audience, one third of which are noticed as "Mormons" *convicted of living with their wives*, the balance serving sentences for various crimes and misdemeanors, all wearing the garb of convicts, these services being designed to make them consistent and better Christians.

Lorenzo Snow

(To be continued.)

As the result of Apostle Snow's surrender to the United States Marshal and his subsequent imprisonment, the Supreme Court at Washington

Photograph of Mormon polygamous prisoners in typical striped prison garb. President George Q. Cannon is top center, and Elder Francis M. Lyman is wearing regular clothes. The author was unable to locate a prison photograph of Lorenzo Snow. (USHS)

advanced his case upon its calendar, as requested. Consequently, the proceedings, instead of being delayed until October, or longer, as might have been the case had he remained at liberty, began before that August tribunal during the closing days of April.

On the tenth day of May, 1886, the Supreme Court of the United States rendered its decision in the Snow case, argued before that tribunal on the 28th and 29th of April. The Court held that it was without jurisdiction in this class of cases, and therefore dismissed it.[4] At the same time, in order to be consistent, it reconsidered its action in the Cannon case, decided some months before, recalled the mandate issued in that case, and dismissed it likewise for want of jurisdiction.

The belief that the Supreme Court, in so deciding, had, for political reasons, evaded the issue and shirked a grave responsibility was very general. Though technically correct, as many conceded the opinion to be, it created much surprise that the Court of last resort, after considering and deciding the Cannon Case of the same class as this—should, in May 1886, conclude it had no jurisdiction in such cases, and instead of sacrificing a technical point in order to rescue an oppressed community from the grasp of a tyrannical and rapacious horde of adventurers, practically hand over to them, bound and helpless, the people of the fairest and richest of American Territories, to be robbed and trampled on at pleasure.

Governor Caleb West, who had lately arrived in Utah, succeeding in office Governor Murray, twice visited Lorenzo during the first part of May, his purpose being to mediate and seek a presidential pardon if Lorenzo and the other Mormon prisoners would agree to stop practicing polygamy and renounce their plural wives.

Apostle Snow, in his third letter to his family, recounts his first interview with the Governor:

> Utah Penitentiary, May 28, 1886.
>
> To my family:
>
> I have had two interviews with C. W. West, our newly appointed Governor, the first two or three days after his arrival in Utah, the other on the 13th inst. The last one has been reported in the local papers.
>
> I will describe the first interview. The gentleman was accompanied, on his visit, by Arthur Pratt, J. Burnett, and Boliver Roberts. When he was admitted through the gate into the prison yard, I was engaged in conversation with two of my daughters in the reception room.
>
> On their departure I returned to the yard and was here accosted by the Warden who informed me that the Governor wished to see and

speak to me. Upon being introduced we indulged at considerable length in conversation mutually agreeable and interesting the substance of which I give as follows:

The Governor remarked that he had frequently heard my name spoken of in respectable circles, was pleased to meet me, should have preferred, however, that his interview had occurred previous to my trial and conviction, as he believed had it so been this imprisonment might have been avoided. I replied, that I appreciated my present condition with a fair grace, feeling quite contented and tolerably comfortable, being conscious that I was innocent of crime or any wrong doing; deprived of my rights and liberty by a wrong interpretation and unjust administration of the law. He regretted, he said, that there existed such an unpleasant state of affairs in Utah, but believed there was a remedy at hand, and he hoped that these difficulties would be amicably adjusted.

He thought it would be wise and politic for our people, at once, to place themselves and our institutions in harmony with the laws of our country, and thought this was our duty as good American citizens and thus provide against all future trouble by securing the aid and protection of the Government.

I infer from your remarks, said I, that you now recommend the abandonment of our doctrine of plural marriage, and the abandonment of our wives. But as that doctrine is a fundamental principle of our religion, we having rescued a knowledge of its divine origin, we could not consent to relinquish it through any force of circumstances.

He replied there was no occasion to renounce our religious belief and opinions it was the practice only which was in conflict with the expressed wishes of the nation; that in the war between the North and South, he, and his political friends held to certain views regarding State rights, but thought it just and politic to yield obedience to the laws, yet they still held the same opinions.

I think Governor, said I, that yourself and your political friends acted wisely; but our cases are widely different. Your belief of State rights was of human source and direction, whereas our doctrine of Celestial marriage is divine, revealed to us from heaven. The Governor said, he did not wish to bring religion into the question as he was not familiar with theology, had always figured as a politician; he wished himself and my people to see and understand our situation—that it was our best policy as well as our duty, as good citizens to submit to the expressed will of some sixty millions of people—that we were but few and our religious opinions were in opposition to those of the entire Christian World; and that we had become now an object of judicial attention, that it was nearly the universal feeling of the nation and the determination of the Government to enforce an obedience to its laws.

I said I perfectly understood the force of his remarks regarding the peculiar position in which we stood religiously compared with the Christian World, and as being antagonistic to a certain enactment of Congress called the Edmunds Law. As to that law, we believed it unconstitutional, but we had not opposed its administration; and however unjust its application, we had always submitted to its punishments and never been defiant. True, we were a feeble minority, but we had accepted certain truths revealed from heaven which would alternately prevail, and become the popular and dominant religion. This would not be the first instance in the world's history, that true principles when first revealed, had but few adherents, and they obscure, but after struggling through fire and blood, those principles spread and multiplied votaries until princes, kings and emperors became their supporters.

Governor, I continued, our people are but little known and, as you say, are comparatively few and the nation is rising in its might to destroy us and blot out our name and memory, but these sacred truths and doctrines will pass the fiery ordeal, and time will mark their onward march until similar results follow.—As I before stated, I was ultimately acquainted with Joseph Smith, the Prophet, and know him to be man of God and he testified to the truth of these principles, and I know them myself through a knowledge from God.

The Governor intimated again that he did not wish to introduce religion into the discussion.

But Governor, I remarked, you are a Bible believer, a Christian, I presume? "Yes" he replied, "but cannot believe that God interferes now with the affairs of men; our safety and welfare now depends upon our obedience to the Nation's will, as expressed in its laws and I hope, Mr. Snow, that you will see things in this light and allow me to persuade you to employ your influence to bring your people to this conclusion."

I thank you, Governor, said I, but having adopted sacred and holy principles for which we have already sacrificed property, home, and life on several occasions in their defense, we do not propose, at this late hour, to abandon them because of threatened danger. Now, Governor, I continued, suppose we adopt your suggestions and relinquish plural marriage, what guarantee have we of enjoying peace, and from being molested in our religious rights and liberties? "Oh," said he, "I will pledge, my word and honor you shall not be disturbed." Well, I will give you credit Governor, said I, for sincerity; but this would not be the first instance in our history when a Governor has pledged his word, in case too, where life and death were at stake, and broke his sacred pledge resulting in the massacre of our Prophet and Patriarch; this occurred in the state of Illinois, and our people were broken up and driven out of the State.

"Well, but I am positive," said he, "that your trouble if any, would be from a few unprincipled persons whose aggressions would be punished when brought to the attention of the Courts; the laws would protect you and the Government would give its aid in enforcing them in your behalf in every emergency."

But, I replied, it was the State, the whole State with its Governor that mobbed us and drove us out of Missouri and on application for redress to Van Buren, President of the United States, he admitted our cause was just but had no authority to protect us, and you must remember, Governor, our doctrine of Plural Marriage, at that time was not taught or known. Therefore it could not have been the cause of the popular feeling and prejudice which inflamed the passions of our enemies. This seemed to annoy the Governor a little and disturb his usual equanimity; and he contented himself in still persisting that we certainly would be protected in the Courts they being impartial and unprejudiced.

"Governor, said I, all we now ask is an unprejudiced and a correct interpretation and impartial administration of the laws; but you are aware, as well as ourselves this is far from the facts which is forcibly demonstrated in my own case as well as in many others." "But," said he, "if in such cases the law has been wrongly interpreted and applied, there is a remedy—the Supreme Court of the United States where your case is now being investigated; surely in that Court prejudice or partiality cannot appear—the decisions will be just and should be honored and obeyed by all good citizens." "But," said I, "our past experience in that Court has shown quite the contrary, and yours also Governor."

When the matter was referred to that Court which of the two candidates had been elected, President Hayes and Lilden? the notorious vote of eight against seven, inspired a powerful conviction in the mind of yourself and your Democratic friends, that political aims could find place and way and influence, even in that high tribunal of justice. This provoked a laugh among the listeners at the Governors expense. The interview though sharp and pointed in many parts of the conversation, was pleasant and interesting throughout.

After a cordial handshaking the Governor took his leave under the powerful cheers delivered by the joint efforts of the entire inmates of the Penitentiary—signifying a gracious acknowledgment, he passed from the prison yard.[5]

Lorenzo Snow

The second widely-reported visit (May 13) consisted of further verbal sparring in which the Governor had no chance considering his counterpart and a proposal from the Governor to work for a pardon for them if they met his terms to stop practicing polygamy.[6]

While there is no doubt that Governor West, in making his proposition, was partly actuated by humane and magnanimous feelings such as many newcomers to Utah feel until the local anti-Mormon virus has entered their souls and imprisoned their better natures, it is also probable, from what is now known of the defunct official, that the vain desire to exhibit himself in the supposedly heroic role of a would-be solver of the Mormon (polygamy) problem likewise animated his breast. The inconsistency of his request, that men convicted without a shadow of evidence should promise to obey a law "as construed by the courts," when the constructions of said courts were as various and changeable as the colors of the chameleon and when even the highest tribunal of the land appealed to for a definite construction of the statute had repeatedly failed to furnish one, is too apparent to require comment.

From an editorial in the *Deseret Evening News* of May 14, 1886, is excerpted the following, on the subject of the preceding day:

> The Governor's principal conversation was with Apostle Lorenzo Snow. His case illustrates our argument. The evidence for the prosecution showed conclusively that he had only lived with one wife for several years. By mutual arrangement this was with a wife who bore him children. The others he provided for, but did not live with. He only cohabited with one woman but was convicted for cohabiting with more, the court ruling that it was to be implied that he cohabited with his first wife though the evidence showed that he had not. What would be the meaning of his promise to obey the law as construed by the courts? He had done so, strictly, as construed by Judge Zane in the Musser case.
>
> But suppose he is to keep the law as construed by Judge Powers in his own case. How can he do that? He must not live with any but his first wife. But in one indictment it was ruled that Sarah Snow was his first wife, and in another indictment that Adeline Snow was his first life. Must he live with both? If so he can be entrapped again. If he lives with Sarah only he can be caught on the ruling that Adeline is his first wife. If he lives with Adeline he can be ensnared on the ruling that Sarah is his first wife. And under the ruling of Judge Zane in the latest case, if he lives with one and steps in to see another when dangerously ill, he

could be sent again to the Penitentiary. Notwithstanding his pardon or any amnesty that might be extended. If Governor West will study the Snow case he will see one very urgent reason why the prisoners cannot consistently agree to obey the law as construed by the courts.[7]

Chapter 8

Enduring Prison Life with Grace and Dignity

Four days had elapsed since the visit of Governor West and his party to the Penitentiary. We refer to the second visit of His Excellency, on which occasion he laid before the imprisoned elders his conditional offer of amnesty. A meeting of the Brethren had been called for the purpose of considering the propriety of answering in a formal manner the governor's proposition.[1] This meeting of the Brethren in the "Pen" was held May 17th, 1886, and the outcome was a decision to write a declaration formally declining the governor's offer. Lorenzo was the guiding influence of the meeting, although all present had their say. He moved that a committee be appointed to draft the response, which met to consider the best way to do so the next day. A committee was then nominated, which included Elder Snow.[2] After several meetings and due deliberation, a draft was eventually completed:

> Utah Penitentiary, May 24th, 1886.
> To His Excellency Caleb W. West,
> Governor of Utah.
>
> Sir:- On the 13th inst. you honored the inmates of the Penitentiary with a visit, offered to intercede for the pardon of all those enduring imprisonment on conviction under the Edmunds Law, if they would but promise obedience to it in the future as interpreted by the Courts.
>
> Gratitude for the interest manifested in our behalf claims from us a reply. We trust, however, that this will not be construed into defiance, as our silence as already been. We have no desire to occupy a defiant attitude towards the Government or to be in conflict with the nation's laws. We have never been even accused of violating any other law than the one under which we were convicted, and that was enacted

purposely to oppose a tenet of our religion. We conscientiously believe in the doctrine of plural marriage, and have practiced it from a firm conviction of its being a divine requirement.

Of the forty-nine Elders of the Church of Jesus Christ of Latter-day Saints now imprisoned in the Penitentiary for alleged violation of the Edmunds Law, all but four had plural wives from the time of its passage to thirty-five years prior thereto. We were united to our wives for time and eternity by the most sacred covenants, and in many instances numerous children have been born as a result of our union, who are endeared to us by the strongest parental ties.

What the promise asked of us implied you declined to explain just as the Courts have done when appeals have been made to them for an explicit and permanent definition of what must be done to comply with the law.

The rulings of the Courts under the law have been too varied and conflicting, heretofore, for us to know what may be their future interpretation.

The simple status of plural marriage is now made under the law material evidence in securing conviction of unlawful cohabitation, thus independent of our acts, ruthlessly trespassing upon sacred domain of our religious belief.

So far as compliance with your proposition requires the sacrifice of honor and manhood, the repudiation of our wives and children and the violation of sacred covenants. Heaven forbid that we should be guilty of such perfidy; perpetual imprisonment with which we are threatened, or even death itself would be preferable.

Our wives desire no separation from us, and were we to comply with your request they would regard our action as most cruel, inhumane and monstrous, our children would blush with shame, and we should deserve the scorn and contempt of all just and honorable men.

The proposition you made, though prompted, doubtless, by a kind feeling, was not new, for we could all have avoided imprisonment by making the same promise to the Courts. In fact, the penalties we are now enduring are for declining to so promise rather than for acts committed in the past.

Had you offered us unconditional amnesty it would have been gladly accepted, but dearly as we prize the great boon of liberty we cannot afford to obtain it by proving untrue to our conscience, our religion and our God.

As loyal citizens of this great Republic, whose Constitution we revere, we not only ask for, but claim our rights as free men, and if from neither local nor national authority we are to receive equity and mercy,

> we will make our appeal to the Great Arbiter of all human interests, who in due time will grant us the justice hitherto denied.
>
> That you may as the Governor of our important but afflicted Territory aid us in securing every right to which loyal and peaceable citizens are entitled, and find happiness in so doing, we will ever pray, as witnessed by our hands. (The prisoners signed the document.)

Weeks lengthened into months, and still our Apostle, wearing a convict's garb and classed with criminals of the deepest dye, remained behind prison walls.[3] Since the decision of the Supreme Court at Washington dismissing his cases, Lorenzo had reconciled himself to the belief that no further effort in that direction would avail and that he was fated to serve out the full term of his triple sentence. With characteristic patience and a calm, even cheerful stoicism, he resigned himself to what he deemed the will of God.[4]

The extreme rigor of the crusade was now beginning to abate. The tidal wave of persecution, which for more than a twelve-month period had been sweeping over and submerging in sorrow fair Utah, having spent its force, and reached for the time being its highest point, had begun to recede, and the first faint signs of an ebb in the angry waters now appeared. It was noticeable that, at rare intervals, a Mormon, sentenced in the district courts for polygamy or unlawful cohabitation, escaped the maximum penalty for his offense and was treated more like other offenders—with an occasional show of something akin to leniency. It was rumored that some of the more prominent crusaders were becoming weary of ill-doing, and not finding "Mormonism" any nearer to its end than when they had first set about its destruction, were desirous of adopting a policy more humane, and at the same time more effective, for the solving of this vexing problem.

Hence, the overtures of peace through Governor West—in which Messrs. Zane and Dickson joined to Apostle Snow and his fellow prisoners in the month of May.

Prior to that time, however, there were indications of the breaking up of the ice-flow of popular hatred as expressed in this persecution.

On March 16th of that year—1886—Governor Eli H. Murray, one of the most unscrupulous enemies of Utah and the Mormon people, had been removed, and his place filled, as has been stated, by the appointment of Governor West, who arrived in Salt Lake City on the 5th day of May. The cause of this change was Murray's malicious and unreasonable course in vetoing the most important measures passed by the legislature, which had just adjourned, as well as his tyrannical conduct in general toward the people he had been sent to govern.

Less than a month after Murray's removal, the press announced the lopping off of two other heads of the local anti-Mormon hydra. One of these was no other than Judge Orlando W. Powers, who had tried and sentenced Apostle Snow in the district court at Ogden. His cunning scheme for place and power had failed. Providence, which had permitted the Apostle Lorenzo to be thrown into a felon's cell, in order that he might, like Paul of old, be "brought before Caesar" to testify, had not designed that his enemies should reap any advantage from the issue. The confirmation of Judge Powers, as associate justice of Utah, during the whole time of his incumbency, had been pending in the United States Senate, that body hesitating to confirm him, owing, it is said, to his malodorous political notoriety.[5]

In order to influence congress and secure his confirmation, Judge Powers, it is believed, became the willing tool of a conspiracy—if indeed he did not conceive it—to entrap and imprison Apostle Snow that he might offer him a captive in exchange for an office and a ransomed reputation. How far the scheme succeeded has been shown. Fate now interposed a barrier to his triumph. "Thus far, but no farther," had been decreed concerning "Judge Powers, and the golden fruit of a glittering prospect now turned to ashes upon his lips."

On the 12th of March, 1886, Lorenzo Snow entered the Utah Penitentiary. On the 12th of April, one month later to a day, the nomination of Orlando W. Powers as associate justice of Utah was withdrawn.[6] The other official, whose head, figuratively speaking, had fallen into the basket, was Marshal E. A. Ireland, an official whose petty tyrannies, servile submission to the anti-Mormon ring, and general smallness of soul, had won for him the contempt of nearly all classes. A full account of the outrages heaped upon the suffering citizens of Utah by Ireland and his horde of heartless hirelings, may possibly never be written. One of his latest exploits had been to purchase the betrayal of President George Q. Cannon. After raiding the Gardo House on the 8th of February, in fruitless quest of Presidents Taylor and Cannon, the marshal proceeded to put a price upon the latter's head, offering five hundred dollars for information of his whereabouts. As a result, President Cannon was betrayed into the hands of his enemies. He was arrested at Humboldt, Nevada, on the 13th of February, while on his way west over the Central Pacific Railway. He was surrendered by Marshal Ireland into the custody of Captain

Penny and a squad of thirty soldiers, who conveyed him a prisoner to Salt Lake, where he was required to give bail in the excessive sum of $45,000. Failing to appear for trial on the day set—March 17th—his bail was at once declared forfeited. Ireland was superseded in office the same day that the nomination of Judge Powers was withdrawn, Frank H. Dyer being appointed his successor as United States Marshal of Utah. It was not until about the middle of June, however, that the new marshal entered upon the duties of his office. On the 13th of that month, Apostle Snow penned the following note to a member of his family:[7]

> With the exceptions of some ten days with a severe cold,[8] soon after my introduction into the prison, my health all along has been universally good, better I believe, than at any time during the past two years. The medicines you kindly put into my trunk, I have had no occasion to use. Every day I make it a practice to take exercise by walking around the yard, from a mile to a mile and a half. Nine times round the yard make one mile. I am considered one of the finest and fastest of walkers, and am constantly tendered compliments on my remarkably healthy appearance, and buoyant spirits; in fact I am a surprise to myself. I feel that I owe much of this to the faith and prayers of the Saints, and feel very grateful to them and the Lord. . . .
>
> Sister Eliza, Franklin S. Richards, his wife and mother called last week; we had a half hour interesting visit, they left me crackers, candy, sweet cake, and a can of jam.[9] I do not infrequently have little knick-knacks sent me by friends. Some time ago a nice chest was sent me, and today a pretty little stand to write on, with drawers, and key to lock up.
>
> "Rudger" bestows a pie now and then which helps materially in the eating department.
>
> God bless you,
> L. Snow

On the first day of July, Apostle Snow wrote two more letters to his family, further descriptive of his prison experiences. The first of these was in the regular course of his correspondence; the second evidently an afterthought, inspired by an interesting interview that took place that day between him and the new marshal, Mr. Dyer. We give the letters in their order:

> Utah Penitentiary, July 1st, 1886
> To my family:
>
> Some time has passed since I wrote you, and I am somewhat at a loss to know where to begin or what would prove most interesting.
>
> There are some scenes in prison experience, occurring now and

then, which may be anything but agreeable, yet even here we find no cloud so perfectly developed in blackness but it may bear a bright and silver lining; no picture so dark and somber but has some redeeming feature, some bright and beautiful point which may be seen here or there when very closely observed. This observation is truly applicable to us in our experience of prison life. I will relate some incidents embracing the two opposites light and shade, seen in the picture of life in the Utah Penitentiary. . . .

Many of our fellow prisoners have associates outside of the marriage relation, are suffering for crimes of different shades, from the stealing of a calf to that of the terrible crime of murdering their fellow man. Some of these and even the last mentioned, have shown that they still possess some good and redeeming qualities; one and all have exhibited kindness and respect toward myself and the brethren. In some cases at least their punishment seems cruel and severe in the extreme. I listen now and then to a few of their unhappy tales which awaken feelings of interest, sorrow and sympathy. One, a man of some thirty years of age, while wandering in the mountains and in distress for food, killed a calf for which he was sentenced to seven years imprisonment.

An Indian boy poisoned a man for having murdered his father, and although he declares himself justified in committing the act, the poor fellow is now serving sentence for perpetual life imprisonment.

A young man has been sentenced for five years in the Penitentiary for stealing a colt which he declares was his own property.

Now and then some scenes occur within these gloomy precincts which, to say the least, are rather sad and painful to witness. They generally happen at the first meeting between husband, wife and children. On first seeing the fond husband and father issuing from his prison through the ponderous iron gated door, his head closely shaven, attired in the convict's garb, then and there are too often heard the sighs of pain and anguish and bitter tears are seen coursing down the cheeks of the grief stricken wife and sorrowing children.

An incident is told that the father on returning into the prison, at the close of an interview, with his family, while passing through the door, the child cried out in a pleading voice, "Do come home with ma now won't you, Papa?" Another instance a little boy and his mother standing upon the wall of our prison yard, while looking down into the enclosure, suddenly the little fellow espied his father, and reaching out his little arms cried out in the most beseeching tones, "O Papa! Come up here! O, do come to me!" It is quite easy to imagine, and appreciate in such cases, the feelings of parents by any one not devoid of sensibility. It is not uncommon to see women come upon the walls, stand a few moments gazing down upon the imprisoned inmates, then quickly depart with eyes overflowing with tears. One woman when looking from the walls and first seeing her husband dressed as a convict, fainted away and had to be cared for by the Warden. Too many similar scenes which occur here could be told, but the above is sufficient to illustrate this class of prison experience.

While taking my accustomed exercise around over the hard beaten gravel path, lying alongside my prison walls, nine rounds of which are equal to one mile, I am not un-frequently reminded of the caged animals I have noticed in a menagerie ever tramping to and fro, around within his iron bars or wooden cage.

However, there are some interesting points in this enclosure, from which we secure fine views of the mountain summits, some clothed in their lively and beautiful virtue of charming green, while others are seen mantled and glistening in beautiful snow.

As we gaze with rapturous delight upon this lively scene, so grand and picturesque we forget for the moment that we are convicts, torn from our families, our sacred liberties and divine rights wrenched from us by the fierce unrelenting hand of cruel oppression. But as we turn from this lovely enchanting scene, we are quickly reminded of our situation, as our eyes rest upon the dark and somber walls by which we are environed and gaze upon the iron bars of our prison, and away aloft we notice our guards upon the watch towers, or treading to and fro upon the walls, armed with loaded guns, while at the same time our eyes saluted with the heavy and clanging sounds of the ball and chain dragging along the gravely ground then again when we notice ourselves dressed as convicts, we are brought to a full sense of our strange and singular condition, and yet we feel that we are innocent of crime that our motives have been pure, our conscience clear, and that during many long and weary years, we have sacrificed the enjoyment of loved and happy homes, of loving wives and children, often jeopardizing our lives in order to engage in awaking people sitting in darkness from their sleep of death, and point them to the way of life, to our Father, God to the fountain of intelligence to everlasting peace and exaltation; and notwithstanding we have been thrust into prison by the will and sanction of the people in whose interests we have made many sacrifices, suffered these deprivations, yet our intentions are still to labor for their good and we feel we cannot do it more successfully in any other way than we are now doing; therefore we accept this class of gospel labor resignedly and cheerfully knowing that the eyes of the world, of angels, the eyes of God and the heavenly hosts are upon us: and the attention of the wicked Lucifer, and his hosts of evil spirits likewise are directed toward us, and they fear and tremble in view of the results from the maintenance of our integrity, devotion and fixed resolutions to honor our God, our holy religion and priesthood, notwithstanding the forbidding prospects of lifelong imprisonment. Says the prophet Isaiah: "How beautiful upon the mountains are the feet of him that bringeth good tidings, that publisheth peace; that bringeth good tidings of good that publisheth salvation, that saith unto Zion thy God reigneth." And I will add: How beautiful to contemplate our Elders of Israel in the Penitentiary of Utah, in the prison at Boise, and at Detroit, Michigan; though suffering a lingering martyrdom, yet smiling at their sufferings and rejoicing that they are accounted worthy to be thus persecuted, as were the ancient saints, for religious belief, for the love of God and the testimony of Jesus.

There is one important sentiment entertained by our brethren here, regarding which, I believe there are no exceptions, I often hear it expressed viz.: that our confinement, as it regards ourselves personally, we care not a fig, it is only our families, their anxieties and the inconveniences they suffer, that we care for and which give us any uneasiness. I certainly feel proud of my noble associates, high priests, seventies, of their devotion and heroism, willing martyrs for the glory of God; and I pray earnestly that I may be strengthened in heart to accomplish my share of the peculiar gospel labor, magnify my Apostolic Priesthood, and fail in no particular in doing whatever is required for promoting and sustaining the purposes of our Heavenly Father in the interest of His Church and people.

Lorenzo Snow

Utah Penitentiary, July 1st, 1886

To my family:

I was called out this afternoon to have a conversation with Marshal Dyer. We took seats beneath some poplars, protecting us from the scorching sun, and forming a pleasant and cooling shade. He was pleased, he said, to notice that I was looking so well and enjoying health. Thanking him for his kind expressions, I said that I considered that I had no reason to complain and felt quite reconciled to my situation. Had made up my mind from the moment of my arrest to accept, without worry, whatever might be the results; being convinced that important good would surely come of it both to myself and the Great Cause, to promote which, during the course of fifty years, I had been industriously engaged. He said that he regretted very much that these difficulties now existed, creating so much ill-will, causing crimination and recrimination between the two parties "Mormons," and "Gentiles"; that he had done business with our people for some ten years, and very pleasant and satisfactory had been his business relations; that now having assumed the office of Marshal, he felt greatly the delicacy and peculiar responsibilities of his position. He wished to do his duty, he said, expected to, but the lookout was somewhat unpleasant, fearing it impossible to avoid making enemies. I replied that I felt as he did. His duties as a Marshal, in many respects were of an unpleasant nature, and no doubt that in discharging them, his motives in some cases would be more or less misapprehended, and cause censure, but so far as our people are concerned he need entertain no fear of injustice while he confined himself to the legitimate sphere of his office, and employed only decent and respectable deputies; and that in making arrests and treating prisoners, it be done in a proper and humane manner. We have no disposition, Mr. Dyer, to blame you or any one for discharging his whole duty as a public officer. A man can do this and be sustained and respected by the great majority of our people. Warden Dow might be sighted as instance illustrating this fact. He discharges his official duties faithfully and energetically, no infraction of prison rules or discipline is permitted to pass unpunished, yet he regards his prisoners, not as brutes, but men possessing some rights belonging to human beings in the image of God, and he treats them in a spirit of humanity, thereby gaining their love and respect. He said that he intended to do his duty firmly without bias, and would not be influenced by party spirit or prejudice; but still that he much feared his ability to make his official labors even satisfactory to himself.

He said he had experienced so much pleasure in his business intercourse, with our people, and been treated with such kindness and courtesy, that now if these difficulties between our people and the Government, could be harmonized by a personal sacrifice of one years' salary, that he would give it gladly; but thought, he continued, that it would not be long before we should conclude it policy to accept a compromise and so settle the question. I replied that such a proposition, on more than one occasion, had been suggested and urged by prominent officials, but declined in positive terms—indeed it could not be entertained a moment. The Authorities, nor the people, have any such right, plural marriage was instituted by God, and revealed from heaven, and it cannot be repealed; and Mr. Dyer, God does not conform His institutions to human enactments to suit the ideas of any man, legislators or nations. Mr. Dyer said that he differed with me in opinion; he did not believe in present revelation and he thought his belief ought to be a proper offset against my belief. Possibly so, Mr. Dyer, said I, if both parties were depending on belief, as one opinion would be as weighty as another if equally supported by argument; but in this question I possess knowledge, you only belief. By taking certain steps divinely pointed out, I secured this knowledge through direct revelation to myself. In belief a man may be mistaken, but in knowledge he cannot me mistaken. Your belief is of human reason, it is of man and not sustained by scriptural evidence; my knowledge is of God and is supported by scripture. Well, he said, it is the fixed determination of the Government to enforce obedience to its laws, and he thought that under the circumstances it would be good policy and we would be justified, even allowing our principles to be true, and abandoning, at least for the time being, our practice of plural marriage. My. Dyer, I replied, you are comparatively a young man, apparently have a good constitution with prospects of living many years, which, if so you will witness a mighty revolution in public opinion regarding this "Mormon Question"; the public sentiment now so bitterly opposed to us, is molded chiefly by ignorance and prejudice, stimulated by politicians, the public press, Christian Ministers, so called, to accomplish private ends; but these false views and misrepresentations will be dispelled through enlightened opinion, and you will see the so called "Mormons" religion better understood and its people honored and respected. It has fallen to my lot, Mr. Dyer, and a few others to manifest our sincerity, integrity and devotion by suffering unjustly the deprivation of our liberty, and God being our helper, we shall not falter in doing our duty, though at the cost of a lifelong imprisonment, as the prospects of some of us now seem to appear.

But, Mr. Dyer, I continued, the ultimate issue of this business and the final triumph of "Mormonism" so called, depends wholly whether it be a fact that Joseph Smith was authorized of God, through the administration of Peter, James, and John, to administer the ordinances of the Gospel and promise the Holy Ghost, and organize His Church. If so, then we are His people and He will sustain us, and the powers of earth will not prevail against us. I have received a divine knowledge of the truth of the gospel we preach, and tens of thousands bear a like testimony, and, having been blessed with this knowledge, God requires us to stand by it at whatever cost, or personal sacrifice, like a beacon of light firm upon its rocky basis amid the howling storms and dashing waves; yet calm and unmoved, its glittering light directing the observant Mariner with unmistakable certainty to the desired haven of safety and rest.

So stood, in days of old, the Saints, the Prophets, the Apostles, and Jesus Christ the Son of God.

Various subjects were discussed during this interesting interview, which I do not care to mention, suffice it however, to say, that I was favorably impressed with the spirit manifest by Mr. Dyer, and am satisfied, if he carries out his present intentions and present views without allowing himself to be led astray by evil council and influences, he will prove a very fair Territorial Marshal.[10]

Lorenzo Snow

Chapter 9

Preaching and Prophesying among the "Spirits in Prison"

The author's [Orson F. Whitney's] personal acquaintance with Elder Snow began in the month of July 1886, three days after the interview with Marshal Dyer, detailed in the preceding chapter. Though familiar with his figure in public for many years and partly informed, by reading, of some of the principal events of a life which it has since been our good fortune and pleasure to more thoroughly peruse, I had never until then stood face to face and conversed with him, "as one man talketh with another."

This is mentioned, not because of my public interest attaching thereto aside from a little incident that happened that day, which possibly may edify some, but to honor the request of one whom we have learned to regard with feelings of more than ordinary friendship and esteem.

It was Sunday, July 4th, the Nation's Birthday. One hundred and ten years before had been given to the world the declaration of American Independence—the axe laid at the root of the tree of despotism, and the inalienable rights of man to life, liberty, and the pursuit of happiness, unmolested by his fellow man, thundered in the startled ears of the world's tyrants. Yet here, on this day of days, the anniversary of freedom's birth, in the dawn of the second century of Columbia's proud career, in the Utah Penitentiary, guarded and imprisoned as convicts, were men, some of them descendants of the pilgrims and patriots, whose only crime, for which they were now suffering a living martyrdom, had been the innocent and harmless exercise, in all good conscience, of the rights asserted by the Declaration.

The theme was a suggestive one, and in the Sabbath meeting inside the prison—it being the first or "Mormon" Sunday of the month—the Elder [Whitney] sent to conduct the services and "preach to the spirits in prison," did not fail to take advantage of it. His subject was "man's inhumanity to man," and the ultimate dawn of a day of liberty, when the rights guaranteed by the Constitution would be enjoyed equally by all, when to worship God according to the dictates of conscience would no longer be considered a crime, and when the Gospel of Christ, "the perfect law of liberty," would be everywhere honored and extolled, and not, as now, hated and condemned because of ignorance and prejudice, and its disciples immured in dungeons or driven into exile for its sake.

The auditors—prisoners, guards, and all—listened with rapt and respectful attention to the Elder's discourse.

In an interview with Apostle Snow, held a few minutes later, outside the prison, in an apartment used for such purposes, the writer, during the course of the conversation, and while still under the influence of the spirit poured out so plenteously upon the meeting, was constrained to predict that the Apostle would not finish the term of his sentence in prison.

"Well, I came here with that expectation," he said, smiling, half in sadness.

"You will not, though," was the reply, "I feel satisfied of it."

They parted, after further good words of cheer, and a mutual "God bless you"; the one to accompany his party back to the city, the other to rejoin his comrades within the prison walls.

Seven months later the writer had the happiness of grasping his revered friend and brother by the hand, a free man, reminding him of the prediction, and receiving his gracious acknowledgment of the fact, with the declaration that the words spoken had been inspired of God. . . .

July 5th was a day long to be remembered by the inmates of the Utah Penitentiary. The "Nation's Birthday," which, as stated, fell that year upon the Sabbath, was celebrated by the prisoners on the following Monday, with every demonstration of rejoicing that their condition and circumstances would allow.[1] That same day, one of the true convicts, a burglar named "Nosey" Banks, stole a suit of clothes from President Snow and escaped. The next day he was captured in a drunken stupor in a saloon, brought back to the prison, and put in a "sweat box" as punishment.[2]

On the 24th of the month, it being the day celebrated in Utah Territory as the anniversary of the Pioneers entering the Salt Lake Valley, the Mormon prisoners engaged in an unusual exercise—a vigorous rendition of the "Hosanna Shout," a sacred traditional shout usually employed in modern times at temple dedications. In this case, it gave many of the imprisoned brethren a sense of inspired exultation.

Some fifteen years later, Elder Rudger Clawson shared his memory of the occasion:

> I am reminded by the remarks of President Snow of my experience in the Penitentiary at the time of his incarceration. I remember with at great deal of pleasure and satisfaction my association with him there. I came there before him and remained after he had left. I will give you some of my impressions of him. He seemed to accept the situation with the most sublime patience. Though it was a trying time yet he was ever cheerful and ready to offer words of comfort and encouragement to the brethren who were with him. Without flattery, and I am not given to that, I can say that I think and feel that our President accepted this experience and trial as an angel of God. On one occasion it so happened that all the brethren at that time in the Penitentiary had assembled in one room. There were none others gathered with us; for once we were alone, President Snow made a proposition to us that was startling in its nature. He asked each one of us separately to express himself on that proposition. He said we were confined here for conscience sake, to defend the Gospel of Christ. Now the proposition was something which perhaps never before had been made in an earthly prison house. He said: I propose that in this prison, behind these prison walls we shall offer up the sacred shout. It is possibly against the rules of the prison and were it known we might not be permitted to do so, but I propose it as we are here in the defense of one of the principles of the Gospel of the Son of God. The brethren, some thirty or forty in number, all spoke, one after the other, and each expressed himself as highly in favor of the proposition. A few moments were then spent in training as it was new to some of us and we had to learn it. President Snow gave us the training. He said: I want it understood that if you undertake to do this you must lift your voices to the very heavens, put your whole souls into the shout, raise your voices and send it into the very heavens. We agreed to this, took our handkerchiefs and waved them and raised such a shout from that prison house as was never heard there before. It seemed as if the building would be lifted from its foundations, and the very walls trembled. The very souls of the men incarcerated in that prison went into that shout. As I now remember it, it was a most extraordinary experience never to be forgotten. It was sacred and glorious. The sequel also seems extraordinary. I don't remember that any inquiry was ever made because of that shout. There were guards on the walls and rough men, criminals, in near proximity, but I do not remember that any inquiry

was ever made or that any of them ever asked what was meant by that shout. It is something I never could account for: never an investigation, never an inquiry! It was a glorious privilege to us that must have been acceptable to the Lord.[3]

The meager facilities of the Utah Penitentiary, and the consequent privations and sufferings of the hopeless inmates, especially during the extremes of midsummer and winter, after being repeatedly brought to the attention of Congress, at length induced that body to make an appropriation for some much needed improvements at the poverty-stricken institution. On the 19th of August, it was visited by a Congressional party who came to inspect the grounds inside the enclosure with a view to providing plans and specifications for a new building to be erected there.

In a letter to his family written on that day, Lorenzo thus describes this visit:

Utah Penitentiary, Aug. 19, 1886

To my family:

Today we were visited by a party of Gentlemen, twelve in number, most of whom for the purpose of inspecting the grounds with a view of furnishing plans and specifications for the erection of buildings for which Congress has made appropriation. Three strokes of the bell announced their arrival, when all the prisoners immediately retired to the upper end of the enclosure, where they remained until the party withdrew.

After their entrance I was told by the Warden that my presence was desired. I noticed all eyes were directed toward me as I approached and joined the party. Marshal Dyer saluted me cordially and directly introduced me to Colonel Williamson, who, in turn, made me acquainted with Senator Ferry and several other strangers.

Col. Williamson opened the conversation by the remark that this interview has been solicited rather from curiosity—having heard my name often mentioned and noticed it associated very prominently with the affairs and history of our people.

"Well, gentlemen," I replied, "if I can minister in any form to the stratification of your curiosity, I imagine I ought to esteem it both a pleasure and honor."

This remark, though somewhat of a dubious or twofold meaning, seemed to have a salutary effect and it was pleasantly received. After a few words with the Senator, the Colonel asked me to sit down with him for a private conversation, remarking he felt no particular interest in the "plans and specifications." Accordingly we took seats, when he began by saying he was connected with the Department of Justice, was Government Inspector for which business he was now engaged—was a member of Congress when Captain Hooper was Delegate and formed an intimate acquaintance with him. He was a nice intelligent and interesting gentleman. "I suppose, Colonel," said I, "it is the intention of the administration to prepare a way for the admission of Utah into the Union, and that looking to this object, it is intended to remove the present Republican Officials and supply their places with Democrats?" "Yes," the Col. replied, "this is the intention," and he trusted the difficulties in the way of our entering into the Union, an independent State, would soon be adjusted, and believed they would. That he supposed we would be satisfied if there was nothing operating antagonistic against our religion.

Yes, I answered, that is now our cause of complaint—that we had been in the practice of plural marriage many years before any law existed against it; that it was a fundamental principle of our religion, and we felt that the law was enacted purposely to deprive us of our religious rights guaranteed by the Constitution. That we regarded this doctrine of Celestial Marriage a divine principle revealed from heaven

Well, he said, it appears that the Government has committed itself, has decided to abolish polygamy and does it seem probable it would be disposed now to withdraw from its position that is now publicly announced? Colonel, said I, please allow me to illustrate the situation by supposing a case viz.: that Abraham, Isaac, and Jacob in the practice of polygamy having previously received a revelation from God that He sanctioned and required it, the Government to which they belonged had afterwards passed a law against it, which in the end would be compelled to abandon its position? The position of those holy men represents exactly ours; the position of the opposite party represents precisely the position assumed by the U.S. Government. The former is divinely authorized and will be sustained by the Almighty; the latter is of man's wisdom, antagonistic to God's institutions and ultimately must succumb. It is impossible for us to compromise, but we would suffer death or rot in prison rather than turn traitor to our religion and our God. Having been over fifty years, and traveled over a large portion of the globe promulgating this doctrine, I do not, at this late period of my life, propose to abandon my faith, heavenly knowledge and future prospects. Thousands and tens of thousands of our people, both men and women, are imbued with like feeling and resolution. Many have had a divine knowledge regarding the doctrine of plural marriage, and having entered into its practice with this knowledge in the honesty of their hearts, and with the purest of motives, therefore they will go to their death before consenting to renounce this principle.

My seven wives with the exception of one, with whom I have been living since the enactment of the Edmunds Law, are past the age of child bearing, their children grown up and many of them married. During my trial not one scintilla of evidence was produced against me by the prosecution. The jury had been selected by an open venire, purposely to convict, many of them being of a notoriously bad reputation. One glance at those jury-men, as they took their seats, showed at once it was useless to expect justice.

I appealed to the Supreme Court of the Territory, and thence to the U.S. Supreme Court, at Washington, where through the most convincing, powerful and incontrovertible arguments, were shown the illegal, ridiculous rulings and decision of the Utah Courts. The judge perceiving no way of escaping the responsibility of reversing those decisions, decided that the court had no jurisdiction and admitted having made a mistake in deciding a similar case some time before, called the Cannon case, and consequently annulled that decision. My case, Colonel, affords a fair specimen of the ridiculous and conflicting rulings of the Utah Courts. I had seven wives married to me for time and eternity. In order to ensure a verdict of conviction, Judge Powers, in his charge to the jury, said that Adeline, one of the seven, was my legal wife; Zane, the Chief Justice in the Supreme Court differed with Powers, and decided that Sarah Ann, another one of the seven, was my legal wife, and according to The Edmunds Law, under which I was declared guilty; also according to Judge Zane's declaration on two different occasions in open court, Minnie, another of the seven, was a proper wife to live with. Now, Colonel, which one of these wives when I leave here would you advise me to live with, in order to escape future imprisonment? At this part of the conversation the party signified they had completed their inspection and were now ready to retire; the Col. arose from his chair laughingly, shook hands warmly and thanked me for the pleasure enjoyed in the interview. Senator Ferry and acting Governor Thomas approached, shook hands, then all withdrew through the gate of the prison yard.

Aug. 24th, 1886

I was called to the reception hall this morning to have an interview with Mr. Forwood, Mayor of Chester City, Penn. He was accompanied by Apostle H. J. Grant and Junius F. Wells—introduced to me by the former with an explanatory remark that the Mayor had desired this interview for the purpose of gratifying his curiosity in seeing and conversing with a modern Apostle. I observed that I trusted Mr. Forwood was not surprised to find an Apostle in a Penitentiary in convicts attire, that had he lived in former times and sought to interview an Apostle, very likely he would have found him, not in a Penitentiary perhaps, but in some prison bound with chains or at the whipping-post in the hands of an infuriated mob, or possibly in the arena engaged in a deadly struggle with wild beasts. He seemed a little dazed and made no response to this observation. Chairs were furnished and the Mayor seated himself beside me. The conversation was continued between him and myself chiefly during the allotted half hour, while Brother Clawson entertained Brothers Grant and Wells. The conversation throughout was lively and interesting, and at the close, I feel assured, I had produced a very favorable impression and awakened in the Mayor's mind a deep interest in this subject of "Mormonism," modern prophets, apostles, and present revelation. During the interview I bore a strong and powerful testimony of the divine knowledge I had received concerning the restoration of the gifts and powers of the gospel, and the law of Celestial Marriage, and fixed resolve to adhere to our principles though at the cost of liberty and life. Though fifty millions of people had opposite sentiments and the Government had undertaken to overthrow us, and extirpate [destroy] our principles and the opposition might seem appalling, yet we felt calm, unmoved and confident. We know it is God's work and cannot be overthrown, though the whole world combine for this purpose. He asked various questions and seemed much interested and satisfied with the explanations and answers. On replying to his inquiry regarding the number of polygamists compared with the entire Mormon population, he spoke feelingly and in the most positive terms against the undemocratic and shameful injustice of disenfranchising so large a community to punish so small a minority.

The expiration of the allotted half hour being signaled by the guard, the Mayor shook hands and retired to ponder over the subjects of conversation, having, no doubt had his curiosity gratified in a manner he little expected.

Lorenzo Snow

October came; seven months had flown. For more than a third of his triple term of imprisonment had the Apostle Lorenzo been a patient, uncomplaining inmate of that den of wretchedness—the Utah Penitentiary. How he passed his time since last accounts may be gleaned from a perusal of the epistles with which he continued from time to time to supply his anxious household. The next two letters of his family series were as follows:

Utah Penitentiary, Oct. 9, 1886

To my family:

Monday Sept. 20th, 1886, Marshal Dyer called at the Penitentiary accompanied by Judge R. W. Morgan of Memphis, Tenn., and Col. W. H. Selden of the Metropolitan Hotel, Washington, D.C. I was immediately called and the Marshal at once introduced me to the gentleman.

Their fine intellectual features, genial manners, dignified deportment, and commanding presence impressed me at once very favorably that they were no ordinary interviewers.

As it appears to be the practice to point me out to all visitors who secured passes to the Penitentiary as one of its principle curiosities on exhibition, therefore through my respect to Marshal Dyer, who treats me kindly, I endeavored to show myself to as good of advantage as possible under the peculiar circumstances, consequently in an easy and pleasant way I lead my interviewers directly to the favorite, all absorbing question of the hour, viz.: What is Mormonism? Why am I a Mormon? And myself and brethren in the Penitentiary? The Marshal remained a listener to our conversation. After a few moments spent in preliminary questions Judge Morgan began as follows: Mr. Snow, said he, hesitatingly, we do not wish to ask questions which would appear impertinent or indelicate. Oh, not at all gentlemen, I said, ask any questions you see proper. Well, said the Judge, if it is not an improper question, I wish to inquire, how many wives, Mr. Snow, have you, and your number of children?

It was shown in the court at my trial, I replied, that I was the husband of seven wives now living, and two dead. My children, living and dead number over forty. After a few other questions relating to the family, he inquired regarding the family of Pres. Young. I stated that I was not fully posted, but he had, when living, quite a number of wives and a numerous family of children. After a few other questions and answers given, I turned the subject with the observation, that my incarceration was purely on account of my religion; that myself and brethren here had espoused the same religion—the same Gospel as the ancient Saints and Apostles, and were now passing through the same ordeal, the same suffering and persecutions as they were forced to experience.

I have been over fifty years, gentlemen, actively engaged in bearing witness of my knowledge respecting the divine authenticity of what is called "Mormonism" and have declared the principles of my religion, and borne my testimony of them through various portions of my own Country, also in Great Britain, Wales, Ireland, France, Italy, Switzerland, Austria, Germany, Turkey, Land of Palestine and on the Islands of the sea. These arduous and sacred responsibilities, would never have been ventured by me without first knowing this religion, this gospel, and the authority to preach it, had come direct from God to Joseph Smith, pure and unadulterated; not simply a belief, but a knowledge direct to me from God Himself.

Mr. Snow, if I may be allowed to inquire, said the Judge, what you mean by the term knowledge, is I presume, a conviction arising from an internal feeling or inward light. I wish now, he continued, it to be distinctly understood, Mr. Snow, that we are in the pursuit of information not of indulging in criticisms.

Judge Morgan, said I, in speaking of knowledge I employ the term in its literal sense. I mean a physical demonstration, not belief alone, a feeling arising merely from mental enlightenment, as you mentioned, but a physical knowledge, through the organ of the senses, of a nature which could never be questioned or doubted by its possessor while life or memory exists.

Would you object, Mr. Snow, said the Judge, to explain, and fully describe the nature of that knowledge, and the precise manner in which it was given? I shall be happy gentlemen, to do so, but you must allow me time, and to approach the question in my own way, a little circuitously. The following circumstances, gentlemen, led me to investigate what is called "Mormonism."

While attending College at Oberlin, Ohio, in the spring of 1836, I had occasion to visit Kirtland, some 60 miles distant, where two of my sisters were residing. At that time this was the principal settlement of the "Mormons." Joseph Smith, his Counselors, and leading Elders, then had their homes in that locality and the Saints had just completed a beautiful edifice, called a Temple. I became acquainted with Joseph Smith, his counselors and a number of the prominent leaders. I attended several of their meetings at which it was their custom for lay members both men and women to speak—give their experience, and testify regarding the extraordinary Spiritual Manifestations. I talked with these people, their prominent Elders; with Joseph and his aged father, the Patriarch of the Church. I marveled and was exceedingly astonished while listening to what they solemnly declared regarding their wonderful experiences.

The strange things I heard and saw at their prayer and testimony meetings, these marvelous experiences as related my men and women whose sincerity and honesty I could not doubt, and as they asserted, these were the natural and legitimate fruits of obedience to what they called the restored New Testament Gospel, together with a Priesthood which held the keys of right to administer its ordinance of baptism for the remission of sins and the laying on of hands for the reception of the Holy Ghost; these things, as I said, overwhelmed me with astonishment. Joseph Smith assumed this position which no false prophet would dare—viz.: that he had received the visitation of three angels, Peter, James and John who in the name, and by the command of the Son of God, authorized him to preach the Gospel, administer its ordinances and promise the Holy Ghost which would impart a knowledge of his authority and divine mission, and his right to organize the Church of God on the earth to prepare a people for the second advent of the Son of Man. Under these circumstances, gentlemen, I could not otherwise then believe that Joseph Smith was honest, sincere, and I knew that his statement was of that peculiar character in which, with him, there could be no chance of deception; and such testimony, if false, could be no less than positive villainy. In view of these facts, gentlemen, I felt it my duty to accept this Gospel—and would you not yourselves? Being at that time a young man full of worldly aspirations, with bright prospects and means to gratify my ambition in acquiring a liberal Collegiate education; also having a host of wealthy, proud aristocratic friends and relatives watching eagerly for my achieving high honors in life; of course you can easily understand that it was a great trial and required the strongest effort to form a resolution to abandon those prospects, disappoint expectations, join the poor, ignorant despised "Mormons," and become a follower of "Old Joe Smith, the money digger," as he and they were regarded.

Had I then understood, as I now know, the ultimate results of obedience to the Gospel, a life of purity, and after its close and exaltation to the fullness of the Godhead, I should then have been ashamed to call it a sacrifice. But in my ignorance, at that time, of its blessings and glories, it proved the fiercest struggle of heart and will I ever experienced before or since.

But through the help of the Lord, for I feel certain he must have helped me, I laid my pride, worldly ambition and aspirations upon the alter, and as humble as a child went to the waters of baptism, received the ordinance administered by an Apostle and afterward the laying on of hands.

One evening, a few days after this, when alone, engaged in earnest prayer, the heavens were opened, the veil was rent from my mind, and then and there I received the most wonderful manifestations, grand and sublime, I believe, as man was ever permitted to receive, and beyond the power of language fully to describe. It was shown me in that vision that there truly existed a Son of God—that Joseph Smith was really a prophet of God.

The first intimation of the approach of that marvelous vision, was a sound just above my head like the rustling of silken robes, when immediately the Holy Spirit descended upon me enveloping my whole person, filling me from the crown of my head to the soles of my feet, which was a complete baptism as tangible an immersion in a Heavenly principle or element—the Holy Ghost—infinitely more real, physical in its effects upon every part of my system than was the immersion when I was baptized in water. That night after retiring to rest the same wonderful manifestations were repeated, and continued to be several successive nights. From that time to the present on numerous occasions, miraculous manifestations of the Divine power have followed me and my administrations of the Gospel ordinances. Judge Morgan, I continued, I profess to have and actually do have, the right and authority from God to administer this Gospel and promise the Holy Ghost and divine knowledge to follow all who accept it with sincerity and purity of heart. I was intimately acquainted with Joseph Smith many years previous to his martyrdom. He introduced and explained to me, personally in a private conversation these principles of Plural Marriage, for complying with which I am now incarcerated. He told me that God commanded him to obey this Law of Marriage, which if he disregarded, he would not only incur his displeasure but must suffer the severest penalty.

Gentlemen, we will never give up these sacred principles, abandon our wives and nullify our Holy Covenants. Sooner than be thus guilty, prove recreant to our religion and our God we will suffer a lifelong imprisonment and should our persecutors then go so far in their fierce cruelty as to deny us the right of a decent Christian burial, they may bury us beneath these prison walls, because most assuredly we know, and we clearly see in the bright prospects after death that which will infinitely repay the sacrifice.

Government need not cherish the expectation that they can ever force us to renounce our Holy Religion. We are prepared to die in supporting it and its interests, but not to compromise its principles. If God will allow them, of course they may accomplish the former, they can slay us, but in the latter as God lives they will fail. Our prospects and promises of eternal glory, happiness and everlasting exaltation in the Celestial world, in God's presence are too precious to be forfeited for a few brief days of liberty and sufferance of life, secured so disgracefully, so servile, and so sinfully.

At this part of the conversation, it being signified the time had come for leaving, they arose, having listened with the deepest interest, shook hands thanking me in the warmest and most expressive terms for the great pleasure I had afforded them in my plain, and intelligent answers, and explanations given during the very interesting interview.

As they left, Judge Morgan said if possible he should like to avail himself of the privilege of another interview and renew the conversation.

I replied that it would give me pleasure, and if he called again, and would spend a couple of hours I felt certain I would make the time both interesting and profitable. After inscribing, by request, their names and residences—repeating their feelings of thankfulness they withdrew attended by the Marshal.

Lorenzo Snow

Utah Penitentiary, Thur. Oct. 7, 1886

To my family:

The Marshal accompanied by Governor West and Sc. Thomas called at the Penitentiary. Not caring for another interview with Gov. West unless particularly requested I took my chair and writing materials and withdrew to a place in the yard farthest from the gate where they entered. I had been in my place of seclusion but a few moments, however, when I observed the Governor slowly wending his way, circuitously around in the direction I was sitting. As he drew near I arose and saluted him with a cheerful greeting, shook hands cordially with the remark: why, Governor, you fail to visit us now as often as formerly; though, as I now remember you have been some length of time from the Territory. "Well, Mr. Snow," said he, "the fact is I experience no pleasure in my visits here, they always impart feelings of sadness." Why, Governor, I said, you surprise me by that remark. "Well," said he, "I suppose so; but, Mr. Snow, it is witnessing your sufferings that I think are entirely unnecessary; and I regret sincerely that you and your people disincline to allow us to assist you out of your present difficulties." We feel that we are right and that God approves, justifies, and requires the course, I replied, therefore we feel resigned and cheerful, and though obliged for your expressions of sympathy, Governor, yet I can scarcely believe you have discovered any sign among us to cause such feelings, you see no sign of it in me do you, Governor?

"Well, Mr. Snow," said he, "perhaps not as regards your outward appearance; of course I admit you may succeed in concealing your sufferings, but still they are there inwardly. You are deprived of your liberty, the society of family and friends; now, Mr. Snow, permit me to say, though I admit your sincerity, I believe you are wrong, all wrong, in this matter."

Governor, said I, while I believe you also are sincere in your views regarding us and the policy we should adopt, yet I do positively know you are in error in this matter which will be shown in the outcome.

Well now, Mr. Snow, you and your people have been expecting to return to Jackson County, but you have not succeeded and I am sure you cannot while continuing in your present course in standing out against the laws of the land; now we are willing and anxious to help you, if you will agree to conform to the laws which you certainly will be forced to do eventually. Through a prudent and wise policy and exercise of patience, showing a proper submission to the Government, a time may come, Mr. Snow, when things may change, laws may change and your condition and prospects as a people assume a brighter aspect. Governor, said I, the condition on which you have been pleased to offer us liberty, we feel that we cannot conscientiously accept; you require a promise to obey the law in the future—the "Edmund's Law," which would bind us as honorable men, to yield blind submission to the multifarious, contradictory interpretations already given that law, or still may be, according as the Utah Courts are inspired by their bigotry and cruelty.

Now, Mr. Snow, said the Governor, if you and your people would but manifest some disposition to do your share in removing the cause of these perplexities, what you complain of, would all be arranged satisfactorily.

Governor, I said, you require impossibilities. You demand obedience to a Statute, inconsistent, wrong and unconstitutional, enacted purposely to prevent our obeying a command of God previously given; to obey a law of man when in conflict with a known law of God, is against our conscience and religious conviction. Mr. Snow, said he, I cannot believe that God ever requires a people to disobey a law of their country, or justifies them in such disobedience. Well, Governor, said I, you reason and draw your conclusions from your stand point. I from one quite different, I will now illustrate our position. When Nebuchadnezzar, as history tells us, sat upon his throne ruling the nations of the Earth, he enacted a law, affixing a fearful penalty to be executed upon whosoever dared disobey. This law was in direct conflict with a law of God; one law could not be obeyed without disobeying the other. The King had erected a golden image of himself, and commanded all people to worship it on certain occasions. A law of God had been given previously forbidding such worship. The Princes, the Governors, the Generals, the Captains, and all the Kings subjects but three Hebrews, obeyed the law of their country, the law of the Empire in preference to honoring God in obeying His Law.

There were two great laws in conflict, one the law of man, the other the law of God. Now, Governor, will you please answer me this question? Had you been one of those Governors of Provinces, as you are now Governor of Utah, which law ought you to have obeyed, the law of the Empire or the law of God?

Notwithstanding the Governor's usually masterly command over his feelings, he scarcely concealed his annoyance at this pointed question; and though I insisted on an answer, and pressed it as far as courtesy would allow, yet to no purpose, but his Excellency intimated, be the object of the question.

Soon after this interview closed and the Governor retired after shaking hands and a few friendly expressions.

Lorenzo Snow

The object in calling attention, at the opening of this chapter, to the fact that our Apostle had served more than a third of the time for which he was sentenced to prison, was to emphasize an event that occurred in the latter part of October, the final result of which was Lorenzo's liberation.

Chapter 10

The US Supreme Court Overturns Segregation Law

On the 22nd of October, Lorenzo Snow's able attorney, F. S. Richards, made another effort for his client, which, unlike so many previous ones put forth with equal zeal and ability, was ultimately fruitful of success. It was the filing in the Third District Court of a petition for a writ of habeas corpus in behalf of Apostle Snow, who, it was held, having served a six-month term of imprisonment—the maximum penalty of that nature for unlawful cohabitation—was now illegally detained in custody.

In answer to a question by the Court as to the object of the petition, the reply was that the design was to test the legality of the segregation process, which had not yet been passed upon by the court of last resort.

Mr. Richards said the reason the case had been brought before Judge Zane was that the statute required application to the most convenient court. The petitioner did not ask a review of the case in this court or the United States Supreme Court. The only question was whether the court exceeded its jurisdiction in passing additional judgments after the petitioner had been sentenced once for the offense.

Judge Zane, however, refused to issue the writ, and exception to the ruling was taken by counsel for the petitioner.

On the 25th of October, an appeal from Judge Zane's decision was allowed, and the case was carried up to the Supreme Court of the United States.

The final letter—No. 9—of the series written by Apostle Snow to his family while he was in prison bears the date of December 3, 1886, and runs as follows:

Utah Penitentiary, Dec. 3rd, 1886

To my family:-

The wonderful dinner so magnanimously supplied us on Thanksgiving Day, by the Young Ladies Mutual Improvement Association of Brigham and Willard City, was a grand surprise and astonished everybody.

One of the oldest inmates of the prison, of some seven years standing, was the same as many others, in perfect ecstasy and declared both long and loud, that nothing since the day of his incarceration had ever witnessed the like before, as regards variety, richness and vastness of supply, which sentiment was enthusiastically endorsed by the entire crowd of participants.

In the afternoon we had a musical entertainment by several prominent Ladies and Gentlemen from Salt Lake City.

Since I addressed you my last communication I have had several interesting interviews with Ladies and Gentlemen from different parts of the Union, and some from Europe. In every instance persons of education and Official or such as occupy important positions in high circles of society, have always treated me as kindly and listened to me as attentively and respectfully as though I had been some distinguished Congressman. Of course at these interviews, I feel perfectly at home and quite easy in my conscience, and feeling entirely foreign to those of a convict guilty of a crime, which was seen, and I presume impressed my visitors, as they showed they regarded me and my brethren in the light of convicts guilty of crime. . . .

Lorenzo Snow

A correspondent of the *New York Tribune* visited the Penitentiary about this time and interviewed Apostle Snow and Elder Nicholas Groesbeck Jr. From the letters which appeared in the columns of that journal in relation to his visit, we excerpt the following:

One balmy afternoon when the air was tingling with the ozone which is so abundantly generated in the superb climate of Salt Lake, armed with my permit, I started with a clerical friend, a priest connected with a new Catholic College of the Hollows, for the Penitentiary. He wished to see a murderer who was confined there, and who has since been released—by a bullet. I was bent on seeing Apostle Snow and the layman Groesbeck.

After three miles' driving, at a pace which afforded abundant opportunity for enjoying the orchards, flecked with sunshine and shadows, rich wheat crops and long stretches of meadow land, we drew up at the Penitentiary. The place was anything but inviting. The inmates did not add much to stone for the lack of brightness. Slowly circling about in the space between the buildings or in the large area beyond were men in striped dingy clothes. Some were gathered into little knots and a few were sitting apart by themselves as if communing with their thoughts. While I was hastily taking in these details from the parapet above the enclosure and asking questions of a man with a gun, a stentorian voice right beneath me shouted into the yard: "Snow and Groesbeck!" "Snow!" and he an Apostle. The doughty guardian angel on the wall called the names again in even gruffer tones, bawling them out to the prisoners below. Hearing my card sent in, as it were, in this way, I hurried down the steps to the court which was the reception room to meet the gentlemen when they should come out. I had not waited more than a moment when the creaking of two iron-barred gates was heard and "Snow and Groesbeck" appeared.

Mr. Snow led the way. I recognized him at once from a steel engraving which I had seen. He was a spare man with an olive-tinted complexion and wore a snowy beard. His calm, brilliant eyes looked from beneath the heavy eyebrows like polished agate. There was a dignity in his expression which could not fail to impress even the most unsympathetic observer. Strikingly ascetic in his appearance, the Apostle betrayed intellectual force and a commanding self-possession. I felt myself in the presence of a Mormon Chrysostom.

Mr. Groesbeck was the exact opposite of Mr. Snow. He was nearly six feet high, strongly built, his plump round legs and arms filled his striped suit completely, and his round, hearty face was in keeping with his perfect health. He was bourgeoned . . . to the bone. I stepped forward and introduced myself, as they stood looking to see who had called for them. They shook hands heartily with me and seated themselves on the rough bench against the wall while I took a chair just in front of the them. At our left the good father was engaged in conversation with the murderer whom he had come to talk with. The turnkey hovered in the neighborhood to see that his protégés were not smuggled off.

"I have been looking into your church," I said then, "during a stay of some months in Salt Lake, and as this institution has acquired an incidental connection with it on account of so many of its prominent members being imprisoned here, I thought I would round off my study of it by calling on you. Do you find it very hard here?"

"The hardest part is in not being free," said Mr. Snow a little drearily.

"How are you treated? Are the officials kind and considerate?"

"Oh yes!" replied Mr. Snow. "They are gentlemanly and treat

us fairly. We treat them like gentlemen and they do the same by us." "And the diet?" I inquired.

"Good enough. It is plain, but solid and substantial," returned Mr. Snow.

"And the sleeping quarters?" I went on as if I were a Health Inspector.

"They are not quite as neat as they might be," said Mr. Groesbeck, "but there is nothing very disagreeable in the accommodations. Oh," he added cheerfully, "I've been in worse places than this. We are allowed books and papers, and can receive fruit and delicacies from friends. The mail comes regularly to us. Perhaps I feel it a little more than Brother Snow, who has been accustomed to a sedentary life."

"Yes, I have traveled about a great deal," said Mr. Snow. "During the fifty years I have been a Mormon I have gone over 150,000 miles in my evangelical work."

"What is it that you would have to do to be free?" I inquired.

"We have simply to assent to what they demand," answered Mr. Snow. "I could bring myself to submit to the Edmunds Law without any difficulty, if the courts did not vary so in their interpretation of it that a man can hardly know how to keep it to their satisfaction."

"But as soon as you were out, could they not re-arrest you again?"

"It seems so. A lawyer told me that I might pass the rest of my days in the Penitentiary if the courts segregate the counts. Well, it is no more than the saints had to endure of old for religion, and we shall look back on this time with satisfaction.

"I have had numerous introductions to various persons visiting here, and often enjoy long conversations with them. They are pleasant and agreeable. In fact, the Marshal seems to take much pleasure in gratifying the visitors' curiosity by allowing interviews with the imprisoned Mormon Apostle. Ladies and gentlemen, tourists from various parts of the United States and Europe, solicit these interviews, and I think Marshal Dyer granted them in every instance. Among the callers have been several United States Judges, Congressmen, military officers, and other prominent people. One of the pleasantest interviews I have had was with Chief Justice Waite, of the Supreme Court, a short time ago. Governor West has also had several interviews with me, and the officials in the prison always treat me with kindness and courtesy."

I remarked at the time how moderate and resigned they both were. There was not any rancor in their words. They bore their imprisonment with philosophic (or was it religious?) calm. The robust Mr. Groesbeck was occasionally led into some touch of dry humor accompanied by his snug smile. They both seemed to enjoy being called out for a talk much

> as boys at a boarding school like to be sent for by a visitor. It was not long, however, before the practical turnkey rattled his keys as if itching to turn them on his prey, and said briskly: "Time's up." We shook hands warmly and I expressed the hope that if I should meet them again it might be under more congenial conditions. As they meekly passed through the two iron barred doors into the yard of the "Pen" I ran up the steps and took a parting glance at the place. The convicts were taking their supper, and through the open door I saw them at plain tables sitting on benches and drinking tea from tin dippers. Mr. Snow and Mr. Groesbeck disappeared through the door in quest of their modest reflections. I was somewhat disturbed by the thought that possibly my detaining them might unpleasantly curtail their meal, and eased my mind by asking the warden when I got down stairs if they would have time enough for their supper. I was relieved to hear him say: "Oh, yes; they'll get it all right."

From the general spirit of these interviews, with people from various parts of the nation and from Europe, it was evident that the tone of public feeling was moderating and that sentiments more liberal and humane than those which had recently prevailed so widely in relation to the people of Utah were gradually gaining ground. That Apostle Snow's conviction and imprisonment, with his heroic conduct from the beginning of his trial until now, had had much to do with this revulsion of feeling, is beyond question. Who shall say that this was not the purpose in his imprisonment? Not the first time was it that the sacrifice of one had saved the many.

The end of his imprisonment was drawing nigh.

Proceedings in the Snow habeas corpus case, on appeal from the Third District Court of Utah Territory to the Supreme Court of the United States, began before that august body on Thursday, January 20, 1887. The appellant was represented as before, by F. S. Richards and George Ticknor Curtis, as was the respondent by Assistant Attorney General Maury.

It lacked but half an hour of 4:00 p.m., the time at which the court closes each day, when Mr. Richards, who made the opening argument, began his remarks. After starting the case as disclosed by the record, he called the attention of the court to the fact that the case involved two distinct propositions, on either or both of which they relied for a favorable decision from the court.

The first and least important was that the judgment was void because of its uncertainty. The second point was that three sentences were sought to be imposed upon the prisoner for a single offense.

Mr. Richards was continuously interrupted by interrogations from the court—an evidence always of interest in the case on the part of the bench.

At the conclusion of Mr. Richards's argument, Assistant U.S. Attorney General Maury began speaking, and made his case, also being interrupted with considerable questions.

George Ticknor Curtis closed the case. He was not interrupted by the court (save once, when a short query was put to him). He talked quietly and clearly to the points, emphasizing those already advanced in favor of the petitioner. It was evident that the court had taken the view advanced by Apostle Snow's counsel and the failure of Mr. Maury to even attempt the explanation of the proposition so repeatedly put to him could serve only to convince them of the hopelessness of his case. "With great respect for the counsel on the other side," said Mr. Curtis, "it seems to be nonsense to talk about this being three judgments."

Mr. Maury: I don't think I said that.

Mr. Curtis: It was one judgment. With regard to the second point, there can be nothing plainer than that the time during which this offense lasted has nothing whatever to do with a quantity of punishment. That is fixed by the statute. There certainly was but one offense committed by this man. Argument and further discussion will not elucidate the matter anymore. I leave it on the face of the judgment.

Mr. Curtis thus closed, not seeing fit to occupy all the time remaining to him, so confident did he feel that the court had taken the view of the case presented by him and his colleague. There was no attempt at eloquence. It was altogether a plain and logical statement of legal facts, relieved and brightened by the pungent and frequent inquires from the bench.

At the conclusion of the arguments the court took the case under advisement. That the decision, when rendered, would be favorable to the appellant, was regarded as all but a foregone conclusion.

Chapter 11

The U.S. Supreme Court Frees Lorenzo Snow

The hour had come . . .

> Washington, D.C., Feb. 7, 1887
> Franklin S. Richards:-
> Snow released. Mandate ordered. Thanks to God! George Ticknor Curtis John T. Caine

Such was the announcement, brief but thrilling, contained in a private telegram to Hon. F. S. Richards, who had returned to Utah from the nation's capital soon after the Snow case was submitted to the Supreme Court. It had come at last. The thunder bolt of justice, long delayed, had fallen and the splintered fragments of the iniquitous decisions of the district court in regard to "segregation," lay quivering before the startled eyes of their amazed and confounded authors. The Supreme Court of the nation had set the seal of its disapproval upon the acts of injustice and cruelty that disgraced the annals of the Federal tribunals in the Territories. It was no longer "good law"—Zane, Dickson, Powers, Boreman, and their ilk to the contrary notwithstanding—to punish a man, even a Mormon polygamist, twice, or more than once for the same offense. The decision of the District Court in the Snow habeas corpus case was reversed, and the prisoner ordered to be discharged from custody.

The following special dispatch to the *Deseret Evening News* appeared in that journal on the day the decision was rendered:

> Washington, D.C., 3:30 p.m.
> February 7th, 1887
> The Supreme Court today reversed the decision of the Utah court

in the Snow case. The syllabus set forth that where a district court in the Territory of Utah refuses to issue a writ of habeas corpus involving a question of personal freedom, an appeal lies to this court from its order and judgment of refusal. The offense of cohabiting with more than one woman, created by the act of March 22nd, 1882, is a continuous offense and not one consisting of an isolated act. After giving the history of the case, the Court says; "On appeal to this court it is held—first, there was but one entire offense for the continuous time; second, the trial court had no jurisdiction to inflict a punishment in respect of more than one of the convictions; third, as want of jurisdiction appeared on the face of the proceedings, the defendant could be released from imprisonment on habeas corpus; fourth, the order and judgment of the court below must be reversed and the case remanded to that court with direction to grant the writ of habeas corpus prayed for.

The court's opinion was delivered by Justice Blatchford. The rejoicing among the friends of truth and justice, and the corresponding chagrin and discomfiture of the enemies of right, when the decision of the Supreme Court became known, may better be imagined than described. There was but one opinion among fair minded people, and this that justice had been done, though it had cost months of mental suffering and privation to secure it. In the eyes of the Mormon people the Supreme Court had measurably redeemed itself for its former action, or want of action, in the Snow and Cannon cases, and a more hopeful feeling than had existed for many months was manifested throughout the community.

Apostle Lorenzo Snow emerged from the Utah Penitentiary on the 8th of February, the day after the decision was rendered, he having been an inmate of the place since March 12th of the preceding year; thus serving eleven months, lacking four days, of his eighteen-month term of imprisonment.

The release took place at 4 o'clock p.m. His feelings on regaining his liberty, of which he had been wrongly and unjustly deprived, and the hearty and whole-souled reception given him by the friends who assembled outside the walls to welcome him back to freedom are described by the Apostle in a letter to his family, written from Salt Lake City the day after his liberation. It must be remembered that up to the moment of his release, owing to a rule excluding all late local papers from the prison, no tidings of the decision of the Supreme Court had reached him. Said he:

"Eleven months I had been incarcerated within the walls of a gloomy prison! Imagine for yourselves, how like a dream it seemed, when, suddenly and unexpectedly the prison gate flew open, and clad in

Lorenzo Snow (USHS)

my striped convict suit, I was at once ushered into the presence of a multitude of warm-hearted friends, anxiously awaiting my appearance. Oh, what warm clasping and shaking of hands! What hearty greetings and expressions of congratulation!

Having gone the rounds of this animating introductory scene, I repaired to the tailor's department of the prison, and donned a new black broad-cloth suit and "Richard was himself again."

Amid the soul-enlivening and heart-cheering gaze of my numerous friends, I was conducted by Hon. F. S. Richards to a carriage and seated with my daughter Eliza S. D., my son Alvirus, and son of Hon. F. S. Richards.

When we started for Salt Lake City, it was a matter of astonishment that so large a gathering should put in an appearance on the spur of the moment. Included in the number were Heber J. Grant and John W. Taylor, of the Quorum of the Twelve Apostles, Hon. F. S. Richards wife, Abraham H. Cannon, representing the Seven Presidents of Seventies, John Nicholson and George C. Lambert, representing the *Deseret News*, a representation of the *Salt Lake Herald*, President L.W. Shurtliff of the Weber Stake, and many others—ladies and gentlemen—noble men and women of God, of whose society I am justly proud.

The same evening, after his arrival in the city, Apostle Snow attended, by special invitation, a pleasant party given in the Social Hall under the auspices of the Tabernacle Choir. At 10:00 p.m. there was an intermission in the dancing and a brief concert program was rendered, in the course of which Brother Evan Stephens, by request, sang a greeting to Brother Snow—"Home Again"—with chorus by the choir. The honored guest responded with a few appropriate remarks and after another chorus, dancing was resumed.

Greetings and congratulations, personal and epistolary, now poured in from all sides upon the venerable Apostle, who was kept busy for the next few days, receiving and answering his voluminous correspondence.

His first letter home after his restoration to freedom:

> The past and present still seem to me as a dream, I mean the last eleven months more especially; and reaching back to that ever memorable, extraordinary, and never to be forgotten scene that occurred on the occasion of my arrest.
>
> What agonizing feelings, what blasted hopes, and bitter disappointment; what terror depicted in the pale faces of the Dear Little Ones! Well, thanks be to our Heavenly Father, it has ended for the present honorably and gloriously. Our persecutors are discomfited, dishonored, and ashamed. Our holy religion vindicated and God glorified, and made me his unworthy servant, to pioneer the opening of the prison gates to my brethren, the Spirits in prison. 'Well, I am now out of prison, I know not what course I will take in the future; but it will be shown me plainly. One thing, though, is quite clear, like the Savior, I have no home to go to, but from the bottom of my heart I thank God my wives and family have comfortable homes, and I hope they will not indulge in feelings of complaint if I do not meet and greet them as would be desirable. I suppose, for the present I must assume the life and habits of the bachelor. It is my wish at present to go to Brigham next week and hold forth at the Tabernacle, if it should not be considered unwise, unsafe, or imprudent. Yet the thought is humiliating—going there and not being allowed to meet or visit my wives—after so long absence, and it is possible I may change my mind and not go at present. I shall never consent for a wife of mine to give up her home to me and move out of her house, I will go back to my prison first, though I feel obliged, honored and grateful for the offer, but it will not be accepted. I am told here, if I am seen to speak to my wives on the street, I am liable to be arrested, and sent back to the Penitentiary. How would it seem, and how would I feel to meet a number of friends at the depot in Brigham and among them a wife or wives, and refuse to shake hands, or speak to them? Such thoughts come into my mind, and are anything but agreeable, or consoling. I am now stopping at Eliza's[1] though I was very kindly offered a home at the Gardeau [Gardo] house, but only stayed one night, Eliza told me all about Le Roie's [LeRoi's] and Mabel's excited demonstrations of gladness, and Mabel's proposition, to come after me, and keep house. God bless their little hearts; I'll not forget such manifestations, nor the kind letters of welcome to liberty, but O what liberty!!"

On the Sabbath following his release from the Penitentiary—February 13—Apostle Snow addressed the congregation at the Salt Lake Tabernacle.

> The rage of the anti-Mormons at the manifestly just decision of the Supreme Court, liberating Apostle Snow and other victims of their malice, was expressed in various ways. Firstly, in the reluctance with which the Prosecuting Attorney and his confreres, yielded to the requirements of the court's mandate and consented to the release of the unlawfully detained captives. Secondly, in the spiteful conduct of that official toward Mormon defendants and witnesses in the courtroom, where he, far more than the judge on the bench, or the jury in the box, had long been recognized as the ruling power.
>
> Like hungry tigers robbed of their prey, seemed the whole ring of the Federal officials and their minions, at this interesting period of their unsavory career.
>
> Indeed, it had appeared, ever since the beginning of the proceedings that resulted so overwhelmingly in their discomfiture, as if the conspirators, fearing the ultimate issue, had resolved to wreak vengeance before hand, on the still helpless victims of their hate. Deputy Marshals continued their midnight raids, terrifying helpless women and children in the absence of their male protectors, who were "wanted" by these ruthless invaders of social and domestic peace. In more than one instance women were grossly insulted, and others, while in delicate [pregnant] condition, fleeing precipitately from their pursuers to escape arrest, met with injuries that resulted fatally.

For prudential reasons, Apostle Snow reconsidered his intention of returning immediately to Brigham City, and in lieu of going north, accepted an invitation to visit Sanpete, and attend a conference of that stake of Zion, which convened on the 19th of February.

Accompanied by his little son LeRoi, a lad of ten years, who had come to Salt Lake from Brigham City to greet his sire, Apostle Snow, on Friday the 18th of February, set out on his journey southward. He arrived in Manti in time to be present at the opening of the conference, which was held there on Saturday and Sunday.

His cordial reception by the warmhearted Saints of the south, and his labors in their midst during this brief, but pleasant period, are thus reported in his letters home:

> Fort Ephraim, Feb. 21st, 1887
>
> I have only a moment to write. We are all well—LeRoi is a little

gentleman—I introduced him on the stand to the conference as my Danish boy, to the great amusement of the people, since which he has taken off some attention and interest which otherwise, no doubt, would have been bestowed upon the writer.

I preached four discourses at the conference. Tonight I have a meeting here; tomorrow at Spring City at 1 p.m.; and in the evening at Mount Pleasant; the next evening at Moroni, where we take the train to Nephi, thence to Deseret, and from there we go on Friday to Fillmore, to attend conference, by the urgent request of the president of that Stake. Expect to return to Salt Lake about the following Wednesday.

We are having a perfect ovation wherever we go. The most intense interest and the warmest greetings and congratulations are everywhere manifesting in the most pronounced manner, and God is with me and His Holy Spirit is richly poured out on speaker and people; so you see I am wonderfully blessed.

Roi [LeRoi] keeps a journal, and is both interesting and interested, and insists on attending all my meetings. We had our pictures taken in Manti. We visited the Temple and went through it. It is much richer and grander than the Logan Temple.

His next letter dated the 25th, was from Salt Lake City. In it he said:

On arriving at Nephi yesterday I received a telegram from here, to come direct to the City, where I arrived last evening. I was thus obliged to forego my journey further south, and to disappoint my friends at Fillmore.

In all my travels and preaching among the Saints I have met with enthusiastic feelings and warm hearts and congratulations. In every place the houses have been crowded to excess, night and day, even at the shortest notice, and at unusual hours of meetings. Bands of music in several instances saluted us at our approach. When relating my situation, and my inability or right to visit my home and family without rendering myself liable to be sent back to the Penitentiary, and that my little Danish boy now sitting behind me on the stand was the only member of my family I had seen with but one exception (Alvirus) etc., etc., well I awakened sympathy.

Roi [LeRoi] is well and full of life, and joy. He has attended every meeting and been properly introduced, and has been an object of attention and admiration by the vast crowds of people, forming our enthusiastic congregations night and day, and not infrequently embraced and fondly kissed by the sisters at the close of the meeting. So you see the little fellow has made a decided impression among his Scandinavian relatives, not easily forgotten, and added much to the interest of the occasion.

Sister Madson, when at the Penitentiary on Thanksgiving Day, spoke about offering me a room in their building. Which would be the best, for me to accept that, or the place kindly offered me by Joseph and Lucy?

I intend, after preaching in the Tabernacle there, to travel and preach through the various settlements of the Stake, if nothing prevents. And it now seems to me I shall prefer to return to Brigham unannounced and without any demonstration.

Pursuant to this resolve, Elder Snow, after dispatching the business in Salt Lake that had recalled him thither proceeded quietly to his home in the north. Among the letters he received about this time was the following epistle from the Presidency, still in exile:

Salt Lake City, Feb. 17th, 1887
Elder Lorenzo Snow,

Dear Brother:

We cannot express to you the pleasure and the thankfulness we have had at your deliverance from prison, and being once more free. We have taken great interest in the reports which have reached us concerning your health, your contentment, and the equanimity and resignation which you have manifested in bearing the unjust punishment inflicted upon you. It is evident the Lord was with you, and that He has given you strength and grace to bear your trials with patience and serenity; and it is plain that it is He who has delivered you, and we feel to praise Him therefore. We trust your health has not been impaired, and that you will now be able to enjoy to the fullest extent, liberty and freedom of action which has become so precious among us of late. The enclosed letter explains itself; it is sent to you that the matters therein mentioned may be examined by you and be reported to us.

We shall be glad to hear from you, and it would give us much pleasure to see you. With love, and praying the Lord to bless you and preserve you from every evil,

We remain,
Your Brethren,
John Taylor,
George Q. Cannon

In his answer to this letter, on March 12th—the anniversary of his incarceration—Elder Snow, after reporting to the Presidency the results of his examination into the business hinted at in their epistle, added:

"I feel thankful that my course and labors of the last year have met your approval, which you expressed in your communication; and any counsel you may be pleased to give regarding my future action will be thankfully received.

"Unless otherwise counseled, I have thought I would now employ my time in visiting the principal settlements of the Saints, as I almost or quite feel it a duty to do so, under the peculiar circumstances, not being certain how long I may have this favorable opportunity."

The full sanction and approval of the Presidency having been obtained, Apostle Snow began making arrangements for an extended tour through the settlements of the Saints.

He was now back at his home in Brigham City, or, rather, *not at home* in that place. For obvious reasons he made his abode for the time being at the residence of his brother-in-law Joseph Jensen, pending the fitting up of other apartments where his protracted experience as a bachelor—though with a large and interesting family—was about to begin.

Sunday, March 6th, 1887, was made memorable to the good people of Brigham City, by the public appearance, after an absence of nearly a year, of their beloved leader and friend. It having been reported about town, and given out in the Sabbath Schools that Apostle Lorenzo Snow would be present at the afternoon meeting in the Tabernacle, a vast throng, mostly devout worshippers of the same faith, assembled there to see and hear him.

Elder Snow's discourse on that occasion was one of the most impressive and powerful from him on record. "I have been engaged in promulgating the principles of the Gospel for the past fifty years," he stated, "and I have received for myself a perfect testimony that this is the power of God unto salvation." He related some humorous incidents from his prison experiences, though he indicated he did not want to return. He recognized that the locals would be participating in an election the next day, and stated, "I have nothing to say in regard to this matter. Every man and every woman should do that which seems right to his or her sight in this matter as well as in any other." Despite the bigoted crusade against the Church (and plural marriage) instigated by those that imprisoned him and others and the misinformed feelings of the masses that supported them, he said: "I have no feelings against those who are not of us [our faith]. I have no ill feelings towards them, because I know they are the children of God. I know the world is naturally prejudiced against us. Still, if we go and sit down and talk with them, we find that their prejudice gives way, and that they have hearts after all. I say this because I know that when [such] people pinch us we are very apt to pinch them back, and to have feelings against them." They were blinded by the subtle craftiness of men (Doctrine and Covenants 123:12), and he knew it, but he also knew Him whom he served, as did others of his brethren: "We understand that those who are not of us do not understand these things; they do not know that God has spoken from heaven, and that He has appeared and manifested Himself to men who are now living." He mentioned Joseph Smith and Oliver Cowdery being visited by the risen Christ in the Kirtland Temple (see Doctrine and Covenants 110), but he could also have had in mind a few of the current Twelve Apostles; perhaps even himself. He testified: "I know that these things are things that are true as God is true. But the nations of the earth are not aware of it, that Jesus, the Son of God, has come and appeared to man, and clothed them with authority to preach the Gospel and to promise the Holy Ghost to all who will believe and obey. . . . God bless the Latter-day Saints and pour out His Spirit upon you."[2]

Lorenzo Snow (USHS)

Lorenzo Snow, 1878 (USHS)

Lorenzo Snow (CA)

Lorenzo Snow, age 78 (USHS)

Lorenzo Snow (CA)

Lorenzo Snow (CA)

Lorenzo Snow (CA)

Lorenzo Snow, shown here with mirror reflection in the Salt Lake Temple (USHS)

Lorenzo Snow (CA)

Lorenzo Snow (USHS)

Lorenzo Snow, age 72 (USHS)

Chapter 12

Serving as the Senior Member of the Quorum of the Twelve

A few days after speaking in Brigham City, Apostle Snow received and accepted a cordial invitation to be present at the semiannual conference of the Young Men's Mutual Improvement Associations of Utah Stake, to be held at Provo on the 26th and 27th of March.

The third day of April, 1887, the seventy-third anniversary of the birth of the venerable apostle was celebrated by his family and friends at the Third Ward Meeting House in Brigham City.

Early in April the following communication came to hand:

> Salt Lake City, April 5th, 1887
>
> Elder Lorenzo Snow,
>
> Dear Brother:-
>
> As circumstances prevent the First Presidency of the Church from attending the Annual Conference to be held on the 6th of April at Provo, we think it proper to address you this letter and request you, as the senior Apostle who is at liberty to attend that conference, to take charge of the meetings and preside over the conference.
>
> If there should be any special business that we wish to bring to your attention, and through you at the conference, we will communicate it to you. Before the close of the conference we shall have our Epistle ready and forward it to you in time to have it read to the Saints who shall be present.
>
> The question will naturally arise as to how long the conference should be kept in session. This you will be in a position to judge of better than we can. It is not well to prolong conferences to too great length; but the Spirit of the Lord will manifest to you the proper course to take upon this point.

Interior of the Provo Tabernacle (1926). This is where Lorenzo Snow presided over and conducted general conference in 1887–88 when the First Presidency was in hiding. (USHS)

> With kind regards and praying the Lord to bless you and all the Elders who may be selected to speak to the people by the inspiration of the Holy Ghost, and to bless the people, with hearts to receive your instructions. We remain your brethren,
>
> John Taylor, George Q. Cannon

The Fifty-seventh Annual Conference of The Church of Jesus Christ of Latter-day Saints convened at Provo on Wednesday, April 6, 1887, Apostle Lorenzo Snow presiding. There were present also of his quorum, Apostles Franklin D. Richards, John Henry Smith, Heber J. Grant, and John W. Taylor. The remainder of the Twelve, with their counselors and the First Presidency, were away on missions or in exile on the underground.

The meetings were held in the new stake tabernacle, a handsome and commodious structure, which, though the interior was yet in an unfinished state, had been fitted up very comfortably for the occasion.

The conference throughout was one of the most enjoyable ever held in the Church. The weather was delightful, being clear and pleasant up to a short time previous to the final adjournment, when a brisk shower fell, cooling the air, settling the dust, and rendering travel all the more enjoyable. The fine new stake tabernacle, though not large enough to contain all who wished to attend, was very comfortable and admirably adapted for all hearing what was said; the Saints of Provo were untiring in their efforts to entertain their visitors; the Holy Spirit was poured out in a rich degree upon speakers and hearers, and the Saints separated at the conclusion of their conference feeling spiritually refreshed and better prepared for the future journey of life.

Conference being over, Apostle Snow proceeded to carry out his project of visiting the settlements of the Saints. Leaving Salt Lake one Thursday evening in the latter part of May, he arrived at Deseret, 150 miles distant, at one o'clock the next morning. Alighting from the train, which had brought him thus far on his journey, he found a brother waiting with a buggy, to which was attached a wild "bronco," that required, said the Apostle, "the skill and physical force of two men to keep him in position till I had ascended and planted myself squarely in the seat, disagreeably unconscious as to how long I could successfully retain it.

"The driver—the bronco plunging meanwhile to the right and

The Provo Tabernacle was constructed in 1885 and then was partially destroyed by fire in 2010. In 2011 it was announced it would be reconstructed as a temple. (USHS)

left—gave the work to the two men to look closely and see that the rigging was all right, then 'let her go.' The animal took the hint and bounded off with a speed rather more admirable than agreeable, being heightened no doubt by the whistle of the engine that struck up at that moment. It was dark; no moon to shed its benign light over our course, which led a long distance close beside the railway track; and every moment expecting the train to follow us. We had to cross the track somewhere, and the driver not being well acquainted with the road, or the place to cross, we danced and bowled along watching our opportunity to find a crossing before the train rushed upon us. At last it was discovered and we were enabled to clear ourselves from the predicament, and its possible results had the iron monster overtaken us.

"For a while I fancied that my change of situation from the Penitentiary to the present one was not adding much to my enjoyment, nor my personal safety. Well, after tearing along through the darkness over a wild path, crossing several streams over dilapidated bridges, a distance of nearly two miles, I was safely landed at Bishop Black's, and received a hearty welcome. He had been sitting up waiting for me. He furnished me a good bed and I slept nicely the remainder of the night. In the morning he took me in an open carriage to Fillmore, 35 miles, where I am now comfortably domiciled and well cared for."

The letter from which the foregoing extract was taken bore the date of May 22, 1887. The writer of it added:

"Our conference has just closed. An excellent spirit prevailed. I delivered two discourses, and all seemed satisfied and highly pleased with the meetings. . . ."

Monday morning according to program, Apostle Snow left Fillmore by team, this time behind a span of sturdy, steady-going steeds, at the safe rate of four miles per hour, affording a striking contrast to his experience with the frisky bronco, whirling him through the midnight darkness from the railway station at Deseret. After dinner and a very interesting meeting at Holden, he was driven on to Scipio, where he held a meeting and tarried overnight. Next morning he set out for Salina, twenty-five miles away, where he preached that evening.

At this point he encountered Bishop E. F. Sheets, "on the underground" and traveling under an assumed name, who took him in his buggy, next day, to Richfield, where a meeting was held in the evening. Crowded houses and attentive congregations greeted him everywhere. His health continued good, notwithstanding the rough and rugged travel, which administered needed exercise and lent enjoyable zest to his slumbers, and the Spirit was poured out richly upon him in his public and private teachings.

One feature of his experience that especially pleased him was to observe, as he passed along, the remarkable improvements made since he last went through that part of the country. Said he, "Many of the towns and cities are built up with nice and beautiful edifices, private and public, and laid out with fine streets and ornamented with beautiful shade trees along the sidewalks. It cheers my heart to see the great blessings the Lord is bestowing upon His people in these lovely mountain valleys of Ephraim, and I often ask the Saints if they appreciate them and realize that it has been through the love of God that they have been given these great favors and their happy condition."

In company with Bishop Sheets, Apostle Snow pressed on to Panguitch, holding meetings en route at Monroe and Circleville, Thursday and Friday, and reaching the first-named town Saturday, May 28. Here the Sabbath was spent and several meetings held.

Monday morning found our tourist again on his travels. That evening he reached Upper Kanab, forty miles distant, and the next day rode another forty miles to a place called Johnson's; there he met Apostle F. M. Lyman and John Henry Smith, who were on their way to Old Mexico, to be gone for several months. After meeting, which convened at nine o'clock next morning, the apostles bade each other adieu and pursued their respective ways. It was twelve miles from Johnson's to Kanab, where Apostle Snow preached in the evening and where he parted company with Bishop Sheets, who was traveling on Church business and was now obliged to take another direction. The Bishop's nice and easy conveyance, driven by his son Heber, was a luxury Brother Snow had highly appreciated, and from which he was now somewhat loath to part. The Bishop, as stated, was going under an assumed name, and owing to the prevalence of spies, traitors, and deputies, had not deemed it prudent to attend any of the meetings held by Brother Snow.

Our Apostle's next destination was Orderville, where the Kanab Stake Conference was to be held on Saturday and Sunday, the 4th and 5th of June. He reached there the evening before the conference, after a warm and wearisome ride of twenty-five miles, over and through deep, sandy roads and rough canyons, and that night addressed the stake gathering of the Young Men's and Young Ladies' Mutual Improvement Associations.

The weather was now becoming very warm, as he advanced toward

"Dixie" and caught a slight cold, the result of exposure in the grateful night air after a heated meeting. He was nevertheless able to preach three discourses at the conference, which were listened to with the same eager interest everywhere elicited.

Orderville, where the conference was held, was the former headquarters in that region of the "United Order," from which the town derived its name. The members of the organization, however, had divided up their property and decided to await the dawn of a more auspicious day to practice the great principle of consecrations and stewardships.

Another ride of forty miles, through the blazing sun and burning sands of "Dixie," brought our Apostle to his extreme southern destination—St. George. He arrived there on Friday the 10th of June and slept that night in the temple, where he had the happiness of striking hands with his old-time friend, Apostle Wilford Woodruff, the President of his quorum. The meeting of the two veterans within the peaceful and sacred precincts of the house of God, after so long a separation and so many trying vicissitudes, was one which both could well appreciate.

Apostle Snow attended the St. George Stake Conference on the 11th and 12th, bade the Saints of that city adieu and rode to Toquerville (twenty-five miles), where he addressed another meeting. The next day found him at Cedar, fifteen miles distant, where he held two meetings and tarried a couple of days at the hospitable home of Patriarch Henry Lunt. Twenty miles further on the return trip, he attended; on the 18th and 19th, the stake conference at Parowan. At this place the children of the Sabbath School, with their teachers and superintendent, led by the president of the stake, came out to meet him, and he was repeatedly honored, during his stay, by delightful serenades from the Parowan string band. They also presented him with a $20 gold piece, with the remark that he had refused to accept that sum from "Uncle Sam,"[1] they would not consent to his refusing it from them.

The day after conference he rode thirty-five miles to Beaver, and resting overnight, held a meeting Tuesday evening. Wednesday he went on to Cove Creek, twenty-five miles. On the following day he reached Elsinore, in the Sevier Stake, where he held one meeting, and next day rode on to Richfield. He there reorganized the Sevier Stake of Zion, setting apart Brother A. K. Thurber as president of the stake, with Wm. H. Seegmiller and W. H. Clark as his counselors. He also ordained a patriarch and organized a bishopric. The reorganization of the stake was in compliance with a special request of President Taylor, transmitted

Eliza R. Snow (USHS)

to Apostle Snow while on his journey.

Leaving Richfield on Saturday, June 25, he held a meeting that night at Redmond, twenty-two miles away, and filled a similar appointment on Sunday at Gunnison.

Apostle Snow then boarded the Utah Central train at the nearest convenient point, and the beginning of the week found him once more treading the streets of Salt Lake City.

Thus ended this interesting tour of the Apostle Lorenzo, a period to him, notwithstanding the arduous labors it entailed, of great social and spiritual enjoyment, and nonetheless interesting and happifying to the hospitable and warmhearted Saints of the south.

Only a few weeks had elapsed after the return of Apostle Snow, from his southern tour, when an event occurred which caused all Israel to mourn. It was the death of Zion's chieftain, President John Taylor, who passed away in exile, at five minutes to eight o'clock on the evening of Monday, July 25, 1887.

The obsequies of the deceased President took place at the tabernacle, in Salt Lake City, on Friday the 29th of July. Prior to the services, the body lay in state in the great building from 7:00 a.m. till half past 11:00, during which time the calm features of the dead were gazed upon by reverent thousands. The interior of the Tabernacle was draped in mourning. The stand of the First Presidency was vacant, but in the one next below were seated Apostles Lorenzo Snow, Franklin D. Richards, and Heber J. Grant, the only members of their quorum—excepting Apostle John W. Taylor, who sat with the mourners—not in exile.

The closing month of the year 1887 witnessed another event similar in character to the one just chronicled; an event that, though it saddened the hearts of thousands throughout Israel, was regarded in the light of a happy release of a noble soul from the toils and trials of mortality. On Monday, December 5, at five minutes past one o'clock a.m., the spirit of Eliza R. Snow Smith, sister to the Apostle Lorenzo, and one of the noblest and purest of women, forsook its mortal tenement and passed beyond the portals of the spirit world.

The news of her decease, though causing a natural and widespread sorrow, created little surprise in the community of which she was a member, it being generally known that for a year past her health had been gradually failing. It was a simple decline and final dissolution of the physical powers, resulting from old age, while her mind remained intact, unshattered and unshaken to the close. Up to within an hour or two of her death, she smiled and spoke cheerfully and was conscious to within five minutes of the end.

Between Sister Eliza and Brother Lorenzo, there had always existed the purest and most exquisite affection; a brotherly and sisterly love worthy of so noble a pair. During her illness he was with her a great deal and watched at her bedside while she breathed her last. She died at her apartments in the Lion House, Salt Lake City.

The obsequies over the remains of Sister Eliza were held in Salt Lake Assembly Hall on Friday, December 7.

When President John Taylor died and Wilford Woodruff became the leader of the Church by virtue of his position as President of the Quorum of the Twelve Apostles, Lorenzo Snow found himself the senior member of that body, under President Woodruff. He also found a quorum of men in disarray and disunity. This state of affairs is little known today but is of such importance that it requires appropriate notice here and at later key points in Lorenzo's life.

The death of President Taylor caught most of the Twelve by surprise, since many of them were hiding on the underground and had been unable to communicate effectively or meet as a full quorum for almost three years. His condition was also being kept confidential to avoid undue concern amongst members.[2] Taylor's First Presidency itself had not been together for almost the same length of time. George Q. Cannon, a counselor in the First Presidency, had been with President Taylor during his last declining months and had been forced to make some difficult financial decisions. He also endured public scandal involving his eldest son, John Q. Cannon.

John Q. served a mission to Switzerland and Germany, and not long after his return had begun a promising career in business and Church affairs, becoming an editor for the *Deseret News* and a counselor in the

Presiding Bishopric at age twenty-seven; he was also a member of the territorial legislature and the Salt Lake City council. But despite his inimitable family name, education, and natural talents, his personal weaknesses kept him from living up to his potential. He committed adultery with his wife's sister, assaulted the *Salt Lake Tribune* reporter that exposed him, was excommunicated after a public confession, and was soon thereafter found to have embezzled at least eleven thousand dollars (and probably more) from tithing and temple funds to pay his gambling debts. President Cannon had repaid the stolen Church funds from his own personal resources, but the timing and circumstances of John Q.'s indiscretions and his father's quick and quiet methods of resolving them were of concern to some of the Twelve, who wanted full and detailed disclosure—especially Elder Heber J. Grant.[3] Rumors of scandal, along with miscommunication and dissatisfaction with the previous Church administration, especially on financial and administrative matters, had taken a heavy toll on the Quorum's sense of unity and purpose.

Historian Ronald W. Walker has written of this period: "To one degree or another, [these] views [of Elder Grant's] were shared by several other members of the Quorum—second generation leaders like Francis M. Lyman, John Henry Smith, and especially the outspoken Moses Thatcher. These four men, along with the more seasoned Quorum member, Erastus Snow . . . felt uneasy about the influence and personality of George Q. Cannon in the leading councils of the Church. They also were reacting to the last years of the administration of President John Taylor, which they saw as peremptory and imperious."[4] Further, "While President Taylor was a man of undoubted talent, especially with the written and spoken word, his personality and administrative style was stern. . . . It was said that he carried himself stiffly, which probably had less to do with his attitude toward the office he held than with his natural and native English reserve. And he could be firm to the point of stubbornness."[5] Continuing, Walker wrote: "While Taylor was still alive, his First Presidency typically did not inform or consult with members of the Twelve—or invite their recommendations. That complaint probably could have been also leveled in some measure against Taylor's predecessors, but Taylor seemed unusually aloof, impatient—and at times impersonal."[6] As a consequence, "By summer 1887, a majority of the Quorum, probably a consensus, felt the role of the Twelve needed redefinition."[7]

The Quorum that Elder Lorenzo Snow served with was made up of frontier-born and tested men—authentic apostles it is true—but still

Photograph taken in the yard of the Beehive House in 1868. Left to right: Orson Hyde, Orson Pratt, John Taylor, Wilford Woodruff, Ezra T. Benson, Charles C. Rich, Lorenzo Snow, Erastus Snow, Franklin D. Richards, George Q. Cannon, Brigham Young Jr., and Joseph F. Smith. Front: George A. Smith and Brigham Young. (USHS)

independent-thinking, strong-willed, self-made men. As an example of the dynamic that had been in place in the quorum during the Taylor presidency, one of the Twelve, John Henry Smith, recorded:

> Yesterday in the meeting of the Presidency and Twelve President John Taylor presented an article that he had written. . . . Joseph F. Smith objected to its being published and Moses Thatcher and myself also concurred with him by speaking against certain items in the article. The other brethren were more noncommittal but felt as we did. No vote was taken. The president asked the opinions of the brethren present. . . .
>
> At 2 p.m. we met in Council. . . . President Taylor had his article . . . read again and with slight changes it was approved. Bro. Taylor then went for those who had spoken against his article the day before and he showed much feeling. . . . Some mutual explanations were made and all felt well. . . . I was somewhat surprised to see the president attempt to bull down the Council after giving them the utmost liberty to speak and he will find such talk will never hold the present Council in awe.[8]

Elder Smith recorded his thoughtful and almost prophetic conclusions from these meetings: "I am satisfied that before another President over our Church is sustained the Twelve Apostles will be compelled to have an understanding in relation to the duties of their respective quorums. The first President takes the whole business in his hands."[9] Lorenzo Snow, by then the senior and most experienced man among them, shared in the worries of his younger Quorum associates when it came to the financial methods of President Cannon but felt much less concern in relation to other issues, such as succession. Yet the problems existed and ran deep—so deep that they affected the internal relationships among the leading councils for years to come.

"Including the death of Joseph Smith," Ronald Walker further wrote, "there had been only two previous successions, and neither had gone smoothly. After Smith's death, Brigham Young had delayed reorganizing the First Presidency three and a half years due to the uncertain times of post–Joseph Smith Nauvoo, the Church's Exodus to the West, and the lack of a consensus within the Quorum. When he finally forced a decision in December 1847, it was done despite a lack of enthusiasm on the part of some Quorum members. Taylor's succession had also been somewhat uncertain. . . . Therefore, three years passed before Taylor was formally sustained as President. With such an uncertain pattern in the past, some ambiguity about the process of succession remained."[10] The present and future role played by President George Q. Cannon in Church affairs also continued to be a worry for these men. "The problem lay not so much with settling past grievances as with planning for the future. . . . Sensing the divisions among them, the Quorum for the time being was content to endorse Woodruff's letter to the Church proclaiming an apostolic rule. But what was to be done about Cannon? . . . [H]e might, some feared, dominate Church affairs as First Counselor to an aging and perhaps too pliable Woodruff."[11]

Lorenzo had a front-row seat from which to observe the internal Quorum dynamics—the strife and bickering—that took place, especially over the next two years. He witnessed the discord this caused and did not like it. In the midst of this dissonance (kept from the general knowledge of the Church), because he had his personal liberty (freedom from arrest for unlawful cohabitation), he was able, as mentioned, to preside in place of the First Presidency at the April 1887 general conference. Scheduled around conference sessions were Quorum meetings, where President Woodruff was attempting to unify this group of men that seemed more interested in getting answers to their many questions and concerns about President Cannon and how a new First Presidency would treat the Quorum if it were reorganized, than in reorganizing it.

Matters were discussed and deliberated, thoroughly and over again. Six months later (October 1887), one of the office staff members taking minutes of the meetings commented in his journal: "Conference convened this morning at 10 o'clock in the Tabernacle. The brethren who could not attend [because of anti–plural marriage laws] were at the office. Elder Lorenzo Snow presided [at conference]. The council of Apostles met at 7 o'clock at the President's office. I met with them. The ill feeling among some of the quorum was spoken of by President Woodruff very forcibly. I never attended such a meeting."[12] It was a tough but decisive period for the Quorum.

Elder Snow was again assigned to preside at the 1888 general conferences, due to the continuing possibilities of arrest for members of the First Presidency.

In early August 1887, a Council meeting was held in which the relative position of the Quorum of the Twelve to the First Presidency was deliberated, and the feelings of some of the Twelve about President Cannon's past actions were again aired, and after considerable discussion, he was accepted back into his normal place of seniority in the Twelve.[13]

In September financial issues were discussed, including the living allowance received by the senior Brethren: "The Committee on Wages

The apostles in 1898. Left to right, back row: Matthias Cowley, Owen Woodruff, George Teasdale, Francis M. Lyman, John Henry Smith, Heber J. Grant, John W. Taylor, Marriner W. Merrill. Front row: Brigham Young Jr., Franklin D. Richards, President Lorenzo Snow, George Q. Cannon, Joseph F. Smith, and Anthon H. Lund. (USHS)

reported and the report was read and received. Bishop William B. Preston made a recommendation that the Twelve be put on the same footing as to pay. After consideration, the allowance for the Twelve and Bishopric was fixed at $3,000 each [per year]."[14] Some years later this matter would again be given further scrutiny and adjustment. Members of the leading church councils were not spendthrifts but had greater expenses than is often realized. Many were supporting multiple plural families in separate homes, losing business income because of long absences on missions, traveling throughout the stakes, and loaning money to the Church—all were financially draining.

October of 1887 and February and March of 1888 saw further questioning of President Cannon, with some bad feeling but eventual forgiveness and resolution among the Apostles.[15] President Cannon, who kept one of the finest journals in all of Church history, used it on occasion to defend his actions before his Brethren. In a February meeting, "Bro. Cannon read at some length from his private journal his reflections and action in the arrangements effected by him and others . . . to save the properties of the church [in danger of escheatment by the government] as directed by the Trustee-in-trust President John Taylor—all of which elicited extensive range of conversation, explanation, and criticism from some members not then present."[16]

In mid-March, President Woodruff spoke privately with Elder Franklin D. Richards, asking him, as Church Historian, to prepare the draft of a dedicatory prayer suitable for the upcoming dedication of the Manti Temple, and also mentioned he hoped to reorganize the First Presidency by April conference time.[17] On March 20, President Woodruff, "called for the report of the committee on a new system to run Church affairs and also said he thought it was about time to organize the First Presidency. Lorenzo Snow spoke in favor"—but since some others were not, on the next day further problems pertaining to President Cannon were discussed.[18] A couple of days later they met again; President Cannon expressed his sorrow at how deeply the conflicts had hurt him personally, and President Woodruff became rather exercised and emphatic about settling things and moving forward, pushing again for reorganization of the First Presidency, but without success: "The Quorum was badly split. As usual Cannon lay at the center of things. Everyone understood that Cannon would probably be selected as Elder Woodruff's First Counselor, and this hard fact prevented resolution. . . . It was clear that matters were worse, not better. 'The more we tried to get together the wider apart we were,' wrote the despairing Woodruff. 'I never saw as much bitterness manifest against one good man by five Apostles since the days of the Apostate Twelve against the Prophet Joseph in Kirtland.' In the heat of emotion, Woodruff was satisfied that those opposing Cannon were dictated by simple jealousy. 'Any acts of President Taylor that five of the Twelve did not think was right was laid to George Q. Cannon,' he complained. With such disunity present and with no solution in sight, on the evening of March 23, [1888] Woodruff withdrew his proposal."[19] President Woodruff's apt use of the analogy of dissension among the Quorum of the Twelve in Joseph Smith's day was not lost on Lorenzo, who referenced it himself a number of times while he led the Quorum.

At their next meeting three days later, they "finally came to an understanding and forgave each other."[20] Still later another major hurdle was cleared when a committee recommended and President Woodruff and all the Twelve "agreed that the Presiding Bishop should be the custodian of all church funds."[21] This unusual move placated some of the Twelve with their concern that one man, though he be the President of the Church, not have unlimited control over tithing funds, business income, and expenditures of the Church. This policy was reconsidered toward the end of President Woodruff's administration and reversed.

Dedication of the Manti Temple

May of 1888 saw the dedication of the Manti Temple in Manti, Utah, to the south of Salt Lake City.[22] There was no First Presidency at the time and a number of the leading Brethren were being sought by the law, so preliminary dedication meetings were held privately. President Woodruff met with a number of the Twelve, including Elder Snow, at 10:00 a.m. on the sixteenth to finalize arrangements for the dedication of the temple. The dedicatory prayer prepared by Elder Richards at President Woodruff's request was read and approved for use by those present; a temple president and assistants were selected, as well as a recorder. The number of temple workers that needed to be called and set apart was estimated. After lunch, the Brethren assembled again and President Woodruff indicated that he would like to meet the next morning for a private prayer circle that would include those general and local authorities that could assemble; he also determined that a private dedication would take place at noon.

The next morning (the seventeenth) President Snow met in prayer at 10:00 a.m. with the others invited and then reassembled together in the celestial room, where President Woodruff offered the dedicatory prayer (officially dedicating the building to the Lord) and made some general remarks about temple work to those assembled.[23] Those present then gave the Hosanna Shout, and President Snow, along with a few other senior apostles, spoke for about ten minutes to about thirty specially invited guests.

For two days prior to the Manti Temple dedication, the Sanpete Stake Conference was in session at Manti, Elder Lorenzo Snow presiding. Part of the time overflow meetings were held, in addition to the main gathering, and still many hundreds were unable to find even standing room in the commodious yet crowded halls. The Spirit was poured out richly upon these meetings, which no doubt paved the way for the remarkable spiritual manifestations experienced during the dedication.

Monday morning broke bright and beautiful, promising an ideal day for the dedication, a promise that was in every way verified. The Saints, long before the opening hour, began climbing the Temple Hill and swarming round the doors leading to the interior of the sacred edifice. It was a May Day in the people's hearts, as well as throughout the wide domain of universal nature.

The east doors of the temple being thrown open, the vast but orderly throng surged into the great audience hall in the upper part of the building, the seating capacity of which was soon filled. Admission tickets had been previously distributed, in equal numbers to the seats to be occupied, and the same plan was adopted for the days following.

On the twenty-first the first main public dedication was held, with Elder Lorenzo Snow presiding (President Woodruff could not be present for worry of arrest). He told the large assemblage in attendance that "The Prayer given in the Kirtland Temple, 27 March 1836, was given by revelation from the Lord to the Prophet Joseph Smith. The prayer we are now about to offer is inspired and was written by Holy men who now live, and whom we know. Let all the people bow and hear and join with us while we offer the prayer." He then read the dedicatory prayer (this took thirty-eight minutes), after which several other Church authorities spoke and hymns were sung, as directed by Elder Snow. He also led them in the Hosanna Shout, traditionally given at temple dedications. This pattern was repeated for three sessions, May 21–23, with Elder Snow presiding and reading the prayer twice, and also speaking.[24]

The dedication was a spiritual feast for those attending, with many accounts on record wherein patrons witnessed miraculous manifestations: "During the services and on each of the three days there were spiritual manifestations enjoyed by some of the saints present. . . . A bright halo of light was seen by a number of persons over and around the heads of the following speakers—Lorenzo Snow, Jacob Gates, Robert Campbell, John Henry Smith, Francis M. Lyman, John W. Taylor and A. M. Cannon. . . . While the public dedicatory prayer was being offered by Brother Lorenzo Snow, near the middle of the prayer, during a pause, the words 'Hallelujah, hallelujah, the Lord be praised,' was uttered by a voice in a very soft and melodious tone, heard by Brother Lewis Anderson, one of our assistant recorders here."[25]

On the third day, President Snow, after the dedicatory prayer, which was delivered by Apostle F. M. Lyman, reminded the assembly that that was the closing day, that the Spirit of the Lord had been enjoyed to a marked degree during the past two days and that it was the privilege of those present to have another spiritual feast of a similar nature. Addresses were then made by Counselor D. H. Wells, Elder Henry Beal, Elder Lorin Farr, Apostle John W. Taylor, Elder Milando Pratt, Apostle H. J. Grant, Elder Anthon H. Lund, Apostle F. D. Richards, Chief-mason Edward L. Parry, Elder W. H. Seegmiller, Apostle John Henry Smith, Elder David M. Stuart, and Apostle Lorenzo Snow. The latter spoke of the glorious time enjoyed and the rich outpouring of the Holy Spirit manifested. Reminded the Saints of the visits of the Savior and of angels to the Kirtland Temple, and that there was no reason why such visits should not be received here. Was assured that the Lord had accepted the present Temple. Exhorted his hearers to make new resolves to be faithful, to humble themselves, and to shun temptation. Read from the Doctrine and Covenants a description of the visions beheld in the Kirtland Temple, and said that the promises made by the Savior upon that occasion were equally applicable to the Latter-day Saints and the present occasion. Assured the Saints that the Lord was pleased with their offering and that His blessings would be showered upon them in greater abundance than ever before.

While the dedication of the Manti Temple was in progress, Apostle Erastus Snow, Lorenzo's friend and confrere, at his home in Salt Lake City, lay dying. For many months he had been losing strength, his iron constitution gradually giving way, but only for a few weeks past had he been prostrated. He was very desirous of attending the dedication services, where it would have been a joy to all to have seen and heard the veteran Apostle, but the divine powers had decreed otherwise. Erastus Snow had received his final summons, and was about to pass from earth to join with his fellow Apostles behind the veil, there to worship in a temple "not made with hands."

He died at five minutes to seven o'clock on Sunday evening, May 27, four days after the close of the dedication at Manti. Like President Taylor, who had departed about ten months before, the Apostle Erastus had long been in retirement to evade the unjust enforcement of the Edmunds Law, though, unlike his chief, he was permitted to pass his few remaining days in his own home, where he died surrounded by his family.

Chapter 13

President of the Twelve Apostles

By January 1889, President Woodruff had made up his mind to once again press for reorganization of the First Presidency.[1] This time he was successful in overcoming enough of the bad feeling and disunity that remained at the time to press forward, and on April 5, before the start of general conference, he convened a special meeting at which the reorganization took place:

> President Woodruff said he felt the time had come that the Church should be fully organized and that the First Presidency should be organized according to the revelations. Called on the brethren to express their feelings.
>
> Elder Lorenzo Snow referred to the days of the Prophet Joseph and the organization of the Church—also to the death of President Brigham Young and when President John Taylor was chosen. Concluded by moving that President Wilford Woodruff be the President of the Church of Jesus Christ of Latter-day Saints, and that he be authorized to nominate his two counselors to form the First Presidency of the Church.
>
> Elder Franklin D. Richards was in favor of the First Presidency being organized and seconded the motion as made by Elder L. Snow.
>
> Elder George Q. Cannon was in favor.
>
> Elder Brigham Young Jr. was in favor.
>
> Elder Joseph F. Smith was in favor.
>
> Elder Moses Thatcher has felt for some time the necessity of a complete organization of the Priesthood. Referred to the organization of the First Presidency at the time when President John Taylor was chosen to preside, was in favor of the motion.
>
> President Woodruff said that Francis M. Lyman had been consulted and had expressed himself as in favor.

Elder John H. Smith was in favor of the motion.

Elder George Teasdale was in favor of the motion.

Elder Heber J. Grant was in favor of the motion.

Elder John W. Taylor was in favor of the motion.

Elder Daniel H. Wells was in favor of the motion.

President Woodruff said. "I have never seen a time when the Church needs the services of the Twelve more than today. Many of us have been tied up—I am thankful for the united feeling which has been made manifest this morning."

On the question of the motion being called it was carried unanimously.

President Woodruff, said, "I have considered this matter for some time and have felt to select and now nominate Elders George Q. Cannon and Joseph F. Smith as my counselors. I am getting along in years and cannot expect to be long with you. I was present when the Prophet Joseph rolled the responsibility of the Church on to the shoulders of the Apostles. I am the oldest member of the Apostles. There should be perfect union among us as Apostles and in this quorum. It is the duty of the Apostles to see that the Gospel is carried to the Nations and their services are very much needed among the Latter-day Saints. . . . We should have no other desire than to labor for the interest of the Church and Kingdom of God."

Elder Daniel H. Wells moved that the nominations as made by President Woodruff be approved. Seconded by Elder John W. Taylor.

Elder George Q. Cannon expressed his personal feelings as to the nomination of himself. He would rather be excused. "I can only accept of this nomination by knowing that it is the will of the Lord, and that it is with the hearty and full approval of my brethren. I trust you will all understand my feelings in this matter."

President Woodruff said, "It has been made manifest to me by the Lord that it is right for us to organize the First Presidency. I can also say that I have prayed over this matter and I know that it is the mind of the Lord, that Bros. Cannon and Smith shall be my counselors."

Elder Lorenzo Snow said he knew that it is the mind and will of the Lord that Bros. George Q. Cannon and Joseph F. Smith should be the counselors to President Woodruff in the First Presidency.

Elder Daniel H. Wells spoke and gave his views. Elder Franklin D. Richards moved that Elder George Q. Cannon be approved and sustained as the first counselor to President Wilford Woodruff in the First Presidency. Seconded by Elder Teasdale.

Elder Moses Thatcher said that "In consequence of the remarks of President Woodruff of the manifestations of the spirit to him, I am ready to vote for Bro. Cannon. I wish I had put myself in such a position as to have had the same manifestations. There has been some matters of his former administration which have not been approved by the Saints but I will let that pass. When I vote for him I shall do so freely and will try and sustain him with all my might."

Elder Lorenzo Snow spoke again.

Elder George Q. Cannon spoke very feelingly and wished the brethren to speak freely.

Elder Brigham Young Jr. could not understand Bro. Thatcher's position. "I know that it is the mind and will of the Lord that Bros. Cannon and Smith shall be the counselors to President Woodruff. . . ."

Elder George Q. Cannon named each of the brethren present and said if he had ever said or done anything to injure or to hurt the feelings of any of you my brethren, "I ask your forgiveness. If there is anything remaining in any of your minds as to what I may have said or done—I ask your forgiveness. I do this as a duty, privilege, and a pleasure."

Elder John H. Smith referred to former meetings of the Council and reconciliations. "I can and shall fully sustain Bro. Cannon."

The question being called, the vote was unanimous in favor.

Moved by Elders Moses Thatcher, seconded by Elder Brigham Young Jr., that Joseph F. Smith be approved and sustained as the second counselor to President Wilford Woodruff. Carried unanimously.

Moved by Elder John H. Smith that Elder Lorenzo Snow be the President of the Quorum of the Twelve Apostles. Seconded by Elder Teasdale and carried.

Moved by Elder John H. Smith that Elder Franklin D. Richards be Historian of the Church. Seconded by Elder Grant and carried.[2]

With the reorganized First Presidency finally in place, Lorenzo Snow, as president of the Quorum of the Twelve Apostles, decided it was time to move forward with a vigorous strategy and goal to achieve the unity and brotherly love among members of the Twelve that he desired so much.[3] With this in mind, he asked President Woodruff for permission for the Twelve to hold their own Quorum meetings quarterly—not for business purposes, but for spiritual matters—to bear testimony and to speak of doctrinal truths, sacred and heavenly things, one with another. He also asked President Woodruff if the First Presidency would meet with the Twelve weekly:

President Lorenzo Snow said the Brethren of the Twelve wished to meet with the First Presidency and consult about the Twelve holding their Quorum meetings and to learn from time to time the wishes of the Presidency, and to know if they can have a room in the Gardo House to meet in.

First Presidency (1889–1898 and 1898–1901) (USHS)

President Woodruff was pleased to meet with the Twelve, and they can have a room in the Gardo House or anywhere else they choose—is in favor of them holding their meetings and wanted them to devote their time among the Saints as much as possible.

It was decided that Prayer Meetings of the First Presidency and Twelve be held at the Gardo House at 2 p.m. on Thursday and at 4 p.m. on Sundays of each week in a room to be prepared for that purpose.[4]

Interior photograph of a room in the Gardo House (that used to be across the street from the Lion House), with architectural design similar to that of the Salt Lake Temple. Before 1893, Church leaders regularly met here for council meetings. (USHS)

Six months later, with the meeting issues settled and moving forward smoothly, President Woodruff moved to fill the vacancies in the Quorum of Twelve. On the afternoon of October 2, 1889, the Brethren "considered names to fill the vacancies in the council of the apostles. The First Presidency recommended Marriner W. Merrill, Anthon H. Lund and Abraham H. Cannon . . . all present approved the nomination." The following day, with a quorum member absent the previous day now present, "a full and united vote was had for Merrill, Lund, and Cannon to fill the vacancies in the Twelve Apostles."[5] Elder Abraham H. Cannon, one of those called, recorded:

> Myself and Bro. Anthon H. Lund . . . were summoned into the presence of the First Presidency and Twelve Apostles. President Woodruff then stated that Bro. Marriner W. Merrill and ourselves had been selected to fill the vacancies in the Quorum of the Twelve. Our selection occurred in this way: The apostles were asked to make suggestions to the Presidency in regard to this matter. Lists were prepared and submitted

> and among the names were ours. The subject was made a matter of prayer and the result was that we were unanimously chosen. We were asked as to our feelings in accepting, and though weak we both felt to accept the great honor, and trust in the Lord to assist us in our labors. Bro. Merrill, through sickness was not present.
>
> At 10 a.m. we went to meeting [general conference] when the first business done was the presenting of the authorities. After the First Presidency and former Apostles were voted in Pres. Woodruff arose and spoke of the intention to fill up the latter quorum. He stated how the selections had been made, and said he had reasons for informing the people that neither he nor his counselors had made the selections proposed. The names of Bros. Marriner W. Merrill, Anthon H. Lund and Abraham H. Cannon were then presented separately, and the vote on each was unanimous.[6]

At about this time President Woodruff also attempted to regain control over tithing funds and Church expenditures. "I went to a council meeting of my Quorum in the Gardo House," wrote Elder Cannon:

> Bros. Thatcher, Teasdale and Merrill were the only members absent. Pres. Woodruff desired the opinion of each member present as to whether we were suited with the present arrangement in regard to finance and as to whether or not he should have an office with clerks and books for the transaction of Church business. The present arrangement, which was adopted some time since on recommendation of a committee of the Apostles, places all funds in the care of the Bishop William B. Preston and they are to be expended only on an order from President Woodruff. Yet within the last month he had paid out several thousand dollars without any order. Of course these amounts were perfectly legitimate, and yet they were paid irregularly. The result of the present plan is that the Bishop has forbidden his agents to pay out anything except on a written order from his office, so that an Apostle in traveling through the country could not be allowed a feed of grain from tithing oats without an order from Bishop Preston. On the other hand the Bishop expends money on repairs and alterations at his office, while anything done for Pres. Woodruff would only by paid for on an order [from] Bishop Preston. Each of the brethren gave expression to his views and they were unanimous in feeling that the funds should only be expended on order from Pres. Woodruff, and wherein the Bishop had done otherwise he should be reprimanded. Opinion however, was divided as to whether the funds should remain in Bishop Preston's care or be in the charge of Pres. Woodruff in his private office. I felt that the

> latter would be proper and Father's view agreed with mine. The First Presidency took the matter under advisement.[7]

The matter of ultimate financial control was not fully resolved until much later in President Woodruff's administration. As mentioned, in 1890, at President Snow's instigation, the Quorum of the Twelve began their own separate (from the First Presidency) Quorum meetings, the purpose, as one member wrote, "being to mutually interchange sentiments, promote perfect union, and derive strength from our Heavenly Father to more fully honor our callings and apostleship."[8] Success was varied, but President Snow would not give up, viewing his aspiration of Quorum union as his greatest purpose as president. Another apostle wrote: "The Council of the Twelve apostles met yesterday as a separate Quorum from the First Presidency for the first time in many years. . . . We were together about 10 hours. We all spoke in turn confessing our sins and expressing our determination to live nearer the Lord in the future."[9] Another account of the same April meeting captured the powerful unifying spiritual processes at work in the Quorum: "President Lorenzo Snow made a lengthy and powerful discourse an hour and more in length, which affected all present and regulated the current of the spirit, cleansing the atmosphere [of the council room]; misunderstandings were adjusted between each other [the Twelve] and between them and the First Presidency. . . . We continued with about an hour's interruption in pouring out our souls to each other till nearly midnight."[10]

President Snow convened two more such meetings over the next several months, and then regularly thereafter. At their August meeting, the Brethren partook of the sacrament ("as the Prophet Joseph taught in his day and way"—the same as done today except for drinking wine and eating an actual meal-sized portion of bread) and then felt to bless each other, and pronouncing apostolic blessings, probably something like patriarchal blessings, on each other: "Lorenzo Snow blessed Abraham H. Cannon and he blessed Lorenzo Snow," stated one account.[11]

Elder Franklin D. Richards, now the senior apostle of the Quorum after its president and also the Church Historian, had learned that a special record or history book of the Twelve had been accidentally destroyed in a fire, and as Church Historian he thought to remedy the loss by having the book rewritten. Therefore in mid-September of 1890, he took the train to Brigham City, and "spent [the morning] deliberating with President Lorenzo Snow about the Record of the Twelve Apostles—had a very enjoyable time indeed."[12]

Chapter 14

Presiding over the Quorum of the Twelve Apostles

The Manifesto

The 1890 October general conference of the Church saw the issuance of the Manifesto by President Wilford Woodruff, now known as Official Declaration 1 in the Doctrine and Covenants. This document became the beginning of the end of the practice of plural marriage within the Church and by those holding the keys of the sealing power. Although the public stance of Church leaders from this time forward was that plural marriages halted with the Manifesto, it is well known they allowed for a slowing trickle of individual exceptions, mostly outside of the United States' geographical boundaries. The practice was fully halted in 1904 by Joseph F. Smith with a document commonly called the Second Manifesto, although this period saw the beginnings of the modern (no longer Latter-day Saint) fundamentalist groups often referenced in news reports for continuing to practice plural marriage.

While most similar declarations and proclamations carry the signatures of the First Presidency and often the Quorum of the Twelve, the Manifesto bore only President Wilford Woodruff's signature, which was all it needed. However, as President of the Twelve, Lorenzo Snow also played an important part in its formal acceptance by the Church, thereby involving in the process the two senior apostles at that time.

The Manifesto was read to an astonished Salt Lake Tabernacle audience, with the Articles of Faith preceding it, for good reason: "The autumn of 1890 saw the issuance of the famous 'Manifesto' relating to plural marriage," remembered Orson Whitney. "In the General Conference I was called upon to read it to the congregation. I also read, by request, the Articles of Faith, to remind the people of the Church's attitude in honoring, obeying and sustaining the law."[1]

When Orson finished reading the Manifesto to the congregation, President Lorenzo Snow offered the following, sometimes called the "Snow Resolution":

"'I move that, recognizing Wilford Woodruff as the President of the Church of Jesus Christ of Latter-day Saints, and the only man on the earth at the present time who holds the keys of the sealing ordinances, we consider him fully authorized by virtue of his position to issue the manifesto which has been read in our hearing and which is dated September 24th, 1890, and that as a Church in General Conference assembled, we accept his declaration concerning plural marriages as authoritative and binding.' The vote to sustain the foregoing motion was unanimous. Salt Lake City, Utah, October 6th, 1890."[2]

President Snow, known as the likely successor to President Woodruff, carried substantial supporting and stabilizing influence. Therefore, by emphasizing President Woodruff's right and authority to make such a declaration, and his own full support of it, he helped the Latter-day Saints accept a sudden and surprising change in practice. The doctrine of the Church did not change—neither President Woodruff, nor President Snow, nor any other modern prophet has had section 132 rescinded or removed from the Doctrine and Covenants—but the authorized practice had been suspended by the one man who held the keys in their fulness and emphatically seconded by the man who would hold them next.[3]

Evidence indicates that President Snow himself lived strictly by the new policy, separate from his plural wives: "At noon I accompanied Pres. Snow to his room [at home in Brigham City] where he lives separate and apart from his family because of the law. His meals are sent to him by his wife Minnie, who lives opposite. It made me feel sad to see him thus banished." So wrote Elder Cannon after a visit.[4] The only exception President Snow seems to have made was with Minnie, when he felt inspired to increase his family.

Little is known about President Snow's movements in 1889–93. Much of what is known related to his position as President of the Quorum of the Twelve has been preserved in the valuable journals of Elder Abraham H. Cannon, who died fairly young in 1896, and that of Elder Franklin D. Richards, a senior member of the Twelve.

President Snow spent most of his time in Brigham City when not acting and traveling in his official Church capacities. He traveled to stake conferences (then held quarterly) to speak and reorganize and ordain as occasion required. In that day there were still few enough stakes that the

First Presidency, the Twelve, and the Seventy could administratively cover them all.

As the years passed, President Snow unwearyingly continued his quest to achieve greater unity among his apostolic Brethren. During one meeting in late January 1889, "We started to talk about the [church] sugar business [company]. Brother Lorenzo Snow said he felt there were some feelings among the Brethren and wanted them settled first, so at it we went. Brothers George Q. Cannon and Moses Thatcher poured out what was in them and agreed to forgive each other."[5] "President Lorenzo Snow read D&C 104:78–86, and thought our case quite analogous to the one in 1834. Also read D&C 115:13 about not going in debt to build [the Lord's] house. He spoke his feelings freely, that if we were all solidly united we could bear off the work triumphantly, and accomplish many great and grand works in the latter days. The question of union arose."[6]

The next day the meeting continued, with the sugar business talk receding and Quorum unity taking the forefront of discussion: "Brother Joseph F. Smith spoke powerfully about our want of respect and deference for each other and bore a remarkable testimony of [Elder Franklin D. Richards'] trials and integrity to the work of God; he said, 'all honor to that man Brother Richards for his steadfastness in all he had passed through' and much more. Brother George Q. Cannon remarked that he had noticed with peculiar pleasure that since President Brigham Young's death, in all our deliberations, he never had known anything to pass [Elder Richards's] lips that would have been unpleasant for President Young to hear. Much precious instruction, exhortation, and explanation was given today."[7]

By the third day's meeting—still continuing consideration of the sugar business questions and the Quorum unity that was needed to make unanimous decisions—"President Woodruff . . . expressed his great joy at the union arrived at in the council and hoped it might continue perfect and perpetual. Much precious instruction [was] given by Presidents Woodruff, Lorenzo Snow, and Joseph F. Smith, and it was finally voted unanimously that the church subscribe [invest fifty thousand dollars in sugar company stock], that it use its credit and influence to borrow the money necessary to carry the enterprise through."[8] President Snow loyally went along with the motion, but likely did not feel himself in complete accord with it.

In late March of that same year, President Snow met Elder Richards at his Brigham City home, to discuss in greater depth the kind of material to include in the *History of the Twelve* manuscript Richards was compiling as

Church Historian. They decided to include some items related to the last days of Elder David W. Patten, one of the early members of the Twelve.[9]

In the July meeting of the Twelve, at which Presidents Cannon and Smith were present, "President Snow stated the nature, object, and success of our meetings which we have held about quarterly the last two years." With the purpose of the meetings being to build and strengthen Quorum unity, President Snow also disparaged the actions of one of the Twelve—Elder John Henry Smith—in partisan political matters, counseling those present not to follow suit.[10]

In late August 1891, the Church negotiated with the federal government in an effort to have returned the money and property that was confiscated by the US Congress under the Edmunds-Tucker Act during past polygamy persecutions. Now that the Church had formally and officially declared polygamy's cessation with the Manifesto, the government, through a "Master-in-Chancery" in court, showed a willingness to cooperate—based on promises to never resume again. Lorenzo Snow was heavily involved as usual. Elder Cannon recorded the discussion in one meeting:

> The matter to be considered was what to do in the Church property case which is soon to be brought before the Master-in-Chancery. The government expects him to suggest some plan by which some $400,000 of property can be disposed of to satisfy the persons who contributed the same. After prayer by Lorenzo Snow, F. S. Richards read a "scheme" which the Church attorneys prepared and proposed to submit to the Master[-in-Chancery], by which the property can be turned over to the Presidency of this Church, and be invested by them according to their best judgment to bring in the largest returns, and all the profits of these investments are to be used for the benefit of the poor of said Church. The Presidency are then to be required to file annually with the Court a statement of all business connected with this fund.
>
> If it were only to secure these funds the brethren all seemed to be inclined to let the matter drop without any protest from us, but it is felt that the situation here demands the saying of something in regard to the Manifesto and our future intentions in regard to polygamy, and hence it is expected that we will prove that the latter is really abandoned. Written questions, which it is likely will be asked in Court, have been sent to all the Twelve for their replies, but only Bros. Snow and Lund have thus far answered them. Some of these are very searching, and almost make us, if we answer them the way it is desired, deny the principle of plural marriage for all time. We all believe that this suspension is merely temporary, and, that God will open the way for his divine revelation to be

> established, but judging from a human standpoint plural marriage is forever stopped.
>
> The questions and answers of Bros. Snow and Lund were then submitted and in general approved, and after considerable discussion it was decided by unanimous vote that Father, L. Snow, M. Thatcher, Bro. Lund and any others whom the Presidency may select, receive our support in going on the witness stand to answer any questions which may be propounded.[11]

Some of the Brethren, including President Woodruff, eventually testified in court and were able to regain some of the Church's property, but much of it had been looted by the crooked court-appointed receiver of properties, Marshal Frank Dyer, and his "legal advisors." The court examination was trying for President Woodruff, who walked a fine line between satisfying the antagonistic government representatives and striving to arrange for the return of desperately needed Church funds. The results were discussed in a November meeting of the Twelve and the First Presidency: "The matter of the Manifesto and the extent of its meaning was then discussed. Pres. Woodruff said that he was placed in such a position on the witness stand that he could not answer other than he did; yet any man who deserts and neglects his [plural] wives or children because of the Manifesto should be handled on his fellowship [disciplined]. Our talk resolved itself into this—that men must be careful to avoid exposing themselves to arrest or conviction for violations of the law; and yet they must not break their covenants with their wives."[12]

President Snow continued his labors with his Brethren. Try as he might, his lofty goal of Quorum unity was sometimes unreachable. A particularly troubling concern that President Snow and his Brethren found intruding upon them in 1891 was the status of Elder John Willard Young, a largely inactive apostle. Elder Young had been a favored son of President Brigham Young and had been ordained at age eleven, an apostle by his father and then later had the ordination reconfirmed upon him at nineteen, a time when two of his brothers were also ordained as apostles.[13] Elder Young, who served for a short time as first counselor in the First Presidency before his father died, had thereafter taken little interest in his religious and ecclesiastical duties, preferring to live in New York or London, where he could pursue his grandiose business plans, live well, and mingle with high society. He possessed a silver tongue and considerable personal magnetism and charm, but evidently little business acumen, as his railroad building schemes usually failed.

Complaints of financial misdeeds and misappropriation of Church funds followed him until he was thrice called up for disciplinary action before the Twelve, and thrice acquitted.[14] He was able to survive the charges simply because there was thought to be a difference between being a failure and being a swindler. Yet his neglect of his Church duties as an apostle, though not a member of the Quorum of the Twelve, could not be ignored.[15] Elder Heber J. Grant summarized the circumstances as he remembered them later:

> I call to mind that the Apostles upon one occasion had a man that they were trying for neglect of duty, and felt that he was unworthy to occupy the position that he did occupy, and he pled and pled for an extension of opportunity to work, and finally a motion was made that he be dropped from the position that he was occupying, and it was seconded, and one of the brethren of the Council of the Twelve made a talk and prophesied in the name of the Lord Jesus Christ and by the authority of the Holy Priesthood that he held, that we would never have to take action against this man, that unless he repented of the methods he had employed in his careless labors, that he himself would cut the cord that bound him to his associates in the Church. Finally, a motion was made that he be given another chance.
>
> Years later the man became very careless and indifferent, and the President of the Church instructed the Apostles who had tried this man to take action, that his carelessness was such we should not endure his occupying a position of trust, and that we should take action. I have never had my faith tried, I believe, in my life, as much as during about three or four hours when the Apostles were in a meeting and the expressed purpose of the meeting was to take action regarding this individual—to think of that marvelous prophecy that was delivered by one of the Apostles years before and which thrilled me from the crown of my head to the tips of my toes like an electric shock, and here we were about to take action against this man, instead of him cutting the cord that bound us together.
>
> We had been discussing another matter, and finally President Lorenzo Snow, who was then the President of the Council of the Twelve Apostles, hit the table and said, "I won't hear one more word. We were sent here by the Prophet of the Lord to take action on a certain individual who has neglected his duty, and here we are talking and talking and talking about an insignificant matter, and I will not listen to another word. We will now take action in connection with the case that has brought us together." A knock came upon the door, the door was

> opened and a letter was handed in. It was the resignation of this man about whom the prophecy had been uttered to the effect that he himself would cut the cord that bound him to a chain with the Brethren.[16]

At the conclusion of this council meeting deciding Elder John W. Young's ecclesiastical status, President Snow again took the opportunity to proffer his usual plea "about union, fellowship and love for each other"—to Quorum members.[17]

If it wasn't money matters, partisan politics could also arouse the ire of the apostles. During a two-day meeting of the Twelve in January 1892, President Snow delivered a warning to his Brethren:

> I know that the Lord is pleased with our meeting together, as are also our brethren of former quorums who have lived and died. I hope that we will be able to keep from us any such spirit as that which took possession of the Apostles and people in Kirtland, when half of the quorum apostatized and the Prophet scarcely dared to go upon the street for fear of being killed. Still the same beginning is being made in our midst today as then existed; the spirit of disrespect for the Priesthood and of disregard of its teachings. If this continues it will lead to apostasy and trouble. We should use our influence to check it. We should never allow ourselves to listen to remarks which are made against any member of this quorum without seeking to check the same. I know the day is not far distant when you brethren will be clothed with great power from God, and you will do things that will astonish yourselves and those who witness them. In view of these glorious things, how careful we should be to do just as near right as we possibly can.

After further like instruction, the Brethren discussed the political activities of democrat John Henry Smith, who spoke highly of his own partisan endeavors. Elder Moses Thatcher, a republican, became annoyed with this recital and interrupted him a few times. Elder Smith defended himself further, but this occasioned a strong rebuke from Elder Franklin D. Richards, the senior member of the Quorum. After these exchanges, President Snow decided to forebear asking for a motion to approve of Elder Smith's political exertions. The Quorum's only possible conclusion—"If John Henry Smith is doing any good, however, we all felt to give him our blessing."[18]

Having performed his duty to rebuke betimes with sharpness, the Quorum president changed tactics for the second day's meeting: "President Snow was uncommonly nice and fine in his instructions to us," wrote Elder Franklin D. Richards. He "read a poem by himself of the sentiment [relationship] of God and man. 'As we are now, so once was he. As he is now, so may we be.' A beautiful collection of thoughts."[19] This was one of many instances when President Snow taught the exalting doctrine that had so many years previously been revealed to him (see also appendix one).

At their next quarterly meeting in April, "after waiting about three-quarters of an hour, we got seven of the Brethren together," reported Elder Cannon. Then, "President Snow arose and expressed his dissatisfaction at our lack of promptness in attending these meetings, and our neglect of them. He felt that we should always be on time, and never allow anything to interfere with our being present at the times appointed. He then continued: 'As for myself I would like to get rid of all financial matters and devote myself to the spiritual affairs of the work. This might not do for my Brethren, but I believe we will yet have to take positions which we do not now understand.'" After this gentle remonstrance, his natural diplomacy took over, and he changed his tone to one of sacred encouragement, testifying, "It is the privilege of you brethren to see the Savior, and thus testify of Him, and that you know He lives." After further remarks, President Snow finished by giving them counsel to promote unity: "Pres. Snow said he felt that when any question came up among us on which the majority were clear, should there be one who did not see as the others, that one should be willing to yield his views to those of the majority, and leave the responsibility of the course pursued with them."[20]

April 6, 1892, saw the laying of the capstone of the Salt Lake Temple. At this meeting, after President Woodruff pressed an electric button that dropped the capstone in place, President Snow led the assembled Latter-day Saints in the sacred "Hosanna Shout." One observer described the occasion:

> Pres. Lorenzo Snow then instructed the congregation in regard to the shouting of Hosanna, when the top stone of the Temple shall have been laid. The Priesthood were arranged in their various orders in the body of the building, and thus left it to march to the place where the ceremonies are to occur. At 11:15 we began the march, and by 12:30 all was ready for the services. Held's band played the Capstone March which had been prepared by C. J. Thomas, and then the choir sang the Temple anthem, the words of which were composed by C. L. Walker and the music by Evan Stephens. Father then exhibited a polished brass plate which was to go beneath the cap-stone. It contained the names of the

> authorities of the Church at the time the corner stone of the temple was laid—April 6, 1853, and the names of the present authorities. Also the names of the architects. The engraving was done by David McKenzie. There were placed in the cap-stone also a full set of our Church Works, photographs of Joseph and Hyrum Smith, Brigham Young, John Taylor, Wilford Woodruff, George Q. Cannon and Joseph F. Smith. Also a picture of the Temple in its present condition.
>
> The prayer was then offered by Joseph F. Smith, and then the cap-stone of the structure was laid by Pres. Woodruff touching the electric button by means of which the stone was dropped into its place. Under the direction of the President of the Apostles, Lorenzo Snow, the assembled multitude, numbering perhaps 40,000, shouted "Hosanna, Hosanna, Hosanna to God and the Lamb, Amen, Amen, Amen." This was done three times, each shout being accompanied by a waving of handkerchiefs, except when the names of God and the Lamb were uttered.[21] (One year later the temple was finished inside and out and could be formally dedicated.)

Later that year in July, the Twelve met again in the upper room of the Church Historian's office. One of the purposes for some of their recent meetings was to listen to a reading of the manuscript *History of the Twelve* that Elder Franklin D. Richards was preparing. He was not present that day so President Snow took the opportunity to air past troubles and again seek Quorum unification. He made two speeches over two days of meetings (summarized):

> [July 12] Pres. Snow said he felt very happy to meet with the Brethren today. It is our privilege and duty to seek for the mysteries of the Kingdom, and to be in advance of those who are around us. It is our labor to bring about the immortality of man, and the more earnestly we are engaged in this labor the more we will be blest in all our affairs. He referred to politics and said the position taken by Bros. Thatcher and Smith had made him think seriously about our condition. He was determined, however, not to let the actions of the brethren divide our Quorum. It is the privilege of the brethren to enjoy the spirit of prophecy and to be guided of the Lord in all the labors required of us. He requested all who engaged in politics to be very careful of the feelings of the brethren. If there are any hard feelings existing among us, this is the time and place to make them known so that they can be settled. Nothing that occurs here should be carried further.
>
> Several of the brethren expressed themselves as having the very best

of feeling for each other, and in this sentiment all the others present acquiesced.[22]

[July 13] I love all my brethren of this Quorum, and I desire to see them united. Before I die I want to see us all unalterably and immovably fixed in the unity of the gospel. If such a spirit was in us we could work wonders, and with the help of God could manage His work as He desires. We should never get into positions where we forget the respect due from one of us to the other. We ought to always cultivate the spirit of kindness and love for our brethren and be careful of the feelings of those around us." He referred to the story of David who would not lift his hand against the Lord's anointed even though that man had sought his life. . . . The lesson he desired to teach us by these examples was that we should not expose the weaknesses of the Priesthood which is over us, if they have weak points, we should try to shield them from the gaze of the unbelieving or scoffing attitude. He especially mentioned the newspaper controversy between Bros. Joseph F. and John H. Smith, and Moses Thatcher. He said that when Pres. Woodruff asks for our views upon any subject, we should express the same fully, but if his advice is contrary to our views we should follow his counsels in opposition to our own feelings if necessary.[23]

Then on December 2, 1892, President Snow was invited, almost casually, by President Wilford Woodruff, to a private meeting or interview—one of the most sacred, important and decisive moments of his life:

Yesterday morning I went to Salt Lake City, where I arrived about eleven o'clock a.m., and proceeded immediately to President Woodruff's office. There were present: President Woodruff, George Q. Cannon, Joseph F. Smith; and F. M. Lyman came in shortly after. George F. Gibbs was also present.

We spent the time in conversation on various subjects till after three p.m., when I arose to leave, shook hands with the brethren and started towards the door, when President Woodruff called me back, saying that he wished to speak with me in private. We went into the adjoining sitting room and took seats on one of the sofas. He said, and spoke with much feeling and energy, "I have an important request to make of you which I want you to fulfill. A few months ago while on a visit to St. George I came near dying. I have no lease of my life, and know not how soon I may be called away, and when I go I want you, Brother Snow, not to delay, but organize the First Presidency. Take George Q. Cannon

> and Joseph F. Smith for your counselors; they are good, wise men of experience."
>
> Of course I was much surprised, and said, "President Woodruff, am I to receive this as a revelation?" I do not call to mind the words of his answer, but they were such as gave me the impression that he wished me to regard it as such. Without thought or considering of the impropriety of such questions, I continued: "President Woodruff, is this the place I am to occupy?" He hesitated a moment, then replied, "It is according to the order." I asked if he had mentioned this matter to his counselors. He said, "No, not to anyone." I told him I wished he would; I understood from his answer that he would do so.
>
> The interview was brief, I think not over five or six minutes. As we arose to return to the President's office he said, "Brother Snow, now do not neglect to organize as I have told you, *it may prevent much trouble*."[24]

This short interview, with its ramifications, made a deep and lasting impression on Lorenzo. He had witnessed firsthand the difficulties experienced with the Quorum by President Woodruff for two years before achieving a reorganization of the First Presidency. He was dealing with occasional problems and tempers within the Quorum himself at the time and knew well that President Woodruff's counsel to reorganize the Presidency quickly after his death was wise and obviously inspired—that following such counsel may indeed "prevent much trouble." Delay could result in further discord, which could lead to additional postponement. Whether it was reasonable or realistic or not, moving forward resolutely and timely to reorganize could result in major advantages: no time for prolonged debate and wrangling.

First President of the Salt Lake Temple

The First Presidency formed a committee consisting of Joseph F. Smith, Lorenzo Snow, and Abraham H. Cannon "to see that the temple in this city is finished: ready for dedication on April 6." Their duties included overseeing the workmen and checking on the quantity and quality of their work.[25] (Finishing the temple in time for the designated dedication day was draining the Brethren and the Church financially, and it would later be mentioned by President Woodruff as one of the causes of the heavy Church debts.)

The Salt Lake Temple was dedicated April 6, 1893, exactly forty years after the laying of the cornerstones. Elder Cannon's journal contains one of the most detailed descriptions of the dedicatory services:

On April 6th the dedication services in the temple were held at 10 a.m. All of the Presidency and Twelve with their families were present, and quite a large number of the Priesthood. The wives of deceased apostles were also present. The assembly room was filled to its utmost capacity. Pres. Woodruff offered the dedicatory prayer. Remarks were then made by himself and counselors. During the time of the services the wind outside blew a perfect hurricane, doing considerable damage throughout the city, and in various parts of the country.

The first service was the pattern for all the other services which were held in the temple, consisting of two sessions a day, and one day three. Also when the Sunday schools were admitted on two different days, three sessions per day were held, at each of which each of the apostles spoke briefly. During the other services the Apostles were called to speak once or twice, and also to read the prayer. . . . The instructions were of a character to teach forgiveness and purity of life. The promise was made that if the Saints would sin no more their past sins would be forgiven of God. It was also said that our enemies would never have so much power over us again as they have had, if we will only be faithful. Many remarkable things were seen and heard in the Temple. Andrew Smith, Jr., said he saw on the stand with the brethren President Young, a number of the Twelve who are dead, and several other brethren whom he did not know.

A little nine-year-old boy also told his mother that he saw angels in the room and on the stand. Numerous parties saw brilliant lights, and heard singing and instrumental music. One rough young man from Brigham City, a son of the late Judge Wright, and the leader in the escapades of the young men at his home, said he saw a bright halo about the head of Pres. Woodruff, and the spirit of the Temple was so strong in him that he went to his home and started a reformation among his companions, which Pres. Lorenzo Snow thinks will affect great good.

Our Quorum held two evening meetings in our room in the Temple in which each of us spoke.

Bro. Thatcher was so seriously ill at one time that we expected every moment to hear of his death. He returned to his home in Logan within a few days after the Temple services commenced. Pres. Woodruff was also taken very sick, and got very low, so that on two different occasions arrangements were being made for his burial. Both of the brethren gradually recovered.

A two-day meeting was held with the General Authorities and the Presidents of Stakes and their counselors on April [blank] and [blank]. There were 115 brethren present. On the latter day we dressed in our priestly robes, formed a circle in the large celestial room, and had

> prayers. Father was mouth in the circle, and Pres. Snow in the opening [prayer]. We then partook of the sacrament in our [temple] robes in the [Council] room of the [First] Presidency. It was a very happy and never to be forgotten time. Our first day of meeting, and part of the second were spent in speaking, each man being asked to express his feelings towards the authorities of the Church, and the Saints generally.[26]

After President Snow read the dedicatory prayer in turn, he "led the congregation" in the Hosanna Shout.[27] Historian B. H. Roberts noted that "Dedicatory services . . . were held daily—at which the dedicatory prayer was always read—from the 6th of April to the 18th of May inclusive. Generally two sessions were held each day, but on the 7th of April, an evening session was added. . . . The attendance at the dedicatory services of the Salt Lake Temple is not definitely known, since many attended more than one of the many sessions held. The attendance of course was by card [recommend], and the least number in attendance was at the evening session of April the 7th—this service being arranged to accommodate the overflow from previous sessions of that day; and even at that session 2,100 were present. At other sessions more than 2,600 passed through the doors. 'Estimating the five children's sessions as being attended by 12,000, half of whom had not attended before,' says the *Deseret News,* editorially, 'it is a thoroughly conservative calculation to say that the dedication services have been attended by 75,000 people.'"[28]

When Lorenzo "was set apart by Pres. Woodruff as president of the Salt Lake Temple, he was then informed by Pres. Woodruff that he had been appointed in the other world [premortal existence] to said position before he came here."[29]

As noted, President Woodruff became very ill after the initial dedication; many supposed his time had come and were pleasantly surprised when he recovered. A few years later, President Woodruff spoke to some of the other Brethren (presumably also President Snow) about a spiritual experience he had during this time:

> President Woodruff remarked that the Lord in the early days of the Church required his servants to make a record of their persecutions and the mobbing they endured from their enemies [D&C 123]. The Lord also told them that angels were waiting to go forth and reap down the earth, but were told to keep back for a season [D&C 38:12; 86:5–7]. President Woodruff said that at the time of the dedication of the Salt Lake Temple, the spirit manifested to him that the Lord was about to send special messengers to the earth for special purposes, and he firmly

> believed as much as he believed anything that some of those messengers had already commenced their work, and that the numerous and great disasters of recent date were the evidences of their presence.[30]

One of President Snow's duties as temple president was to "talk to the workers, and dispel any wrong feelings which might exist. Bro. Snow told them not to impose on the cook by inviting their friends to eat who do not work in the temple. They are not to go out of the door and leave it unlocked in the absence of the door-keeper, and under no circumstances are they to invite strangers into the building."[31] On May 20, the temple workers were set apart.[32]

A great deal of training and instruction was in order for the ordinance workers and others connected to the temple. President Snow organized a temple choir. A temple library was built and furnished in the room behind the sealing rooms adjacent to the celestial room (now the sealer's office) and President Snow installed his son LeRoi (then a teenager) as the librarian.[33]

In 1895, LeRoi invited his nephew and friend Chauncey West to visit. Chauncey "was still only a teacher in the Aaronic Priesthood, but [his] Grandpa (Lorenzo Snow) was president of the Salt Lake Temple, so Chauncey was ordained an elder and received his endowments. He also participated in baptisms for the dead. He enjoyed almost a unique opportunity to examine the interior of the Temple." Chauncey's journal stated, "We started to see the interior of the Temple at one o'clock and went in the six towers as far as we could safely get. We went almost to the top of the west, middle tower, up past the last strait projection. I never care to be in a nicer place than the Temple. When we came back down, I sat in the chair made for the President of the Temple (my Grandpa). It was as soft and easy as life could wish to rest upon. I walked over the top of the Temple. We came out after 3 hours of walking and seeing. I went through as thoroughly as anybody and more than visitors and workers."[34]

Spending so much time in the holy temple placed the saintly Lorenzo where the veil was thin and heaven close. Under these circumstances, he learned that his family was not yet complete. His granddaughter wrote:

> As President of the Salt Lake Temple, Grandfather often lived in the temple for months at a time. On one occasion he was awakened during the middle of the night by the voice of a baby calling "papa, papa, papa." Arising from his cot he walked out into the corridors leading from the Celestial Room. All was dark and still. Thinking he must have been mistaken about the voice, he soon was settled back in his room and had

> fallen asleep. Three times during that night he was awakened by the same baby voice, calling him. The following morning, with the events of the previous night still fresh on his mind, he left the temple and went home to share this strange occurrence with his wife. He told her, "Minnie, there is another very special spirit waiting to come to us." For the first time in her life she was speechless. Then after assuring him that it was quite impossible considering their ages of 42 and 82 he replied, "Now Minnie, we might be sure of the impossibility of the situation, but you shall see, it will happen, another spirit will come to us."

A few months later, Minnie was pregnant. Rhea Lucille Snow was born November 5, 1896, in Cardston, Alberta, Canada, where Lorenzo and Minnie traveled so she could deliver the baby away from prying eyes and gossiping tongues, resulting from persecution caused by prejudice against plural marriage. Rhea was given her baby blessing by her father in the Salt Lake Temple. "When grandfather saw his baby girl he was so proud. This baby was the joy of his old age," wrote his granddaughter.[35]

When the temple opened in 1893, the First Presidency and Twelve began holding their meetings there in preference to some of the other locations where they had met, such as the Gardo House. At one such meeting in October, President Snow spoke to members of his Quorum: "He said it is our privilege to receive great revelations in our meetings, and we should seek for knowledge and instruction whenever we come together. We may not get any very great physical manifestations, but we can enjoy the things of the Spirit. God will try us till He knows our hearts, and finds us worthy to suffer all for His sake."[36] Later that year, James E. Talmage brought his little brother Albert, who had been accidently blinded by a miss-aimed pitchfork, to the temple to receive his endowments. Brother Talmage wrote that, "After the endowment [ordinances] he was taken into Pres. Snow's room and there administered to, . . . Pres. Snow himself being mouth, and his counselors, Bros. Winder and Madsen, also father and myself assisting. Albert was promised the blessing and favor of God, according to his faith; he was urged not to give up, but to keep his hopes and faith strong before the Lord."[37]

Raising the Dead

While serving as President of the Twelve, President Snow was involved with a miraculous priesthood administration, in which he blessed his deceased niece, Ella Jensen, to return to life. Ella had contracted scarlet fever, and for some time had weakened, until March 3, 1894, when she passed away and entered the spirit world where she remained for about three hours. After being blessed by President Snow and stake president Rudger Clawson, she returned to life and was able to describe her sojourn in the spirit world in some detail.

The patriarchal blessing that Lorenzo Snow received from Joseph Smith (Sr.) or "Father Smith" as President Snow and many others referred to him, had stated that Lorenzo would be involved with miracles such as raising the dead: "Thou shalt become a mighty man. Thy faith shall increase and grow stronger until it shall become like Peter's—thou shalt restore the sick; ... The dead shall rise and come forth at thy bidding." The *Improvement Era* contains the entire account, of which excerpts are included below:

> The parents were called and as they entered the room the daughter told them that her Uncle Hans, who was dead, had suddenly appeared in the room, while she was awake, with her eyes open, and told her that messengers would be there at ten o'clock to conduct her into the spirit world. The father and mother feared that the girl was delirious and tried to get her to be quiet and go to sleep. She knew their thoughts and said: 'I know what I am talking about. No, I am not going to sleep any more. I know I am going to die and that they are coming to get me.' . . .
>
> Towards ten o'clock, Uncle Jake, the father, who was holding his daughter's hand, felt the pulse become very weak. A few moments later he turned to his wife saying: "Althea, she is dead, her pulse has stopped." The heart-broken parents wept and grieved at the loss of their beautiful daughter. . . .
>
> We talked the matter over and wondered what we should do. I told my wife that I would go to town, more than a mile from home, and see President Snow, tell him about her death and have him arrange for the funeral.
>
> I . . . got [Presidents Clawson and Snow] and took them both down to my home, about a mile and a half south of Brigham City. We went into the house. My wife and children were there. After standing at Ella's bedside for a minute or two, President Snow asked if we had any consecrated oil in the house. I was greatly surprised, but told him yes and got it for him. He handed the bottle of oil to Brother Clawson and asked him to anoint Ella. [President Snow] confirming the anointing.
>
> During the administration I was particularly impressed with some of the words which he used and can well remember them now. He said: "Dear Ella, I command you, in the name of the Lord, Jesus Christ, to come back and live; your mission is not ended. You shall yet live to perform a great mission."

He said she should yet live to rear a large family and be a comfort to her parents and friends. I well remember these words.

[President Clawson said:] "As we entered the home we met Sister Jensen, who was very much agitated and alarmed. We came to Ella's bedside and were impressed by the thought that her spirit had passed out of the body and gone beyond.

Turning to me President Snow said: "Brother Clawson, will you anoint her," which I did. We then laid our hands upon her head and the anointing was confirmed by President Snow, who blessed her and among other things, used this very extraordinary expression, in a commanding tone of voice, "Come back, Ella, come back. Your work upon the earth is not yet completed, come back." Shortly afterward we left the home."

Uncle Jake, Ella's father, continues his account: "After President Snow had finished the blessing, he turned to my wife and me and said; "Now do not mourn or grieve any more. It will be all right. Brother Clawson and I are busy and must go, we cannot stay, but you just be patient and wait, and do not mourn, because it will be all right." . . .

Ella remained in this condition for more than an hour after President Snow administered to her, or more than three hours in all after she died. We were sitting there watching by the bedside, her mother and myself, when all at once she opened her eyes. She looked about the room, saw us sitting there, but still looked for someone else, and the first thing she said was: "Where is he? Where is he?" We asked, "Who? Where is who?" "Why, Brother Snow," she replied. "He called me back."

We explained that Brother Snow and Brother Clawson were very busy and could not remain, that they had gone. Ella dropped her head back on the pillow, saying: 'Why did he call me back? I was so happy and did not want to come back.'"

Regarding the more than three hours that Ella spent in the spirit world she says:

"I could see people from the other world and hear the most delightful music and singing that I ever heard. This singing lasted for six hours, during which time I was preparing to leave this earth, and I could hear it all through the house. At ten o'clock my spirit left my body. It took me some time to make up my mind to go, as I could hear and see the folks crying and mourning over me. It was very hard for me to leave them, but as soon as I had a glimpse of the other world I was anxious to go and all care and worry left me.

"I entered a large hall. It was so long that I could not see the end of it. It was filled with people. As I went through the throng, the first person I recognized was my grandpa, H. P. Jensen, who was sitting in one end of the room, writing. He looked up, seemed surprised to see me and said: 'Why! There is my grand-daughter, Ella.' He was very much pleased, greeted me and, as he continued with his writing, I passed on through the room and met a great many of my relatives and friends. It was like going along the crowded street of a large city where you meet many people, only a very few of whom you recognize.

"The next one I knew was Uncle Hans Jensen with his wife, Mary Ellen. They had two small children with them. On inquiring who they were, he told me one was his own and the other was Uncle Will's little girl. Some seemed to be in family groups. As there were only a few whom I could recognize and who knew me, I kept moving on.

"Some inquired about their friends and relatives on the earth. Among the number was my cousin. He asked me how the folks were getting along and said it grieved him to hear that some of the boys were using tobacco, liquor and many things that were injurious to them.

"This proved to me that the people in the other world know to a great extent what happens here on the earth.

"The people were all dressed in white or cream, excepting Uncle Hans Jensen, who had on his dark clothes and long rubber boots, the things he wore when he was drowned in the Snake River in Idaho.

"Everybody appeared to be perfectly happy. I was having a very pleasant visit with each one that I knew. . . .

"For more than three hours my spirit was gone from my body. As I returned I could see my body lying on the bed and the folks gathered about in the room. I hesitated for a moment, then thought, 'Yes, I will go back for a little while.' I told the folks I wanted to stay only a short time to comfort them." . . .

"It may well be thought that Ella Jensen's work on earth was not yet completed, as indicated by President Snow, for she afterwards became president of the Young Ladies' Mutual Improvement Association in Brigham City. Afterwards she married and became a mother in Israel, and surely a woman can do no greater work in the world than to become a mother of men."[38]

The account in which Ella returned to life after President Snow administered to her became well known as it circulated through various older publications. Evidently this led some to make further inquiry of Ella Jensen Wight, as in the following account, signed by Ella after she related her story to witnesses:[39]

> To whom it may concern:
>
> This happened about 42 years ago on March 3rd on which date I was taken very sick.
>
> For one week I was very ill. On the morning of the 3rd of March I awakened with the impression I was going to die. I could hear beautiful singing and told my parents I was called to go back to the other world. In about 4 hours my spirit left my body. As soon as I caught a glimpse of the other world the knowledge of this world seemed to leave me. I remained in the spirit world for 3 hours. Then I heard Pres. Lorenzo Snow . . . calling me: "Sister Ella, you must come back as your mission is not yet finished here on this earth." The spirit world resembled a large white sphere.
>
> I went thru a long, long, passage way and after I had greeted my Grandpa H. A. Jensen and Uncle Hans Jensen and many others, then I left this sphere and went into another room or place where there was assembled a large gathering of children who were being taught by Eliza R. Snow, who I had known in life. We greeted each other.
>
> Before I entered my body I saw it lying there in its diseased and natural state. I recognized my spirit was in the exact form of my body.
>
> My spirit entered my body again and I opened my eyes and said "Where is Pres. Snow?" My parents informed me he had left the house. They had called him in their sadness and were surprised when he anointed me with the oil and called me and informed them that everything would be alright, to sit and watch my body as he had to return to his meetings.
>
> I was very reluctant about returning to earth [from the spirit world] as it was such a beautiful place far surpassing this world. There was so much love, harmony and peace.[40]

Elder Clawson, after becoming a member of the Quorum of the Twelve, also found occasion to recount this sacred experience: "Meeting at the tabernacle, ... I made remarks upon the subject of signs following believers and related an incident where a young woman [Ella Jensen], who had apparently died, was restored to life and health by the anointing and laying on of hands of President Snow and myself."[41]

Church Financial Situation Worsens

Throughout 1893 and 1894 (and continuing for several years), a severe depression permeated the United States, and Utah was not immune to its effects. A money stringency, or lack of available cash, made it difficult to do business and for the Church to make payroll. About this time, many of the Brethren began to preach tithing payment and its accompanying blessings to the Latter-day Saints, but without consistency and coordination.[42] The financial panic so affected the Church that employees were paid in part with what was known as tithing scrip (orders for goods and foodstuffs from the tithing storehouses).

Arthur Winter, a clerk and stenographer-reporter in the President's Office, described his personal view of circumstances in July 1895, when the economic problems were about their worst: "This is the last day of the month and I have not received from the Church all my wages for June. I never saw such a condition of things as prevails now in financial matters. Banks are breaking on every hand, merchants are failing; thousands and thousands of people are out of employment, and everybody is wondering how it will all turn out. The Church has not enough funds to meet its current expenses and cannot borrow a dollar. Tithing comes in exceedingly slow, and the prospects are that there will be a great falling off this year."[43] Elder Francis M. Lyman recorded the same observations during these years: "Money matters are very tight, banks and mercantile institutions are going broke on every hand."[44]

President Snow continued working for unity within his Quorum as well as between them and the First Presidency. At a meeting in April 1894, he echoed a familiar refrain: "President Snow expressed his pleasure at the union and love which are characteristic of this Quorum at present. He did not believe anything would ever occur to divide us, and hoped such would not be the case. 'I feel that we should get into a condition to know the mind of the Lord at all times. If our eye is single to the glory of God, our whole bodies will be filled with light. If we do everything for the purpose and with the view of forwarding the work of the Lord, we will never fail, but will be successful in everything.'"[45]

Troubling unity issues stemmed from the actions of Elders John W. Taylor and Moses Thatcher. President Snow was asked by the First Presidency to work with Elder Taylor to ensure he spent more time laboring in his ecclesiastical duties and less trying to broker land deals in Canada.[46] Elder Taylor seemed to resent these efforts and "said he did not feel under obligations to sustain the [First] Presidency in anything about which they did not consult him and the Twelve, and he rather complained of their organizing the Utah [electric power] Company for profit, when they had rebuked him for his efforts to make money out of the sale of lands to the Brethren and strangers. Bros. Thatcher and Richards both mildly rebuked Bro. Taylor for the spirit he manifested." After listening to these exchanges, "Pres. Snow spoke of the great apostasy in Kirtland,

and said we must not partake of such a spirit."[47] He would not abandon his quest for Quorum unity. He told them he felt that if any of the Brethren had personal feelings against another Quorum member, they should settle it between themselves without airing it in the Quorum. "He felt jealous of the unity of the Twelve, and hoped we would allow nothing to arise to separate us from the love we should bear towards each other."[48]

Also that October, the First Presidency wrote a letter of instruction to President Snow and the Quorum of the Twelve, requesting them to explore options for educating and training missionaries before their departure into the mission field. The letter admitted, "It is known to all of us who have had experience in the missionary field that there are very many, in fact a great proportion of those who go out, who do not do justice to the message of which they are the bearers." Further, they informed the Quorum, "It is very desirable that something be done, if possible, to make a better impression upon the world through the medium of our elders. The work of God is attracting wide-spread attention, and a different class of people manifest an interest in our doctrines than formerly. The world is also progressing in matters of education." The First Presidency desired the missionary force to be as educated as those they taught—but not in the same sense as Protestant ministers: "There is no reason now why anyone should be ignorant of book learning, and it seems necessary that our elders should keep pace in this respect with the rest of the world. But you will perceive the danger there is of our people falling into the old ruts in which sectarians have been running for a long period of time, and adopting those spirit-killing systems which have prevailed in theological seminaries and other places where men in the sectarian world have been qualified for what they are pleased to call the ministry." This point must be emphasized: "It will be necessary to guard against this evil in any plan which may be decided upon: so that in adopting a system that will afford our elders such a training as is herein indicated, it should be entirely free from any tendency likely to check the Spirit of the Lord or cause men to depend upon their own learning instead of the guidance of the Holy Ghost."[49] As the years passed, the Quorum of the Twelve would experiment with various methods of training missionaries, from instruction in Church colleges and stake academies, to a mission home, to a language training center, to the missionary training centers and stake missionary preparation courses used today.[50]

In April 1895, President Snow spoke at a priesthood meeting and covered several points of counsel, one of which was that short public prayers and sermons were best for the people. A strain of humor showed in his scriptural allusion: "Paul once preached till a young man fell asleep in the window from which he fell and was killed. It might do for Paul to thus prolong his remarks for he had the power to restore the dead to life, but we had better not try to preach so long."[51] That August, President Snow again counseled unity in the quarterly Quorum of the Twelve meeting in the temple.[52]

It was at this time that President Snow first mentioned the idea to the Brethren of sending one of them to Japan on a mission. After some discussion. the matter was tabled, but several years later Elder Heber J. Grant would be called to open the Japanese mission.[53] Another subject that received immediate attention was the method by which the Apostles visited the various stakes for their conferences. Until this point they had either gone where they pleased, or at the request of the First Presidency, or where need dictated—often more than one of them visiting the same stake. As the Church grew and stakes were slowly organized and divided, it made sense to come up with something more systematic: "Heber J. Grant . . . expressed himself as desirous of mingling more among the Saints than he had done, and suggested the apportionment among the Twelve by a committee the various conferences so that we may know for some time ahead what places we are expected to visit. This suggestion met with approval, and Brigham Young, F. M. Lyman and John Henry Smith were appointed such committee."[54] From this time forward, stake conference visiting assignments began to occupy an increasing portion of weekly Quorum council time.

Chapter 15

Unifying the Quorum of the Twelve Apostles

Difficulties and Decisions

The year 1896 became a red-letter year for Church leaders. In response to issues created by the involvement of at least two senior Brethren in partisan politics, the First Presidency and Twelve decided to formulate a document, to be signed by all the General Authorities, that required them to receive approval from the First Presidency before running for office or entering political service. The reason for this was that their general priesthood offices merited first priority in their lives. At the time they accepted their callings, this principle had been explained with clarity to each of them; they had accepted this charge and counsel then, and they were expected to abide by it. None of the General Authorities resisted this "political manifesto" except for Elders Moses Thatcher of the Twelve and Brigham H. Roberts of the First Council of the Seventy.

Elder Roberts desired to run for political office and made political speeches, some of which contained expressions and opinions that were not in harmony with the views of members of the First Presidency. He had been asked and advised both publicly and privately by the First Presidency and other Apostles to alter his course and to sign the political manifesto. He had refused, receiving support for his actions from Moses Thatcher, who also stubbornly refused, feeling it to be an abridgment of his personal rights of conscience.

March 1896 was a critical month for Elder Roberts. On the fifth, "The case of insubordination of B. H. Roberts was taken up, and if he refused to meet the wishes of the Brethren it was decided to suspend him for three weeks, and if he did not then meet the requirement he was to be dropped from his calling."[1] On the nineteenth, "The case of B. H.

Roberts for insubordination was considered . . . . He is to be required to humble himself and put himself in proper shape before the people."[2] On the twenty-sixth, in a meeting, "President George Q. Cannon made the statement that as Bro. B. H. Roberts had not been in harmony with his brethren and that a feeling of dissension had spread through the church on account of some of Bro. Roberts's speeches. That all his Brethren wanted of him was to show a broken heart and contrite spirit, which Bro. Roberts did. We took him into our fellowship. He with the others present shed tears of joy at the change in his spirit."[3] Lorenzo Snow was present for these meetings and in harmony with the decisions and actions of his Brethren to urge a change of heart upon Elder Roberts, though he had less to do with Roberts's situation than with Elder Thatcher's.

It was also at this time that the question of ultimate control of Church finances was revisited by the First Presidency and the Twelve, referencing a previous discussion that had been held by the Brethren seven years before on October 10, 1889. Those intervening years had effectually changed the minds and hearts of certain Quorum members, who now viewed circumstances differently. President Woodruff had given up full authority over major financial expenditures as a concession to certain members of the Twelve in order to facilitate the reorganization of the First Presidency. Now the subject was reconsidered in-depth but carried further, to include a discussion of "Church salaries":

> President George Q. Cannon spoke at some length upon the functions and the office of the Trustee-in-trust for the Church, showing that after the death of President John Taylor, the Trustee-in-trust handled and was responsible for all the funds of the Church. After that event, the Presiding Bishop of the Church was entrusted with the control of the funds of the Church. This left the President of the Church in the position that if he needed any funds for Church purposes, he had to apply to the Bishop, and there was nothing in the office of the Trustee-in-Trust to show what was done with the Church funds except as it was reported by the Presiding Bishop. This was contrary to the custom in the Church from the beginning, and it placed the President of the Church in a fettered and limited position. He thought this was wrong, and that the matter should be set right during the life-time of President Woodruff, so that no precedent should be drawn from the present condition by the Church in future times.
>
> Connected with this subject, President Cannon said, is the question of salaries to the officers of the Church. It had always been a pleasure

to him to know and say that there was no salary attached to an office in this Church. President John Taylor, in consequence of excessive drafts upon the Church by some of the brethren, established a fixed allowance to the Apostles, which was subsequently increased, and the principle was extended to other officers in the Church. This had grown into a system by which a large amount of tithing was consumed in what appeared to be fixed salaries, attached to the several offices. President Cannon considered this improper. There were some of the brethren whose time was given to the Church who should be permitted and were entitled to receive support for themselves and families, while others were in good circumstances, and had little or no need for such assistance. He thought no more should be drawn from the Church by the brethren than was actually necessary, and that the amount should be regulated by their needs, and that should not be in the nature of a fixed salary.

President Woodruff endorsed the remarks of President Cannon, and referred to the time when the change was introduced by a number of the Apostles. He had always felt that it was wrong to transfer the powers of the Trustee-in-trust to the Bishopric, and thought it was like putting the cart before the horse. It was time that the error was corrected. He said further that he had traveled nearly all his life and preached without money and without price; he had never drawn anything from the Church until after the death of President Young. Since then he had received means from the Church, and the brethren had been very kind to him, but he did not believe in the system of stated salaries, and that we ought to go back to the early order of the Church.

Pres. Joseph F. Smith said he did not approve of the new order of things, by which the functions of the Trustee-in-trust was transferred to the Presiding Bishopric, nor of the custom of Church salaries. The Church however ought to support the families of men who devote their entire time to the ministry and need that support; any more than this cometh of evil. If he could get along without drawing a dollar from the Church he certainly would. He did not desire to see changes that would work hardships upon any of the brethren who devoted themselves to the ministry, but he was satisfied that it was wrong to fix salaries to any of the offices of the Church. He believed that the President of the Church should be at the head financially as well as spiritually. At the same time he felt it was right and proper and strictly in accordance with the order of the Priesthood that he and all of the authorities should act together by common consent in the management of Church affairs, not that any one man should act in such matters without the cooperation of the brethren. He thought the hands of the Presidency would be stronger in the management of Church funds with the assistance and

> cooperation of the brethren of the Twelve, or at least a majority of them. President Woodruff endorsed this opinion. President Smith said he had perfect confidence in the Trustee-in-trust, and believed he would have the support of his brethren. He considered that all should be economical and prudent, without extravagance, and so set an example for others to follow.
>
> President Lorenzo Snow said, he had failed to find anything in the Doctrine and Covenants touching on the question of salaries. He had traveled and labored upwards of 40 years without receiving a single cent from the Church, and had supported his family without taking advantage of any individual. He did not know for some time after President Taylor had made an allowance to the Apostles, that there was a sum credited to him. Lately it had been necessary for him to draw on that credit for the support of his family. He would prefer to be entirely independent of the Church in that respect, and felt sorry to say that he was not. He believed however, that all the brethren would see the propriety and advantage of carrying out the suggestion that salaries should not be established. As to the other question, it was the right and duty of the First Presidency to have the control of everything pertaining to the Church, whether spiritual or temporal. As to the present system, he thought the Presidency had only to express their wishes in order to have them carried out. If that was so now and the system worked satisfactorily to them, it would give them more time to attend to spiritual affairs. Elder F. D. Richards expressed himself as being in entire accord with the First Presidency on both questions. He explained the reasons which prevailed at the time when the changes in policy were made, and thought that it was only necessary for the Presidency to indicate that a return to the former practice was desirable, for he could not conceive of anything that pertained to the interest of the Church that did not come under the immediate control of the First Presidency.[4]

The rest of the Apostles then indicated their personal feelings and support of the contemplated changes in financial control and salaries. They wanted the President of the Church to have the purse strings—as long as he consulted with the Twelve on the major business and expenditure questions that arose. Further, some of them needed a living allowance from the Church, since their full time was occupied by their ministries, and they did not have other means of support. After full deliberation, President Woodruff announced that as there was a unanimity of feeling in the Council, the Brethren were no doubt ready for a motion. President George Q. Cannon then offered the following:

"I move, President Woodruff and Brethren of the Council, that there be no credits hereafter placed on the books to any Church official for services rendered in the Church, and that no man in the Church holding official position shall hereafter consider himself entitled to any remuneration for his services as a Church official. I mean all who act in a Church capacity, including Presidents of Stakes and others."

Seconded by Elder Heber J. Grant and carried unanimously.

President Cannon also offered the following motion, which was seconded by Elder Lyman and carried unanimously:

"I move President and Brethren of the Council, that the brethren who have been heretofore in the habit of drawing funds from the Church, or to whom allowances have been made for the sustenance of their families, be entitled hereafter to draw to the same extent as before, and that in the event of their needing anything more at any time, their necessities compelling them to ask for more, that it be done by application to the Trustee-in-trust."

Elder John Henry Smith enquired whether this action was to convey the idea that the Apostles were at liberty to go into business for themselves, and President Joseph F. Smith replied, "Unless we as a body of men act in some concerted movement, I don't consider that any member of this Council has the right to engage in occupations that will absorb his time or take him away from the performance of his duties."[5]

This decision became the beginning of the end of paying stake presidents 10–12 percent of the tithes collected in their stakes for service in their callings, although bishops continued to receive an appropriation of produce as remuneration for handling the tithes, at least through President Snow's administration.[6] While not mentioned in the quoted source, there seems to be little doubt that another reason for the cessation of paying Church officers was the increasing financial stress experienced by President Woodruff, and this was one method that, besides conforming to the principle of no paid LDS clergy, presented an immediate way to increase tithing flow to Church headquarters.

By this time, President George Q. Cannon had drafted the document that would become known as the "New" or "Political Manifesto," and the First Presidency and Twelve met to review it on April 5, which was general conference time.[7] Elder Thatcher refused to sign this paper, and that cost him his apostleship and almost his membership in the Church. The journal history of the Church relates the story:

The First Presidency and Apostles met, as per adjournment, at the President's Office. After some consultation, the First Presidency and those Apostles who were present, signed the document in their order [of seniority]. The Seven Presidents of Seventies and the Presiding Bishops were then invited in. The address was read to this united Council. It was suggested by President Smith that the brethren who had not signed the document have the privilege of talking the matter over among themselves, but the Brethren designated were ready at once to subscribe to the address. After being given an opportunity to make any suggestions for the modification or correction of the language, no change being suggested, all the brethren present signed the document in their order. A space was left for the signatures of Moses Thatcher and Anthon H. Lund, also for John Smith, Patriarch.

President Woodruff expressed his gratification at the union of feeling and sentiment among the Presiding Councils of the Church.

The other brethren having withdrawn, the Presidency and Apostles consulted in reference to Elder Moses Thatcher. It was resolved that President Lorenzo Snow and Elder Brigham Young be appointed to wait on Brother Moses Thatcher, who was too sick to attend Conference, at his residence to present to him the address for his signature. Those brethren went to the residence of brother Thatcher, while the others went to the Tabernacle to attend the Conference.

At 1 o'clock pm, Elder Lorenzo Snow and Brigham Young met the First Presidency at the President's Office and reported that after a pleasant conversation with Elder Moses Thatcher, they presented to him the address, offering to read it to him, but he preferred to read it himself. After doing so, he said there were some grave points embodied in it, and he would like time for further reflection before deciding whether he would sign it or not. They therefore left the document with him on his promise to send it to the President's Office by a safe messenger by half past one o'clock. The brethren expressed their opinion that, much to their regret, Elder Thatcher would return the document unsigned.

At 1:40 pm, the following communication was received from Brother Thatcher:

> April 6, 1896.
>
> President Lorenzo Snow and Apostle Brigham Young,
>
> Dear Brethren:
>
> Having carefully read the document left with me for consideration, I herewith return it as per promise.
>
> There is much of its contents that I could conscientiously endorse by signing it, but there are other portions which I cannot endorse without stultification.

If I was well I might view this most serious matter in another light; or I might do so had I more time to consider it; but as it is, it seems that I must determine now, though I fully realize how sadly long illness has weakened me in every way. In the future the Lord may enable me to define my view and acts as running along those of honor, integrity and truth.

But I can only humbly ask that you act according to the Holy Spirit's dictation as prompted by justice and brotherly love towards your fellow laborer in the cause of our Savior.

Signed,
Moses Thatcher

The Presidency and Brothers Snow and Young went to the Tabernacle, and called together the Apostles to consider what should be done in reference to presenting the name of Moses Thatcher to the Conference with the rest of the Twelve. It was decided not to present his name to be sustained as one of the Twelve Apostles.[8]

To omit the name of one of the Twelve during general conference was a very serious and rare event, and it caused a stir. Arthur Winter commented:

This was the last day of Conference. The meetings were very full. A document, signed by the leading authorities of the Church, and defining the position of the Church relative to the obligations of the officers of the Priesthood to the Church, was read and unanimously accepted by the Conference. This document is intended to set at rest all doubts concerning the rights of officers in the Church to accept other positions, political or otherwise, that would draw their time and attention away from their ecclesiastical duties. It was signed by the First Presidency, the Apostles, the Patriarch, the First Council of Seventies, and the Presiding Bishops. Brother Moses Thatcher of the Apostles declined to sign it, and for this reason his name was not presented this afternoon along with the other Apostles. Brother Thatcher has for a long time now not been in accord with his brethren. He has at different times, rejected the counsel of the authorities, and to those who have been acquainted with his course it has been apparent that he would either have to change or he would lose his position in the Priesthood. His health has been very poor for a long time, and for this reason much consideration and leniency has been shown him. But his refusal to sign this document resulted in his name not being presented for the vote of the people. Brother Thatcher was one of those who supported the Democratic party in the uproar it created during the last campaign in regard to the alleged interference of

> the Church in politics. Brother B. H. Roberts, of the First Council of Seventies, was another, but he, after being labored with very assiduously by the brethren, though their pleadings and entreaties were for some time in vain, finally acknowledged his wrong, and humbly submitted to those who presided over him, and signed the document along with the rest.[9]

Further, "There is considerable excitement in town over what is called the New [Political] Manifesto and the non-submission of Brother Thatcher's name to the Conference. The Gentiles [non–Latter-day Saint residents] do not like it, nor do some of the Mormons."[10]

A special priesthood meeting was held the morning of the last day of conference in the Assembly Hall. President Snow counseled the priesthood about temple work and baptisms for the dead, and then President Cannon gently admonished the assemblage for past breaches of confidentiality with the public, doing so for a reason. He spoke of the decision that had been made in relation to the suspension of Church ecclesiastical officer's salaries, and read them the resolution that had been approved. "He said that men who labored in the ministry and who needed help should receive necessary assistance, but not in the shape of a salary. The resolutions referred to were read again, and unanimously adopted by the meeting."[11] The authorities also directed that the political manifesto be read by local leaders throughout the Church.

Meanwhile, the economic hardships of the Church continued to worsen, and final steps were taken in June to return full control of Church tithing funds from the Presiding Bishop's Office to the Trustee-in-Trust, meaning President Woodruff as President of the Church. It was also suggested that a formal committee be appointed to audit the Church's books, but this was not done in earnest for two more years.[12]

In July 1896, Elder Abraham (Abram) H. Cannon died from a severe ear infection and the primitive medical methods used to treat it. Elder Cannon was the mainstay of his father and over the years had become heavily involved in many business and financial ventures, both his own and also those of his father and the Church.

President Snow had developed a great affection for this youngest of his Quorum and took the loss hard.[13] The funeral was held on the twenty-sixth with President Snow presiding at the services as Elder Cannon's quorum president, and there spoke with tenderness:

> He had been intimate [well acquainted] with the deceased Apostle

> for more than ten years, and more particularly so since his ordination to the Apostleship. A single blot or blemish could not be found on his character. He was perfectly obedient in all things to his father. He was a noble man, heaven had showered gifts upon him; his words had charmed our ears and pierced our hearts. He had come to this earth on a mission, passed through the temptations of mortal life, and returned a virtuous man, who had won a victory. He was not dead, but lived today more than ever. The prospect before him was beautiful, glorious. It would be difficult to find a man who could fill his place in all respects. The speaker invoked the choicest blessings of heaven upon the bereaved family.[14]

On October 1, at the meeting of the First Presidency and Twelve, the matter of the Bullion, Beck, and Champion Mine (B. B. & C.) was brought up. President Cannon felt that if its affairs in stock ownership had been handled properly, the Church would have had sufficient means to run its operations, even during the depression. Because the financial affairs (stock ownership) of the mine occasionally intruded into the deliberations and cohesiveness of the leading councils of the Church, President Snow was sometimes forced to deal with it, especially two years later.

At this meeting, President Cannon explained the Church's involvement with the mine: "President Taylor felt deeply impressed to enter into an agreement to buy the property of John Beck, if he would dedicate three-fifths of it to the Lord. This was done, and three-fifths of the stock was placed in President Taylor's hands and was held by him until his death. When Brother John Beck came home [from Germany] and demanded his stock, President Cannon reminded him of the covenant which had been entered into. His reply was that President Taylor's family and Brother Moses Thatcher had got theirs and he wanted his, and Brother Cannon surrendered the Taylor's family, Thatcher's and Beck's stock, and had kept a strict account with his own."

With these dispersals, the "dedication" of the mine stock for the Lord's purposes ceased. President Cannon turned his portion of the stock over to President Snow in April 1899, at which time further explanation was given to the Brethren (see chapter 19). Elder Thatcher's actions, threats, and attitude toward President Cannon in relation to the B. B. & C. stock grieved the Brethren that knew the circumstances. President Woodruff related that "Brother Moses Thatcher came to him while President George Q. Cannon was in prison [for polygamy], and told him that he was going to sue President Cannon because he held stock and means which belong to him. President Woodruff said he told Bro. Thatcher if he did this it would be the worst move he had ever made."[15]

By the October general conference, both Presidents Woodruff and Snow felt it would be timely and appropriate to inform the Church why Elder Moses Thatcher's name had not been presented for sustaining vote as a member of the Quorum of the Twelve. Their remarks open a window into their feelings about a trying situation that had deeply concerned them for years. President Woodruff spoke first:

> My brethren and sisters, there is something pressing upon my mind that I want to say. We have arrived at a point here with regard to circumstances that it is my duty to take up as the President of the Church. The First Presidency and the Twelve Apostles were never more united as a body than they are today. Our spirits are united. We believe together, we work together, we pray together; and we believe in each other, because we are all trying to do the will of God. This is the case with all of us, with one exception. That exception is Brother Moses Thatcher. A great many people marvel and wonder why something is not done with him. Some have said we were afraid of Moses Thatcher. I am not afraid of Moses Thatcher, nor of any other man who breathes the breath of life, when it comes to a matter of duty. But I am afraid to disobey God, or to not perform my duty in any position that I am called to in the Church. There has been a great deal said with regard to Brother Moses Thatcher, and many have wondered why something was not done about him. Well, I will say that this is a matter that belongs to the Twelve Apostles. He is a member of that quorum, and of course it is their duty to take hold of that work and attend to it until it is settled. But I have felt, as the President of the Church, it is my duty to not let this conference pass without saying something upon this subject. . . .
>
> What is the difficulty with Brother Thatcher? The difficulty is, he has not been with his quorum in spirit for years. He has not been united with them hardly, I may say, since the death of President Taylor. It is not his declining to sign this declaration of principle [the political manifesto] that was brought up at the last conference by the leaders of Israel. This is a matter of comparatively small consequence. I say here—and I say the truth—Brother Thatcher has not been in fellowship with us for a series of years. He has not met with his quorum. . . . There is a spirit affecting him, and not a good spirit either. With regard to his standing with his quorum, he should have met with them and talked these things over; but he has not done it. He has met with them comparatively few times since President Taylor's death.

> Brethren and sisters, these are truths. The Apostles know that he has neglected to meet with them at times when he could and should have done so. He has been at difference with them in many things that have transpired. He has been by himself in his labor, and for himself, and not for the Church. Now, I want to say that neither Moses Thatcher nor any other man on the face of the earth can stand in the way of this Church.[16]

Then President Snow followed with some explanations of his own, opening his heart to the people and his Quorum regarding his unrelenting quest for unity among them. Few sermons such as this had ever been heard in the tabernacle:

> As the President of the Quorum of the Twelve Apostles, of which Brother Thatcher is a member, I want to say a few words in connection with this subject that has been introduced by President Woodruff. I feel it my duty, however unpleasant that duty may be to me, to testify to the truth of what President Woodruff has said in reference to the fellowship existing between Brother Thatcher and our quorum. I think it was seven years ago when the present Presidency of the Church was organized, and I then was appointed to preside over the quorum of the Apostles—a duty and an obligation that I felt the utmost incompetency to discharge; and yet believing and knowing that it was my duty to accept that position, I was satisfied that the Lord would aid and assist me in accomplishing the duties pertaining to that sacred office. I have labored actively from that day to the present to do that which I considered my duty, to accomplish a perfect union between every member of that quorum, and a perfect union also with the First Presidency. I felt the importance of this when I took the position as President of the Twelve, and I asked the Lord to let me live until these duties were accomplished—until I could see and feel that every member of the quorum of the Twelve Apostles was in perfect fellowship with each other and with the First Presidency. The brethren of the Twelve can answer now whether that has been accomplished, and how far it has failed. It has failed in only one single instance, and that has been presented to you by President Woodruff. There are now of the Quorum of the Twelve ten members sitting here upon these stands. With these ten brethren there is now a perfect union between themselves and with the First Presidency.

President Snow went on to speak of a fund-raising meeting held in the temple one year before its dedication at which President Cannon had stood and informed those present (about 150 people) that the First Presidency was in perfect unity with each other. "After he got through, I dare say that the people there—I thought so, at least—expected that I would arise and say something in reference to the union of the quorum of the Twelve Apostles. I did not do it. I sat there in silence. And I never explained the reason to the quorum of the Twelve, that I have any remembrance of, why I sat there in silence. I am now going to explain it. I thought my brethren had reasons to expect that I would arise and speak in reference to union. I could have spoken as loudly and as effectively in reference to the union of our quorum as Brother Cannon in reference to the union of the First Presidency, with but one single exception. That exception, I regret to say, was Brother Moses Thatcher." President Snow spoke of a long conversation he had with Elder Thatcher while traveling to Brigham City on a train, and also of working at another meeting "to bring Brother Thatcher into a union with us, hour after hour, till about two o'clock in the morning. I labored diligently. I always thought a good deal of Brother Thatcher. He and I always got along lovingly together; and he knows and will state it if he ever comes to address the people, that Brother Snow was one of his particular friends and felt an interest for him as deep as any man in the quorum. We labored there with only one object in view—to bring one member of our quorum into a perfect union with ourselves and with the First Presidency."

President Snow spelled out other efforts, all of which had been unsuccessful. He then changed subjects and introduced a note of humor into this somber story, telling of a reported incident from the lives of two other Brethren: "I am reminded of a little anecdote I heard of Brother Erastus Snow, which illustrates a principle. Brother George A. Smith was speaking to an 'outside' audience one night, and Brother Erastus fell asleep. When he got through preaching he sat down and elbowed Brother Erastus, and requested him to bear his testimony. It was thought that Brother Erastus had scarcely heard a word; but he arose and said, 'My friends, every word that my brother here has said is God's truth.' Now, why did he say so? There was a reason for this. Why, he knew Brother George A. Smith; he had heard him preach a hundred times, and he knew that he was a man of inspiration, and that he would never say anything but that was true."[17]

Thereafter, the Latter-day Saints collectively knew why Moses Thatcher had not been sustained with the rest of the Quorum of the Twelve, and they also had the benefit of some historical background as to why. This public knowledge proved advantageous later, as Thatcher sought publicity for his cause and made an issue of it in the press. That November, the

Quorum of the Twelve met and proceeded to review and discuss Elder Thatcher's standing among them, as directed by President Woodruff:

> President Snow called the meeting to order. A few minutes before that hour a son of Bro. Thatcher came to the room bearing a letter to President Snow from his father. After President Snow had opened it and read its contents, he then expressed himself to the effect that evidently Brother Thatcher did not want to meet with his quorum, and by way of informing the brethren present of what had passed between himself and Brother Thatcher in the shape of written communications, he requested Elder Richards to read the following letters, which explain themselves: . . . [several letters were then read].
>
> President Snow then remarked that the case was now before the Council, and it was for the Council to take such action as was proper and right. As for himself he had very little faith in Brother Thatcher's sincerity, as the spirit of technicality was plainly manifest through all his correspondence; but he had chosen not to meet with his quorum. Pres. Snow said that he did not think anything would be gained by communicating any further with him, and all that was left for the quorum to do was to proceed and take action in the case. He closed by frankly admitting that he did not think the Lord was pleased with them as a quorum for the way in which they had temporized with Brother Thatcher, allowing him to go so long in his downward course without dealing with him. He added that he knew the feelings of the quorum towards Brother Thatcher, as he had been the subject of conversation among themselves for such a length of time; but it was for each one now to express himself freely as to the action to be taken.
>
> Each one of the brethren present then spoke briefly, all agreeing with President Snow that if they had erred at all in the consideration of Brother Thatcher's case, as doubtless they had, they erred on the side of leniency. They all expressed themselves prepared to vote, and endorsed what President Snow had said in his opening remarks.
>
> After each one of the brethren present had spoken, President Snow said that he had little thought when the present First Presidency was organized that this quorum would be called upon to sever from it one of its members. We never imagined such a thing possible. Ever since the first meeting Pres. Snow said he had felt moved upon to show his brethren the necessity of establishing a perfect union among themselves as a quorum, and the necessity also of being perfectly united with the First Presidency. At that time a perfect union did not exist among them. He had sometimes thought that his reference to this subject so often since then had become somewhat tedious to some of the members of

> the Council; but he said he had been impressed to speak upon it in the hope that at least he would succeed in effecting a thorough and perfect union in the quorum. The last conversation he had with Brother Moses Thatcher was on the train between Salt Lake and Brigham City, during which he reminded Brother Moses that this was the day and hour of his trial, and he asked him saying, "Bro. Moses why is it that you cannot see it, and why is it that you will not let your brethren help you to see it?" He felt truly sorry; he loved Brother Thatcher, and it was because of the love he had for him he undertook to make one last effort to save him and to draw him to this council. He knew a man who had a great deal of love for Brother Thatcher, a man who had already done all he could to help him to see the position he was in, and he sent this brother to him to see if it was not possible to prevail upon him to come to this meeting, and to show him that the way was perfectly clear before him, and that nothing would be expected of him in order to regain the fellowship of his quorum more than any other member; but it was no use, everything had failed, and it remained for the quorum now to do its duty.[18]

Some little time was then occupied informally by the Brethren discussing the form of motion or resolution to be introduced expressing the mind of the Council, it being the unanimous feeling of the Brethren that they could not do less than drop Brother Thatcher from the quorum and deprive him of his priesthood. Brother Grant then moved that this be the decision of the Council; it was seconded by two or three of the Brethren and carried unanimously. It was then moved by Elder John Henry Smith, and seconded by Elder F. D. Richards, that President Snow be requested and authorized to prepare a card (announcement) signed by himself as President of the Twelve Apostles, informing the officers and members of the Church through the *Deseret News* of the action taken in Brother Thatcher's case.[19]

The following day the First Presidency informally commiserated over Moses Thatcher's stubborn rebelliousness, though they realized it was inevitable: "President Woodruff expressed his regret at the course pursued by Brother Moses Thatcher, leading to the unfortunate condition in which he has placed himself. President Woodruff said he felt that Brother Thatcher had gone too far and indulged too long the spirit of opposition to his brethren to be able to repent."[20]

A week later, on Thanksgiving day, a special meeting was held at the President's Office to discuss Moses Thatcher and his political ambitions. Attending the meeting were the First Presidency, President Snow and several of the Twelve, and a few others. Comments made by some of the Brethren on this occasion, including President Snow, give insight into the internal dynamics of the Quorum of the Twelve over many preceding years; this in turn contributes to a fuller understanding of President Snow's goals and efforts as the President of the Twelve. A glimpse of President Woodruff's dry wit is also evident:

> The subject of the indisposition of many of the Latter-day Saints to be guided by the authorities of the Church in matters not regarded as spiritual was considered. The followers [supporters] which Moses Thatcher appeared to have [in northern Utah], particularly in politics, was also dwelt upon, and all present took part in the conversation. The course pursued by Moses Thatcher in reference to Pres. George Q. Cannon was also ventilated [reviewed].
>
> President Woodruff stated that ever since the death of President John Taylor Brother Moses Thatcher had been influenced by an apostate spirit. It took Brother Thatcher about a week to confess Brother Cannon's sins for him, without making any confession whatever of his own. He had indulged that spirit more or less ever since. During those trying times he [President Woodruff] was closely associated with President Cannon and he could testify that the spirit which animated Brother Cannon was a righteous and forgiving spirit, and the spirit which animated Brother Thatcher was of the evil one. Brother Thatcher undertook to control the Apostles and run things generally, and was able for a while to influence two or three of the Twelve. Brother Thatcher had come to him when Brother Cannon was in prison and declared he was going to sue Brother Cannon before the law. Such an expression from an Apostle struck him (Brother Woodruff) like a clap of thunder. But it showed the spirit Brother Thatcher was of. He told Brother Thatcher that if he carried out his threat, it would be the worse pill he ever took in his life. The unfortunate part of it was that Brother Thatcher never repented of it.
>
> President Snow said what President Woodruff had stated was true, and the brethren of the Twelve understood that President Woodruff had sounded the key note of Brother Thatcher's apostasy. He believed firmly that all the trouble that had come on Brother Thatcher had arisen in consequence of his spirit and conduct toward Brother Cannon. President Snow said he thought the course pursued by Brother Thatcher in the Bullion-Beck business ought to be fully exposed. . . .
>
> Elder Heber J. Grant confessed that he at one time had been led by Brother Thatcher into a wrong spirit, and that Elder Erastus Snow, who at first seemed to favor Brother Thatcher's views, emphatically warned

> Moses Thatcher and himself (Brother Grant) that unless they repented, the spirit they were of would lead them away from the quorum of the Apostles. From that very time, brother Grant said, he had avoided being led by the spirit that was in Brother Thatcher, whom he had learned to love and in whom he had placed great confidence. But, Brother Grant said, Brother Thatcher was a covenant breaker. . . .
>
> The subject of Brother Thatcher's candidacy for the United States Senatorship was fully considered, and it was unanimously decided that it would be a calamity to have Brother Thatcher elected to that position upon the platform which he had put forth, in opposition to the Church and its discipline, and as an advocate and representative of that opposition.[21]

As President Snow entered his last two years as President of the Twelve Apostles, business moved forward as usual, including the meetings of the Twelve together. The Quorum still had occasional struggles, but also periods of sublime success.[22] At an early April 1897 meeting, one of them recorded: "We talked over many matters. We also partook of the sacrament and the Holy Spirit was with us in great power."[23]

Two days later, the Holy Spirit was again present and manifest to an unusual degree. On April 3, for President Snow's birthday, the Salt Lake Temple workers organized a "tribute" gathering (really a fast and testimony meeting) for him in the temple: "Many bore testimony. A good spirit was present," wrote one in attendance. Such was the spirit of the occasion that both President Cannon and Elder John Henry Smith stood and "testified we had seen the Savior," at previous points in their lives.[24] One of the temple workers present, Joseph Dean, recorded further details of what he heard and experienced in this meeting: "I never felt a more heavenly influence in my life, especially the last hour. We did not get away until 12:30. The last hour our hearts were so melted that the most of us were sobbing and weeping for joy. Pres. Geo. Q. Cannon began to speak at 11:30. He was saying or began to say that he knew that Jesus was the Christ, for he had seen his face and heard his voice. His emotions here overpowered him, and he had to stand and say nothing for a few moments until he could control himself. He also testified that he knew that God lived for he had seen his face and heard his voice. He also knew that the Holy Ghost was a *living being* for he had heard his voice."[25]

Later that day, President Snow visited with his ailing apostolic associate, Elder Brigham Young Jr., who struggled with poor health often.

Lorenzo "spent some hours with me in my room," wrote Elder Young. "Our conversation was pleasant and I enjoyed myself. Brother Snow seems like another father to me."[26] Three weeks later, Elder Young's health had not improved—"Miserable days, pain and insufferable itching, sleepless nights, and sick to my stomach. . . . President Lorenzo Snow came in and said, 'why can't I place my hands on your head and under God heal you?' 'I have not the faith, [I said], but I will try if you will bless me.' He did so and I have felt a new man ever since. Our conversation was of the choicest brotherly kind."[27]

In late September, two new Brethren were called into the Quorum of the Twelve. The First Presidency and President Snow gathered names (written on slips of paper) for candidates from the Twelve and then prayerfully considered them for several hours together, although one selection had actually already been made a year earlier.[28] The Quorum of the Twelve normally had a great deal of influence in selecting those called to join their Quorum, but in this case President Wilford Woodruff had previously written a letter to his counselors and President Snow specifically asking that his son Abraham Owen Woodruff be chosen to fill a vacancy. "I have a request to make of you, my brethren," he wrote. "There is a vacancy in the quorum of the Twelve Apostles, through the death of Abram H. Cannon, and it is our duty to fill it." He went on to explain how seven members of the First Presidency had been privileged to have a son called into the Quorum of the Twelve and reviewed his own lengthy apostolic service of fifty-four years. Then, he wrote: "Now I ask of my counselors George Q. Cannon, Joseph F. Smith, Lorenzo Snow, and the Twelve Apostles that you will grant me the same great blessing that my predecessors have had before me, that when I get into the spirit world I can look back to the church and kingdom of God on the earth and behold one of my own posterity mingling with the Twelve Apostles, building up the Kingdom of God on the earth and preparing for the coming of the Son of Man. I would not ask this favor at your hands if I did not believe you would grant it, and that it is the will of God, which I am thoroughly satisfied it is."[29]

This request was granted, although Owen was only twenty-three at the time. Matthias Cowley (father of Matthew Cowley) was the other new apostle called.[30] These men took the places of Moses Thatcher and Abraham H. Cannon. Not all members of the Twelve were thrilled with Owen's selection, he being so young and inexperienced, but as the years passed, Owen was able to give a good accounting of himself in the ministry, filling some of the more physically demanding assignments that the older members could not undertake, until he suffered an untimely early death from smallpox.[31]

At the October conference, the new apostles were sustained, and during the priesthood meeting of that conference, President Snow, speaking in his capacity as President of the Salt Lake Temple, became somewhat firm in directing bishops and stake presidents to exercise appropriate care with those recommended to attend—he had "found a beer bottle" in a temple patron's satchel and was not pleased.[32]

In late 1897, discussions intensified among the leading councils of the Church in relation to the increasingly poor financial circumstances of the Church, including its mounting debts, and what could be done about it. President Cannon was urging the Brethren to hire his son Frank J. Cannon to act as Church agent with capitalists in the eastern United States in obtaining a two-million-dollar loan. It was felt this money would assist the Church with consolidating its debts, but the interest rate would be high—*if* anyone would consent to loan the money. Further complicating the situation, some of the Brethren strongly opposed using (paying) Frank Cannon to operate as a middleman, or Church agent.[33] In urging Frank Cannon's hired services, President Cannon again put himself in an awkward position with his associates. Some of the Twelve, observing Cannon's maneuvering, became concerned. During meetings held in December and in January 1898, they made their feelings known. Elder John Henry Smith (four entries) and Brigham Young Jr. (one entry) recorded the following:

> Lorenzo Snow, Heber J. Grant and I called at Brigham Young's home. We had a long talk over the financial condition of the Church. We also determined to insist that under existing conditions that the Councilors of the President must consult the apostles on leading questions.[34]

> At 10 a.m. Lorenzo Snow, F. D. Richards, Brigham Young, Myself, Geo. Teasdale, Heber J. Grant, John W. Taylor and Abraham O. Woodruff met in the Apostles' room of the Temple. We spent the day talking over the relative positions of the First Presidency and Twelve Apostles on all great questions in the Church. All spoke and gave their views.[35]

> We [the Twelve] are all thoroughly convinced that Presidents Woodruff and Smith are all right [with finances] but President Cannon is wrong in many things in financial business. I proposed that we trust the [Latter-day Saint] people with the labor of helping the church out of its indebtedness. . . . It was agreed that President Snow lay our feelings before the

First Presidency for we feel that President Snow and one or two others of the Quorum should be in perfect harmony and knowledge [with the First Presidency] of financial affairs.[36]

All of the Apostles . . . met at the Temple. . . . At 11 a.m. all of the First Presidency came in. President Lorenzo Snow asked the Presidency as to the duties of the Apostles in connection with the Presidency in the financial affairs of the Church. All of the Apostles present spoke very plain and Elder Brigham Young [Jr.] made a very sweeping statement in which he said President George Q. Cannon was the cause of the great indebtedness of the Church.

All three of the Presidency said it was their view that the two Quorums should be united in the consideration of the more weighty problems that affect the whole Church. President George Q. Cannon felt very much hurt over the remarks of Elders Brigham Young and Heber J. Grant.[37]

All of the First Presidency and most of the Apostles . . . met at 12 noon in the Apostles' room in the Temple.

After some explanations of yesterday's sayings, President Franklin D. Richards moved we forgive each other for harsh words spoken and that we partake of the sacrament. President Joseph F. Smith seconded the motion and said it now being about to be determined by vote of the joint Councils of the Presidency and Twelve that they shall act together upon all questions of great moment to the Church, he felt to add his hearty endorsement of this action.

The vote was unanimous. We partook of the sacrament together. After the Presidency withdrew, President Lorenzo Snow said, "brethren, the Lord approves of our action and in the future the Quorums will understand each other better."[38]

It was evidently during this January 7 meeting, in the context of his ongoing effort to fully unite the Brethren, that President Snow uttered what has become one of his more well-known introspective observations (thoughtfully recorded at the time by President Cannon): "I saw Joseph Smith the Prophet do things which I did not approve of; and yet . . . I thanked God that he would put upon a man who had these imperfections the power and authority which he placed upon him . . . for I knew I myself had weakness and I thought there was a chance for me. These same weaknesses . . . I knew were in Heber C. Kimball [as well], but my knowing this did not impair them in my estimation. I thanked God I saw these imperfections."[39] (Lorenzo was no fool, and he knew God used weak, imperfect, and very mortal men and women in His service—including himself.)

The Twelve together seemed determined to proceed with deliberate caution where financial matters and President Cannon and his son Frank were concerned.[40] Exactly how fully settled these financial agreements became during 1898 is questionable. Other sources indicate that later in July and August President Cannon again asserted himself forcefully with the Twelve (including President Snow), rebuking them for their desires to meddle in those financial affairs he felt were the province of the First Presidency alone.[41] The Cannons were able to only temporarily persuade the others to let Frank act on the Church's behalf to seek to secure a loan from Eastern financial institutions (in July 1898), but they were eventually reversed.[42]

As 1898 began and President Woodruff continued to age and become more reliant on President Cannon for counsel, the financial concerns of the Twelve intensified, and further meetings were held. At one in late March, "Pres Snow . . . said that we [should] bury the past in these [contentious] matters and hold ourselves humbly before the Lord to do his will." Then later after a mid-July meeting of the Twelve, Elder Young recorded his personal observations and thoughts:

> President Snow opened with a stormy [emphatic] reference to our financial condition. Others followed in the same line. President Cannon . . . will not trust the Twelve in financial matters. . . . While we all believe in the integrity of President George Q. Cannon, still, we believe that he has nearly ruined the credit of the church with schemes which have failed, and the responsibility rests upon President Woodruff. . . . The Twelve should now enter fully into the councils of the First Presidency. It has been delayed too long and now necessity demands that this reform be inaugurated.[43]

Chapter 16

The President of the Church

President Woodruff enjoyed comparatively decent health (for a man of his advanced age) for years, right up to his passing.[1] He had suffered innumerable aches, pains, broken bones, accidents, and illnesses throughout his long life—some of them almost snuffing it out—but he continued to amaze his friends and colleagues with lengthy episodes of robust health. In April 1893, he had come close to death (as he had on another occasion previous to that) but had rallied back to full service.

In March 1894, an employee in the President's Office attended President Woodruff's eighty-seventh birthday party and noted: "President Woodruff is in remarkably good health. He is a wonderful man for his years."[2]

Such vigor made what happened later something of a surprise. In August 1898, President Woodruff traveled to California with President Cannon: "The President had suffered occasionally from asthma and from kidney and bladder troubles, but when he left for the coast on the 13th of August, he was well and cheerful, and in fact remarked to a friend, 'I wish President Cannon was as well as I am.' At a dinner given in his honor . . . at San Francisco, a few evenings before his death, and of which no man under eighty was permitted to partake, Pres. Woodruff, though in his 92nd year, was voted the smartest of the party. The day before he died he was talking about going out fishing."[3]

Then President Woodruff had a "sudden" attack, and doctors were called, but to no avail. He died September 2 after sleeping peacefully all night. "Word reached the President's Office today that President Wilford Woodruff died this morning, at 6:40, in San Francisco. The news was very unexpected and spread very rapidly through the city."[4]

President Joseph F. Smith, the second counselor in the First Presidency, "at once notified the Apostles, most of whom were absent from the city, and requested their presence here [at headquarters] at the earliest possible moment; . . . Pres. Lorenzo Snow received the word at Brigham City."[5] According to President Snow's son LeRoi, "The telegram was delivered to him on the street in Brigham. He read it to President Rudger Clawson, then President of Box Elder Stake, who was with him, went to the telegraph office and replied that he would leave on the train about 5:30 that evening. He reached Salt Lake City about 7:15, proceeded to the President's office, gave some instructions and then went to his private room in the Salt Lake Temple." Again, according to LeRoi Snow:

> President Snow put on his holy temple robes, repaired . . . to the . . . sacred altar [in the Holy of Holies], offered up the signs of the Priesthood and poured out his heart to the Lord.[6] He reminded the Lord how he plead for President Woodruff's life to be spared, that President Woodruff's days would be lengthened beyond his own; that he might never be called upon to bear the heavy burdens and responsibilities of the Church. "Nevertheless," he said, "Thy will be done. I have not sought this responsibility but if it be Thy will, I now present myself before Thee for Thy guidance and instruction. I ask that Thou show me what Thou wouldst have me do." After finishing his prayer he expected a reply, some special manifestation from the Lord. So he waited,—and waited—and waited. There was no reply, no voice, no visitation, no manifestation. He left the altar and the room in great disappointment. Passing through the Celestial room and out into the large corridor a glorious manifestation was given President Snow.

The manifestation received at that time by President Snow was no less than the visit of the resurrected, glorified Son of God, Jesus the Christ, who had come to personally instruct his servant, the prophet Lorenzo Snow—herein given as related by "Allie" (Alice Armeda Snow Young) Pond, who carefully recorded the incident as told to her, on the advice of her mother, Celestia Armeda Snow, soon after hearing it. She wrote:

> One evening while I was visiting grandpa Snow in his room in the Salt Lake Temple, I remained until the door keepers had gone and the night-watchmen had not yet come in, so grandpa said he would take me to the main front entrance and let me out that way. He got his bunch of keys from his dresser. After we left his room and while we were still in the large corridor leading into the celestial room, I was walking several steps ahead of grandpa when he stopped me and said: "Wait

Alice Armeda Snow Pond (1876–1943)

a moment, Allie, I want to tell you something. It was right here that the Lord Jesus Christ appeared to me at the time of the death of President Woodruff. He instructed me to go right ahead and reorganize the First Presidency of the Church at once and not wait as had been done after the death of the previous presidents, and that I was to succeed President Woodruff."

Then grandpa came a step nearer and held out his left hand and said: "He stood right here, about three feet above the floor. It looked as though He stood on a plate of solid gold."

Grandpa told me what a glorious personage the Savior is and described His hands, feet, countenance and beautiful white robes, all of which were of such a glory of whiteness and brightness that he could hardly gaze upon Him.

Then he came another step nearer and put his right hand on my head and said: "Now, granddaughter, I want you to remember that this is the testimony of your grandfather, that he told you with his own lips that he actually saw the Savior, here in the Temple, and talked with Him face to face."[7]

In later years, Alice Pond and her husband, Noah S. Pond, often discussed her visit with her grandfather Snow in the temple. After her death, Noah Pond recorded his own memories of what she had told him, presenting a second account witnessing to its truth:

We talked about the great privilege that was hers in visiting her grandfather, President Lorenzo Snow, in the Salt Lake Temple on the memorable evening of his narrative of the Heavenly visitation of the Savior to him and the instructions given him to proceed forthwith in the reorganization of the First Presidency of the Church.

The reason for Allie going to the Temple [was] . . . the taking of the "Gruel," a favorite food item of the President. On the Evening of the occurrence he had taken time to tell her many interesting experiences

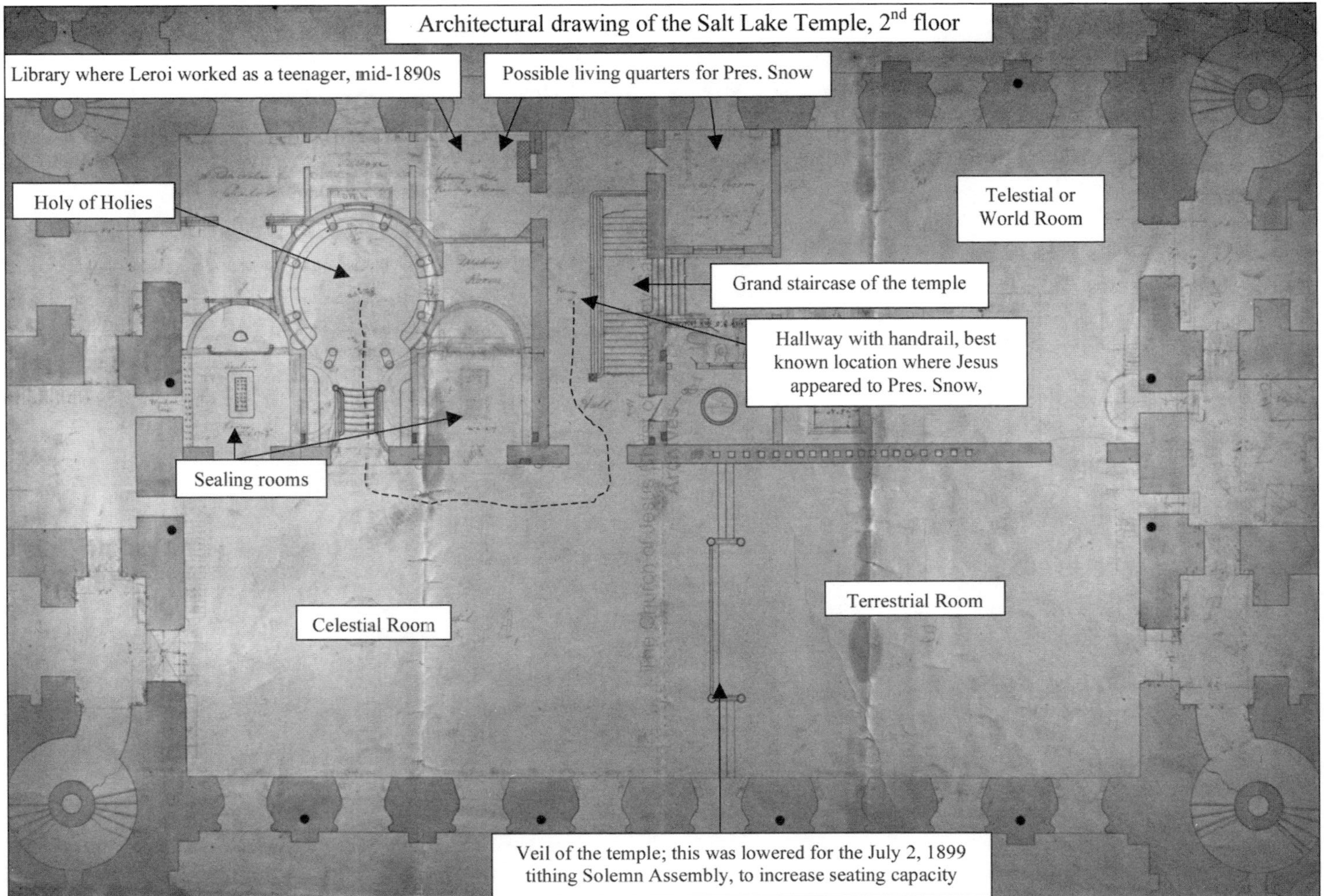

Architectural drawing of the Salt Lake Temple, 2nd floor

> and the hour became late, so late in fact that the watchman had locked the doors and the Temple was silent with only the two within.
>
> President Snow led Allie to the large front door, and in passing from his room he halted at the designated spot, and placing his arm on her shoulder he said, "I want you to remember, my daughter, that here the Savior appeared to me in answer to my prayers, and instructed me to proceed with the reorganization of the First Presidency. That this was pleasing to the Lord and Blessings upon the Church would follow President Snow's administration."
>
> President Snow's statement was very definite that he saw the Savior, and heard his voice.[8]

President Snow himself disclosed a less-detailed account to his apostolic Brethren in the temple, the day he was sustained by them as the President of the Church. President Snow said that, "He knew the action taken by the Council was according to the mind and will of the Lord, who had shown and revealed to him several days ago that the First Presidency should be organized before the next conference. He had been feeling a little gloomy, and perhaps a little discouraged at the prospect, and the vast responsibility that would naturally fall upon him as President of the Twelve Apostles, and with this feeling he went before the Lord, offered up the signs of the Holy Priesthood and called upon Him to let light come to his mind. His prayer was answered, the Lord manifesting unto him clearly what he should do; also in regard to the counselors he should select when he became President of the Church."[9]

Others present on this occasion also verified President Snow's testimony. LeRoi Snow wrote of them:

> During the June conference in 1919 at an M. I. A. officers' meeting in the Assembly Hall I related the above testimony [quoted from Alice Pond]. President Heber J. Grant immediately arose and said:
>
> In confirmation of the testimony given by Brother LeRoi C. Snow quoting the grand-daughter of Lorenzo Snow, I want to call attention to the fact that several years elapsed after the death of the Prophet Joseph before President Young was sustained as the president of the Church; after the death of President Young, several years elapsed again before President Taylor was sustained, and again when he died several years elapsed before President Woodruff was sustained.
>
> After the funeral of President Wilford Woodruff, the apostles met in the office of the First Presidency and brother Francis M. Lyman said: "I feel impressed, although one of the younger members of the quorum,

> to say that I believe it would be pleasing in the sight of the Lord if the First Presidency of the Church was reorganized right here and right now. If I am in error regarding this impression, President Snow and the senior members of the council can correct me."
>
> President Snow said that he would be pleased to hear from all the brethren upon this question, and each and all of us expressed ourselves as believing it would be pleasing to the Lord and that it would be the proper thing to have the Presidency organized at once.
>
> When we had finished, then and not till then, did Brother Snow tell us that he was instructed of the Lord in the temple *the night after* President Woodruff died, to organize the Presidency of the Church at once. President Anthon H. Lund and myself are the only men now living who were present at that meeting. . . .
>
> A few days after the M. I. A. conference, in an interview with President Lund in his office, he retold the incident to me as given by President Grant regarding the meeting in the office of the First Presidency on Tuesday morning, September 13th, 1898, at which Lorenzo Snow was chosen President of the Church. He also said that he heard father tell a number of times of the Savior's appearance to him after he had dressed in his temple robes, presented himself before the Lord and offered up the signs of the Priesthood.
>
> I related this experience in the [Salt Lake] Eighteenth ward sacramental service. After the meeting Elder Arthur Winter told me he also had heard my father tell of the Savior's appearance to him in the Temple instructing him not only to reorganize the First Presidency at once but also to select the same counselors that President Woodruff had, Presidents George Q. Cannon and Joseph F. Smith.[10]

LeRoi Snow also quoted President Cannon's confirming statement: "President Snow, clothed in his priestly robes, presented himself before the Lord, in the temple, and the Lord instructed him to organize the First Presidency and revealed to him who his counselors were to be."[11]

The accounts all bear irrefutable witness that the Lord Jesus Christ appeared to President Snow and told him to proceed with the reorganization of the First Presidency at once, before general conference. From the various statements we also learn that President Snow was told to select counselors and who they should be; also that blessings would follow his administration. But seldom is the question asked—*why* did Jesus Himself visit His prophet on this occasion? Perhaps other methods of revelation, such as an angel, or the voice of the Spirit, would have sufficed. Outside of descriptions in the standard works, few occasions are known in which the

Son of God has personally appeared and instructed His mortal servants, with no veil between them. So *why* did He do so on this occasion?

The reason derives from material found in chapters 12 through 15 of this work and is hinted at in other pages. Disunity and discord had unfortunately entered the apostolic councils of the Church on too many past occasions. Resentment and jealousy had been present with some. Desire for change of policy and influence over Church finances had been sought and granted in order to achieve a measure of peace and unify the Twelve enough to sustain and set apart President Woodruff and his counselors—after two years of occasional contention. President Woodruff—foreseeing the possibility of future similar complications—had then instructed President Snow to reorganize without delay after his death because "it may prevent much trouble."[12] What trouble?—the same troubles that had and might again come with delay. If President Woodruff had been able to manage a reorganization of the First Presidency quickly, in his time, he may have prevented much trouble also. President Snow had witnessed all of this from a front-row seat and, being wise and inspired, had worked persistently and effectually to unify his brethren—but now it was his part to make the final decision. He beseeched his Heavenly Father in mighty faith and the Lord Jesus answered personally. He came Himself to ensure that His prophet knew that he was to move quickly so no troublesome delay could intervene and interfere. And He wanted to establish a precedent and pattern. Further, He wanted no more disunity and strife within His called and ordained Quorum of Twelve Apostles. This is the reason President Snow was given such specific and pointed instructions at that time by the second member of the Godhead.

At some point either just before or more likely soon after this sacred visitation, "President Lorenzo Snow said to me," remembered Joseph F. Smith, that "'it will be our duty to proceed as soon as possible to reorganize the Presidency of the Church.' As you are aware, after the burial of the remains of President Woodruff, he proceeded at once to do this. In this connection I may tell you another thing. President Snow said to me, 'you will live to be the President of the Church of Jesus Christ of Latter-day Saints, and when that time comes you should proceed at once and reorganize the Presidency of the Church.'"[13] President Smith's son, Joseph Fielding Smith, shared further insight into this prophecy, indicating that, "President Snow said to Joseph F. Smith that the Spirit whispered to him that Joseph F. Smith would succeed him as President of the Church. This statement President Smith recorded in his journal at that time."[14]

The funeral of Wilford Woodruff in the Salt Lake Tabernacle, September 8, 1898 (USHS)

The morning after Jesus spoke with President Snow, he and the Twelve held a meeting with President Woodruff's sons to make some preliminary burial arrangements for President Woodruff's remains.[15] The next few days were filled with further meetings regarding formal funeral arrangements, culminating with a decision to hold it the following Thursday, September 8.[16] President Snow also sent a telegram to presidents of distant stakes, authorizing them to hold their own stake memorial services for President Woodruff if they were not able to attend the main service in the Salt Lake Tabernacle.[17] Of the funeral, one observer wrote: "Today the body of President Woodruff was consigned to the tomb. The funeral services were held this morning in the Tabernacle, which was very much crowded. The speakers were President Joseph F. Smith, President Lorenzo Snow, Apostle Franklin D. Richards and President George Q. Cannon. The Tabernacle was draped in white, and the floral decorations were very beautiful."[18]

In his talk, after speaking feelingly about his predecessor:

> President Snow spoke of the vacancy in the Presidency caused by the death of President Woodruff. Many people, said he, had been led to wonder and imagine how the affairs of the Church were to be carried on. The Gospel in its completeness, said the speaker, made

> provision for these changes. The work would roll on uninterruptedly as it had done, succeeding the death of the Prophet Joseph and those of Presidents Brigham Young and John Taylor. On the death of the President of the Church, the responsibility fell upon the Quorum of the Twelve Apostles, and so it was on this occasion and ever would be. The Quorum of Apostles, said President Snow, was never as able to handle such a responsibility as it was at the present time. It was fully organized, and the Brethren were in perfect union and accord with each other, and faithful and devoted to the trust reposed in them. Presidents Cannon and Smith were men of God, full of faith and devotion to the cause, and their work in rolling on the kingdom would be greatly appreciated and felt. There was no danger as to the outcome of the work of God. It had been established for a purpose and that purpose would be accomplished, and the Church progress and increase in the earth, no matter how many of the authorities were called to another sphere.[19]

Evidently President Snow felt some need to comfort and assure the Latter-day Saints regarding matters of succession at that time, as other prophets have also. The next day (September 9) a meeting of the Quorum of the Twelve was held in the temple. Several things were accomplished in this meeting, though not the reorganization of the First Presidency. "Lorenzo Snow, Franklin D. Richards, Geo. Q. Cannon, Joseph F. Smith, Brigham Young, Francis M. Lyman, John Henry Smith, Geo. Teasdale, Heber J. Grant, John W. Taylor, Marriner W. Merrill, Anthon H. Lund, Matthias F. Cowley and Abraham O. Woodruff," were all present, with "President Lorenzo Snow presiding."[20] "George Q. Cannon and Joseph F. Smith were received back in the quorum by vote and took their place with Brigham Young Jr. above Joseph F. Smith. This was afterwards commented upon and it was said by President Brigham Young Jr. that [he] Brigham out-rated [out-ranked in seniority] Joseph, while President John Taylor said Joseph F. Smith out-rated Brigham Young Jr."[21] (This issue of seniority would be resolved later.)

At this point:

> President Snow, by the action of the Council, was placed in charge of all Church affairs until the First Presidency should again be organized. . . .
>
> President Snow spoke, referring solemnly to the absence of Pres. Woodruff, whose death had disorganized the first quorum of the Church. He suggested the possible presence with them on this occasion of Joseph Smith, Brigham Young, John Taylor, Wilford Woodruff, and other departed leaders, and spoke of the great responsibility which had

> now fallen upon the Quorum of the Twelve. He felt thankful beyond expression for the union that existed in the Council of the Apostles, and he believed, and in fact knew, that by each one laboring unselfishly for the cause of Zion, their labors would be crowned with success, and they would triumph. He exhorted the brethren to be charitable to each other, and to accept their new duties and responsibilities in all humility as servants of the Lord Jesus Christ. He offered to vacate his position as President of the Twelve, and thus give place to anyone else who might be the unanimous choice of the Council.
>
> Joseph F. Smith moved, and several of the brethren seconded and it was voted heartily and unanimously that Lorenzo Snow be sustained in his position as President of the Council of the Twelve Apostles.
>
> George Q. Cannon spoke briefly but feelingly of the present happy state of love and confidence in the Council, in contrast with past embarrassments, and expressed hope and faith of an honorable and happy outcome through a continuance of the love and union alluded to by President Snow. He invoked the blessing of the Lord on the President and the Council, to enable them to safely bear off the work of God.
>
> Brothers Cannon and Smith were requested, by vote of the Council, to furnish a report showing the condition of the Church's finances.
>
> The Council, by unanimous action, then accepted the responsibilities of the Presidency of the Church.[22]

The Quorum made a present of a fine desk to President Snow that he had been given earlier by them and had used since becoming temple president. He used it the rest of his life; however, on his death his estate took possession of it and then ended up selling it back to the Church at a private auction.[23] "Before dismissing" the meeting, "it was voted that the widows of President Woodruff receive $50 a month, each, until further orders."[24]

The next day, President Snow had a talk with a few of the Apostles about Church finances—a subject that would become President Snow's obsession for much of his administration.[25] Also, at this point President Snow had apparently told no one about his sacred experience with Jesus in the temple and the instructions he had been given.[26] If a timely chance had presented itself to reorganize the First Presidency during the September 9th meeting, he had not taken advantage of it but said little except to offer to vacate his position—an offer that was rejected.

This meant the issue of immediate or delayed succession was yet undecided and not broached. Arthur Winter, a clerk employed in the President's Office, shared the perspective of one positioned close to weighty matters, but who still knew little. He thoughtfully mused: "There is no

First Presidency now, and it seems peculiar to us at the office. Presidents Cannon and Smith have taken their places in the Quorum of the Twelve, and the Twelve from present indications, are going to manage the affairs of the Church for some little time to come. President Snow is the head of the Quorum, and as such presides over the Church until the First Presidency is reorganized. President Woodruff several times requested the Twelve to not let the Church be long without a First Presidency after his death, and he has in public expressed the hope that when he died the Church would not be long without a First Presidency; but what President Snow will do in relation to this is impossible for me to tell."[27]

On the morning of September 13, another meeting of all the Twelve was held for the purpose of financial discussion, specifically to determine whether to give further consideration to seeking a loan from eastern financiers or to find another solution to the severe debt problems the Church faced:

> At 10 o'clock this morning the Council of the Apostles met at the President's office, according to appointment. . . . . On motion of Elder F. D. Richards, Elder George F. Gibbs was appointed secretary and stenographer of the Council, on the same terms as made by the late First Presidency.
>
> It was agreed by the Council to begin the approaching General Conference of the Church on Thursday morning, October 6th.
>
> The special object of this meeting was to hear a report from Senator Frank J. Cannon [son of George Q. Cannon], relative to the matter of borrowing for the Church the sum of $1,500,000, for which purpose he had been East. . . . Senator Cannon thought the death of President Woodruff might have the effect of somewhat delaying the present negotiations, as the question of legal ownership of Church property, in consequence of succession to the Presidency, would have to be discussed.

The question now arose as to what was necessary to be done by the Council to satisfy the moneyed parties, in view of the changed conditions consequent upon the death of President Woodruff. The original document forming the basis of these negotiations had been given by the Trustee-in-trust, and it was evident to the Council that nothing could be done legally by way of continuing the negotiations without a new Trustee-in-trust.

At this point Frank Cannon was dismissed from the meeting and asked to wait in the sitting room outside the President's Office.[28] Further discussion then ensued:

Elder Lyman, speaking to this question, said he was reminded of the time when the Council was together after the death of President Taylor, and the feeling of President Woodruff at that time; he was also reminded of President Woodruff's feelings, as expressed on different occasions during his administration, to the effect that whenever he died, the First Presidency of the Church should be organized without delay. "And if the Lord should manifest to you, President Snow, that it was the proper thing to do now, I am prepared to not only vote for a Trustee-in-trust, but for the President of the Church." Brother Lyman added that he saw no reason why this action should not be taken at the present meeting, giving the President time, if he desired it, in which to choose his counselors. He remarked that after the death of Joseph Smith, three years elapsed before the First Presidency was organized; after the death of President Young, it also took three years to organize the First Presidency; after the death of President Taylor, eighteen months elapsed, and the speaker believed that if the Council had then been in harmony, no such interval would have occurred, but the Presidency would have been organized earlier. He believed the right thing to do now was to organize the First Presidency, and this act would tend to create confidence at home and abroad.

Bro. Grant remarked that the present time was just as opportune

George Q. Cannon, Lorenzo Snow, and Joseph F. Smith in 1900 (USHS)

as any other, and that he could sustain Pres. Snow with all his heart as President of the Church.

Bro. Young remarked that Bro. Grant had expressed his feelings exactly. He felt that this was the way out.

Bro. Teasdale said that he was in perfect harmony and accord with the feelings of the brethren.

Joseph F. Smith said: "I move that that be the sense of this meeting."

The motion was seconded by Bro. Cowley.

President Snow asked if there were any further remarks. Several of the brethren called for the question, whereupon Pres. Snow asked Elder Joseph F. Smith to put the motion. This being done, it was carried unanimously, and Lorenzo Snow was thus sustained by the Council of the Apostles, as President of the Church of Jesus Christ of Latter-day Saints.

Pres. Snow then arose and said: There was no use in his making excuses as to inability, etc., to assume the vast responsibilities involved in the position to which he had been elected [sustained]. He felt that it was for him to do the very best he could and depend upon the Lord. He knew the action taken by the Council was according to the mind and will of the Lord, who had shown and revealed to him several days ago that the First Presidency should be organized before the next conference. He had been feeling a little gloomy, and perhaps a little discouraged at the prospect, and the vast responsibility that would naturally fall upon him as President of the Twelve Apostles, and with this feeling he went before the Lord, offered up the signs of the Holy Priesthood and called upon Him to let light come to his mind. His prayer was answered, the Lord manifesting unto him clearly what he should do; also in regard to the counselors he should select when he became President of the Church, "and" said he, "In accordance with the light given me, I now present to you the name of George Q. Cannon as my first counselor, and that of Joseph F. Smith as my second counselor."[29]

Several of the brethren, speaking at the same time, seconded the choice of counselors, and the brethren named expressed themselves upon the subject—Bro. Cannon to the effect that he was willing to act in this capacity, or any other, if he could have the love and confidence of his brethren, and Bro. Smith to the effect that since the Lord had manifested his will in this matter, he had nothing to say, except that he was perfectly willing to act in this or any other position, and would do all he could to sustain the hands of the President in righteousness before the Lord.

Pres. Snow, before calling for the vote, said, "I have not mentioned this matter to any person, either man or woman. I wanted to see what the feelings of the brethren were. I wanted to see if the same spirit which the Lord manifested to me was in you. I had confidence in you that the Lord would indicate to you that this was proper and according to his mind and will. I do not feel that I should be over-anxious in regard to anything pertaining to the work of the Lord. I had one revelation or manifestation in my early career which became my star, so to speak, and which I have always had before my mind. I put the meaning of it into couplet form, as follows:

'As man now is, God once was; As God now is, man may be'.

That was revealed to me with power; the Holy Ghost was upon me for a long time, and I knew it was my privilege to be like Him whom I afterwards knew was my Father and God. As John the Apostle says, "We are now the sons of God; when He shall appear we shall be like Him," etc. We must act as far as we possibly can like God while we are in the flesh, and I know we can reach that degree of perfection [eventually]. Now brethren, I shall do the best I can, as God shall give me wisdom and power. I sense keenly my own weakness and inability, but I appreciate the fact that God can make me strong. If I know my own heart, the administration about to be ushered in shall not be known as Lorenzo Snow's, but as God's, in and through Lorenzo Snow. As to things which have happened in the past, I do not want to talk about them; it will become us as servants of the Lord to go to work and meet the difficulties before us, as the Lord shall aid and assist us. I feel to say in my heart, God bless you, and I invoke the blessing of the Lord upon myself in the discharge of the obligations resting upon me."

The vote was then taken approving the President's choice of counselors.

M. F. Cowley now moved, and the motion was carried, that Lorenzo Snow be sustained as Trustee-in-trust for the Church of Jesus Christ of Latter-day Saints.

Pres. George Q. Cannon suggested that the President of the Twelve Apostles be appointed, and on motion of F. M. Lyman, Franklin D. Richards was unanimously sustained to act in that position.

Pres. Cannon suggested that Frank J. Cannon be at liberty to continue negotiations with the Eastern parties on the loan question. . . . Senator Cannon, who was in the adjoining room, was sent for, and this information was imparted to him. [This decision was later changed, much to Frank Cannon's disappointment.]

On motion of Bro. Grant, it was decided to make public, in this evening's paper, the action of the Council, in organizing the First Presidency and appointing the Trustee-in-trust and the President of the Twelve Apostles.

The Council then adjourned.[30]

After meeting, the First Presidency and Twelve met together at the photography studio of Charles Savage, at the time run by his son Ralph, and had their picture taken as a group.[31]

When the actions taken during the meeting to organize the First Presidency were announced, pleasant surprise was the common reaction, as the move was not expected, given precedent. Arthur Winter's comments from his perspective of close observation are telling: "At a meeting of the Twelve Apostles this morning, held at the President's Office, the First Presidency was organized, with President Lorenzo Snow as President, and George Q. Cannon and Joseph F. Smith as his Counselors. This action was a surprise to all, as so speedy a reorganization was totally unexpected. The Apostles themselves, when they went into this meeting, had no idea of taking such action, but in their deliberations the Spirit of the Lord moved upon them to organize the First Presidency at once. This result was very gratifying to all at the office."[32]

The following day, another meeting was held in which the "general situation" of the Church was discussed by the Brethren.[33] There is little doubt that most of the time was devoted to finances and financial policy, which President Snow now oversaw. Then on September 15, President Snow took time to write answers to some questions submitted by a reporter for the *New York World* magazine, supposedly curious about possible changes in the Church under the new First Presidency. Some of President Snow's answers convey something of the prophetic in his thinking:

> What sort of revelation is responsible for your appointment?
>
> A revelation given March 28th, 1835, which clearly defines the relationship the Twelve Apostles bear to the First Presidency. When a vacancy occurs in the Presiding Council, such as has occurred by the death of President Wilford Woodruff, the Twelve Apostles become the Presiding Council of the Church, and it has been the rule for the President of that body, if he be the senior Apostle by ordination, to succeed to the Presidency, when the Council of Apostles decided that the First Presidency should be reorganized. He, with two counselors whom he may select, are then presented to the body of the Church in General Conference. If accepted by the Church, they become the First Presidency thereof. In this manner I have been selected as the President of the Church.
>
> What is the future of the Latter-day Saints?
>
> Their mission is to preach the Gospel of Jesus Christ as restored by divine revelation, to all the world; to gather the Saints, and prepare

> for the advent of our Savior, who will then become King of kings and Lord of lords. They will become a great and powerful body of religious worshippers. They will sustain the constitution and laws and institutions of the United States, and be the champions of liberty and of that constitution when its integrity shall be threatened. Their future will comprehend the fulfillment of the predictions of the prophets of God concerning the redemption of the earth and its inhabitants.[34]

After being nominated and sustained as President of the Church by his fellow associates of the Twelve, President Snow gave his first major discourse to the Salt Lake Stake in the Tabernacle. He then referenced those recent actions, noting with gratitude the special spirit and unity that had been present:

> It is a matter of great rejoicing and satisfaction to me to behold the unity and brotherly love and perfect oneness of feeling existing with the Twelve and which was manifested a few days ago when they met in council and the First Presidency of the Church was reorganized. Every one of the Apostles expressed himself on that occasion, and they were perfectly agreed; the Spirit of the Lord rested upon them and prompted them in that which was done. It was not expected when they met on that occasion that this result would be accomplished. But the conditions and circumstances surrounding the Church rendered it necessary that something should be done in order that its affairs might be properly conducted, and when it was proposed that the First Presidency should at once be appointed, everyone who was present was inspired by the same spirit and it was unanimously decided that this was the right thing to do. We all felt that this was the will of the Lord. There was no dissenting voice. When sustained by my brethren, the Apostles, as President of the Church, I selected as my counselors Presidents George Q. Cannon and Joseph F. Smith and they were unanimously accepted and sustained by the Twelve. I can assure you, my brethren and sisters, that it made me feel very humble. I realize the responsibility that rests upon me and my brethren of the First Presidency, but I know that the blessings of the Lord have attended me in the past in the discharge of duties placed upon my shoulders. . . .
>
> I can assure you, brethren and sisters, that I had no ambition to assume the responsibility which now rests upon me. If I could have escaped it honorably I should never have been found in my present position. I have never asked for it, nor have I ever asked the assistance of any of my brethren that I might attain to this position, but the Lord revealed to me and to my brethren that this was His will, and I have

The Lion House, left; the President's office, center; and the Beehive house, right, in 1906, approximately five years after President Snow passed away. (USHS)

> no disposition to shirk any responsibility nor to decline to occupy any position that the Lord requires me to fill.[35]

President Cannon also addressed the stake, using the occasion to explain the matter of the unusually quick reorganization: "Referring to the organization of the First Presidency, I may say that there never was a more united, spontaneous and hearty co-operation of a body of men than the action of the Apostles a few days ago in the confirmation of President Lorenzo Snow as President of the Church, and the selection by him of his two counselors. The reorganization of the First Presidency has been accomplished sooner than most of the people anticipated, for it had become almost an established precedent to wait for some time after the death of the President of the Church before the appointment of another President." He then spoke of the time periods between the deaths and First Presidency reorganizations of past presidents of the Church and continued:

> And thus, it might be said, a precedent had been established, and the general feeling was that no immediate action would be taken in organizing the First Presidency. But on September 13th, at a meeting of the Apostles, while discussing the necessity for the appointment of a Trustee-in-trust for the Church, the necessity also of organizing the First Presidency appeared clear to the brethren, and one after another of the Twelve spoke in favor of such action being taken at that time. After hearing their views, President Snow then arose and stated to the brethren that he had, since the death of President Woodruff, felt led to present himself before the Lord, clothed in his priestly robes, in the Temple, and the Lord had revealed to him that the First Presidency should be organized, and also revealed to him who his counselors should be. He did not give any expression to this, however, until after the Apostles had spoken on the subject. This statement of President Snow was evidence

> to them that the Spirit of God had inspired the remarks which they had made, and approved of the work which they had proposed to do, and it caused them to rejoice greatly.

President Cannon then testified to the members of President Snow's prophetic call:

> President Lorenzo Snow was called of God to occupy the position in which he stands today, and he will be sustained by the Lord as His mouthpiece to the Church, and also by his Counselors and the Apostles, and the whole Church will approve of the action taken and sustain it fully. I think I am safe in saying that a thrill of joy went through the entire Church when the word was sent out that the First Presidency had been reorganized and that Lorenzo Snow was the President. . . . I can say that President Wilford Woodruff, shortly before his decease, expressed his desire that there should be no delay after his death in perfecting the organization of the Presiding Quorum. The action taken was inspired of the Lord, and it is a matter of gratification and rejoicing that this has been so soon accomplished.[36]

The next weekend, President Snow traveled to Brigham City to speak at the Box Elder Stake conference, telling them that "one of the objects of his visit was to solicit the faith and prayers and support of the Saints in Brigham City in the discharge of the important and sacred duties that seemed to have fallen upon him." He said that he "could see clearly that there are great rewards held in reserve for the Latter-day Saints. A glorious future awaits the righteous. Many in the congregation had received in the Temple the highest blessings ever given to man, and many others would receive them." After being called from Brigham City to become the President of the Salt Lake Temple in 1893, he "had been happy in recommending them [the Box Elder Saints] to President Woodruff for choice blessings—the highest ever conferred upon men or women since the formation of the earth." Then he again mentioned his new position of President of the Church: "He said he felt his weakness and inability. He, however, had the consolation that God had always given him strength to fulfill every duty thus far in life, and he had faith to believe that such would be the case in the future." He told them that, "When the Twelve met recently they had no idea of organizing the First Presidency, but the Spirit of the Lord made it plain that the time was at hand."[37]

A couple of weeks later, young Bishop David McKay (whose son would many years later become President of the Church) called on President Snow on behalf of the Weber Stake Academy (which would become Weber State University) and asked for financial help. The academy was almost twenty thousand dollars in debt and was being pressed by creditors for payments that they could not make. President Snow had to tell Bishop McKay that he could not help them at present but hoped to find a way soon—other Church organizations were suffering in the same way and would be helped when he could.[38]

At the meeting of the First Presidency and Quorum of the Twelve held on Wednesday, October 5, before the start of general conference, President Snow brought up the need to fill the vacancy in the Quorum of the Twelve: "President Snow then invited each of the Apostles to hand in at their leisure, the names of persons from which a selection might be made to fill the vacancy. He went on to say that he had deep feelings while beholding the faces of his Brethren around the sacramental table. He could not help but believe that the Prophets Joseph, Brigham, John, Wilford and others were cognizant of this meeting, and watched with deepest interest the deliberations and actions of the Council. He invoked the blessing of the Lord upon all present, and besought the Brethren to be humble in their callings and hold themselves in readiness to conform their wills to the will of God." He also had a gentle warning for them, "never to be over-anxious to have their own way, but learn to listen with unbiased feelings and conclusions; leaving the mind free to be operated upon by the Holy Spirit. In this way the will of the Lord would be done in the Council. He had felt sometimes that brethren were more anxious to sustain a speaker who expressed their own mind and conclusions, than they were to obtain light, and he felt to caution the brethren against this spirit." His feeling was that "there was nothing more glorious to behold than unity, a complete union among the Priesthood of God, and if they persevered, determined to sacrifice their own feelings in order to accomplish the Lord's purposes, great would be the results and great would be the joy of this body of men."[39] At this meeting, Elder Brigham Young Jr. unwittingly committed an error in suggesting a new apostle: "I seemed to have made a blunder," he wrote, "in suggesting—all things being equal—I would love to see President Snow represented in the Twelve [by a son]. Afterwards his counselors took me to task for such an unwise suggestion; said I placed President Snow in a very embarrassing position. I could not see it."[40]

The next day, the October general conference began (Thursday through Saturday), but did not proceed entirely free of controversy—the first real administrative issue that President Snow had to deal with as president.

One of the members of the Twelve, Elder John W. Taylor,[41] referred to rumors he had heard of immorality problems among the young people in a local Utah community and also among some members of the Tabernacle Choir. These references caused something of a stir, and so President Snow asked George Q. Cannon, whom he knew to be perhaps the most capable speaker in the Church at that time, to smooth the ruffled feathers. President Cannon did his best, diplomatically seeking to soften the impact Elder Taylor's talk had had, but he was only partially successful.[42] When a summary of Elder Taylor's remarks were printed in the evening paper, Taylor went to the newspaper's office and asked that a full and complete account of his discourse be published, hoping that such would clarify and diminish concern.[43]

On the morning of the Saturday general session of conference, President Snow convened a general priesthood meeting. Evidently feeling inspired and humbled by the high and holy office which had come to him, he shared his personal view of how the assembled priesthood stood, stating (in summary) that:

> There was no question in his mind but what the Lord was looking upon this congregation; that Abraham, Isaac and Jacob were looking upon it; that Joseph Smith, Brigham Young, John Taylor and Wilford Woodruff were also deeply interested in this body of men, because of the great authority entrusted to them. God had called this class of men, though unlearned and comparatively uneducated, to assist him in the redemption of his family. He himself felt keenly the weight of the responsibility resting upon him in being called to preside over the Church. . . . He referred to his early career. . . . He was [then] exceedingly anxious to know without doubt that Joseph Smith was a true Prophet, and when he received the Gospel, he obtained that knowledge, and was perfectly satisfied in relation to the matter. Everything he had thought about in a religious way was changed; every part of his system was convinced by the power of the Holy Ghost that God was his Father, that Jesus Christ was his elder brother, and that Joseph Smith was a prophet of God. Soon afterwards he was called upon a mission, and just before starting received a revelation which he put into the following couplet: "As man now is God once was; As God now is man may be." The light imparted to him through this revelation prompted him to purify himself that it might take possession of his whole soul. Referring to the new position which he had recently been called to occupy as President of the Church, Bro. Snow said: "Brethren, I am at your service; if you desire to approve the action of the Apostles, I will try with them to carry out the purposes of God."[44]

After the priesthood meeting and regular conference session, the First Presidency and Twelve met in the celestial room of the temple, and President Snow asked them to turn in their suggested names for the new member of the Twelve. The First Presidency then withdrew to consider the names, and "upon the return of the Presidency, President Snow said that it was a very solemn thing to fill a vacancy in the Quorum of the Apostles. Our union for many years has been of the most perfect kind, and we hope it will continue to be perfect in the future. Said that he and his Counselors had met and read the names of those suggested to fill the vacancy in the Quorum of the Apostles. We are perfectly united. He was sure we would want the man whom the Lord approved of and that none of us desire that our own judgment shall prevail. Said: I know that we have the mind of the Lord, and I know it just as perfectly as I have ever known anything. The man we have chosen, and upon whom we are perfectly united, is Rudger Clawson. President Franklin D. Richards moved that we sustain the choice of the Presidency and the motion was unanimously sustained."[45]

That afternoon, the General Authorities of the Church were presented for sustaining vote. The conference reporter wrote: "The meeting was a Solemn Assembly, the Priesthood occupying the body of the hall in their quorum capabilities, and voting as such on the First Presidency and Twelve, after which the remaining authorities were submitted in usual form. It was a very impressive sight to see quorum after quorum rise to their feet and vote."[46] During the sustaining, some opposition was manifest toward Elder Taylor for his remarks the previous day. According to the official report:

> All the voting was unanimous, and it was so announced, until the negative vote upon sustaining the members of the Quorum of the Twelve Apostles was called from the Elders. Two of these arose to their feet. President Cannon addressing them, asked who they objected to and for what reason?
>
> Each of these two Elders said he objected to John W. Taylor, and the reason was certain objectionable remarks made by him in Conference on Friday, October 7th.
>
> They were asked if they would come to the stand at the close of the session and see whether Brother Taylor could make the matter right with and satisfy them. Both replied that they were willing to do this.
>
> The voting for members of the Quorum of the Twelve Apostles then went forward uninterrupted and was unanimous, until the negative vote of the entire congregation was called for. At this point a number of

members of the Tabernacle choir, probably from twenty to twenty-five of both sexes, arose to their feet.

On being asked by President Cannon who they objected to and the reason for it, they replied that they objected to John W. Taylor on account of some disparaging remarks he had made in Conference regarding the choir, on Friday, October 7th. They were asked if they were willing that Brother Taylor should personally meet with the choir and endeavor to make the matter right to their satisfaction. They signified that this arrangement was agreeable to them.

It was then announced by President Cannon that a vacancy had been created in the Quorum of the Twelve Apostles by the removal of President Snow from it to assume the position of President of the Church. It had been decided that this vacancy should be filled, and announced the name of Rudger Clawson for the position. The mind and word of the Lord had been obtained upon the selection of Brother Clawson for this office.[47]

After the sustaining vote, the new apostle, Elder Clawson, briefly spoke of the sacrifices he had been called upon to make in his life to that point, and then President Snow addressed the congregation:

I never felt more humble than I do on this occasion. It is, as was said by President Cannon, a serious ordeal through which we have to pass from time to time to be presented here before the people, and all of our past acts and doings viewed by them, and we depend upon their sanction and approval or rejection. This belongs to them. . . . There may be some things that the First Presidency do; that the Apostles do, that cannot for the moment be explained; yet the spirit, the motives that inspire the action can be understood, because each member of the Church has a right to have that measure of the Spirit of God that they can judge as to those who are acting in their interests or otherwise.

Now, brethren, this much I say, and I say it in the name of the Lord: I will endeavor to be devoted to your interests and the interests of the kingdom of God. I will serve you to the best of my knowledge and understanding, in reference to that which will promote your interests in connection with the interests of the Almighty. I will do this, the Lord being my helper. . . .

We are a mighty people, and growing mightier as trials and difficulties arise. I can imagine that at some future period, in the other life, we will pass through an ordeal [of judgment] that will be as close and as serious to us as we have passed through today; for our past course and conduct will be fully understood. . . . You who are seated here will have

The First Presidency surrounded by the Quorum of the Twelve (CA)

> opportunities of standing in the presence of multitudes, and I can easily imagine, yonder in the next life, after we have passed along perhaps a thousand years or more, that many of you who are here today will have an audience before you of your own posterity. I am as sure of it as I am that I am talking to you; I know it just as well as I know anything.[48]

The next Monday morning, October 10, the First Presidency and Twelve met at the President's Office and then went together to a local photography studio (Fox and Symons) to sit for a group photograph. At noon they met again at the office, where President Snow and the other Brethren circled around Rudger Clawson and ordained him an Apostle and set him apart as a member of the Council of the Twelve Apostles, President Snow voicing the blessing.

Then President Snow, at his request (having only been sustained to this point), was set apart as President of the Church, with George Q. Cannon acting as voice. He was blessed, among other things, to "be entitled to the revelations of the Lord Jesus and give the mind and will of God to the Church; to impart unto them from time to time that knowledge concerning the will of God that shall be communicated to them." He was blessed "with increased power to go forth and magnify [his] calling in the midst of the Church of Christ . . . and that the Lord will communicate with [him] from time to time everything necessary for the perfect government of his Church."[49] When finished, President Snow in turn set George Q. Cannon apart as his First Counselor, specifically mentioning a blessing of improved physical health, and then set apart Joseph F. Smith as his second counselor. Upon both men was bestowed all the blessings, gifts, rights, and privileges necessary for their calling as Counselors.

Finally, Franklin D. Richards was set apart as President of the Quorum of the Twelve Apostles with President Cannon again acting as voice. At this point the Brethren took their seats and listened as President Snow delivered the "Apostolic Charge" to Elder Rudger Clawson. The Charge, traditionally given to every new member of the Quorum, dated back to the days of the original Twelve, when Oliver Cowdery, at the behest of the Prophet Joseph Smith, taught them their duties and responsibilities in the apostleship and the Quorum.

The Charge consisted of several parts: to keep themselves pure and unspotted from the world; to consecrate their all to the cause of the Church and Kingdom of God; to perform to the best of their ability the assignments that came to them; to speak their mind fully and frankly in council but to accept the decision of the majority even if it was contrary to their own opinions; and most important, to bear witness to all the world that Jesus is the Christ, the Son of God.

In Elder Clawson's case, being the newest member of the Quorum, he was told by President Snow, "You will, of course, not feel it your duty to take up all the time, but let others speak. Let those who have had long experience speak when it comes to matters of high importance, and you listen. Do not occupy too much time at first." Presidents Cannon and Smith also each took opportunity to add to what President Snow had said. The counsel contained in the Charge also served as a reminder for the other apostles assembled. President Smith told Elder Clawson that "one of the great callings and special duties of an Apostle is to become a living witness of the Lord Jesus Christ; to know him and be able to testify that he is the Son of God and the Savior of the World. From then on, his highest loyalty would be to his quorum and the First Presidency."[50]

Chapter 17

A Plethora of Problems Greet the New Prophet

With formal administrative protocol taken care of, President Snow launched himself into the work of his new position as President of the Church, and he was not reticent about moving forward with faith and zeal. A variety of problems and issues of all sizes instantly greeted him—financial (by far the largest), business, political, publishing, temple work-related—and he struggled and worked to resolve them as he encountered them, seeking and implementing inspired and practical solutions.

Not long after the meeting at which he had been set apart as President of the Church, Elder Francis M. Lyman of the Twelve took the initiative to speak privately with the new prophet: "I met and conversed freely and confidentially with President Snow. I drew his attention to the fact that there has been in the administration of each one of the presidents some particular and peculiar phases of their mission to emphasize their administrations, and that I was satisfied that the important measure in his life would be to get the Church out of debt; that he would live to see it accomplished. He said he had prayed and labored to bring the Quorum [of the Twelve] to oneness and had succeeded. Now his prayer and labor would be to see the Church free from debt."[1] With all the other issues of importance that he encountered and dealt with, this goal became President Snow's greatest obsession—as it did for others of the Brethren as well.[2]

Elder Brigham Young Jr. likewise sought the Prophet with a similar thought in mind, noting: "I had a private and pleasant interview with President Lorenzo Snow on the [subject of the] United Order. I believe the Lord has something for us concerning this principle for Pres. Lorenzo

Snow is well qualified to be the medium to His people in beginning to establish this order preparatory to redeeming Zion. God grant we may have a little of this principle as we can stand it, and work into it understandingly."[3] (While a program as expansive as the United Order itself was not then instituted, the preparatory principle of tithing soon received renewed emphasis and attention.)

With Utah politics a continual battleground, rife with accusations and rumor, President Snow gave an interview to a reporter from the *Salt Lake Herald*:

> "President Snow," said the reporter, "there is much misunderstanding in Weber county over the position of the First Presidency in regard to the senatorial candidates. The impression is abroad that you are being represented by [Stake] President [Lewis] Shurtliff as desiring the success of Senator [Frank J.] Cannon. . . . Will you not state if it be true or not true?"
>
> "Well, I can explain my own position in short order. I have never been in politics. I want to keep entirely out of it, and am not in now. I never have said a word to any man to influence his political choice or action. I never have tried to influence his political action in any way. I don't want to. I want people to choose for themselves. That's how I feel on it, no matter how the others feel or what they have said."
>
> "If, then," said the reporter, "President Shurtliff or any other person represented that it is the wish, disposition and desire of the first presidency that Senator Cannon be returned to the senate, he was mistaken?"
>
> "Yes, sir. If any man says I ever did aught [anything] to influence his political choice he says that which is not so. I want the people to be free about such things."
>
> "You favor then the keeping up of party lines?"
>
> "Yes, certainly I do. If we had not we would not have recommended it. I think it is too bad that we have to be continually answering that question. We have said so times enough already. We have other things to think about and to do; at least I have."
>
> "Your statement is then that the [present] First Presidency, as an ecclesiastical body, has no wishes and has had no wishes to communicate regarding politics or political action?"
>
> "That's it."
>
> "And if any stake president is pretending to express the wishes of the First Presidency in such matters his representations are unauthorized?"
>
> "Yes, sir; I believe I have said that three times already."
>
> "May I make your statements public in this matter?"

> "As public as you choose—tell it to every man, woman and child in the world, if you please."[4]

It is well to keep this statement in proper perspective. As was well known, President Snow had decades earlier served for a lengthy season in the territorial legislature and had been its president for a time, but he obviously did not equate that experience with the main issue the reporter inquired about. And he did give strictly personal support to Thomas Kearns, a non–Latter-day Saint mining magnate, for his senate candidacy—always clarifying that such support was his own, and not the Church's or the First Presidency's.

Many years later, in 1911, Frank J. Cannon, who had long since completed his descent into apostasy and deep bitterness toward the Church and its leaders, produced an anti-Mormon memoir. Therein he claimed that President Snow had summoned him to a late-night, clandestine interview at his home, in which the prophet supposedly sought to persuade Frank (an incumbent seeking reelection) to give up further senatorial ambitions so that his father George could become the favored candidate. The story was repeated as being essentially true, though undoubtedly twisted, in a 1982 biography of President Snow.[5] (In order to unblock a stymied state legislature, the Brethren did briefly agree to push George Q. Cannon's name, but when it was learned he did not have enough votes, the idea was quietly scrapped.)[6] As for this story and for Frank Cannon's vengeance-motivated exposé, a review of relevant portions indicates that his assertions of motivating influences and conspiracies attributed to President Snow's administration were usually either unsupported or contrary to other more reliable sources. Determining how much of his narrations and conclusions have elements of truth and how much are fiction would entail a volume in itself.[7]

One of the first matters to come to President Snow's notice was the precarious condition of the Church-owned newspaper, the *Deseret News.* For some six years it had been leased by the Deseret News Publishing Company, a business owned by President George Q. Cannon. His sons John Q. and Abraham H., among others, had been operating it.[8] Abraham had since passed away, and John Q. had proven unreliable. The paper had not received adequate attention and was suffering both editorially and financially.

The problems were brought to President Snow's attention when a policeman called at the President's Office on a Monday morning to complain about a story that had appeared the previous Saturday evening, accusing the police of not sufficiently cracking down on illegal gambling in Salt Lake City. President Snow protested that in truth they were giving the matter special attention and a high priority.

President Snow therefore asked George F. Gibbs, secretary to the First Presidency, to investigate the origin of the offending article. Gibbs learned that the writer was a new employee; that he had relied on someone else for his information; that he was "a drunkard"; and that as a result he had "been locked up by the police quite a number of times." The last time he had threatened to "get even with" the police and had taken this method of doing so. Further, Gibbs reported there was no formal managing editor in place at the *Deseret News*; an able employee had stepped in to do the best work he could without authorization, but things were a mess and would probably remain so unless changes were made.[9]

Two days after the investigation, President Snow convened a meeting to elect officers to constitute a board of directors for the Deseret News Company (the *Deseret News*'s property had recently been transferred from Cannon's company, to a Church holding company with a similar name). During the discussion, one of the proposed directors recommended that the holding company be dissolved and the paper transferred to direct Church ownership. This was agreed, and then President Snow "inquired into the financial condition of the Deseret News Company, and after an extended discussion of the subject, he concluded that there was no other alternative but for the Church to take possession of the property and shoulder its immense indebtedness." A temporary supervisor was also appointed until further action could be taken.[10]

A week later, President Snow and his counselors discussed "the selection of an editor for the *Deseret News*, remarking that he had concluded in his own mind that Bro. Charles W. Penrose was the best man at the command of the Church for that position." With that choice approved, they also considered someone for a business manager but decided nothing.[11] The following day at a meeting of the First Presidency and Twelve, President Snow told the Brethren of his choice of Penrose to head the editorial side of the paper and received their approval. It was also decided that the *Deseret News* columns should be nonpartisan regarding politics. Then President Snow asked the Twelve for names of someone to hire as business manager. "He said that before making the appointment he would like to know the man and everything about him. The President also stated that . . . Bro. Horace G. Whitney had been recommended to him as a suitable person for the place." Then, "Elder Heber J. Grant spoke in favor of Bro. Whitney."[12]

Many years later, Heber J. Grant related further details of how it was decided to hire Horace G. Whitney to manage the *Deseret News*: "On one occasion President Lorenzo Snow sent for me and, referring to the fact that during the time I owned control of the *Salt Lake Herald* it had been successful, he said: 'Our paper, the *Deseret News*, has lost us [the Church], in the last few years, over one hundred thousand dollars. Give me a leaf out of your book so that we can make the *News* a success financially.' I replied: 'President Snow, it will break my heart to tell you how to do it, but I can tell you.' 'Well,' he repeated, 'how can I do it?' I answered, 'Steal the manager of my insurance business, Horace G. Whitney; and I pledge you my word he will make your paper a success.' And during his management of the *Deseret News,* he did succeed in accumulating several hundred thousand dollars for the institution."[13] Whether this interview between Grant and Snow happened before or after the meeting with the Twelve, where Elder Grant favored Whitney, is not known. Horace proved unusually competent, rescuing the *Deseret News* from financial woe and keeping it profitable. It was also around this time that President Snow hired and appointed Orson Whitney as an assistant Church Historian, taking Charles W. Penrose's place.

By mid-month, President Snow decided to personally resolve other financial problems at the *Deseret News*, and upon walking over to their office, he "had a talk with the employees, in relation to the indebtedness [back wages] due them . . . and had an understanding with the employees about settling the same, much to their satisfaction."[14] They would be paid part in tithing office produce and part in cash, "which was gladly accepted by all."[15] Several days later, President Snow arranged to pay another newspaper debt and then signed the "legal papers transferring the *Deseret News* Publishing Company's business to the Trustee-in-trust. At the same time the Trustee-in-trust signed obligations assuming the indebtedness of the *Deseret News* Publishing Company, amounting to $108,325.08."[16] Also during November, he was able to travel to his beloved Brigham City and speak again to the people he had known so well for so long (here summarized): "Our spirits are immortal, our identity can never be destroyed. We will always have our agency, and after a time we shall have perfect control of our bodies. Men whom the Lord had selected to do his work in the world were not great in learning; they were not the mighty and the wise in scientific knowledge; Joseph Smith, the great prophet, was not an educated man when God chose him and made known to him his mission. The Lord bestows spiritual gifts and knowledge upon the unlearned, and the greatness of the kingdom is made known to them by the power of the Holy Ghost, and they gradually become great in the knowledge of the things of God. He referred to the sacredness of the marriage contract and the sublime possibilities unfolded by the Gospel. It was revealed to him that as man now is, God once was; as God now is, man may be. He knew these things were true."[17]

In December, as a Christmas present to the Church (specifically the Salt Lake Temple fund), President Snow accepted the donation of an accumulation of nickels from the Salt Lake Stake's Primary Associations, amounting to fifty dollars. In reply to their generous communication, President Snow wrote: "This is very kind and thoughtful and is doubtless the result of what your teachers have taught you. Not only does this offering appear in your credit upon the records of our sacred Temple, but angels too have record borne."[18]

In early January President Snow was approached by Joseph F. Smith, who asked him for permission to take a long vacation (for health reasons for a wife). "That day President Snow gave him no answer, but the next morning when he came to the office, President Snow said to his second counselor: 'Well, Joseph, last night when I got home and thought of your going away I felt like crying. I depend upon you to help me, you understand things and I need your help. You are not afraid to speak your mind before anyone, therefore you are a helpful counselor, and I rely upon your integrity and your judgment. Still, if you have made up your mind and feel clear that you will be all right on the sea, and the voyage will do your wife good, all right.'"[19] President Smith left in January, during which month it was officially announced to the Church that the *Deseret News* was once again its official organ and that the Latter-day Saints should subscribe to it and otherwise support it.[20]

It was also in January that President Snow was obligated to deal with certain book publishing questions, and with defining the relationship of the authors to the Church. Brother James E. Talmage met with the First Presidency in consultation regarding doctrine contained in a series of public lectures he had given on the Articles of Faith. When the doctrinal points were settled, Brother Talmage was informed that President Snow had approved the suggestion of the reading committee (that had reviewed his work): let the Church itself publish the lectures in book form.[21] Elder

Talmage recorded some of the discussion regarding a doctrinal point on the personage and personality of the Holy Ghost:

> One of the questions referred to the First Presidency by the Committee was, as to the advisability of reprinting the lecture entitled "The Holy Ghost" which appeared in the *Juvenile Instructor* soon after its delivery in the theology class at the Church University. I remember that considerable discussion attended the reading of the lecture before the former committee prior to its delivery. The question hung upon the expediency and wisdom of expressing views as definite as those presented in the lecture regarding the personality of the Holy Ghost, when marked ambiguity and differences of opinion appeared in the published writings of our Church authorities on the subject. The lecture was approved as it appeared in the *Instructor*. I have incorporated it in the prospective book in practically an unaltered form. President Snow took the article under advisement today. In conversation President George Q. Cannon supported the view of the distinct personality of the Holy Ghost, and stated that he had heard the voice of the third member of the Godhead, actually talking to him.[22]

President Snow had also enjoyed a special experience with the Holy Ghost completely enveloping him, shortly after his baptism (see appendix 2), and was therefore well qualified to make such a determination. A few days later, Brother Talmage again met with the First Presidency regarding the content of his Holy Ghost chapter. There, "President Snow announced his unequivocal approval of the lecture on the 'Holy Ghost'; and directed its insertion. The preliminaries relating to publication were furthered."[23] President Snow would not let Talmage put "Elder" in front of his name on the title page, but instead directed that his academic title of "Dr." be used, doing this in hopes that the book might be more inviting to non–Latter-day Saint readers.[24] By January 17, President Snow had decided that the Church would publish the book, something that had never been done before under those circumstances regarding one author's doctrinal work, but it was felt that such an action would "give the book greater prestige." Brother Talmage was asked to select the type font and oversee other publication details for his book, for which a first edition of ten thousand copies was scheduled for printing and binding by the *Deseret News* press. Talmage had refused a royalty and given the copyright to the Church. On March 10, President Snow had an official announcement inserted in the *Deseret News*, part of which read: "The lectures were prepared by appointment of the First Presidency, and the book will be published by the Church. . . . The work has been approved by the First Presidency, and I heartily commend it to the members of the Church."[25] This statement of approval indeed gave the new book a unique and lofty standing, but did not qualify it as scripture; nor was it ever formally canonized as a standard work of the Church.

As the end of the month neared, President Snow received an inquiry regarding the possibility of temple ordinances being performed in behalf of a person that had committed suicide: "President Snow decided that in this and in all like cases, where persons committed suicide in an unsound state of mind, temple work might be done for them."[26] A couple of days later, an unusual request came to President Snow from an "invalid" woman, who was unable to do her own temple work, and "wanted to know if it would be proper for her to receive her endowments by proxy. Presidents Snow and Cannon consented to this being done, but expressed a desire that the matter be not talked about [locally]."[27] Two months previously, Elder Owen Woodruff had sent a telegram to President Snow, also related to temple work. In it he inquired whether he could perform sealings for young people outside the temples, asking—"Shall I do it? Reply at once." In response President Snow replied, "Such authority cannot be given at present. Lorenzo Snow."[28]

Meanwhile, another publishing question surfaced. Andrew Jenson, an assistant Church Historian, had finished extensive work on the second edition of a book filled with Church history information and data, titled *Church Chronology*. He had proposed to donate the copyright to the Church, with a generous plan that sales profits be used to build a new Church Historian's office and fireproof records-storage building (he thought the current office and storage conditions severely deficient). In May 1898, the First Presidency and Twelve had formally approved his idea, and on July 16, the First Presidency (then consisting of Wilford Woodruff, George Q. Cannon, and Joseph F. Smith) had endorsed and recommended the book to the Church as a "valuable work of reference" in the *Deseret News*.[29] In late September, Presidents Snow and Cannon received a letter from Jenson, "asking the Church to handle the sale of his work entitled *Church Chronology*. . . . The matter was presented to Presidents Snow and Cannon, who expressed themselves decidedly against using the Church authorities for the purpose of selling this or any other work. They thought the *Church Chronology*, like other Church works, should sell on its own merits, and that the most the Church could undertake to do was to recommend it."[30] This they soon did; in December 1898, the Lorenzo Snow First

Presidency recommended the book in a signed statement printed in the same newspaper: "We commend *Church Chronology* to the kind consideration of the Saints, and trust it will meet with the success it merits, and that the presiding officers and leading men in all the Stakes of Zion will favor the work with their aid and influence, so that the purpose for which it is being published may be successfully carried out."[31]

By late February 1899, the book was ready to be printed and bound. Jenson, thinking he had sufficient permission to include a statement in the book that it was a Church production, visited the President's Office to get final approvals, unprepared for what happened next. "Brother Andrew Jenson of the Historian's Office presented to Presidents Snow and Cannon the title page of the second edition of his work *Church Chronology*, in which it was stated that the author and compiler had turned it over to the Church. President Cannon expressed his sentiments very freely to President Snow in the presence of Brother Jenson regarding the matter. He was opposed to the Church accepting this work for the purpose of building a new Historian's office." President Cannon reasoned that after Jenson's death, his heirs might institute legal claims against the Church and its property (something that other employees' heirs had done); also, that it was the Church's responsibility to build and pay for its own offices, not Jenson's. "Brother Jenson here reminded President Cannon that the Church had accepted the copyright of his work and that he had used time in compiling this work which belonged to the Church, he being one of its paid employees. He maintained that the Church ought to accept this work from his hands, as things had gone so far and his honor was at stake." Jenson and others had been promoting it with the understanding that it was a Church-owned and endorsed production, and profits would go for the new office—as the signed *Deseret News* endorsements had said. "President Cannon admitted that in his opinion a mistake had been made in accepting the copyright, but maintained that this and all the other matters mentioned might be corrected and Brother Jenson's honor" saved. President Snow had listened to part of this conversation, but had been interrupted with another matter. Jenson continued to press his case with Cannon, "remarking that the work would be out in a few days," and wanting to know "what he should do about it. President Cannon answered that he had now expressed himself" and told Jenson to ask President Snow. "Brother Jenson turned to President Snow, who was at his desk, who referred him back to President Cannon," telling Jenson that anything Cannon told him to do would meet with his approval. Obviously flustered and frustrated, Jenson turned back to Cannon, and Cannon proceeded to assist Jenson "in correcting the title page, by striking out the line 'published by Franklin D. Richards, Historian for the Church of Jesus Christ of Latter-day Saints.' This left Brother Jenson to publish the work himself and be responsible for it. He now withdrew, and President Snow remarked to President Cannon that he endorsed his views entirely," on the matter.[32]

But the story was not yet complete. Prophets can change their minds and reconsider, and in this situation, they did. The first copies of *Church Chronology* were issued in May, and in October a circular letter was composed in the President's Office, that again endorsed the book and the originally planned use of profits. It read:

> We heartily recommend to the Saints the *Church Chronology* recently issued from the press. As a work of reference on matters pertaining to the history of the Church, it is exceedingly valuable. And since the proceeds accruing from the sales are to be used towards the erection of a new Historian's Office and a fire-proof structure in which the valuable records and documents of the Church can find a safe home, *Church Chronology* ought to meet with universal favor throughout the entire community. We trust presiding officers and leading men in all the settlements of the Saints will place the matter before the people and take such steps as they may deem proper towards obtaining the popular sales advocated in the printed circulars previously forwarded. Your Brethren, Lorenzo Snow, Joseph F. Smith.[33]

While the book was not as successful as Jenson hoped, its profits did eventually enable him to donate $3,000 toward the desired new historian's office.[34]

In mid-March, a meeting of the First Presidency and Twelve was held, in which a proposal began to take shape of somehow having a "History of the Church" written and published. However, there were competing internal interests desiring the rights to prepare such a work. The meeting began with Elder John Henry Smith making some remarks about men "betraying the confidence of the brethren" and suggesting that something ought to be done to "guard against such things." In response President Snow—letting his dry sense of humor show—said, "he thought the only way it could be done would be by giving men new bodies and eliminating all the material of which they are at present composed." According to President Smith, who had returned from Hawaii by then, the "matter had been discussed by the General Board of the Y.M.M.I.A., and it was decided to publish it in the *Improvement Era*." President Cannon objected, saying "that Elders Charles W. Penrose, editor, and Horace G. Whitney, manager, claimed that it was clearly the right of the *Deseret News* to publish the Church history." Then Franklin D. Richards chimed in, "very much in favor of the suggestion, but thought it ought to be published in book form rather than in a magazine. [He] thought that the history as given in the [*Millennial*] *Star* including the revelations should be followed." Although different methods had been suggested, enthusiasm was building quickly for the idea: "Pres. Cannon was very much interested in the subject, and thought enough attention had not hitherto been given to the writing of our history. Great care should be taken and all important facts fully explained, and when necessary amplified." President Snow was just as eager. He "endorsed [the] remarks of previous speakers, and suggested that the matter be gone right into and a history of the Church be published in book form—[with a] cheap binding . . . that it might be within the reach of all." Money was a huge consideration—"The Church has but little means to put into this enterprise, but, if we are united, a great deal can be accomplished." President Snow desired a committee to be appointed to "take charge of the work." Elder Clawson "moved that it be the sense of the meeting that we accept the suggestions of Pres. Snow and that the Presidency be authorized to select the committee." Then, "President Joseph F. Smith asked if the motion carried with it the understanding that the history should be published by the *Deseret News*. President Snow answered yes and said that the committee appointed would be held responsible to see that the work is speedily and correctly done. The motion was then put and carried by unanimous vote."[35] Thus was launched the first major Church-endorsed historical publishing project, though the final details of production evolved over time.

In early March, LeRoi Snow returned from his mission, and his father quickly employed him as an assistant and chief tithing clerk in the President's Office. Arthur Winter, a seasoned employee, recorded, "Yesterday, while I was absent, LeRoi Snow commenced his labors in the office. This morning I instructed him concerning the method of receiving tithing, etc."[36] In early April President Snow received a visit from the Manti Temple president and gave him instructions in relation to temple finances. Later that day, "the first two hundred volumes of Dr. James E. Talmage's new church work *The Articles of Faith*, were issued from the *Deseret* bindery. . . . The first half dozen books turned out [finished], in several elegant styles of binding, were laid upon the desk of President

Snow, who expressed himself as highly pleased with the workmanship."[37]

April 1899 turned out to be a busy month for President Snow, outside of the signal decision to travel to St. George (reviewed in chapter 18). On the twelfth B. H. Roberts discussed with the prophet his fight for his seat in the United States Congress, to which he had been duly elected by the people of Utah, but which was eventually denied him by the anti-Mormon elements permeating Congress. President Snow told him "that it was not clear to him whether Brother Roberts would or would not secure his seat, but it was clear to him that the purposes of the Lord would be accomplished through him trying to get it."[38]

The next day in the regular meeting of the First Presidency and Twelve, an extended discussion took place in relation to using such terms as "ordain" and "set apart" when advancing men in the priesthood to various positions. The question had arisen because Elder Anthon H. Lund had been assigned to ordain Joseph W. McMurrin as one of the First Council of the Seventy, and he was worried because he had neglected to use the term "ordain," replacing it with "set apart." After the vigorous discussion, mostly between the members of the First Presidency, President Snow declared the act valid since Elder Lund had used language conveying all the rights, privileges, and powers of the office upon him. "He favored the use of the word *ordain* in Brother McMurrin's case, but at the same time held that the conferring of all the rights, keys, and powers of the office was equivalent to an ordination, and the term used really embodied all the meaning that the word ordain could convey. He thought that it would be very unwise to question the ordination."

President Cannon incidentally mentioned that "he was told by the late Apostle Parley P. Pratt that the first Elders of the Church, in confirming new members, laid their hands upon them and confirmed them, but that the language used was not spoken audibly, and that the Prophet Joseph told them they had better speak audibly. But the people received the Holy Ghost all the same." President Smith then asked a question, to which President Snow replied that the main necessity was "bestowing all the rights, keys, and powers of the office intended to be bestowed upon the person. Such language, with the intent, would in the judgment of the President be all sufficient." President Smith made some further explanation on the subject as did a few other apostles, but evidently President Snow thought the discussion was deteriorating into argument, because he put a stop to it, indicating he felt that "no further light would be obtained by discussing the question any longer at the present time, and remarked that if the Council preferred the First Presidency to further consider the matter, it would be done."[39]

The next day, President Snow received a visit from two missionaries traveling to Samoa, Edward J. Wood and William G. Sears. They wanted Presidents Snow and Cannon to speak into "a graphophone, or talking machine" so a personally recorded message from them could be delivered by them to the Samoan Latter-day Saints. "They consented, the machine was brought in, and after President Cannon had spoken, President Snow spoke as follows":

> My dear brethren and sisters in Samoa: I have just heard what President Cannon has said to you, and I hope you will not forget it. I should be pleased to have the privilege of seeing you, and talking to you face to face, but hardly expect to have this opportunity; but I say to you, if you will live faithful and keep the commandments of the Lord and follow the counsels of the Elders who we send to you, I shall have the pleasure of meeting you and talking with you in the other life. The Elders we send to you you can trust; they will tell you what is for your best good, and you will be perfectly safe and be greatly blessed in following their counsels. We are very much pleased at hearing from you from time to time, and learning you are faithful in keeping the commandments of the Lord and treating his servants so kindly. I constantly keep you in my mind, and pray for you at the family altar; and hope to have your prayers and faith to sustain me in the high and sacred position which the Lord has called me to occupy. God bless you, Amen.[40]

On the nineteenth, "Elder Seymour B. Young, the senior President in the First Council of Seventies, called and saw President Snow about the matter of Elder Joseph W. McMurrin's ordination as one of that body, the subject so exhaustively considered at the last meeting of the Apostolic Council. Brother Young wanted to know if Brother McMurrin had been actually and properly ordained, since the word 'ordain' was not used, but the words 'set apart' at the time of his ordination. President Snow explained to Brother Young that inasmuch as the intent was to ordain Brother McMurrin, and the words used on the occasion not only set him apart, but conferred upon him all the authority, keys, and privileges of the office and calling, it was a complete and valid ordination, and had been so decided by the Presidency and the Apostles in council. At the same time, President Snow remarked that if it had to be done over again, his mind would be that the word *ordain* should be used."[41]

Also during April, President Snow had two long talks with President

Cannon about special "dedicated" stock that Cannon held in the infamous Bullion, Beck, and Champion mine. The history of this mine and its relationship to members of the First Presidency and Twelve had become a resurfacing source of controversy within the leading councils. In brief, President John Taylor had felt inspired to buy stock in a mine owned and operated by a Church member named John Beck. He and George Q. Cannon, along with a few other Brethren, invested considerable amounts of money purchasing mine stock, which was considered "dedicated" to the purposes of the Lord's kingdom. If the mine became profitable, President Taylor desired to use the proceeds for special purposes such as buying land for a temple in Jackson County, Missouri, for court costs defending the Brethren in their plural marriage trials, and other like expenses where it was felt best not to use tithing funds if possible. Although more complicated than reviewed herein, in general, most investors understood that their stock was specially dedicated and any profits were to be used for Church purposes. However, after President Taylor died and the Utah economy worsened, some investors decided to pull their shares out of the dedicated stock pool, then controlled by President Cannon at President Taylor's behest. President Cannon was therefore forced to surrender portions of the stock to others. He also found himself needing to use his share for personal, family, and Church needs—an unanticipated move. These factors, combined with mine mismanagement, negligent bookkeeping, misunderstanding of President Taylor's intent, miscommunication about stock purposes, the bankruptcy of John Beck, stock price miscalculations, and President Cannon's secretive stock oversight, became one of the principal causes of occasional strife and contention within the Quorum of the Twelve and First Presidency.[42]

Presidents Snow and Cannon were attempting to settle the issue once and for all, and in doing so wanted to involve the Council of the Twelve:

> This afternoon, from about 4 to 6 o'clock, President Snow was engaged in private conversation with President Cannon upon the subject of the turning over by the latter of the "dedicated" Bullion-Beck mining stock and the accounting for dividends upon the same. President Snow, after President Cannon had gone for the night, informed Secretary Gibbs that he had told Brother Cannon that he would prefer the tender of the stock and the accounting to be submitted to the Council of the Apostles, or to such of the Apostles as Brother Cannon might name, and that if they accepted of the same he would agree to accept of it. President Snow also stated that President Cannon expressed a desire to

have this "dedicated" stock used for the purpose of covering the losses sustained by the Church in the Sterling mine [a failed investment initiated by Cannon]. This proposition was to be considered.[43]

In consequence, on the twenty-seventh, the First Presidency and Twelve met at the President's Office to discuss the B. B. & C. mine stock business:

President Cannon was asked to state the object of the meeting. He said that he had felt impressed for some time, and especially since President Woodruff's death, to transfer to President Snow as Trustee-in-trust what is known as the "dedicated stock" in the Bullion-Beck mine. He had therefore drawn out a statement concerning it, including the amount received by him in the shape of dividends, the disposition he had made of these funds and what remained in his hands. When this was proposed to President Snow he felt disinclined to accept such a statement at once, taking time to consider the matter a little further; afterwards, a week ago today, they had a meeting at which the affairs of the Sterling mine were investigated; a meeting which the speaker [Cannon] said he was very desirous should take place, for one reason particularly—to clear up the relationship of the First Presidency to that mine, and he was pleased with the result. When thinking about it afterwards, it occurred to him that there was something necessary for him to do in relation to this other [B. B. & C.] matter. President Snow having taken into consideration the expense of this mine, the Sterling, he (President Cannon) felt to propose the turning over of the "dedicated stock" in the other mine, on behalf of the late First Presidency, to liquidate the obligation [debt] assumed by them in connection with the Sterling property; and he subsequently proposed this to President Snow. The latter desired to submit the matter to the Twelve, and expressed the wish that nothing be done in the premises until he had thought more about it. This meeting was the result of a proposition to turn over the dedicated stock to the Trustee-in-trust.

President Snow then said that he would like to have the proposition read, and President Cannon thereupon read a statement that he had had prepared in book form, giving the history of the dedicated stock and accounting for the dividends received by him from the same and the disbursements that he had made. [Various figures given] . . . President Cannon now proposed to turn over to the Trustee-in-trust the house and lot known as the Cannon House, [and other securities and cash amounting to the same figure of just under $180,000 equaling the worth of the B. B. & C. stock].

President Snow asked the brethren present to express themselves. [Which they did] . . .

President Snow stated [the question] to be: Will the brethren accept from President Cannon this dedicated stock and the accounting he makes of its dividends. He said that if all the earnings of the stock were to be turned over in cash there could be no question in receiving the trust; but the question was whether the brethren could accept of it for the Church in the condition [mostly assets] in which it now came. He had previously remarked that it was a very serious matter, more serious than the Council might imagine, and he did not feel to accept of this accounting, in fact could not conscientiously do so, as representing the Lord, without first laying the matter before the Apostles and the Presiding Bishopric. He did not propose to express any opinion upon it at present, but it became a serious matter when looked at in its full light. This fund was created by revelation given to President Taylor, who received another revelation confirming the former one, and to the effect that a portion of the fund should be used to assist President Cannon on a certain occasion. It was a holy and sacred trust to President Taylor, and whether it would be right to blot out the fund entirely, so that it would cease to exist after his death, was a grave question, and one for the Council to decide. Whatever the spirit suggested, he for one would accept without hesitation.

President Smith said that the dedicated stock concern was one of those things that perhaps had never been heard of before, and whose parallel would never be heard of again. It never pretended to stand upon business principles. It was something that originated with President Taylor and the Lord. He went on to give President Taylor's reasons for establishing the fund, a fund that might be used as the tithing could not be used. This fund consisted of three-fifths of the Bullion-Beck mining stock, and its object was to protect the liberties of our people; also to purchase the Jackson County Temple lot, the Kirtland Temple lot and other properties which had been in possession of the Church; but the upshot came when President Taylor's heirs, John Beck and others drew out of the combination. President Smith favored President Snow's receiving this trust from President Cannon, without going into its history or the merits of the case, thus leaving the latter responsible for its past use, President Snow to become like responsible for it and free to use it as he might deem proper.

Brother Lyman and Brother John Henry Smith both agreed with President Smith that President Snow should accept of President Cannon's tender of this fund. . . . [Elder J. H. Smith] thought that the fund should never have been in the hands of anyone but the

> Trustee-in-trust, who had been given a bond in connection with the Bullion-Beck mine's troubles, a proceeding to which he and other Apostles objected at the time, until President Taylor told them that it was the will of the Lord. . . .
>
> Brother Merrill said . . . he could not see why President Cannon should contribute this means to the Church, and all the rest go free; he thought President Cannon was just as much entitled to his share of the fund as the others.
>
> President Snow (to Brother Merrill): "But you did not understand anything about the dedication, while President Cannon understood all about it, and he dedicated this means to the Lord through President Taylor."
>
> President Cannon: "Yes, this stock is dedicated, and is the Lord's, and you President Snow can make use of it as you please."
>
> President Smith then made the following motion: "I move that in consideration of the facts set forth and involved in the evidence, . . . that it be the sense of this Council that this property is dedicated property, and was absolutely put into the hands of President Cannon to do with as he pleased, without being questioned or asked to give an account of it to anybody, the Church or anybody else; that the property being absolutely his, to do with it as he pleases, we therefore accept of his tender of this property for the use and benefit of the Church.
>
> The motion was seconded. . . .
>
> President Cannon reminded the brethren of the circumstances under which this fund was turned over to him. President Taylor and he were alone, so to speak; President Smith not having returned from the [Hawaiian] Islands, and none of the Twelve being at hand. President Taylor, who had brought him up, and was his uncle by marriage, had entire confidence in him, and knew, from his past course, as chief executor of President Young's estate, that he desired to respect the rights of the Church. . . .
>
> After some further talk, President Snow put the motion, which was carried unanimously.[44]

Little more is known of the B. B. & C. mine stock as it affected Church leadership. Meanwhile, a few days before President Snow left with his party for St. George, Orson Whitney stopped by the President's Office to read him an article on "Utah and the Mormons" that he had prepared for the *Deseret News*.[45] Then the day before they left (May 15), Elder J. Golden Kimball of the First Council of the Seventy visited at the office and counseled with President Snow about his own personal financial woes.

He recorded: "I called at the President's Office to see President Joseph F. Smith. He was absent but I met President Lorenzo Snow. I placed before him what I had done in the bankruptcy case. I explained the circumstances. Bro. Snow said 'what you have done is all right.' I stated that I desired to be honest as my father [Heber C. Kimball] was. He replied, 'your intention and desire is to be honest and you are as honest as your father.' Being sustained by the prophet of the Lord is a great comfort to me."[46]

Chapter 18

Church Financial Distress and the Revelation Reaffirming Tithing

In order to grasp the enormous impact and success resulting from the Lord's revelation to President Snow commanding a renewed emphasis on payment of tithing by faithful Latter-day Saints, the severity of the debt problems of the Church in the 1890s must first be reviewed and sufficiently understood. This biography is not the best place to trace the multiplicity of complicated movements and maneuvering of Church leaders and other forces that eventually led to the fiscal crisis; however, a brief summary of the major issues in play may serve to assist in underscoring the magnitude of the problem.[1]

Origination of the Debt

The main factors contributing to the Church's crushing debts were the following:

(1) The escheatment (confiscation) of Church property by the federal government, under the provisions of the Edmunds-Tucker Act. As part of its persecution of Mormons for practicing polygamy, the United States Congress passed this and other laws meant to financially cripple or destroy the Church. The main receiver of these properties, US Marshal Frank Dyer, stole from these funds while in his control, and much less was eventually returned than was originally taken. Part of the problem is that the Church was charged exorbitant rents to use its own confiscated properties, although the price wasn't high enough for the anti-Mormon elements in the government at the time. Other related issues developed which also drained Church resources.[2]

(2) Temple construction. Generous donations from the general and local authorities necessary to finish the interior of the Salt Lake Temple by April 1893 had the effect of draining the personal financial resources of most Church leaders. Their commitment to consecration was highly commendable but personally crippling. For example, Elder Heber J. Grant found himself nearly bankrupt and some years later had to ask President Snow to forgive his "IOU" commitment toward temple construction. Elder Francis M. Lyman was likewise affected. Reflecting on his own donations, he wrote: "The possibility of losing all my earthly possessions by endorsing with the Church, troubles me only so far as it may hurt people I am owing, and thus cast a blemish on my good name and credit. I thank the Lord it was all done to uphold the First Presidency and the Church; I rejoice that I have placed it upon the right altar. If it be necessary that I must be sacrificed, I do now and for all time to come acknowledge the hand of the Lord in taking it from me, as freely as I acknowledged His hand in receiving it from Him."[3]

(3) The financial panic of 1893–95. This nationwide severe depression and accompanying money-shortage affected the Utah Territory as much as elsewhere, with banks failing, personal and institutional bankruptcy rampant, and great personal financial embarrassment to the trustee-in-trust (President) and other high Church leaders. Even President George Q. Cannon's supposed wealth was often an illusion; the panic had hit his businesses particularly hard, and he often could not pay his creditors.[4]

(4) A steady decrease in tithing payments by individual Church members, watching their freewill charitable contributions flow into corrupt government hands and disappear. Church leaders understood this and sympathized and may have had a hard time remonstrating the poorer Saints until agreements were reached and the government returned what remained after the looting.

(5) The financial policies of the former First Presidency. While there is some debate as to where blame might be placed for the deficit spending and investment policies of the Woodruff presidency, some members of the Twelve unabashedly charged President George Q. Cannon with excessive spending on investment schemes that usually failed.[5] Railroad building, sugar, salt, mining, and electric power companies took serious capital to start and operate, and *if* they turned a profit, it was usually much later. Two

of the major enterprises that needed large amounts of money to organize were the Pioneer Electric Power Company, in which the Woodruff First Presidency guaranteed an investor's note for $1,500,000; and the Sterling Silver mine in Nevada, in which their capital investment of $180,000 was lost when the mine failed to produce.[6] As for the electric company, it became the single greatest investment risk the Church had ever taken, and it was done at a point the Church could least afford it.[7] Elder Abraham H. Cannon described the 1895 meeting in which it was decided to legally guarantee the investor's note; a decision in which his father's (George Q. Cannon) feelings carried a great deal of weight:

> In the afternoon at two o'clock [I] was at the President's Office at a meeting. Present: All of the Presidency [Wilford Woodruff, George Q. Cannon, Joseph F. Smith], Lorenzo Snow, F. D. Richards, John Henry Smith, Heber J. Grant and myself: John R. Winder and George Gibbs. The President stated that the Pioneer Power Co. of Ogden had expended over $50,000 on its property, which amount had been raised on the individual credit of the directors. The control of the Company is in the hands of the Presidency of the Church, and they desired to carry the work through to completion, because they believed it would be a benefit to Zion in whose interest they were working in this enterprise. The Company had unsuccessfully tried to sell its bonds, till now they have an offer from Mr. Banigan [an eastern investor], . . . [He] is to buy the $1,500,000 of bonds at 80 cents on the dollar, and the interest and principal of the same is to be guaranteed by the Church. His demand is a very heavy one, but there is no likelihood of our being able to do better. Pres. Woodruff desired to know if the brethren would approve of the endorsement of the Church on these bonds. The matter was considered at some length, resulting in all of the brethren voting for the motion which was made by Pres. Lorenzo Snow, and seconded by F. D. Richards, that we do give the Presidency our full support and faith in signing these bonds, and that we stand behind them in the doing of the same. John Henry Smith said he voted for the motion, though his conscience and judgment did not approve of the course which it was decided to take. He feared the credit of the Church might be injured by this action. Both he and F. D. Richards urged that we defer action till the majority of the Quorum are together, and thus get them committed to the policy, but the necessity for immediate action on this matter was urged, hence it was decided to take the vote of those present, and see others of the Quorum thereafter, and try to secure their sanction. Pres. Snow remarked that the [First] Presidency

> would have the support of the Quorum of the Twelve in whatever they decided to do, even though the course they took resulted in financial failure. Father said he saw light in taking this course, and felt easy; this was also the feeling of Pres. Woodruff, which was the reason for his change of heart on the matter, for when the matter of endorsing the paper was first mentioned he repelled it instantly. . . . Pres. Woodruff evidently felt that this was the thing that ought to be done, and was very much relieved in his feelings when the vote of the brethren was in favor of the proposition.[8]

So great was the First Presidency's stake in the enterprise that they officially endorsed and commended the project to Church members and the people of Utah, hoping to ensure its success.[9] (The story of how the Church was miraculously delivered from this entanglement is noted in chapter 20.)

Carrying the Debt

Over the years, the stress caused by the debt problems was felt by all the leading Brethren, troubling them deeply. One of them wrote: "The pressure upon the Church is very great just now. The Lord will have to come to our assistance or we will be driven to bankruptcy."[10] An occasional flash of positive thinking was eagerly accepted by them. Elder Abraham H. Cannon wrote (in 1893): "At two o'clock I went to a meeting of my Quorum in the Temple. . . . President Snow made a few remarks. . . . He spoke of our present financial difficulties, and though our lack of wisdom may be blamed for some of our troubles, he felt that we will be delivered this once there from, and prosperity will shine upon us. His words were very encouraging for us."[11] President Snow was six years early with his prediction. The financial problems continued and then worsened, affecting the day-to-day operations and decisions of the Church. Money problems were the never-ending constant: "At 1 o'clock the Presidents of a number of the stakes in close proximity to this city met in the President's office, where the financial condition of the Church was clearly stated to them by several of the brethren, and they were asked to use their influence to obtain relief for the Church by the collection of tithes, offerings for the temple, and also by making loans for the Church at the rate of 10% per annum. All present held up their hands in token that they will do their best to relieve the Church, and help it to pay its debts."[12]

President Woodruff's journal indicates his level of anxiety. On August 8, 1894, he wrote: "I don't sleep nights and am weary by day. As

Trustees-in-trust and the presidency of the church we have taken such a load upon us it is difficult to carry it." Then the next day: "There is a heavy load resting upon us in church affairs, our debts are very heavy." In September 1896 the Journal History of the Church noted: "The First Presidency were all at their office today, and were much perplexed on monetary affairs, creditors of the Church pressing for payment and means not being at hand to meet those obligations."[13] A few weeks later at a meeting of the First Presidency and Twelve in the temple, "President Woodruff expressed his feelings in regards to the burden of indebtedness which he was carrying as Trustee-in-trust for the Church, and which had borne very heavily upon him of late."[14]

Then again on December 30, 1896, President Woodruff noted: "The presidency of the church are so overwhelmed in financial matters it seems as though we shall never live to get through with it unless the Lord opens the way in a marvelous manner. It looks as though we shall never pay our debts."[15] Again in the April general conference of 1897, "I spoke of this financial condition of the church, explained the action of the government officials in starting our debts. I did not want to die until the church and myself as Trustee-in-trust are out of debt."[16] President Franklin D. Richards commented on the substance of President Woodruff's message in his journal: "President Wilford Woodruff: The Lord has designs concerning this work and they will not be thwarted. The indebtedness of the Church has been the greatest burden on his mind that he has experienced in all his life. He then related circumstances that led up to our present condition—giving into Marshal Dyer's demands and conditions of compromise. . . . [rents to the government on church properties] . . . Several millions are invested in our temples. . . . If something can be done to help meet this indebtedness we can begin to look up. He has lost his sleep, it has worn upon him but he has not wanted to die with such a debt on his name as it is contrary to his way of doing all through his life."[17]

President Snow related his observations of President Woodruff's stressful circumstances to Elder Clawson: "Wilford Woodruff was not promptly and fully posted in advance as to the time when the Church obligations fell due for payment, and it became a source of great worry and anxiety to him, and doubtless shortened his life. . . . Surprises were often of common occurrence. The Chief Clerk [James Jack] would come into the President's private office and say that he must have $20,000 at once to meet an obligation due that day; or at another time it may have been $40,000 or $50,000, etc. President Woodruff would ask why he had not been notified of this before so that he might have had time to arrange for the payment. He did not appreciate such surprises."[18]

It was under this burden that President Woodruff died in 1898, leaving the crisis to President Snow to solve. The story of finding and implementing that solution is as profoundly inspiring as the debt crunch was overwhelmingly stressful.

Tithing Sporadically Taught

Before relating those events, it should also be recognized that teaching the principle of the payment of tithing to the Latter-day Saints was not new, nor was it neglected as a viable solution; it simply wasn't emphasized and stressed as it might have been.

For example, at a stake conference in Brigham City, Utah, in 1890, Elder Abraham H. Cannon recorded, "I next spoke . . . on tithing, . . . Franklin D. Richards also spoke a short time on the subject of tithing. . . . At the afternoon meeting President Woodruff spoke about an hour. He told of the great financial embarrassments of the Church, and told the people they would be blessed abundantly in paying their tithes."[19]

At the October 1894 general conference, Elder Brigham Young Jr., a member of the Twelve, emphasized tithing: "He felt that it was time for the people to observe the Word of Wisdom and the law of tithing, so that the land may be sanctified to the people. . . . He felt that we had already had talk enough about these principles, and we should now begin to carry them out."[20] At that same conference, another member of the Twelve, Elder George Teasdale, spoke with great earnestness (not unlike his Quorum president, who would likewise speak on the theme some four and a half years later):

> We talk about financial pressure. There never was a time when we ought to be more strict in the payment of our tithing than now. You that are in financial difficulties, I say unto you, that if you will pay your tithing honestly and act acceptably before the Lord, and your offerings for the poor, God will deliver you from your financial difficulties. If you doubt it, try it. "Prove me now herewith, saith the Lord of Hosts, if I will not open you the windows of heaven, and pour you out a blessing that there shall not be room enough to receive it." That is the word of the Lord to the people. The question is, will we do it? The Lord will have our hearts or nothing. If He has our hearts, then He will have everything that we possess. He has given us all that we enjoy today. . . . And I know it is the mind and will of the Lord that the people should repent. These were my feelings under the inspiration of the Spirit that rested upon those who have addressed us.[21]

At the April 1895 general conference, the subject was again referenced at the priesthood leadership meeting. President George Q. Cannon used the occasion to speak frankly to the assemblage about tithing payment:

> An idea prevails that the tithes are not properly used by the officers of the Church, and this is used by some as an excuse for not paying tithing. No faithful Saint will use such an excuse for neglecting a duty. If the Church means are improperly used, those who are guilty will be held accountable. Some ask if they are expected to pay tithing on the increase of cattle which have once been tithed, and that have been fed on hay that has also been tithed. If we are so strict in our dealings with the Lord, we may expect him to be equally close with us. I have not felt it wise to excommunicate non-tithe-payers, but they should be labored with, and made to see, if possible, their duty, and then be encouraged to perform it. Some do not like to pay tithing because it is generally concentrated in Salt Lake Stake, and thus builds it up at the expense of the other Stakes. This is a lame excuse.[22]

Yet without the consistent cohesive efforts of all the Brethren that came later, widespread full tithing payment did not catch fire within Church members.

A Temporary Solution Found—Selling Church Bonds

Facing the heavy debt squarely and with Divine assurance, President Snow immediately set about finding any means he could to begin paying it off. How to accomplish this was not yet apparent and initially took most of his energy and attention.

The first thing he did was to quietly remove President George Q. Cannon from his former delegated position of Church financial policy oversight, in the newly organized First Presidency, and took that obligation completely upon himself. One historian has noted: "In 1898, when Woodruff died, Lorenzo Snow assumed the office of Church President, and Cannon's heavy influence over policy diminished within hours, although Cannon was retained as First Counselor."[23] Supporting this perception is a comment from Elder John Henry Smith of the Twelve (recorded September 6, 1898): "I was sent for by President Lorenzo Snow to go to his room in the Temple. . . . He said he thought the church owed three millions of dollars. He also said he did not agree with President George Q. Cannon's business methods. He said the load seemed more than he could carry."[24] Elder Heber J. Grant recorded a similar remark from President Snow: "President Cannon knows that I do not approve of his methods of running into debt. Nearly all of his schemes where the Church has run into debt there has been a failure, and I have felt that the Lord did not approve."[25]

President Snow also soon found that the financial records of the past First Presidency were in disarray and almost useless to him, so he called for the help of Elder Rudger Clawson, the new member of the Twelve and a friend, protégé, and experienced bookkeeper and auditor: "[I] met [with] President Snow," he wrote. "He said that he wanted me to get up a set of books showing forth the condition of the Church in a condensed form for his personal use, that he might be posted each week as to the exact financial situation. He wanted this work to commence with the beginning of his administration as President of the Church and said that I could get all the information needed from James Jack, head clerk in the President's office. I said in reply that I thought I knew just what he wanted and would be pleased to undertake the work immediately."[26] Very soon President Snow found he needed even more and better information than that: "In a brief interview with Pres. Snow, he said he wished me to leave the work I am at present engaged on and get him up a condensed statement of the entire receipts and disbursements of the Church, commencing with the year 1898, which I promised to do."[27]

The largest immediate measure enacted by President Snow as a temporary solution was to issue bonds in the name of the Church. This move would at least give him time to find better and more permanent solutions for paying off the Church's pressing debts. In a meeting of the leading councils on December 1, 1898, the matter was thoroughly deliberated:

> President Snow submitted for the consideration of the brethren the proposed plan of getting out an issue of $500,000 in bonds to meet a portion of the Church indebtedness. Said bonds to be placed among the Latter-day Saints; payable in 11 years at 6% per annum. A fund to be created to pay bonds at maturity and also to pay the interest half-yearly. The Presidency had given the matter some attention and thought it feasible. . . . Some discussion ensued. It was stated by Bishop John R. Winder upon request for information that the income of the Church at present is about $600,000 and the running expenses about $400,000. President Cannon spoke in favor of the motion as made by himself. President Snow explained the financial condition of the Church, saying that it was heavily involved, the indebtedness being about $1,500,000 and every effort should be made to cancel same. . . . It was moved and carried by unanimous vote that bonds to the amount of $500,000 be issued by the Church.[28]

On January 1, 1899, the first series (A) of the bond issue of a half million dollars arrived at President Snow's office, and the bonds were thereafter quickly sold by the Deseret National Bank. President Snow took part of a day and signed all of them.[29] It was also at this time that he learned for the first time of forty thousand dollars immediately due to English investors in the Church's electric power company, as well as the full scope of the Church's legal obligation:

> President Snow then answered in regard to raising the $40,000, that whatever was right for him to do, he would do, but it was with the greatest reluctance that he entertained the proposition at all. It was a new piece of business to him, something that he did not expect to meet, and he did not think that he should become responsible for this enterprise, as he did not like to take upon himself any more burdens than necessary. But he was willing the matter should go before the Apostles, and whatever was agreed upon in council he would do; but he was not willing to assume the whole responsibility. He felt it to be due to his brethren the Apostles that they should understand this matter, as well as himself, and he felt that the Lord required of the First Presidency that they make the necessary explanations to the Apostles, so that both councils might have a common understanding in relation to the matter, and in fact, all other matters pertaining to the interests of the Church. Referring to the means about to be realized from the sale of the Church bonds, the President said that he had made up his mind that these proceeds should not be used for any other purposes than the debts of the Church.[30]

At a second follow-up meeting of the First Presidency and Twelve on the fourth, it was decided to pay the forty thousand owed; also,

> President Snow stated that it was thought to be desirable to make a second issue of bonds to the amount of $500,000. The first issue had been rapidly taken up, and the second issue, if made, would doubtless find a market. The money, he said, would be needed by the Church. The matter was then submitted to the Brethren. It was moved by Elder John H. Smith and seconded by that the second issue of bonds for $500,000 be made. Carried by unanimous vote. Pres. Snow stated that the Church would be called upon tomorrow . . . to pay $45,000 interest on certain bonds of the Pioneer Power Co. After some explanations were offered showing the relationship of the Church to said company, it was decided by unanimous vote to pay said amount.[31]

A previously formulated plan had been for President Cannon's charismatic but erratic son Frank J. Cannon to act in behalf of the Church in selling the proposed bonds to eastern capitalists, an idea that some thought would be more successful than trying to sell the bonds "at home" in Utah. Some of the Brethren, including Elder John Henry Smith and President Joseph F. Smith, strongly disagreed. President Smith's son Joseph Fielding Smith wrote of the incident from his perspective:

> At this particular time a certain unscrupulous person who had the ear of some of the authorities and the possession of an oily tongue, tried to convince the brethren that these bonds could not be sold locally and would have to be disposed of in the east to certain financial firms. He volunteered his services to sell these bonds, but of course, with the understanding that he was to receive a very handsome commission. By his energy and flattering persuasion he almost accomplished his purpose and was able to convert many of the brethren to his way of thinking. To this proposition President Smith strenuously objected, taking the ground that there was no reason to fear that these bonds could not be sold at home and that too without paying any man a commission. "I opposed it," said President Smith, "and voted against it. I was opposed to giving a commission at all, and thought the bonds should be sold at home." Notwithstanding his strenuous objection, action was taken and it was agreed that this proposition should be accepted. Later, by earnest pleading, President Smith convinced President Lorenzo Snow that such a course was erroneous and it would be well to first try his plan, that of disposing of the bonds at home.[32]

With the million dollars' worth of bonds sold, President Snow had on hand enough money to meet the immediate debt payments hanging over his head as Trustee-in-trust for the Church, but he knew well that the real solution was yet to be found; the problems had only been postponed by the bonds. At a January 5 temple meeting of the Brethren, a suggestion was made by one of the apostles that the financial condition and circumstances of the Church be shared with the membership assembled in general conference, something that had been done to some extent in the past by Presidents Young and Taylor, but that had ceased with the polygamy persecutions. President Snow, while in favor of careful auditing and financial controls, and with generalized disclosures, did not agree with informing members of the Church of the specifics:

> President Snow remarked that he was glad this matter had been brought up. He thought it of the highest importance that an auditing committee should be appointed, not only in justice to himself, but in justice to the

> Church. He held that at the close of every [presidents] administration of this Church the financial affairs thereof from the beginning to the end of that administration should be audited. He would most assuredly expect this to be done at the end of his administration and this Council to judge of them righteously and generously. He thought, too, that the Lord required that such a committee be appointed. But as to presenting the affairs of the Church before the general public, that was another question entirely. [He felt] The committee might go before the people and speak in general terms of the Church's condition. The President went on to say in further justification of the appointment of an auditing committee, that things which could be satisfactorily explained while men were living, might be very difficult to explain after their death. He himself was to a certain extent in the dark regarding the Church's financial condition, and he thought nobody could be hurt, but great benefit derived from the appointment of such a [auditing] committee.[33]
>
> (President Snow named several of the apostles to comprise the committee, to review and clarify the Church's financial books. Elder Clawson did most of the work.[34])

The subject then changed to methods that were being implemented by President Snow to reduce Church expenditures:

> The question of the recent reduction in salaries of Church officials and employees was also discussed, and the reasons given why such a step had been deemed necessary. The present limits had been set for the sake of retrenchment [spending cutbacks] and to assist in getting the Church out of debt. Speaking upon this subject, President Snow said that while he understood the Apostles' salaries were to be reduced, he also understood that they were not to be reduced below what was actually necessary for their support; and now, he added, "Whenever any one of the Twelve Apostles come to the Presidency and tell them that what they are receiving is not enough, their wants will be supplied at once." He believed that where brethren gave their time to the Church, their needs should be supplied. Retrenchment should be made in the building of churches [meetinghouses], etc., and not in what men needed to eat.

President Joseph F. Smith also spoke in favor of the committee, giving as reasons "the protection of President Snow. . . . [And] for the protection of the ex-First Presidency. No doubt mistakes had been made—the building of Saltair [a resort located at the South end of the Great Salt lake] for instance; but he would say that the object in building that resort was that the Latter-day Saints might have a place of recreation under their own control."[35] President Smith went on to explain that he had been paid a thousand dollars a year for eight years of work done in the Church's employ, but mistakes in the accounting books showed him owing all the money back. He "also referred to the defective manner in which the books of the Trustee-in-trust were kept." Further, "He did not think that the office of Apostle should call for a certain salary, but he did think that the Apostles should be compensated by the Church and that each one should know what he could expect to receive, and govern himself accordingly."[36]

The Revelation on Tithing

The precarious financial condition of the Church continued to be the main concern and priority of the First Presidency and all of the Brethren. Many hours and meetings were spent pondering and praying and searching for solutions and relief. Then a sign came that the tide was about to turn. During an early April 1899 quarterly meeting of the Quorum of the Twelve, at which the First Presidency was not present, Elder Francis M. Lyman, one of its senior members, "said the way would open up for the relief of the brethren from financial embarrassment and also that the Church would be relieved. Said he felt that there was going to be a great change in the financial condition of the Church. The stand that Pres. Snow is taking is the beginning of a great revolution. It will be but a little time when we may look for an increase of faith in the hearts of all. There will be an increase in the tithing. A wonderful change is coming." Such a positive prophecy during a time of gloom was unlooked for, yet heartening to those present. At this same meeting, Elder Clawson stated: "The Spirit bore testimony to me that the prophecies uttered by the brethren while we have been together would be fulfilled."[37] A transformation was coming, and they felt an assurance.

A few days later at the conclusion of the April 1899 general conference, President Snow addressed a special meeting of the General Authorities and stake and ward leadership, telling them, "The Church was in debt, and it was for the Church to get out of debt as soon as possible, and remain out." Stake presidencies were told "that it would be expected of such brethren that they would work for the interest of the Church as much as possible without compensation; but in cases where they needed assistance it was expected that they would write to the First Presidency, stating how much they would need, and provision would then be made for them to draw accordingly."[38] After the meeting President Snow invited this same group, with their wives and families, to Saltair beach for some recreation and relaxation.

Later in the month, the First Presidency and Twelve met in a special meeting to consider whether to sell off some Church-owned real estate and discussed the advisability and feasibility of owning properties that, though they may have some investment potential, were not central to the main purposes of the Church. "His view," President Snow said, "was similar to that of the brethren—we should hold on to our enterprises." But at the same time, "The present indebtedness of the Church, he remarked, amounted to about $2,000,000 and in order to meet this stupendous obligation, matters would have to be managed carefully."[39] Further, he said, "The question was, how much [land] should we have and try to get today. With regard to holding on to the properties under consideration, the only question with him was, were we able to do it. . . . The Lord had said it was not right to run into debt, even to build temples. . . . [President Snow] did not like this way of doing business, that is, by going into debt, for it placed us in the power of men who might injure us, if they felt so disposed. He believed in holding on, but he did not believe, while holding on like grim death, in getting more and more and getting so much as to be obliged perhaps to let everything go at a sacrifice. His great aim and object was to get the Church out of debt, and being imbued with this feeling he shrank from taking upon himself further responsibilities, unless it was absolutely necessary to do so."[40] Part of the reason President Snow expressed himself so strongly on this point was to curb the ambitious instincts of two of the Brethren, President Cannon and Elder Heber J. Grant, who were both adept at finding ways to spend a dollar, even if it meant borrowing it.

By April 26, an inspiration had come to President Snow.[41] He sent for Presiding Bishop Preston, and "informed the Bishop that he had concluded to visit the [Southern Utah] settlements by carriage conveyance as President Young used to do, and asked him to see what would be necessary in the line of furnishing carriages to go as far south as St. George."[42] (During the 1860–70s, Elder Snow had been on many excursions through Southern Utah with President Young.) At the May 4 meeting of the First Presidency and Twelve, President Snow told the Brethren he had received an invitation to dedicate a new stake tabernacle in the Summit [Coalville, Utah, area] Stake, and had decided to accept. He also "stated a trip by the Presidency and some members of the Twelve through the southern settlements to St. George was in contemplation."[43]

Plans were underway and invitations extended. Not everyone President Snow invited was able to go, so eventually a smaller party was assembled than originally anticipated. LeRoi C. Snow had just returned from his

The Summit Stake Tabernacle in Coalville, Utah. It was completed and dedicated in 1899 but torn down in 1971. (USHS)

mission in early March and had been put to work as a private secretary or assistant to his father, and also as chief tithing clerk in the President's Office.[44] For this trip he also functioned as a "special correspondent" (meaning a temporary reporter) for the *Deseret News*. His shorthand reporting skills would prove valuable in providing the newspaper with verbatim accounts of his father's and other General Authorities' talks.

Orson Whitney found a way for his own son to be included: "I introduced my son Horace to President Snow, at the latter's home, and seconded a request from the *Salt Lake Herald* that he be allowed to accompany the President and his party on their contemplated trip to St. George. The President kindly consented."[45] Horace (or Race) had been working at the paper for only three months, but the arrangement proved successful.

Arthur Winter, a young clerk and reporter in the President's Office, was also assigned to accompany the Brethren. He recorded: "Sunday, May 14, 1899; I took the 7 a.m. train for Coalville where conference of Summit Stake is to be held today and tomorrow. President Snow, President Richards, Brother George Teasdale, LeRoi C. Snow and myself constituted the visiting party. We reached Coalville at 10:15, and went directly to the Tabernacle, which was dedicated this morning by President Snow. It is just completed after being in the course of construction for over 20 years. It is now one of the best meetinghouses in the Church. . . . President Snow and a party of brethren and sisters (of which I expect to be one) expect to leave tomorrow evening on a trip to St. George and other southern settlements, and on this account President Snow found it impracticable to remain over at Coalville for tomorrow's meetings. He, President Richards, LeRoi Snow and myself left Coalville at 11 o'clock this evening."[46]

Since Arthur Winter's journal account of the trip south is the most detailed and explanatory available, we quote further from it:[47]

> [Monday, May 15, 1899] At 5:30 this evening I started with President Snow and party on a trip to St. George. The party consisted of President Snow and wife and son (LeRoi), President Joseph F. Smith and wife, President Franklin D. Richards and wife, Apostle Francis M. Lyman and wife, Apostle Abraham O. Woodruff and wife, President Seymour B. Young, Presiding Bishop William B. Preston, William B. Dougall and myself. Horace Whitney (son of Bishop Orson F. Whitney) was also along as a representative of the *Herald*. A Pullman car (the first, it is said, that was ever on this line) was specially attached to the train, so that we could have sleeping berths if we desired. We rode in that, and were very comfortable. Sister Taylor, who keeps the eating house at Juab, telegraphed an invitation for the party to stop at Juab and eat. When we arrived there, at 9 o'clock, we found an excellent meal prepared.
>
> [Tuesday, May 16, 1899] We arrived at Modena (which is on the new Utah and Pacific line) at 8:15. This is the end of the railroad part of our journey. We found awaiting us teams and carriages from St. George, also three teams and carriages which had been sent on ahead from Salt Lake. Brothers McHenry, Reese and Kingsbury were along to drive the last mentioned teams. We breakfasted in the section cars, and at 9 o'clock started on our journey by team.
>
> We reached Fort Hamblin at 12:30. I rode in a covered spring wagon, with Horace Whitney, our driver being a young man named West. Just before we got to Hamblin we changed our team, and Brother Isaac West, of Washington, (uncle to our first driver) took charge of us. We stayed at Hamblin upwards of an hour, and had dinner at Sister Canfield's. Resumed our journey at 2 o'clock. . . .
>
> It was quite cold when we left Modena, but as we traveled along it became warmer. We reached St. George at 7:30 p.m., having made the trip with nine hours of actual traveling. . . . The road was pretty good, except the last ten miles. The last four or five miles the road was very dusty and rocky. We got literally covered with the red dust of "Dixie."
>
> The whole trip from Salt Lake to St. George occupied 26 hours. It has never been done before in that time, so far as anyone knew. We found the weather quite pleasant in St. George. They have had it very warm, but a cool spell is on now, for which we were not sorry. It is very dry, and has been a long time. We were glad to get to bed and rest, for the journey was quite fatiguing.[48]

The visit of President Snow and the accompanying party of General Authorities had been advertised in St. George, and for many of these settlers it was the "most notable event in the history of this stake." Businesses were closed, streets were lined with wagons from outlying settlements, and

The St. George Tabernacle was completed in 1875 and built of red sandstone by the architect Truman O. Angell. It was restored in 1993. (USHS)

the day was made a general holiday. "The President's journey from Salt Lake in twenty-six hours is the one subject discussed by old residents," the *Herald* noted, "The time was never before equaled."[49]

The next morning, May 17, the first session of stake conference started at 10:00 a.m. The St. George Stake Tabernacle was filled to capacity. Because of their revelatory and historical importance, events of this meeting are here recounted as thoroughly as possible. There was an opening song, prayer, and another hymn. Then President Snow spoke to the people for forty-seven minutes.[50] It was while giving this sermon that he received a spiritual manifestation, probably in the form of a vision,[51] in which the Lord mainly reaffirmed the commandment that every member of the Church should pay a full and honest tithe, though further related concepts were conveyed.

No prophet receives such a revelation without the powerful presence of the Holy Ghost, but the records are not uniform as to whether President Snow himself may have been transfigured or otherwise spiritually illuminated before some in the congregation.[52] (His son LeRoi recorded nothing about witnessing such a scene at the time, but it is evident that by thirty-five years later he believed his father was transfigured during a pause in his remarks.[53]) Involvement in such matters is often directly correlated to the spiritual maturity of those in attendance and can vary widely. In this case, the diverse experiences and feelings of the assembled witnesses to his talk cannot now be known.

No complete verbatim record of this talk is known to exist (nor is there any known formally prepared description of the manifestation); however, minutes, summaries, and brief quotations from it were written by various attendees and preserved; from these can be assembled a partial account of what President Snow said on this now-famous occasion.[54]

Below is the best possible amalgamation of the discourse from available sources:

> [Minutes] President Lorenzo Snow had not words to express his gratitude for this privilege, his first visit for thirteen years. He could scarcely express the reason why we came, yet he felt reassured the Lord would have somewhat to say to us. He was pleased that there were no rich men

The interior of the St. George Tabernacle during a meeting. Imagine President Snow speaking at the pulpit. (USHS)

here. He referred to the manner Pres. Young called such as were wanted to come to settle this land and it is a pleasure to think of the many obstacles that had been overcome, and how much has been accomplished. Spoke of deprivations endured and successes realized of far more value than temporal riches.

[*Deseret News*] President Snow, the first speaker, said he had not words to express his joy in visiting the people here. It is thirteen years since he was here. He and his brethren had come to visit the Saints, and in the name of the Lord to instruct the people, and tell them the will of the Lord.

[*Herald*] "I remember well the settlement of St. George. A sturdy people was needed to contend with this rough region and every man who came through the inspired selection of Brigham Young was rough and ready, sturdy and strong. It is a satisfaction to behold those same faces today never wavering in their glorious faith. You were not expected to become rich but you have made a great success. You are nearer a celestial world perhaps than those Saints of any other part of the world in proportion to your number."

[*Deseret News*] "I am glad," said the President, "that there are no rich men among you. I remember well when President Young called some of the best people among us to colonize these parts. You were not sent here to get rich, but to prepare yourselves to enter the kingdom of God. To go to heaven we must first learn to obey the laws of heaven and we shall approach God's kingdom just as fast as we learn to obey his laws. We are going back to Zion, but we must first establish Zion within our hearts before we can go there. We must learn to pay a full and honest tithing. If all the Saints would do this we should not hear a cry for employment and in doing this we shall be making the preparation that the Lord requires of us."

[Minutes] He referred to parties leaving here but except they have been properly called, those staying will be better off. To honor our beings we must obey the voice of the good spirit and thereby prepare ourselves to inherit the highest degree of glory. In our present lives immense and glorious chances to acquaint ourselves with those doctrines which will prepare us to act consistently before heaven are given. Soon some of us may be called to build up the center stake and from some of the present cities of Zion will there be so many called to that work as St. George and this locality. Speaker wanted the people around here to prepare to go [to] Zion.

[Annals] President Lorenzo Snow greeted the assembly. Stated he was here thirteen years ago. Dwelt upon the theme of going to Jackson County. He declared there was no region where so large a proportion of

> the Latter-day Saints will be called to go to that favored land as would be called from this Southern Mission. He said, "I want the people of St. George to prepare themselves to go to Jackson County"
>
> [*Herald*] Continuing he said we are surely going to Zion in Jackson county sooner than some of us anticipate. There is no doubt about it. The time is close at hand and I want you to prepare yourselves. The call may be limited but no city or settlement will provide more men than St. George if you remain faithful.

(It seems plausible that at this point in the discourse, President Snow received the revelation from the Lord regarding reemphasis on the payment of tithing.)

> [Minutes] The poor are found on tithing books to be the most generous—he believed that those in this vicinity pay the highest amount. Touched upon the selfishness of the saints in this matter in the early history of the Church. He was astonished at the present reticence in this respect even in the most exemplary wards. He wished a strict observance of this principle—the payment of a full tithing. This is an essential preparation for Zion that our enemies may not be suffered again to drive the inhabitants. As the stones were each fitted to take their place in the temple of Solomon, so must those be fitted to take their place in the building of the Center Stake.
>
> [*Herald*] The president referred to the necessity of paying a full tithe and congratulated the community upon its past record which he hoped would be maintained.
>
> [Annals] He dwelt upon the principle of tithing and declared, "The poor people are the most faithful in paying their tithing, according to their means." He said wards, as a rule, pay, not to exceed one-half tithing.
>
> [Minutes] He deprecated the incongruities found in the society of the saints—some rich some poor—the former living in affluence, the other in apparently adverse circumstances. It will not be so in Zion. The Lord is coming soon and he wanted to see the people prepared for Him.
>
> [Minutes] This is the word of the Lord to all the people of this church. He asked God's blessing upon us.
>
> [*Deseret News*] The President invoked the blessings of the Lord upon the people.[55]

After a rest hymn, A. Owen Woodruff, Franklin D. Richards, and LeRoi Snow were the final speakers at that session. It is not known whether President Snow spoke to any of the other Brethren specifically about his

Interior of the St. George Tabernacle, with a view from the pulpit that President Snow would have had. (USHS)

revelatory experience between sessions, but at the 2:00 p.m. meeting, President Joseph F. Smith spoke for a half hour on tithing, as did Presiding Bishop Preston, with a few other Brethren closing out the remarks. Either something was said, or these leaders had the sense to recognize, build upon, and echo the concluding point about tithing that President Snow had made.[56]

That night President Snow (who stayed at the stake president's home) had time to ponder on the revelation he had been given and more fully comprehend and appreciate the message—the marvelous solution—it contained. The next day he met in the tabernacle with the Sunday School, addressing them briefly.

"President Snow wished the little ones to regularly attend to prayers and 'if at any time absent from father and mother difficulties surround you or you may lack understanding on any matter apply to our Father in heaven and obtain what you seek. Always obey father and mother no matter how old you may be. I shall shake hands with each and all children present so that they may be able to say that they have shaken hands with a man who has shaken hands with a man who saw God face to face while in the flesh, Joseph Smith, the prophet standing at the head of this dispensation.' The children marched single file by classes, by President Snow, each one shook hands with him and glancing upward saw his face. He kissed the babies. 836 persons passed by in thirty minutes."[57]

At the 10:00 a.m. session, Arthur Winter spoke, recording that "President Snow called upon me to speak first. I was very much surprised and somewhat embarrassed, but I spoke about ten minutes and felt pretty well."[58] Then Elder Lyman spoke on tithing, followed by President Richards. A comment in President Richards's talk assists with further identification of when the revelation came to President Snow: "I have been deeply interested, as no doubt you all have been, while listening to the very interesting remarks that have been made. As a people we have been passed in review, by which we have been enabled to notice and consider several different phases of our existence both as a Church and as individuals. . . . We want to be true and faithful on this subject of tithing; and, as President Snow *presented to us yesterday morning* in such lovely terms, we want to get up to this line of paying an honest, straightforward tithing. He wants to see it in all Israel, you and I want to see it."[59]

"At the close of morning service," the *Annals of the Southern Utah Mission* tell us, "Presidents Lorenzo Snow and Joseph F. Smith, Presiding Bishop Preston, and the Presidency of the St. George Stake went into the Stake Office, where President Lorenzo Snow set apart" some priesthood leaders for various local stake purposes.

At 2:00 p.m. on May 18, the final session of the stake conference convened. William Dougall spoke first and was followed by President Lorenzo Snow, who then gave perhaps the most influential address of his prophetic ministry and probably his life. (The published report does not mention it, but his forty minute discourse was evidently interrupted at some point with a solo sung by a local member.[60]) President Snow began by referring to the revelation in the Doctrine and Covenants reviewing the occasion wherein the resurrected Jesus appeared to Joseph Smith and Oliver Cowdery in the Kirtland Temple in 1836. He referred to the blessings God had poured out upon the Saints and also to the sacrifices they must be willing to make—following the example of Jesus who suffered more than all others for our sins. Then he came to the heart of the subject:

> I come here now with my brethren that you may understand what is required of you as a people under the peculiar conditions in which the

> Church is now placed. It is the word of the Lord to you, my brethren and sisters, that you should conform to that which is required of you as a people who have these glorious prospects of exaltation and glory before you. What is it? Why, it is something that has been drummed into your ears from time to time until you perhaps have got tired of hearing it. I need the faith and the prayers of every Latter-day Saint; no man needs them any more than I do; and it is unpleasant for me to say things that would in any way diminish the exercise of your faith and prayers in my behalf. But the Lord requires me to say something to you, and since I commenced to labor in His interest, I have never failed, thank the Lord, to do that which He has required at my hands; and I shall not do it today, nor any other day, the Lord being my helper. The word of the Lord to you is not anything new; it is simply this: THE TIME HAS NOW COME FOR EVERY LATTER-DAY SAINT, WHO CALCULATES TO BE PREPARED FOR THE FUTURE AND TO HOLD HIS FEET STRONG UPON A PROPER FOUNDATION, TO DO THE WILL OF THE LORD AND TO PAY HIS TITHING IN FULL. That is the word of the Lord to you, and it will be the word of the Lord to every settlement throughout the land of Zion. After I leave you and you get to thinking about this, you will see yourselves that the time has come when every man should stand up and pay his tithing in full. The Lord has blessed us and has had mercy upon us in the past; but there are times coming when the Lord requires us to stand up and do that which He has commanded and not leave it any longer. What I say to you in this Stake of Zion I will say to every Stake of Zion that has been organized. There is no man or woman that now hears what I am saying who will feel satisfied if he or she fails to pay a full tithing.[61]

After this powerful pronouncement, President Snow went on to counsel the children to be taught to pay their tithing, and the Lord would bless them to live long lives; and he also spoke about plural marriage, forcefully denying that he had authorized any plural marriages whatsoever during his administration as President of the Church. (The *Herald* report missed the import of the tithing emphasis and lead with a headline about the prophet's denial of further plural marriages.[62]) President Snow had now had time enough to fully comprehend what the Lord wanted him to tell the Latter-day Saints. The main published report of the conference in the *Deseret News* and *Millennial Star* was taken down by LeRoi Snow in shorthand.

Arthur Winter, also present and also adept at this form of speed-writing, recorded a slightly different version of the main capitalized statement:

"The word of the Lord is now for every Latter-day Saint who calculates to be prepared for the future and to hold his feet strong upon a proper foundation, to do the will of the Lord and to pay his tithing in full."[63] Since Winter was the officially assigned Church reporter and stenographer, a strong case could be made that his version, rather than LeRoi's (from the *Deseret News*), represents the authorized wording of the announcement, although the accounts are so close it matters little.

President Snow was followed by President Smith, and then the session closed. Arthur Winter wrote his impressions of the meeting and perhaps some further insight he had obtained: "At this meeting President Snow told the people plainly that the word of the Lord to every man, woman and child of the Latter-day Saints was to pay a full tithing. The Lord had made this manifest to him, and he gave it to the saints as the word and will of the Lord, which would be carried to every Stake in Zion."[64] At a meeting held a week later in the small town of Holden, Utah, President Snow clarified *when* the revelation was given to him: "When we left Salt Lake we did not know just what we were going to visit these southern settlements for, but it was *clearly manifested in the first meeting* in St. George. The Lord has sent us here for a special purpose."[65] The reason such timing clarification becomes significant is two-fold: First, the June 2, 1899, edition of the *Deseret News* in which the full discourse was published contained a typo that dropped a *1*, turning May 18 into May 8. That error was perpetuated in the Church's European periodical, The *Latter-day Saints' Millennial Star*, and has since regrettably been carried into many published histories and articles mentioning this tithing revelation episode.[66] Secondly, LeRoi Snow's published accounts of the trip to St. George contain some substantial inaccuracies and narrations that, according to the best contemporary evidence available, cannot be corroborated and in some instances are contradicted.

The Movie *The Windows of Heaven*

These historical problems have been magnified and continued over generations of Latter-day Saints' perceptions because they were woven into the screenplay and plot of a well-known and oft-seen Brigham Young University–produced movie titled *The Windows of Heaven*, that used LeRoi Snow's articles as its research and information basis. The most egregious issue is that this film, as well as LeRoi's articles, contains recurring references, as a major subplot, to an unsubstantiated prophecy, or promise, allegedly uttered by President Snow during this conference.

LeRoi Snow wrote in a *Church News* article: "President Snow told the people that if they would observe the law of tithing, from then on, and pay a full tithing, that they might go ahead, plow their land and plant the seed; and he promised them, in the name of the Lord, that the clouds would gather and rains from heaven descend, and their lands would be drenched, and the rivers and ditches filled, and they would reap a bounteous harvest that very season."[67] Some four and a half years later, in an *Improvement Era* article, LeRoi wrote that his father said on this same occasion, "That if they would observe the law of tithing from then on, and pay a full and honest tithing, that they might go ahead, plough their land and plant the seed. And he promised them, in the name of the Lord, that the clouds would gather, the rains from heaven descend, their lands would be drenched, and the rivers and ditches filled, and they would reap a bounteous harvest that very season."[68] Three years later, in another *Church News* article, he quoted again the same words from his *Improvement Era* article.[69] Other unsubstantiated elements from the articles and film include President Snow praying earnestly when it did not rain soon after his return to Salt Lake City; that he had St. George area weather reports brought to him daily, that LeRoi received a telegram meant for his father announcing that it had rained in St. George (on August 2); that the rivers and ditches had been filled with heaven-sent rainwater; and that in response to this good news, his father had uttered a humble prayer of gratitude that his prophecy had been vindicated—prayers LeRoi somehow could quote verbatim over three decades later.

The trouble is that most of these mentioned items almost certainly never took place, at least as portrayed by the movie and in LeRoi's writings. President Snow did indeed receive a powerful manifestation from God regarding tithing payment; a worrisome and lengthy drought was in progress; President Snow's traveling party did observe the dry and arid ground as they crossed it, noticing that livestock and crops were dying off; and it *was* a major topic of local concern. But no reliable contemporary record of this alleged prophecy has been located for that conference or with such details. In his writings, LeRoi did not place quotation marks around these "tithing-for-rain" statements, as he did the quotations he could verify from extant records. The only prophecies that can be located in President Snow's addresses to the people during May 17 and 18, 1899, relate to the Lord sanctifying the land to the people, returning to Zion, God's forgiveness of past sins of neglecting to pay tithing, and general prosperity if the people will repent and begin paying their tithing; also, a prophecy of a railroad eventually being built from Salt Lake City to St. George.

A little rain did fall in the area on June 2, and more fell on August 2 (about two inches), but this resulted in only slight and temporary relief from the drought—and thankfully allowed for a few crops to be harvested that year, though it was 30 percent worse or more than the average yield.[70] But rivers and ditches were not filled; the rains did not continue; a bounteous harvest was not reaped that year. As the August 2 newspaper report indicated (that LeRoi himself quoted), "every drop . . . went into the parched earth." That particular drought cycle continued for twenty-one more months before a sizeable amount of snow and rain fell, and even then dry conditions returned.[71] St. George is located in a desert climate and normally receives arid, desert-like moisture amounts, some years receiving more precipitation, others less.[72]

Having corrected the record, it should be noted that President Snow did make some limited general prophecies or promises at various times to the Latter-day Saints relative to strict tithing payment, obedience to the commandments, repentance, and faith in God, and their likely reception of the blessings of moisture, crops, and spiritual and temporal prosperity—even to the St. George Saints.

The following March—nine months later—when President Snow learned during a meeting of the First Presidency and Twelve that a member of the First Council of the Seventy had been assigned to visit the St. George Stake for their upcoming conference, he uttered the closest thing to a prophecy of temporal betterment based on faithful tithing payment (for that stake) that can be found. In a meeting, "It was stated that Elder Seymour B. Young [later changed to Joseph McMurrin] would be present at the St. George Conference and President Snow stated that he desired that one of the Brethren of the Apostles also go to that conference. The southern country had been afflicted with drought, so much so that not only have they raised no crops, but their cattle have died for the lack of drinking water. Brother Lyman signified his willingness to go. The President then told Brother Lyman to tell the people not to waver in their faith, but to pray fervently to the Lord for the necessary moisture, and he believed that the Lord would hear their prayers inasmuch as they strictly adhered to the law of tithing."[73]

After the conference, the *Herald* reported that in St. George, "The stake quarterly conference closed yesterday, after a series of very interesting meetings. Apostle Francis M. Lyman and President Joseph W. McMurrin of the seventies quorum were present, together with the members of the stake presidency. . . . The St. George stake has made considerable advance in the matter of tithing. . . . The drought was a special topic and the greatest economy was urged and the people were told to be of good faith, that the county was to yet be a place of great fruitfulness and productivity, and it was stated that President Lorenzo Snow looked for a bright future for this section, and that the Prophet Brigham Young was not mistaken when he undertook to settle Dixie."[74] Back in Salt Lake City in the meeting of the First Presidency and Twelve, "Elder Francis M. Lyman reported his visit to the St. George Stake Conference. He said the people had suffered greatly from drought, but the people, with but few exceptions, were feeling remarkably well."[75]

Some two years after President Snow's visit to St. George, at a birthday celebration for President Snow, the St. George Temple president, David H. Cannon (a younger brother of President George Q. Cannon), in making brief comments in company with several other guests, was reported by one of the other Brethren present to have remembered that, "Pres. Snow had promised the people of the St. George country that, if they were faithful in honoring the law of tithing and other commandments of God, they should be visited by the early and latter rains [an allusion to James 5:7]. This promise had been literally fulfilled, for a recent drought of some 5 years had been broken by copious rains."[76] Without verification of wording, date, and circumstances, this later third-hand remark remains indefinite and inconclusive.

CHAPTER 19

TEACHING TITHING IN SOUTHERN UTAH AND SALT LAKE CITY

Preaching Tithing on the Return Trip to Salt Lake City

After the meeting" in which full tithing payment was so forcefully taught, recorded Arthur Winter, "we went down to the temple and passed through the building and on to the roof, from which we got a splendid view of St. George."[1] The much longer journey back to Salt Lake City is recounted best in newspaper reports and Arthur Winter's journal. It is not an easy trip to track, with some changes in plans, impromptu meetings, a buggy race with the Prophet, and over two dozen meetings in the small towns and settlements dotting the long road home. The first stop was "at Washington while President Snow shook hands with the children and people, and then proceeded on to Leeds, where we stopped again for President Snow to shake hands with those gathered. Continuing our journey, which was very dusty, we reached Toquerville at 12:40. The children were formed in line as we entered the principal street, and as we passed they shouted in chorus, 'Welcome to President Snow and company.' The weather turned quite cool, and a little rain fell about 2 o'clock. Meeting was held here at 3 o'clock. The speakers were President Snow (for a half hour, on tithing), President Richards, President Smith, F. M. Lyman and A. O. Woodruff."[2]

Here, among other remarks, President Snow advised, "When we call you to the ministry, or to take charge of a ward, or a stake, or any matter of importance, we want to ask you if you have paid your full tithing, and we want to hear the answer that you have."[3] He also said: "Many of the Saints have neglected to pay tithing and it is my duty to talk upon this principle, and I want you to understand exactly what I mean. The Lord wishes you to pay your tithing. We have glorious prospects. We should prepare ourselves for the other life. There is not a long distance between here and heaven; we must first establish heaven within our hearts before we arrive there. I expect to see you and rejoice with you after this life."[4] President Franklin D. Richards also spoke, referring to one of the main reasons tithe payment had stopped in the Church: "When our property was being taken from us, many said they would pay no more tithing to go out of our hands; there is no such excuse now. The Saints are now gaining confidence in the use that is made of the tithing. We should have perfect confidence in each other and in God. The time will come when men will not be placed in responsible positions unless they pay an honest tithing. In paying tithing we should be honest to ourselves and honest to God. I received this same principle from the Prophet Joseph himself."[5]

Continuing, "We left Toquerville this morning promptly at 8 o'clock. The road was very rocky and rough as far as Belleview. We reached Kanarra at 12:30. The Sunday school children were out to greet the party. Held meeting here until 4 o'clock, when we started for Cedar City. Just before we reached Cedar City a body of horsemen met the party and escorted us into town, where the Sunday school children were lined up on either side of the street." This was one of many occasions when local Church members had made plans that President Snow felt to change, from entertainment to the newly commanded tithing meetings: "An entertainment and social had been arranged for this evening in honor of President Snow and party, and I went to the tabernacle shortly before 9 expecting to participate in it, but to my surprise I found a regular meeting being held and President Smith talking. It appeared that a change had been made at the last moment."[6]

Along with the twenty-five horsemen, a band met and escorted them into town. Crowds thronged the roads, cheering and waving flags and banners as they rode through town. Meetings were held there and at Kanarra.[7] "Tithing is the principal topic of every meeting, and President Snow gives the word of the Lord to the people on this subject. Left Cedar for Parowan at 3:30. . . . At Summit the children were out and shook hands with President Snow. We reached Parowan at 6 o'clock, sooner than we were expected, and too soon for a reception by the Sunday school children that had been planned."[8] The journey (or mission) continued: "Started soon after 8 for Beaver. . . . Reached Beaver about 2 o'clock. There was quite a demonstration on our arrival. The Sunday school children were out, and a brass band. . . . Meeting was held at 7:30 p.m. An overflow meeting was also held, there not being enough room in the tabernacle to hold all the people."[9] At Beaver President Snow spoke to the people with frankness and power as he immersed himself in his newly commissioned errand:

> We cannot expect success without the Spirit of God in every condition of life. I am thinking much of going to Zion, and I expect to go, even if I have to return from the other life to do so, for that will be the headquarters of the Church of Jesus Christ. There are some things that must be done before we can go to Jackson County, and we want to talk to you tonight about the necessary preparation. There are many things that we do not practice now that we must practice before we can go there. There is one thing that is sadly neglected, and that is the principle of tithing. It is not pleasant to me to talk upon. The Saints are commanded to observe this law and the Lord said those who do not shall not live among the people. The Lord commanded me to present these things to the people. We shall build a temple in Zion and many of them all over this continent; but we cannot go to Zion unless we observe this law. How many of the people here are prepared to go now? Too few. . . .
>
> We have been educated in the law of tithing for sixty-one years, but have not yet learned to observe it. We are in a fearful condition and because of it the Church is in bondage. The only relief is for the Saints to observe this law. I never before thought it to be as I know it is now.
>
> When Solomon's Temple was built, no sound of a tool was heard, everything was prepared beforehand, a long ways off, to lay in place. No Latter-day Saints will go to Jackson county who are not fully prepared beforehand. The time is near when people will be called to go and build up a mighty city. Jesus will come and talk to the people in the Temple there.
>
> We are a strange people and have disturbed the whole world. We must keep the law of tithing to prepare us for the United Order, and until then there will be poverty. In the past men who have never paid tithing have received recommends to the House of the Lord, but they should not in the future. Form a strong resolution to do better in the future, and may God bless you.[10]

Others among the traveling party began to feel a portion of the spiritual power resting upon President Snow. Elder Francis M. Lyman, who had four decades before lived for a time in Beaver, recorded: "I was awakened in the night and the Spirit of the Lord came upon me, bringing to my mind a flood of light and inspiration; unfolding before me my former life and labors in Beaver and in Fillmore with their remarkable experiences. It seemed as if the Spirit would consume my veins within me. I wept tears of joy for a long time until the Spirit withdrew so that I could go back to sleep. I was led to wonder how much joy one could endure in the flesh."[11]

The strenuous pace of the trip continued: "We left Beaver about 8:30

for Kanosh. . . . We lunched at Cove Creek Ranch. There a fort is erected, the like of which I have not seen in this country. . . . Reached Kanosh, about 50 miles from Beaver, about 4 p.m. We found the roads pretty good, and the weather was quite pleasant. . . . Meeting was held at 7:30."[12] "[Then we] left Kanosh about 8:30 for Meadow, about 6 miles north, which place we reached at 9:30 and held meeting at 10. At this meeting President Snow called upon me and told me to say as much as I could in ten minutes. . . . Left Meadow at 1:30 for Fillmore, about 8 miles. Reached there shortly before 3, and had scarcely time to brush up before meeting commenced. The meeting was held in the old State House, which was built, I believe in 1856, when Fillmore was the capital city of Utah. . . . Another meeting was held at 7:30."[13]

The last part of the road to Fillmore was a little more eventful than the other buggy rides had been, though a wearisome pace had continually been maintained: "In all the party traveled 345 miles by rail and about 312 by team; a total of 657 miles with stops of two hours to two days at every town or hamlet on the route. Most of the travel by team was over a rough and untrained country and not one day elapsed that the company did not travel at least thirty miles," reported LeRoi in the *Deseret News*. "Yet President Snow, now in his 86th year, declares that he is in better health than before the journey; that its effect was positively refreshing. . . . The success of the tour has led President Snow to hope that before many weeks the northern settlements, both in Utah and Idaho, will have received the same attention as those of the south." With such positive thinking among the group, President Snow found a competitive spirit rising within him:

> He led the procession of eight or ten conveyances with a spanking team of blacks [horses], the best in the outfit, shipped from Salt Lake. As a rule, the party had some difficulty in maintaining the pace, but upon this occasion the presidents' carriage was jogging along at a most comfortable rate.
>
> President Joseph F. Smith, who was second in line drove alongside the president and suggested: "Perhaps it would be as well to go a trifle faster over these good roads President Snow." "Very well," was the answer, "just follow us." President Snow gave his teamster a knowing nudge and in another minute both teams were on a forty-mile gait over sagebrush and ditches and those behind saw only a cloud of dust with now and then a glimpse of something resembling a buggy top. On and on the horses dashed and the excitement of the occupants increased with every leap; it was invigorating.

> The horses had traveled neck and neck for two miles or more. The eyes of the aged leader flashed like diamonds as he rose in his seat and watched the progress of the race. "Go, go," he shouted, "never mind the ruts. We'll get beat. Go!" And the driver did so. President Smith's team was slightly outclassed and the other managed to maintain the lead. Clumps of sagebrush and five-foot washouts were as pebbles to these venerable leaders, now thoroughly enshrouded in their boyhood days. Up in the air and down, touching a high place here and there, the contest lasted for fifteen miles and President Snow loves to relate how his team came out victorious, though the honors are disputed by President Smith.[14]

Continuing from a *Deseret News* account: "President Snow's party arrived in Fillmore yesterday at 3 pm and was met by several committees from the city and the Church authorities here. . . . A general meeting convened at 3:30. Many of the people could not be accommodated in the meeting house. Tithing was the main principle discussed. The speakers were very plain and free in all they said." Another "meeting commenced at 10:20" the next day. "President Snow said he had been inspired by the Lord to present the law of tithing to the Saints and he intends to visit all the Stakes in Zion and awaken the people to their duty in this regard. The 119th section of the Doctrine and Covenants was read to the meeting. 'If the people whom we have visited will observe this law my life will be preserved and I shall see you all again but if you do not I shall not see you again.'"[15] When interviewed by Race Whitney, "President Snow . . . remarked today that he has not met a man older than himself in the south—insists that he is holding up better than anybody, and his appearance bears out the assertion. If solicited as to his welfare, he will cheerfully reply: 'Never mind me; I am old and tough, and can stand it; But,' he will add, 'do look after these young people. We do not want them sick on our hands.'"[16] They left Fillmore at 8 o'clock and traveled ten miles to Holden.

> President Snow's party was met yesterday morning, on approaching Holden, by an escort of horsemen, who welcomed the President into their town. . . . The building was crowded when meeting commenced at 10 o'clock. During his remarks President Snow said: "When we left Salt Lake we did not know just what we were going to visit these southern settlements for, but it was clearly manifested in the first meeting in St. George. The Lord has sent us here for a special purpose. There is one important command that was given to the Latter-day Saints that has not been observed; it is the law of tithing. Jackson county must be built

up by the Latter-day Saints and the most glorious temple that has ever been erected, where the Lord will talk to His people. You are here not to gain wealth, but to raise families and properly educate them. It is of the highest importance that we are properly educated and prepared to go to Jackson county. Some of the Saints once settled there but because they did not observe the law of consecration, they loved their money much." President Snow read from Sec. 101 of the Doctrine and Covenants: "It is the command of the Lord," continued President Snow, "that we remind the Saints of their duties, I know this. We must pay a full tithing, and we will prosper. If you pay your tithing I know I shall have your prayers; the Lord will sustain me and I shall come and see you again."

After meeting the party took lunch and left at 1:30 o'clock for Scipio, fifteen miles distant. The drive was the first unpleasant one of the entire journey. The wind was so strong that we were riding in clouds of dust almost the entire distance. Notwithstanding the wind, all the children of Scipio, and most of their parents, had gathered along the street to welcome President Snow and his party, who arrived at 3:30. The President paid no heed to the wind but got out of his carriage and shook hands with all of the children, much to their delight.

The evening meeting commenced at 7:30.

During his remarks, President Snow thanked the people for the token of respect they had paid his party in the demonstration they made this afternoon. Reference was made to the importance of punctuality.

"The law of tithing is one of the most important ever revealed to man," said the President; "It was given over 60 years ago. There are certain blessings accompanying the obedience to each principle of the Gospel, while a penalty will follow disobedience. The penalty following disobedience to the law of tithing is that the disobedient shall not live among the people of God. But through obeying this law the blessings of prosperity and success will be given unto the Saints. I wish you to pray for me, because I need your prayers as much as any man living. May God bless the people in this valley."[17]

President Snow's party left Scipio Friday . . . at 8 o'clock. The weather being favorable and the roads smooth, the drive was an enjoyable one. . . .

At 2:30 o'clock the President's party was met by a large body of mounted horsemen and the Nephi brass band, and was escorted into the city. . . .

They then entered the main assembly room which was crowded with children. It was a beautiful sight. After the opening exercises, President Snow arose and said:

> "My dear children, I am overwhelmed with surprise because of the grand reception you have given us, I am satisfied that you will accomplish a vast amount of good. If I can have your faith, I know as well as I know anything that the Lord will bless me and sustain me in discharging the great responsibilities that rest upon me. I love the Latter-day Saints. I love you and have not words to express my gratitude to you. Listen to and respect your teachers in the Priesthood and you shall become great in the Kingdom of God. You have been sent into the world to accomplish great things. Be good, my dear children, honor your parents and many of you will live to be 100 years. Whoever lives twenty-five years will see many very aged people. May the Lord bless you."
>
> President Richards promised the children that some of them, if they would keep the commandments of God, would live to see the Savior.
>
> The evening meeting commenced at 8 o'clock. President Snow was the first speaker. He thanked the people for the great respect they had paid him and his party: "We wish to talk plainly to you as we have certain things to tell you. I wish you to distinctly understand we shall not find fault with you, we do not wish to tell you anything unpleasant, and yet you have been neglectful in one regard. It is in regard to the law of tithing and it is a matter of the highest importance that you understand and obey this law. . . . This law is very plain and simple and yet it has not been conformed to by the Saints. True the Lord has blessed us wonderfully in the past, not because of our disobedience, but we were being educated and the Lord did not expect full obedience to this law in the past; now, however, He does. He requires it of us. I feel that you will follow these sacred instructions."[18]

President Snow also told them: "Men and woman have gone into the holy temple who have never paid one cent of tithing; the Bishops have given recommendations to such persons; and when men have paid only half of their tithing, and perhaps less, and perhaps a little more, they have gone into the temples and administered for their dead friends. Now, we would like to please the people as we have done in the past, and let these things go; but the Lord will not suffer us to do this. He has manifested to us most clearly that this law must be taught to the Latter-day Saints and they must obey it."[19]

The prophet's love and affection had grown for each member of the party throughout their journey. "After this [meeting]," wrote Arthur Winter, "the Tabernacle was cleared, and the company alone had one of the most delightful meetings that I ever had the privilege of being present at. Nephi is the last place we expect to visit on this trip, which will be memorable as the time when the Lord gave his word and will concerning the payment of tithing, and President Snow expressed a desire to have all the company together before we separated for home. The Spirit of the Lord was poured out in power, and the remarks made by President Snow touched every heart. He asked the forgiveness of the Brethren and sisters if he had said or done anything that in any manner hurt them, and said he should expect every one of us to be witnesses that the word and will of the Lord had been given through him on this trip. He expressed the pleasure he had had in our society, and felt to bless us all."[20] At this meeting, President Snow said:

> I do not feel satisfied, my brethren and sisters, to close our visit and scatter without saying a few words. We have had a glorious time, and the Lord has been with us. Now, if anything has been said or done by myself that has not been altogether pleasing to you, I want you to forgive me. The Lord has been with us greatly and manifested His holy will. We have had a revelation from the Lord since we left Salt Lake City, as you all understand. This manifestation that the Lord has given to me, and that you have received and borne testimony to, can never be forgotten. I know it just as well as I know anything that I ever did know. There are different ways in which persons may receive revelations. One way is to receive it powerfully by the Holy Ghost falling upon us. Then there is another way that comes to us just as clearly and just as fully as the way in which the Lord bestowed upon us this revelation, when the Spirit of the Lord rests upon us and fills us from the crown of our head to the soles of our feet. Now, this which I have received was not with the power of God resting upon me from the crown of my head to the soles of my feet, as it was when He gave me a knowledge of this Gospel, or when He gave me a knowledge of this principle, "As man now is God once was; as God now is man may be." That came to me powerfully and suddenly, and I saw it just as clearly as I see this bench or see your faces. This revelation that was given to me in regard to this matter of tithing that we have talked about in the different settlements, was given to me just as fully and I know it just as clearly as any manifestation the Lord ever gave me. And this has got to go through all the Stakes of Zion, and you brethren and sisters will be called upon from time to time, perhaps, to bear testimony to this manifestation. It has got to go through every Stake in Zion, and brethren will be called upon to assist in teaching the Latter Day Saints in reference to this law of tithing. The Lord requires it of us now to go to and perform those sacred duties that

> He required of us in the beginning. He has not urged it upon us in the past as He has some revelations, perhaps, but He requires it now of us. This visit of ours, there is something marvelous about it, from the day we commenced to talk upon this matter in St. George throughout all the settlements. This will be a matter of record that will go down to generations to come; it will be eternal and everlasting. Every one of you that has been a member of this company will have this matter renewed to you, and you will see it clearly; and you will see one of the greatest revolutions that has ever been made since this Church was organized, in this matter. There are things connected with it that I can see in the future. President Smith has made some explanation in regard to what is needed through this awakening of the people, but it is not policy for us to say very much about it—that is, some things—as it may be by and by. I want to say, God bless the members of this company, every one of you, that we may never forget what the Lord has manifested to us, and that which we shall see clearly. God bless you, Amen.[21]

"We left Nephi at 6:40 this morning," wrote Arthur Winter, "and reached Salt Lake at 9:35. It was raining heavily. . . . This has been a delightful trip. In every meeting President Snow has given to the people the word and will of the Lord concerning the payment of tithing. He has announced that the time has now come when the Lord requires the Latter-day Saints to pay their full tithing. This has been the message to every settlement on this trip, and all the speakers have dwelt upon this subject. There has been an excellent feeling between all the members of the party, and we have enjoyed ourselves immensely. We come back full of the spirit of tithe-paying, and ready to bear witness that the word of the Lord has been given through President Snow.

"President Snow, though 85 years of age, has stood the journey remarkably well, as well as any of us. The trip has been the hardest on Brother Richards and wife. They have not been at all well."[22]

A *Deseret News* reporter interviewed President Snow upon arriving home in Salt Lake City: "Are you satisfied, President Snow, with your visit in the south?" "I am highly satisfied," answered the President, "and so is every member of my company; we all say it is the most enjoyable trip we have ever made."

"How were you received by the people?"

"With the warmest manifestations of joy and appreciation of our visit."

"How did you find the condition of the people generally?"

"Well, they are living in comfortable homes, they are particularly well dressed, and appear to have plenty of the good things of the earth to eat and drink. In the St. George Stake the people are suffering from the severe drought, the severest one that has ever visited the country, but they have faith that they will soon have moisture. I am so pleased with the result of this visit that I contemplate traveling through all the Stakes in Zion, in the near future."

"You appear to have stood the journey remarkably well," added the reporter. "Yes, so they all say," remarked the venerable President: "the trip has done me good. I never felt better in my life. I feel that the Lord sustains me in answer to the prayers of the Saints."[23]

Preaching Tithing to the Stakes of Zion

The day after returning from southern Utah, Sunday, May 28, President Snow found the general Mutual Improvement Association (MIA) meetings were about to start. (At that time they were a much larger and more organized and distinct group than modern Young Men and Young Women activities.) This gathering of young people and their leaders caused President Snow to take advantage of the timing of the meetings, and he spoke to them three times in three days. "I have just returned from a journey to the south," said President Snow, "having been absent eleven days. I made twenty-four addresses to the people and held twenty-six meetings. There were about twenty brethren and sisters with me. The Lord blessed us very much. All the brethren and sisters who accompanied me said that they never enjoyed the Spirit of the Lord more than they did during this visit. . . .

"There are many important things that we have to do and to take into consideration. Some things we have sadly neglected in the past and it will be necessary to present these things unto you. We must arouse the people who gather in these meetings, to the necessity of taking hold and fulfilling those things that have been neglected."[24]

In his remarks on Monday, May 29, in the Assembly Hall to the YMMIA, President Snow said: "We are going to visit you in your stakes and tell you what the Lord has put in our hearts to tell you. Spoke upon the law of tithing, and said, if we don't obey it, this will not be a land of Zion to us. We don't half obey it. If the saints had paid an honest tithing during the past two years, there would be a million dollars in the treasury of the Church that is not there now. It is a question, he said, whether people who don't pay an honest tithing are entitled to go into the temple and receive blessings there. In conclusion he invoked the blessings of the Lord upon the young men present."[25] Later that afternoon, "An officers meeting of the Young Men was held in the Templeton Building. General topics of interest were talked on. President Snow talked tithing and impressed us all that he was inspired of God, and was a prophet of the Lord."[26]

For the third meeting on Tuesday, the editor of the *Improvement Era* observed that President Snow "seemed to realize keenly the heavy burden resting upon him" as he spoke to the Young Men's MIA officers [adult leaders] conference.[27] It is evident that an unusual Spirit was present during this meeting, which had not been present the previous day (for reasons mentioned):

> I feel, brethren, that I am addressing an important body of men whom the Lord has blessed with understanding and with wisdom, and with long experience, as many of you have had. . . . Some of you are fine speakers, especially in politics, if you will excuse me for saying it. You are men of intelligence and will understand what is required of you.
>
> There are hundreds of thousands of dollars in notes that are coming up now for payment, and we have no reserve at all, but I am just as sure that we will be able to settle our troubles here in regard to the debts of the Church, just as sure as I see you here, but it will not be done without exertion in reference to the paying of tithing.
>
> President Smith, President Richards, Brother Lyman, Brother Woodruff, Brother Seymour Young and some others, were with me in the south. We talked plainly to the people, and we had the Spirit of the Lord. There was not a difference of opinion among us, as was shown among you today, we all saw the point exactly alike and we talked plainly upon it. We hoped to present it yesterday morning to the young people, but I do not know why it was, we did not have the spirit that we hoped to have. I understand however that there were persons in the meeting who were making sport, and were not united with us.
>
> Now, brethren, we shall visit all the stakes in Zion and we shall see you again in the parts where you reside. We wish you to consult yourselves and the Spirit of the Lord in reference to this principle. People who have never paid a cent tithing go into the temples. This law of tithing is one which if it is not kept, the land shall not be sanctified unto those who disobey it, and it shall not be a land of Zion unto them. . . .
>
> I have given myself to this work, and I do not propose to turn away from the Lord, neither shall I neglect my duty even if it is unpleasant to talk about these things, but I hope it is not unpleasant to you. . . .
>
> I am surprised that I am in this position. I am not a speaker. I used

> to, when I was younger, try to take up a text and to talk upon it, but I was not very successful. But I can tell what the Lord wants of me, and I know what my duty is . . .
>
> I have taken an interest in you and prayed for you and for those who have the direction of your affairs. Now that I see what you are doing I feel that you are strong and that you will do as the Lord requires you to do. God bless you.

During this talk, one of the MIA general board members, Elder B. H. Roberts, had quickly composed an impromptu resolution. Evidently he had by then sat through enough frank and forceful sermons on tithing over three days that he understood something special was happening. Therefore,

> At the conclusion of President Snow's address the following resolution was presented by Elder B. H. Roberts: Resolved: That we accept the doctrine of tithing, as now presented by President Snow, as the present word and will of the Lord unto us, and we do accept it with all our hearts; we will ourselves observe it, and we will do all in our power to get the Latter-day Saints to do likewise. The resolution was unanimously adopted by all present rising to their feet and shouting "Aye."
>
> Apostle Francis M. Lyman then arose and said: "President Snow: I believe this body of men are about as clear upon this law and have about as faithfully met their obligations in regard to tithing as any body of men in the Church. It is a splendid thing, brethren, for us to be always in shape to accept the will of the Lord when it comes."
>
> Visibly affected, the President then arose and said: "Brethren, the God of our fathers, Abraham, Isaac and Jacob bless you. Every man who is here, who has made this promise, will be saved in the Celestial Kingdom. God bless you. Amen."
>
> Not a person in the large congregation, the cream of the young men of Zion, but felt the solemnity of the occasion, and was thrilled with the significance of the glorious promise. Many expressed themselves afterwards that such a blessing from the mouth-piece of God was worth every sacrifice that could be made.[28]

After speaking to the MIA conference, President Snow went back to the office to catch up on business that had accumulated during his trip south. Around noon that Friday (June 2) President Snow decided, on the spur of the moment, to go to Deseret [about 140 miles southwest of Salt Lake, by Delta, in Millard County, Utah] to attend their stake conference. Once there, he and all the speakers preached tithing, and their new meetinghouse was dedicated.[29] "The President promised the Saints that if they would observe this law that they would be greatly prospered and become a rich people. . . . President Snow said: 'We come here to tell you of things that we know to be of the highest importance to you, and one of these things is the law of tithing. We have been very careless in observing this law, for which we are all to blame, but the Lord has now called a halt, and from now on He desires us to be honest in observing this law.'"[30]

On the return trip, wrote Arthur Winter, "We drove over to Abraham, about 10 miles distant. This is a place where some few years ago some of our most prominent men took up land with the view of developing the country. The late First Presidency were interested in it, and they with others of the brethren have spent many thousands of dollars in getting water on to the land. There is a vast area of country hereabouts. We rode around, went to the reservoir and dam which have been constructed, and before we got back to Oasis [the nearest railroad to Deseret] we had traveled about 25 miles. . . . After supper several hours were spent in music and singing, when Presidents Snow and Smith and wives retired to the private car for the night."[31]

Then President Snow called two special priesthood meetings with the Salt Lake Stake, "to lay before the priesthood of this stake the mind and will of the Lord concerning tithe paying, as he has been doing in the Stakes south."[32] At the regular Thursday meeting of the First Presidency and Quorum of the Twelve, President Snow "said that he had been impressed to call the presidents of stakes and bishops of wards throughout Zion to meet in the temple, fast day, July 2nd, 1899, and there present to them the law of tithing."[33] The other Brethren quickly supported him and decided that all General Authorities, stake presidencies, and bishoprics would be invited to attend, and notices were sent out the next week.

That Sunday President Snow went to Centerville, Utah, for the Davis (County) Stake conference with President Smith and some other Brethren and preached on tithing; the next day President Snow went to Brigham City.[34] Later that month, at a special business meeting of the First Presidency and Twelve, a financial deal the former First Presidency had made with an investor to finance a new electric power company was discussed. As mentioned in the previous chapter, the Church had guaranteed the investor's loan for 1.5 million dollars; this guarantee, over the signature of the Trustee-in-trust, obligated the Church for an enormous sum—especially considering its poor financial health—in the event of fiscal disaster (failure of the new company). The investor had since died, and other capitalists interested in the matter were making trouble. An arrangement was considered and approved, with the Church offering to pay $250,000 in installments and interest to the investor's heirs, and then the offer was sent by telegraph.[35]

President Snow then turned their attention to another serious matter.

Chapter 20

Teaching Tithing throughout Zion

The "Tithing" Solemn Assembly in the Salt Lake Temple

After the return from St. George, President Lorenzo Snow was instructed by the Lord to call the memorable Solemn Assembly," wrote LeRoi Snow. "It was shown to him in vision. One day he took Brother William [H.] Salmon, the temple custodian, into the Celestial room [of the temple]. The President looked [around] and walked about the room. A worried expression came over his face, whereupon Brother Salmon asked: 'What is the matter, President Snow? Is something wrong?' 'Yes, yes,' was the reply, 'this is not what I saw. I saw more [room for] people here than I now see,' (There was no one else in the room.) 'This is not right. There is something wrong about it.' Brother Salmon quickly said: 'We can easily fix that, President Snow. We can take down the curtains and remove the veil.' He then went to the curtains and pushed them aside. President Snow looked through into the Terrestrial room and back again into the Celestial room and said: 'Yes, Brother Salmon, that is what I saw. That is all right. See that it is so arranged,' and he [left] . . . leaving Brother Salmon standing in astonishment."[1] The first solemn assembly in the Salt Lake Temple was then planned.

"Pres. Snow said that the meeting called for next Sunday at the temple would be a very important one," Elder Clawson recorded, "if not the most important we have had for years. It is to be called a Solemn Assembly and surely will be one. . . . The meetings will be held in the Celestial and Terrestrial Rooms. The object to be accomplished is twofold, namely, to get those who attend the meeting to pay a full tithing, and through them, to get those over whom they preside to do the same. I know [said President Snow] the brethren feel impressed with the importance of this meeting, and I want you to pray for the Spirit to rest upon all who attend. There will be no time for long sermons, but we want to hear from the Presidency, the Twelve, the Seven Presidents, and very briefly from the presidents of stakes. I will keep the time."[2]

The solemn assembly in which the principle of tithing payment was taught with renewed emphasis to most of the priesthood leadership of the Church took place on July 2, 1899.[3] Arthur Winter described the occasion:

> Today will be a memorable day in the history of the Church. A Solemn Assembly was held in the Celestial Room of the Temple here. 623 persons were present, consisting of the First Presidency, the Twelve Apostles, the Patriarch, the First Seven Presidents of Seventies, the Presiding Bishops, the Presidencies of Stakes, the Bishops of Wards, and other invited brethren. There were a few sisters present also. I was there as the reporter. The Temple choir furnished the singing. The meeting was called to order at 10:20 a.m. and was in session till 7:20 p.m., with the exception of a little over an hour (3 to 4:15) when we all partook of lunch in the upper room of the temple, known as the assembly room. All the First Presidency, all the Twelve, the Presiding Bishop and Elder LeRoi C. Snow spoke, and the subject dwelt upon the law of tithing, in the same strain as it was set forth on the trip to and from St. George. It was an inspiring sight to see all the leading officers of the Church gathered together in the Temple of the Lord, and there appeared to be a perfect unanimity of feeling among those present. I do not remember ever having to write shorthand longer at a stretch than at this meeting. We were in meeting five hours before recess was taken, and at least four of those hours were occupied by the different speakers. And we were fasting too; for this is fast day, and it was the understanding that all should go to the meeting fasting.[4]

Andrew Kimball (a stake president and the father of President Spencer W. Kimball), along with others in attendance, recorded some of the proceedings: "[We were] admitted about 9:00 a.m. passed around the yard and entered the west door of the Temple. At a little after 9 a.m. we were seated in order [and] met in the Celestial and Terrestrial rooms with [the] veil taken down. The Presidency [were seated] behind the stand, [with the] Apostles and Patriarch John Smith on the right [and] The Seven Presidents of Seventy on the left. Immediately in front came Presidents of Stakes and their Councilors; then Bishops and invited guests. . . . It was the largest body of Presiding priesthood ever met at one time as such."[5] There was an opening song, prayer, and another song. President Snow then addressed the group for an hour, the below excerpt being the only sizeable verbatim fragment available to researchers:[6]

> The Lord has shown me most clearly and distinctly that this is what I should say to you. The Lord testified to me while we were in St. George, before the conference there, that this is what we should tell the people. We did not know what we went to St. George for, but when we got there the Lord showed me most plainly in the first meeting, why we were there. We told the people just what they were to do and we now tell it to you. All through "Dixie" we found everything [crops and livestock] dying, many [people] moving away and everybody discouraged because of the terrible drouth.
>
> Then, there are other troubles. Our enemies calculate to get the next Congress to [pass a constitutional amendment to] disfranchise us, and the whole nation is aroused against us. Well, we have found in our experiences that when we kept the commandments of God we could rely upon His promises. He has said that He will preserve us, and this shall be a land of Zion unto us, if we will observe this law of tithing.
>
> Well, the Latter-day Saints are a good people and the Lord loves us. He loves us because we are His sons and daughters. Because He loves us He has forgiven us our forgetfulness of this holy law in the past; but He will not forgive you and me any longer. I say it in the name of the Lord, He will not forgive this people any longer should we continue this dilatory way of paying tithing. Just as sure as you and I live, unless we honor this law of tithing fully, as a people, the Lord will never allow us to go back to Jackson County. I know that those who are within the sound of my voice, with very few exceptions indeed, will listen to the voice of the Lord that comes through me and my brethren. The sacrifices which the Latter-day Saints have made are marvelous. God has been pleased with us, and has forgiven us, but He will not forgive us any longer, so far as the law of tithing is concerned. God bless you. We feel to bless you all the time, and we are willing to sacrifice ourselves and do all we can for you.
>
> There is just one thing that a Latter-day Saint, an Elder in Israel should never forget; it should be a bright, illuminating star before him all the time—in his heart, in his soul, and all through him—that is, he need not worry in the least as to whether he should be a deacon or president of the Church; it is sufficient for him to know that his destiny, through his faithful obedience to all the laws and commandments of the gospel, is to be like his [Heavenly] Father, a God in eternity. He may not only be president of a church, but he may see himself presiding over a kingdom, president of worlds, with never-ending opportunities to enlarge his sphere of dominion [see JST Revelation 2:26–27].

> God lives. We must teach the people this law of tithing—first by paying tithing ourselves. Just as sure as we live, if we do not honor the law of tithing, we will never possess the land of Jackson County, except it be by the shedding of blood, but it will not be by the shedding of blood because you will listen to my voice and the voice of my brethren. We are the sons of the prophets and the sons of God. The Lord will not send hornets to drive the people out of Jackson County, as he promised to drive the people out of the land of promise before the children of Israel, but he will send cyclones, earthquakes, and pestilences.[13]

After President Snow, Elder Matthias Cowley spoke, and then at 3:00 p.m. the entire group walked to the large upper assembly room to break their fast and eat lunch, after which they returned to the Celestial and Terrestrial rooms for further instruction.[14] President Snow then called on his son to speak, at which point LeRoi bore testimony of tithing.[15] Then George Teasdale, Joseph F. Smith,[16] John Henry Smith, Francis M. Lyman,[17] and George Q. Cannon all spoke. Some of President Cannon's remarks were unusually memorable for many in attendance. He did not hold as closely to the subject of tithing as most. Andrew Kimball summarized:

> After 16 speakers it would require patience to listen to him. Bore testimony to the truth of the remarks made by Pres. Snow. Said he never had ambition for office, but had an ambition to see this church on top. Spoke of the confidence shown in us by English Capitalists. We should avail ourselves and enjoy the honor. Spoke against Populism and all socialists of the kind. [Said] That God had organized a perfect system. Three times now he [Pres. Cannon] had consecrated all he had [to the Lord]. Bore testimony to the correctness of the principle of Tithing and that we will be blessed. God will make us as copartners with him. We should make our means a ligament to tie to the church and tie us to the Lord. Quoted Pres. Taylor speaking of the phonograph [recording machine] and said: This was a correct idea that we would record our own deeds, our record would be in our minds. . . . There are descendants of the old prophets in here, there [are] descendants of the Christ here."[18]

The last portion of this account was also the main point caught by others listening. Anthony Ivins recorded President Cannon as saying: "There are men in this congregation who are descendants of the ancient Twelve Apostles, and I shall say it, of the Son of God Himself; for he has seed, and in time they shall be known."[19] Elder Clawson's account stated: "There are those in this audience who are descendants of the old

I saw this principle after being in the Church but a short time; it was made as clear to me as the noon-day sun, and I expressed it in this language: 'As man now is, God once was; As God now is, man may be.' This thought in the breasts of men filled with the light of the Holy Spirit tends to purify them and cleanse them from every unholy ambition or improper feeling.

This glorious opportunity of becoming truly great belongs to every faithful Elder in Israel; it is his by right divine. He may be a God in eternity; he may become like his [Heavenly] Father did before him, and he cannot be deprived, except by his own unfaithfulness, of the opportunity of reaching this exalted state.

I never sought to be a Seventy or High Priest, because this eternal principle was revealed to me long before I was ordained to the Priesthood. The position which I now occupy, as President of the Church, is nothing as compared with what I expect to occupy in the future [eternities].[7]

President Snow, according to available records, was followed by Presiding Bishop Preston.[8] Then speaking briefly were Elders Abraham Owen Woodruff, Franklin D. Richards,[9] Brigham Young Jr., Rudger Clawson, Marriner W. Merrill,[10] Anthon H. Lund, and Heber J. Grant.[11] After Elder Grant's talk, Presiding Bishop Preston and some helpers passed the sacrament to the assemblage. Then President Snow spoke further, the two paragraphs below representing the most complete accounts available for these remarks:

President Snow read from sec. 86, D&C 8th verse. If the people were not a good people we would not be here in this house; Holy to the Lord; where He has been in times past, and He has forgiven us heretofore but He will not forgive us longer. The man who fails to pay his tithing hereafter I could not recommend to the House of the Lord. Let every president of a stake pay his full tithing. Let every bishop do so. If people have been remiss in the past they may make it good if they desire but we shall not say anything about the past. The Lord will send cyclones, whirlwinds, and devouring fire and the way will be prepared for the fulfillment of his purposes.[12]

President Snow read Sec. 86, Book of D.&C. Said, we are the sons and daughters of God, and descendants of the prophets and apostles. Said, the Lord has forgiven us for our carelessness in paying our tithing in the past, but he will forgive us no longer—and if we do not obey this law, we will be scattered as were the saints in Jackson County, and this by reason of the knowledge we have attained to. What I say is as true as

12 Apostles and, shall I say it, yes, descendants of the Savior himself. His seed is represented in this body of men."[20] Orson Whitney wrote: "Pres. Cannon said there were descendants of the old Prophets, and of the Savior himself in the congregation."[21] (President Cannon had many years before been told by President Heber C. Kimball that he himself was one of those descendants.[22])

After President Cannon's remarks, President Snow again spoke briefly in conclusion, saying: "I feel we have said enough. I understand from the spirit we all feel we are well paid for meeting together. Be ambitious in the sowing seeds of this principle."[23] "[President Snow] said he hoped the brethren would take the spirit of these meetings home with them and impart the same to the people."[24] He then asked for a sustaining vote on their teachings regarding tithing: "[He proposed that] we would set the example ourselves, and then we would teach it to the people and ask them to follow us. We had a rising vote, and every man there raised his right hand and solemnly testified before the Lord that he would reform and pay his tithing."[25] Arthur Winter stated: "a motion was unanimously carried to the effect that we accept the word of the Lord as given through President Snow on the law of tithing, and that we covenant to obey it fully and completely."[26] After the vote on the resolution, President Snow "stepped up on an elevation above the stairs and swinging his handkerchief led us in the [hosanna] shout."[27] After a song and prayer, the meeting closed.

The sacred event left a deep impression on those attending. Elder J. Golden Kimball wrote: "The meeting was all it was intended to be, a Solemn Assembly. A stillness pervaded the whole house. There was no very great manifestations of the Spirit, and yet every man there will be held responsible and accountable to live the law of Tithing and teach it to the people, and to their families. . . . The impression this meeting has made upon me shall never be forgotten."[28] Elder John Henry Smith summarized his impressions: "We were together for about ten hours. . . . It was a splendid day."[29] Elder Merrill wrote: "Had an excellent time and a refreshing from the Lord and all enjoyed the day."[30] Elder Lyman predicted wonderful benefits resulting from the meeting: "There has never before been such a gathering in the Church; its effects will be potently felt throughout all the stakes and wards; the result will be the rise of the Church financially and a closer union between all its members."[31]

President Snow shared his reactions to the meeting with a reporter for the *Salt Lake Herald*:

> President Snow, when seen last evening, was not so fatigued as might be expected. He talked freely of some matters pertaining to the assembly, which he refers to as a grand success.
>
> "The addresses made," said he, "were substantially the same as those delivered in the south on our recent tour. General subjects of interest to the church were discussed, tithing forming one theme, and what was said, I presume, will be echoed in the pulpits of the church in all directions.
>
> "I was astonished to see with what readiness the authorities assembled this morning. The hour set was 10:30, but upon my soul," laughingly the president declared, "both rooms were literally packed when I entered with my counselors an hour beforehand. Only two presidents of stakes were absent, and they, I believe, were represented by counselors.
>
> "We had a glorious time, and I do not hope to experience any gathering more harmonious, peaceful and full of good will. I believe everybody there feels well repaid for their attendance."[32]

Preaching Tithing in the Stakes of Zion

A few days after the solemn assembly, word came that the Church's offer to buy out Joseph Banigan's investment in the new electric power company had been accepted by his heirs and the Trustee-in-trust would therefore be freed from its largest single financial obligation, for an amount much less even than they had hoped for:

> President George Q. Cannon explained to President Snow and President Smith the result of the late deal between the Church, with the English people connected with the Union Light and Power Company, and the Banigan heirs, as follows: The Trustee-in-trust is to pay $25,000 within thirty days; give secured note for $200,000, payable in one year, at 5% [interest]; also guarantee interest on $250,000 of preferred stock for ten years at 2%, amounting to $50,000, being five thousand dollars for ten years, which it is understood the company will be able to meet. For the foregoing we get the following: Release from guarantee of one and a half million dollars; 658,500 shares of preferred stock in the Union Light and Power Company, including the control of the company. We also get eighty 4% bonds, and thirty-nine prior lien 5% bonds, with 80,000 shares of preferred stock, on which the company says 2% will be paid. This we get for paying $180,000 or $190,000, two years interest on the Banigan bonds.[33]

When this was announced to the Twelve at their regular Thursday temple meeting, the Brethren were almost giddy with relief and gratitude:

> Brother Lyman observed that . . . The Lord was overruling things in a remarkable manner, and in a few years, he believed, we would be relieved from our present debt, and be better prepared for new [financial] burdens.
>
> President Snow's face brightened, as he here remarked that he felt especially happy and thankful for what had been accomplished in the way of getting rid of the Church guarantee, as had been explained by President Cannon, and he was rather astonished to learn that the Banigan heirs had consented to its relinquishment on the terms agreed upon.
>
> President Cannon, in response to a desire expressed by some of the brethren, then made quite a lengthy report of the matter touched upon, showing how the deal was accomplished and giving the results, as recorded. . . . After President Cannon had finished, Brother Grant moved that the Council be very happy, which brought forth smiles from everybody.
>
> President Cannon expressed himself as desirous of having his report approved, and Brother Grant felt that we should not only approve the report, but express our gratitude to the Lord for the marvelous overruling. All the brethren united in Brother Grant's sentiment and seconded his suggestion, and a motion covering the subject was carried unanimously.[34]

At their next meeting, so that they might all be united, the Twelve by themselves and later with the First Presidency and the First Council of Seventy, discussed at some length the correct interpretation of the law of tithing. President Snow told the assembled Brethren how grateful he was for the unity that prevailed in the leading councils of the Church and hoped it would continue. He then sat down, but immediately arose again to speak further, with great earnestness, "saying that the Lord had revealed to him that it was his duty, and the duty of his brethren, to stir up the people from the bottom of their hearts, in relation to one of the laws of heaven, which they had failed to keep. Unless this law was obeyed the Church could not exist financially, nor could we exist as a people for the want of His blessing. He referred to the law of tithing. The Lord had promised that we should be preserved from our enemies if we observed this law, but that if we rejected it we should be cursed. This was the word given to the Church in early days, and it applies to us today. If the Saints had observed this law, the Land of Zion would have been sanctified, and their enemies could not have dispossessed them. . . . There was safety in strictly adhering to the Lord's commandments, and this applied to officers as well as to lay members of the Church."[35] After settling on a standard interpretation of tithing the meeting closed.

The following week, President Snow traveled to Richfield, in Central Utah, to dedicate their new Tabernacle during their stake conference, "a beautiful structure, so far as the exterior is concerned; the outside appearance I like better than any other stake tabernacle I know of; but the interior is not equal to some of the others," said one of the party.[36] President Snow used the occasion of the dedication to preach about tithing:

> There is one subject that I wish introduced to you; it is the law of tithing. . . .
>
> Everyone who has any knowledge at all of financial affairs must understand that such a body of people as we are cannot carry on business without money. Here are four temples. It takes somewhere in the neighborhood of $50,000 or $60,000 a year to keep them going. We have the poor to sustain, which takes about as much. We have numerous other things that require means. . . .
>
> Now, I tell you Latter-day Saints—I tell it to you in the name of the Lord—that you and I have no promise of being defended from our enemies and remaining here in peace, so long as this law of tithing is not observed. The promise is, if we observe this law, we shall be defended from our enemies, we shall be greatly and abundantly blessed, and this land shall be sanctified, that it shall be most holy. . . .
>
> How do you suppose it would look for a Bishop to give a man who did not pay his tithing a recommend to the holy temple of the Lord, there to receive the highest blessings that can possibly be conferred upon man, notwithstanding he had ignored this law? . . .
>
> The Church is badly in debt. What is the cause of our present financial condition? Well, the Lord will never allow us to get out of debt unless we pay a proper tithing and do what we ought to do. I fully expect the Latter-day Saints will from this time forth pay their tithing as they ought to pay it. Then we will be blessed. I say to you, in the name of the Lord God of Israel, that the Lord will not allow this people to pass along as we have been doing in matters of tithing, without trouble following us. . . .
>
> If I were going to my death one hour from now, I would talk to you more strongly than I now do, if the Lord would give me the power to do it, and I would tell you just precisely what I am telling you now. I would leave it as my last dying testimony. For I know the Lord is calling upon us now to remedy wherein we have been faulty. . . . Pay our debt to the Lord, if we never pay another debt. What the Lord requires of us is to

> pay our tithing now. And He expects every person in the future to pay his or her tithing. . . .
>
> I think I have said enough for you to understand me distinctly. I have spoken plainly, and I say it comes from the Lord what I have said to you in regard to tithing. You act now according to the Spirit of the Lord, and your eyes will be opened.[37]

Two months after receiving the revelation in St. George, President Snow showed no sign of slowing, feeling under Divine obligation to teach tithing to the people whenever and however he could. After returning to the President's Office in Salt Lake City, President Snow met again with the Brethren in the Thursday temple meeting. It was there mentioned that a prestigious speaking invitation had been sent to the First Presidency, and he was asked if it should be accepted. In reply, "President Snow did not see that he could respond to the invitation in person. He had firmly made up his mind to attend as many stake conferences as he could during the warm weather [to preach tithing], as he could not venture out in cold weather; but he would like Presidents Cannon and Smith to respond to the invitation in behalf of the First Presidency."[38]

On the weekend preceding Pioneer Day (July 24), President Snow took his counselors and a few of the other Brethren with him to the Provo Stake conference. During that meeting (at which they were disappointed with the poor attendance), "President Snow said that in attending this conference he had a special object in view, and desired to speak on a subject of the highest importance to the people of the Church, namely, the law of tithing. He urged the people to obey this law; he spoke of the blessings derived from such obedience; dwelt at length on the negligence of many, and read from the Doctrine and Covenants on the duties of Latter-day Saints in this respect. In closing he said: 'And I now say to you that the Lord will not be so lenient with you in the future as he has in the past, but will require you to observe this law in its fullness or you will not enjoy his blessings.'"[39]

The work of teaching tithing payment continued, though other business was also considered. Arthur Winter, for instance, was pleased when Church employees were given half-Saturdays off by President Snow.[40]

Next came the Weber Stake conference in Ogden, Utah. Here President Snow said:

> I have found in my study of human nature that money is the great difficulty we encounter in obeying the Lord. For example, in paying tithing:

> Many poor people pay an honest tithing but when they accumulate means their tithes decrease. . . .
>
> After this law is clearly explained unto you, and it will be during this conference, then there will be but one way in which you can obtain promises upon which to depend to secure and hold this land; that way is through observance of this law. . . .
>
> It costs about $50,000 a year to carry on our temples. Many poor people go into these temples; their tithing goes to support this work, and they receive the highest blessings. Others go into the temples who never pay a cent of tithing; they also receive promises of great blessings, but I shall not venture to say that they are worthy of or do receive those blessings. From now on if Bishops recommend non-tithe-payers to the House of the Lord, they themselves must take the responsibility.
>
> The Lord has whispered to me through His Spirit, that He requires me and my brethren to talk to you in regard to this subject. I ask the Lord to let His Holy Spirit rest upon you, and I ask you to talk to your friends who are not here today, upon this important law, it is your duty to do so.
>
> Conform to this law in the Spirit of the Gospel and you will be mightily blessed of the Lord; He will enable you to settle your debts, we shall be a free people, and the Church will be free. Brethren and sisters, I plead with you to do this and I ask you in the name of the Lord to do so.[41]

Elder Francis M. Lyman followed and stated: "It has fallen to the lot of President Lorenzo Snow to take up this mission, as it has not been taken up before. This is the burden of the word of the Lord unto him. We know that the Lord has manifested himself unto President Snow, in this direction. When he first made known the word of the Lord to the people in St. George, it flew as with the wings of air, all through Zion. . . . Through observing this law we shall be astonished at the manner in which the windows of heaven will be opened unto us." Elder Lyman followed that with a comment that he later had to clarify at the next general conference: "It has been promised by the Apostles that anyone who has weaknesses that he has not been able to control will be given power to overcome them, and his past transgression will not only be forgiven him by the Lord, but will be forgotten that it will not burn in his memory, if he will fully observe this law of tithing."[42] It was evidently felt that this latter statement had overstepped the promises given by President Snow as part of the revelation, and Elder Lyman clarified that:

> Since President Snow has been talking so plainly upon this subject, there have been a class of people who have undertaken to take advantage of his promise to the Latter-day Saints in regard to this law, that if for the future they would observe this law faithfully the past should be forgiven. There have been men guilty of breaches of the laws of morality and honesty who have claimed that if they now pay their tithing all their sins will be forgiven them. President Snow never announced any such doctrine as that. He could not announce such a doctrine as that. But the Lord is perfectly able to say to us that if we will observe this law of finance, which we have been under now for over sixty years, for the future and keep this commandment our past negligence of the law of tithing will be forgiven. He is competent also to say that if we will repent of our sins and serve God with all our hearts for the future, our sins will be forgiven us; but not otherwise. The forgiveness of sins is predicated upon faith in God, repentance and reformation and baptism. Sins are not forgiven through the payment of tithing, nor through the partaking of the sacrament, nor observing the Word of Wisdom, or prayer. There are blessings attached to each of these important requirements of the Gospel; but if a man would have his sins forgiven, and be allowed to enter into the Church, he must have faith in God, and in His Son Jesus Christ and in the Holy Ghost, he must repent of all his sins, turn unto the Lord with full purpose of heart and sin no more. Then God will forgive him and redeem him from his sins; but not by paying tithing.[43]

Next came the Logan Stake conference. President Snow again took a number of the Brethren with him, traveling by train. The Logan stake had an unusual situation at the time in that their stake president had become desperate over heavy financial losses due to commodity speculation, some of them involving others, and had gone to the Alaskan gold rush in hopes of finding quick financial salvation there. He returned later having had no success, but in the meantime was not present, and everyone expected a new stake president to be chosen at that conference. Between that drama and the visit of the President of the Church, they had the largest attendance ever recorded to that point for that stake.

In the morning President Snow spent over an hour shaking hands with 2,324 children and then spoke to them:

> I wish to say a few words to you that you will never forget. You have advantages that I never had, and you therefore can receive certain blessings that I could not obtain. You can live to a much older age than I expect to. This you can do by being faithful in keeping the

The Logan Tabernacle, 1884. The Logan Temple can be dimly seen, upper left. (USHS)

> commandments of God; especially learn obedience to your parents; love and respect them; do this every hour of your lives and the Lord will bless you greatly for it. There is a great future for you; you will receive the choicest blessings that God has ever given to His people. When I shake hands with you I want you to look up into my face, that you may always remember me. Now I am not any better than many other men, but the Lord has placed great responsibilities upon me. Ever since the Lord made Himself known unto me, most perfectly as He did, I have endeavored to perform every duty resting on me. It is because of the high position that I occupy that I wish you to remember me, remember that you have shaken hands with the President of the Church of Jesus Christ. I hope you will not forget to pray for me and for my counselors.

Later, in the regular session, "President Lorenzo Snow spoke while the Sacrament was being passed. During his remarks the President said: 'I have something to say to you that is of great importance; and the time will come, if you accept this message, when you will be thankful for this day.'" Continuing, he said:

> There has been a certain neglect among the Latter-day Saints in the past. The Lord always speaks plainly to His people. There have been times in the past when the Lord has sent His servants to remind the people of their duties. This is exactly the condition of the Latter-day Saints today. You have been blessed wonderfully in this Stake, but there is one law that you, as well as the people in other Stakes, have not fully observed. . . .
>
> That this land may be a land of Zion unto us, it is absolutely necessary that we observe this law of tithing. I say unto you, and I say it in the name of the Lord, that from now on He requires us to pay an honest tithing on all our increase.
>
> The Church is in debt. I do not propose to borrow money and thereby increase this debt. I shall do no such thing. It is the duty of the Latter-day Saints to pay tithing, and if they do so, the obligations of the Church, which are the obligations of the people, will be liquidated.
>
> I never had a more perfect revelation than I received on this subject of tithing while I was in St. George. The people are now getting an understanding of this law, and are commencing already to observe it more fully.

Elder Lyman then spoke to the unsettled question of calling a new stake president:

> I hear that you are anxious to know who will be your next Stake president. As soon as the Lord makes known who it shall be, President Snow will tell you. There are two counselors in this Stake, and in the absence of the Stake president, it is their duty to look after the people; this work devolves upon them. To reveal the word of the Lord unto you, for which President Snow has come, is more important than naming a Stake president, and you should be thankful that his word has been delivered unto you.

Then President Snow, in his closing remarks, said:

> We have now said all that we had to say to you. I shall never come up here again to talk to you upon this subject. It is because the Lord loves you that He has required us to say these things. If it had not been the requirement of the Lord, and of vital importance to the Church, we should not have said these things unto you. You are a good people and the Lord loves you. I say to you in the name of the Lord God of Israel, if you will pay tithing from now on, the Lord will forgive you for all the past [neglect] and the blessings of the Almighty will be poured out upon this people, and the Church will progress with a force and rapidity that has never been experienced before.[44]

During stake conference visits, President Snow usually stayed at the home of the stake president and often took his wife Minnie and son LeRoi with him, or a daughter. Other Brethren were likewise assigned to stay at the home of some local priesthood leader, thus relieving them of boarding expenses. During the meetings, President Snow would call on whomever he felt so inspired to name to speak. Not everyone appreciated this method; yet the subject was always clear. "The payment of tithing has been the topic of this conference, as it has been of all the conferences since the word of the Lord was first announced at St. George," wrote Arthur Winter, "President Snow directs the speakers to make the principle of tithing their subject."[45]

The Wasatch Stake conference in Heber City was the next stop, with President Snow telling them: "I promise you if you will observe this law conscientiously that all past neglect will be forgiven you."[46] After that President Snow visited the Bannock Stake in Soda Springs, Idaho. There, "President Snow said he had come for a special purpose. A subject had been given to him of the Lord—a subject of interest to every man and woman. It is the law of tithing. The books show that not one-half of the tithing is paid. The Lord has shown [President Snow] that the people must pay their tithes, or great calamities will come upon them. He then read the law of tithing, Doctrine and Covenants 119, and said, 'Keep and observe this law, and greater blessings shall follow, than we have ever had.' . . . President Snow summed up with: 'The Lord wants you to pay a full tithing.'"[47]

President Snow next visited the Bear Lake Stake; there he observed:

> When we visited the Saints in St. George we found that they were suffering greatly, because of drought. Their crops were almost a failure, they were not blessed as you seem to be, but the Lord required us to present the law of tithing to them for their observance. He requires the same of us in visiting you. . . . The Lord has given the Latter-day Saints a law whereby we can obtain possession of the land and be preserved against our enemies. . . . There is but one way in which we can sanctify the land and make it a land of Zion unto us, and that way is by observing the law of tithing. When we were in St. George, the Lord revealed most clearly unto me His will concerning this law. It is that it must be observed faithfully by the Saints. Now, if you will commence and from now on fully observe this law, I say, in the name of the Lord, that you shall be forgiven for all past neglect. I think you will do this, for you are a blessed and a good people. Our prospects are grand and glorious,

but if we obtain the blessings promised us it will be through observing the law of God.[48]

In the last meeting, he also testified: "I know this to be the word of the Lord. If you will accept and obey it, all your past neglect will be forgiven you. I shall never visit you again to talk to you upon this subject. I do not know how long I shall live, but I should like to live to see the Saints observe this counsel. I hope the Lord will let me live to visit these conferences again when I can come and congratulate the Saints in having observed the law of tithing, and I, myself, should like to see the grand blessings that are sure to follow this observance."[49]

At the Sanpete Stake conference in Mt. Pleasant, Utah, President Snow echoed the same theme: "As I told you yesterday, we came here for a special purpose; we have accomplished what we came here for. We shall never come here again to talk upon the subject of tithing. I knew in St. George that the Lord required this of me. I of myself am nobody. I never sought this position as President of the Church of Christ, but now that I hold it I am going to perform my duty with the help of the Lord. I do not care what man may think of it."[50] President George Q. Cannon confirmed President Snow's teachings: "President Snow has been moved by the Spirit of God to teach tithing. This is preparatory to something much greater. President Snow is desirous that we observe more advanced laws. It is foolish to talk about the United Order until we can observe the lesser law—that of tithing."[51]

At Manti, in early September, President Snow bore further witness of his tithing revelation: "I have something to tell you; it is my duty to do so; the Lord requires it of me, and I wish you to hear and pay attention to what I shall say unto you. A few months ago, when I was in St. George, the Lord manifested to me, most clearly, that I should present this thing to the Latter-day Saints. I have now, in company with several of my brethren, visited many conferences and talked upon this subject, and the Lord has been with us in this thing. It concerns a law which is as important as any law that God ever revealed to the people. It is the law of tithing. This law has been sadly neglected by the people in general. Now, we have not come to find fault with you but simply to tell you your duty in the future, and this we shall do most clearly. The salvation of this people and our preservation from our enemies depends upon an honest observance of this law."[52]

From Manti they returned to Salt Lake and spoke more about tithing. Then on to the Davis Stake conference, held in a bowery in Farmington. At that meeting, President Cannon again confirmed the revelation received by President Snow, even though he had personally not been present to witness events on the St. George trip: "The Lord has communicated His mind and will to His servant Lorenzo Snow, and commanded him to make known this message unto the people. The Lord has also inspired His other servants to testify to this word." President Snow followed: "The Lord has revealed unto me a certain principle concerning our neglect regarding the law of tithing. You little children bear a part of this responsibility and I ask you to observe this commandment; when you get a dollar pay ten cents of it to the Lord."[53]

With the passing of September, general conference convened. Tithing payment was a major subject. At the special priesthood meeting of General Authorities and stake and ward leadership, President Snow "addressed the meeting in a very impressive manner. His subject was, Obedience of the Priesthood to the Law of Tithing. He had done, he said, all that he could do consistently, to reflect [convey] the mind and will of the Lord, as pertaining to this matter, and he gave the assembled priesthood to understand that the Lord would now hold them responsible for the continuation of this work among the people. It was for them to strictly observe the law themselves, and thus become imbued with its spirit, that they might impart the same to the people."[54] Another account contains a clearer statement from the prophet: "Upon the presidencies of stakes and bishoprics of wards, I place the responsibilities of seeing that the counsels given at conference concerning tithing and other matters are carried out by the people."[55]

At the end of October, President Snow returned to Logan for the Cache Stake conference to reorganize the stake presidency as formerly promised (on August 7). Orson Smith, the stake president, had suffered severe losses in some financial speculations, and out of desperation had left the stake and gone to Alaska for six months in a vain effort to find gold. "President Snow, however, visits the Stake this time for the purpose of putting in a new President. Rather unexpectedly, Brother Orson Smith returned home last Friday, and there is considerable querying in the minds of the people as to what will be done now that Brother Smith has returned."[56] President Snow asked Orson Smith to resign, which he did in his opening remarks at the conference. Elder Marriner W. Merrill of the Council of the Twelve was then sustained as the new Cache Stake President (see the following chapter under the same date for further details). Although the stake reorganization was the main drama among the people, President Snow had other things in mind and again preached tithing:

> You have heard what President [Orson] Smith has told us and I think you unite with me in sympathizing with him as we do. I do not feel to find fault with Brother Orson Smith or with anyone else. I think he has done the very best that he could do under the circumstances. Now we do not feel to cast him off but to do that which will be the very best for him and for the interests of the Cache Stake. It is indeed unfortunate that things have gone as they have. But under the circumstances we know that what President Smith has done in tendering his resignation is the very best, both for him and for the people. Any of you who can be of any assistance to Brother Orson Smith you should do so, and I would say to his creditors, be very lenient with him and give him an abundance of time and I feel that he will do all in his power to liquidate all his debts.
>
> Considering the failure of your crops this year, it is truly remarkable what an increase there is in tithing this year over last year. In July this year the people of Cache Stake paid four times as much as in July of last year. . . . You have done much better than I could have anticipated to live to see. Now, I say to you, in the name of the Lord, that your prospects for a rich harvest next year are of the brightest character because of your great obedience.
>
> The Lord has manifested to me most clearly that a time of great prosperity awaits the Latter-day Saints. It is a joy to me to be able to come here and speak of these things that you have done. Continue to do so. God bless you. Let me beg of you, Latter-day Saints, do not go into debt. Live within your means. Don't go into debt. Let me beg of you keep out of debt. I have about as large a family as anyone, but there is only once that I have ever gone into debt; that was when I went on a mission. I borrowed $60, the only time that I was ever in debt in my life. If I could call to all Israel I should say, Don't go into debt. It is an unfortunate thing to do. We have a sad example here before us today, and there are many others. Many men who are just as good as he are in a much worse condition. Now, I repeat, God bless you and He will. And I say the Lord will give you a president with whom you will be well pleased.[57]

As President Snow and the other Brethren continued to emphasize tithing throughout the Church, conditions began to improve; tithing contributions flowed into headquarters accounts at increasing rates, and President Snow began to find some relief for Church indebtedness, although it came slowly. In early November 1899, one of the Brethren commented that, "The president has a heavy strain on him to meet all these [financial] demands upon him."[58]

Brigham City Tabernacle, built in 1868 (USHS)

Later that month, President Snow traveled to Brigham City to reorganize the stake. Elder Rudger Clawson had been splitting time for a year with duties as an apostle, bookkeeper, and auditor of Church finances; and as Box Elder Stake president. Further details of this reorganization are also given in the following chapter; but again, President Snow spoke on tithing:

> There are some things that I wish to say to you. This is the largest congregation that has ever gathered in Boxelder Stake. Though it is somewhat unpleasant, I feel it my duty to address you upon the subject of tithing, as this is my first opportunity since I commenced speaking upon this subject. While in St. George it was manifested to me most clearly that this law of God had been sadly neglected and that it was my duty to try to work a reformation in this regard. . . .
>
> Now, I tell you, in the name of the Lord, that it is your duty to obey this law, and if you do not, this shall not be a land of Zion unto us. I saw this most clearly while in St. George. Obey this word and I shall visit you again and congratulate you upon your improvement. If you do this from now on, pay your tithing honestly, all your past neglect will be forgiven you. I know this. During the last four months the people have paid $100,000 more than during the same four months of last year. . . . Here is a promise which we all may receive through obedience to this law. The Lord will rebuke the devourer that is among us and your crops will be increased. I expect that you will do as well as other Stakes are now doing, because I believe you are just as good as the people in other Stakes. I want you to read and re-read the 119th section of the Doctrine and Covenants. We ask nothing more of you than what the Lord requires you to do. I pray you to observe this law, and I promise you the blessings. If all is well, we shall reorganize this Stake tomorrow.[59]

As winter approached, President Snow spent more time in Salt Lake City at the office, feeling less able to visit the stakes in cold weather. Yet the revelation he had received regarding tithing was still present in his mind.

Interior of the Brigham City Tabernacle, 1899. Lorenzo Snow, age eighty-five, is speaking at the funeral of Alvin Nichols, whose portrait is above Lorenzo. (CA)

At a meeting of the First Presidency and Twelve in early spring of 1900, he "requested the brethren, in their visits to the Stakes, to hold meetings with the Bishops and their counselors and the Stake Presidencies, and urge upon them the necessity of their taking up a private labor themselves with the non-tithe payers of their several wards, and not leave such matters to the ward [home] Teachers."[60] A week later, at the next council meeting, voluntary Church contributions of various kinds became a subject of discussion.

> President Cannon stated that there were two things that could be consistently taught and they were tithing and fast offerings for the support of the poor, and if the Saints would faithfully do this the Church could afford to defray the temple expenses, and he felt that the poor of the Church were entitled to the benefits of the ordinances of the Church without charge. . . .
>
> President Snow emphasized President Cannon's remarks on the subject of donations. The question of tithing was a serious matter. Referring to a Tithing record book that Bishop Preston had taken to the office, President Snow said that when he saw the size of the book [he]

> thought it was that of the tithe payers but to his astonishment it was the lists of non-tithe payers and about 10,000 names were in the record. He had learned that there were some names on the book which should not appear there, as the parties were on missions, and he believed that one half of those recorded in the book would not be there if Bishops and Stake presidents had done their full duty towards those whose names were on that record. He advised the brethren in attending conferences to take a list of the names of non-tithe payers of the Stakes they visit and confer with the Stake presidencies in regard to them with the view of taking up a labor with such individuals.[61]

Though it took time, the results of President Snow's determined efforts became apparent. In a conversation with Elder Lyman in January of 1901, "President Snow told [Elder Lyman] we would have all the Church obligations paid off by next January, except the bonds. . . . I reminded him of my feeling that he would live to see the Church entirely out of gambling. He was delighted with our prospects financially."[62]

About five months before he died, President Snow was deeply gratified to view the results of his labors and the consequent response of members paying tithing. Elder Rudger Clawson and President Snow reviewed the state of the Church finances, as well as its reasonable prospects for the future under the improved circumstances: "I, therefore, assured President Snow that, if he should live until the close of 1904, he would see the church free from every obligation. He was very much gratified with the statement and remarked that, if he were living at that time and the church were free from the bondage of debt, there would most assuredly be a big jubilation in the temple."[63] The Lord, through His prophet and the willing sacrifice of the Latter-day Saints, had solved the debt problems of His Church.

CHAPTER 21

GUIDING, BLESSING, AND SERVING THE LATTER-DAY SAINTS

Soon after President Snow's return from Southern Utah, feeling inspired and pleased with the enormously hopeful and positive results of his trip, President Snow talked further with James Talmage about his having freely given his book *The Articles of Faith* to the Church. Brother Talmage related the circumstances:

> There was some hesitation on the part of the First Presidency in accepting the gift, partly owing to a request of mine that the book be sold strictly at cost, and partly because of Pres. Snow's statement that a proper payment ought to be made. The first edition of 10,500 copies has been sold, and copy for a second issue is now in the [works]. . . . Several times I have been called into conference with the publication committee and with the Presidency relative to the transfer of my copyright to the Church; this the authorities desire, and for the same the Presidency declare a payment ought to be made. The brethren have urged the matter with such kindness that I could not well do otherwise than express acquiescence. I was asked to name a sum that would be satisfactory; this I declined to do, saying that I had offered the work as a gift. President Snow replied that it had been accepted as a gift, but they desired to make me a present in return. Today President Snow informed me of the decision reached, and I was handed a check for fifteen hundred dollars. I made the legal transfer of copyright to the work and assigned all claims incident to the first edition.[1]

President Snow's summer entailed the usual routine office business, but the prophet's main focus was forging ahead—preaching tithing to the Church, mostly through visits to stake conferences. Evidently President

Snow was showing some strain from his efforts and age. He suffered some kind of illness or other ailment in mid-June, and six weeks later, one of the Twelve indicated that he thought "President Snow looks worn tired out," and commented, "God help him for his load is great."[2]

On July 13, President Snow again invited the First Council of the Seventy to meet in council with the First Presidency and the Twelve. Elder J. Golden Kimball recalled: "We all assembled and were received very kindly by the Brethren. President Snow, and others, spoke on tithing, and also some of the missions." They discussed some names for a new president of the Cache Stake but were unable to come to agreement then.[3]

President Snow also gave thought to changing his residence. The rented home he had lived in for some years was proving inadequate, and he had been urged by some of the Brethren to move into the Beehive House on the block east of Temple Square, a large and commodious mansion built by Brigham Young. It was convenient since the President's Office was nearby in the Lion House. After mulling over whether to rent someplace else or to build or to buy, in September President Snow made up his mind and decided to live there. He hesitated because of the expense of keeping up such a place, but he finally decided it would make a good official residence for the President of the Church (as had Brigham Young). After waiting a week for renovation and repair work to be completed, President Snow moved in on June 23. A front east room was designated as an office for the First Presidency.[4]

In late October President Snow decided to call Elder Marriner W. Merrill of the Twelve as the president of the Cache Stake in Logan to replace Orson Smith. With the confusion resulting from the financial problems of the former stake president and his prolonged absence, President Snow evidently decided it would be beneficial to have an apostle running the stake, a move he admitted was by that time somewhat unusual.[5] Elder Merrill wrote: "I attended private meeting with President Snow and Apostles Lyman and John Henry Smith this evening to decide who my Counselors were to be, and the Presidency and Twelve in their meeting in the Salt Lake Temple last Thursday, October 26th, decided that I should preside over the Cache Stake of Zion."[6]

At the stake conference, President Snow asked the stake president to resign (which Smith did in his opening talk), accepted it, and then said: "I suppose most of you are anxious to know who will be your president in this stake. Well, you should not be anxious; why should you worry about it? . . . Some want this man; others want another; but I don't care

Lorenzo Snow (USHS)

what his name is, just so he has the necessary qualifications. . . . Now, I wish to select such a man for you, . . . Remember that you, yourselves, are not perfect and therefore do not expect to find perfection in your president. I now present to you the name of the man who is best fitted for this position: it is Apostle Marriner W. Merrill. We think you are worthy of an Apostle, although it is a little out of our regular order. Now it is for you to either accept or reject this man, just as you please."[7] (Elder Merrill only served for a few short years as the calling put a strain on his time and health; he was also serving in the Twelve and as the president of the Logan Temple.)

At this same time, President Snow learned that one of his oldest and dearest friends and associates, President Franklin D. Richards, had suffered a severe setback in his health and become nearly comatose. With this news provoking deep sorrow within him, he also learned that President Cannon, on a business trip to the Eastern United States, had developed pneumonia and for a few nights was in critical condition. President Cannon got well, but President Richards did not and died that December.[8]

While attending a temple council meeting in early November, President Snow decided to reactivate the practice of holding prayer circles at those meetings; this tradition had been temporarily suspended when President Woodruff's health made it inconvenient for him to participate. President Snow also decided to buy the President's Office and Lion House properties from the heirs of Brigham Young.[9] Later that month, President Snow traveled to Brigham City to install a new stake president to take the place of Elder Rudger Clawson, who had been called to the Twelve the year before. This visit turned into a major stake reorganization and evidenced the reason for one of President Snow's oft-spoken counsels—be careful and wise and seek inspiration when calling men to prominent priesthood leadership offices. Elder Clawson recounted events: "Before the opening of the morning meeting Apostle John Henry Smith and myself had a talk with President Snow in relation to the reorganization of the stake presidency" and determined their course. They held a "meeting of the . . . named brethren at President Snow's home after the morning session of the conference. President Snow stated the object of the meeting and asked the brethren, each one, if they were willing to accept the appointments [in the new stake leadership]. Each expressed his willingness to do so and would endeavor to magnify the same." At this point, a certain bishop was asked to speak with President Snow:

> Pres. Snow explained to Bishop _____ that it was deemed advisable to make a change in the bishopric of the Willard Ward and felt that it would be for the best good of all concerned—for himself and for the people—if he would resign. He [Lorenzo Snow] said that affairs in Willard were not satisfactory. He did not wish to go into details, unless Bp. _____ desired it. He had no desire to find fault, but would be content in the statement that he, Bp. _____, probably lacked some of those qualifications that were indispensable to a successful bishop.
>
> Bp. _____ seemed to feel that he was entitled to know the exact cause for asking his resignation. Pres. Snow, thereupon, called upon me [Elder Clawson] to make a statement. I complied by saying that the Willard Ward was not up to the standard of the other wards of the stake; that the tithing was not properly looked after; that, speaking of tithing, the presidency of the stake a year or two ago called Bp. _____ and counselors together and stated clearly and strongly that the tithing was not properly cared for and demanded stricter attention to this matter, but no improvement had since been made; that the Willard Ward, the largest in the stake, paid less tithing than the Brigham City 4th Ward—a ward of widows and orphans; that Willard was always slack in meeting the apportionments made by the Presidency of the church and the presidency of the stake (which Bp. _____ now admitted); that aside from the matters herein specified, many complaints concerning the bishop's neglect had come to the presidency of the stake from the people of the ward; that Bp. _____'s counselors had threatened to resign because of the unsatisfactory condition of affairs. Brother Chas. Kelly endorsed my statement as being correct.
>
> Bp. _____ said he was willing to do anything Pres. Snow desired and, if his resignation was wanted, it would be forthcoming, but he was now taken by surprise and, therefore, asked a few days for consideration. Granted.

In his public remarks that day, Lorenzo indirectly alluded to his experience with the unsuccessful bishop:

> President Lorenzo Snow was the speaker of the afternoon. . . . I suppose you are anxious now, he said, to know who shall be president of the stake. Don't worry about it; you shall know in good time. Said the brethren called will be set apart to these positions. How long will they act? Forever, no, perhaps not. It depends on circumstances. They may be called to other positions; they may be released, possibly, for lack of qualification as the future may develop. He spoke of one of the presiding bishops of the church, who was successful in a small way, but when he came to be Presiding Bishop and had to deal with large concerns, he measurably failed. Referred to the case of a leading man in one of the southern stakes, who was called to preside over a stake because of certain qualifications the brethren thought they discovered in him, but after awhile there was trouble. He failed to visit among the people, to get acquainted with them. For this and other reasons he was asked to resign and it was right to do so.[10]

As legal Trustee-in-trust of the Church, President Snow was vested with final authority for all significant financial decisions and approved all regular expenditures. This duty kept him busy and obligated him to become sufficiently conversant with a wide array of economic aspects, including stock and real estate.[11] December 1 saw the annual tithing settlement instruction circular sent to bishops of all wards in the Church. Among other things, it asked that all *cash* received as tithing be sent immediately to President Snow; he desperately needed it for debt payments as produce and livestock were little help unless they could be sold. (Only around 30 percent of tithing was then paid in cash; the rest was *in-kind*—produce, livestock, real estate, stock, and so on.) Also, a confidential list with names of non-tithe-payers in each ward was requested and prepared. This list was meant to be used privately to invite lax members to repent.[12]

One day in early December, President Snow's business acumen was tested at the same time as his innate Christian love for his fellowmen. He met with a man from Cedar City about selling some property that the Church held a past-due note on. At some previous time the man had been excommunicated and later rebaptized by Elder John W. Taylor. This man did not like the course of the conversation in settling the property issues and indicated his displeasure. Then:

> President Snow replied that he would not like to promise not to dispose of the note to a third party, nor to foreclose the mortgage, as it would all depend upon circumstances. He said further that he considered that

> he had given very fair terms, which could not possibly injure or hamper Brother Thomas Taylor in the sale of his property.
>
> The latter now arose and was about to leave the office, his manner indicating that that was an end to the business. As he moved to go, he said with much feeling and even bitterness that he did not owe this money anyway.
>
> President Snow told him that as Trustee-in-trust he was but doing his duty to the people over whom he presided, and that Brother Taylor, one of the people, should not allow ill feelings to enter his heart against him. So saying the President shook hands with him, and Brother Taylor departed, with the remark that this was only a repetition of his former experiences, that is, whenever he got ready to sell his property, this thing was brought up to hamper him.

Thomas Taylor left unhappy, but after talking further with Church legal counsel, he consented to sell his property, saying that he'd had some information clarified.[13] President Snow was very careful with the Church's tithing funds, but also as charitable toward people as circumstances allowed.

On December 12, President Snow attended President Franklin D. Richards's funeral, and after speaking in glowing terms of his deceased friend, "he related an incident that occurred in the days of the [Mormon] reformation when some thought that the priesthood should be taken from a great many men in the church. Brother Franklin D. Richards and himself went to Pres. Young and tendered to him their priesthood, if he felt they had not magnified it. President Young replied: 'Brothers Lorenzo and Franklin, you have magnified your priesthood to the satisfaction of the Lord. God bless you.'"[14] A touch of mirth is evident in another comment: "I am not surprised at the calling away of President Richards at this time; but had the idea of President Richards passing away been presented to me about the time when he went with us to St. George, some five or six months ago, I should have been surprised, because in looking upon Brother Richards at that time and for many years before, my idea was that he was just as likely to live as any member of the Quorum of the Apostles, and more so, I might say, than one or two whom I might mention."[15]

A few days later in their regular council meeting, the idea of the Church starting a life insurance company was discussed, but it received mixed reaction: "President Snow observed that as this was a new idea to the Council, he thought each member might ponder it over for himself and discuss it further at some other time."[16] The idea would not become reality until President Heber J. Grant's administration.

Just before Christmas that year (1899), while the First Presidency were busy working in their office, President Cannon engaged President Snow in a personal discussion about tithing payment. The discussion sheds light on their relationship:

> President Cannon informed President Snow that he desired to pay a certain amount on account of tithing, but he did not have the money, and therefore proposed to pay it in Grand Central Mining stock at six dollars a share.
>
> President Snow hesitated, for the reason that he did not know the value of such stock.
>
> President Cannon remarked that he did not have to pay it, perhaps, but in order to satisfy his feelings he felt that he ought to do so.
>
> President Snow answered that he did not see why President Cannon should pay tithing unless it was a tenth of his income.
>
> President Cannon explained that his practice had been, whenever he was in a tight place, to overpay his tithing, and he had found that in doing this he had been prospered.
>
> President Snow: "Then, President Cannon, you make the Lord your debtor, and obligated to you."
>
> President Cannon: "No, not in that light."
>
> After further talk on the subject President Snow said that he should leave such matters to President Cannon himself, as he knew what to do, and did not need any counsel from him.
>
> President Smith, however, saw no reason why the Church should not receive President Cannon's tithing in this stock.[17]

Between the holidays, a recently returned missionary visited the President's Office to report his mission and to give President Snow an unusual coin that he himself had earlier been given: "Brother Richard M. Robinson, of Grantsville, called, having just returned from a mission to Florida. He exhibited a gold coin, a little larger though a little thinner than our ten cent silver coin, and containing well marked characters. He stated that this coin had been found by Brother I. N. Carlton of Casey Settlement, Camden County, Georgia, while plowing in his field at that place. It was situated on the St. Mary River, which divides Georgia from Florida. The coin was plowed up last spring, and was given to Brother Robinson in the latter part of August. He now presented it to President Snow, as head of the Church, hoping that it might be found useful in helping to establish the authenticity of the Book of Mormon, or for some other sacred purpose."[18] Brother Robinson later wrote a long narrative explaining that he thought the coin was of Nephite origin. (Neither this coin nor any other has ever been substantiated as such—if the Nephites even had "coins." Most likely it was of Spanish or Roman mint.)[19] Further, in a story that seems to have improved with the passage of time (thirty-five years), he remembered:

> [December 29, 1899] In the office of the First Presidency there were President Lorenzo Snow, President Joseph F. Smith, [and Francis M. Lyman]. After reporting my mission, I took the coin out and showed it to them. . . .
>
> The coin had not tarnished and the characters looked as if they had been stamped. The coin was about the size of the five-dollar Gold piece, eight-cornered and about as thick again as common tin. It was stamped on both sides, the characters running around the outside. The characters were small, somewhat like script or cursive writing. . . .
>
> I was asked what I intended doing with the coin and I turned to President Snow and told him that I was making him a present of the coin; that [Mission] President [Ben E.] Rich had told me that that was the proper thing to do and that I was following his instructions.
>
> President Snow put his arm around my shoulder and said, "Brother Robinson, you have been faithful and have kept the pledge." He then went and got the . . . Seer Stone and said, "This is the Seer Stone that the Prophet Joseph Smith used. There are very few worthy to view this, but you are." He handed the Seer Stone to me and I couldn't express the joy that came to me as I took that stone in my hands. Words are not equal to the task of expressing such a sublime joy. He then told me to hand the Seer Stone to my wife and I handed it to her. He then blessed us with the greatest blessing I have ever heard fall from the mouth of man.
>
> The Seer Stone was the shape of an egg though not quite as large, of a gray cast something like granite but with white stripes running around it. It was transparent but had no holes, neither in the end or in the sides. I looked into the stone, but could see nothing. . . . President Snow blessed us that day and to this day, his promise that we should never suffer for bread has been valid.[20]

The seer stone mentioned has long been a subject of curiosity and scholarly investigation since the Prophet Joseph Smith is thought by many to have used it along with the Urim and Thummim in translating the Book of Mormon from gold plates by the gift and power of God.[21] After falling into President Brigham Young's possession, the stone was put up for sale (along with other relics) by his heirs upon his death. One of President Young's daughters wrote: "I refer to some very sacred articles I bought at the sale of my father's personal effects, articles that never should have been given up to the idle gaze; but being brought out, my mother and myself felt it a wish of our hearts to get them, that their sacredness might not be sullied. They are: two seer stones and an arrow point. They are in the possession of President Woodruff now, and very properly too, but I feel, dear cousin, that they should ever be the property of the President of the Church, and not of individuals; that at his demise, they are not retained as they were before among personal effects, but considered ever the legitimate property of God's mouth-piece. Do I feel right about this? I trust you will make this a matter of history. For having once possessed these holy relics, I desire to leave on record what is right concerning them."[22]

Apparently Robinson was shown one of the two seer stones mentioned here that passed from Zina Young Card to President Woodruff.[23] In showing the seer stone to select and worthy visitors, President Snow followed the example of President Woodruff.[24] Evidently showing the treasured seer stone to others was a purposeful method of strengthening their faith or rewarding loyalty and served as a kind of physical or emotional tie to Joseph Smith.[25]

That same December day, President Snow met with most of the Twelve and his counselors in the President's Office, where a proposed constitutional amendment to outlaw plural marriage was discussed, with President Snow remarking that "he was not disturbed in his feelings over the present situation, but felt perfectly calm. [He] thought we should do what we could in wisdom to forestall threatened evils." Then mentioning the promised blessings associated with tithing payment, he observed: "The saints [are] now doing better than heretofore. One third more tithing has been paid during the past 5 months than during the same period last year. If the saints continue in a more faithful observance of this duty, the Lord will not permit our enemies to bring evil upon us—only so far as it will accomplish His purposes."[26]

On the thirtieth, the First Presidency and Twelve continued their meeting, this time discussing plural marriage as it related to the Manifesto and the commitments that President Woodruff had made to the government and courts relating thereto. "President Lorenzo Snow considered that what President Wilford Woodruff had said in the Court of Chancery in regard to Co-habitation was binding on us." Some emotional discussion followed, since some of the brethren did not want to live apart from plural wives that still wanted children; yet they were willing to follow the prophet's counsel. At this point the newest and youngest apostle, Elder Owen Woodruff, became a little exercised on the subject, feeling they were betraying the principle of plural marriage: "President Snow asked him if he thought his father had done right in giving the manifesto? He said that he believed his father was inspired of God in doing so. President Snow asked which was worse: the abrogation of polygamy or the counsel to abstain from having children? (President Snow is taking the same view on the manifesto as President Woodruff stated publicly was his.) . . . Owen Woodruff wanted to get up and speak but the President said: 'Never mind. You are a young man yet. Let some of your seniors speak.' It was a hard rebuke for poor Owen. He is such a good fellow and what he said he meant, but not in a way to go against the President."[27] Evidently Elder Anthon H. Lund, who wrote the foregoing account, did not capture the full extent of the "rebuke," for in his own journal, Elder Woodruff indicated that President Snow "gave me the most complete sitting down I ever got in my life."[28] President Snow could be firm and unequivocal with the Brethren when necessary.

Chapter 22

Keeping the Church and Its Affairs on Course

In early January 1900, President Snow had an official statement printed in the *Deseret News*. While he himself did not compose it, he did approve and sign it, thereby taking ownership for it. It dealt with the cessation of plural marriages, especially during his administration:

> Polygamy and Unlawful Cohabitation—From the reading of the various editorials and articles of the public press it is evident that there is much misconstruction and misunderstanding as to the present attitude of our Church respecting the subjects of polygamy and unlawful cohabitation; and, believing that many good and conscientious people have been misled and much adverse criticism occasioned thereby, I feel it but just to both "Mormons" and non-"Mormons" to state that, in accordance with the manifesto of the late President Wilford Woodruff, dated September 25th, 1890, which was presented to and unanimously accepted by our General Conference on the 6th of October, 1890, the Church has positively abandoned the practice of polygamy, or the solemnization of plural marriages, in this and every other State, and that no member or officer thereof has any authority whatever to perform a plural marriage or enter into such a relation. Nor does the Church advise or encourage unlawful cohabitation on the part of any of its members. If, therefore, any member disobeys the law, either as to polygamy or unlawful cohabitation, he must bear his own burden; or in other words, be answerable to the tribunals of the land for his own action pertaining thereto.
>
> With a sincere desire that the position of our Church as to polygamy and unlawful cohabitation may be better understood, and with best wishes for the welfare and happiness of all, this statement is made,

Lorenzo Snow (USHS)

and is respectfully commended to the careful consideration of the public generally. Lorenzo Snow; President of the Church of Jesus Christ of Latter-day Saints. Salt Lake City, January 8, 1900.[1]

That month President Snow also visited family in Brigham City. On his return, he met with the First Presidency and Twelve in the temple at what he felt to be a highly spiritual meeting. To those who held the apostleship seated before him, he talked tenderly about the necessity of unity in their Quorum—"although we . . . had met with all kinds of troubles, had suffered from heart burnings, and had been called upon to make all sorts of sacrifices, yet we had never lost hope of arriving in due time at a state of perfect union." He then spoke of deeply sacred feelings within him. The Lord "had sustained his servants and given them grace sufficient to meet and overcome every trial and trouble. This being the fact, he for one, could look into the future with the greatest assurance. He did not feel to worry one particle as to the present or the future. . . . With such feelings as we have here we could not but feel that our Lord and Master is very near to us, and that holy beings are in our presence. With these thoughts in his heart, the President said that he felt to bless his brethren, and he hoped they would continue in the line of salvation and perfection." After the closing prayer, one of the Twelve asked President Snow whether "it was wise for the brethren to speak from the public stand on the principle of plural marriage. President Snow answered that the subject should be let alone and that there was too much being said about it already." He then issued a caution to the Twelve: "Without reference to anyone present, he said, that there were brethren who still seemed to have the idea that it was possible under his administration to obtain a plural wife and have her sealed to him. He authorized and requested the brethren present to correct this impression wherever they find it. He said emphatically that it could not be done. President Cannon moved that this be accepted as the mind and will of the Lord. Seconded by Brother Lyman and carried unanimously."[2]

About this time—January 1900—a smallpox scare gripped some areas of Utah, and therefore President Snow cancelled some stake conferences and temporarily closed the temples; they were reopened in mid-February.[3] At the end of January, President Snow received a visit from the owner of the local telephone company (telephones were still fairly new in Utah at that time), asking if the Church would invest in his company and also wanting to buy the Church's telegraph company. President Snow eagerly accepted the offer to sell, but not to buy, "stating that the Church was not investing any means, but on the contrary was getting out of debt as fast as possible."[4]

In early February, James Talmage visited with Presidents Snow and Cannon about his assignment to divide the Pearl of Great Price into chapters and verses. He desired to provide footnotes and was informed this was acceptable as long as they were limited to cross-references to other verses, and not doctrinal commentary.[5]

Three days later, Elder B. H. Roberts "called and had a talk with President Snow regarding his political troubles and President Snow advised him to settle down to his ecclesiastical duties and cease fighting the inevitable; he had done all in his power and had made a courageous and proper fight in his endeavor to retain his seat in the National House of Representatives, and had accomplished all he, President Snow, thought was possible for him to accomplish, and the President believed that great good would come out of it."[6]

During February, the First Presidency and Twelve considered an unusual proposition that two emissaries from the "Hedrickite" or "Church of Christ, Temple Lot" splinter group brought them. These "Hedrickite" elders wanted to form a non-binding committee made up of representatives from their church, from the Reorganized Church of Jesus Christ of Latter Day Saints (sometimes also called the "Josephites"; now known as the Community of Christ), and the Utah Mormons (LDS). The committee, to consist of four representatives from each church, would explore possible ways to unite the three faiths and also seek a way to build a temple in Jackson County on property they owned. President Snow took their proposition seriously, giving the men a complete hearing and asking many questions. From the start it was apparent that much bad feeling had arisen that would somehow need to be overcome if the proposed reunification were possible between the LDS and RLDS. President Snow felt that one of the Prophet Joseph Smith's sons, Joseph Smith III, had some serious repenting to do before a reconciliation could take place, and then there was the RLDS disbelief in temple work to consider. Further:

> President Snow told them that . . . the time was fast approaching, in his opinion, when the Lord would require the building of the Temple at Jackson county, but it would certainly require means to accomplish it. The Latter-day Saints had to some extent been neglectful of the law of tithing and it was through obedience to this law and that of Consecration that the land was to be sanctified, and it would be done in no other way. He was happy to say that there had been a marked increase and improvement in this direction among the Saints. The law of tithing he regarded as the stepping stone to the higher law of consecration. Referring to the main question President Snow said that he could not at the present time answer whether the Lord would require of the Saints to see if a reconciliation could be affected between the Church and the Reorganites or not, for his mind was not clear regarding it; but he was not unmindful of the fact that to send four men as a committee to represent us would not in any way commit the Church to anything which might be said or done. He feared, however, that we might just as well undertake to unite with twenty-four of the Utah sectarian ministers as to try to form a reconciliation with the Reorganized church. "But," said he, "as you brethren come in the name of the Lord, I am willing to consider the proposition and see if there be any reasonable chance to act upon it."

When consulted, President Cannon expressed a willingness to try but had little faith in success, since the problem of the RLDS acknowledging LDS authority loomed over the whole issue—although he knew the Lord could overcome anything. President Smith expressed a similar view. At that point in the discussion, "President Snow informed the visiting gentlemen that he did not feel to act in regard to the matter without laying it before the Quorum of the Twelve Apostles. And as it would take about ten days to bring the brethren together this question was postponed until a quorum could be reached, which he thought could not be before the 20th."[7]

Eleven days later, President Snow and his counselors presented the proposition of the Hedrickites to the Twelve for full consideration. He reviewed the issue for all present and then had the two Hedrickites further explain their proposition to the assembled Brethren. More questions were asked by President Snow and were answered. It was clarified that all the Hedrickite men wanted to do was form a nonbinding committee of four men from each of the three churches to try to work out a unity so the temple could be built and the three Churches could seek a way to combine. "President Snow remarked that to his mind it appeared almost an impossibility to create a union out of such discordant elements, but if it were the will of the Lord it would be proper for us to try it."

A lengthy discussion ensued with more questions and answers, some Brethren not feeling satisfied that any real progress could be made with the proposition but still willing to try if the council so decided. "President Snow now brought the conversation to the object of the meeting, and asked the brethren to confine their remarks to it, viz. whether we should send this delegation to Independence, [Missouri,] or not. To do such a thing, he said, could not be done in secret. He did not care about the world knowing it, but the question in his mind was, How would the Latter-day Saints regard it?" This question was then discussed at some length, after which President Snow again spoke:

> He remarked that we believe as the Hedrickites do that in Missouri there was a bad state of things existing when the law of consecration was rejected. We believe also that the law of tithing was given as a substitute, and he was sorry that that law had not been strictly adhered to, but was pleased to say that the people were doing very much better now. He spoke of the late solemn assembly of the Priesthood and the improved state of things was the result of the deliberations of that gathering and the spirit attending. "If the people will now faithfully obey that law," said President Snow, "And we believe they will, it will prepare them for the higher law of consecration; and when that time comes, the people will be prepared to answer any extraordinary call which the Lord may require of them."

Discussion continued, and it was decided to meet later that day without the Hedrickites present, so members of the Twelve could speak their minds freely regarding the proposed venture. When reconvened later that day, "President Snow now declared the meeting open to consider the above question and remarked that he appreciated the spirit in which these men had come to us, but he was not unmindful of the fact that when the Temple should be built at Jackson county, this church would do it. . . . President Snow said because of the innocent persons among these [Independence] organizations, he believed the time would come when those two factions would break up and the majority of them gradually come to us. But the question now was, Shall we send a delegation to Independence?" After further deliberations, President Cannon spoke:

> There is one thought which has passed through my mind which has struck me as being worthy of consideration. Our hearts for years have inclined towards the center stake of Zion. President Taylor wanted to create a fund outside of the tithing, which could be used by himself as President of the Church for any purpose which the Lord might signify to him, which would not trench upon the tithing. He did create such a fund, and the predominant idea in his mind was to watch for a favorable opportunity to buy land in Independence, and we have all felt, no doubt, the desire of that kind. In our deliberations this morning sixty-three acres have been mentioned and it struck him that this conference of committees might result in a way being perceived by which a purchase of that kind might be made. Land might be purchased for us in a way which we could not do ourselves, and that without creating excitement. The speaker said he had heard Presidents Young, Taylor and Woodruff talk in this strain; and the question arose in his mind this morning that perhaps this was an opening for us to accomplish something of this kind. It was plain that the land would have to be purchased, and that we would have to pay for it; it could not be got in another way.
>
> President Snow remarked that President Cannon had expressed his views exactly in relation to the purchase of land. His mind, he said, was tolerably clear in regard to the redemption of Zion in a general way. We are not prepared for it now. We must have money; and if pieces of land could be bought without creating excitement or placing a burden upon us, he would be in for it. If we were to undertake to do this, he feared it would not be kept from the public. We must first get out of debt, and be economical in our affairs; and to do this he asked each person present to keep up the spirit of tithing, to keep the law themselves and to teach others what the Lord requires us to do. We do not ask the rich man to give and make sacrifices, but simply tell the people to pay their honest conscientious tithing. It was clear to his mind it would not take long to create a fund, and when this should be done it would be in order to purchase the land as opportunity presented without creating excitement. In this way, he believed, Zion would be redeemed, as President Cannon had said, by purchase. He was perfectly sure this was the way. The visiting "Brethren" were no doubt excited, and they have no doubt caught the spirit which is now upon the people; but they are sadly out of the way by thinking that this great work was to be done by uniting themselves with the Reorganites and with us. The way this will be done is by the Latter-day Saints paying their tithing; and then there will

> perhaps have to be a change in the government; but this the Lord will attend to. Even if the right men should be sent, he feared that the thing would be made public, and we would be compelled to read things in the newspapers which we would not care to see printed.

At this point Elder John W. Taylor shared his views: he didn't care for the RLDS and was worried that land prices in Independence would become highly inflated if the Church started buying it up. "Elder George Teasdale could not see that any possible good could come out of this thing. The only way to assist the Lord in building up his kingdom was for men to be in harmony with his authority; and, addressing himself personally to President Snow, the speaker said: 'We sustain you as Prophet, Seer and Revelator, and we know who you are; and I do not believe the Lord will pass you by for these men to come and dictate as to appointing anybody to confer with them about the building of a Temple at the center Stake of Zion.'" More discussion ensued, reiterating the feeling that when the temple should be built, the Lord would move upon the President of the Church to do so. If they started buying land in Independence now, and it became public, land prices would skyrocket. Still, some of the Twelve favored sending a delegation while others objected. President Snow then talked further:

> He said he was pleased to hear the expressions of the brethren. He had set no stakes as to what would be proper or improper. He had left the matter unsolved in his own mind until he should hear his brethren express their views, and now, since he had heard them, he could say that he could not feel satisfied to favor sending the delegation to Independence, and he could not think of doing it unless the First Presidency and Twelve heartily approved of it. It would be a mighty up-hill business, he said, and he had not the faintest idea that a union between the Latter-day Saints and the members of the Reorganized church could be effected; in fact such a thing appeared to be entirely out of the question. However, he thought he could see that some possible advantages might arise from such an effort; and yet he had doubted all the time the divinity of the revelation claimed by these visiting brethren that the time had now come for the building of the Temple. He naturally feared some trick being played against us. . . . My mind is now clear, he said, since hearing the brethren talk, that we should not listen to this message. I do not know how we could go before the Lord and say to him that we had sent four of our members on an errand that we did not know anything at all about; and I am sure that we are not prepared, even if we could unite, to carry on the object of the

> visit of these gentlemen. President Snow said he looked for cyclones and earthquakes and the power of the Lord made manifest to make this step. The spirit indicates to me, he said, that the time is speedily coming when we shall build that temple, and when that time comes we will have means to make the necessary land purchases, and means to do the work. My feelings are clear that we should not accept the proposition of these men; but, (addressing President Cannon) he said, I feel that we should pay their expenses while they are here and until they arrive back in Independence.

At this point, "President Cannon moved that this decision be accepted by this Council as the word of the Lord on this subject, and that these brethren be notified accordingly. Seconded by several of the brethren and unanimously carried." It was then decided that "it was also the sense of the Council that President Snow send for these gentlemen and give them their answer. At 4:30 [they] returned to the office, having been sent for. President Snow conversed privately with them and apparently they were quite prepared to receive what he said to them."[8]

Later that March, President Snow's attention returned to the work of publication on the new edition of the Pearl of Great Price. He approved of a permanent, standing committee that could work with Brother Talmage and others involved with such church publications. The committee consisted of two members of the Twelve and a Seventy.[9]

President Snow continued to receive requests for financial assistance from the stakes, often for their educational academies. When representatives from the Oneida, Idaho, Stake Academy sought his help, "President Snow expressed himself in the language of the scriptures: The spirit was willing but the flesh was weak. He regretted very much that as Trustee-in-trust he did not feel himself able to render the school the assistance it deserves, but when he realized the financial condition of the Church and was brought face to face with the many calls upon him for urgent and legitimate assistance, he longed for the day when financial freedom should come to the Church, so that he could be free to bestow help where needed. President Snow, however told [them] not to close the school, but to wait a little while as he intended to see what could be done by way of helping other [church sponsored] schools in the same condition as theirs, and they left in the hope that help would yet be received."[10]

About mid-month, during the regular council meeting of the First Presidency and Twelve, it was learned from Elder Clawson that the Mutual Improvement Association (MIA) was trying to raise money from their members to purchase a monument for the gravesite of President Woodruff.

His will had provided only enough money for a small marker, and the MIA desired to put a larger monument there instead because President Woodruff had been the general president of that organization. It was then suggested that the Church donate to this cause, after which the following solemn but slightly humorous discussion ensued:

> President Cannon remarked that [a small headstone] expressed more the character of President Woodruff, and he would be sorry to see a movement on the part of anyone to erect a costly monument; anyway, it did not seem to him the right thing to do and he was in favor of a modest suitable stone being erected in keeping with the character of President Woodruff, and this ought to be done. President Snow agreed with this.
>
> President Cannon further stated that [purchasing expensive monuments] . . . would create a precedent to be followed by others, and it would only be a question of time when this spirit of monument building would become prevalent. . . . Addressing his remarks to Elder Clawson, President Cannon said he could not favor the idea of calling upon the Mutual Improvement Associations to make collections for monument building, not even for President Woodruff, for whom he entertained the greatest respect and whose memory was very dear to him.
>
> President Snow remarked that if this thing were done for President Woodruff, then it would naturally follow that someone would start the idea to do something in the same way for himself by and by, and so the thing would go on, and neither President Woodruff nor himself cared a fig about a monument. . . .
>
> President Snow stated that President Cannon had expressed his views exactly. He did not believe in building monuments to our leading men, not but what they were worthy of all that we could possibly do by way of perpetuating their memories, for such men were worthy of a world and will be of an eternity of worlds; but it was the example which others would certainly follow.
>
> President Smith inquired if the communications addressed to the various associations on this subject could be recalled?
>
> President Snow did not know, but thought it was time the public was given a rest and calls for money from the public should stop.[11]

Toward the end of March and into early April 1900, President Snow determined it was time to decide a major outstanding point related to succession in the presidency. Brigham Young Jr. had been ordained an apostle by his father before Joseph F. Smith; but Joseph F. Smith, although being ordained an apostle after Brigham Jr., had been set apart as a member of the Quorum of the Twelve Apostles before Brigham. Therefore, the question remained as to which took precedence in determining seniority—the timing of the apostolic ordination or that of being set apart as a member of the Quorum of the Twelve. The issue was becoming increasingly important because the two men senior to them, Presidents Snow and Cannon, were both elderly and gradually declining in vigor. Further, at this time there was not yet a provision established for an "acting" President of the Twelve, so if the next senior apostle after the president of the Twelve was serving in the First Presidency, things became less clear for succession. President Joseph F. Smith described one meeting where this situation was reviewed:

> Presidents Snow, Cannon and I had a confidential talk together, introduced by President Cannon, relative to the choosing of a President of the Twelve. President Snow said: "It is President Cannon's right to stand at the head of the Twelve, but if he did he would have to resign his counsellorship in the Presidency," and plainly intimated that he could do so if he chose. He then said to President Cannon: "If you and I were not here it would be the right of Brother Joseph F. Smith to stand where I am now, and if I were not here, it would be yours right now. President Cannon expressed his desire to possess and enjoy every right that belonged to him but suggested that matters go along for the present as they are and that the Presidency meet with the Twelve and take the lead. Brigham's (Brigham Young Jr.) position in the quorum was talked over and President Snow favored and practically decided that Brigham Young ranked next to [after] me in the council of Apostles. This decided the question, as it was decided by President John Taylor.[12]

President Snow wasted no time bringing up the matter for consideration with the Twelve, but he also lost no opportunity to revisit the subject of tithing. At their council meeting preparatory to the April general conference, "President Snow as Trustee-in-trust presented an elaborate financial report, showing receipts of the Church from all sources during the past year, also the disbursements. On motion the report was received and approved and ordered filed. President Snow made some remarks in relation to the report, and expressed his gratitude that the credit of the Church was so much better now than it was a year ago, because all danger had been removed of creditors making demands that could not be met. The President dwelt on the subject of tithing, and urged the brethren to keep this subject alive in their hearts and among the Saints."[13] After some further discussion about tithing, "Pres. Snow said that it would be necessary to fill the vacancy of the quorum made by the death of the late Franklin

D. Richards and requested the Brethren to hand in two names each for consideration. Apostle Merrill said, speaking for himself personally, that he would prefer to leave the matter with the First Presidency and that he fully believed the Lord would inspire Pres. Snow to make the proper selection. Pres. Snow said that he thought so, too, after the names had been handed in."[14]

President Joseph F. Smith described the next item discussed in the meeting:

> We met with the eleven Apostles and partook of the Sacrament, Brigham Young [Jr.] blessed the emblems. It was unanimously decided that the acceptance of a member into the council or quorum of the Twelve fixed his rank or position in the Apostleship. That the Apostles took precedence from the date they entered the quorum. Thus today, President Snow is the senior Apostle. President George Q. Cannon next, myself next, Brigham Young next, Francis M. Lyman next, and so on to the last one received into the quorum. In the case of the death of President Snow, President Cannon surviving him, would succeed to the Presidency, and so on according to seniority in the Apostleship of the Twelve; that ordination to the Apostleship under the hands of any Apostle other than to fill a vacancy in the quorum, and authorized by the General Authorities of the Church did not count in precedence; that if the First Presidency were dissolved by the death of the President, his counselors having been ordained Apostles in the Quorum of the Twelve would resume their places in the quorum, according to the seniority of their ordinations into that quorum. This important ruling settles a long unsettled point, and is most timely.[15]

That Saturday night, at the general priesthood session of conference, President Snow took occasion to gently reprimand the assemblage for slackness in following up with members of their stakes and wards that had not paid tithing. He exhibited a large book which contained the names of 10,000 non-tithe-payers, and remonstrated that it would have only contained half as many if the local leaders had done their full duty in the matter. He then indicated that "the matter of paying tithing was very important, as among other things the redemption of Zion (namely, Jackson County) would be brought about by purchase with the tithes of the people. In order to improve and correct conditions as they exist at present, he had concluded to divide up the 42 stakes of Zion among the Twelve and make them responsible to look into the matter of tithe-paying."[16]

The next day, before the sustaining vote was taken in general conference, "According to the request of President Snow the members of the Apostles quorum suggested names for the vacancy in their quorum which is to be filled at this conference today. Immediately after the forenoon session today the brethren of the quorum of the Twelve and the Presidency met in the President's Office for the purpose of filling the vacancy. The meeting was short. President Snow informing the brethren that the First Presidency had considered the names suggested and had decided on Elder Reed Smoot to fill the vacancy in the quorum if his selection was approved by the members of the quorum. The nomination was seconded and unanimously carried."[17] At that point:

> Elder Reed Smoot was then called in from an adjoining room and was informed by President Snow what had been decided upon and was invited to express himself regarding the matter. President Snow said further, however, that in calling a man to be an apostle, we take into consideration the man whom the Lord wants, and who will give his heart to the work. We want a man who will be strong in the Lord and will so live that he can have the Spirit of the Lord to give him understanding and judgment in deciding matters of importance that may arise from time to time. We believe that you are such a man. Elder Reed Smoot said he was willing to do anything the Lord required of him, but, nevertheless, he felt his unfitness for the appointment and was very weak. President Snow explained how Moses was called of God to lead Israel. He felt his weakness, but God made him strong. Elder Smoot said he did not know how much help he would be to the quorum, as heretofore he had been engaged more particularly in financial matters. President Snow said in reply, that he did not know either, but felt the Lord could qualify him for the labor. . . . President Cannon said that in case Brother Reed Smoot is ordained an apostle, it is his privilege to see the Lord Jesus, if he so desires and shall live for it, that he may indeed become a special witness of Jesus. This privilege belongs to the apostleship. Warned him against entering into any cabal or association outside of the quorum. We should enter into the quorum or council meetings free from any previous considerations or understandings.
>
> Apostle John H. Smith asked Elder Smoot if he accepted Lorenzo Snow as the leader of the church and as having the right to counsel him in all things. He answered, yes, but further remarked that he was of a positive nature and when he saw and felt a thing to be right, it was hard for him to change and see it differently.
>
> President Joseph F. Smith remarked that the Presidency and Apostles were all constituted that way, but sometimes it became

> necessary to change our views. President Snow said a condition like this has prevailed, namely, that there are men in the church who have stood out against the combined judgment of the First Presidency, the Twelve, the First Council of Seventies, the Patriarch, and the Presiding Bishopric. This, he said, was damnable and has in some measure grown out of the spirit of the devil in politics. . . .
>
> President Snow said, we will present you to the conference, and the church will accept you, of course. Anybody that can pass beyond the scrutiny of the Twelve, can pass into any place in the church.[18]

After general conference, President Snow spoke to a special gathering of local and general Church authorities in the Assembly Hall. He opened his heart to them and spoke candidly. Elder Rudger Clawson reported some of his remarks: "I love you, but that love will not prevent me from telling you your duty." He told those assembled not to go into debt and that the Church was striving to get out of debt. He told them that the tithing payment improvements had helped reduce the Church's monthly interest expenditures. He also spoke of the highest blessings available in the temple and stated, "This blessing is not only intended for the aged, but also for younger men. . . . The privilege should only be given to those who have been tried and tested, being full of integrity and not likely to fall away. In reference to non-tithe-payers, he said we cannot receive them into our temples; and if bishops send people to the temple who have not paid tithing and we find it out, we will send them back and have the bishops reported."[19] President Snow could lay down the law when needed.

On April 9, President Snow was voice as he and his counselors and the Twelve ordained Reed Smoot to the apostleship and set him apart as a member of the Twelve.[20] A few days later the Twelve met together to divide among themselves all of the stakes in the Church for the purpose of "looking into the matter of tithing" as they had been directed by President Snow.[21] Later that month President Snow and Elder Heber J. Grant had a talk, in which it was decided that President Snow would forgive Elder Grant of the obligation to make good on a pledge of two thousand dollars that he had committed himself to some seven years previously, when urgent funds were needed to finish the interior of the Salt Lake Temple.[22] Since then Elder Grant's financial fortunes had suffered to the brink of bankruptcy, and he needed all the relief he could get. The same day President Snow declined an invitation to have the Sanpete Stake Academy change its name to the "Lorenzo Snow Academy" and instead counseled that it be named the "Snow" Academy, after himself and Erastus Snow.[23]

Snow Academy eventually became Snow College, a thriving undergraduate institution.

The month of May began with President Snow attending the funeral of a grandson and asking Elder Clawson, bookkeeper and auditor of Church finances, to work up a report showing how much money the federal government had taken from the Church under the provisions of the Edmunds-Tucker law.[24]

On May 10, President Snow presided at a meeting of the First Presidency and Twelve of some considerable importance to future generations of the Church. On this occasion an extended discussion on the best method of writing the history of the Church ensued. Over a year previously, a Church publication committee was given the responsibility to oversee the beginning and continuation of the project. B. H. Roberts had been chosen and consulted as to his availability to do the work and had agreed. Hundreds of pages of source material had by then been compiled by the Church historian, Elder Richards. President Cannon wanted to know if B. H. Roberts would do all of the anticipated volumes or just the first; this point had not yet been settled. Elder Roberts was then probably the finest and most qualified historical writer in the Church—though others were also known to be skilled with a pen. "President Snow also remarked that the idea was that it would be well to employ Brother Roberts to get out, say, the first volume, and then he might continue his labors unless there should be some reason for a change."

The content and methodology of the work was then considered: whether the narrative would follow the history of Joseph Smith as an outline to be expanded upon or whether Joseph Smith's history should simply be reedited from previously published sources:

> If so, President Cannon was of the opinion that the history of the Church would be a very crude and unsatisfactory work.
>
> President Snow said it was clear to his mind that something ought to be done in this direction, and for that reason he put this committee to work, and he thought too that the history of the Prophet Joseph should be published just as he wrote with the exception of grammatical errors; however, there may be some things that it would not be wisdom to publish in his history, but now was the time to determine the character of the proposed work. He expected that when this committee reported that Presidents Cannon and Smith and the Apostles would be prepared to make their suggestions in regard to it.
>
> President Smith remarked that there was evidently great need for a

> compiled history of the Church, and such a compilation would always be at hand as a basis for a history which might be written by some fairly competent man hereafter.
>
> President Cannon expressed his entire approval of this, also of President Snow's idea about reproducing the history of the prophet Joseph Smith in a revised form, and with that understanding Brother Roberts's duties in this regard would be only to edit the publishing of the proposed work in different volumes, and this could be done in a comparatively short time.

In answer to the question of who Elder Roberts would report to for direction in his work, along with the Committee, "President Snow answered that he thought that would be proper with the understanding of course, that the committee confer with the First Presidency on important matters or matters on which they might be in doubt." President Cannon then talked about the associated problems of historical writing, feeling that one man alone could not write the entire history of the Church, that without material from the Office of the President the history would not be complete. He referenced other collections of correspondence for periods of importance that had not been assembled and inventoried for such use. The brethren then approved type or font styles and sizes for the proposed history. They also formally appointed Roberts "to edit the proposed history of the Church, commencing with the history of the Prophet Joseph Smith, under the supervision of the committee and the First Presidency."[25]

Within several days, further developments concerned with the writing of the history had taken place—Elder Roberts had not been as willing as hoped. Elder Anthon H. Lund of the publication committee had a long talk with President Snow and a few other Brethren about employing Elder Roberts to edit the history of the Church as previously contemplated. Elder Roberts was being paid a living allowance by the Church of $1,200 per year but wanted another $2,500 to do the historical work. President Snow and Cannon "thought this was too much," since it would be compiling and editing documents, not writing original text. Other names were suggested to do the work, but President Cannon's name was also suggested: "at least so far as supervising it was concerned, this desire was generally expressed, President Snow joining in it, but no conclusion was arrived at."

Later that day Elder Francis M. Lyman (chairman of the publication committee) was consulted on the proposed change in direction. "President Snow informed him that during the forenoon some talk was had about having President George Q. Cannon edit the history. Brother Lyman replied that if President Cannon's health would permit of it he would feel free, personally, from responsibility in the matter as he knew of no one more competent to do the work than President Cannon. President Snow then asked President Cannon if he felt that his physical condition would permit him to undertake the task. President Cannon answered that if this was the mind of President Snow and the committee, he had no other alternative than to place himself at their services, and this he did freely and willingly, promising to give the publication of the work his best attention." Elder Lyman indicated that he would let Elder B. H. Roberts know his services would not be needed.[26] That same day President Snow enjoyed his first ride in an automobile (a newer invention), with a Mr. Silver.[27]

About this time, President Snow dealt with further financial difficulties. A prominent Church member that owed the Church a substantial sum applied to the First Presidency with a request that they forgive his debt legally, though he would still consider repayment a moral obligation. He felt this action would improve his business position enough with creditors to enable him to regain his former credit and status. "President Snow stated that he could not feel satisfied or justified as Trustee-in-trust in according to this request; at the same time it was understood that the Church would not press him."[28]

A few days later, the same man again applied to the First Presidency for relief from his substantial debt, saying if he was not excused from it he would soon lose his store to his creditors; but otherwise he thought he could still make it and eventually pay back the church. "President Snow told [him] that he did not feel that he was entitled to the consideration for which he asked, especially in view of the fact that the Trustee-in-trust was compelled to say no to men who had sought for the necessities of life; men, too, who had filled missions and given of their time to the service of the Church and whose families in many instances were suffering." After further deliberation, it was agreed that President Snow would not instigate legal action against the man while he worked with his other creditors to reorganize his business, but if he could not and his business was disposed of, the Church would expect their proportionate share of his remaining assets upon dissolution or sale of his company.[29] With these issues pressing on his mind, President Snow took another automobile ride.[30]

The financial requests did not let up. In one meeting, a proposal was brought to President Snow to remodel the Assembly Hall (on Temple Square next to the Salt Lake Tabernacle) so that it could house the LDS college. The idea never materialized.[31] At the same meeting a decision was made to arrange for prospective missionaries to receive more thorough interviews before being called to service, as occasional unworthy elders were being sent out who were embarrassing the Church with their poor choices and actions. Further, it was decided that funds used for missionaries support should not be tithed.[32]

Two days later, John W. Rigdon, a son of Sidney Rigdon, visited with the First Presidency at their office, and spoke freely with them. He admitted to having entertained doubts about the authenticity of the Book of Mormon for much of his life, but after talking with his father when on his deathbed, his doubts had been partially removed, and now he leaned toward believing it to be true. "He, in talking with his father during his last hours said, 'Father, you are now an old man, and I want you to tell me if you still believe the Book of Mormon to be what it represents to be, and if Joseph Smith always maintained that it was true and a genuine record?' His father answered in the most solemn manner that it was a true and genuine record, and that Joseph Smith always maintained its genuineness, and that he translated it by the gift and power of God from the gold plates shown to him by the angel. John Rigdon said he had come to believe the Book of Mormon, but his wife and children did not and were now antagonistic to the Church and the Book of Mormon. He said his father died an unhappy man, but in hopes and assurance of a glorious resurrection."[33]

As time passed, the First Presidency, and President Snow himself, entertained a wide variety of visitors. President Snow's youngest daughter Rhea Lucille remembered occasions when important guests met with her father: "Sometimes I was sent by Mama into the President's Office to tell Papa dinner was ready, when he was having an important conference. Great dignitaries might be there. . . . They always wanted to meet Papa. He heard my knock and said, 'Come in,' so I could. He always stood up then, and . . . would say 'Gentlemen, this is my little daughter Lucille. May I now be excused. Minnie, my good wife has prepared the meal and it is ready to serve; I never keep her waiting.'" He would then pick his daughter up and take her to the dinner table. Afterward he would often hold her and stroke her hair with his old, gnarled hands.[34]

June and July of 1900 were trying months for President Snow. He suffered with pain in his legs and lower back. On June 6, he was only out of bed long enough to open his mail. By June 12, a doctor tried to relieve his pain, likely with morphine injections, and he received a blessing.[35] On the night of June 28, "he did not rest well and vomited considerably in the night."[36] The next day, President Snow was feeling so much pain that he could not attend his son LeRoi's wedding in the temple, so President Cannon substituted for him as officiator.[37] During the first week of July, President Snow took several automobile rides to relieve his cabin fever, but he felt miserable and spent the rest of his time in his room in bed.[38] On July 7, "President Snow walked into the office for the first time since he was confined to his bed; however, he spent no time in the office and later in the day he went for a drive."[39] Finally, President Snow's condition started to improve enough that by mid-July he was able to greet and briefly visit with some members of the First Presidency and Twelve at the President's Office.[40]

On July 11, the Apostles, in their council meeting, decided that President Snow should "be asked to provide a suitable receptacle for church relics and that the same as fast as gathered be deposited in the temple."[41] (This enigmatic note likely referred to such items as the seer stones and original manuscripts of revelations, and was probably a precursor to what eventually became known as the First Presidency's vaults, now located in the Church Administration Building and the Granite Mountain Vault.)

The next day, "President Cannon informed the council that President Snow came into the office yesterday, and in chatting with him desired the minutes of the Council of April 5th last passed upon, he having heard of them and approved of them himself. The minutes referred to the succession in the presidency and seniority of the Apostles quorum; and on motion of President Joseph F. Smith, and seconded by Elder Brigham Young, the minutes were unanimously approved."[42] Evidently, during his lengthy illness, the imminent possibility of his own death caused him to be mindful of the attendant succession consequences. Indeed, this particular illness had been severe and prolonged enough that it could be thought a more logical and natural time for the aged President Snow to die than when he actually did a year and a half later, evidencing the fact that Higher powers were directing his ministry. President Snow continued to suffer pain for a few more weeks in his legs and was only intermittently able to work in the office or attend meetings with the Twelve.

> I was called to the presidency of the church, which will explain in part the necessity for the presence of the Twelve at home. The financial situation of the church was deplorable. I remember as I was leaving to attend the first general conference held after I was sustained as president—or rather the general conference at which I was sustained—Brother [James] Jack came to me and said that a certain man, whom the church was owing, wanted $10,000 immediately and the balance due him shortly after. The church actually could not pay it. This was the first intimation I had of the real condition of affairs. I found that the church was obligated for about $4,000,000—$2,500,000 of direct indebtedness and $1,500,000 of guaranteed indebtedness. Frank J. Cannon was sent East to borrow $1,500,000 pledging the church property as security, and he couldn't get it. Had the people we were owing at that time come against us, this church would have been bankrupt. Such was really the case. To relieve the situation it was decided to bond the church for $500,000 and later for another $500,000—making a million dollars in all. The bonds found ready sale at home, and we had money to meet our pressing obligations.
>
> The question arose as to how we were going to pay off the church indebtedness. During my trip to St. George last year, the Lord manifested to me that it was to be done through the tithing of the people. This message was carried to the saints by the First Presidency and Twelve, and with splendid results. . . . We are not borrowing money and do not need to. The brethren of the Twelve have assisted us in bringing about this condition. Through the blessing of the Lord, the guaranteed indebtedness of $1,500,000 has been removed from the church, which is miraculous in our eyes.[14]

Another account of these remarks from President Snow includes these details:

> Insomuch as we are united, we can say to the Lord, What do you want us to do? No matter what it might cost us or what the sacrifice might be, whatever was required of us we could do. "I say again," said he, "We are not going to be idle; the Lord has conferred upon us the highest Priesthood upon the earth and will not let us stand idle. We will have something to do requiring great faith and the manifestation of the power of God to accomplish it. I am sure of this, Amen."

The thoughts and feelings expressed at this time by President Snow became the underlying impetus for the gradual spread of missionary work across the earth as seen by the Church throughout the twentieth century.

President Snow then "asked President Cannon to address the brethren as he might be led." President Cannon then expressed his feelings and impressions along the same vein as that which President Snow had:

> There was one thing near his heart which had occupied his mind a great deal of late and that was the opening of the foreign missions. When he thought of the lands unvisited and the great work yet to be done by way of preaching the Gospel before the coming of the Lord, it opened up to his view a mighty field which meant work and perhaps much sacrifice; but he felt that every one present should be able to feel that he had done his full duty by way of preaching the Gospel to people who had been praying for the Gospel, and he believed there were many people in the same condition and that it was the duty of the Twelve to see to it that the Gospel of the Kingdom is preached to all nations, and if he were a member of that quorum he would not rest without breaking through the routine labor now being done and penetrate new lands. . . . Although his physical condition was not as good as it had been and therefore he felt embarrassed somewhat in speaking in this way, however if called he would willingly go forth to open up some of these fields. These feelings had been strongly working in him for a long time, and he hoped that no exceptions would be taken to what he had said.

This was exactly what President Snow wanted to hear and what he wanted the Twelve to hear and internalize, and he told them so. Some of the Twelve began making suggestions of how to begin missionary work in foreign nations, expressing their willingness to go if called, and recommending that prospective missionaries should study the languages of foreign countries before leaving for service. "Elder Brigham Young . . . said it was very evident to him that there was something before us [the Twelve] of an unlooked for character, and when President Snow mentioned this, the spirit in him bore witness of it. The feeling of his fellow Apostles was that they hold themselves in readiness to go or come at the bidding of the Presidency. Every member of that quorum had stated while they had been together in their own meeting that they were in perfect harmony with the First Presidency, and if the Presidency say, 'Go abroad to the Nations of the earth, there was not a man of the quorum but what was ready to go at an hour's notice.'"[15]

After this meeting, it was again time for general conference. In his first talk, President Snow returned to a theme that had marked his private efforts in presiding capacities for a dozen years:

> Here are my counselors. We are one. We are united. We do not quarrel with each other. We speak well of one another because we ought to do it, and we think we are worthy of being well spoken of by each other. And here we have twelve men sitting in front with us—Twelve Apostles. There are many of these that you know. You know them from hearing what they have accomplished. You have a personal acquaintance with some of us. Now they are with us heart and soul. We are united together. We do not quarrel with each other. We do not slander one another, but we go where counsel requires and we are heart and soul together. What for? Not to make ourselves rich, not to make ourselves wealthy, but to see what we can accomplish in the interests of the people, and we are laboring continually to see what we can do. We come together every week and we talk about what we can do for the people. What can we do for these forty-two or forty-three Stakes of Zion? . . . We talk these things over. We study and consider them. . . . We are not idle in these things.[16]

President Snow was at last willing to state publicly and with conviction that the leading councils of the Church were unified, a goal he had sought with steady diligence for so many years. Then President Snow addressed the priesthood leadership of the Church, reminding them of their place and purpose and work, according to revelation that had come to him:

> He said he was sure he was standing before an audience composed of the greatest men on the earth who had a great work to accomplish. Wherein, he asked, was our greatest?
>
> The answer comes to us all with no uncertain sound, in the Priesthood we hold, as without this there is very little to any of us. Speaking personally he said, aside from the Priesthood which God has bestowed upon him there was not much to him, and in speaking thus of himself he thought it would apply to everyone present. Our true greatness lay in our magnifying the priesthood. He appreciated the fact that he was standing before men who would in time be gods, but our glory, after all, would depend entirely upon ourselves and our faithfulness. If we fail to magnify our Priesthood it would have been better if it had never been conferred upon us. He had not been long in the Church before the Lord revealed to him this grand and mighty principle, and he expressed it in a couplet composed by himself. "As man now is, God once was; as God now is man may be." Jesus was god before he came into the world, and yet his knowledge was taken from him as it has been taken from us. He did not know his former greatness, neither do we know the greatness we had attained to before we came here; but He had

> to pass through an ordeal as we have to without knowing or realizing at the time the greatness and importance of His mission. We should appreciate the fact that we are the sons of God, and that it is our father's children who are placed under our charge.[17]

Toward mid-October, President Snow again became ill, this time with a cold that he caught while visiting at President Cannon's home a day or two before.[18] He also paid John W. Rigdon (a son of Sidney Rigdon) for a manuscript he had written on Church history. President Snow "felt that the manuscript was of no particular benefit to the Church" but felt charitably toward Mr. Rigdon who was a poor man, and therefore gave him three hundred dollars for it.[19]

That month President Snow also received and accepted an offer from a wealthy Latter-day Saint of twenty-five thousand dollars of real estate for the Church. However, when the man's family found out he had willed this property to the Church, they protested and threatened legal action. President Snow had not known of the inheritance issues and quickly reversed himself and refused the offer, unless the matter was completely and satisfactorily settled by the family first.[20]

Work on the newly commissioned Church history progressed, with a title being approved of *The History of The Church of Jesus Christ of Latter-day Saints*. It was decided that "the history will be printed from the journals kept by the Prophet and his clerks with notes and additions in the form of footnotes, it having been previously agreed to follow the account as recorded in the manuscripts on file in the archives of the Church, which will compose four or five volumes [actually seven] when published. President Cannon suggested that there be a preface written explaining that part of the work known as the 'History of Joseph Smith,' these being the personal writings of the Prophet or his dictations to his scribes or clerks. This was approved." At this point, it seems evident that Anthon H. Lund and his staff were doing most of the work, under President Cannon's supervision.[21] In another meeting on the same subject, "The question was raised by President Cannon whether in the publication of the 'History of the Church' about to be published, should he divide the history into chapters and verses, also the revelations as now published in the Doctrine and Covenants; or follow the method of the publication of the 'History of Joseph Smith' as published in the *Millennial Star* which is not so divided. It was decided that the divisions both in the history as to chapters and verses and in the revelations into verses should be made in the publication, which would make it more interesting."[22]

Later that October, President Snow visited family in Brigham City and on his return found that two RLDS missionaries desired to visit with him. They "had a long interview with President Snow in regard to plural marriage and other doctrines of the Church. President Snow gave them his personal testimony of the teachings of the Prophet Joseph Smith to himself on the subject of plural marriage."[23]

Little is known about President Snow's movements in November. It is assumed that he followed the regular routine of office work, mainly making financial decisions and attending meetings. On the thirtieth he toured the Deseret Museum with Dr. James E. Talmage.[24] In early December, his plural wife Sarah A. Snow passed away while he was at her bedside—Lorenzo was not spared the heartaches and grief attendant to mortality.[25] December passed with President Snow catching another cold a week before Christmas, forcing him to remain at home in bed. He did go to the office long enough to hear President Joseph F. Smith's report on his trip to Mexico to disband the BYU Zarahemla Expedition. After Christmas he was well enough to attend the meeting of the First Presidency and Twelve before the start of the new year.[26]

January 1 was an important day for the prophet. He took the unusual step, on the first day of the new century, of preparing a formal address to be delivered in the Salt Lake Tabernacle that he entitled, "Greeting to the World." Read by his son LeRoi on account of illness, President Snow reviewed the wonders of the past century; spoke with optimism of the next; offered solutions for the common problems of mankind; and testified that the Heavens had opened to the Latter-day Saints.[27]

President Snow seized the moment and spoke in his prophetic capacity to the world, whether anyone listened or not. He himself had entered the last calendar year of his life; he had little more than nine months to live; and he had no fear of what the world thought of him. His last months would be blessed with some of the most powerful and personal discourses that he ever delivered. He constantly sought to bring the Latter-day Saints up to the higher spiritual plane upon which he himself stood. The eyes of his understanding had been opened; he had gazed into eternity; henceforth, he stubbornly sought to impart his prophetic vision to those who had ears to hear and eyes to see.

Yet as prophet, president, and Trustee-in-trust of a growing church entering a new century becoming filled with inventions like telephones and automobiles, President Snow was forced to focus on the mundane and temporal. In January he received a request for information and illustrations from a publisher, which he reviewed and granted on recommendation from the manager and editor of the *Deseret News*. When several senior brethren went to see an invention being promoted by Frank J. Cannon, President Snow did not accompany them—"President Snow did not feel so sanguine over the matter."[28] (The invention failed.) It was a strange dichotomy; President Snow was increasingly uninterested in temporal things, yet was obligated to deal with them almost daily. The day after opting out of the excursion to examine the invention, he appropriated two thousand dollars to the "Snow" Academy (later Snow College).[29]

The next month, financial matters continued to occupy him. Representatives from another stake academy called at the office asking for financial help for their school. President Snow asked them to do all they could for themselves financially and he would help if he could, promising them a thousand dollars a year.

President Snow felt to pay off the mortgage on a home for a widow of President Richards. This decision was in response to a complicated financial situation involving the Richards family, the Utah Bank and Trust of Ogden, and Elder Abraham Cannon. As explained to Lorenzo by President Richards's son Franklin S., the Church attorney:

> President Franklin D. Richards, together with his sons Franklin S. and Charles C., borrowed money for the purpose of starting the Ogden Loan and Trust Company, which ended in failure; but before it failed, and when the bank was considered in good condition; Abraham H. Cannon desired to control it in connection with a railroad scheme, and President Richards and his sons sold to Brother Cannon. They were invited to either buy out other stockholders or to sell, and not being able to buy they sold, realizing but sixty cents on the dollar, or a loss of some three thousand dollars on his investment, and this balance had been carried by him and his sons. During his lifetime he spoke to President Snow about this matter, feeling quite disappointed that the late First Presidency could not see their way clear to help him as it was the first time he had ever asked the Church for financial aid. President Cannon now informed President Snow that when Brother Richards made the application he was sorry it could not be granted, but that it was purely on account of the financial pressure at the time, but that he certainly favored it then and does now. Presidents Snow and Smith were of the same mind so the appropriation was made.[30]

A wide variety of matters continued to involve President Snow. He dedicated a new building for the LDS Business College.[31] He granted a one-year extension on some notes for land being developed by Mormon settlers in Alberta, Canada, since they could not then be paid off.[32] He listened as the editor of the *Deseret News,* Charles W. Penrose, read a proposed editorial about controversial vaccination legislation vetoed by the governor of Utah:

> He had not read very far before President Snow stated that he thought it wisdom not to say anything in the way of criticism of the Governor's attitude. Brother Penrose thereupon, out of deference to President Snow, decided that it would be better not to publish the article, although he was of the opinion that it was clearly the duty of the *News* to meet some of the arguments in the Governor's veto favoring compulsory vaccination. Later in the day President Cannon came to the office and Brother Penrose was sent for and again submitted the article, but President Cannon concurred in the expression of President Snow.[33]

(Penrose's views were later vindicated as on February 21 the Utah State Senate overturned the governor's veto and the bill became law.)

By mid-February, an earlier discussion regarding sending missionaries to foreign-language missions bore its first fruit, as the First Presidency decided to open a mission in Japan and called Elder Heber J. Grant, who had no inkling of the Japanese language, to go.[34] The call happened like this:

> Two days after his return from California, during the General Authorities' regular temple meeting, he heard George Q. Cannon, First Counselor in the First Presidency, announce the decision to open a new mission in Japan. "The moment he made this remark," Grant later recalled, "I felt impressed that I would be called to open up this mission." This prescience, however, brought a flood of reasons why he should reject the call. The Panic of 1893 and its subsequent depression had crippled his finances. He calculated his net worth to be a negative $30,000. Moreover, he had co-signed financial notes making him responsible for another $100,000 in non-personal debt. Because of his strained circumstances, neither of his wives had a home of her own, while his mother's house was mortgaged to assist with his obligations.
>
> As President Cannon continued for twenty-five minutes, Grant quietly weighed financial and religious commitments. Then came the call he expected from Cannon: "We hear that Brother Grant has overcome all his great financial difficulties and has announced that he is

> going to take a trip around the world to celebrate his financial freedom, and we have decided to stop him half way around at Japan, to preside."
>
> Having extended a call to Grant, President Cannon yielded to President Lorenzo Snow, who, since becoming the Church's prophet, seer, and revelator in 1898, had slashed at every unnecessary expenditure to save money. Fearing that Elder Grant's precarious finances might somehow encumber the Church, President Snow had some specific questions in mind. First he wanted to know whether President Cannon had accurately quoted the Apostle about touring the world.
>
> "Heber, did you make that statement?"
>
> "Yes, I did, but there was an extra word in it, and the word was 'if.'" Grant had no plans to leave if he was unable to retire the rest of his debt.
>
> "Well, then, you are not free?"
>
> "No, I am not free, I owe a few dollars."
>
> President Snow wanted specifics. "Well, what are you making?"
>
> "A little better than $5,000 a year."
>
> "Can you afford to lose that $5,000 for three years while you are in Japan?"
>
> "Yes, I can."
>
> In later years, Grant's memory of this incident remained very much alive. "[President Snow] tried for ten minutes to get something out of me [about my debts] and could not do it," Grant remembered.
>
> Finally I said, "President Snow, with the blessing of the Lord I think I can arrange all my affairs to go on this mission, . . . and it will be time enough for me to come and tell you I cannot when I feel in my heart I can't."
>
> "The Lord bless you, my boy," said President Snow, obviously pleased. "We will give you a whole year. You go right to work and fix up your affairs to go on this mission."[35]

President Cannon's formal issuance of the call of Elder Grant to Japan turned out to be one of his last major acts. Cannon's health had been perceptibly declining for years and more so for months, and by March he had reached such a state that he felt the need to do something drastic. So he "had a private talk with President Snow, after which he bid President Snow and the other brethren who were in the office goodbye as he intended to leave for the West in a day or so. For some time he has not been well and feels now that he is in a precarious condition and that the climate of California will benefit him."[36] He left two days later, and that was the last time President Snow saw his first counselor. President Joseph F. Smith was also ill at the time.[37] This kept President Snow busy in the office until his birthday on April 3, when he received a telegram of congratulations from President Cannon, whose health had continued declining since leaving.

At the next council meeting, held the day before general conference started, a proposal was made to increase the compensation or living allowances of the seven presidents of Seventies. Recent tithing payment increases had been wonderful, but so deep had been the mountain of debt piled on the Church that options were still limited: "President Snow said that nothing could be done in the matter at present. We have not arrived at a point where we can say to the General Authorities of the church: 'Give up all your financial affairs, devote your whole time to the work, and the church will provide fully for you; but that time is coming.'"[38]

While the conference continued, good financial news reached the prophet: "Word comes to the brethren of the Twelve from President Snow that he has just received the guaranty given by the church to secure payment of the 1500 $1000 bonds (or $1,500,000) of the Pioneer Electric Power Co. It cost the church $225,000 to secure the return of said guaranty, but it is felt by the brethren, notwithstanding the heavy actual cost ($225,000) to the church, that the Lord has removed from our path a threatening danger of great magnitude. The church at the present time is rapidly being freed from debt, but was liable at any moment, through the guaranty, to be engulfed in a further indebtedness of $1,500,000."[39]

President Snow again spoke to the priesthood leadership meeting, where plain counsel was given to bishops, stake presidents, and General Authorities. He told the stake presidents to exercise great care in recommending people to the temples to receive the highest blessings available there. He spoke of tithing: "No one can get a remission of his sins except by baptism, and so no one can secure the blessings of the land he occupies except by observance of the law of tithing." President Snow then "blessed the brethren and authorities present. Said that it was a wonderful blessing to receive and hold a portion of this sacred and all-powerful priesthood. . . . The church can pay all of its obligations as they fall due, or may arise, and we do not have to borrow money for that purpose."[40]

Only a few days later President Snow received a telegram that grieved him deeply: "George Q. Cannon died at 1:20 am at Monterey California," it said. "President Snow was deeply impressed [moved] when the information of President Cannon's death was communicated to him as was also President Joseph F. Smith. The news was not, however, unexpected as every indication and telegram for days past intimated that death was approaching."[41] President Snow had not cared for President Cannon's financial methods and decisions, and he probably imputed at least some portion of blame to Cannon for the Church's debt mess that he was cleaning up. But he also had been in close association with Cannon for two and a half years, and had come to appreciate his sound counsel; often commenting in meeting, after President Cannon had given his views, that they represented his own exactly. President Snow ran his own course as Trustee-in-trust with Church finances, but he valued his first counselor's knowledge and experience in most other areas. They had become unified and close in their work and Quorum counsels. At his funeral on April 17, President Snow had his son LeRoi read his prepared remarks, since he himself was then ill.[42] In those remarks, President Snow "testified to the faithfulness, integrity, and humility of Pres. Cannon as his first counselor and as a Latter-day Saint."[43] Further, he stated: "I wish it to be distinctly understood that no one in my position ever had a counselor who displayed less of such a spirit or disposition [of arrogance or self-sufficiency]. In our councils, whatever might be the matter under consideration, although my decision was sometimes opposed to his views, he invariably yielded his point gracefully and gave me his most loyal support."[44]

President Snow would not move to replace Cannon for nearly six months. Before the funeral President Snow had asked the Twelve "to administer to him as he had not been feeling well for several days past."[45] President Snow felt sick enough to remain home the next day during the regular meeting of the First Presidency and Twelve, which President Joseph F. Smith was obliged to conduct in the absence of both other members of the First Presidency. At this meeting the question "'Can anyone receive another wife in any other country?' was discussed. President Lorenzo Snow says no. Joseph F. Smith said he could not say otherwise."[46]

Perhaps feeling blue from the death of his first counselor and also feeling the effects of his own considerable age and mortality within himself, President Snow expressed some hesitation with allowing his good friend Elder Lyman to depart for Europe to become the mission president there. "'I regret that you must go now,' he reflected, as if he knew it would be a final parting so far as this world is concerned, 'But it's all right,' he added, after more reflection, and told F. M. to go with his blessing."[47] President Snow would thereafter communicate with him by letter.

By the end of April, President Snow had become well enough that he was able to attend council meetings and deal with financial matters, one of them being a decision to have the Mormon Tabernacle organ refurbished. He released Elder Marriner W. Merrill from his duties as president of the Cache Stake, and it was divided into three stakes. He also attended the funeral of Elder Rudger Clawson's baby.[48]

Chapter 24

Concluding Scenes of a Holy Prophet's Ministry

In the first apostolic meeting of May, not skipping a beat, "President Lorenzo Snow instructed the quorum of Apostles to preach tithing until all non-tithe payers were converted."[1] It was a busy time as usual. President Snow was appointed the Superintendent of the Deseret Sunday School Union and General Superintendent of Sunday Schools of the Church (succeeding President Cannon). He hired an artist (John Hafen) to paint likenesses of the Brethren and other scenes for display in the temple and other buildings.[2]

On May 23 at the regular weekly temple meeting, "President Snow stated that the writing of the church history had been placed in charge of President George Q. Cannon, but now that he was gone, it would be necessary to make other arrangements. After some discussion it was decided by unanimous vote that Brother B. H. Roberts be employed to do the work under the direction, advice, and assistance of Apostle Anthon H. Lund, church historian."[3] In commenting on his responsibilities regarding the history, Elder Lund wrote: "B. H. Roberts was appointed to take hold of the work of publishing the History of Joseph Smith and I suggested that he be attached to the Historian's Office. I was told that the responsibility would be upon me to see that the work was pushed. Bro. Lorenzo Snow is very anxious about having the work progress."[4] Elder Roberts was soon suggesting some minor changes to the typesetting design of the history: "Today Presidents Snow and Smith conferred with Elder Brigham H. Roberts, who is editing the *History of the Church*, and decided to print the revelations in a smaller type than that used in the text and that notes be added and a still smaller type be used for them."[5] These changes reflect the look of the volumes as they were eventually published.[6]

President Snow spent the next few days visiting with Senator Thomas Kearns, for whom he had developed a friendship and become a benign political supporter, and went an excursion to Saltair, the popular Church-run resort on the south edge of the Great Salt Lake, in celebration of President Brigham Young's birthday.[7] Mid-June saw Presidents Snow and Smith traveling to Ogden for a reunion of the Weber Stake leadership of past years. A promising young bishop named David O. McKay was also in attendance.[8]

More than once in his last few months of life, President Snow spoke to various congregations of his early Church experiences and personal revelations. Along with carrying the prophetic mantle and holding the directing priesthood keys of the Church, he constituted one of the last and best living ties to early Mormonism and the Prophet Joseph Smith. For these reasons and others, the Latter-day Saints had come to love and revere him.

A few days later, President Snow dedicated a new ward meetinghouse and then attended the regular meeting of the First Presidency and Twelve, where a discussion of educational matters and Church schools took place. After this, he attended a reception for Elder Heber J. Grant and the three other missionaries soon leaving for Japan. This was another special occasion where President Snow opened his heart to his associates. His remarks at this event constitute one of the most candid and personal witnesses and testimonies of the resurrected Christ on record from President Snow: "President Snow arose and said, I desire to bear my testimony. I know that Jesus lives. Many of you who are here tonight will see him; you will see that he is a noble looking man, and you will feel like going to him and shaking hands. . . . I bear this testimony for I know it is true."[9] A second account from another apostle present stated: "I went to a reception given by Pres. Joseph F. Smith to Bro. Heber J. Grant and his companions for Japan. President Snow said: 'Some of you will live and see the Redeemer, and you will find him a beautiful person so attractive that you will be drawn towards him.'"[10] These were not such unusual declarations to make since President Snow was addressing a group of men that included apostles and two future presidents of the Church.[11]

Six days later the MIA sponsored its own parting reception for the "Japanese" missionaries. Of this occasion, the Journal History records: "The reception at the Beehive house . . . in honor of Apostle Heber J. Grant and his companions to Japan, was a most enjoyable occasion. President

Snow was in a very happy mood and one of the most active ones present. The guests began to assemble at 4 o'clock and were graciously received by Mrs. Lorenzo Snow [Minnie], Miss Mabelle Snow and Mrs. LeRoi C. Snow."[12] Again, President Snow spoke to them of their mission and duty with deep feeling:

> When the Lord first sent forth his elders in this generation, very little was known as to what their labors would be and what they could accomplish. They failed in some respects, but they did not fail in one thing: They did their duty. Apostle Orson Pratt and others were sent to Austria to open a mission there, but, by reason of the rejection of their testimony, they did not succeed. Nevertheless they did their duty and were blessed. Noah preached one hundred and twenty years; he was a grand man; he did his duty, but failed, and it was because the people rejected him. However by doing his duty, he secured to himself exaltation and glory, while those who rejected his testimony were held in prison for two thousand five hundred years. Moses in leading the children of Israel to the promised land, failed to accomplish what the Lord wanted by reason of the Israelites. Moses himself, through faithfulness has attained to the Godhead. There is no doubt of this. As to these brethren who will shortly leave for Japan, the Lord has not revealed to me that they will succeed, but he has shown me positively that it is their duty to go. They need not worry concerning the results, only they should be careful to search the Spirit of the Lord, and understand its language to see what it indicates to them. Do not be governed by your own wisdom but by the wisdom of God. When you return, we will come together, perhaps as we are together today, and will rejoice in your faithfulness. God bless you, and may our Holy Father in heaven open the way before you, and may you succeed in converting many of the Japanese people.[13]

During this same week President Snow donated money to some "colored" gentlemen to build a church, and he heard arguments from the faculty of the University of Utah that Church academies should only teach high school curriculum and leave the college-level courses to them.[14]

July saw progress on the *History of the Church*, with Historian's Office staff, including B. H. Roberts and Church Historian Anthon H. Lund, assembling and comparing and arranging material for the lengthy project.[15] Also with July came excessive heat, which was hard on the aging President, possibly giving him heatstroke on one occasion. In an effort to find cooler living quarters, especially at night, President Snow began spending most of his evenings in accommodations at Saltair resort, hoping the lake breezes would help.[16] Weakening and sickness caused by the overpowering heat initiated the slide toward his eventual demise three months later. While at Saltair, President Snow met with the Relief Society, although because of his exhausted condition, his son LeRoi read his speech for him.[17]

On the fourteenth, President Snow was able to deliver a powerful and poignant talk to the Millcreek Ward in which he reviewed in some depth early scenes from his own life: the spiritual experiences he received after his baptism, of receiving the gift of the Holy Ghost, and of a vision of man's possible eternal destiny—that he could become a god like unto his Father in Heaven. He also recounted some early missionary experiences.[18]

In mid-July, the First Presidency and Twelve decided that a standardized method be used in the stakes and wards when sustaining general and local Church authorities. After the meeting in which that decision was approved, President Snow set apart Elder Heber J. Grant for his mission to Japan.[19] It had only been five months since the formal call was issued, but his financial circumstances had improved miraculously during that time.

As the end of the month neared, a small incident occurred that gave impetus to the eventual formation of a Church "Bureau of Information" and later the visitors' centers that have long inhabited Temple Square. Non-Latter-day Saint buggy or "hack" drivers were showing tourists around the most notable sites in downtown Salt Lake City, including Temple Square and nearby locations where the President's Office and other "attractions" were located. According to LeRoi Snow:

> In the latter part of July, 1901, a great many tourists passed through Salt Lake City on their way to attend the convention of the Epworth League in California. I was standing near the Eagle Gate when a party of tourists drove up and stopped within a few steps of where I was standing. The hack-driver then commenced telling his stories. After telling a lot of other falsehoods he continued:
>
> "This is the Bee Hive House, where Lorenzo Snow, the president of the Church lives. The building is kept closed from the public. No one is ever permitted to go in there. We do not know what goes on there."
>
> I stepped up to the driver, thanked him kindly for repeating in my hearing the stories which had been prepared for the tourists, and then I turned to the strangers, introduced myself, and invited them to go through the Bee Hive House with me and to meet my father, the President of the Church.
>
> They appeared very much surprised and undecided just what to do. I assured them that they would come out alive and that no harm would

> come to them. Here the driver interrupted, saying: "Oh, come on. We have a lot of places to go, and we must be on our way." This settled the matter with one of the party who replied: "Oh, I don't know, we are paying you for your time, and I presume we can use it as we wish. I, for one, want to accept the invitation." The other members of the party immediately expressed their desire to go also. The driver, who showed very plainly that he was very greatly displeased, was told to remain until the return of the party.
>
> I took the good people through the Bee Hive House, introduced my mother to them and answered their many questions which proved to their interest. We then went into the President's office where they met my father and had a short visit with him. I told him of the incident which had just occurred outside, to which one of the gentlemen added: "Yes, I can see that we have been very much mis-informed about the 'Mormons' and I should like to know the truth about you and your city." As we returned to the carriage I again spoke to the driver, saying: "I want to thank you again for letting me know what kind of information you hackmen are giving to the tourists, and I shall not rest until I do all in my power to see that this work is taken out of your hands and that steps are taken to give visitors to Salt Lake reliable and truthful information about our faith, people and Church." The party expressed appreciation for their visit.[20]

With Salt Lake City temperatures reaching ninety-eight degrees as July turned into August, President Snow continued to stay nights at Saltair. Sometimes he came into the downtown President's Office; other times he had the secretary to the First Presidency, George F. Gibbs, bring him his mail.[21] On the eighth he managed to attend the regular council meeting but left shortly after.[22] Our best summary of President Snow's activities that summer comes from a letter he wrote to Elder Francis M. Lyman, then serving as the European mission president:

> *The Articles of Faith* by Brother Talmage is now the property of the Church, Brother Talmage having freely turned over the work to us; we saw fit, however, to compensate him for it. The work of revising [proofreading, dividing into chapters and verses, and footnoting] the Pearl of Great Price is about completed, and we look for a new edition in the near future. Brother Roberts, as you no doubt know, is carrying on the work of preparing the manuscript for the *History of the Church*, taking it up where President Cannon left it. We have accepted of suggestions of Brother Roberts to give side headings to the work, thereby greatly enhancing its value as a work of reference; also to allow the revelations

> as they appear from time to time to be printed in a little smaller type than the body of the book which gives it a nice and more striking appearance. . . .
>
> I close by saying to you and the faithful men laboring under your direction, that inasmuch as they shall continually seek unto the Lord in humility, having an eye single to His honor and glory, and desiring in their hearts the salvation of the souls of man, and doing all they can to bring about their salvation, they shall have joy beyond expression in their labors in the flesh, and shall at last be made partakers with the Father and the Son of things too great and glorious for mortality to conceive or contemplate.[23]

On August 13, President Snow received word that Elder Grant and his companions had arrived at Japan. The same day a representative of a midwestern newspaper, the *Chicago Chronicle*, visited with President Snow, the prophet presenting him with a copy of his biography.[24] The next evening President Snow attended an army reunion and the theater.[25] A couple of days later, he was again at Saltair, this time for a special meeting of Scandinavian Latter-day Saints. His son LeRoi again read his remarks because he was too weak to make himself heard.[26] Then the weather cooled sufficiently that President Snow was able to sleep at home again, and he worked in the office and appropriated needed funds for various Church-related uses.[27]

President Snow was in a council meeting on August 22, talking further about the duties of the Apostles:

> President Snow made remarks and said in substance that he doubted whether we were justified in keeping the Twelve Apostles and Seven Presidents of Seventies at home as much as we do. Their special calling is to preach the gospel to the nations, and he felt that a great work must be accomplished in this regard before the coming of the Savior. The president of the Twelve should think about this matter, should pray about it, that his mind might be broadened to comprehend what is needed. It is a matter worthy of thought and consideration. Referring to the 130 quorums of seventies, remarked that he didn't know how far we are justified in waiting for the young men of the Mutual Improvement Associations to be instructed and qualified to do this work, and leaving the members of the quorums inactive.[28]

He said: "It seems to me that the quorums of the Priesthood will have to receive attention, the actual work that is being done appears to be in the direction of the Mutual Improvements, but the quorums are not doing much."[29] As fine of an organization as the MIA was, President Snow felt that the priesthood, meaning the men of the various priesthood quorums holding authority to act in the name of God, should be performing necessary labors in the kingdom. He impressed this thought strongly on the Twelve.

Though feeling poorly, President Snow attended the meeting of the First Presidency and Twelve near the end of August. The confusion surrounding the office of Seventy was again addressed. An idea had developed in some minds that the Presidents of Seventies were apostles, and this was causing some misunderstanding:

> It having been remarked that a certain brother who held the office of a Seventy declined to be ordained a High Priest, President Smith said that if the Seventies generally could be convinced that they were simply elders with a special calling as aids to the Apostles in preaching the Gospel in foreign lands, and their minds could be disabused of the idea placed there by the teachings of the late Elder Joseph Young, President of the Council of Seventy, to the effect that the Seventies were Apostles, some of them would not perhaps feel as they do now.
>
> Brother Cowley related a conversation he once had with the late President John Taylor, to the effect that a man holding the office of an Elder has all the authority necessary to preach the Gospel, and believing this to be true, though the Elders should not be ordained Seventies in a wholesale way as they were now being ordained, but that they should be chosen according to their fitness to become aids to the Apostles.
>
> President Snow remarked that when elders were ordained Seventies no more Priesthood was conferred upon them, but that they were merely called to work in a special field.[30]

On September 2, President Snow presided and spoke at the funeral for Zina D. H. Young, a plural wife of President Brigham Young and influential leader among the women of the Church. Among other things, he said: "We ought to feel in our heart that God is our Father and that while we make mistakes and are weak yet if we live as nearly perfect as we can all will be well with us. This sister has lived in this way. When she was suddenly stricken with the blow that took her consciousness away, she was prepared to go and meet her Maker. Now I say to all you brothers and sisters, do likewise."[31] By the ninth, word reached Salt Lake City that US President William McKinley had been shot and was dying. President Snow spoke in eulogy about him at the Salt Lake Stake conference. McKinley died on the fourteenth.[32] President Snow had again been staying at Saltair, but bad weather forced him to move home again. At the President's Office, President Snow met a group of Catholics and offered them free passes to the amusements at Saltair.[33] The last month of President Snow's life was busy. He attended the opening of the Granite Stake Academy; he increased the cash portion of the salaries of Brigham Young Academy teachers; he negotiated with the Oregon Short Line Railroad for them to lease the upper floor of the *Deseret News* building, since their own offices had burned down; he attended meetings of the Church sugar company; and he sent official condolences to Mrs. William McKinley.[34]

Such an energetic flurry of activity would be his last. On September 17, the record states: "President Snow was not very well today having contracted a cold on his lungs and he does not feel like attending to official duties."[35] He went to the office the following morning, but felt "quite unwell." The severe cold caused him to miss the memorial service for President McKinley that he had authorized to be held in the Tabernacle.[36] During the last week of the month, he was able to receive a few visitors but do little else.[37]

On the twenty-sixth, he attended the routine council meeting of the Twelve and First Presidency, summoning up enough energy to give some pointed direction to the Twelve on their responsibilities:

> I want to say, here's the Apostles and the Seventies; their business is to warn the nations of the earth and prepare the world for the coming of the Savior. They have been engaged in this more or less, but now we find ourselves in a compact gathered condition, the Church is divided into Stakes, and we come together from time to time in a council meeting to consider the interests of the cause generally and make appointments for brethren to visit the stakes when holding their conferences. It looks to me that our minds ought to extend somewhat, and we should get out of our beaten track, and a little change be made. For instance, we have started in this direction by sending Brother Heber J. Grant over to Japan, but his is only a start. Things seem to be going on favorable with him; and whether he will accomplish much or not, it matters little in one sense; it is for the Apostles to show to the Lord that they are his witnesses to all the nations, and that they are doing the best they can.[38]

President Snow was not letting the Twelve relax. His repeated encouragement and prodding on this issue, including his final general conference address, became the spark that lit the flame of missionary activity in the Church for the next century and beyond.

Chapter 25

A Prophet's Passing and Legacy

The president of the Quorum of the Twelve, Brigham Young Jr.—an emotional and blunt man, who loved President Snow dearly—felt impressed to ensure that he had provided the temporal necessities of life for himself and his wives and family: "Met in the temple [meeting]," he wrote. "President Snow was present." He then said, "I have had a talk with President Snow and have begun to try to get the brethren all interested in having President Snow become the owner of a house and lot, as he is a poor man." President Young then "asked President Snow what his aged widows would do if he were taken [died]. He said, 'three of them would [have to] go out to beg.' I begged of him to provide for these and all helpless members of his family in need, while he was able to do so. He said, 'I am doing so as fast as I can.'"[1]

A few days later, the Quorum of the Twelve, at their own council meeting preparatory to the October general conference, turned their collective attention to the temporal condition of their prophet and his family. President Young said he had felt moved in relation to President Snow's personal temporal condition:

> Apostle Young was the first speaker and said in substance that he had good reason to believe that if Pres. Snow should pass away suddenly [he was dead nine days later], he would die a poor man financially and his family would be left in need. He felt that Pres. Snow should take steps, while living, to provide for his family that they might be made comfortable in a time to come. If the brethren approved of it, he would like so to express himself to President Snow, and he believed that the President would appreciate the good feelings of his brethren.
>
> Apostle Smith expressed his approval of the suggestion and said

> it would be in harmony with the course taken by Presidents Brigham Young, John Taylor, and Wilford Woodruff, who each in his time provided for their families while yet they were with us. If we were living in the United Order, these matters would be properly adjusted. The families of our leaders—especially their widows—should be cared for within reason, but of course they should be frugal and industrious. He also felt to endorse the idea and proposition that if any wife of an apostle (be the apostle alive or dead) be found lacking in those things needful for her comfort, provision should be made in such case that it shall not be necessary for her to call upon the bishop each week of her life.
>
> Apostle Teasdale said that he was in harmony with the views expressed. He felt that there was no need for a wife of the President or an apostle to suffer for the necessities of life.
>
> Apostle Taylor felt that Brother Brigham's suggestion was inspired of the Lord, and it, therefore, had his hearty approval. Apostle Lund said that he felt to be one with his brethren in this matter. Apostle Merrill felt that Brother Brigham's suggestion came as an inspiration. Apostle Woodruff said that he felt that the wives of our leading men should not be left to suffer for the common necessities of life. . . .
>
> Apostle Young said that he would submit the matter to President Snow.[2]

With that matter settled, President Young turned to the next subject of importance—the charge that President Snow had laid upon the Quorum to investigate the possibilities of opening new foreign fields for missionary work:

> Spoke in reference to the duty of the Twelve in opening the door of the gospel to the nations of the earth. Said that President Snow's mind of late had been impressed with the importance of this obligation which rested upon his brethren, and he had several times within a recent period expressed a wish that they should take the subject into consideration. Brother Brigham felt that the question we should now seek to answer is this: where are the nations, not already visited, to whom the gospel might be carried by the Twelve? His mind, he said, had rested upon South America, and possibly fields might be opened up in Brazil, the Argentine Republic, La Plata, Montevideo, and other places. It was thought that at the close of the war South Africa would be a good field.
>
> Apostle Smith said that he would feel a little chary [reticent] about recommending himself or any member of the quorum for a mission, as he conceded that this right belonged to the First Presidency. The apostles are here and are ready to go to the ends of the earth at their bidding.

> Apostle Young explained that President Snow did not expect the apostles to call themselves to fill missions, but simply desired them to suggest new fields for missionary work. Upon the recommendation of Apostle Taylor, it was decided that an atlas be secured for reference and that a goodly portion of the time tomorrow be devoted to this subject.[3]

Two days later President Snow met for the last time with his Brethren of the First Presidency and Quorum of the Twelve. President Snow received a note of thanks from the family of the late United States President for expressing condolences.[4] After a slight reprieve in which his illness had relented enough to allow him to work in the office for a couple of days and attend meetings, October 4 saw a change for the worse: "President Snow was not feeling well at all this morning; he is suffering from hoarseness and has a cold on his lungs. He requested that word be sent to President Joseph F. Smith to the effect that he would not be at the opening session of the General Conference and for President Smith to take charge."[5]

Thereafter, President Snow stayed in bed, husbanding his strength in determination of speaking at conference. After the last morning session on October 6, he sent for Elder Rudger Clawson of the Twelve to come to his bedside:

> I called at the Bee-Hive House to inquire after President Lorenzo Snow's condition, as he had not been able to attend any of the conference sessions, up to that time.
>
> As I went into President Snow's room he said: "Brother Rudger, I am a sick man. I should not go to the meeting this afternoon but I have some important business to present to the conference and I feel that I must go. I need another Counselor in the First Presidency and I feel impressed that it should not be put off any longer. I have chosen you to be my Second Counselor."
>
> In astonishment I replied: "Why, President Snow, this is like a thunderbolt from a clear sky. I am greatly surprised. There are others of the Twelve Apostles who are much older than I am, who have had a great deal more experience and are better qualified for this responsible position. If I am chosen I fear it may create some jealousy or perhaps dissatisfaction."
>
> "It is not only that I have chosen you," President Snow said, "but it is also the will of the Lord. So, go now and have your lunch and then come back and ride with me in my carriage to the Tabernacle." This I did.
>
> After President Snow had finished speaking to the people he turned

The First Presidency for four days in October 1901: Joseph F. Smith, Lorenzo Snow, and Rudger Clawson. (USHS)

> to President Joseph F. Smith, saying: "Brother Joseph, please present the names of the General Authorities for the vote of the congregation. Present your own name as my First Counselor and Brother Rudger Clawson as my Second Counselor." This was done and all the names were sustained unanimously by the conference.[6]

Before the sustaining vote was taken, President Snow gave his final public discourse to the Latter-day Saints. In his message, he touched on points that had occupied his mind the most during his illness and that he had been impressing upon his associates so forcibly:

> I have had a distressing cold the last eight or ten days, which has made me very hoarse, and I feared that I would not be able to appear at all during this conference. . . . The Apostles and the Seventies, it is their business by the appointment of the Almighty, to look after the interests of the world. The Seventies and the Twelve Apostles are special witnesses unto the nations of the earth. . . . You presiding officers of the various Stakes of Zion, the time is coming when you will not have to call and depend so much upon the Twelve Apostles. They will be directed in other channels, and I want you to distinctly understand it; and do not seek to throw responsibilities that belong to you upon these Twelve Apostles and upon the Seventies. . . .
>
> There is still one matter that I might speak of. I am going on pretty fast toward my eighty-eighth year; I will soon be eighty-eight years old; and I have been laboring now for some months with but one counselor—President Joseph F. Smith. I feel as though I wanted a little more help—another counselor; and I have selected one, (through, I believe, the manifestations of the Lord), who, I think, will be energetic and strong, will serve the people, and help me and President Joseph F. Smith along in a proper way; and I hope you will sustain and support him. God bless you, Amen.[7]

The next morning (Monday), "President Snow thought he felt a little better . . . but did not feel well enough to attend the priesthood meeting of General Conference." At the priesthood meeting, "President Smith informed the brethren present that the Church was fast getting into good shape financially, and he felt hopeful, if the Saints continued to observe the law of tithing, that the Church would soon be financially free, and have means to spare to devote to purposes which it was not able to do at present." Later that afternoon, a delegation of returned Polynesian missionaries went to the President's Office to pay their respects to Pres. Snow and present him with a fine ornate walking cane as a token of their esteem.

"President Snow, who, on being informed came into the office from the Beehive house and was introduced to them." One of them made a speech while presenting him the cane. "President Snow received the gift and bade [the Sister] to thank the donors in his behalf, and to say that he would cherish it as long as he lived in remembrance of them."[8] This occasion was probably President Snow's final formal interaction with guests.

Lorenzo Snow (USHS)

The following morning (Tuesday), Elder Clawson recorded, "President Snow sent for me and said he designed my first official act as his counselor to be an act of charity. He instructed me to obtain full information regarding the widows of the following named brethren with special reference to their means of support: Heber C. Kimball, Orson Hyde, John Taylor, Orson Pratt, Parley P. Pratt, and Daniel H. Wells. The purpose of this mission, now given me, was not stated, but from the views expressed at one of the meetings of the Presidency and Twelve, I had every reason to believe that President Snow designed rendering assistance from the church to the widows of these brethren in all cases where help was needed."[9]

Rudger Clawson's temporary call into the First Presidency is highly unusual in that he was called, sustained by the Church in general conference assembled, and served for a few days in the new capacity. However, he was never set apart as the second counselor in the First Presidency. Standard Church histories that bear on the subject all designate him as a second counselor to President Snow even though it lasted only four days.[10]

Tuesday night and Wednesday morning saw President Snow decline: "He spent a very bad night, vomited considerable and is feeling badly today. He has been confined to his bed," noted the Journal History.[11] Elder Matthias Cowley, present to witness parts of President Snow's final few days, wrote that President Snow was still able to do a few things connected with his prophetic calling: "Forty-eight hours before passing away he signed the appointments of fifty-eight members of the Young Men's Mutual Improvement Association to go on missions, and only twenty-seven hours before his death, he presided at a meeting of his business associates [directors of the Salt Lake and Los Angeles Railway Corporation], thus showing how unimpaired were his faculties up to the last."[12] But the "last" came nonetheless, and quickly:

> At 5 o'clock in the afternoon Sister Snow informed Brother George F. Gibbs that she was alarmed at President Snow's condition, he having just come out of a sinking spell. She expressed a desire to have President Smith administer to him. President Smith and a number of the brethren were in the office at the time for the purpose of holding the regular weekly MIA meeting and he and brother John Henry Smith went to President Snow's bedside and administered to him. Afterwards President Smith received permission to send for a physician and Dr. Joseph S. Richards was sent for and when he arrived pronounced President Snow's ailment Pneumonia. Sister Snow had already consulted Dr. Wilcox. The physicians gave no hope for the President's recovery, unless a sudden change for the better set in.[13]

Elder Clawson reviewed his movements with President Snow: "Thursday morning a messenger came to my home and notified me that President Snow was much worse. I immediately went to his bedside and found the President in a very serious condition. President Smith, and the apostles, and members of his family had been summoned to his bedside, and responded with the utmost dispatch. President Snow's condition was so critical, that we administered to him at once, without waiting for President Smith. Apostle Cowley anointed, and I confirmed the same. We were assisted by Apostle Woodruff and LeRoi C. Snow. President Smith and a number of the apostles came in a little later. Pres. Snow's condition was quite critical all the morning."[14]

President Joseph F. Smith, among others, described what he knew of President Snow's last day of mortality:

> During that night and early the next morning [Wednesday night to Thursday], and again later, about 9:30 o'clock, the President showed signs of sinking, but still he appeared to believe that he would get over it. At twelve minutes past noon, while myself and the Apostles were in council meeting in the temple a messenger was admitted to the room bearing the news that the President was rapidly sinking. We at once adjourned our meeting and repaired in a body to the bedside of our beloved leader, where we found that many of the family had already

> gathered. Until within a couple of hours of his death the President was quite conscious and self-possessed, but not at all communicative. Besides members of his numerous family we found in the sick room the temple choir who, it appears, had been sent for the purpose of rendering a couple of favorite selections in keeping with a request said to have been made to Sister Minnie J. Snow by the President a few days before his death. As some questioned the propriety of the choir singing at that particular time, the President was asked if he wished to hear the choir sing. He unhesitatingly replied in the negative, but invited them to sing at his funeral. After this he called for members of his family at different times and with much difficulty tried to make himself understood, but afterwards his speech became less and less coherent until he failed entirely to do so, and at 3:35 that same afternoon the spirit of him who fully expected to tarry with us until at least certain undertakings should be completed and accomplished, passed from mortal life, and we were left appalled at the change so suddenly wrought, which may be better imagined than described.[15]

President Clawson's account gives other details: "At this point Brother Arthur Winter came in and notified the brethren that President Snow was much worse, and a moment later Brother L. John Nuttall brought the same message." They quickly closed their meeting in the temple. "The brethren immediately repaired to the Beehive House. We found President Snow's symptoms very alarming. By direction of President Smith the brethren and all present knelt around his bed, and I was mouth in offering prayer. The President steadily grew worse as the day wore on, and at 3:35 p.m., Thursday, Oct. 10, 1901, he breathed his last. His final moments appeared to be free from pain."[16]

Practical considerations were then put in place: "Elder Joseph E. Taylor, the undertaker, was sent for and took charge of the remains. President Smith then invited the sons of the President to meet with him in the back parlor to have an understanding regarding the funeral arrangements. This resulted in the selection of Elders Abraham O. Woodruff and Rudger Clawson as a committee representing the Apostles, to confer with them, the sons, in regard to the matter. A cable message announcing the death of President Snow was sent to Elder Francis M. Lyman in Liverpool and to Elder Heber J. Grant in Yokohama. Telegraph messages were also sent to the outlying Stake Presidents announcing the time of the funeral services which, it was decided, would be held at 2 o'clock Sunday."[17]

The day after President Snow's passing, "A meeting of the Apostles was arranged for this morning at 10 o'clock at the office. . . . The object of this meeting was chiefly to arrange for the pallbearers and speakers at the funeral services. It was decided that no special speakers be named, but that the time be occupied by several of the older Apostles who should make brief remarks. . . . President Smith sought the mind of the brethren as to whether it would be proper for the Apostles to now act as the presiding quorum of the Church, or the counselors, until after the burial. The brethren generally accorded to the counselors the right to act until after the funeral services, and this according to precedent."[18]

That Sunday, October 13, 1891, President Snow's funeral took place in the Tabernacle, and his remains were then transported by rail and wagon to Brigham City for interment.[19] After the funeral, Joseph F. Smith moved to immediately reorganize the First Presidency, as President Snow had counseled him. That duty having been accomplished, a special general conference was called for November 10, wherein the assembled Latter-day Saints could formally sustain the action. At this conference, President Smith said:

> It is only recently that we held our semi-annual general conference, which was largely attended, and at which, on the last day, we were privileged to hear the voice of President Lorenzo Snow, who spoke to us for the last time in the flesh, and left with us his instruction and counsel in relation to some of the most important matters that pertain to the continuance of the ministry and the labor of the Apostles of Jesus Christ throughout the world. We little supposed then that it would be the last time he would appear before us, or that we would be favored with his presence, his counsel and wisdom; but the Lord has taken him from our midst. He has finished his mission here, and the labor now devolves upon us who survive.[20]

He then reviewed some succession history with previous presidents of the Church, being careful to omit the reasons *why* his predecessors (except President Snow) had waited or "hesitated" to immediately reorganize; he also mentioned *why* he himself had moved forward without such hesitation. Further, he said:

> As soon as the news reached us of the death of President Woodruff, who was in California at the time, President Lorenzo Snow said to me, "it will be our duty to proceed as soon as possible to reorganize the Presidency of the Church." As you are aware, after the burial of the remains of President Woodruff, he proceeded at once to do this. In this

Lorenzo Snow's funeral procession (CA)

> connection I may tell you another thing. President Snow said to me, "you will live to be the President of the Church of Jesus Christ of Latter-day Saints, and when that time comes you should proceed at once and reorganize the Presidency of the Church." This was his counsel to me, and the same was given to the Twelve Apostles. In accordance with this principle and with the injunction of President Snow, within one week after his death the Apostles proceeded to designate the new Presidency of the Church, and we did it strictly in accordance with the pattern that the Lord has established in His Church, unanimously.[21]

President Joseph F. Smith felt a great loyalty in most matters toward his predecessor, realizing in humility that he had enormous shoes to fill; President Snow's ministry had indeed been "the Lord's ministry in and through him."[22]

Both Presidents Snow and Smith knew well that the time of President Snow's passing was likely to come in the not-too-distant future and had evidently discussed the matter between themselves. President Smith informed one mourner that "such changes are in the course of nature and might naturally be expected; in fact the President himself looked forward to the change, but, like the rest of us, did not expect it to come so suddenly."[23] President Smith had been sustained as President of the Church shortly after the funeral of President Snow. Having moved forward as such, he now felt the weight of the prophetic mantle fall upon himself. A sobering and sensitive letter to Elder Francis M. Lyman (then serving in Europe) speaks to this growing awareness:

> When confronted by the stern reality of the situation, I hardly know how to express the feelings of appreciation which well up in my heart; for I now keenly realize, as others have before me, that the eyes of the Lord, and those whom we have been wont to look up to, who are now on the other side of the veil, as well as my associate brethren in the flesh, are now directed towards me, as they have been towards my predecessors. But in contemplating the seriousness of the responsibility imposed upon me by the Lord and my brethren, its burden is at once comparatively lightened in the realization of the fact that you and I are the servants, servants of Him whom we have listed to obey; that the kingdom is the Lord's, and that it is for Him to guide and direct, and us to follow. . . . My mind naturally runs backward at times; and the men who have figured prominently in their time now appear to be nearer and stand out more clearly and conspicuously, perhaps, than ever before; and I cannot help but wonder at the things which have been accomplished through them when the conditions surrounding them are considered.[24]

President Snow's family sold many of his possessions after his passing, with the new First Presidency acting through their secretary to obtain a few of them that were felt to be special to the Church: "$117.50 was appropriated to pay for the desk of the late President Snow, which was bought at the private auction sale of his personal effects this morning by George F. Gibbs. The desk was presented to President Snow by the Apostles when he was their president, and was used by him in the temple when he was

President Snow's horse-drawn hearse arrives at the family burial plot. (CA)

The Snow family burial plot in Brigham City (CA)

President of his quorum, and afterwards by him at the President's Office when he became President of the Church. Also five dollars was appropriated to pay for a round-headed cocoanut wood cane which was presented to President Snow by the Sabbath School children of Samoa through a delegation about a week or ten days before his death."[25]

As for President Snow's legacy, much could be said. Elder Brigham Young Jr. felt that "his last days have been the most important," and this seems a well-considered conclusion. His last fifteen years of life were filled with two overriding concerns, with both of which he achieved remarkable success: unity in the presiding councils of the Church and abolishment of Church debt. His life was filled with many other great and remarkable things, but those stand out as the preeminent successes—he was the right man for the right time and did the right things under the blessing and guidance of his Lord.

Elder Heber J. Grant, on becoming President Heber J. Grant with the death of President Joseph F. Smith, reminisced about the hard work and successes of President Snow and paid due tribute:

> It is stated that men do not amount to much after they pass fifty, and that when they are sixty you ought to get some kind of a drug and put them to sleep, and that when they are seventy they are simply useless. But Lorenzo Snow came to the presidency of the Church when he was eighty-five years of age, and what he accomplished during the next

> three years of his life is simply marvelous to contemplate. He lifted the Church from the financial slough of despond, so to speak, from almost financial bankruptcy—when its credit was hardly good for a thousand dollars without security, when it was paying ten per cent for money—he lifted the Church out of that condition and made its credit A No. 1, so that people solicited and asked for the privilege of buying the bonds of this Church at six per cent. Ten per cent is sixty-six and two-thirds per cent more than six per cent, and in three short years this man, beyond the age of ability in the estimation of the world, this man who had not been engaged in financial affairs, who had been devoting his life for years to laboring in the temple, took hold of the finances of the Church of Christ, under the inspiration of the living God, and in those three years changed everything, financially, from darkness to light.[26]

Elder Clawson, who had been of such critical assistance to President Snow in providing him accurate information regarding past and current Church finances, met with the new First Presidency that November to bring them up to speed on current conditions:

> Having completed the statement of assets and liabilities of the church, showing the financial condition thereof at the beginning of President Joseph F. Smith's administration, and also showing incidentally what had been accomplished during President Lorenzo Snow's incumbency in office during the past three years of his life, I submitted the same to the First Presidency, going carefully over every detail. . . .
>
> The report, which covered eleven sheets of extra large ledger paper, was listened to with rapt attention by the First Presidency, who were greatly surprised and gratified with the excellent showing made and marveled at what had been accomplished in so short a time by Pres. Lorenzo Snow under the special blessing of the Lord: for it will be seen that the assets of the church had not only increased in value to the extent of $111,879.62, but that the church indebtedness had been decreased $687,283.80. In addition to this, it will also be seen that the contingent indebtedness of Feb. 18, 1899, amounting to $1,568,954.29, had been entirely wiped out, while the net assets of the church jumped from $82,628.40 in Feb. 1899 to $881,791.82. And such was the glorious work accomplished by President Lorenzo Snow and the saints under divine favor in the short period of three years. The reason I use the word saints is this: the saints listened to the voice of counsel in respect to the payment of their tithes and thus opened up the way, through the wise and prudent management of affairs, for substantial and permanent relief to the church.[27]

Latter-day Saints arrive at the Salt Lake Tabernacle for general conference, April 6, 1906. At the conference one year later, President Smith announced the Church financially solvent to the extent it did not owe a dollar it could not pay immediately. (USHS)

By early 1904, President Lund took pleasure recording a welcome exercise undertaken by the First Presidency: "The forenoon [morning] was spent in counting the [first issue of redeemed] Church bonds and then destroying them. We burned nearly half a million [dollars] in bonds. We felt happy that we had been able to do this and thus save the Church $30,000.00 per year in interest. We kept a bond for each of the Presidency and the Twelve and the Patriarch as a souvenir."[28]

Only a few years later, the second bond issue received like treatment. Leslie Thomas Perry (the father of L. Tom Perry) related an experience he shared with President Joseph F. Smith:

> I well recall one evening after coming to the Beehive House (in early 1907) President Smith returned home rather late—I had been doing some chores and was in the family dining room. I soon knew the cause of his elation; he remarked to his wife, "Julina, I have brought home the last of the bonds of the church—evidence of the church indebtedness—I desire to destroy them." I was asked to make a fire in the fireplace, and after it was burning vigorously, sending its warmth in the room, and its glow in the walls, President Smith took from his briefcase a few instruments and thrust them into the fire. The expression on his face, the twinkle in his eye, the intense feeling in the room, revealed to me his thoughts. . . . It

> was an occasion for elation, thanksgiving to the Lord. I surmised what he was thinking as I watched the fire consume the last evidence of an obligation of the Church of Jesus Christ of Latter-day Saints.[29]

Such became the fate of the bonds issued by President Snow to save the reputation and credit of the Church—he had done a mighty work.

Confirming this, in the April 1907 general conference of the Church, President Joseph F. Smith stated: "I want to say another thing to you, and I do so by way of congratulation, and that is, that we have, by the blessing of the Lord and the faithfulness of the Saints in paying their tithing, been able to pay off our bonded indebtedness. Today the Church of Jesus Christ of Latter-day Saints owes not a dollar that it cannot pay at once. At last we are in a position that we can pay as we go. We do not have to borrow any more, and we won't have to if the Latter-day Saints continue to live their religion and observe this law of tithing. It is the law of revenue to the Church."[30]

Epilogue

The abundance with which the Lord continued to bless the Church following President Snow's administration proved to be unprecedented. In about 1917 Charles W. Nibley, then the Presiding Bishop of the Church, wrote: "In the eleven years that I have been in the [Presiding] Bishop's office a great many material improvements have been effected. Eleven years ago all of the Church employees were paid mostly in tithing scrip. I immediately took up a labor with the Presidency and got them to pay cash and to call in all the outstanding scrip." After listing a number of large building projects completed, including the Church Administration Building, two temples, the Hotel Utah, and others, Bishop Nibley concluded: "The Church has never been so prospered, either in a material way or spiritual way as it is now." Nibley also mentioned that the Church's purchase of stock in two sugar companies became profitable, explaining: "I estimate that the Church cleaned up a large amount of means in this transaction, running up to several million dollars. . . . Never in the history of the west, I think, has such a large deal been turned and out of which so much money has been made by everybody concerned. All who became interested in it made money out of it. I cannot say that it was through my ability or acumen or better judgment that this great beneficial investment was turned over to us. It was really through the blessing of the Lord. In fact, I have said hundreds of times that it was simply shoveled into my lap. Therefore, let the Lord be praised for His goodness and mercy in so many, many ways."[31]

Another major step in the Church's financial affairs occurred in 1990, when Church leaders announced a decision to eliminate budget assessments on member families, proclaiming instead that "we have reached this tremendously significant day when in the United States and Canada all costs of operations, in terms of physical facilities for wards and stakes and missions, and a reasonable activity program will be financed from the general funds of the Church"—funds deriving from the tithes and offerings paid by faithful members.[32] Elder Glen L. Rudd, a member of the Quorums of the Seventy at the time, recorded details of a visit he received from President Gordon B. Hinckley:

> On November 17, 1989 . . . President and Sister Hinckley stayed with . . . me in our little condo in Sydney, Australia. I was quite interested in President Hinckley's first announcement to me. He seemed to be all smiles and was truly happy when he told me about the last thing he had done before leaving his office in Salt Lake City: He had signed an official letter that abolished ward budgets and other financial assignments with the exception of tithing and fast offerings.
>
> He then prophesied that tithing and fast offerings would increase tremendously and that the Saints would be greatly blessed because of this new policy change. For more than a half century, the Brethren have had a strong desire to relieve most of the financial burdens from the Saints and have been hoping for this day to arrive. President Hinckley participated time and time again over the years in raising money for welfare farms, chapels, seminary buildings, etc.; and signing the letter was a very happy and momentous event for him.[33]

Appendix 1

"As man now is, God once was. As God now is, man may be."

When Latter-day Saints remember President Lorenzo Snow today, they often remember him for two reasons: tithing emphasis and the couplet he formed and often expressed: "As man now is, God once was. As God now is, man may be." Yet with time, memory of this doctrinal teaching has faded. Critics and enemies of the Church have recognized it as a deeper doctrine they seek to manipulate to weaken the faith of the unprepared—to give gospel meat to spiritual babies, as it were. Others have noticed that it is rarely taught in the Church in the couplet President Snow formed and often repeated. Chapter one herein contains a narration from President Snow explaining how this revelation was received. Several other accounts of this experience from President Snow are found throughout the main biographical text, in addition to those recounted below.

In 1997 a reporter asked President Gordon B. Hinckley about the couplet and the doctrine it teaches. In response, President Hinckley is purported to have said: "I don't know that we teach it. I don't know that we emphasize it. . . . I haven't heard it discussed for a long time in public discourse. I don't know. I don't know all the circumstances under which that statement was made. I understand the philosophical background behind it. But I don't know a lot about it and I don't know that others know a lot about it." The reporter also wrote that President Hinckley "sounded uncertain."[1] Critics have sought to use this quotation to cast the Church, its doctrine, and its prophet in a bad light before the world, which does not understand the couplet and is not prepared for it.

Knowing that such deception would be attempted, President

Hinckley referred to the incomplete publication of the interview in general conference: "The media have been kind and generous to us. This past year of pioneer celebrations has resulted in very extensive, favorable press coverage. There have been a few things we wish might have been different. I personally have been much quoted, and in a few instances misquoted and misunderstood. I think that's to be expected. None of you need worry because you read something that was incompletely reported. You need not worry that I do not understand some matters of doctrine. I think I understand them thoroughly, and it is unfortunate that the reporting may not make this clear. I hope you will never look to the public press as the authority on the doctrines of the Church."[2]

Two concepts need to be clearly understood when grappling with this kind of situation: (1) As a generality, many reporters are not simply seeking truth and facts and context for their stories—especially when a person being interviewed claims to be a prophet or apostle. They are seeking angles and sensationalism that will increase readership of their piece and consequent advancement of their careers and readership. Many reporters are not Christian, belong to no organized church, have not read the Bible or other LDS scriptures, and have little or no religious background or knowledge. Such questioners may not care whether something might actually be true or not; it is the sensational nature of it (in their minds) that motivates asking about it and printing it. They themselves disbelieve it and know many of their readers will also, but to them it makes a great story for public consumption. In the past, most news organizations and media outlets sought to provide objective, professional, factual, unbiased news reporting to the public. Today, this goal often gives way to entertainment, opinion, agenda, and bias. 2) President Hinckley knew all of this. He knew that some reporters asking questions were seeking the most unconventional or fantastic answers they could get for their stories.

So how should he, as the President and chief spokesman for the Church, answer such questions? As an experienced and savvy communicator, he gave the least amount of supposedly "unusual" information possible for others to make mischief with. If the reporter was correct that President Hinckley sounded hesitant, it wasn't because he did not fully understand and believe the doctrine, it was because he was placed in the uncomfortable and distasteful role of being asked to "cast pearls before swine." It was a no-win question and high-risk situation in some respects, and he gave probably the best answer possible.

This kind of background and context, which leads to clearer and more accurate understanding, undermines the goals of the critic, so the critics are necessarily ignored or dismissed in favor of those tactics that further their cause with the unwary.

President Hinckley, however, was correct when he indicated that the couplet is not referenced much in the Church today in its complete and original form, as rendered by President Snow. The fact that it is buried in old records and publications not commonly read today by Latter-day Saints has much to do with this, as does the truth that some members are spiritually unprepared to understand and accept it. The doctrine it teaches, therefore, is often expressed using other language and different quotations—but it is all the same revealed truth. President Hinckley's main point should not be lost or forgotten in the confusion and wrangling emanating from critics and unbelievers—the public press is not a source of authoritative Church doctrine.

In late 2009, a few reporters and bloggers claimed they found evidence that Lorenzo Snow may not have been the originator of the famous couplet, but that Brigham Young may instead have been the author. Someone had stumbled onto some expressions of President Young, found in a recent publication, and jumped to the conclusion that something was fishy or confused. President Young is alleged to have said:

> Brother Lorenzo Snow made some remarks on the character of Jesus Christ, and asked for light. I replied—While on a mission to England, the following came forcibly to my mind—'As God was, so are we now; as he now is, so we shall be.' Our Father was once born of parents, having a father and mother the same as we have. He is the very eternal Father, because of the creation of God. He is the Savior of the world, the root of spirit and the offspring of flesh, the Only Begotten of the Father in the flesh. The Father came down and begat him, the same as we do now, and Jesus was the only one.[3]

These expressions, designating who spoke, in what setting, and whether the wording is accurately transcribed and completely quoted, are by no means clear and unambiguous. To extrapolate from this muddled talk that President Young came up with the couplet seems both unwarranted and insufficient. A better scenario is simply that Lorenzo Snow received the vision he claimed he received, with the accompanying doctrine, as he said he did; that he then went to England on a mission and shared the doctrine (in couplet form) with Elder Brigham Young, at that time as he said he did; and that is why Brigham is alleged to have said, "The following came forcibly to my mind" while in England. Brigham was deeply impressed with the doctrine Lorenzo shared with him then, pondered it, believed it, and repeated it on that occasion; possibly as a reminder to Lorenzo Snow of their past conversation. Such seems to be a better scenario when compared with other relevant records, although others could be postulated.

Below are quotations taken from incidents where President Lorenzo Snow taught the doctrine contained in the couplet to various gatherings, given in chronological order:[4]

At the Brigham City Tabernacle, January 10, 1886, just prior to his sentencing to prison for polygamy:

While thus living we may look forward far away into the spirit-land, with full assurance that when reaching that happy clime, we shall be crowned with the sons and daughters of God, and possess the wealth and glory of a Celestial kingdom.

Apostle Paul in his time, taught the Saints to have the same mind in them as was in Christ Jesus, who, finding Himself in the form of God, thought it not robbery to be equal with God. Apostle John, on the same subject says, "When Jesus appears we shall be like Him." "Every one that hath this hope in him, purifieth himself even as God is pure."

As man now is, God once was—even the babe of Bethlehem, advancing to childhood—thence to boyhood, manhood, then to the Godhead. This, then, is the "mark of the prize of man's high calling in Christ Jesus."

We are the offspring of God, begotten by Him in the [premortal] spirit world, where we partook of His nature as children here partake of the likeness of their parents. Our trials and sufferings give us experience, and establish within us principles of godliness.[5]

In a meeting of the Council of the Twelve:

He [President Snow] said the Lord revealed to him that as man is God once was and that [as] God is man will [may] be.[6]

In the October 1894 general conference:

In the revelations which God has given, we find what a person can reach who will travel this path of knowledge and be guided by the Spirit of God. I had not been in this Church more than two years when it was clearly shown to me what a man could reach through a continued obedience to the Gospel of the Son of God. That knowledge has been as a star continually before me, and has caused me to be particular in trying to do that which was right and acceptable to God. . . . It is a long time since the knowledge of which I speak was communicated to me in a vision. But it has not been forgotten. When it was first shown to me it was personal property; I dared not communicate it. It was something that I had never heard before. Now, however, it is public property. . . .

Now I will say what I received in vision, which was just as clear as the sun ever shone. The knowledge that was communicated to me I embraced in this couplet:

As man now is, God once was.

As God now is, man may be.

That is a very wonderful thing. It was to me. I did not know but that I had come into possession of knowledge that I had no business with; but I knew it was true. Nothing of this kind had ever reached my ears before. It was preached a few years after that; at least, the Prophet Joseph taught this idea to the Twelve Apostles. Now, however, it is common property; but I do not know how many there are here that have got a real knowledge of these things in their hearts. . . . Now, we are the sons and daughters of God. He has begotten us in His own image. He has given us faculties and powers that are capable of enlargement until His fulness is reached which He has promised—until we shall sit upon thrones, governing and controlling our posterity from eternity to eternity, and increasing eternally. That is the fact in regard to these matters, and there are some people who understand distinctly what I am saying.[7]

A meeting of the Council of the Twelve:

There was a man who stood near Joseph, whom I asked for certain counsel. While he spoke I saw this beautiful principle contained in the following couplet which I made: As God was—so man is. As God is so man may be. I saw it like a revelation. I told it to my sister. I went to England and saw Bro. Brigham Young to whom I told this. He said he believed it. A couple of years afterwards Joseph preached the same. The revelation had this effect upon me that I saw what God had prepared for man and what the latter can attain to if he lives up to the principles which God reveals and what he knows to be right.[8]

First public address after becoming President of the Church, given to the Salt Lake Stake in the Tabernacle:

That exalted position was made manifest to me at a very early day. I had a direct revelation of this. It was most perfect and complete. If there ever was a thing revealed to man perfectly, clearly, so that there could be no doubt or dubiety, this was revealed to me, and it came in these words: "As man now is, God once was; as God now is, man may be." This may appear to some minds as something very strange and remarkable, but it is in perfect harmony with the teachings of Jesus Christ and with His promises. . . . This is the high destiny of the sons of God, they who overcome, who are obedient to His commandments, who purify themselves even as He is pure. They are to become like Him; they will see Him as He is; they will behold His face and reign with Him in His glory, becoming like unto Him in every particular.[9]

Second major discourse after becoming President of the Church, given in Brigham City, Utah:

President Snow spoke of the destiny of man. The time will come, he said, when we shall be like our Father in Heaven. This had been revealed to him early in his experience. He referred to the saying of John, that when Christ shall appear we shall be like Him; also to the angel that John the Revelator fell down to worship.

We are told that Abraham, Isaac and Jacob are Gods in eternity. We can attain to this condition by purifying ourselves as God is pure.[10]

Related at the October 1898 general conference:

I devoted myself to be worthy to receive something that no mortal man can receive except through the spirit and power of the Holy Ghost, and the Lord has shown me things and made me to understand them as clearly as the sun at noonday in regard to what shall be the outcome of those Latter-day Saints that are faithful to their callings.[11]

At a priesthood meeting after the October 1900 general conference:

He [Pres. Snow] appreciated the fact that he was standing before men who would in time be gods; but our glory, after all, would depend entirely upon ourselves and our faithfulness. If we fail to magnify our Priesthood it would have been better if it had never been conferred upon us. He had not been long in the Church before the Lord revealed to him this grand and mighty principle, and he expressed it in a couplet composed by himself. "As man now is, God once was; as God now is man may be." Jesus was God before he came into the world, and yet his knowledge was taken from him as it has been taken from us. He did not know his former greatness, neither do we know the greatness we had attained to before we came here; but He had to pass through an ordeal as we have to without knowing or realizing at the time the greatness and importance of His mission.[12]

To a reunion of Weber Utah Stake authorities (in Ogden, Utah), held on June 12, 1901:

You will all be great some day: as great as you want to be. I remember an incident which occurred in Kirtland when I received my first patriarchal blessing from Father Smith. A better man never existed, nor was there a man better loved than he. I was introduced by my sister Eliza R., though at that time I was not a Latter-day Saint and had no idea of becoming one. He said to me: Don't worry, take it calmly and the Lord will show you, and you will want to be baptized. He told me another thing that greatly surprised me. He said, you will be great, and as great as you want to be, as great as God Himself, and you will not wish to be greater. I could not understand this, but years after in Nauvoo while talking upon a principle of the Gospel the Spirit of God rested powerfully upon me and showed me more clearly than I can now see your faces a certain principle and its glory, and it came to me summarized in this brief sentence: "As man is now, God once was; as God is now man may be." The Spirit of God was on me in a marvelous manner all that day, and I stored that great truth away in my mind. I felt that I had learnt something that I ought not to communicate to others; but I told it to my sister Eliza R. Three or four weeks after that I was called to go upon a mission to England, and I went. As I said, I did not understand Father Smith at the time, but I studied the principles of the Mormon people, and went to their testimony meetings in Kirtland, and what I heard there was marvelous to me. Brethren and sisters would get up and testify of experiences which they had enjoyed, such as I had never heard of before. . . .

[After President Snow finished] President Joseph F. Smith addressed the Saints in effect as follows: Beloved brethren and sisters, it is with feelings of humility that I arise before you. I have listened to many interesting things this morning, among them the early experiences of President Lorenzo Snow and the moving influence of his life, the Holy Ghost, which has directed his efforts in assisting to establish Zion. . . . It is impossible at this moment to speak upon any particular subject, but I call your attention to the man who took down his patriarchal blessing and to the remark of the Patriarch when the blessing was read over that he, this brother, had been so long steeped in the traditions and prejudices of the sectarian world that it was difficult for him to comprehend what was said. I'm sorry to say that I have witnessed the same thing in many men connected with the Church, but who have been born, reared and educated in the sectarian world, to such an extent that notwithstanding they have become Latter-day Saints, have been born again under the new covenant, they were yet so imbued with the traditions of the fathers that it was difficult to get the truth fully into their minds. I had an old friend, for many years a Bishop. We buried him a few days ago. There was no better man according to his understanding and according to the desires of his heart, but when he preached and how he prayed, whether at home or in public, you could see the horns of sectarianism sticking out all over him and bristling in him. There is too much of this among us. We have heard the remarks of President Snow, of the revelation that came to him in respect to our relationship to God, and His to us, as expressed by President Snow in the words, "As man now is, God once was, and as God now is man may be." It is hard to get this idea into the heads of many of the Latter-day Saints, and it is almost an impossibility to get it into the minds of the people of the so-called Christian world.

President Smith then talked on the God-head and showed plainly that as Christ, the Son of God, came to earth, born of His mother, perhaps the least of all men, descended below all things, and rose to become the Redeemer of the world, the Son, the very Eternal Father of this heaven and this earth, so we could rise; notwithstanding the God in Him, having power of life within Himself and power to defy death, He still died for us. This was the Son of the Eternal God and who sits enthroned on His right hand possessed of everlasting power and dominion. What is more natural than that as God is man may become if we take Jesus Christ as an example. We are like Him now, but in embryo, while He has developed and advanced and sits upon His throne and reigns. This truth has been revealed to President Snow and it ought to appeal to every human being on earth, and particularly should it appeal to us because of the greater light that has been received by revelation through the Prophet Joseph. Here President Smith read a verse in Eliza R. Snow's poem:

I had learned to call Thee Father,
Through Thy Spirit from on High;
But until the Key of Knowledge
Was restored, I knew not why. In the heavens, are parents single?
No. The thought makes reason stare.
Truth is reason: truth eternal
Tells me I've a mother there

When Jesus was on earth He had a mother there as we have. We are built on the same plan as God our Father. Our destiny is the same as His, for we are formed in His likeness, and nothing is more natural than that as He is we may become. For this the world calls us blasphemous, because they worship a nonentity, a nondescript, without body, parts and passions, whose circumference is everywhere and whose center is nowhere. Yet there is no truth that has been revealed to us that is more simple and plain than this. God grant that we may all understand this principle and cling to it and never yield it while life shall last. God bless you. Amen.[13]

From a discourse delivered at the Millcreek Ward meetinghouse, July 1901:

Now, I have told you what Father Smith said to me, that I should become as great as I could want to be, even as great as God Himself. About two years and a half after, in Nauvoo, I asked Elder Sherwood to explain a certain passage of scripture, and while he was endeavoring to give an explanation the Spirit of God fell upon me to a marked extent, and the Lord revealed to me, just as plainly as the sun at noonday, this principle, which I put in a couplet;

"As man now is, God once was; As God now is, man may be."

That fulfilled Father Smith's declaration. Nothing was ever revealed more distinctly than that was to me. Of course, now that it is so well known it may not appear such a wonderful manifestation, but when I received it, the knowledge was marvelous to me. This principle, in substance, is found also in the scriptures. The Lord said to John as recorded in the third chapter of his Revelation:

"To him that overcometh will I grant to sit with me in my throne, even as I also overcame, and am set down with my Father in His throne."

Have you ever heard the ministers of the day preach a doctrine of that kind? They read it, but do not believe it. Paul says in his second epistle to the Corinthians, 12th chapter:

"I knew a man in Christ above fourteen years ago, (whether in body, I cannot tell: or whether out of the body I cannot tell: God knoweth)

How that he was caught up into paradise, and heard unspeakable words which it is not lawful for a man to utter."

This same Paul, writing to the Philippians says:

"Let this mind be in you, which was also in Christ Jesus: Who, being in the form of God, thought it not robbery to be equal with God."

Do we ever hear ministers try to explain that? But these things are undoubtedly clear to your minds, I say to you sister, your husbands, if they are faithful, will be Gods in eternity. After we have passed through the various ordeals of life and go to the other life, where our Father dwells, even the God of heaven the promise is that we shall be like Him. The Apostle John says:

"Beloved, now are we the sons of God, and it doth not yet appear what we shall be; but we know that, when He shall appear, we shall be like Him."

As an illustration, here is an infant upon its mother's breast. It is without power or knowledge to feed and clothe itself. It is so helpless that it has to be fed by its mother. But see its possibilities! This infant has a father and a mother, though it knows scarcely anything about them; and when it gets to be quite a little boy it does not know much about them. Who is its father? Who is its mother? Why, its father is an emperor, its mother is an empress, and they sit upon a throne, governing an empire. This little infant will someday, in all probability, sit upon his father's throne, and govern and control the empire, just as King Edward of England now sits upon the throne of his mother. We should have this in mind; for we are the sons of God, as much so and more, if possible, than we are the sons of our earthly fathers. You sisters, I suppose, have read that poem which my sister composed years ago, and which is sung quite frequently now in our meetings. It tells us that we not only have a Father in "that high and glorious place," but that we have a Mother too; and you will become as great as your Mother, if you are faithful.[14]

At a fast meeting in the Salt Lake Temple, one of the last occasions of President Snow speaking in public before his death:

I know the destiny of the Latter-day Saints. I know my destiny, providing I keep in the path the Lord has marked out. I know what you—brethren and sisters—can reach. We are all the children of God—all that live upon the earth. God loves us all. When Jesus died, he died for the whole human family. He died that we might become Gods and Goddesses in eternity. Latter-day Saints are tried, have their troubles and disappointments. We cannot obtain a fullness of joy in this world. It was not intended that we should. Some will secure a fulness of glory hereafter, and others will receive it in part. There are three glories and other conditions that are not so glorious, and the Lord will bring his children into those conditions. As to the Latter-day Saints, the Lord designs that they shall receive a fullness of Celestial glory, and they are destined to become Gods in eternity. Jesus was God before he came into the world and he was God after he came, while a babe in Bethlehem, but he did not know it.[15]

From a poem entitled "Man's Destiny" written by President Snow:
Dear Brother:
Hast thou not been unwisely bold,
Man's destiny to thus unfold?
To raise, promote such high desire,
Such vast ambition thus inspire?
Still, 'tis no phantom that we trace
Man's ultimatum in life's race;
This royal path has long been trod
By righteous men, each now a God:
As Abra'm, Isaac, Jacob, too,
First babes, then men—to gods they grew.
As man now is, our God once was;
As now God is, so man may be,
Which doth unfold man's destiny.
For John declares: When Christ we see
Like unto him we'll truly be.
And he who has this hope within,
Will purify himself from sin.
Who keep this object grand in view,
To folly, sin, will bid adieu,
Nor wallow in the mire anew;
Nor ever seek to carve his name
High on the shaft of worldly fame;
But here his ultimatum trace:
The head of all his spirit-race.

Ah, well: that taught by you, dear Paul,
'Though much amazed, we see it all;
Our Father God, has ope'd our eyes,
We cannot view it otherwise.
The boy, like to his father grown,
Has but attained unto his own;
To grow to sire from state of son,
Is not 'gainst Nature's course to run.
A son of God, like God to be,
Would not be robbing Deity;
And he who has this hope within,
Will purify himself from sin.
You're right, St. John, supremely right:
Whoe'er essays to climb this height,
Will cleanse himself of sin entire—
Or else 'twere needless to aspire.
Lorenzo Snow.[16]

From "Characteristic Sayings" of President Snow:
Man may become like his Father, doing the works which his Father did before him, and he cannot be deprived of the opportunity of reaching this exalted state.
The destiny of man is to be like his Father—a god in eternity. This should be a bright, illuminating star before him all the time—in his heart, in his soul, and all through him.
As man now is, God once was:
As God now is, man may be.
As son of God, like God to be,
Would not be robbing Deity.[17]

Appendix 2

Lorenzo Snow's Testimony

Various accounts related by President Snow of the testimony he received shortly after his baptism and conferral of the Holy Ghost upon him. Several others are found in the main text:

I laid my pride, worldly ambition and aspirations upon the altar, and as humble as a child went to the waters of baptism, received the ordinance administered by an Apostle and afterward the laying on of hands.

One evening, a few days after this, when alone, engaged in earnest prayer, the heavens were opened, the veil was rent from my mind, and then and there I received the most wonderful manifestations, grand and sublime, I believe, as man was ever permitted to receive, and beyond the power of language fully to describe. It was shown me in that vision that there truly existed a Son of God—that Joseph Smith was really a prophet of God.

The first intimation of the approach of that marvelous vision, was a sound just above my head like the rustling of silken robes, when immediately the Holy Spirit descended upon me enveloping my whole person, filling me from the crown of my head to the soles of my feet, which was a complete baptism as tangible an immersion in a Heavenly principle or element—the Holy Ghost—infinitely more real, physical in its effects upon every part of my system than was the immersion when I was baptized in water. That night after retiring to rest the same wonderful manifestations were repeated, and continued to be several successive nights. From that time to the present on numerous occasions, miraculous manifestations of the Divine power have followed me and my administrations of the Gospel ordinances.[1]

Having become convinced by reasoning, and by listening to the testimony of others who had received these principles, I became satisfied that it was my duty to experiment upon these principles, that I might be able to test the results. This I consequently did, and there followed the same testimony and the same experiences, so far as the knowledge of the divinity of these principles was concerned, as followed obedience to this Gospel as proclaimed by the apostles in former times. And this knowledge could not be disputed. It was not only acknowledged intellectually, but the inspiration of the Holy Ghost imparted to me a knowledge as physically and as demonstrative as that physical ordinance when I was immersed in the waters of baptism; that as I had passed through the atmosphere into the element of water, so my experience, knowledge and testimony was full and complete, so complete, indeed, that from that day till the present moment, through all of the vicissitudes of life through which I have passed, I have no more doubted the truth of these principles than I do now that I behold this audience, and I never can doubt it. As long as memory continues and reason shall assert its throne, I never can permit the powerful testimony and knowledge that was communicated to me to remain silent. It was revealed to me. The heavens were opened over my head, and the power of God and the life of the Holy Ghost descended and elevated my whole being, and gave me the most perfect knowledge that Jesus was the Son of God. It was not the result simply of opinion or belief, as is the case in many other things, but it was a knowledge far beyond that of belief or opinion. I knew that God had sent His angels and restored the fulness of the Gospel as taught in ancient times; that He sent angels to authorize Joseph Smith, and gave him authority to administer in the ordinances of the Gospel, and to promise the Holy Ghost to all who would be obedient.[2]

Brethren and sisters, my testimony is that this is the work of God in which we are engaged. I had not been in this Church two weeks when the Lord revealed to me a knowledge that He was God, and that He sent His Son into the world to be crucified for the sins of the world. No man ever did or ever could receive a more perfect knowledge in regard to the existence of God and of the truth of this work than God gave to me by revelation and the opening of the heavens.[3]

And now I will close my remarks by bearing my testimony to the knowledge of God that I have received in relation to this work. It is true.

I received a knowledge of the truth of this work by a physical administration of the blessings of God. And when receiving the baptism of the Holy Ghost I knew I was immersed in a divine principle that filled my whole system with inexpressible joy; and from that day to the present has blessing crowned my labors.[4]

We know from our experience that the foundation upon which we have placed our faith is grand and glorious. I know this for myself. I had been in this Church but a short time when I succeeded in securing the most perfect knowledge that there was a God, that there was a Son, Jesus Christ, and that Joseph Smith was acknowledged of God as His prophet. It was a knowledge that no man could communicate. It came through a revelation from the Almighty.[5]

I had been a member of this Church but a short time when I obtained, by a divine manifestation, a clear, explicit and tangible demonstration of the truth of this work.[6]

[In council meeting] "Brother John Henry Smith remarked that a man named Samuelson had approached him, saying that he had given some thought to the subject of the Godhead. It was represented in one place, in the Prophet Joseph's lecture on the subject, that the Father is a personage of spirit, and in another place that He has a body of flesh and bones, also the Son. [Bro. Smith] thought it would be a good thing for young theological students if there could be a reconciliation of these two statements.

President Snow believed that the best thing to do with such matters was to let them alone. He thought it proper to make necessary explanations when it was wise to do so, but there were some things that could not be reconciled to man's present finite understanding. The President then referred to the subject of the Holy Ghost and invited the brethren who had definite ideas regarding it to express themselves. In confirming members of the Church, it was customary to say to them "Receive the Holy Ghost." And yet we are told that the Holy Ghost rested upon Jesus in the form of a dove. Speaking of his own experience when confirmed, President Snow said that he felt a burning sensation running from his head to his feet, and he now asked the brethren if they thought that was a personage of spirit that was resting upon him.

Brother Lyman answered, "No, that it was the power and spirit of the

Holy Ghost." And Brother Lund added that when a person received the Holy Ghost, it was its power that he received, even the spirit of light and truth.[7]

The President then related his doubts caused by his not having any great manifestation at the time of his confirmation. He felt that he had made great sacrifices in becoming a Mormon and in blighting his prospects as a young man, but he was ashamed now that he had ever called it a sacrifice. It is inconsistent, he said, for any of us to call our losses for the Gospel's sake a sacrifice. He related his visit to his many relatives after he became a Mormon and how he had gained light and knowledge of the truth after being thus disturbed in his mind by not receiving the gift of tongues or prophecy when confirmed; and how the spirit had come down upon him once when kneeling in prayer with a power that had passed through his body and had given him an absolute knowledge that God lived, that he was our Father and that Jesus was his son and had come to earth and talked with the Prophet Joseph, receiving a perfect knowledge of the truth of this work. "I shall never forget it," the speaker said, "so long as I draw breath."[8]

[Published interview by a non-Latter-day Saint reporter and writer] I had an hour's chat here with the venerable Lorenzo Snow, the President of the Church of Jesus Christ of Latter-day Saints, and the leader of the three hundred odd thousand Mormons who are scattered over the United States. Mr. Snow is now eighty-six years of age. . . .

President Snow told me there was no doubt in his mind that the Father and Jesus Christ really appeared in person to Joseph Smith while he was upon earth, and that Joseph Smith had frequent and full directions for all things connected with the Church from on high. He said such revelations were manifested today, and I thereupon asked him point blank if he himself had ever had a revelation or direct manifestation from God.

"I know that I have, and that several times," replied the President of the Mormons, "The first one was when I was a boy. My parents were very well to do. They sent me to college at Oberlin, Ohio, but I found the professors, they were Congregationalists, insisted I should believe as they did, and I left and went to Kirtland. There I met Joseph Smith and the Mormons. I attended their meetings and saw the brethren and sisters prophesying, speaking strange tongues, and giving forth the revelations they received from God. I was converted by them. I believed they had the true religion, and I joined the Church. So far my conversion was merely a matter of reason. I had had no manifestation, but I expected one.

"It was about two weeks later, when I went out in the woods one day to pray, that it came. I was on my knees when I heard a rustling like that of a silk dress, and something came down upon me and enveloped me. I can't describe it, but I knew it was from the Lord. I was filled with ecstasy, and my sins seemed to have passed away. I was immersed in the presence, which stayed with me for perhaps an hour. It came again at night when I was in my bed. After that I had the power of conversion, and of healing by the laying on of my hands, and parties have told me that when my hands were placed upon them they experienced the same feelings I had in the woods. That was many, many years ago. I have been a Mormon ever since."[9]

One Sunday the Prophet Joseph arose in the pulpit just before the meeting closed and said, "A young man by the name of Lorenzo Snow wishes to be baptized, and Brother John Boynton (who was then one of the Twelve Apostles) will baptize him." I was baptized in the stream that ran through Kirtland, and hands were laid upon me by Hyrum Smith and some others. I received no special manifestation at that time, but I was perfectly satisfied that I had done what was wisdom for me to do under the circumstances. I had studied the scriptures and was convinced that the Gospel as preached by the Latter-day Saints was in accordance with that taught by the Son of God and by His Apostles in former days. A peaceable, good spirit came upon me that I had never experienced before, and I felt satisfied at the sacrifice I had made. . . .

About two weeks after that, Elder Sherwood, at that time one of the right hand men of the Prophet's, said to me, "Brother Snow, have you received the Holy Ghost since you were baptized?" That question struck me almost with consternation. The fact was, while I had received all I needed perhaps, I had not received that which I had anticipated; and after Brother Sherwood put this question to me I felt dissatisfied, not with what I had done, but with myself. With that feeling I retired in the evening to a place where I had been accustomed to offer my devotions to the Lord. I knelt down under the shade of a tree, and immediately I heard a noise over my head like the rustle of silken garments, and there descended upon me the Spirit and power of God. That will never be erased from my memory as long as memory endures. It came upon me and enveloped my whole system, and I received a perfect knowledge that there was a God, that Jesus, who died upon Calvary, was His Son, and that Joseph the Prophet had received the authority which he professed to have. The satisfaction and the glory of that manifestation no language can express! I returned to my lodgings. I could now testify to the whole world that I knew, by positive knowledge, that the Gospel of the Son of God had been restored, and that Joseph was a Prophet of God, authorized to speak in His name, just as Noah was in his day.[10]

Other testimonies born by President Snow

In reference to John, who bore testimony to the Son of God, I never heard his voice; I never had the pleasure of shaking hands with him. But Joseph Smith I was familiar with. In the year 1832, if I mistake not, I first saw him and heard him preach. And from that time on, with the exception perhaps of a couple of years, I was intimately acquainted with him. I have conversed with him many times. I have heard him preach many times. I have sat at his table at various times. I knew him to be a man of God, full of the spirit of his calling—a man whose integrity could not be disputed, and who was honest in all his endeavors. No one that was as intimately acquainted with him as I was could find any fault with him, so far as his moral character was concerned.[11]

Now, I know of the things of which I speak. A little spiritual knowledge is a great deal better than mere opinions and notions and ideas, or even very elaborate arguments; a little spiritual knowledge is very important and of the highest consideration. We have received that knowledge, and we will stand by it, the Lord being our helper.[12]

There is no man that knows the truth of this work more than I do. I know it fully; I know it distinctly. I know there is a God just as well as any man knows it, because God has revealed himself to me. I know it positively. I shall never forget the manifestations of the Lord; I never will forget them as long as memory endures. It is in me.[13]

The Lord is a consistent being. He does not require the people to do that which is improper, nor does he expect of them anything unreasonable. He gives us a knowledge of what we shall do, inasmuch as we are willing to sacrifice our lives rather than go contrary to that knowledge. He opens to us the secrets of the celestial kingdom, and he is constantly communicating to us things that we never knew before. This knowledge and intelligence is growing upon us continually.[14]

Appendix 3

Teachings about Temple Work for the Dead & Salvation for Wayward Children

It is possible that Lorenzo Snow spoke more about the salvation of wayward or rebellious children of faithful temple-endowed and sealed parents than any other modern prophet. One reason for this may have been because, as some sources hint, certain of his own children and descendants had not followed his example and teachings of faithful discipleship as much as he hoped.[1]

Elder Orson F. Whitney, in an oft-quoted general conference address, stated the following:

> The Prophet Joseph Smith declared—and he never taught a more comforting doctrine—that the eternal sealings of faithful parents and the divine promises made to them for valiant service in the Cause of Truth, would save not only themselves, but likewise their posterity. Though some of the sheep may wander, the eye of the Shepherd is upon them, and sooner or later they will feel the tentacles of Divine Providence reaching out after them and drawing them back to the fold. Either in this life or the life to come, they will return. They will have to pay their debt to justice; they will suffer for their sins; and may tread a thorny path; but if it leads them at last, like the penitent Prodigal, to a loving and forgiving father's heart and home, the painful experience will not have been in vain. Pray for your careless and disobedient children; hold on to them with your faith. Hope on, trust on, till you see the salvation of God.[2]

The exact quotation from Joseph Smith that Elder Whitney references has not been located by the Church's historians, although some with similar wording and meaning have been found.[3] With this uncertainty involved, it is possible that Whitney had in mind doctrine that Joseph Smith had personally taught to Lorenzo Snow, or that had been otherwise conveyed from the Prophet to him—and that Lorenzo had then taught the same doctrine to Orson. Though speculative, this linkage would explain why President Snow and Elder Whitney were such advocates of the concepts taught below. These summaries and quotations from President Snow were found in a variety of sources, are given in chronological order, and provide an overview of his views. They do not, however, provide a complete perspective of authoritative doctrinal teachings available on this subject.[4]

From a meeting of the First Presidency and the Twelve:

A faithful man, though he may have wayward wives or children, will doubtless have the power hereafter given him to bring them up to a plane of happiness and to exaltation, even though he may have no influence with them here. God has a right to suspend His law, as He has done in the inspiration under which Pres. Woodruff wrote the manifesto, and as the Savior did when He suspended the law of Moses and permitted the disciples to pluck corn on the Sabbath day when they were hungry. The very important law concerning baptism is at times suspended as in the case of married women whose husbands are opposed to the gospel, or minors whose parents object to the baptism of their children. I can see great good and no inconsistency in this matter.[5]

From a general conference talk:

The work that has been accomplished in the nations of the earth and the islands of the sea is grand and glorious. And this is not all; within the last few months thousands of persons in the spirit world have been placed in a condition that they may receive the word of God and be saved, through the ordinances that have been administered in these four temples in this Territory. A wonderful work is being accomplished in our temples in favor of the spirits in prison. I believe, strongly too, that when the Gospel is preached to the spirits in prison, the success attending that preaching will be far greater than that attending the preaching of our Elders in this life. I believe there will be very few indeed of those spirits who will not gladly receive the Gospel when it is carried to them. The circumstances there will be a thousand times more favorable. The brethren are laboring in these temples with their hearts and souls in the interest of the dead. The Savior said on a certain occasion, "Verily, verily, I say unto you, the hour is coming, and now is, when the dead shall hear the voice of the Son of God;" and He continued and made this remarkable expression: "and they that hear shall live." I believe there will be very few who will not receive the truth. They will hear the voice of the Son of God; they will hear the voice of the Priesthood of the Son of God, and they will receive the truth and live. These brethren and sisters that are laboring so industriously in the temples will have the honor of being, as it were, saviors to their kindred and friends in whose favor they administered these ordinances. . . .

When the gospel was preached, those who believed were promised that they might know for themselves whether it was true, and whether the men who preached it had authority from God. They were promised that they should receive the Holy Ghost, which should be a revelation to them, and upon that they should be founded; and they should build their spiritual house upon it, and when the storms came, and the rains descended, and the floods came, and the winds blew, they should not be driven from this position. If we are in this condition, the trials and afflictions that we have to pass through will not have power to move us, because we are founded upon the revelations of the Almighty. God has fulfilled His promises to us, and our prospects are grand and glorious. Yes, in the next life we will have our wives, and our sons and daughters. If we do not get them all at once, we will have them some time, for every knee shall bow and every tongue shall confess that Jesus is the Christ. You that are mourning about your children straying away will have your sons and your daughters. If you succeed in passing through these trials and afflictions and receive a resurrection, you will, by the power of the Priesthood, work and labor, as the Son of God has, until you get all your sons and daughters in the path of exaltation and glory. This is just as sure as that the sun rose this morning over yonder mountains. Therefore, mourn not because all your sons and daughters do not follow in the path that you have marked out to them, or give heed to your counsels. Inasmuch as we succeed in securing eternal glory, and stand as saviors, and as kings and priests to our God, we will save our posterity. When Jesus went through that terrible torture on the cross, He saw what would be accomplished by it; He saw that His brethren and sisters—the sons and daughters of God—would be gathered in, with but few exceptions—those who committed the unpardonable sin. That sacrifice of the divine Being was effectual to destroy the powers of Satan. I believe that every man and woman who comes into this life and passes through it, that life will be a success in the end. It may not be in this life. It was not with the antediluvians. They passed through troubles and afflictions; 2,500 years after that, when Jesus went to preach to them, the dead heard the voice of the Son of God and they lived. They found after all that it was a very good thing that they had conformed to the will of God in leaving the spiritual life and passing through this world. God will have His own way in His own time, and He will accomplish His purposes in the salvation of His sons and daughters.[6]

From a meeting of the First Presidency and Twelve:

Pres. Snow said, and Pres. Woodruff coincided with the view, that very, very few of those who die without the Gospel will reject it on the other side of the veil.[7]

From a meeting of the First Presidency and Twelve:

Pres. Snow said that he gleaned from the remarks of the Presidency at the office a few days ago that where a man is faithful to all his covenants, he will not lose his wife in the world to come even though she obtain from him a divorce in this life. Where men are untrue to their families and their God they will be left without wife or child in the future existence . . . .[8]

From a Salt Lake Stake Conference meeting:

When two Latter-day Saints are united together in marriage, promises are made to them concerning their offspring that reach from eternity to eternity. They are promised that they shall have the power and the right to govern and control and administer salvation and exaltation and glory to their offspring worlds without end. And what offspring they do not have here, undoubtedly there will be opportunities to have them hereafter. What else could man wish? A man and a woman in the other life, having celestial bodies, free from sickness and disease, glorified and beautified beyond description, standing in the midst of their posterity, governing and controlling them, administering life, exaltation and glory, worlds without end![9]

From a special priesthood meeting held in connection with general conference, in the Assembly Hall:

President Lorenzo Snow spoke on the subject of Temple work. He showed the importance, and benefits to the living, as well as to the dead. The spirit prevailing in the Temple was carried by the workers into their several wards. The expense of the Temple was just as great when few attended as when it was crowded. President Snow promised heads of families that if they would worthily attend to their duty for the dead, they should be successful in drawing their posterity to them.[10]

Appendix 4

Lorenzo Snow's Patriarchal Blessings

Blessing given by the Patriarch Joseph Smith (Sr.), December 15, 1836

Brother, in the name of the Lord Jesus Christ and by the authority of the Holy Priesthood which God has conferred on me and by the Holy Anointing I lay my hands on thy head and give thee a father's blessing. I ask God the Eternal Father who has called me to the office of the priesthood to open the visions of my mind and give me the Holy Spirit. I ask him to have mercy on thee who art but a youth—thou hast been diligent and ardent in the application to thy learning. God has looked upon thee from all eternity—has been propitious, has been born I feel in his gifts—given thee. Intelligence, talent and great faculties of mind that though mightiest be useful in his cause. Thou hast a great work to do in thy day and generation. God has called thee to the ministry, thou must preach the gospel of the Savior to the inhabitants of the earth. Thou shalt become a mighty man in the earth—thou shalt have great faith—even like that of the brother of Jared. Thou shalt have power to translate thyself from one planet to another. Power to go to the moon if thou shalt desire it. Power to preach to the spirits in prison; power like Enoch to translate thyself to heaven. Thou shalt have power to rend the veil of heaven, and see Jesus standing at the right hand of His father. There shall not be a mightier man on earth than thou. Thy faith shall increase and grow stronger and stronger. It shall be like that of Peter. Thy shadow shall rest over the sick. The diseased shall send to thee their handkerchiefs and aprons and by thy touch their owners shall be healed. Thou shalt have power over unclean spirits, at thy command the powers of darkness shall stand back, and devils shall flee away. If it be expedient the dead shall arise and come forth at thy bidding; even those that have long slept in the dust shall come forth to life. Thou shalt have long life. Thou shalt live to the age of Moses, yet not be old for old age shall not come upon thee; the vigor of thy mind shall not be abated and thy vigor and strength of thy body shall be preserved. Thou shalt have power to stand in the flesh and see Jesus come in the clouds. No power shall take thy life so long as it shall be useful to thy fellow men. Thou shalt preach the gospel as long as there shall be an ear to hear or an heart to believe. Thou must open thy mouth and the Lord will fill it with arguments; thy voice shall cause the earth to tremble. Thou must pray for thy kindred and be diligent and thou shalt see all thy kindred shall be brought into the kingdom and have a Celestial Glory. Though art of the house and lineage of Abraham. Thy descent is through the loins of Joseph and Ephraim and art entitled to the Priesthood. God will give thee of a companion of thy heart's desire. Thou shalt have posterity; thy sons shall be large in stature like unto the Jaredites. Their strength shall be like the strength of Samson. Thou shalt sit in council with the one hundred and forty-four thousand and shall stand with the Lamb on Mount Zion and shall be able to sing thy song. This is thy Blessing. In the name of Jesus Christ I seal them on thy head and by the authority of the Holy Priesthood I seal thee up to eternal life. Even so Amen and Amen.[1]

Copy of a blessing conferred on Lorenzo Snow
by Isaac Morley, Patriarch, December 19, 1843

Brother Lorenzo I lay my hands on thy head in the name of Jesus thy Redeemer. I seal and ratify the blessing that has been conferred upon thee by the authority of the Everlasting Priesthood. I seal upon thee the blessings of Abraham and equal blessings with Isaac and Jacob. Thy name is registered in heaven. Thy offering and thy sacrifice is accepted before the Lord, and for all thy labors and sacrifices, thy toils, thy travels (travails?), and fatigues shall blessings from on high be poured out upon thee. Thy Creator has given thee a mind capable of reception and of expanding within eternity. And it shall be thy gift and blessing to receive the Comforter even the Spirit of Truth which shall lead and guide thee into all Truth. Thou hast the gift and blessing of discernment of spirits to detect error and embrace truth. (Ask?) and thou shalt receive the gift and blessing of a white stone in that stone a new name written that no man knoweth save him to whom it is given. And through and by that blessing thou shalt attain to the faith once delivered to the Saints. Prisons shall only cause thee to smile to see the follies of men. Power from on high shall be given thee and clear thy way before thee. Remember thy calling that thou art called to prune the Vineyard of the Lord in this last Dispensation. The heavens above are stored with blessings for thee. The Earth will (?) its treasures to thee and to thy Posterity after thee. And thou shalt have the blessing to win thousands unto Christ. Thy love and thy labor in the Gospel of Jesus that is past will be realized and blessing will follow it to the latest ages of Posterity. Thousands will honor thee and claim thee their Father in the Gospel. Thou hast a spirit and principle in thy bosom that cannot be subdued or conquered by wicked men. And thou shalt have the blessing to stand in the ranks when one shall chase a thousand and two shall put their ten thousand to flight. The principal of love shall cast all fear from thy mind and thine enemy shall ever flee from before thee and thou shall yet wear the laurels and crowns of victory upon thy brow. Thou shalt ever be admired by all who are lovely and enjoy the society of Kings and Nobles. Brother Joseph shall be thy Prophet and Friend. The fidelity of thy heart shall cause many to rejoice because thou will never deviate by influence of flattery and deceit. Ask and thou shalt receive length of days until thou shalt be satisfied with life and see the kingdoms of this world of our Lord and our God and no good thing shall be withheld from thee. Ask and thou shalt receive the Anointing and the ordinance in the House of the Lord. Thy Posterity shall be as numerous as was promised to Abraham because thou hast the blood of Joseph who was sold into Egypt. The blessing to be in the same Everlasting Covenant I know ask God the Eternal Father to let his holy spirit rest down upon thee that it may perform its proper office in bringing to thy mind and thy memory all things that are necessary for thy present and thy everlasting welfare, and in the name of Jesus I seal the blessings of Eternal Life upon thy head. Amen and Amen.

Appendix 5

Autobiographical Synopsis by Lorenzo Snow

I was born April 3, 1814. My father's name was Oliver Snow, who was the son of Oliver.

My Mother's maiden name was Rosetta Pettibone, whose Father married Rosetta Barber.

My Father with his family moved from Becket Berkshire County, Massachusetts, when about 30 years of age and settled in Mantua, Portage County, Ohio, which was the place of my birth.

My parents had seven children, namely, Abigail Leonora, Eliza R., Persia Amanda, Melissa, Lorenzo, Lucian A., and Samuel.

My parents were Baptists, but they left their children to adopt such religious views as they saw proper, and were very strict in teaching and impressing the observance of moral principles. I had an opportunity of becoming acquainted with several religious persuasions, but through a disgust to their inconsistencies and opposing principles I never attached myself to any religious society. Through the good instructions of my parents, and the blessings of the Lord, I was prompted to keep a guard continually upon my conduct, having the fear of God before me so that I was kept in the path of virtue and established in the principles of morality.

When the Book of Mormon was first read at my father's house, I was favorably impressed and afterwards on hearing Joseph Smith bear his testimony to its truth, by the power of the Holy Ghost, a light arose in my understanding which has never been extinguished. I had an ardent desire to obtain an education; being the oldest son and my father having a large family to provide for, and having to draw his profits from his farm, as he managed it himself, my labors were therefore needed, and I had no opportunity of acquiring much knowledge, only some of the common branches of education taught in district schools. Therefore I decided to devote my time to study as soon as I could command my own time. This favorite object I so long had cherished gave a tendency to check the growth for a while of the good seed sown in my heart and operated to prevent my obedience to the gospel when I first heard its announcement. I continued to work for my father until I arrived at the age of 21 years, soon after I made arrangements to enter upon my favorite pursuit. I proceeded to Oberlin College, a Presbyterian institution and commenced my course of studies. I very soon became disgusted with their system of intolerance, religious tyranny and bigotry, and as I felt to proclaim and report the principles of Joseph Smith as far as I knew them, which all were bitterly opposed to, therefore my removal from the college was warmly recommended by the authorities. I did not wait for an action on their part, but after a stay of about six months, I returned home with the intention of going to some eastern college where religion would not be made the exclusive object of education.

On reaching home I learned from my sisters that Hebrew was being taught in a school at Kirtland and I concluded I would improve the opportunity of acquiring a knowledge of that language, and also put myself in the way of becoming more acquainted with the Latter-day Saints. My sister Eliza R. Snow resided in Kirtland, and I had all along kept up an interesting correspondence with her by which many acts were presented to my notice, that had transpired among the saints which greatly awakened my curiosity. On repairing to Kirtland I took up my abode with my elder sister Leonora who was keeping house with her two daughters Cornelia and Lucia. My sister Eliza was teaching a family school at Joseph Smith's which afforded me an opportunity of forming an intimate and familiar acquaintance with him and his family.

In June 1836 I was baptized by John Boyington [Boynton] and confirmed by Hyrum Smith. I received a knowledge of the divine authenticity of the gospel in the most happy and glorious manner. The Heavens were opened and the Holy Spirit descended upon me and I tasted the joys of eternity in the midst of the power of God. Those manifestations have never been effaced from my memory. A high school was established at Kirtland, and by President Rigdon's request I continued my studies. But a change had come over my feelings which took away my desires and interest in my favorite pursuit and I desired ardently to preach salvation to the children of men. But my extreme diffidence seemed a mountain of difficulty. But my path of duty being clearly pointed out by the Spirit which was upon me, I determined to persevere in overcoming this weakness by the power which I believed might be enjoyed in the Priesthood. The following winter I was ordained an elder under the hand of father Oliver Beman, president of the elder's quorum and received my washing and anointing.

In the spring of 1837 I took my valise and went forth preaching from house to house and holding meetings every opportunity. I labored faithfully and perseveringly as the Lord gave me ability and was much blessed in my administration. I held large public meetings in my native town and in the adjacent townships obtaining the privilege of school houses and in several instances Baptist and Methodist meeting houses and bore a faithful testimony to my neighbors and acquaintances. I baptized a number of my relations, school fellows and acquaintances: in many instances I was insulted, mobbed and threatened with tar and feathers. I felt a growing determination to lift my warning voice and proclaim the gospel more effectually at all times and in all places according to the increasing grace of the Lord upon me. I preached in several of the northern and middle counties of Ohio in the latter part of summer and fall and baptized a number in those sections of the state.

In the spring when the saints removed from Kirtland, I assisted my father in moving his family to Missouri. We settled in Daviess County, in the neighborhood of Adam-ondi-Ahman, where my father purchased several land claims with considerable improvements, from which he was subsequently driven by the persons from whom he purchased. I had a severe sickness of fever and ague, and before I had fully recovered I started upon a mission through the south of Missouri for the purpose of preaching the gospel and aid in allaying a mob excitement which was then spreading like wildfire through every part of the state and mobs were gathering various directions to plunder and destroy our people. I found a bitter and murderous feeling in the minds of the people in many places and after laboring faithfully some weeks, the excitement was so great that I deemed it wisdom to change the direction of my travels and I proceeded into the southwest part of Illinois where I preached and baptized a number. I then went to Washington County, Kentucky, where I preached till the latter part of winter; then went to Ohio, settled up my business, and went to Nauvoo where I enjoyed the happiness of meeting my friends after their expulsion from Missouri.

This season (fall of 1840) I was appointed on a mission to England and previous to my leaving I was ordained a high priest under the hands of Don Carlos Smith, being then a member of the seventies through an ordination that I had received in Kirtland under the hands of Elder Henry Harriman. The latter part of this summer I left Nauvoo and arrived in Liverpool the forepart of November.

At Manchester I had a pleasing interview with presidents Brigham Young, Heber C. Kimball, and others of my acquaintances. I was appointed to labor in connection with Elder Alfred Cordon in Birmingham and West Bromwich, and early in the following spring I was appointed by President Young to labor in London and its vicinity. Here I met with, and for a few days enjoyed the society of elders Heber C. Kimball, and Wilford Woodruff, by whom I was introduced to the saints in London, numbering about 40, and through Elder Kimball was introduced to the acquaintance of many persons in various parts of the metropolis, who were favorable to our principles and whose acquaintance he had procured through much toil and perseverance and proved of great service to me in carrying forward the gospel in that city.

I labored principally in London, Woolwich and Bedford while I remained in England, and before I left this field of my mission, there were added to the church under my administration about five hundred members.

The forepart of January 1843, I left Liverpool having under my charge a large company of saints. We had a pleasant passage, and after some little detention at New Orleans and St. Louis, I arrived with my company at Nauvoo about the middle of April, and on landing had the pleasure of being cordially welcomed by President Joseph Smith and many friends who stood on the bank to welcome my return.

This season I performed a mission to Ohio and returned late in the fall and in the spring following was appointed to go to Ohio to present before the people the claim of President Joseph Smith for the presidency of the United States. While thus engaged I received the heartrending news of his massacre and then returned to Nauvoo.

The next fall I went to Ohio on church business and returned about the beginning of winter, was married shortly after and receive my anointing and sealings in the temple some few weeks following.

The 9th of February 1846 I left Nauvoo with my family in company with President Young to seek an asylum of peace beyond the Rocky Mountains. I arrived in Mount Pisgah, a small settlement sometime in June, where I was taken severely sick and did not fully recover till late in the fall. Next spring I was appointed to take the presidency of the settlement, in which office I continued till the next year when I left with a portion of the settlement and joined President Young and company some 30 miles west of Council Bluffs en route for Great Salt Lake. Our companies were organized at the Horn, I was appointed to take charge of the advance company of one hundred wagons which left the Horn June 1st, I arrived in the valley the later part of September and was ordained into the Quorum of Twelve on February 12, 1849.

Note: Elder Matthew W. Mansfield, of Teasdale, Utah, writing to President Snow under date of 27th, after stating that he had been ordained a high priest under his hands on the 24th of June, 1887, asks how the priesthood came to him, and desired this information traced back to the Prophet Joseph Smith. The matter was referred to the historian for the information, and Brother Andrew Jenson, after searching the record made answer as follows:

President Lorenzo Snow ordained an Apostle February 12th, 1849, by Heber C. Kimball, who was ordained an Apostle, February 14th, 1835, under the hands of Oliver Cowdery, David Whitmer and Martin Harris, Who were "blessed" to select and ordain the "Twelve" by Joseph Smith the Prophet, who was ordained to the Apostleship by Peter, James and John, who were called and commissioned by Jesus Christ. (Matthew 10th chap.)

On the above being read to President Snow this 8th day of March, 1901, the president remarked that Heber C. Kimball no doubt was mouth [voice] on the occasion, in fact, there was no doubt whatever existing regarding it, but at the same time he himself had no private record of it, neither was he able to remember who was mouth in his ordination, but he distinctly remembers that he was ordained under the hands of Brigham Young, Heber C. Kimball, Willard Richards and some other of the Apostles, among them he thought was John Taylor. (George F. Gibbs; placed here by Anthon Lund)

Note: Excerpt from the "Manuscript History of Brigham Young, 1847–1850." (Available in *Manuscript History of Brigham Young*, ed., William S. Harwell [Salt Lake City: Collier's Publishing Co., 1997], 148–52.)

Appendix 6

President Snow's St. George Tithing Discourse

given May 18, 1899, in the St. George Tabernacle

The following discourse was delivered by President Lorenzo Snow at St. George, Utah, on Thursday, May 18, 1899.

Brethren, sisters and friends, I wish to read to you this afternoon what occurred in the Temple of the Lord at Kirtland about sixty-three years ago. I was intimately acquainted with the parties concerned. It is a vision manifested to Joseph, the Seer, and Oliver Cowdery, in the Kirtland Temple, April 3, 1836:

"The veil was taken from our minds, and the eyes of our understanding were opened.

"We saw the Lord standing upon the breast work of the pulpit, before us, and under His feet was a paved work of pure gold in color like amber.

"His eyes were as a flame of fire, the hair of His head was white like the pure snow, His countenance shone above the brightness of the sun, and His voice was as the sound of the rushing of great waters, even the voice of Jehovah, saying—

"I am the first and the last, I am He who liveth, I am He who was slain, I am your advocate with the Father.

"Behold your sins are forgiven you, you are clean before me, therefore lift up your heads and rejoice.

"Let the hearts of your brethren rejoice, and let the hearts of all My people rejoice, who have, with their might, built this house to My name.

"For behold I have accepted this house, for My name shall be here, and I will manifest Myself to My people in mercy in this house,

"Yea, I will appear unto My servants, and speak unto them with My own voice, if My people will keep My commandments, and do not pollute this holy house,

"Yea the hearts of thousands and tens of thousands shall greatly rejoice in consequence of the blessings which shall be poured out, and the endowment with which My servants have been endowed in this house;

"And the fame of this house shall spread to foreign lands, and this is the beginning of the blessing which shall be poured out upon the heads of My people. Even so. Amen."

I might well say that I am fully satisfied and delighted with the visit that I have had with the Saints in this Stake of Zion, having enjoyed the privilege of shaking hands with your beautiful boys and girls and of kissing your babies. One might suppose that I could go home perfectly satisfied, and I might think so myself; but there are some things that I feel under the most sacred obligation to say to you.

It is a wonderful pleasure to speak upon the great things that God proposes to bestow upon His sons and daughters, and that we shall attain to if we are faithful. The ultimatum of our travel in this path of exaltation will bring to us the fulness of our Lord Jesus Christ, to stand in the presence of our Father, to receive of His fullness, to have the pleasure of increasing in our posterity worlds without end, to enjoy those pleasant associations that we have had in this life, to have our sons and our daughters, our husbands and our wives, surrounded with all the enjoyment that heaven can bestow, our bodies glorified like unto the Savior's, free from disease and all the ills of life, and free from the disappointments and vexations and the unpleasant sacrifices that we are making here. We portray in our minds the glories that are before us, and we know that if we are faithful there will be no disappointment in the securing of these blessings. The power to prevent us from receiving these things is not in the hands of any man; it lies within ourselves. What I have read to you shows that Jesus, the Son of the living God, has been among the children of men. He has talked with them, and they have seen His glory. I am ten times more sure of this than I am in reference to what we read about that which transpired in the land of Judea when the Son of God was there. I knew Joseph Smith and Oliver Cowdery. I know that they were men of honor, honest, full of philanthropy, and served the Lord. Joseph Smith and his brother Hyrum served the Lord faithfully through all their lives, and died as martyrs to the principles we now believe in. We have established our faith upon a sure foundation, and there is no power beneath the celestial worlds that can take it from us. Everyone has the right to secure, and I hope has secured, this principle of revelation upon which we are founded, each for himself or herself. We have made a discovery in regard to the path that leads to this honor and glory, and we feel as the Savior expressed it on one occasion when He was with the people in Judea. He said:

"The kingdom of heaven is like unto treasure hid in a field, the which when a man hath found, he hideth, and for the joy thereof goeth and selleth all that he hath, and buyeth that field.

"Again the kingdom of heaven is like unto a merchant man, seeking goodly pearls:

"Who, when he had found one pearl of great price, went and sold all that he had, and bought it."

So with ourselves; we have found the treasure in the field, we have found the pearl of great price, and now we have got to give all that we have for it, at one time or another. The Lord has said that He will prove us even unto death, to see whether we will stand by the covenants we have made with Him. Some Latter-day Saints have things in their possession which are so valuable to them that they would prefer death to the loss of those things. We have to deal with facts, not a mere ideal. In one sense, it is a hard thing for us to sell all that we have that we may secure these glories that have been opened to our view; but it will pay us in the end. Jesus, the Son of God, was sent into the world to make it possible for you and me to receive these extraordinary blessings. He had to make a great sacrifice. It required all the power that He had and all the faith the He could summon for Him to accomplish that which the Father required of Him. Had He fallen in the moment of temptation, what do you suppose would have become us? Doubtless at some future period the plan would have been carried out by another person. But He did not fail, though the trial was so severe that He sweat great drops of blood. When He knelt there in the garden of Gethsemane, what agony He must have experienced in contemplating His sufferings on the cross! His feelings must have been inexpressible. He tells us Himself, as you will find recorded in section 19 of the Book of Doctrine and Covenants, that His suffering was so great that it caused even Him "to tremble because of pain, and to bleed at every pore, and to suffer both body and spirit: and would that He might not drink the bitter cup, and shrink." But He had in His heart continually to say, "Father, not my will, but Thine be done." It was a dark hour for Him:

and every man and woman who serves the Lord, no matter how faithful they may be, have their dark hours; but if they have lived faithfully, light will burst upon them and relief will be furnished.

For a portion of our lives we do about as we please and move along in a way that is rather gratifying to ourselves, no particular call being made up on us; but there are times when the Almighty requires certain things at our hands, and we cannot dodge them. At such times we receive the advantages of a past pure life, having kept the commandments of God and prepared ourselves for such calls. To illustrate: We call, say twenty young men from here, ten from another place, thirty from another, to go upon missions abroad; and in more instances than one these calls are made without giving time to make proper preparation; but, it is gratifying to say, there is scarcely a single instance, out of the thousands that are called, where an unfavorable response is made. The party says, "Yes, I will respond to the call. There are difficulties in the way, but I will try to remove them, and will be on hand at the time specified." It is glorious to think that among the thousands of calls that are made upon our young men to go upon missions, I do not remember of a single instance where the call has not been responded to favorably. Here is an instance right before us. When the people were called by President Young to establish themselves in this locality, it was a very great trial to them; but those who accepted the call, you see how they have been blessed and how God has honored them. He has honored them in giving them sons, grandsons, and daughters, and various ways the blessings of God have come upon them. What is greater than all, they have so conducted themselves that these wonderful prospects have been kept bright before them. When they view the course that they have taken in the past and the glorious prospects of the future, they derive great consolation there-from.

The Latter-day Saints have done wonders; but they cannot cease from doing wonders in the future. There will be greater things demanded of the Latter-day Saints than has ever been demanded since the organization of the Church. The Lord has determined in His heart that He will try us until He knows what He can do with us. He tried His Son Jesus. Thousands of years before He came upon earth the Father had watched His course and knew that He could depend upon Him when the salvation of worlds should be at stake; and He was not disappointed. So in regard to ourselves. He will try us, and continue to try us, in order that He may place us in the highest positions in life and put upon us the most sacred responsibilities. When we were placed in certain circumstances with our wives and children, and the nation was pursuing us with the intention of destroying us, the Lord opened our way in a manner that we never expected. Very few indeed thought our deliverance would come in the way which the Lord saw proper to bring it. A sacrifice had to be made—a greater one than had ever been made before. The Church itself depended upon the Saints acting in a wise and prudent manner, and making the sacrifice that was required at that time. The word of the Lord came to President Woodruff. When that Manifesto was issued, you knew what it meant. Some were alarmed. They thought the Church would go to pieces; thought they were breaking their covenants; thought the Lord had withdrawn from them. But that Manifesto was issued by the command of the Lord; and the Saints humbled themselves before the Lord and bowed to the requirement. The heavens rejoiced and God smiled upon us. He blessed His people, and delivered us from our enemies, and they were brought to shame and disgrace. They thought to destroy the Latter-day Saints, but they failed in their attempt. Nevertheless, we had to make the sacrifice, and it was right that we should. The Lord could have delivered us in some other way, had He so wished; but He knew best, and that was the course He required us to pursue and the sacrifice He desired us to make. We made it, and He has blessed us wonderfully from that time to the present. He has given us power among the nations, and in various ways the people have been raised in the estimation of the world. Men of great wisdom have looked upon us, though they may have been silent, and they have honored the course we have taken. The Lord required that of us.

I come here now with my brethren that you may understand what is required of you as a people under the peculiar conditions in which the Church is now placed. It is the word of the Lord to you, my brethren and sisters, that you should conform to that which is required of you as a people who have these glorious prospects of exaltation and glory before you. What is it? Why, it is something that has been drummed into your ears from time to time until you perhaps have got tired of hearing it. I need the faith and the prayers of every Latter-day Saint; no man needs them any more than I do; and it is unpleasant for me to say things that would in any way diminish the exercise of your faith and prayers in my behalf. But the Lord requires me to say something to you, and since I commenced to labor in His interest, I have never failed, thank the Lord, to do that which He has required at my hands; and I shall not do it today, nor any other day, the Lord being my helper. The word of the Lord to you is not anything new; it is simply this: THE TIME HAS NOW COME FOR EVERY

LATTER-DAY SAINT, WHO CALCULATES TO BE PREPARED FOR THE FUTURE AND TO HOLD HIS FEET STRONG UPON A PROPER FOUNDATION, TO DO THE WILL OF THE LORD AND TO PAY HIS TITHING IN FULL. That is the word of the Lord to you, and it will be the word of the Lord to every settlement throughout the land of Zion. After I leave you and you get to thinking about this, you will see yourselves that the time has come when every man should stand up and pay his tithing in full. The Lord has blessed us and has had mercy upon us in the past; but there are times coming when the Lord requires us to stand up and do that which He has commanded and not leave it any longer. What I say to you in this Stake of Zion I will say to every Stake of Zion that has been organized. There is no man or woman that now hears what I am saying who will feel satisfied if he or she fails to pay a full tithing.

I could reason with you upon this, but what need is there of showing why we should do these things. We receive from the different Stakes of Zion requests for help, some to build meeting houses and some for other purposes. Well, we feel that we ought to help them, because they are deserving of help; but we cannot do it. I do not think I will say much about the financial condition of the Church. The Church, of course, is very much in debt. And I do not know that anybody is to blame for it being in debt. It has been partially explained today by the brethren, and I will leave it in that way. But we are going into debt no longer. All the enterprises that we have gone into, have been for the benefit of the people. Well, I do not care to talk about this. It is sufficient to say to the Latter-day Saints that we must now pay our tithing. I have scarcely ever talked about tithing. I have said it was the duty of the Latter-day Saints to pay tithing, but I have never made it a business like some of my brethren have. You will not hear much from me now in regard to tithing. I simply tell you the truth straight out; and I have faith in the Latter-day Saints to believe and know that they will respond to this.

Brethren and sisters, I feel and know that you are a good people. I do not flatter you when I say this. I simply tell the facts. The Lord has helped you, as He has helped other portions of the people in Zion. He has done this, not because they have done right under all circumstances, not because they have paid their tithing properly, but because they have paid it partially and have done some good. But when the voice of the Lord comes to us and His will is expressed, then is the time for us to act.

Now, I have shaken hands with over 800 children, and I want to see those children grow up and become 80, 90, 100 or 140 years of age; and this will surely be the case if you will teach them these things that I am talking to you about today. Teach them to pay their tithing while they are young. You mothers, teach your children that when they get any money they should pay one-tenth of it to the Lord, however little it may be. Educate them to pay their tithing in full. Then we will have a people prepared to go to Jackson County. President Smith was talking yesterday about the land of Zion. Yes, surely, this entire continent is the land of Zion, and the time will come when there will be Temples established over every portion of the land, and we will go into these Temples and work for our kindred dead night and day, that the work of the Lord may be speedily accomplished, that Jesus may come and present the kingdom to His Father. He is coming soon, too. But we will not hear His voice until we build up Jackson County. Now we should make the preparation for this. We are not only going to have Zion throughout this continent, but we will have it over the whole earth. The whole earth is the Lord's. The time will come when it will be translated and be filled with the spirit of the Almighty. We will breathe that Spirit instead of the atmosphere that we now breathe. But now it is for us to make the preparation, that we may be worthy to be called into the house of the Lord and receive our second blessings. I do not want the presidents of Stakes to send any person to our Temples to receive the highest blessings that have ever been bestowed upon man since the world began, until it can be said of him, "He pays his full tithing." When you find an honest, faithful Latter-day Saint who is worthy of receiving His blessings, send him along. I do not care how fast they come. The time is now at hand when the Latter-day Saints can be greatly and abundantly blessed, so that they can make the preparation in its fullness.

Now, if I say anything more, I am afraid you may forget what I have said—I will take that back; I said it without thought. You will not forget, you cannot forget what I have said to you here. I do not know how soon we may be called to build up Jackson County; but I feel it is nearer at hand than Latter-day Saints generally believe. When you look upon Jackson County and its surroundings at the present time, it looks like an impossibility. There are perhaps thirty thousand people settled there, adjacent to the Temple location, and they are doing business very extensively. Looking at it naturally, it would seem as if a favorable arrangement for us to go back there could never arise. But when the Lord sets about to accomplish His purposes, He finds it easy to make it effectual. It will be so in this. I can imagine several ways in which the road would be perfectly clear, and the people be very glad for the Latter-day Saints to go back to Jackson County. As I said yesterday, establish the principles of Zion in your hearts, and then you will be worthy to receive Zion outside, with beautiful houses and castles, and lovely surroundings, and by and by go into a city the streets of which will be made of pure gold, where everything will be just as good and grand as the experience of millions of years has given to those who have to do with such buildings. Just read the last chapter in the Bible and see what a glorious city Latter-day Saints will have the privilege of living in, if they are faithful. And we will be able to build cities of our own after a time. It may be thought that I am going away into the future; but I do not say any more to you than I can find in the revelations of the Lord in the Doctrine and Covenants and in the Bible. It is all there; but only those can understand it who have the Spirit of the Lord.

I want to say a word or two on another subject. I understand that there are in St. George about eighty widows and about one hundred marriageable sisters, and there seems to be considerable lamentation in regard to this condition. There is no need of this particularly. A lady came into our office the other day and asked to see me on a private matter. She informed me that she felt very badly, because her opportunities for getting a husband had not been favorable. She was about thirty years of age, and she wanted to know what her condition would be in the other life, if she did not succeed in getting a husband in this life. I suppose this question arises in the hearts of our young people, especially the marriageable sisters and the young widows; and some very foolish doctrine has been presented to some of the sisters in regard to this and other things of a kindred nature. I desire to give a little explanation for the comfort and consolation of parties in this condition. There is no Latter-day Saint who dies after having lived a faithful life who will lose anything because of having failed to do certain things when opportunities were not furnished him or her. In other words, if a young man or a young woman has no opportunity of getting married, and they live faithful lives up to the time of their death, they will have all the blessings, exaltation and glory that any man or woman will have who had this opportunity and improved it. That is sure and positive. Faithful Elders in the Church have died without having married. You that have been in the temple of the Lord understand the arrangements that are there made for such persons. Where we have the names of husbands and wives who lived a thousand years ago, they having been married according to the laws then in force, we consider that those parties have a right to all the blessings that they would have if they were living now, because if they were honest and honorable they did all that the Lord required of them under the circumstances. The Gospel was not then being preached; therefore they could not receive it; but they raised families, and that was the very thing that the Lord commanded in the Garden of Eden. The first commandment given was to multiply and replenish the earth. Now we make these relations sacred over our altars. People who have no opportunity of marrying in this life, if they die in the Lord, will have means furnished them by which they can secure all the blessings necessary for persons in the married condition. The Lord is merciful and kind, and He is not unjust. There is no injustice in Him; yet we could scarcely look upon it as being just when a woman or a man dies without having had the opportunity of marrying if it could not be remedied in the other life. There would be injustice in that, and we know that the Lord is not an unjust being. My sister, Eliza R. Snow, I believe, was just as good a woman as any Latter-day Saint woman that ever lived, and she lived in an unmarried state until she was beyond the condition of raising a family. She was sealed to Joseph Smith, the Prophet; but she had not children to bear her name among the children of men. I cannot for one moment imagine that she will lose a single thing on that account. It will be made up to her in the other life, and she will have just as great a kingdom as she would have had if she had had the opportunity in this life of raising a family.

As to plural marriage, I want to say a few words; for I may not have the opportunity of bearing my testimony to you again. There is no man that lives that had a more perfect knowledge of the principle of plural marriage, its holiness and divinity, than I had. It was revealed to me before the Prophet Joseph Smith explained it to me. I had been on a mission to England between two and three years, and before I left England I was perfectly satisfied in regard to something connected with plural marriage. When I returned to Nauvoo with my company of about 250, it was made manifest to me in reference to the truth of this principle. I was at Joseph Smith's one afternoon on a visit, and after conversing upon different subjects he asked me to walk out with him, as he wished to speak to me privately. We went down to the banks of the Mississippi River and sat down on a log that lay there in the sand. Then and there he explained to me the principle of plural marriage most perfectly and clearly; he told me in regard to the angel coming to him and making this principle known to him, and what would follow if he did not practice it. He informed me that my sister Eliza R. Snow had been sealed to him, and also mentioned the names of others. In that conversation, which lasted about half an hour, he told me all about it, and referred to his brother Hyrum.

I know this principle is true, pure and sacred, and I want everyone to understand my testimony that it is true as the Lord is true. Yet the Lord has seen proper that the principle of plural marriage should no longer be practiced. Therefore that Manifesto was issued. I will say now before this people, that the principle of plural marriage is not practiced. I have never, in one single instance, allowed any person to have that ceremony performed, and there are no such marriages at the present time, nor has there been during the time of my presidency over this church. There is no man or woman that can ever say that any such thing as this has been done. The Lord has commanded it, and I see that it is carried out. Such marriages are not done. There has been an impression in the minds of some that such marriages have been done in the Temple at Salt Lake City; but not a single marriage of the kind has ever been performed in that temple, nor in any other temple. I want this to be distinctly understood.

Now brethren and sisters, God bless you and pour out His Spirit upon you. This may be the last time that I may have the opportunity of speaking to you; yet there may be other opportunities. President Smith thought he would not prophesy, but he might just as well have done so, and I would have sustained him in it—that there will be a spur of the railroad right through here, that you may go right up; to Salt Lake City, and then to Brigham City if you want to, on the railroad. If you do as I have told you, the blessings of the Lord will be upon you, and He will open your way in a manner that will astonish you. Be of good cheer. Everything is going along, and prosperity will attend the exertions of the Latter-day Saints, victory will be ours, and we shall accomplish the very things for which we have come into the world, and be exalted and glorified in the presence of God, if we are faithful. Amen. (*Millennial Star*, August 24 & 31, 1899, and *DN*, June 2, 1899.)

As a matter of related interest, the below letter, written upon his return by (second counselor) President Joseph F. Smith, to two of his sons, represents something of an itinerary of the St. George tithing-revelation trip taken through southern Utah by President Snow and his party.

May 27, 1899
Joseph R. and Joseph F. Smith Jr.
My dear sons:

I have just returned today from an absence of two weeks visiting our southern settlements, going from here on the 15th last, by railroad to a station called Modena on the Utah & California Railroad where we left the road and with horse teams proceeded to travel fifty five miles over dry, dusty and rocky roads to St. George, making the fifty-five miles in one day's drive. We spent the 17 and 18th holding meetings and visiting the people in this place and had a very pleasant time. On the 19th inst. we came to Toquerville, a distance of twenty five miles from St. George, passing through Washington, Harrisburg and Leeds on the way. At all of these places the Sunday School children and people generally turned out *en masse* to welcome the president and his party. At Toquerville we held two meetings, and on the 20th inst. we journeyed over very rough roads for thirty five miles to Cedar City, stopping at Kanarra for noon where we held meetings and also meeting with the people at Cedar. At both of these places we were greeted as before. On Sunday, the 21st, we held Sunday School and two meetings at Cedar and travelled fifteen miles to Parowan where we again held meeting in the evening, and remained over night. On the 22nd inst. we traveled forty miles to Beaver, and here held Relief Society, YLMIA meetings and a general meeting in the evening and also an overflow meeting, the largest meeting house not being sufficient to accommodate the multitudes who turned out. On the 23rd we had an eight o'clock start and traveled fifty miles to Kanosh, Millard County, nooning at Cove Creek Fort, near the sulphur bed. This was the next longest drive of the trip and exceedingly dusty and rather warm. At Kanosh we held meeting and rested for the night. Next morning drove six miles to Meadows, held meeting from ten to twelve, got our dinners, drove fifteen miles to Fillmore and held two meetings; first from three to five o'clock in the evening and second from 7:30 to ten o'clock at night with a woman's meeting sandwiched between. Here also we rested for the night, we took supper with Melissa Callister and lodged at Thomas O's. Following morning we came ten miles to Holden and held meeting. While, in all the former settlements President Snow and his company had been greeted by all the school children, their teachers and the populace, a new feature was introduced at this place. Here, at Holden, the children were drawn up in two lines before the meeting house and the path between them was strewn with wild flowers forming a mat or carpet for the President to walk upon while shaking hands with the children, meantime two young ladies with violins and others with mandolins and other instruments discoursed sweet music. After meeting here we drove fifteen miles in a heavy windstorm which blew the dust so that often we could scarcely see our teams and made the journey exceedingly unpleasant, between Holden and Scipio. At this place we also had a royal reception and attended meeting in the evening, and on yesterday we drove from Scipio to Nephi, forty miles, resting at Juab for dinner. At Nephi we were met by the entire populace of the town with bands of music and beautiful banners and songs of welcome. President Snow shook hands with over five hundred children who filed into the meeting house and were there addressed by a number of the brethren briefly, after which the party were invited to partake of a sumptuous banquet which had been provided for them in the music hall, where some hundred and fifty people sat down to an excellent feast. After the feast all again gathered to the meeting house for our last meeting on the trip. All the way through the President's party enjoyed excellent health and joyful spirits and although traveling over three hundred miles by team not an accident occurred throughout nor did we miss an appointment or fail to fill each one punctually according to the program. The people were greatly delighted with our visit and the principal there dwelt upon in all the settlements was obedience to the law of tithing, the word of wisdom, and making preparations for the redemption of the center stake of Zion when that time should come. We remained over night at Nephi. I having lodged at Aunt Asenath's. This morning at 6:40 we boarded the cars for home reaching here at 9:45 in a drenching rainstorm. (Source: CHL, MS 1325, Bx 33, fd 2; available in *Selected Collections*, vol. 1.)

Appendix 7

Reminiscences of the Prophet Joseph Smith & Elder David W. Patten

Reminiscences of the Prophet Joseph Smith

by President Lorenzo Snow

The first time I saw the Prophet Joseph Smith I was about eighteen years of age. It was about the year 1832, in the fall of the year. It was rumored that the Prophet was going to hold a meeting in Hiram, Portage county, Ohio, about two miles from my father's home. Having heard many stories about him, my curiosity was considerably aroused and I thought I would take advantage of this opportunity to see and hear him. Accordingly, in company with some of the members of my father's family, I went to Hiram. When we reached there the people were already assembled in a small bowery; there were about one hundred and fifty or two hundred people present. The meeting had already commenced and Joseph Smith was standing in the door of Father Johnson's house, looking into the bowery and addressing the people. I made a critical examination as to his appearance, his dress, and his manner as I heard him speak. His remarks were confined principally to his own experiences, especially the visitation of the angel, giving a strong and powerful testimony in regard to these marvelous manifestations. At first he seemed a little diffident and spoke in rather a low voice, but as he proceeded he became very strong and powerful, and seemed to affect the whole audience with the feeling that he was honest and sincere. It certainly influenced me in this way and made impressions upon me that remain until the present day.

The Prophet's Geniality and Kindness

Not long after this meeting he baptized my mother and two of my sisters, Laura and Eliza R. Snow into the Church, generally known as the Mormon Church. Soon after this Joseph Smith and Sidney Rigdon were dragged from their beds at night by a mob; both were inhumanly whipped and tarred and feathered.

Luke and Lyman Johnson, with whom I had been intimately acquainted all through my boyhood days, received the Gospel and were ordained Apostles. After this I attended high school and college and partially forgot the effect of the meeting described, as my mind was diverted in other directions.

The next time I saw the Prophet was at his own house in Kirtland. After I was introduced to him he invited me to take dinner with him. He seemed to have changed considerably in his appearance since I saw him before. He was very ready in conversation, and had apparently lost that reserve and diffident feeling, that he seemed then to partake of. He was free and easy in his talk with me, making me feel perfectly at home in his presence. I remember this meeting and conversation as if it were but yesterday. He sat down at one end of the table and I sat next to him. I felt as free with him as if we had been special friends for years. He was very familiar. During my stay in Kirtland, in the fall and winter of 1835 and 1836, I attended the high school, meeting the Prophet Joseph very often and under many circumstances, sometimes at his home, sometimes on the street, sometimes at the close of meetings shaking hands with him and at other times while he was overseeing public business.

I will relate an instance which goes to show one of his traits of character that I learned later to be very strong—his deep feelings of kindness towards animals. There was a steep hill in Kirtland which was being leveled, and quite a number of workmen were engaged. President Smith was there and I met him with his first counselor, Sidney Rigdon. The Prophet was overseeing the work. One of the brethren came up to the Prophet, carrying a nest full of young mice. He showed them to Joseph, who after looking at them, seemingly with great interest, said to the workman: "Pretty little innocent things, take them back and put them where their mother can find them."

I attended the meetings in the Temple regularly and heard the Prophet discourse upon the grandest of subjects. At times he was filled with the Holy Ghost, speaking as with the voice of an arch-angel and filled with the power of God, his whole person shone and his face was lightened until it appeared as the whiteness of the driven snow.

His Dislike of Assumed Sanctity

One time when the Temple walls in Nauvoo were about fifteen feet high, (it was on Sunday morning,) President Smith came up to the meeting grounds accompanied by a tall, fine-looking gentleman, well proportioned and about six feet high. He was a Presbyterian minister, as I learned later. They both came into the Temple and walked up the aisle together. There was a large crowd of people present. He gave the gentleman a seat on the stand and then sat down beside him. The minister seemed very peculiar, and a pious appearance, seemed not to move a single muscle, and was intensely solemn. When anything was said that created merriment or laughter among the people, the minister remained perfectly quiet, not even showing the least change of countenance. The Prophet felt very well that morning and made a fine appearance as he walked up to the stand. He noticed there was some confusion among the people in getting their seats because of the crowd. He saw the marshal sitting on the wall with his chin resting upon his cane, who seemingly had forgotten his duties. The Prophet called out, "Mr. Marshal, please take that cane away from your mouth and come down here and help these people to get their seats, and if you don't do it I shall walk down the aisle myself and swing my hands from side to side until there is room for the people to pass through the crowd and get their seats." This, of course, caused some laughter among the people, but the minister was as solemn and still as a statue. After the opening of the meeting President Smith got up and I never heard him speak with more power than on this occasion. The people were delighted, he was filled with the Spirit of God and spoke with great force and eloquence. At times he spoke lightly, and at other times he explained the mysteries of the kingdom. The change was so noticeable that it seemed he was elevated into heaven while addressing the people who were on the earth, and then returned again to more familiar themes.

Frequently Told Amusing Anecdotes

The Prophet was always very pleasant and at times he was given to telling anecdotes. I will relate one in his own words as nearly as I can remember them:

"Now this anecdote that I am going to tell you is not for the purpose of casting reflections upon the Irish people, so if there are any Irish brethren and sisters here I don't want them to take any offense, for the Irish people, as a rule, are always willing and ready to act, and are often better prepared to meet an emergency than either the English or American people. I wish to say this much in behalf of the Irish. There are some people, some ministers of the Gospel, who feel that they ought always to be solemn and have a holy appearance and to present their religious views to everyone they meet, wherever or whenever it may be, and to try to force their belief upon others. I don't feel this way myself. If a person desires to hear what I have to say, I am pleased to bear my testimony but I never feel to force my views upon anyone. I have heard of a minister who was traveling in a buggy on a turnpike road in Vermont. He overtook an Irishman, stopped him, alighted from the buggy and approached the Irishman in this way: 'My dear friend, O my dear dying friend,' he said in a mournful voice, 'Do you know the awful state you are in?' 'Och, yis sor,' said the Irishman, 'to be sure I do sor. I'm in the Shtate of Verrmont.' Then the minister answered in his grave way: 'O, but, my dear dying friend, you do not understand me, I'm afraid you have lost your way entirely. 'Och, no indade,' rejoined the Irishman, 'bedad an' I'm sure I have not sor, how kin a mon lose his way on a turrunpoike road sor?' 'But,' answered the minister, 'you do not understand me. Have you made your peace with Jesus?' 'No sor,' said the Irishman, 'indade Oive no nade for that same, for Jasus an' I have niver had inny fallin' out, sor.'"

The Council with Indian Chiefs

I once met the Prophet at his home when he was being visited by a council of Indian chiefs who had been sent by their tribes from Georgia, having heard of the Prophet and that he was a man of God, they called upon him for counsel and advice. He was engaged in council with them when I called. The Indians knew him to be their true friend. I waited until he had finished his conversation and the Indians left the room. They were as fine looking Indian chiefs as I have ever beheld. They were perfect types of health, and attired in full Indian dress. After their departure, Brother Joseph told me who they were and for what purpose they had come. He told me with tears in his eyes that he was unable to help them. He seemed very much affected and very sorrowful during the entire time of our conversation which followed.

Another strong trait in the Prophet's character was his innocent confidence in mankind. I will relate an incident that I remember, illustrative of this: One morning as he was walking along one of the streets in Nauvoo he met a brother who seemed very much distressed about something. He looked to be in great trouble. The Prophet addressed him in a friendly way, asking him what troubled him. The man said, "Yes, I am in great trouble, I am in debt to a man who is suing me, and I haven't a cent to pay him." The Prophet asked him the amount of his debt. "Twenty-five dollars," replied the man. "Oh, is that all?" asked the Prophet, at the same time putting his hand into his pocket and giving the man twenty-five dollars, saying, "Here, pay your debt, and God bless you." The Prophet asked no questions regarding the debt as most people would have done, but when he saw the man in distress his sympathy was so perfect that he was pleased to be able to assist him without asking any further questions.

Increase of His Power and Influence

Toward the latter part of his life Joseph Smith became a master of strength and influence over his fellows. This fact was brought very vividly to my attention on my return from a mission to Europe. I noticed and even remarked to him that he had changed very much since I last saw him; that he had become stronger and more powerful. He admitted this and said that the Lord had endowed him with additional portions of His Spirit.

One day he called the brethren of the Twelve Apostles together and other prominent Elders of the Church to appoint them to their several labors and missions. Each sat and waited with much anxiety to hear the word of the Prophet concerning his future duties. They felt that they were in the presence of a superior being. While in Kirtland the Prophet did not seem to possess that strength and power, and some of his brethren were not afraid to oppose him and even to threaten him. A mob gathered to do him injury and he had to flee for his life, but in later years he had become so strong in the power of the Lord that the people felt it. It was so on this occasion. The Elders realized his superior strength. "Brother Brigham," he said, "I want you to go east and attend to the affairs of the Church in the Eastern States, and Brother Kimball may accompany you." Turning to another he said, "You turn your attention to the publication of our paper," and thus appointed each one to his special mission; all accepting his word as the mind of the Lord.

On another occasion, Joseph Smith had indulged in playing a game of ball with some of the young men in Nauvoo. When his brother Hyrum saw it he wished to correct the Prophet and even rebuked him, saying that such conduct was not becoming in a Prophet of the Lord. The Prophet answered in a mild voice, "Brother Hyrum, my mingling with the boys in a harmless sport like this does not injure me in any way, but on the other hand it makes them happy and draws their hearts nearer to mine, and who knows but there may be young men among them who may sometime lay down their lives for me."

The Magnetism of His Presence

The Prophet had the power to impress in a remarkable manner all who approached him. There was something about him which went to their hearts. This was particularly the case with brethren when receiving from him their appointments to go forth and preach the Gospel. The inspiration that flowed from him possessed their souls and his words penetrated to the innermost recess of their being. They loved him, and believed in him, and were ready to do whatever he directed for the furtherance of the work of God. He filled them with the power of his presence, and thrilled them with the testimony of his prophetic mission. There are many people in the world who possess an extraordinary spirit of magnetism and warmth that everyone feels who meets them. I have met many such men, but never yet have I met another person in whose company I felt the peculiar and powerful influence that I felt while in the presence of the Prophet Joseph Smith. It was due to the great portion of the Spirit of God that he possessed, merely the shake of his hand would cause a person to become filled with this influence, and any sensitive nature would know that he was shaking the hand of an extraordinary person.

The Prophet Joseph on Plural Marriage

I wish to relate in full a conversation that I had with the Prophet Joseph Smith concerning the principle of the celestial marriage. I feel it my duty to do this as there are now but few persons living who heard from the Prophet's own lips his views and testimony concerning this principle. By doing so, however, I do not wish to convey the idea that plural marriages are now being contracted in any place in the world by the Church of Jesus Christ of Latter-day Saints, but to the contrary, I do most solemnly testify that during my administration as President of the Church no such marriages have been contracted, neither to my knowledge have any such marriages been contracted since the Manifesto was issued by President Wilford Woodruff.

In the month of April, 1843, I returned from my European mission. A few days after my arrival at Nauvoo, when at President Joseph Smith's house, he said he wished to have some private talk with me, and requested me to walk out with him. It was toward evening, we walked a little distance and sat down on a large log that lay near the bank of the Mississippi river; he there and then explained to me the doctrine of plurality of wives.

He said that the Lord had revealed it to him and commanded him to have women sealed to him as wives; that he foresaw the trouble that would follow and sought to turn away from the commandment; that an angel from heaven appeared before him with a drawn sword, threatening him with destruction unless he went forward and obeyed the commandment.

He then told me that my sister Eliza R. Snow had been sealed to him as his wife for time and eternity.

He further said that the Lord would open the way, and I should have women sealed to me as wives. This conversation was prolonged, I think, one hour or more, in which he told me many important things.

I solemnly declare before God and holy angels, as I hope to come forth in the morning of the resurrection, that the above statement is true.

I know that Joseph Smith was a true Prophet of the living God. I testify that he saw and spoke with God and with His Son Jesus Christ. The Lord gave me this living testimony and it has been burning within my soul ever since I received it. I now give it unto the whole world. I not only testify to all mankind that Joseph Smith was sent of God and the work that was established through him is the work of God, but warn all the nations of the earth concerning the predictions made by the Prophet, and testify in the most solemn manner that I know them to be true.

Lorenzo Snow

(*Deseret Semi-Weekly News,* December 29, 1899)

Testimony on Life of David W. Patten

Salt Lake City, Utah, February 6, 1900.

To the Reader:

All the circumstances of my first and last meeting with Apostle David W. Patten are as clear to my mind as if it were an occurrence of but yesterday, and yet it took place some sixty-four years ago. He appeared to me then to be a remarkable man, and that impression has remained with me ever since.

We traveled together on horseback from my father's home, at Mantua,

Ohio, to Kirtland, a distance of perhaps twenty-five miles, he on his return from some missionary labor, I to commence a course of studies at Oberlin College.

On the way our conversation fell upon religion and philosophy, and being young and having enjoyed some scholastic advantages, I was at first disposed to treat his opinions lightly, especially so as they were not always clothed in grammatical language; but as he proceeded in his earnest and humble way to open up before my mind the plan of salvation, I seemed unable to resist the knowledge that he was a man of God and that his testimony was true. I felt pricked in my heart.

This he evidently perceived, for almost the last thing he said to me, after hearing his testimony, was that I should go to the Lord before retiring at night and ask him for myself. This I did with the result that from the day I met this great Apostle, all my aspirations have been enlarged and heightened immeasurably. This was the turning point in my life.

What impressed me most was his absolute sincerity, his earnestness and his spiritual power; and I believe I cannot do better in this connection than to commend a careful study of his life to the honest in heart everywhere.

Lorenzo Snow

(Circular letter, located in the CHL, Salt Lake City; as quoted in Clark, *Messages of the First Presidency* 3: 324–25.)

Key to Note Abbreviations

Abbr.	*Full Source*	*Location*	*Also Available*
AHCJ	Abraham H. Cannon Journal	L. Tom Perry Special Collections, Harold B. Lee Library, Brigham Young University, Provo, Utah	Dennis B. Horne, ed., *An Apostles Record: The Journals of Abraham H. Cannon* (Clearfield, UT, 2004)
RCJ	Rudger Clawson Journal	Rudger Clawson Collection, Special Collections, J. Willard Marriott Library, University of Utah, Salt Lake City, Utah	Stan Larson, ed., *A Ministry of Meetings: The Apostolic Diaries of Rudger Clawson* (Salt Lake City, 1993).
JGKJ	J. Golden Kimball Journal	Church History Library, Salt Lake City, Utah	Selected Collections, MS d 1354; bx 1, fldr 7, vol. 14; Book no. 15
AHLJ	Anthon H. Lund Journal	Church History Library, Salt Lake City, Utah.	John P. Hatch, ed., *Danish Apostle: The Diaries of Anthon H. Lund* (Salt Lake City, 2006).
MWMJ	Marriner W. Merrill Journal		Melvin C. Merrill, ed., *Utah Pioneer and Apostle Marriner Wood Merrill and His Family*, 2nd ed. (Marriner Wood Merrill Heritage Committee: 1980).
LJNJ	L. John Nuttall Journal	L. Tom Perry Special Collections, Harold B. Lee Library, Brigham Young University, Provo, Utah and Church History Library, Salt Lake City, Utah	Jedediah S. Rogers, ed., *In the President's Office: The Diaries of L. John Nuttall* (Salt Lake City, 2007).

Abbr.	*Full Source*	*Location*	*Also Available*
JHSJ	John Henry Smith Journal	Church History Library, Salt Lake City, Utah (originals), and Special Collections, J. Willard Marriott Library, University of Utah, Salt Lake City, Utah (photocopies)	Jean Bickmore White, ed., *Church, State, and Politics: The Diaries of John Henry Smith* (Salt Lake City, 1990).
JETJ	James E. Talmage Journal	L. Tom Perry Special Collections, Harold B. Lee Library, Brigham Young University, Provo, Utah	*Selected Pages from the Journals of James E. Talmage* (limited edition; no publication or editor information given)
AWIJ	Anthony W. Ivins Journal	Unpublished document, "Notes from the diary of Anthony W. Ivins" (Church History Library, Salt Lake City, Utah, (MS d 3957)	
FMLJ	Francis M. Lyman Journal	Church History Library, Salt Lake City, Utah	All quotations herein found in Albert R. Lyman, Biography: Francis Marion Lyman, Apostle (Delta, Utah: Melvin A. Lyman, 1958).
FDRJ	Franklin D. Richards Journal	Church History Library, Salt Lake City, Utah	Selected Collections; also Scott G. Kenney Collection, University of Utah Library, Special Collections, MS 587.
BYJJ	Brigham Young Jr. Journal (son of President Brigham Young)	Church History Library, Salt Lake City, Utah	Scott G. Kenney Collection, University of Utah Library, Special Collections, MS 587.

Abbr.	*Full Source*	*Location*	*Also Available*
OFWJ	Orson F. Whitney Journal	Orson F. Whitney Collection, 1855–1931; Church History Library, Salt Lake City, Utah; MS 599 [or MS d 1302]	
AWJ	Arthur Winter Journal	Church History Library, Salt Lake City, Utah	
JH	Journal History of the Church	Church History Library, Salt Lake City, Utah	Selected Collections
GC	General Conference		Available online, in paperback reprints, and in *Collected Discourses*, often also referenced as CR in publications.
JD	*Journal of Discourses*	26-volume set containing stenographically reported discourses of prominent church leaders from the 1850s into the 1890s; originally published in Liverpool, England.	Reprint editions of this set are available in many public and private libraries, in bookstores, and online.
CD	*Collected Discourses*	5-volume set containing stenographically reported discourses of prominent church leaders 1886-1898. This collection takes up where *Journal of Discourses* leaves off.	Brian H. Stuy, ed., *Collected Discourses*, 5 Vols. (Burbank, CA: B.H.S. Publishing, 1992), Vol. 5 used herein.
DN	All variations of the *Deseret News*, the Church-owned newspaper, such as *Deseret Evening News*, *Deseret Semi weekly News*, etc.		Scanned images available online at the *Deseret News* website archives, and other sites.
SLH	The *Salt Lake Herald* newspaper		Scanned images available online

NOTES

FOREWORD

1. *Teachings of Presidents of the Church: Joseph Smith,* 40.
2. Unpublished biography of Minnie J. Snow.

INTRODUCTION

1. Quotation taken from Matthias F. Cowley, Univ. of Chicago, Oct. 6, 1925, n.p. These reminiscences about President Snow by Elder Cowley were not included in his biographical account as published in Matthias Cowley, *Prophets and Patriarchs and Cowley's Talks on Doctrine*, 86–98, perhaps because he wrote them twenty-five years later.
2. Orson F. Whitney, *Through Memory's Halls*, 191–92.
3. "[LeRoi] took up shorthand and typewriting when twelve years of age and held the position of public stenographer and typewriter with Judge Coombs in Brigham City. While thus engaged he copied Orson F. Whitney's *Latter Leaves*" ("LeRoi C. Snow", entry in Jenson, *LDS Biographical Encyclopedia* 3: 716-17).
4. See Orson F. Whitney Collection, 1855–1931; Located at CHL XMSF 599 [or MS d 1302, roll 1]; used by permission; courtesy of the Church Archives, The Church of Jesus Christ of Latter-day Saints.
5. Matthias F. Cowley, Univ. of Chicago, Oct. 6, 1925, n.p.
6. As quoted in Thomas C. Romney, *Life of Lorenzo Snow*, 14–15.
7. DN, October 10, 1901 [editorial].
8. SLH, October 11, 1901 [editorial].
9. *Salt Lake Tribune* report quoted in JH, July 12, 1899. Angus M. Cannon, a brother of President George Q. Cannon, was the president of the Salt Lake Stake, and carried an influence some historians have thought to be almost on par with members of the Quorum of the Twelve of that day. To arrest and imprison him was a coup for the anti-Mormon element seeking to damage the Church by prosecuting polygamists.
10. DN, January 5, 1900; interviewed by Frank Carpenter, December 15, 1899.
11. While researching this biography, I often thought Lorenzo resembled President Gordon B. Hinckley in temperament, personality, and humor.
12. As quoted in LeRoi C. Snow, "Lorenzo Snow Biographical Index, 1950," 1.

13. JH, April 14, 1900.
14. AHCJ, April 3, 1894.
15. See the text of the Second Manifesto in Clark, *Messages of the First Presidency* 4:84. LDS Church members entering into plural marriages after this official declaration became subject to Church disciplinary procedures. Modern so-called "fundamentalist" groups that practice polygamy often trace their roots to disobedient Latter-day Saints living at this time that still wished to continue performing polygamous marriages after being directed to cease by those in authority. Uninformed media outlets often confuse such groups with members of The Church of Jesus Christ of Latter-day Saints.
16. BYJJ, March 13, 1901; as quoted in Hales, *Modern Polygamy and Mormon Fundamentalism*, 60.
17. See Hales, *Modern Polygamy and Mormon Fundamentalism,* 59–61. Historians examining these issues are often forced to use qualifiers such as "probably" and "may have" when discussing the subject from the limited and scanty sources available. This dearth of certainty does not tend to engender confidence that sufficient understanding and knowledge of such a complex issue has been achieved. Further, some historians, or critics who style themselves as historians, examine the sources with only a negative bias, seeking to discover the sensational, not searching for truth in motivations nor acknowledging or allowing for divine intervention.
18. AHCJ, July 15, 1886. Elder Cannon only lived for ten more years.
19. JH, March 11, 1897; see also AHCJ, October 1, 1895.
20. The current prevailing teachings and example of the First Presidency and Council of the Twelve on scriptural interpretation should be followed in all doctrinal matters; safety is found by staying in the doctrinal mainstream of the Church.
21. Matthias F. Cowley, Univ. of Chicago, Oct. 6, 1925, n.p. President Harold B. Lee taught: "How do we measure whether or not one's teachings are true or false? If anyone teaches beyond what the scriptures teach, we may put it down as speculation except one man who has the right to bring forth any new doctrine—that is the one man who holds the keys—the prophet, seer, and revelator who presides in that high place. And no one else. If anyone presumes to bring forth what he claims to be new doctrine you may know that it is purely his own opinion and you label it as such regardless of his position in the church. If it contradicts something that is in the scriptures, you may label it immediately that it is false. That is why we call the scriptures, our four Standard Church Works. They are the standards by which we measure all doctrine and if anything is taught which is contrary to that which is in the scriptures, it is false. It is just that simple" ("Viewpoint of a Giant," Summer School Devotional Address, Department of Seminaries and Institutes of Religion, Brigham Young University, July 18, 1968, 6).
22. JH, March 1, 1900 (see also AHCJ, October 1, 1890). As stated, they are personal views (of only historical curiosity today), but likely influenced the prevailing understanding of the time:

> President Snow, commenting on this subject, said that he asked President Brigham Young on one occasion, why it was that millions and millions of people were cursed with a black skin, and when, if ever, this curse would be removed?

> President Young explained it in this way—but whether he had it revealed to him or not, President Snow did not know—when Cain slew Abel he fully understood the effects of the killing of his brother, but that it extended to the spirits in eternity. He said that in the spirit world people were organized as they were here. There were Patriarchs standing at the head of certain classes of spirits, and there were certain relationships existing which affected their coming into the world to take tabernacles. For instance, when Abel came into the world it was understood by Cain that the class of people which he presided over as a prince, if they ever came into the world in the regular way, they would have to come through him. So with Cain, he was a prince presiding over a vast number of a certain class of spirits, and it was natural that they should come through him, if at all, and therefore when Cain slew Abel he understood that the taking of his brother's life was going to deprive the spirits over whom he (Abel) presided from coming into the world, perhaps for thousands and thousands of years; hence the sin was immense because the effects were immense. Then there was this understanding when the Lord executed judgment upon Cain: The spirits under his leadership still looked up to him, and rather than forsake him they were willing to bear his burdens and share the penalty imposed upon him, and it was understood that this curse would remain upon his posterity until the class of spirits presided over by Abel should have the privilege of coming into the world and taking tabernacles, and then the curse would be removed" (JH, March 1, 1900).

It is highly likely that the date on which Elder Snow talked to President Brigham Young about this issue and received the given explanation was February 13, 1849 (the day after he was ordained an apostle); see Ronald K. Esplin, "Brigham Young and Priesthood Denial to the Blacks: An Alternate View," 394–401, esp. 395.

23. This philosophical commonality among legitimate historians is also defined in a quotation found on the LDS Church's official website (newsroom page: mormonnewsroom.org) in an article by Elder Marlin K. Jensen (the former Church Historian) addressing the broader subject of polygamy: "As thoughtful historians know, a serious study of history does not impose contemporary understandings and sensibilities onto an interpretation of earlier time periods." (See mormonnewsroom.org/commentary/polygamy-then-and-now.) Such a practice among those wishing to manipulate the unwary for private purposes is often called "presentism"—seeking to influence a modern reader by using their present feelings or beliefs of how *things should be*, with a non-contextual, unfounded description of how *things once were*—that were different or opposed to those present feelings; if a negative reaction from the reader about the issue is achieved, their purposes are accomplished, although honest historical inquiry is cheated.

24. The First Presidency gave a leather edition of Eliza's book as a Christmas present to Church employees in 1999, but this was a specialized and limited printing. As of this writing, several websites contain scanned pages of Eliza's "public domain" book in its entirety.

25. See Hedges and Holzapfel, eds., *Within These Prison Walls: Lorenzo Snow's Record Book, 1886-1897.*

26. See Bibliography for these works.
27. For these quotations, see Hedges and Burrup, "Shaping the Stones: Lorenzo Snow's Letters to Priesthood Leaders of the London Conference, November 1842", 11, 24-25n.30.
28. On Whitney's first draft title page, the title is given as "Later Leaves in the Life of Lorenzo Snow." When Thomas Romney used a few excerpts from it, he titled it, "Later Leaves of Life of Lorenzo Snow." The entry on "Orson F. Whitney" in Jenson's *LDS Biographical Encyclopedia* (1:679) gives the title as, "Later Leaves from the Life of Lorenzo Snow." I have simply changed *later* to *latter*, reflecting the scope of this work.
29. Those wishing to study Whitney's draft in its entirety can inspect the original, available in the LDS Church History Library archives. Whitney's title page included the following: "A Sequel to the *Biography and Family Record of Lorenzo Snow*, comprising the four years of his life from 1885–1889, and embodying a successive history for that period of the principal events of the Utah anti-polygamy crusade." Then, after the word "Prefatory" [preface], Whitney wrote: "It is the purpose in these pages, while detailing the individual experience of President Lorenzo Snow, the later chapters of whose life I have undertaken to write, to review some of the leading events of that period of tribulation through which the Church of God has passed, and is still passing, since the enactment of the Edmunds Law of 1882.
"A full history of the wrongs and cruelties heaped upon a patient and suffering people during this season of sore distress cannot now be given. They are a volume in themselves; a chapter of infamy; a page of pain and tears; adding one more leaf to the world's crimson record of religious persecution, and leaving a blot upon the annals of this Christian nation that will yet win the wonder and contempt of lovers of liberty the world over; and, in years to come, bring the blush of indignant shame to the burning cheek of America's patriot posterity.
"The present narrative will necessarily be confined to such events of the 'crusade' as may properly come within the scope of this biography. The Author; May 1890."
30. I have also placed in the notes of the Whitney-produced chapters some relevant material from the prison journal of Abraham H. Cannon, in order to provide wider background and perspective on President Snow's own prison experiences.
31. I was told a version of this story by a couple of descendants of President Snow and two other Snow researchers that had heard of it. If true, it explains the apparent lack of personal sources about President Snow. See also AHLJ, October 21, 1901.
32. From a letter preserved in the manuscript of *Latter Leaves*, it is known that as late as 1885 President Snow was making daily entries in a diary, the whereabouts of which is now unknown, if it still exists. One might logically deduce from his lifetime diary writing habit that he probably continued to do so the rest of his life when time allowed.
33. When dealing with such sources, even those taken from records created by shorthand experts, quotations should not always be viewed as precise word-for-word utterances; sometimes they are very close, even exact; other times they are summaries of what was said; many times it is impossible to tell the difference.
34. See Bibliography for a list of these articles.

35. See LeRoi C. Snow, "Lorenzo Snow Biographical Index, 1950," in the Bibliography, Unpublished Materials.
36. See the discussion of LeRoi Snow as a suspect source in Beecher, Newell, and Avery, "Emma and Eliza and the Stairs," 89–91.
37. AWJ, under date given.
38. OFWJ, January 3, 1899.
39. DN, January 20, 1872.
40. DN, October 10, 1891.

INTRODUCING ORSON F. WHITNEY

1. Throughout this volume the designation OFWJ, followed by a date, is used to identify material from Whitney's journals as found in Orson F. Whitney Collection, 1855–1931; CHL, MS 599 [or MS d 1302].
2. Elder Whitney enjoyed his literary work editing the European mission periodical, the *Millennial Star*, but behind-the-scenes issues in the mission office troubled him. He was almost sent home early because of his poor health, and to make matters worse, the mission president, Albert Carrington, was carrying on with the mission home maid, the two occasionally being caught by headquarters staff in compromising positions. Years later, Carrington was excommunicated for committing adultery with several different women, but he was rebaptized before he died. One suspects Elder Whitney was relieved to be removed from proximity to an evidently awkward situation at mission headquarters.
3. "Charles Whitney, a younger brother of Orson's, committed suicide day before yesterday by shooting himself through the head. The coroner's jury state that it was done during a fit of temporary aberration of the mind" (AHCJ, August 6, 1886).
4. See FDRJ, January 30, 1888.
5. For further information about Eliza R. Snow Smith, who was also a plural wife of Brigham Young (for time only), see *Eliza R. Snow: The Complete Poetry*, ed. Jull Mulvey Derr and Karen Lynn Davidson, eds. (Provo and Salt Lake City, Utah: Brigham Young University Press and University of Utah Press, 2009), xiii–xxxvii.
6. As quoted in Clark, *Messages of the First Presidency* 3:200.
7. JGKJ, September 8–9, 1898.
8. Jenson, *Autobiography of Andrew Jenson*, 207.
9. In 1900, Orson also repented of some false doctrine that he had privately entertained for a number of years. In a personal letter to his friend President Joseph F. Smith, he wrote: "I have pondered and prayed much over the matter of the written statement that I made to you in May 1898, the subject of which need not now be mentioned. That statement I wish to withdraw. I have banished the subject from my mind. I no longer believe as I did, and I wish that nothing shall remain to perpetuate the matter either in my own memory or others. While I do not admit that my faith in the Gospel and my loyalty to the Priesthood have ever wavered—for I know that they have not—I do acknowledge that I have been mistaken, honestly mistaken in certain things, and I desire to rectify that mistake" (OFWJ, July 1, 1900). For further information regarding this matter,

see AHCJ, August 15, 1895; September 5, 1895; October 24 & 27, 1895; OFWJ, June 3 & 8, 1889; July 27, 1900; see also Lorenzo Snow's discourse in general conference, April 1901.

10. In relation to the mentioned sustaining vote, Andrew Jenson, an assistant Church Historian that worked in the same office with Whitney, described some of the difficulties that he experienced with decisions that had been made about his being formally sustained in general conference—Jenson himself resenting it when he was not. He wrote: "Since Bro. Lund was appointed Church Historian in 1900 no assistant historians have been sustained. This was according to the plan of the late President Lorenzo Snow, but was not in harmony with the feelings of Bro. Joseph F. Smith, who considered, as I now understand, that I, who was the only one of Bro. Richards's assistants left, was treated unjustly [in not always being presented for a sustaining vote]. This was also what I thought, . . . but now, after being acknowledged and sustained in the position I think I am entitled to, I shall once more throw my whole soul into the work at the Historian's Office" (as quoted in Perkins, "A Study of the Contributions of Andrew Jenson to the Writing and Preservation of LDS Church History," 60). Jenson also felt confused (and underappreciated) over whether being sustained as an Assistant Church Historian meant he became a General Authority entitled to certain privileges. In a 1915 letter to President Joseph F. Smith, he wrote: "I believe you will understand me and have sympathy with me when I in the midst of my best endeavors have been turned down, especially when your predecessor, President [Lorenzo] Snow, turned me down through the influence of [George Q. Cannon]. I am frank to acknowledge to you that I have felt slighted on many occasions, and have been made to feel the sting of it most keenly. I both am and am not one of the General Authorities of the Church. I am just outside the circle. When the question is up for transportation—something that I need as much as any man in the Church—I am just outside the limit. If any invitations are issued for the General authorities to attend [events], I am again just where I am missed. If I attend any stake conference or any other important meeting, I am simply tolerated" (Scott G. Kenney Collection; folder 4: Andrew Jenson, letter to JFS, 1 January 1915, 6 pages; Andrew Jenson, Correspondence, 1906–1915).

11. B. H. Roberts, Correspondence (1928–1929) B. H. Roberts, letter to Reed Smoot, 5 July 1929, 2 pp, Scott G. Kenney Collection, folder 18.

12. AHLJ, October 14, 1909. Lund's October 20 journal entry states: "Our meeting at the Temple lasted five hours. The statement as to our position on the Origin of Man was read and sanctioned by the Twelve."

13. Clark, *Messages of the First Presidency* 4:205 (200–206). Some have speculated that in preparing this statement, Whitney drew upon wording from an earlier article he had written entitled, "Man's Origin and Destiny" (see *Contributor*, Vol. 3, No. 9 [June 1882]). If so, this was and is common practice among speakers and authors—to reuse, revise, or refine their own material; yet here it becomes irrelevant since the final document became the authoritative position and voice of the First Presidency, not of Orson Whitney. Yet, there is little wonder that President Smith would often draw on the talents of this exceptional apostle, as Whitney had become one of the finest and most persuasive writers and speakers in the Church.

14. AHLJ, November 3, 1902.

15. An in-depth examination of Orson F. Whitney's writings can be found in Thomson, "Orson F. Whitney: Mormon Writer," unpublished Master's Thesis, University of Utah, 1949.

CHAPTER 1

1. Unless otherwise noted, all material in this chapter is taken from Eliza R. Snow Smith's *Biography and Family Record of Lorenzo Snow.*
2. Other biographical sketches of Lorenzo Snow's life can be found in Arrington, *Presidents of the Church*, 144–78; Nibley, *The Presidents of the Church*, 171–222; and [CES], *Presidents of the Church*: Student Manual, 125–147; *Presidents of the Church Student Manual*, 2003, 75–92.
3. "Testimony on life of David W. Patten," [February 6, 1900], as quoted in Clark, *Messages of the First Presidency* 3:324–25.
4. Lorenzo's own account of this time, written much later, includes the idea that he was already desiring to proclaim Mormonism as a missionary: "I proceeded to Oberlin College, a Presbyterian institution and commenced my course of studies. I very soon became disgusted with their system of intolerance, religious tyranny and bigotry, and as I felt to proclaim and report the principles of Joseph Smith as far as I knew them, which all were bitterly opposed to, therefore my removal from the college was warmly recommended by the authorities. I did not wait for an action on their part, but after a stay of about six months, I returned home with the intention of going to some eastern college where religion would not be made the exclusive object of education" ("Synopsis of Lorenzo Snow's History", as cited in *Manuscript History of Brigham Young*.) The authors of the article on Lorenzo Snow in *The Encyclopedia of Mormonism* wrote: "Lorenzo's sister Eliza, in her biography of him, claims to have whetted his interest in Mormonism while he was at Oberlin, his own account tells of hearing the Book of Mormon being read in his home in Mantua and of later meeting with the Prophet at Hiram in 1831" (Cited in Maureen Ursenbach Beecher and Paul Thomas Smith, "Lorenzo Snow." *Encyclopedia of Mormonism*, vol. 3:1367).
5. DN, "The Grand Destiny of Man," July 14, 1901.
6. LeRoi C. Snow, quoting Lorenzo's journal in "How Lorenzo Snow found God," in *Improvement Era*, February, 1937. This material is also found in Thomas C. Romney, *The Life of Lorenzo Snow*, 23–25, though with an incorrect *Improvement Era* volume number given (should be 37 not 40).
7. DN, June 15, 1901. Eliza explained Lorenzo's reaction: "Unenlightened as his mind was at the time, the foregoing saying of the Patriarch was a puzzle which my brother could not comprehend, as will be seen by the following expression from his journal:

> The old gentleman's prediction, that I should ere long be baptized, was strange to me, for I had not cherished a thought of becoming a member of the "Mormon" Church; but when he uttered the last clause, I was confounded. That, to me, was a big saying, and, I then thought, approaching almost to blasphemy. And why not? After years of study and diligent search after knowledge, in that which most intimately concerned

> me— "From whence came I?" "Why am I here?" "What is my future destiny?" In all this, I was profoundly ignorant. As yet I had received no key that could unlock those mysteries—that could make known, to my satisfaction, my relationship to Him who controls the universe.
>
> I looked at Father Smith, and silently asked myself the question: Can that man be a deceiver? His every appearance answered in the negative. At first sight, his presence impressed me with feelings of love and reverence. I had never seen age so prepossessing. Father Joseph Smith, the Patriarch, was indeed a noble specimen of aged manhood.
>
> But with all my favorable impressions of the Patriarch, that big saying was a dark parable. The prediction that I should soon be baptized was fulfilled in two weeks from the time it was spoken, and in about four years from that time I was reminded of the foregoing prediction by a very wonderful revelation on the subject in which the principle, as well as the promise, was made clear to my understanding as the sun at noonday. (*Biography and Family Record*, 9–10)

8. This journal reference is from *Biography and Family Record*, 7–9. Lorenzo later left this record: "One Sunday the Prophet Joseph arose in the pulpit just before the meeting closed and said, 'A young man by the name of Lorenzo Snow wishes to be baptized, and Brother John Boynton (who was then one of the Twelve Apostles) will baptize him.' I was baptized in the stream that ran through Kirtland, and hands were laid upon me by Hyrum Smith and some others. I received no special manifestation at that time, but I was perfectly satisfied that I had done what was wisdom for me to do under the circumstances. I had studied the scriptures and was convinced that the Gospel as preached by the Latter-day Saints was in accordance with that taught by the Son of God and by His Apostles in former days" (DN, "The Grand Destiny of Man," July 14, 1901).

9. DN, "The Grand Destiny of Man," July 14, 1901. Another account of this experience related by President Snow gives Oliver Cowdery as the man he asked counsel from about whether or not to go to college: "I desired to obtain a perfect education before receiving the Gospel. I heard some missionaries returning and gave their happy experiences. Tho I got the spirit of it Joseph Smith got up and said that such young men as wanted to be ordained Elders should come forth. I among others presented myself. This is the only office I have sought. I went to a school of young men. I heard the testimony of my comrades. I was getting out of the notion of going to College and wanted to bear my testimony. I asked Bro. Oliver Cowdery's opinion. He said I think you ought to get your education. I kept thinking and for once I felt to resist the counsel. I felt to go out without purse and scrip. It is the only time I have not followed counsel. I have not regretted it, though I have been in circumstances where I have wished I had had more education" (AHLJ, March 30, 1897).

10. DN, "Notable Reunion of Weber Stake: A reunion of the authorities of the Priesthood in the Weber Stake of Zion, June 12, 1901," June 15, 1901. The blessing is introduced with the following notation: "At a patriarchal blessing meeting held in the Lord's house in Kirtland this the Fifteenth day of December 1836.

Joseph Smith Sr. the Patriarch of the Church of Latter-day Saints being present and holding the meeting. A patriarchal blessing was conferred on the head of Lorenzo Snow son of Oliver Snow born in Mantua Portage Co. State of Ohio the 3rd of April 1814." Further information on patriarchal blessings given by Joseph Smith (Sr.) can be found in Mark L. McConkie, *The Father of the Prophet: Stories and Insights from the Life of Joseph Smith Sr.* (Salt Lake City: Bookcraft, 1993); and Earnest M. Skinner, "Joseph Smith Sr., First Patriarch to the Church," unpublished master's thesis, BYU, 1958; see especially pages 118–21.

11. It is unknown whether Oliver Snow was baptized, although he and his wife received patriarchal blessings from Father Smith, in which Oliver was encouraged to join the Church. See Cheryl McClellan, "Staying Connected: The Snow Family of Ohio," 7–8, unpublished paper delivered to the Mormon History Association in Vermont in 2004; copy in author's possession. Cheryl McClellan is an Ohio Period, Snow family researcher and authority.

12. Correspondence, Lorenzo Snow to his Father and Mother, London, November 11, 1941; CHL, MS 1330 1; letters and patriarchal blessings 1836–1843.

13. Correspondence, Lorenzo Snow to "Sister" (likely Eliza), London, January 4, 1842; CHL, MS 1330 1; letters & patriarchal blessings 1836–1843.

14. A good review of Elder Snow's mission in England is found in Andrew H. Hedges and Jay G. Burrup, "Shaping the Stones: Lorenzo Snow's Letters to Priesthood Leaders of the London Conference, November 1842," *BYU Studies*, Vol. 38, no. 4 (1999), 6–25.

15. For the full quotation, see the last half of President Snow's tithing talk in Appendix 6.

16. This is a direct quotation from *Biography and Family Record*, 69–70. Eliza quotes further from Lorenzo's journal of the time: "At the interview on the bank of the Mississippi, in which the Prophet Joseph explained the doctrine of Celestial Marriage, I felt very humble, and in my simplicity besought him earnestly to correct me and set me right if, at any time, he should see me indulging any principle or practice that might tend to lead astray, into forbidden paths; to which he replied, 'Brother Lorenzo, the principles of honesty and integrity are founded within you, and you will never be guilty of any serious error or wrong, to lead you from the path of duty. The Lord will open your way to receive and obey the law of Celestial Marriage.' During the conversation, I remarked to the Prophet I thought he appeared to have been endowed with great additional power during my mission in England. He said it was true; the Lord had bestowed on him additional divine power" (70).

17. For a list of these wives and their children, see Francis M. Gibbons, *Lorenzo Snow, Spiritual Giant, Prophet of God* (Salt Lake City: Deseret Book, 1982), 208–9.

18. A biographical record written by a descendant states: "In the Nauvoo Temple, January 17, 1846, Harriet was sealed to Lorenzo Snow for time and all eternity by President Brigham Young. The marriage was witnessed by Willard Richards and Amasa M. Lyman" (Harriett died May 12, 1890). (Cited in "Harriett Amelia Squires Snow," unpublished two-page sketch written by Maude R. Sorenson [a granddaughter], CHL; MS 12144).

19. List provided to the author by Cynthia Snow Banner, great-great-granddaughter of Lorenzo Snow (email 12/10/2010); this list has been combined with information taken from the Lorenzo Snow family ancestry webpage. http://www.our-genealogy.com/Latter-Day-Saint-Families/Snow-Family/lorenzo_snow.htm, accessed 8/23/2010.
20. See Hedges and Holzapfel, *Within These Prison Walls: Lorenzo Snow's Record Book, 1886-1897*, xxviii and 157–59.
21. AHCJ, April 5, 1894.
22. Further information about Mt. Pisgah can be found in Leland H. Gentry, "The Mormon Way Stations: Garden Grove and Mt. Pisgah," *BYU Studies*, vol. 21 (1981).
23. Further details about Lorenzo's Iowa travels can be found in Maureen Ursenbach Beecher, "The Iowa Journal of Lorenzo Snow," in *BYU Studies*, vol. 24, no. 3 (Summer 1984), 261–73.
24. "Oliver Jr., age seventy, was displaced physically, emotionally and spiritually. In Ohio, he had been a popular, prosperous farmer, surrounded by his family. In Illinois, he was unknown, poor, and far from his family. He was grieving the recent deaths of many of them. Oliver Jr's. disposition may also have been affected by illness, since his death occurred a year later." Many years later, in the 1870s and 1880s, when Lorenzo and Eliza's Mormon fame and names had become well-known, their Ohio relatives forgot their bitterness and resentment toward Joseph Smith and their Mormon relatives, and they welcomed them back with friendliness, although they would not join the Church (see Cheryl McClellan, "Staying Connected: The Snow Family of Ohio," 12–20).
25. Quoted from "Elenor Houtz Snow," unpublished nine-page manuscript, CHL; MS 12145. Elenor was Lorenzo's fifth wife. She was born August 14, 1831, and died September 14, 1896, in Brigham City, Utah, of heart disease (age sixty-five).
26. Lorenzo's own autobiographical record states: "The 9th of February 1846 I left Nauvoo with my family in company with President Young to seek an asylum of peace beyond the Rocky Mountains. I arrived in Mount Pisgah, a small settlement sometime in June, where I was taken severely sick and did not fully recover till late in the fall. Next spring I was appointed to take the presidency of the settlement, in which office I continued till the next year when I left with a portion of the settlement and joined President Young and company some 30 miles west of Council Bluffs en route for Great Salt Lake. Our companies were organized at the Horn, I was appointed to take charge of the advance company of one hundred wagons which left the Horn June 1st, I arrived in the valley the later part of September and was ordained into the Quorum of Twelve on February 12, 1849" (Harwell, ed., *Manuscript History of Brigham Young*, 152).
27. JD 26:366. Further information on Elder Snow's apostolic ordination is found in the *Manuscript History of Brigham Young*: "Note: Elder Matthew W. Mansfield, of Teasdale, Utah, writing to President Snow under date of the 27th, after stating that he had been ordained a high priest under his hands on the 24th of June, 1887, asks how the priesthood came to him, and desired this information traced back to the Prophet Joseph Smith. The matter was referred to the historian for the information, and Brother Andrew Jenson, after searching the record made

answer as follows: President Lorenzo Snow ordained an Apostle February 12, 1849, by Heber C. Kimball, who was ordained an Apostle, February 14, 1835, under the hands of Oliver Cowdery, David Whitmer and Martin Harris, who were blessed to select and ordain the Twelve by Joseph Smith the Prophet, who was ordained to the Apostleship by Peter, James and John, who were called and commissioned by Jesus Christ.

"On the above being read to President Snow this 8th day of March, 1901, the president remarked that Heber C. Kimball no doubt was mouth [voice] on the occasion, in fact, there was no doubt whatever existing regarding it, but at the same time he himself had no private record of it, neither was he able to remember who was mouth in his ordination, but he distinctly remembers that he was ordained under the hands of Brigham Young, Heber C. Kimball, Willard Richards and some others of the Apostles, among them he thought was John Taylor" (Harwell, ed., *Manuscript History of Brigham Young*, 152).

CHAPTER 2

1. *Manuscript History of Brigham Young*, 245.
2. Further comment on Elder Snow's Italian missionary activities can be found in Michael W. Homer, "The Church's Image in Italy from 1840s to 1946: A Bibliographic Essay," 83–114.
3. "Elenor Houtz Snow," unpublished manuscript, n.p.
4. "Lorenzo Snow: Some of His Outstanding Characteristics," *Improvement Era*, December 1929; ostensibly quoting from the August 1899 *Improvement Era*, although it is really a summary of a slightly longer and more detailed earlier history.
5. See "Territory of Utah: Legislative Assembly Rosters, 1851-1894," compiled by the Utah State Archives staff, 2007. Accessed at http://www.archives.state.ut.us/research/guides/legassembly1-10.htm on December 20, 2010.
6. For further information on this important phase of Lorenzo's life's work, see Arrington, Fox and May, *Building the City of God: Community & Cooperation Among the Mormons*, 111–33. See also Arrington, *Great Basin Kingdom*, 324–41; Arrington, "Cooperative Community in the North: Brigham City, Utah," *Utah Historical Quarterly*, 33:3 (Summer 1965), 199–217.
7. As quoted in Romney, *The Life of Lorenzo Snow*, 206–7.
8. "Notable Reunion of Weber Stake," DN, June 15, 1901.
9. LeRoi C. Snow "Lorenzo Snow Biographical Index, 1950," (June 8, 1870), 154 ,also 127.
10. LeRoi C. Snow, "Lorenzo Snow Biographical Index, 1950," 142; see also JH, May 8, 1867. Amasa Lyman was the father of Elder Francis M. Lyman, also of the Quorum of the Twelve, and a friend to Lorenzo.
11. For further information on the School of the Prophets, see Patrick, "The School of the Prophets: Its Development and Influence in Utah Territory," 23 and 142 for dates of the Brigham City organization. Also of interest is the following *Church News* article: "Brigham City—An historical document signed by Brigham Young was discovered recently in the wrecked ruins of the old Lorenzo Snow residence

across the street west from the Central School in Brigham City. Roy Winders . . . discovered the manuscript when an old closet in the house was torn down. The old home was being razed so that the space could be utilized as additional play area at Central School. The manuscript was found in a hand-made envelope addressed to 'Miss Birdie Snow, Box Elder County, Utah.' The envelope, mailed from Salt lake City, was postmarked February 9, 1890, and contained other personal letters, one of which was from a relative in Springville and was dated 1882. The manuscript outlining 17 rules to be observed by the first class of the School of Prophets, apparently was written by a secretary, as was the endorsement on the outside which read, 'Elder Lorenzo Snow is hereby authorized to organize a school of the Prophets in Brigham City.' This statement was signed by Brigham Young." ("'School of the Prophets' Manuscript is Discovered" DN, *Church News* section, August 7, 1954.) See also JH, August 24, 1868.
12. JH, April 10, 1899.
13. LeRoi C. Snow, "Lorenzo Snow Biographical Index, 1950," 148; see also JH, September 3 and 5, 1869, and Evans and Anderson, *Ezra T. Benson: Pioneer, Statesman, Saint*, 319–20. Elder Benson was the grandfather and namesake of President Ezra Taft Benson.
14. LeRoi C. Snow, "Lorenzo Snow Biographical Index, 1950," 150 (October 9, 1869). LeRoi named an Ezra C. Robinson and Florence Truelson as his main sources for this story. He also wrote, "I have heard a number of accounts of this experience, but have not been able to definitely verify the date." Substantiating the severe canyon winds in the Davis County, Utah, area, President Charles W. Penrose told a story from his own life of severe hardships dealing with high winds in Farmington (see "Graphic Glimpses of Pioneer Life," *Improvement Era*, July 1925).
15. See LeRoi C. Snow, "Lorenzo Snow Biographical Index, 1950," 156.
16. As quoted in Norlyn Snow Torres, "History of Minnie Jensen Snow," unpublished manuscript, December 1, 1982, n.p.. Of her marriage to Lorenzo, Minnie later said: "An unkind word has never passed between us." See also LeRoi C. Snow, "Lorenzo Snow Biographical Index, 1950," (June 12, 1871), 156.
17. Gene Sessions, ed., *Mormon Democrat: The Religious and Political Memoirs of James Henry Moyle* (Salt Lake City: Signature Books, 1998), 297. Concerning LeRoi, James Moyle, who served at times as President Snow's legal counsel, said: "He [Lorenzo] had the boy sit on the highest seats of the Tabernacle at General Conferences as an aide. It was common talk that the President wanted him made an apostle, and why it did not go farther I do not know. He had never done anything to indicate that he was apostolic timber. He is, however, a very fine Church member. One thing is generally understood, namely that the apostles were opposed to LeRoi's appointment or it is believed the appointment would have been made" (297–98).
18. DN, January 20, 1872.
19. For a review of this trip and its dedicatory purpose, see Blair G. Van Dyke and Lamar C. Berrett, "In the Footsteps of Orson Hyde: Subsequent Dedications of the Holy Land," *BYU Studies*, 47:1 (2008), 57–93; esp. 65–72.
20. For an abridged collection of these letters by Elder Snow, see *Biography and Family Record*, 496–581.
21. As quoted in Durham and Heath, *Succession in the Church*, 73.

22. See Durham and Heath, *Succession in the Church*, 73n.7. See also *Biography and Family Record*, 497.
23. See LeRoi C. Snow, "Lorenzo Snow Biographical Index, 1950," 131 (September 1, 1864).
24. See LeRoi C. Snow "Lorenzo Snow Biographical Index, 1950," 133 (July 15, 1865); see also JH, July 15, 1865.
25. For reference to Elder Snow's connections to the Logan Temple, see Nolan P. Olson, *Logan Temple: The First 100 Years*, 11, 22, 32, 33, 39, 56, 139, 141, and 161.

CHAPTER 3

1. Other attempts to prosecute polygamists under the Edmunds Law had been made prior to this, in several of which women suspected to be plural wives were imprisoned, one of the them with an infant in arms, for refusing to answer questions before the Grand Jury relative to their family affairs; but the Clawson case was the first that came to trial and resulted in a conviction.
2. The Federal Court of this District was held alternately in Ogden and Provo, the latter the county seat of Utah County.
3. See revelation given through President John Taylor, October 13, 1882.

CHAPTER 4

1. The account of this short mission is found in the original draft of Whitney's *Later Leaves in the Life of Lorenzo Snow* manuscript, but it was removed from herein for space purposes.
2. The Constitution of the United States declares that no person shall be subject for the same offense to be twice put in jeopardy of life or limb.
3. Another account of President Snow's arrest is found in a statement from LeRoi C. Snow, November 20, 1885: "After the officers had searched the house until they decided father was not there and were about to leave, one of their guards outside the house reported that he had noticed the watch-dog sniffing at a small ventilator grating in the foundation of the house. The officers returned to the bedroom over that grating and finally discovered hinges under the carpet and opened a trap-door in the floor which lead to a small room where father was hiding. They called to father and he came out" ("LeRoi C. Snow Statement," n.p.).

CHAPTER 5

1. A note of commentary from the journal of Elder John Henry Smith is relevant: "I went by the U.C. train to Ogden. I attended Court and heard the pleas of the lawyers in Bro. Lorenzo Snow's case. It was a great farce and the third trial was much more of a farce, no evidence being given. I spent the evening with Bro. Lorenzo Snow and found him cheerful" (JHSJ, December 31, 1885).
2. One of President Snow's friends, Elder Matthias Cowley, later shared his opinion of this speech: "During the Anti-Mormon crusade, Pres. Snow was sent to the Penitentiary for keeping the commandments of the Lord. Each of

the brethren at the time of his sentence was invited by the judge to make any statement he wished to the court. I have read many of these addresses given in court by the brethren and have always considered Pres. Snow's speech to the court the greatest of all, and next to it, the speeches of Elders Rudger Clawson and Francis A. Brown" (Matthias F. Cowley, Univ. of Chicago, Oct. 6, 1925). Elder Cowley was impressed enough to include the entire speech in his biographical account of President Snow, found in Cowley, *Prophets and Patriarchs and Cowley's Talks on Doctrine*, 91–94.

3. Attorney F. S. Richards, prior to the speech of Elder Snow, had dwelt upon the general good character of the defendant, and requested that the age of his client and the fact that he had been convicted on three separate indictments, might be taken into consideration by the court in pronouncing sentence.

CHAPTER 6

1. For a general review of Mormon prison life, see Bashore, "Life behind Bars: Mormon Cohabs of the 1880s," *Utah Historical Quarterly* 47.1 (1979): 22–41. Two book-length treatments about other Mormons that were sent through a similar judicial farce and then to prison are Van Orden, *Prisoner for Conscience's Sake: The Life of George Reynolds*, and Larson, *Prisoner for Polygamy: The Memoirs and Letters of Rudger Clawson at the Utah Territorial Penitentiary, 1884–87.* Elder Abraham H. Cannon, serving his own sentence for polygamy, observed: "Apostle Lorenzo Snow today voluntarily delivered himself up to the U.S. Marshal for confinement in the Pen so that his case, now pending before the U.S. Supreme Court might be advanced on the calendar. His case is to test the validity of the segregating process now in vogue and to see whether a man must publicly announce that he is keeping the Edmunds Laws in order to avoid prosecution" (AHCJ, March 12, 1886).

2. It may be that President Snow did have to allow his beard to be trimmed to some extent. Elder Cannon's journal includes this note: "Bros. Snow and Dinwoodey are to be cropped close. All our 'fresh fish' were shaved clean" (AHCJ, May 14, 1886).

3. Another favor shown President Snow, the most prominent prisoner at the time, were his sleeping accommodations: "There are only two bunks containing but one person each: Bros. Lorenzo Snow's and A. Miner's" (AHCJ, March 17, 1886).

CHAPTER 7

1. Commenting on Elder Snow's deportment in prison, and on conditions there generally, Elder Abraham H. Cannon wrote the following description to Matthias Cowley: "Bro. Snow, though so aged, bears up remarkably well and sets an example of patience and goodness which we all can follow with profit. Not a single word of complaint have I heard him utter since I came here. Indeed all the brethren seem to be perfectly contented. And why should they not be so? They are not conscious of having sinned against their God, their families, or their fellow men. . . . Of the prison and its management I have not the least complaint to make. Our warden, Mr. G. N. Dow, is a kind-hearted, genial gentleman who

does all in his power to make things agreeable to the prisoners under his care. He does not inflict any punishment except such as may be necessary to maintain discipline. There is not a prisoner here, as far as I know, but what speaks well of him and would like to see him retain his position indefinitely" (correspondence, Abraham H. Cannon to Elder M. F. Cowley, April 27, 1886; available in CHL).

2. For example, Elder Cannon recorded that "During the evening I was studying and conversing with Bros. Snow and Clawson" (AHCJ, April 20, 1886).

3. The afternoon of April 6th became one of these occasions, with President Snow giving a speech to Mormon prisoners being released that day (see AHCJ, April 6, 1889). Two days later: "[The *Deseret*] *News* of the 6th having come to our hand I read aloud to the brethren in [Bunkhouse] No. 3 the epistle of Pres. Taylor and Father to the saints, read at conference. It was the best of the kind ever written, and at its close we all arose to our feet and under Bro. Snow's direction repealed a fervent Amen three times" (AHCJ, April 8, 1886; for the full text of the epistle, see Clark, *Messages of the First Presidency* 3: 45–71).

4. Elder Cannon commented thus: "News was received from Washington today that the U.S. Supreme Court had decided that the Snow appeal case was out of their jurisdiction and belonged solely to the lower courts. This virtually gives the officers in this Territory power to segregate cohab cases as much as they like and imprison a man for life as well as rob him of all his property. It also decided that even if a man lives with only one woman but holds the others out as wives, he can be prosecuted and punished for cohab. Bro. Snow seemed to take the decision quite calmly though it must be a severe blow to a man of his age to think of remaining here still a solid 13 months" (AHCJ, May 10, 1886).

5. Elder Cannon also described this first meeting of West and Snow: "About 2 p.m. our new governor West, Arthur Pratt, B.H. Roberts, and Jo Barnett accompanied by the Warden came into the Pen. After looking through the buildings a number of the 'Mormons' were called out to talk with him, I being among the number, being introduced to him by B.H. Roberts. He talked about the situation here and seemed very anxious to argue us into the belief that it was proper for us to yield the promptings of conscience to the dictates of our law makers. He said, 'As sure as the sun shines in yonder heavens your system of marriage will not be tolerated in this country.' When asked what he would do if he placed himself in our position, he said, 'Why I would yield my principles and submit to the laws.' 'But,' it was remarked, 'all laws are not proper and just;' to which he replied, 'they are so until repealed.' Bro. Snow met him ably at every point, and it was evident the Governor did not desire to get involved in a discussion for fear of being worsted. As it was he jumped around from one subject to another wherever he thought he could get in a telling blow" (AHCJ, May 9, 1886).

6. For an account of this interview, see Larson, ed., *Prisoner for Polygamy: The Memoirs and Letters of Rudger Clawson at the Utah Territorial Penitentiary, 1884–87*, 111–18. See also SLH, May 14, 1886; all Salt Lake City newspapers reported the lengthy interview.

7. That same day Elder Cannon recorded his own observations: "The interview had with Bro. Snow and the brethren yesterday by the Gov. and party was published in full in the morning's *Tribune*. After making his proposition to Bro. Snow yesterday and it was refused, the Governor said, 'Well if your people do

not accept our offer you surely cannot call the consequences persecution.' 'No,' replied Bro. Snow, 'no more than we call that persecution which was heaped upon the Savior by the Jews, or upon the early Christians by the Romans.' The *Tribune* calls the Gov's visit a fruitless one and blames Bro. Snow mostly for its failure, though the fact is that the latter did not utter a word either for or against the proposition" (AHCJ, May 14, 1886).

CHAPTER 8

1. Space limitation precludes inclusion of the full minutes of this meeting; however, those interested in viewing them can find them in the original and complete version of Whitney's *Latter Leaves* manuscript.
2. Elder Cannon's record of this meeting states: "At 3:30 p.m. a meeting of all the brethren was held in [bunkhouse] No. 3 when the Governor's offer of pardon to us was considered, and also the advisability of replying in writing to the same. A number of the brethren spoke, and I also made a few remarks advocating the sending of a brief concise and pointed reply. Bro. Snow also favored the proposal. A few of the brethren were opposed to it" (AHCJ, May 17, 1886).
3. Elder Cannon recorded a summary of some of President Snow's remarks to his fellow prisoners, shared at around the same time the document answering Governor West was being formalized: "During the evening I was listening to the testimony of Bro. Snow concerning Plural Marriage. He states that the Prophet Joseph Smith himself related the revelation to him in April of the year 1843 in July of which year it is purported to have been given. Bro. Snow's Sister, Eliza, was one of several other wives which the Prophet had previous to that time" (AHCJ, May 22, 1886).
4. Yet not all news was bleak. Perhaps unknown to Orson Whitney, good news secretly reached President Snow in early June: "Word came from F. S. Richards to be communicated only to Bro. Snow and myself so that it would be kept in the greatest secrecy, that the segregation subject will be brought again before the U.S. Supreme Court in the Autumn, and it is thought that the decision cannot be anything but favorable to us, as there are some circumstances connected with the affair which cause him to believe such will be the result. These reasons could not be now explained" (AHCJ, June 1, 1886). Soon thereafter further hopeful news came: "Word has been received from lawyers that when Bro. Snow has served six months of his time an effort will be made to have him released on a writ of *habeas corpus*" (AHCJ, June 17, 1886).
5. A notoriety that Judge Powers's Utah record, especially during the Ogden and Salt Lake election campaigns of 1889–90, has done nothing to diminish.
6. It is said that President Cleveland, learning more of the man Powers than he knew when he appointed him to office, and doubtless well aware of his Utah record, took him by the forelock and withdrew the nomination before it should be rejected by the Senate.
7. Along with writing letters to family and friends, President Snow also felt to celebrate holidays to the extent allowed: "Bro. Snow called some of us brethren together to consult about exercises for the Fourth of July in the yard" (AHCJ, June 12, 1886).

8. Elder Cannon recorded: "Bro. Snow is quite sick today with a cold and headache," and "Bro. Snow is still quite unwell" (AHCJ, March 25 & 26, 1886).
9. Of this visit from President Snow's sister and friends, Elder Cannon wrote: "I was called outside together with Bros. Snow and Stuart, to see Sister E. R. Snow Smith, F. S. Richards and wife and Sister Jane Richards. All were well and report everything progressing satisfactorily on the outside. Bro. Richards speaks in the highest terms of George Ticknor Curtis who assisted him in Bro. Snow's case before the Supreme Court. Sister Smith is looking remarkably well considering her great age of nearly 80 years" (AHCJ, June 8, 1886).
10. Elder Cannon also described this meeting of Dyer with Snow: "Marshal Dyer had a long conversation with Bro. Snow in the afternoon in which he remarked that he intended to do what he could towards granting passes to plural wives until he received other advice from Attorney General Garland. Bro. Snow gave him a testimony of the truth, and was much pleased with the way in which Mr. Dyer questioned and listened. I believe that Mr. Dyer at present desires to do what is right by everybody" (AHCJ, July 1, 1886). Not long before this meeting, Dyer had made his first visit to the prison, for which he was now responsible: "Between one and five p.m. three bells drove us back into the yard and our new marshal Dyer, who took his place yesterday, entered and inspected the various buildings. He called Bros. Snow, Dinwoodey and Cooper and spoke a few words with them. He spoke very kindly and promised to see if he could not favor us with the local papers" (AHCJ, June 18, 1886).

CHAPTER 9

1. Activities of the celebration were detailed in the *Deseret News* (See Clawson, *Prisoner for Polygamy*, 122–23, 138n.1).
2. See AHCJ, July 5–6, 1886.
3. "Notable Reunion of Weber Stake," DN, June 15, 1901. Other historians have pointed out that Clawson's account improved with age and retelling, with the main element improved being the feelings of some few of the other Brethren present, who were less enthusiastic, feeling it perhaps unwise to take part in such a sacred ceremonial act inside the walls of a filthy and degrading prison. Elder Cannon was one of these: "We had a meeting of the brethren in a room in the afternoon . . . Bro. Snow read the history of the celebration of the 24th of July in [18]76. . . . Bro. Naisbitt also read a poem about our imposition entitled 'An Angel on the Wall.' Bro. Greenwell sang a song after which at Bro. Snow's suggestion we all arose to our feet and shouted "Hosanna, Hosanna, Hosanna, to God and the Lamb. Amen, Amen and Amen." Into this latter I could not enter with spirit and I felt badly about it because I thought my heart was wrong, until on speaking with Geo. Lambert, Royal Young and others I found their feelings were like mine in this matter. This comforted me" (AHCJ, July 24, 1886). By mid-August, Elder Cannon had finished serving his term and was released: "At night a sort of ovation was held in our room in honor of my expected departure. The speeches made were all made up of praises for me. Mr. Johnson, while acknowledging his prejudice against our people and religion, said that I would stand among the first

on the list of those whom he thought were trying to approach the example set by our great Master. He made many other expressions of the highest praise. . . . Bros. Snow, Naisbitt, Lambert, Clawson, Foulger and others all gave me words of encouragement and praise. I made my valedictory in which I thanked all for their kind feelings. I do not believe there is a man in the yard but what feels kindly towards me" (AHCJ, August 17, 1886).

CHAPTER 10

None

CHAPTER 11

1. His daughter, Mrs. Dunford.
2. Quotations taken from March 6, 1887, discourse given in the Brigham City Tabernacle, as cited in *Millennial Star*, vol. 39, no. 16 (April 18, 1887), 241–46; also found in CD 1:23–29.

CHAPTER 12

1. Elder Snow, on leaving the Penitentiary, declined the customary twenty dollars provided by the Government for liberated convicts, with the remark to Marshal Dyer that "Uncle Sam" would need it before he got through his work of putting down Mormonism.
2. See Walker, *Qualities that Count*, 212. In a letter dated June 28, 1887, to President Joseph F. Smith, then in Hawaii on the underground, President Franklin D. Richards wrote, "It has been known some time past that the President [John Taylor]'s health was failing—that at times his mental faculties refused to act or if at all but very sluggishly—with almost entire loss of memory of what had been recently transpired" (as found in Scott G. Kenney Collection, MS 587, Box 4; fdr. 1). The letter also requested President Smith to keep the health information confidential.
3. The matters involving John Q. Cannon's troubles are much too complex to detail here. Those wishing to explore the subject further should see Cannon, "The Tragic Matter of Louie Wells and John Q. Cannon," 126–90; and Horne, *An Apostle's Record*, 38, 84–86, 91.
4. Walker, *Qualities that Count*, 195–96.
5. Ibid., 201.
6. Ibid., 201.
7. Ibid., 202.
8. JHSJ, January 4, 1882.
9. JHSJ, October 16, 1882.
10. Walker, *Qualities that Count*, 208–9.
11. Ibid., 213. In relation to President George Q. Cannon, Walker wrote: "The personalities of John Taylor and George Q. Cannon created their own social

discord. Cannon, who bore the brunt of the succession controversy, had great intellectual and administrative gifts, as well as Christian virtue. Nevertheless, he lacked the politician's easy, personal touch that might have allowed many of his associates to like him as much as they admired him. Yet, as Woodruff observed, the charges brought against Cannon mainly concerned 'personality' and not 'substance.' The most potentially serious accusation was his gaining control of the Bullion-Beck consecrated property [stock] during Taylor's decline, the full details of which still wait extended historical analysis. However, in Cannon's defense, the matter was investigated during the Woodruff succession, and no charge of wrongdoing was leveled against him, then or later" (*Qualities that Count*, 222). At President Franklin D. Richards's funeral, President Cannon himself publicly alluded to past relationships with Richards and other quorum members: "I think I ought to appreciate Brother Franklin D. Richards more than anyone else. There are many reasons for this. I was his junior in the Quorum of the Twelve Apostles. Some years ago I was called upon to stand in the First Presidency. This brought me into relations with the older members of the Quorum of the Twelve that were very peculiar. Now, I cannot recall any incident where Brother Franklin ever showed any feeling but that of great respect to me. . . . I need not mention the other brethren now and their conduct, but I can dwell upon his, and it has left an impression upon me that can never be eradicated" (DN, December 16, 1899).

12. LJNJ, October 6, 1887.

13. JHSJ, August 3, 1887.

14. Ibid., September 9, 1887.

15. Ibid., October 5, 1887.

16. FDRJ, February 27, 1888. Historian Davis Bitton has written of President Cannon: "His critics in the Church, especially in the 1890s, considered his financial judgment faulty, and that case can be made." However, "when charges of wrongdoing were leveled, he did not run for cover or start shredding documents. He brought forth his diary and explained what he had done and with whose approval he had done it" (Bitton, *George Q. Cannon: A Biography*, 455–56).

17. See FDRJ, March 14, 1888.

18. JHSJ, March 20 & 21, 1888, and FDRJ March 21 & 22, 1888.

19. Walker, *Qualities that Count*, 216–17; see also JHSJ, March 23, 1888 and FDRJ, March 23, 1888—"President Wilford Woodruff decided no First Presidency now!"

20. JHSJ, March 26, 1888

21. JHSJ, March 27, 1888.

22. Along with the references given below, further information about the dedication of the Manti Temple can be found in Glenn R. Stubbs, "A History of the Manti Temple," and Hargis, "A Folk History of the Manti Temple: A Study of the Folklore and Traditions connected with the Settlement of Manti, Utah, and the Building of the Temple."

23. Elder B. H. Roberts also mentions the following in connection with the dedication: "One item mentioned by President Woodruff about the private dedicatory services at Manti is of more than passing interest. 'Before leaving,' he writes, 'I consecrated upon the altar the Seer Stone that Joseph Smith found by revelation some thirty feet under the earth (ground), and carried by him

through life.' This is the very Seer Stone that the Prophet Joseph Smith used part of the time when translating the Book of Mormon; the one he took from the well he was digging with his brother Hyrum, near Palmyra . . ." (Cited in Roberts, *Comprehensive History of the Church* 6:230). It is not currently known how or why President Woodruff consecrated the seer stone at this time and place. Further information on this seer stone, which had evidently only recently come into the possession of President Woodruff, is found in chapter 21.
24. These summaries and quotations are cited in Rasmussen, *The Manti Temple*, 45–56; see also Roberts, *Comprehensive History of the Church* 6: 230. Elder John Henry Smith noted that after the service, those in attendance were allowed to go "through the building"; also that "It was a day never to be forgotten by those present" (JHSJ, May 21, 1888). His comments for the session held on the twenty-third were likewise ecstatic: "The people passed through the rooms of the house. 2,200 persons were said to be present. The heavens were opened. Sacred choirs sang, Angles were seen, Hallo's of light encircled the head of the Priesthood and joy filled our hearts. It was the day of days and none present will ever forget it" (JHSJ, May 23, 1888). Likewise, Elder Francis M. Lyman wrote his view that it was "the most impressive and the most important since the dedication of the Kirtland Temple. . . . I never before felt so plainly the power of the Holy Ghost. The heart of every Saint was convinced beyond a doubt that the dedication was acceptable to the Lord, that He has placed His name upon it." (FMLJ, 120–21).
25. Roberts, *Comprehensive History of the Church* 6:231.

CHAPTER 13

1. "Last evening Pres. Woodruff told me that he purposed to bring before the Apostles before next conference the question of organizing the First Presidency" (LJNJ, January 23, 1889).
2. LJNJ, April 5, 1889. Elder John Henry Smith's shorter account states: "President Wilford Woodruff stated he felt it was time to organize the First Presidency. Lorenzo Snow spoke and moved that Wilford Woodruff be president and name his Counselors. All present spoke in favor of organizing the presidency and Bro. Wilford Woodruff was unanimously sustained. He chose for Counselors George Q. Cannon and Joseph F. Smith. After a few explanations by some of the brethren they were both unanimously accepted. Bro. Lorenzo Snow was made President of the Twelve and Franklin D. Richards Historian of the church" (JHSJ, April 5, 1889).
3. Further explanation comes from Elder Clawson's journal: "Apostle Teasdale spoke briefly and said he very much regretted the absence of Pres. Brigham Young [Jr]. When these meetings were first inaugurated, the Apostles were not fully united and Pres. Snow's purpose was to unite the brethren that they might be presented to the Presidency as being of one heart and one mind. Upon a certain occasion at the close of one of our quarterly conferences, he presented the quorum of apostles to the Presidency as being fully united and said that in this the desire of his heart had been gratified. It would be a calamity, said Apostle Teasdale, if this body of men were divided" (RCJ, April 2, 1902).

4. LJNJ, April 10, 1889. See also JHSJ, April 9, 1889.
5. FDRJ, October 2 & 3, 1889. Elder John Henry Smith recorded: "President Wilford Woodruff presented the names of M. W. Merrill, A. H. Lund and A. H. Cannon to fill the Quorum of Twelve and all present did endorse them" (JHSJ, Oct. 2, 1889).
6. AHCJ, October 6, 1889.
7. Ibid., October 10, 1889.
8. FDRJ, April 9, 1890.
9. JHSJ, April 9, 1890.
10. FDRJ, April 9, 1890. Elder Abraham H. Cannon's account of this meeting and President Snow's remarks to the Quorum is the most detailed available: "At 7 p.m. I met in the Historian's office, where President Lorenzo Snow had requested our quorum to meet. . . . Bro. Snow stated that he desired the quorum to meet together occasionally to talk over different matters and to unite our hearts and feelings together. Where ill feelings existed we should express them and have our differences amicably arranged. The brethren all felt that the union which should prevail in our quorum did not exist, and were glad that President Snow had been moved upon to call such meetings as were suggested. It was thought best for us to fast and meet tomorrow, and spend the day in expressing ourselves fully and freely. At this John W. Taylor arose and said he could not meet as he had hard feelings against Father [George Q. Cannon], because the latter had expressed his disapproval of the settlement that was made with John Beck in the [B. B. &] Champion mine affairs, and John W. felt that Father had accused him of misappropriating funds and he would not rest easy under the imputation. Bro. Thatcher felt that John W. should visit and talk with the offender privately in this matter, and seek reconciliation between themselves. In this view all agreed and John promised to see if this matter could not be settled in the morning before 10 am. to which time we adjourned" (AHCJ, April 9, 1890; see also Horne, *An Apostle's Record*, 144–48).
11. FDRJ, August 6, 1890.
12. See FDRJ, April 8, 9, and September 15, 1890.

CHAPTER 14

1. Whitney, *Through Memory's Halls*, 203.
2. See Doctrine and Covenants: Official Declaration 1; see also Clark, *Messages of the First Presidency* 3:195. A second account, from the journal of Abraham H. Cannon, said: "The Church authorities were presented and sustained. O. F. Whitney then read the Articles of our Faith and on motion of Franklin D. Richards they were accepted by the Church as its rules of guidance. Pres. Woodruff's manifesto was then read, and Lorenzo Snow moved that recognizing Pres. Woodruff as the only man who now holds the keys of the sealing ordinance upon the earth, we sustain him in his action in this matter. The vote was unanimous" (AHCJ, October 6, 1890).
3. For some discussion on Quorum deliberations about the manifesto, See FDRJ, September 24, 25, 30, 1890 and AHCJ, same dates.

4. AHCJ, October 27, 1890.
5. JHSJ, January 28, 1891.
6. FDRJ, January 28, 1891.
7. Ibid., January 29, 1891.
8. Ibid., January 30, 1891.
9. Ibid., March 28, 1891.
10. "Regretted Brother John Henry Smith having as he thought to take the stump on politics and hope that no other of us might find it necessary to do so" (FDRJ, July 9, 1891).
11. AHCJ, August 20, 1891.
12. AHCJ, November 12, 1891; see also AHCJ, October 20, 1891.
13. President Young's ordination of his eleven-year-old son as an apostle was likely more of a father's patriarchal blessing and is unique in the history of the Church for age. John W. was not then or later set apart as a member of the Quorum of the Twelve, and when it was decided by President Snow and the other brethren that the time of entrance into the Quorum of the Twelve fixed the date of seniority, John W. had no claim to succession. See note 15 below.
14. See AHLJ, October 18, 1901, for a short description of John W. Young and rumors of financial malfeasance.
15. For a review of Elder John W. Young's circumstances, see Todd Compton, "John Willard Young, Brigham Young, and the Development of Succession in the LDS Church," 111–35, especially 125. See also Travis Q. Mecham, "Changes in Seniority to the Quorum of the Twelve Apostles of the Church of Jesus Christ of Latter-day Saints," USU Master's Thesis, 42–53.
16. Remarks of Heber J. Grant, cited in Joseph Anderson, *Prophets I have Known*, 39–40. Another account of this meeting in relation to Elder Young, but which excludes the reference to President Snow's remarks, is found in AHCJ, October 3, 1891: "Pres. Snow was just about to give his views when the Presidency entered, and upon hearing what was under discussion Father [G. Q. Cannon] read a letter which he received yesterday from John W. who is in London. Therein he expresses his faith in the success of his plans, but regrets that unforeseen difficulties prevented their consummation at an earlier date. He expresses a wish that his name be withheld at Conference, and that for the present he be relieved of his position. It was therefore unanimously decided that this course be taken and a statement be made that at his request his name is not presented."
17. FDRJ, October 3, 1891.
18. AHCJ, January 12, 1892.
19. FDRJ, January 13, 1892. It is likely that Elder Richards recorded the gist of President Snow's couplet, but mixed up the words slightly while retaining the correct meaning.
20. AHCJ, April 1, 1892
21. Ibid., April 6, 1892; see also Roberts, *Comprehensive History of the Church*, 6: 232–33.
22. Ibid., July 12, 1892.
23. Ibid., July 13, 1892.
24. Lorenzo Snow, Brigham City, Dec. 3, 1892, "An Account of a private interview with Pres. Woodruff, Brigham City 1892, Dec. 3" [date recorded]

CHL, MS 3558 [An account of a private interview with Pres. Woodruff, Dec. 2, 1892, at Salt Lake City], emphasis added; see also Durham and Heath, *Succession in the Church*, 103–4. The Durham and Heath account omits the last five words of the final sentence.
25. AHCJ, March 21, 1893.
26. AHCJ, May 18, 1893. Elder Marriner W. Merrill wrote the following of this occasion (April 20): "I met with the Priesthood, First Presidency, Twelve, Presidents of Stakes and Counselors, and Presiding Bishopric, in the Temple at 10 a.m. today, all fasting. We remained in the Temple until 6 p.m. All joined in the Prayer Circle clothed (115) in the Celestial Room, the largest Circle ever convened or got together in the Church. All of the Twelve present and Presidents Cannon and J. F. Smith spoke today, President Woodruff and Apostle Moses Thatcher both being sick and not able to be there. We had a glorious time and all felt well and all testified at these meetings to sustaining the First Presidency in all things, political as well as all other matters" (MWMJ, April 20, 1893).
27. Jenson, *Autobiography of Andrew Jenson*, 205.
28. Roberts, *Comprehensive History of the Church* 6:236.
29. RCJ, April 3, 1901.
30. JH, May 28, 1896.
31. AHCJ, June 23, 1893. These instructions were given before the sealing annex was built, and there was evidently no security personnel beyond a doorman that checked recommends.
32. AHCJ, May 20, 1893.
33. "From 1893 to 1896 Bro. [LeRoi] Snow acted as librarian in the Salt Lake Temple" (as quoted in Jenson, *LDS Biographical Encyclopedia* 3:717).
34. As quoted in Bitton, "Six Months in the Life of a Mormon Teenager," *New Era*, May 1977, 45. It now requires First Presidency permission to tour the temple.
35. As quoted in Torres, "History of Minnie Jensen Snow," December 1, 1982. Rhea died in 1976. As for Rhea's mother, Minnie got something in her eye while traveling on a train, which eventually caused a malignant cancerous growth resulting in severe eye pain for years, as early twentieth-century medical skill was incapable of resolving the problem. Eye cancer was the cause of her death on January 2, 1908.
36. AHCJ, October 3, 1893.
37. JETJ, December 6, 1893.
38. This account concludes with the statement: "Ella Jensen was born August 3, 1871. The experience related in this article occurred March 3, 1891, in her twentieth year. She married Henry Wight, March 20, 1895. They are now living in Juniper, Idaho. Of their eight children six are living and they have six grandchildren" (Snow, "Raised from the Dead," *Improvement Era*, October 1929).
39. The following document is prefaced by this introduction: "The miracle of the return of the spirit of Ella Jensen Wight, formerly of Brigham City, Utah, who on Feb. 5, 1934 related to Flora Belnap & Dr. George Ramsey in the Celestial Room of the Salt Lake Temple the enclosed statement that Pres. Lorenzo Snow administered to her dead body saying, 'Ella come back' and left the house telling her parents to watch her. When her spirit entered her body she opened her eyes and said, 'Where is President Snow?' Ella J. Wight and her husband Henry Wight

at the time of this narration by Mrs. Wight. Flora Belnap." Also a location and date: "Salt Lake City, Feb. 5, 1934" ("Ella Jensen Wight," CHL, MS d374).
40. The document concludes with the following signatures: "Signed, Ella J. Wight, Juniper, Idaho, wife of Henry Wight. In the presence of Flora Belnap, Dr. George Ramsey; 50 No. West Temple, Salt Lake City. Harriet A." ("Ella Jensen Wight," CHL, MS d374).
41. RCJ, October 14, 1900. Further authentication and details of this miracle can be found in Romney, *The Life of Lorenzo Snow*, 406–16, especially 416.
42. See for example, the remarks of Elder George Teasdale, who taught the law of tithing with vigor in general conference, October 6, 1894; cited in DN, December 7, 1894.
43. AWJ, July 31, 1895.
44. FMLJ, August 3, 1893, 138.
45. AHCJ, April 3, 1894.
46. Ibid., April 2, 1894.
47. Ibid., October 3, 1894. At another meeting a few weeks later, politics became the provoking issue; see AHCJ, October 25, 1894.
48. Ibid., January 17, 1895.
49. As quoted in Clark, *Messages of the First Presidency* 3:265–66.
50. For an early result of President Snow's response to the letter from the Woodruff presidency, see Clark, *Messages of the First Presidency* 3:323–24, where in 1899 prospective missionaries are requested to enroll for a year's worth of instruction at a Church college.
51. AHCJ, April 20, 1895.
52. "Pres. Snow spoke for a short time. He felt that these meetings should be most sacred to us, and nothing should be allowed to interfere with our prompt attendance at them. Bro. Thatcher would be better in his health if he would attend the meetings of his Quorum. Bro. Merrill has no reasonable excuse for his absence. The early apostles of this dispensation on many occasions quarreled, and were not united; so was it also with the apostles in the time of Jesus; but God has given us a union which I hope will ever continue. We must not oppose the authorities over us, but do as David said was right—not raise our hands or voices against the Lord's anointed" (AHCJ, August 6, 1895).
53. For further information regarding Elder Grant's Japanese mission experience, see Walker, *Qualities that Count*, 231–62.
54. AHCJ, August 8, 1895.

CHAPTER 15

1. JHSJ, March 5, 1896.
2. Ibid., March 19, 1896.
3. Ibid., March 26, 1896.
4. JH, April 2, 1896. During these years the living allowances of the First Council of Seventy were also reviewed. J. Golden Kimball recorded: "On May 4th had written the Presidency asking for an [monetary] appropriation. While doctoring my foot this morning, received the following letter from Bro. George Reynolds:

Dear Bro. Golden:

Please call on Bro. [James] Jack. The First Presidency inform me that permanent arrangements have been made regarding allowances to the members of the First Council, and that Bro. Jack has been given full instructions in relation thereto.

I was in a wonderful [distressed] state of mind, knowing that if any radical retrenchment was made in my case I could not make ends meet.

At once went to Bro. Jack and learned that $100 per month was the maximum, and we were to do on as much less as possible.

No more appropriations were to be made, but we were to call on Bro. Jack, the treasurer.

Felt very much better although it is close picking when you get T.O.S. [tithing office scrip] and everything [priced] so high" (JGKJ, May 5, 1898).

5. JH, April 2, 1896; see also JHSJ, April 2, 1896.

6. Evidently the First Presidency and Twelve felt there was a definite difference between a *fixed church salary* for stake president's and bishop's regular continuous service in their callings, which was here abolished, and a remuneration for the specific duty of handling the tithes paid by ward members at the year-end tithing settlement. The "General Instructions" for the annual tithing settlement sent by the First Presidency to all stake presidents and bishops for 1899 and 1900 indicate that bishops and stake tithing clerks divided between them 10 percent of the tithing collected from ward members, for "handling the tithes," none of which was actual cash, since *all* cash was to be forwarded to President Snow. At this time, most tithing was paid in-kind, meaning livestock, produce, and other such farm-produced commodities. The 1900 instructions stated: "Respecting the 10 per cent which was authorized by the late President John Taylor, as compensation to the Bishops and Clerks, the Presidency and Bishops of each stake will please meet at the first convenient date in the new year, when a careful estimate should be made of the value of the services rendered by the Stake Tithing Clerk in compiling the annual Stake reports, which should be mutually agreed upon between the Stake Presidency and the Bishops. In making said allowance, *no services should be considered other than for compiling the annual reports as stated above.* After his salary has been determined upon, it should be deducted from the 10 per cent and the balance distributed to the Bishops according to the amount and value of the services rendered in handling the tithes of their respective wards. In making this distribution, consideration should be given as to the kinds of tithes received in each ward and the labor necessary to handle same to the best interests of the Church" (as quoted in Clark, *Messages of the First Presidency* 3:332; see also 322, emphasis in original). As for stake presidency "salaries" (10–12 percent), by April 1898 they were being paid strictly in produce. A letter from President Woodruff to one stake president said: "The sum of $1000 has been appropriated in favor of your Stake Presidency to be drawn in whole or in part by them during the current year in *equitable produce* at tithing office prices, and you are authorized and requested to place the same to their credit, as follows: Orson Smith, $600; S. M. Molen, $200; Isaac Smith, $200. At the close of the year please report the amount drawn by each of the brethren on account of this appreciation, and a regular order will be issued to cover the same" (ibid., 297–98; emphasis in original).

7. JH, April 5, 1896.
8. Ibid., April 6, 1896. Elder Abraham H. Cannon's journal provides some background on Elder Thatcher's past history with his quorum: "Pres. Woodruff said LeGrand Young had suggested that the Twelve issue a document containing the statement that the Saints are politically free, but it was felt that we had already done enough of this kind of thing, and the fear was expressed that even were we to do as suggested, Moses Thatcher might refuse to sign with us. Pres. Woodruff said that Moses Thatcher's discontent began at the death of Pres. Taylor, when he sought to rule the Twelve, at which time he also attacked Father in a vicious manner, and charged him with great wrongs, which he had never done. Heber J. Grant said he had seconded Moses' efforts to down Father at that time, but he had since seen the error of his ways, and repented of them, which Moses had never done" (AHCJ, October 17, 1895; see also AHCJ, December 12, 1895).
9. AWJ, April 6, 1896.
10. Ibid., April 7, 1896.
11. JH, April 7, 1896.
12. Ibid., June 4, 11, 1898.
13. Ibid., July 19, 1896. Arthur Winter wrote of him: "He was only 37 years old, and was the youngest member of the Quorum of Apostles. He had a splendid physique, and to all appearances looked as if he would live a long time. But he was an untiring worker and was loaded down with business responsibility. From early morn till late at night he worked at a rapid pace, and without doubt it has told on his system. He was greatly beloved by the people. I esteemed him as a very noble man and one where life was full of great promise. His father, President George Q. Cannon, as well as his family and kindred, will no doubt severely feel the blow" (AWJ, July 19, 1896; see also JH, July 20, 1896).
14. Ibid., July 26, 1896; see also AWJ, July 26, 1896. For a biographical review of Elder Abraham H. Cannon's life, including his last days, see Horne, ed., *An Apostle's Record: The Journals of Abraham H. Cannon*, 29-52.
15. Ibid., October 1, 1896; see also JH, April 24, 1899.
16. Wilford Woodruff, GC, October 5, 1896.
17. Lorenzo Snow, GC, October 5, 1896.
18. This unnamed "brother" sent as a last-ditch attempt to rescue Moses Thatcher may have been Elder B. H. Roberts.
19. JH, November 19, 1896.
20. Ibid., November 20, 1896.
21. Ibid., November 26, 1896. Elder Brigham Young Jr.'s diary indicates that in August 1897 Moses Thatcher "acknowledged that he published President Snow's [private] correspondence [to him] to retaliate for the First Presidency and Twelve speaking about him at conference in explanation of our dropping his, Moses', name from his Quorum the previous conference" (BYJJ, August 7, 1897). More in-depth historical review of Moses Thatcher's troubles with the brethren can be found in Godfrey, "Moses Thatcher in the Dock: His Trials, The Aftermath, and His Last Days," 54–88.
22. President Snow had little trouble with one member of the Twelve in particular. After a meeting of the Twelve in which his actions at a particular stake conference were called into question, Elder Francis M. Lyman recorded: "President Snow

reproved me, and so did Brother Brigham [Young Jr.], for which I thanked them and will profit by it. . . . This has been a glorious day for me—it has taught me humility, a lesson that will last me all my life" (FMLJ, 143). Angus M. Cannon, younger brother of George and president of the Salt Lake Stake (the largest and most influential stake in the Church) was a different story: "In conversation with President Lorenzo Snow, Angus stood his ground when President Snow reprimanded him for being too harsh with one of his members. Said Angus, 'I believe you would be quite as impatient as I am.' President Snow replied, 'I might be worse than you' " (from the Journal of Angus M. Cannon, February 15, 1899; as cited in Cannon, "Angus M. Cannon: Pioneer, President, Patriarch," in Whitaker and Cannon, eds., *Supporting Saints: Life Stories of Nineteenth Century Mormons*, chap. 14).

23. JHSJ, April 1, 1897.

24. Ibid., April 3, 1898.

25. George Q. Cannon journal, as quoted in Bitton, *George Q. Cannon: A Biography*, 415; emphasis in original. In his journal, under November 4, 1889, President Cannon wrote (in reference to his remarks at a meeting held in Cardston, Alberta, Canada): "I testified that the Lord Jesus lived, for I had seen Him and heard His voice, and I had heard the voice of the spirit, speaking to me as one speaketh to another" (ibid., 415, 523n.33).

26. BYJJ, April 3, 1897.

27. Ibid., April 27, 1897.

28. Ibid., September 30, 1897.

29. Correspondence, President Wilford Woodruff to George Q. Cannon, Joseph F. Smith, Lorenzo Snow, and the Twelve Apostles; Salt Lake City, Utah, October 26, 1896; copy in author's possession. The letter went on to state: "I have several sons, any of whom I believe would magnify the Apostleship, if called to it, but I have my mind especially upon one son, and I believe it is the will of God that he should occupy that position. He is a young man, but he is sound, he is virtuous. . . . His name is Abraham Owen Woodruff. . . . Now brethren, I leave this matter with you for your decision, and that you may be directed according to the mind and will of God, is the earnest prayer of Your Brother, Wilford Woodruff [signed]."

30. JHSJ, September 30, 1897.

31. Elder Brigham Young Jr., for instance, found himself praying that God would help him over his feelings of rebelliousness at Owen's call (see BYJJ, September 30, 1897).

32. FDRJ, October 7, 1897.

33. JHSJ, December 23, 1897. If President Cannon had a failing, it was his near blindness when it came to the faults of his children, and he seemed unable to fully recognize or acknowledge to himself how morally weak his son was—Frank was the opposite of Abraham in virtue and most of the Twelve knew it. Even Davis Bitton, President Cannon's biographer, acknowledged that Cannon's contemporaries noticed this tendency: "As some of his children, especially John Q. and Frank, became assertive adults with their own careers, they created opponents, who in turn looked upon George Q. as blind to the faults of his own family"—*very* generously put (Bitton, *George Q. Cannon: A Biography*, 455–56).

34. JHSJ, December 26, 1897. Of this meeting and his personal feelings, Elder Young's diary noted: "Note from President Lorenzo Snow informed me that John Henry Smith and Heber J. Grant would call [on me] at noon. Our chat was a long one. Decided that the First Presidency should admit us (the Twelve) into their confidence. Pres Cannon carries [influences] President Wilford Woodruff [to agree] with him; Joseph F. Smith is [then] obliged to succumb [concede] to what he believes to be wrong in financial matters. It is our [the three men meeting] opinion that President Cannon will bankrupt the Church if allowed to proceed with Frank J. Cannon and Nephi Clayton as aids [agents]. These men he [Cannon] places before all others in money matters and they have more say in the disposition of church funds than everybody else combined. I believe the Lord desires those upon whom the burden will soon fall [the Twelve] to regulate this matter. If the Quorum of the Twelve and First Presidency were going to remain it would be a different thing, but a short time and the Twelve will be the presiding authorities. . . . God help us or we are financially ruined. President Cannon's wild schemes have done it" (BYJJ, December 26, 1897). It should be remembered that Elder Young evinced an emotional temperament, and often disagreed with President Cannon's financial policies. See below note also.

35. JHSJ, January 4, 1898. For this meeting Elder Young recorded: "President Snow called upon Brother Owen Woodruff, followed by Brother Taylor [to speak]. Then President Snow spoke on the condition of the First Presidency, followed by Brother Teasdale (who was in favor of our minding our own business); John Henry Smith, Brigham Young Jr., and Franklin D. Richards all had complaints to make. I wanted a Trustee-in-trust appointed to relieve [replace] President Woodruff and for the First Presidency to correct all mistakes, especially President Cannon, so that he would not be humiliated when the First Presidency was dissolved. John Q. Cannon and Frank J. Cannon would be relieved as soon as the Twelve arranged matters [when presiding]. Brother Richards did not agree with me. I related a dream about relief coming to President Woodruff" (BYJJ, January 4, 1898).

36. BYJJ, January 5, 1898.

37. JHSJ, January 6, 1898.

38. Ibid., January 7, 1898.

39. Lorenzo Snow, as quoted in George Q. Cannon Journal, January 7, 1898; CHL; as cited in Kimball, *Heber C. Kimball: Mormon Patriarch and Pioneer*, XVn.1; ellipses in original.

40. "Called upon President Lorenzo Snow; had conversation on situation. We agreed perfectly . . . the Twelve are united" "Temple Meeting of the Twelve: little business was done . . . harmony prevailed but still there is a strong feeling that reforms in expenditure of money is an absolute necessity" (BYJJ, January 9 & 13, 1898).

41. See Bell, "The Windows of Heaven Revisited," 52n21, for a recounting from extracts of President Cannon's journal wherein he is reported to have taken the Twelve to task with vigor for desiring input into church financial matters. These journal extracts cannot at present be verified because the Cannon journal is not available to researchers at this time.

42. JHSJ, July 29, 1898.
43. BYJJ, July 12, 1898.

CHAPTER 16

1. LeRoi Snow wrote, without substantiation: "For some time President Woodruff's health had been failing. Nearly every evening President Lorenzo Snow visited him at his home. This particular evening the doctors said that President Woodruff could not live much longer, that he was becoming weaker every day. President Snow was greatly worried. We cannot realize today what a terrible financial condition the Church was in at that time—owing millions of dollars and not being able to pay even the interest on its indebtedness. My father went to his room in the Salt Lake Temple, dressed in his robes of the Priesthood, knelt at the sacred altar in the Holy of Holies in the House of the Lord and there plead to the Lord to spare President Woodruff's life, that President Woodruff might outlive him and that the great responsibility of Church leadership would not fall upon his shoulders. Yet he promised the Lord that he would devotedly perform any duty required at his hands. At this time he was in his eighty-sixth year" (Snow, "An Experience of my Father's"). LeRoi Snow was on a foreign mission (from March 1896 to early March 1899) during President Woodruff's last years and did not personally witness anything related to President Woodruff's health, his death, or his father's experiences becoming President of the Church. LeRoi's account was published thirty-five years after the events he is allegedly describing, and they are not corroborated by other sources; especially concerning President Woodruff's health before his passing. However, it should be noted, for what it is worth, that LeRoi could have learned the details of President Snow's actions from him by letter, or conversation upon his return, or have had access to Lorenzo's personal records, though such is speculative.
2. AWJ, March 1, 1894.
3. JH, September 2, 1898. Another account relates: "Presidents Woodruff and Cannon went to San Francisco two or three weeks ago, and stayed at the residence of Colonel Isaac Trumbo, President Cannon had to return home on account of the sickness of his daughter Vera, but went back again after a day or two here. He said then that President Woodruff was in good health and spirits and enjoying himself very much. Later in the day it was learned that President Woodruff was taken sick somewhat suddenly on Wednesday, but it was not thought to be serous until yesterday. Trouble with his urine was the cause of his death. There is a general feeling of regret that he died away from home" (AWJ, Friday, September 2, 1898).
4. AWJ, September 2, 1898; see also JH, September 1, 1898.
5. JH, September 7, 1898.
6. One confused source, ostensibly traceable to articles by LeRoi Snow, relates that, "For three days and nights, fasting, he supplicated the Lord and waited for an answer" (in Smart, "Lorenzo Snow: Mighty Man of God," 222). Which three days these are supposed to have been is not indicated, if such actually occurred, and becomes perplexing, since the article gives September 2 as the date this "crowning" experience occurred, not three days later on September 5.

Furthermore, Elder Heber J. Grant is twice quoted elsewhere as saying that "Brother Snow told us that he was instructed of the Lord in the Temple, *the night after* President Woodruff died, to organize the Presidency of the Church at once" (see Snow, "An Experience of my Father's," and "From Despair To Freedom Through Tithing," 6). Since President Woodruff died early in the morning of September 2, this would verify that President Snow's crowning experience occurred later that night, but still on the same day.

7. Snow, "An Experience of my Father's"; see also Snow, "The Appearance of the Savior to Pres. Lorenzo Snow." This unpublished version has some serious factual errors not found in the *Improvement Era* version. An abbreviated account is also found in Snow, "From Despair To Freedom Through Tithing," 6.

8. Correspondence, Noah S. Pond to Elder John A. Widstoe, November 12, 1946; located in CHL, unpublished. This visitation by Jesus to President Snow as recorded by Allie Pond and related by LeRoi Snow was officially investigated for verification, resulting in the aforementioned letter in the main text. Elder Widstoe had written the following inquiry to Noah Pond:

"I have been asked by the Council of the Twelve to look into the historical evidence concerning the divine manifestation received by President Snow shortly before his accession to the Presidency of the Church. Your splendid and devoted wife is reported by LeRoi C. Snow to have heard her grandfather tell her in some detail of this manifestation. According to this report, President Snow is reported to have said that he saw the Savior in the passage leading from the Celestial room to his office, now used as the sealing room [office]. Your wife must have told you the story often.

"Would you be good enough to tell me if the report is essentially correct. We all know from unquestioned evidence that President Snow had a divine manifestation in the temple at that time. Did he tell his granddaughter that he actually saw the Savior and where? All this is merely to complete the story for the brethren here and for others who may be interested. It seems to me that you are the best living witness" (Correspondence, Elder John A. Widstoe to Noah S. Pond, October 30, 1946; CHL, unpublished). Alice Pond died in 1943, three years previous to this exchange. Noah Pond's quoted statement, "in passing from his room he halted at the designated spot," is the best verification available of LeRoi Snow's assertions of exactly where in the Salt Lake Temple Jesus Christ appeared to President Snow. This location is thought to be at some midpoint in the large balcony hallway, above the main staircase, between the celestial room and what now serves as a temple sealer's office but in 1898 was probably President Snow's living quarters. See Snow, "An Experience of my Father's."

9. JH, September 13, 1898.

10. Snow, "An Experience of my Father's." Elder Grant's affirmation of this experience is also related in Snow, "From Despair To Freedom Through Tithing," 6. These two accounts originating with Elder Heber J. Grant are the best confirmation we have as to the actual date, September 2, the date President Woodruff died, that Jesus appeared in the temple to President Snow.

11. As quoted in Snow, "From Despair To Freedom Through Tithing," 6.

12. Quotation taken from "An Account of a private interview with Pres. Woodruff, Brigham City, 1892, Dec. 3." CHL, MS 3558.

13. Joseph F. Smith, GC, November 10, 1901.
14. Smith, *Life of Joseph F. Smith*, 324. Further confirmation of President Snow's statement is found in the journal of Elder Rudger Clawson: "[Lorenzo Snow said] I would like to say a few words upon a subject of interest to the Latter-day Saints. . . . [Concerning the passing of President Woodruff] He remarked that it was very sad and, addressing himself to me, said: Brother Joseph, Pres. Cannon will not live to lead the church but you will. I say to you that whenever the First Presidency become disorganized, it is the duty of the Twelve to effect a reorganization at the earliest possible moment. It is the will of the Lord that such action should be taken. Such was the counsel of Pres. Snow, and we have been led to reorganize the First Presidency and fill up the quorum of Apostles, and in all this there has been with us a spirit of unanimity, although some people may find fault with our action and feel that it was premature. There will always be some among us to find fault, I suppose" (RCJ, October 25, 1901).
15. JH, Saturday, September 3, 1898.
16. AWJ, September 4, 1898 and JH, September 4 & 5, 1898.
17. JH, September 7, 1898.
18. AWJ, September 8, 1898.
19. DN, September 8, 1898.
20. JHSJ, September 9, 1898.
21. AHLJ, September 9, 1898. See also BYJJ, September 9, 1898.
22. JH, September 9, 1898. See also JHSJ, September 9, 1898, and AHLJ, September 9, 1898.
23. JHSJ, September 9, 1898; The Journal History states, "A new desk was purchased for the use of President Snow" (September 9, 1898).
24. JH, September 9, 1898.
25. JHSJ, September 10, 1898.
26. See JH, September 13, 1898.
27. AWJ, September 10, 1898.
28. It is interesting to note that Frank J. Cannon, a morally corrupt man, was at this time excused and therefore not present for the highly spiritual discussions and actions which ensued at this meeting. For a review of the life and character of Frank Cannon, see Cannon, "Wives and Other Women: Love, Sex, and Marriage in the Lives of John Q. Cannon, Frank J. Cannon, and Abraham H. Cannon," 83–95. In later years, Frank became arguably the most prominent and visible anti-Mormon and charismatic enemy the Latter-day Saints have ever had.
29. Regarding the selection of counselors, Albert R. Lyman, paraphrasing his father's written journal record of this meeting, wrote: "When they had voted unanimously for Lorenzo Snow, he told them it was as clear to him as anything he had ever seen in his life, that George Q. Cannon and Joseph F. Smith should be his counselors" (Lyman, *Biography: Francis Marion Lyman, Apostle*, 148).
30. JH, Tuesday, September 13, 1898. See also BYJJ & JHSJ, September 13, 1898, and DN, September 13, 1898 (this notice was written by "Geo. F. Gibbs, Secretary. Salt Lake City, Utah, September 13, 1898," with a short biographical notice about President Snow). Another brief account of this historic meeting relates: "Went to meeting at the President's Office. Conference was appointed for Oct. 6th. Bro. Geo. F. Gibbs was appointed clerk of the Twelve. . . . The question

of electing a Trustee-in-trust came up. It was seen at once that we cannot do anything at all without such a man. Bro. Francis M. Lyman said that he had felt that we ought to organize a First Presidency at once. Several brethren expressed the same opinion. Bro. Lorenzo Snow then arose and said that once when he felt the weight of the heavy responsibility which had come upon him he went and offered the signs of the Priesthood and asked the Lord for direction. At once he received an answer to his prayer and it came as clear and with power that he knew the Lord's will. It was that the First Presidency should be organized at once. The motion was then made. He chose George Q. Cannon and Joseph F. Smith for his counselors. The First Presidency was then sustained by unanimous vote of the quorum. Franklin D. Richards was then sustained as President of the Twelve. President Lorenzo Snow was sustained as Trustee-in-trust of the Church. President Lorenzo Snow then told the brethren that he had heard rumors of people thinking that plural marriages could be contracted. He wanted it understood that this cannot be done" (AHLJ, September 13, 1898). An edited version of the Journal History account is found in Durham and Heath, *Succession in the Church*, 108–11.

31. JHSJ, September 13, 1898; see also JH, September 13, 1898.

32. AWJ, September 13, 1898. Elder J. Golden Kimball agreed, writing that "today the First Presidency of the Church was organized. . . . They were unanimous in all that was done. It was very gratifying to learn of their success" (JGKJ, September 13, 1898).

33. JHSJ, September 14, 1898.

34. JH, September 15, 1899. The Journal History further noted: "It is believed that the charges made and published to local Presbyterian ministers in relation to polygamy and its alleged revival in Utah, inspired the solicitation of the foregoing interview." The plural marriage material has been omitted from the text herein.

35. "Unchangeable Love of God," September 18, 1898; as quoted in CD 5: 451–53; see also DN, October 1, 1898, and JH, September 18, 1898. This discourse was printed in both summary and full text form.

36. CD 5:451–53; September 18, 1898; see also DN, October 1, 1898.

37. DN, October 1, 1898; for a description of President Snow's visit and discourse in Brigham City, see JH, October 1, 1898. Later in September, President Snow invited Elder Young into the President's Office for a visit: "Had a chat with President Lorenzo Snow in his office. He said to me 'make yourself at home about this office and about these premises feel perfectly free'" (BYJJ, September 27, 1898).

38. JH, October 3 & 4, 1898. It was also about this time that Elder Brigham Young Jr. recorded further private observations of the challenges faced by President Snow: "I had a long important talk with President Lorenzo Snow. The Lord be with him in his vast labors to correct the gross mistakes which have been made in financial matters. The church is deeply in debt, say $1,500,000, and its moral obligations for loans will be as much more. It stands at the back of the Zion's Savings Bank, and that [institution] seems to have [become] the prey of certain brethren borrowing large sums and depositing worthless mining stock as security. God help us for we are now in the money power of our enemies" (BYJJ, October 1, 1898).

39. JH, October 5, 1898.
40. BYJJ, October 5, 1898.
41. Elder Taylor was a son of President Taylor who had been called (by his father, at age 25) to the Twelve in 1884. In his extemporaneous remarks, he referred to some recent conversations he had had and said: "A gentleman stepped up to me at the Woods Cross station yesterday morning and told me he was going to move to the rural districts and take up land. I want more land, he said, but there is one thing that I do not like to move for, and that it is in the settlement I am going to is in Rhode's Valley, or Kamas Prairie; and I don't like to go for one reason, and that is that I was informed that eight out of every ten of the marriages there have been of such character that the wives have had children before they were married. Now, I CANNOT BELIEVE that in Rhode's Valley the Latter-day Saints are so rotten, as this man stated. I CANNOT BELIEVE that they have so thoroughly rotted in the valley." Further he said: "While conversing with this gentleman another man came up, whose word I could not doubt, and he said: 'I was informed by a lady in Salt Lake who keeps a rooming house, that after the close of practices by the Tabernacle choir, several members come to her rooming house for immoral purposes.' I thought to myself is this possible? Is it possible that we can look upon the beauty of this Salt Lake Tabernacle choir and have a suspicion hanging over them like this? I cannot believe these things'" (October 7, 1898; as quoted in CD 5: 457–62; capitalization in original).
42. President Cannon said: "The remarks which have been made by Elder John W. Taylor have been exceedingly pointed. No doubt there are conditions existing in our settlements, and in this city, that we would be greatly gratified if they could be corrected. It is too true that there are births after the marriage, that are untimely. We have such cases brought to our attention. In some instances the first children are born a little quicker than those subsequently. We deplore this very much, and take every step we can to have a reformation in this respect, for such conduct is not according to Godliness and the principles of the Gospel, as Elder Taylor has told us. But we have regretted—I speak for the First Presidency—that there should be any mention of any particular place as being worse in this respect than others; for we have no reason to believe that this is the case. Therefore, it was with regret that we heard mentioned Kamas Prairie or Rhodes Valley. The Saints from that place—many of whom I know to be good, faithful people—would feel, to a certain extent—I won't say disgraced, but hurt by a public announcement of this kind in this general conference. We think that when the Elders speak concerning sin and evil practices, it is not a wise thing to mention either the names of individuals or of wards or stakes as was done by Elder Taylor. Now, what has been said by him, or that which he had heard somebody say, it may be true, as he says, and it may not. He himself characterized it as an exaggeration, and the mention of the place should have been left alone because it may be an exaggeration, and we have no reason, as the First Presidency to think otherwise—to think that Kamas Prairie is an exception in this respect. Such cases may arise in all the Stakes, but every pain is being taken to repress and correct these, to teach our young people how immoral and how wicked it is to do any such thing" (GC, October 7, 1898; CD 5:463). Further information about this incident can be found in Bitton, *George Q. Cannon: A Biography*, 424.

43. "What Was Said," DN, October 10, 1898; see also JH, October 7, 1898.
44. JH, October 8, 1898.
45. RCJ, October 8, 1898. Rudger Clawson, at that time the President of the Box Elder Stake in Cache Valley Utah, was a protégé of President Snow's, and one of his closest friends. They had served time together in the Utah Penitentiary for unlawful cohabitation and become good friends. Further information about Elder Clawson can be found in Larson, ed., *Prisoner for Polygamy: The Memoirs and Letters of Rudger Clawson at the Utah Territorial Penitentiary, 1884–87.*
46. AWJ, October 9, 1898.
47. CR, October 8, 1898.
48. Ibid., October 7, 1898.
49. JH, October 10, 1898; see also AHLJ, October 10, 1898.
50. Ibid., October 10, 1898.

CHAPTER 17

1. FMLJ, 149.
2. A few days after his visit with President Snow, Elder Lyman wrote in his journal: "We are determined to get out of debt; this is to be the great work of President Snow's administration" (FMLJ, 149). Elder Lyman felt confident enough about his feelings in this regard to state them publicly: "The Lord has been with President Snow. His mission has been a remarkable one. The mission of each of the chiefs of this Church has been emphasized by some very important work. President Snow is to live to see this people made free, and relieved of their embarrassments, financial and otherwise. There is a stride being made by this Church today that has never before been made in its history. . . . And this administration of President Snow shall be made remarkable, as all the others have been" (CR, April, 1901).
3. BYJJ, October 15, 1898.
4. SLH, October 14, 1898.
5. See Gibbons, *Lorenzo Snow: Spiritual Giant, Prophet of God*, 227–28. Frank Cannon's biased and embellished recollection of this purported meeting included the following: "'Last night,' he [President Snow] continued, 'lying on my bed, I had a vision. I saw this work of God injured by the political strife of the brethren. And the voice of the Lord came to me, directing me to see that your father was elected to the Senate.' He studied me a moment before he added: 'What have you to say? . . . I want you to withdraw from the race and throw your strength to your father. It is the will of the Lord that you do so.' 'Have you a revelation to that effect also?' I asked. He answered, pontifically, 'Yes'" (Cannon and O'Higgins, *Under the Prophet in Utah*, 230–31; for the full alleged story, see pages 220–35). Whether or not President Snow really met with Frank Cannon, or told him about an alleged vision, depends on Frank Cannon's reliability as a source, and therefore becomes doubtful.
6. For a review of Frank Cannon's political maneuvering and disappointments, see Bitton: *George Q. Cannon: A Biography*, 428; see also JHSJ, February 23, 1899.

7. While researching this biography, I was unable to find corroboration for Frank Cannon's insinuations and conspiracy theories. President Snow was simply not an unscrupulous manipulator, weaving intricate webs of intrigue and dreaming up political schemes. Rather, it is more likely that Frank Cannon, who lavishly portrayed himself as a hero and political martyr in the face of dastardly hierarchical tyranny, was unconsciously writing a reflection of himself. If judged by either past or contemporary LDS standards, he was morally corrupt (an alcoholic, the father of a child born out of wedlock, and a frequent patron of prostitutes) and also politically ambitious—making him very bitter when he was not supported by Church leaders nor reelected to the Senate. He became especially angry toward President Snow, Joseph F. Smith, and Reed Smoot. Long before he wrote anti-Mormon books, he had been excommunicated and completed his descent into personal apostasy. Thereafter, wielding his articulate and clever pen and tongue, he embarked on a vicious crusade against the Church and its leaders. He wrote anti-Mormon articles for three years for Thomas Kearns at the *Salt Lake Tribune* and then traveled and lectured widely against the Church until he died in the early 1930s. See Cannon, "Wives and Other Women: Love, Sex, and Marriage in the Lives of John Q. Cannon, Frank J. Cannon, and Abraham H. Cannon," 71–130.

8. See Horne, ed., *An Apostle's Record: The Journals of Abraham H. Cannon*, 257 (journal entries dated September 1–2, 1892). See also JH, November 15, 1898. The temporary acting editor was John Jaques (pronounced Jakes), famous in Utah literary circles.

9. Summaries and quotations taken from JH, October 31, 1898.

10. Summaries and quotations taken from JH, November 2, 1898.

11. Summaries and quotations taken from JH, November 9, 1898.

12. Summaries and quotations taken from JH, November 10, 1898. Regarding this same meeting, Elder John Henry Smith recorded: "President Snow said that the *Deseret News* had been turned over to the Church and that Charles W. Penrose had been selected as managing editor. [He] asked [for] an expression of the brethren with reference to the selection. It was moved that he be sustained in this appointment. Carried by full vote" (RCJ, November 10 1898). Penrose would years later be called to the Twelve and then serve as a counselor in the First Presidency.

13. "President Heber J. Grant," remarks quoted in *In Memoriam; Horace G. Whitney: Biographical Sketch, Funeral Ceremonies, Resolutions of Respect, Editorials, Personal Tributes*, 15. This memorial booklet, with no author listed but likely prepared by Horace's brother Orson, also states: "January 1st, 1899, by appointment of President Lorenzo Snow, he took charge of the *Deseret News*, as business manager, retaining that position until April 15, 1920, when failing health compelled him to resign" (ibid., 6). A December 2, 1898, Journal History entry indicates that by late November he had already begun working as manager and was being paid a salary, and a December 9 entry has him meeting with President Snow about important *Deseret News* business model changes. In the book *Life of Lorenzo Snow*, pages 473–75, author Thomas C. Romney includes a story—referenced as being given to him by LeRoi Snow—indicating that "it was in January, 1899, that the President was in consultation with others of the

General Authorities of the Church" regarding the *Deseret News*'s "precarious financial condition," that it was during this time that LeRoi witnessed ("LeRoi Snow who was present, remembered") President Snow interviewing and hiring Horace Whitney to manage the *Deseret News,* including a lengthy conversation and facial expressions. The problem with this recounting is that other sources prove that Horace had already been hired *before* January and started working *before* January 1. Also, Andrew Jenson's reference work *LDS Biographical Encyclopedia* 3: 716-17 lists LeRoi Snow's mission dates as from March 1896 to February 1899 [actually March 4]. This return date places LeRoi as still on his mission for well over a month (probably more than two) after these meetings and the hiring occurred, and he could not have witnessed any of it; thereby casting serious doubt on the story. See also RCJ, May 11, 1899, and DN, April 16, 1920.

14. JH, November 15, 1898.

15. Ibid., November 16, 1898.

16. Summaries and quotations taken from JH, November 21, 1898.

17. Ibid., November 14, 1898.

18. DN, December 23, 1899; communications dated December 22 and 23, 1899. Also at about this time, Elder Brigham Young Jr. ruminated within himself about Church debts and income in his diary: "President Snow gave me private papers to read concerning our indebtedness and moral responsibility for debts. It is a mystery to me where these millions have gone to say nothing of the 6 or 700,000 dollars income we have every year [from incoming tithing] which for years has vanished like the rest. God help us, and I know he will" (BYJJ, December 21, 1898).

19. November 22, 1898; as quoted in Smith, *Life of Joseph F. Smith*, 305–6.

20. Announcement made January 13, 1899; see Clark, *Messages of the First Presidency* 3: 310.

21. In a January 5 meeting of the First Presidency and Twelve, "Brother [Francis M.] Lyman also reported that the committee consisting of himself, A. H. Lund, Karl G. Maeser, John Nicholson, and George Reynolds, appointed for the purpose of passing upon Brother James E. Talmage's new work, 'The Articles of Faith,' had heard the manuscript read, and they decided that it would be a good book to publish as a text book" (JH, January 5, 1899).

22. JETJ, January 13, 1899; see also JH, January 13, 1899.

23. Ibid., January 16, 1899. The Journal History confirms this: "Presidents Snow and Cannon at 1 p.m. were called upon by Brother James E. Talmage, in relation to his work 'Articles of Faith,' which is about to be published. A paper connected with it on the subject of the Holy Ghost had been submitted to President Snow for his consideration, and he now told Brother Talmage that he had read it, and was very much pleased with it, and thought it might with propriety be made a part of the book. Brother Talmage then read a chapter on plural marriage, which it was decided not to publish in this work, which was being issued under Church auspices, lest it might be construed by our enemies as an attempt by the Church to propagate a belief in polygamy" (JH, January 16, 1899).

24. Ibid., April 4, 1899.

25. Ibid., March 10, 1899.

26. JH, January 23, 1899.

27. Ibid., January 25, 1899.
28. Ibid., November 21, 1898.
29. See DN, July 16, 1898. See also Clark, *Messages of the First Presidency* 3: 300–301, where the endorsement is reprinted in full, but with the wrong date of July 9, 1898; and Jenson, *Autobiography of Andrew Jenson*, 391–93.
30. JH, September 30, 1898.
31. See DN, December 3, 1898, for the endorsement by Lorenzo Snow, George Q. Cannon, and Joseph F. Smith. This statement was accompanied by an editorial explanation of the book and the plan for profits from its sale to be used for the purposes stated, building a new historian's office.
32. Summaries and quotations found in JH, February 25, 1899. On October 24, 1901, the *Salt Lake Herald* carried a story that contained similar details: "The last time the question was brought up, about two years ago, Andrew Jenson of the historian's office, publisher of Jenson's *Church Chronology*, offered to put out another edition of his work and devote the profits towards a fund for a new building. The idea was sanctioned by the first presidency and the sale of the book was agitated [promoted] from the pulpit and by influential churchmen in all capacities, who looked upon the move as a most worthy one. Just before the edition went to press President George Q. Cannon took the position that the church should be able to provide its own buildings and could not afford to put itself under obligations to any man in the way proposed, although Mr. Jenson's offer was highly appreciated. The work was issued, but the title page did not name the first presidency as publishers, as had been intended, and the proceeds did not go to the historian's office fund" (SLH, October 24, 1901). The final sentence seems to be in error, since other sources indicate that book sales did provide $3,000 toward an eventual new historian's office, built years later.
33. For the "further endorsement" letter, see Clark, *Messages of the First Presidency* 3:319; and Jenson, *Autobiography of Andrew Jenson*, 394–95. This circular letter was signed by Lorenzo Snow and Joseph F. Smith but not by George Q. Cannon, who was on a trip to the eastern United States at the time. It seems evident that Joseph F. Smith (who was in favor of the profit-donation idea and had personally promoted it in a few sermons), in the absence of President Cannon, was able to convince President Snow to stay with the originally approved project. President Smith had recently been persuasive with President Snow in the matter of the sale of the Church bonds also. President Smith was on vacation until March 4 and therefore not present when Andrew Jenson had his conversation with Presidents Snow and Cannon. For a narration of these events involving Andrew Jenson and *Church Chronology*, see Perkins, "A Study of the Contributions of Andrew Jenson to the Writing and Preservation of LDS Church History," 54–58.
34. See Perkins, "A Study of the Contributions of Andrew Jenson to the Writing and Preservation of LDS Church History," 56. In 1914, still trying to encourage sales, President Joseph F. Smith's First Presidency again endorsed and promoted the book and reiterated that its copyright was owned by the Church, not Jenson (see DN, June 30, 1914; and Clark, *Messages of the First Presidency* 4:309–10).
35. RCJ, March 16, 1899.
36. AWJ, March 21, 1899.
37. JH, April 4, 1899.

38. Ibid., April 12, 1899.
39. Ibid., April 18, 1899.
40. Ibid., April 14, 1899. The whereabouts or existence of this recording seems to be unknown, and it may be the only such voice recording President Snow ever made.
41. Ibid., April 19, 1899.
42. Historian Ronald Walker has written: "As part of President Lorenzo Snow's administrative transition, Cannon was asked to give an accounting of the Beck property stock, which had proven enormously profitable in the 1890s. Since the Woodruff succession, the Beck, Taylor, and Thatcher interests had each forced the dispersal of their portions of the 'dedicated stock' and then used the proceeds for their own purposes. Cannon's share of the pool had earned an impressive $160,000, which he had used for a variety of Church and personal projects, including the quiet repayment of John Q. Cannon's speculations. Snow and Cannon, not wishing any impropriety, agreed that Cannon should surrender assets to the trustee-in-trust to cover all Cannon's private expenditures, plus interest—despite the fact that others involved in the mine had used its dividends for their personal gain. The amount of Cannon's repayment was never announced, nor for that matter was the transfer itself. As enigmatic was the value of the dedicated stock, which by the time of the Snow-Cannon settlement may have become worthless. Thus closed the chapter that Joseph F. Smith called 'one of those things that perhaps had never been heard of before, and whose parallel would never be heard of again.' Whatever its virtues, the Bullion and Beck endeavor had generated more than its share of ill will" (*Qualities that Count*, 224). For further information on the B. B. & C. mine as it relates to these questions, see Bitton, *George Q. Cannon: A Biography*, 286–87. In a note, Bitton explained: "The history of the Bullion, Beck & Champion mining company remains to be written" (510n102). See also Horne, ed., *An Apostle's Record: The Journals of Abraham H. Cannon*, 126–28, 130–31, 136–37, 172n1.
43. JH, April 24, 1899; see also JH, April 14, 1899.
44. Ibid., April 27, 1899; see also Walker, *Qualities that Count*, 206–8.
45. OFWJ, May 13, 1899.
46. JGKJ, May 15–16, 1899. Elder Kimball's bankruptcy was a great personal embarrassment to him. He retrospectively summarized what he felt to be the reason for his financial problems in a July 2 journal entry: "I have paid my tithing for at least seven years in full. Other times I have done so, yet when we sold our Salt Lake City property and received $8,333.00 each we all failed to pay our tithing and thereby transgressed this law, and surely have we paid the penalty, for we lost everything."

CHAPTER 18

1. An extensive review of Church financial history for this period is found in Arrington, *Great Basin Kingdom*, 387–409.
2. See Arrington, *Great Basin Kingdom*, 368–70, 373, 377, 400–401. Marshal Dyer (the federally appointed receiver of escheated Church property), his

associates, and others like him, reasoned that since the ultimate unspoken goal was to financially destroy the Church, then why not line their own pockets in the process. Isaac Trumbo, a politically prominent non–Latter-day Saint friend of the Church, told Elder J. Golden Kimball of his feelings on the matter: "At 2 pm Colonel Isaac Trumbo called to see me. . . . Trumbo talked . . . of the steal that was made by U.S. Marshals from the Mormon people during their persecutions" (JGKJ, September 15, 1898).

3. FMLJ, 139, ca. August 1893. After suffering under a load of personal debt for several years, Elder Lyman was eventually enabled to pay all his creditors and regain a very respectable temporal footing before his death.

4. See, for example, AHCJ, August 20, 1886 & July 13, 1894.

5. For somewhat differing opinions offered by two well-respected historians regarding George Q. Cannon's financial policies and programs, see Bitton, *George Q. Cannon: A Biography*, 419–20, and Walker, *Qualities that Count*, 205–23. Davis Bitton wrote a review of Walker's essays on Elder Grant, although he did not really attempt to evaluate the financial issues therein described (see book reviews section, *Utah Historical Quarterly*, 72:4 [Fall 2004], 386–88).

6. See Arrington, *Great Basin Kingdom*, 402; see also JHSJ, January 5, 1899, and JH, December 2, 1898.

7. See Arrington, *Great Basin Kingdom*, 394–99.

8. AHCJ, December 2, 1895.

9. See Clark, *Messages of the First Presidency* 3:279–80. James R. Clark, a historian of the messages of past First Presidencies, wrote: "The Pioneer Electric Power Company was organized in February, 1896 with a capitalization of $2,000,000. George Q. Cannon of the First Presidency was the president of the company and the L.D.S. Church owned approximately $350,000 of the $400,000 of common stock issued. The company issued 1,500 gold bonds each with a face value of $1,000 and bearing six per cent interest. These bonds were purchased by Joseph Banigan, an eastern financier upon an unconditional and absolute guarantee issued by the First Presidency . . . and Wilford Woodruff as Trustee-in-Trust for the Church" (ibid.). See also Arrington, *Great Basin Kingdom*, 394–99.

10. FMLJ, 138.

11. AHCJ, July 11, 1893.

12. Ibid., August 12, 1893.

13. JH, September 11, 1896.

14. Ibid., October 1, 1896.

15. Clark, *Messages of the First Presidency* 3:304.

16. Clark, *Messages of the First Presidency* 3:304.

17. FDRJ, April 7, 1897.

18. Recollection of (Lorenzo Snow speaking to) Rudger Clawson as found in Clawson, "Reorganization of Financial System at President's Office, Under Administration of Presidents Lorenzo Snow and Joseph F. Smith, (1923)," 1–2; Rudger Clawson Papers, Special Collections, Marriott Library; as quoted in Bell, "The Windows of Heaven Revisited," 51.

19. AHCJ, October 27, 1890.

20. Ibid., October 5, 1894.

21. GC, October 6, 1894; cited in DN, December 7, 1894.

22. AHCJ, April 8, 1895.
23. Walker, *Qualities that Count*, 223.
24. JHSJ, September 6, 1898. A few months later he also recorded that, "Lorenzo Snow said to me and Brigham Young [Jr.] today that he had no confidence in George Q. Cannon" (JHSJ, December 26, 1898; this comment from President Snow probably referred largely to financial philosophies). For further reference to this conclusion, see Gibbons, *Lorenzo Snow, Spiritual Giant, Prophet of God*, 226–27. One might speculate that the only reason President Snow retained Cannon as a counselor was because President Woodruff and Jesus had both told him to do so. For a second, differing, perspective on Cannon's culpability or lack thereof in relation to the financial problems of the Church, see Bitton, *George Q. Cannon: A Biography*, 419–20. Bitton's discussion generally defends Cannon's financial actions and omits or glosses over his difficulties with younger members of the Twelve. Documents indicate no definite number of total Church debt that can be relied upon, and various figures are given depending on the source.
25. Heber J. Grant Diary, January 5, 1898; as quoted in Bell, "The Windows of Heaven Revisited," 51; the date of this statement to Elder Grant is somewhat uncertain, since it is referenced by Bell as 1898, but the wording used to introduce it in Bell's article indicates 1888, and the Grant journals are not available to researchers for clarification; however, I believe 1898 is the most likely correct date.
26. RCJ, Thursday, March 9, 1899.
27. Ibid., Thursday, March 23, 1899.
28. Ibid., December 1, 1898. The account of this meeting as given in the Journal History states: "Pres. Snow then stated that the Presiding Bishopric had been invited to meet with the Council to take part in the consideration of the question of issuing Church bonds. He said he had concluded to try the experiment of issuing bonds to the amount of half a million [dollars], in the hope that our own people will subscribe for them. This matter had been talked over two or three times and a decision had been reached to issue this amount of bonds for eleven years, redeemable in five years, to provide for a sinking fund and to select two persons of good financial reputation to act as trustees. The question was now submitted to the Council, President Snow remarking that the whole matter was open for discussion, as nothing had been determined on that could not be changed. The Form of the bond was then read and Pres. Cannon moved that the amount of the reserve be $50,000 instead of $25,000 as before agreed upon. This, with the interest of $30,000 would make a total fund of $80,000 a year. The motion was seconded by Pres. Smith, and after some further talk and explanations regarding the income of the Church, it was put and carried unanimously" (JH, December 1, 1898).
29. For details of this bond issue, see JH, January 1–2, 1899.
30. JH, January 2 & 4, 1899.
31. RCJ, January 4, 1899; see also JH, same date; and JH, December 16, 1898, where it is mentioned that David Eccles first suggested to President Snow the advisability of issuing a million dollars in bonds instead of the $500,000.
32. Joseph Fielding Smith also wrote: "The blocking of the scheme of this individual [Frank J. Cannon], who hoped to become the agent of the Church in

disposing of the bonds, brought down upon the head of President Joseph F. Smith the wrath of this particular individual, who in later times joined forces with the enemies of the Church in a campaign of bitterness and hate which in some respects surpassed any expression of bitterness ever before manifested against the Church" (Smith, *Life of Joseph F. Smith*, 303–4; see also DN, December 16, 1898). Frank Cannon's silver tongue, literary talent, and powers of persuasion were no myth. Elder J. Golden Kimball recorded his personal impressions of Frank Cannon: "Senator Cannon, was telephoned to, and soon came up. He and I went into a room and conversed for three hours. He spoke of his experience in Congress. We talked of the Authorities and what good men they were; of politics in Utah; about [William] King & [B. H.] Roberts. Not a disparaging word was said by Bro. Cannon. . . . It was a very interesting conversation. I was captured by Frank Cannon. I felt very kindly towards him. He is magnetic, approachable. His spirit is congenial to me" (JGKJ, September 12, 1898). Frank Cannon apostatized after the death of his father George Q. and later became the editor of the *Salt Lake Tribune*, where he spent three years writing vicious anti-Mormon editorials. He did not let up attacking the Church in any way he could until he died.

33. JH, January 5, 1899.

34. "Pres. Snow named the following brethren as said committee: F. D. Richards, F. M. Lyman, J. H. Smith, H. J. Grant, and R. Clawson. Benediction by A. O. Woodruff" (RCJ, January 5, 1899).

35. Quotations and summaries from JH, January 5, 1899.

36. Ibid.

37. RCJ, April 5, 1899.

38. JH, April 10, 1899.

39. RCJ, April 21, 1899.

40. JH, April 21, 1899.

41. Exactly how and when this inspiration was received is not satisfactorily traceable. LeRoi Snow's published accounts do not fully agree, but state: "One morning, as I entered father's room to express the morning's greetings, as was my usual custom, he said he was going to St. George in southern Utah. I was much surprised at the thought of him making this long and hard trip" (Snow, "Special Manifestation of the Word and Will of the Lord," 4); and then eight years later in another article he wrote: "During the night, in the Bee Hive House, the Lord instructed my father to go to St. George, but did not tell him the purpose of the trip. I was the first in his bedroom that morning and I shall never forget his glorious appearance as I saw him sitting upright in his bed. His face was almost white and his eyes shone as I had never seen them before. All he said was: 'I am going to St. George.'" (Snow, "From Despair To Freedom Through Tithing," 6). The second account, written forty-three years after events transpired, includes such details as a "glorious appearance" and living in the Beehive house, not mentioned in the first—but which are likely fictional, since President Snow and his family did not move into the Beehive house until later that year in September.

42. JH, April 26, 1899.

43. RCJ, May 4, 1899.

44. See "Leroi C. Snow" entry in Jenson, *LDS Biographical Encyclopedia* 3:716–17.

45. OFWJ, May 14, 1899.
46. AWJ, under date given. See also RCJ, May 15, 1899.
47. Other journal accounts and newspaper reports also describe the trip adequately, but not with the personal intimacy and detail of Arthur Winter's account; see for example, DN, May 17, 1899.
48. AWJ, under dates given.
49. SLH, May 17, 1899.
50. A period during which President Snow spoke for 47 minutes was noted by President Franklin D. Richards in his journal: "St. George, May 16 [17], 1899: Pres. L.S. 47 min. A.O.W. 11:13 am—15 min. FDR—18 min. LeRoy Snow—11:45 am—12 mins." President Richards's handwriting for this entry was poor, and without careful scrutiny the number could be mistaken as 17 instead of 47. By adding up the total time taken by the speakers, including 47 minutes from President Snow, and then adding time taken by prayers and hymns, there is time for a two-hour stake conference, from 10 am until noon.
51. Several times later in describing the revelation, President Snow used the word "Manifestation"; also, while at another stake conference, President Snow used the phrase, "I *saw* this most clearly while in St. George" (DN, November 20, 1899). This lends weight to the probability that the revelation was given in the form of a vision, and he continually emphasized how "clear" it was.
52. See Bell, "The Windows of Heaven Revisited," 64–65, for a review of various sources (most of unimpressive historical weight) describing a few people's reminiscences of this event.
53. See Snow, "The Lord's Way Out of Bondage," 440, and "Lorenzo Snow Biographical Index, 1950," 3 and 4, for notecards with the typewritten notations: "Transfiguration—Widstoe '93–'94; Sis Gerrard, May 1899." [and] "Transfiguration—St. George Temple [Tabernacle]." See also Snow, "Special Manifestation of the Word of the Lord to Lorenzo Snow," 1, 4, 8. These late printed recollections and notations are insufficient to be considered conclusive of anything except LeRoi's personal position on this question.
54. As noted in the brackets, the minutes of the meeting, newspaper quotations, and an unpublished account kept by James G. Bleak called "Annals of the Southern Utah Mission," provide the best source material. See the following note for source citations.
55. Sources: Copy of Minutes taken in St. George Tabernacle; Wednesday, May 17, 1889, CHL; SLH, May 17, 1899; DN, May 17, 1899; James G. Bleak, "Annals of the Southern Utah Mission, circa 1898–1907," CHL, MS 318 bx 2.
56. Bleak, "Annals of the Southern Utah Mission, circa 1898–1907," lists speakers and topics. There is a question of whether Abraham O. Woodruff spoke after President Snow, as this source indicates he did, but others omit him. See also AWJ, May 17, 1899.
57. Minutes: Thursday 9:00 a.m., May 18, 1899.
58. AWJ, May 18, 1899.
59. May 18, 1899, *Millennial Star*, September 21, 1899; No. 33, Vol. LXI, 593, 596, full discourse 593–97; emphasis added.
60. "Sister Mary Morris sang: 'Hosanna to your King,'" James G. Bleak, "Annals

of the Southern Utah Mission, circa 1898–1907," CHL, MS 318 bx 2; Thursday, May 18, 1899.

61. *Millennial Star*, August 24 & 31, 1899; capital-letter emphasis in original.

62. "NO PLURAL MARRIAGES," SLH, May 18, 1899. See also FDRJ, May 18, 1899.

63. "President Snow at St. George," AWJ, May 18, 1899. See also DN, October 10, 1901.

64. AWJ, May 18, 1899.

65. DN, Monday, May 29, 1899; report from Scipio of a meeting at Holden, held Friday, May 26, 1899; emphasis added.

66. See, for example, Clark, *Messages of the First Presidency* 3:311; Gordon B. Hinckley, *What of the Mormons?: A Brief Study of the Church of Jesus Christ of Latter-day Saints* (Salt Lake City: Corporation of the President, the Church of Jesus Christ of Latter-day Saints, 1947), 213–14; *2001–2002 Church Almanac* (Salt Lake City: Deseret News, 2000), 523. This error is found in all editions of the almanac seen by the author. Other similar sources avoid the erroneous date of May 8 because of the typo but use the sermon of May 18 as the date of the revelation. See Clyde J. Williams, "Lorenzo Snow," in Arnold K. Garr, Donald Q. Cannon, Richard O. Cowan, eds., *Encyclopedia of Latter-day Saint History* (Salt Lake City, Deseret Book, 2000), 1153. Although President Snow surely enjoyed inspiration during his sermon on that day, the first meeting on May 17 remains the correct date and time for the receipt of the main revelation.

67. Snow, "Special Manifestation of the Word and Will of the Lord," 4 (1, 4, 8). This article has a heading that states: "This is the first publishing of this story"—likely so because some parts of it came only from LeRoi's mind. This article—as with the other two—confuses the two separate talks by President Snow of May 17 and 18 as one only, and does not identify which meeting the prophecy was supposed to have been given in, and concludes: "The prophecy was made in the latter part of May and its fulfillment was commenced with the beginning of heavy rains on Aug. 2. Those rains continued. The crops matured and the promised harvest was reaped by the faithful Saints in the St. George stake." These statements are not historically accurate.

68. Snow, "The Lord's Way Out of Bondage was not the Way of Men but Faithfulness to the Law of Tithing Opened the Windows of Heaven," 244–47.

69. Snow, "From Despair To Freedom Through Tithing," 6 (5–7). Other than its inaccuracies related to President Snow's tithing talks in St. George, this article is excellent for covering the highlights of President Snow's life.

70. "Drought Broken at St. George, Aug. 2.—The long and severe drought that Dixie has been suffering from for the last seventeen months was broken this morning, and at noon today one and eighty-nine one hundredths inches of rain fell, every drop of which went into the parched earth. The amount of good that will result will be great. More rain fell than Dixie has had in twenty months. Her grain crops are thirty per cent below the average and the alfalfa is almost as low, while fruit is suffering considerably. Little or no water has been flowing from Pine Valley for three months past and several towns have barely had enough water for culinary purposes." DN, August 2, 1899.

71. See "Southern Utah's Big Snow Fall; long drought broken with a deposit of fourteen inches," DN, February 6, 1901.
72. For an examination of climate, weather, and moisture statistics; a review of most known historical records related to President Snow's visit and talks; problems associated with LeRoi Snow's writings about the St. George tithing revelation and their incorporation into the movie *The Windows of Heaven*, see Bell, "The Windows of Heaven Revisited: The 1899 Tithing Reformation," *Journal of Mormon History*, 20, no. 1 (1994):45–83. Although Bell missed a few sources included in this chapter, his thorough examination of the relevant historical literature, contemporary sources, the scripts, and the many inaccuracies and fictional events and conversations portrayed in the film, make it worthwhile reading for those who wish to review this episode closer. Bell seems to have had some degree of realization that certain of LeRoi Snow's published statements did not mesh with other reliable records.
73. JH, March 8, 1900.
74. SLH, March 13, 1900.
75. JH, March 15, 1900. In January 1901 a news item stated that "John R. Murdock . . . talked interestingly to the *Deseret News* today on the conditions in southern Utah. He says the outlook is not nearly so bright as many people imagine and that the long period of drought that has prevailed in Beaver and other counties has not yet been broken. There was a good rain storm in November and a little snow has fallen since that time though the deposit in the mountains is very meager." DN, January 17, 1901.
76. RCJ, April 3, 1901. For biographical information about David H. Cannon, the St. George Temple president, see Beatrice Cannon Evans and Janath Russell Cannon, *Cannon Family Historical Treasury* (Cannon Family Association, 1967), 238–60.

CHAPTER 19

1. AWJ, May 18, 1899.
2. Ibid., May 19, 1899; see also FDRJ, same date.
3. Ibid., May 19, 1899.
4. DN, May 22, 1899.
5. Ibid., May 22, 1899.
6. AWJ, May 20, 1899.
7. SLH, May 20, 1899.
8. AWJ, May 21, 1899.
9. Ibid., May 22, 1899.
10. DN, Tuesday, May 25, 1899 and DN, Beaver, Monday, May 24, 7:30 p.m. meeting in tabernacle; see also FDRJ, Beaver, May 22, 1899; and AWJ, May 22, 1899.
11. FMLJ, 150.
12. AWJ, Tuesday, May 23, 1899.
13. Ibid., Wednesday, May 24, 1899.
14. SLH, Sunday, May 28, 1899.

15. DN, May 25, 1899.
16. SLH, May 27, 1899.
17. DN, Monday, May 29, 1899; see also AWJ, May 25, 1899.
18. "In Juab and Millard Stakes," DN, May 29, 1899.
19. AWJ, May 26, 1899.
20. Ibid.
21. "Remarks made by President Lorenzo Snow, at Nephi, May 26th, 1899, to the members of the company who accompanied him on his trip to St. George and through the settlements visited from May 15th to the 26th," (AWJ, under dates given).
22. AWJ, Saturday, May 27, 1899. The trip through southern Utah, and the subsequent months he spent traveling to stakes in Northern Utah to preach tithing, was the last major work President Franklin D. Richards did in his ministry. He died about seven months later, after weeks in bed, sometimes in a near comatose condition. President Richards's health infirmities on the trip (largely due to age) were not mentioned in news reports.
23. DN, Saturday, May 27, 1899.
24. "Sunday Morning, May 28th, 1899, Tabernacle," *Improvement Era*, 2:9 (July 1899), 701–4 (esp. 702) and 708–10; see also JH, May 27, 1899.
25. RCJ, 29 May 1899. These are not exact quotations, but contain more detail from the message than any other version located; see also JH, May 29, 1899. Elder J. Golden Kimball left his own observations of the meeting: "The testimony and spirit that accompanied the remarks of our brethren was remarkable" (JGKJ, May 29, 1899).
26. JGKJ, May 29, 1899.
27. *Improvement Era,* 2 (Aug. 1899): 795
28. "Our Work" (May 30, 1899), *Improvement Era,* 2 (Aug. 1899): 795. Elder Kimball's record of this meeting is again instructive: "Pres. Snow then appealed very feelingly to us on the tithing question. We were much affected. We all arose, and cried out 'aye', that we would sustain this principle and the Prophet of God" (JGKJ, May 30, 1899). The reference to President Snow's blessing and promise of salvation in the celestial kingdom is of interest. Matthias F. Cowley recorded a very similar incident from the experience of President Wilford Woodruff: "I was present in the Templeton Bldg, at a Mutual Improvement meeting when President Woodruff prophesied that none of the young men present would ever apostatize; that is now nearly thirty years ago, and up to date so far as I know those present have all been faithful and true to their calling, and I have no doubt that they always will be and thus fulfill the blessed words of this good man of God" (Matthias F. Cowley, at University of Chicago, Oct. 4, 1925).
29. AWJ, June 2–4, 1899.
30. DN, June 7, 1899; from talk given June 6.
31. AWJ, Monday, June 5, 1899.
32. Ibid., June 12, 1899.
33. RCJ, June 15, 1899; see also FDRJ, June 15, 1899.
34. AWJ, Sunday, June 18, 1899; June 19, 1899.
35. The details were much more complicated than here summarized. Rudger Clawson wrote: "The object of the meeting briefly stated was this: the First

Presidency of the Church in the days of Pres. Woodruff, being desirous to see the Pioneer Power Plant enterprise a success and in order to aid said company in securing funds, guaranteed the bond issue, namely, $1,500,000.00, which action, owing to the uncertainty of business enterprises generally, is causing the Presidency and Twelve considerable anxiety. The Pioneer Co. afterwards went into the consolidation known as the Union Light and Power Co. Certain English capitalists, who are also interested in the consolidation, are dissatisfied and are trying to make trouble. Pres. George Q. Cannon, LeGrande Young, and R. S. Campbell have had several conferences with them in Boston and under the authority of Pres. Snow are trying to get the Church released from the guarantee. Pres. Cannon telegraphed that the Banigan Estate, which holds the bonds referred to, would surrender the guarantee upon condition that the Church pay $25,000.00 in 30 days, $200,000 in one year [at 5 percent interest] and guarantee 5% [2 percent] interest on $250,000.00 bonds for 10 years. By accepting this proposition the Church would be relieved of any further liability as against the $1,500,000.00" (RCJ, June 29, 1899).

CHAPTER 20

1. Snow, "From Despair To Freedom Through Tithing," 6; also quoted verbatim in LeRoi Snow's earlier, "Special Manifestation of the Word and Will of the Lord," 8. William Salmon served as a doorkeeper and custodian in the Salt Lake Temple. Since he was alone with President Snow when this happened, it is assumed that Salmon related this experience to LeRoi.
2. RCJ, June 29, 1899. As far as the records show, time did not allow for any stake presidents to speak.
3. Several attendees recorded their experience that day; what was said in summary and their feelings about the experience, as noted below. Among the briefer mentioned accounts are JHSJ, FDRJ, AWIJ, and MWMJ, all July 2, 1899. The Journal History included the following account, which includes a reference to the locations of the full reported discourses: "This being the regular fast day of the Church, and the day set apart by the First Presidency for a Solemn Assembly of the Holy Priesthood at the Salt Lake Temple, meetings were held there accordingly, beginning at 10 a.m., and extending through the day. There were present: The First Presidency, the Apostles, the First Council of the Seventies, the Patriarch, the Presiding Bishopric, stake presidencies, ward bishops, and some other brethren, specially invited. President Lorenzo Snow presided, and various speakers addressed the assembly, all dwelling upon the subject of the law of tithing, the presentation of which to the Priesthood, and the insistence of a stricter observance of the same by the Latter-day Saints, were the purposes of the gathering. A full report of the proceedings, taken by Church reporter Arthur Winder [*sic*], will be found as an appendix to the Journal of the President's Office, kept by secretary George F. Gibbs; and a duplicate copy of the same will be found among the records of the Temple" (JH, July 2, 1899). I was unable to secure permission to view or use Winter's stenographic reports of this meeting from the First Presidency, with the explanation that by policy all

requests for transcripts of remarks made in temple solemn assemblies are denied.
4. AWJ, July 2, 1899.
5. AKJ (Andrew Kimball Journal), July 2, 1901, unpublished; copy provided the author by Edward L. Kimball, Andrew's grandson.
6. See note 3 above. Arthur Winter did enter a very brief portion of President Snow's comments into his personal journal, although it is not known from which of his three talks it comes from: "You want to remember, brethren, that if you live 10 or 15 or 20 years, and perhaps much less than this, perhaps not much over, you will have the opportunity of going to Jackson County. The time is near at hand much nearer than it was 20 years ago. It was said it was rather near at hand in those days, and it is nearer at hand now. And the Lord is going to remove those difficulties that now seem to be so very huge and impossible of ever being removed—He is going to remove those difficulties, and we are going back to Jackson county—a great many of us—such as shall prove worthy." Winter then commented: "The foregoing is word for word what he said upon that point, and is worthy of preservation" (AWJ, July 2, 1899).
7. Snow, "From Despair To Freedom Through Tithing," 7. LeRoi, an expert at shorthand, may have taken down these remarks of President Snow himself, or he may have had access to Arthur Winter's shorthand record. Elder Rudger Clawson also made his own shorter summarized account of President Snow's talk: "It may seem strange, your being called together, but when you understand the object of the meeting you will understand the importance of it. [He] read section 104 and a portion of section 85, D.&C. . . . Read of the troubles and curses that are visited upon apostates. Said he would tell us what the Lord requires of us today. Read Section 119, D.&C. Talked upon the subject of tithing. If the people, he said, had paid an honest tithing for the past year, we would have received $1,000,000 more than we did receive, and if a full tithing had been paid for the past 12 years, we would have received $10,000,000 more than we did receive. Bp. Preston says, and the books prove it, that only about a 50% tithing is paid. A half tithing or a third tithing is no tithing at all, but simply an offering. If we do not observe this law, we have no promise that we shall remain in this land an hour. Said that while visiting in St. George on his recent trip, the Lord revealed to him what counsel he should impart to the people, and the word of the Lord was that the Saints should pay their tithing. Trouble has come upon the people. In the south stock is dying off and crops are drying up, and in the north crops were partially destroyed by frost. An effort is being made to influence the Government to disfranchise the Latter-day Saints by a constitutional amendment. How far this is due to the disobedience of our people in observing the law of tithing, I do not know, but the saints are certainly under condemnation" (RCJ, July 2, 1899). In reference to President Snow's mention of the tithing revelation he received in St. George, Anthony W. Ivins (AWIJ) recorded: "The Lord has told me plainly and most distinctly that the law of tithing should be taught while we were in St. George and he made it just as plain that this is what I should say to you today." Cited in, "Notes from the diary of Anthony W. Ivins"; unpublished; CHL, MS d 3957. Of this same sermon, Andrew Kimball wrote that President Snow said: "Teach your children to observe [the law of tithing]. [He] spoke of dry conditions in Southern Utah; also that the nation was aroused [against the LDS] on account of Elder B.

H. Roberts going to Congress. Pres. Snow said the Lord would forgive us of the past but would not forgive us longer; that the judgments of God would surely follow further disobedience to this law which he said was a perpetual law unto us and must be obeyed" (AKJ, July 2, 1899).

8. RCJ, July 2, 1899.

9. Among other things, President Richards said: "The law of tithing is a law of God to us forever. The gifts of God will be more general among the Saints and God's blessings will be multiplied" (AWIJ, same date).

10. Elder Merrill said: "Non-tithe-payers were on the increase. This meeting has been called that there may be a reformation" (AWIJ, July 2, 1899).

11. Heber J. Grant mentioned that "two dollars are spent in breaking the Word of Wisdom for every dollar paid in tithing" (AWIJ, July 2, 1899).

12. AWIJ, July 2, 1899.

13. RCJ, July 2, 1899.

14. For a chronological narration of these movements, see AWIJ, RCJ, and AKJ, July 2, 1899.

15. Elder J. Golden Kimball, not one to soften his perspective, wrote: "LeRoi C. Snow, a boy of Pres Snow's, was called up to speak. Some were amused and surprised. He is a son of a favored wife and his father's pet. Men are sometimes great and mighty, and the Lord loves them, yet they will exhibit just such weaknesses [favoring his son], as was presented today. This young man will no doubt be an apostle, if Pres. Snow has his way. This part of the meeting was unpleasant to me, although the young man may be favored of God" (JGKJ, same date). LeRoi was never called as a General Authority, although many years later he served on the General Board of the YMMIA and also worked in some capacity with the Church Historian's office.

16. A few notes of President Joseph F. Smith's remarks on this occasion have been preserved: "The latter, in speaking of tithing, said, the books should record not only what we do, but what we ought to have done and did not do. A man is in a poor business as president or bishop of a ward who says to the people, do as you ought to do, not as I do. The poor of a ward—widows and orphans—all should pay their tithing" (RCJ, July 2, 1899). Also: "Pres. Joseph F. Smith read from the Bible. God once cleansed the earth with water. He will cleanse it with fire. Just as sure as we live, just as sure as you hear the sound of my voice, unless we honor this law of tithing we shall never get back to Jackson County unless we go there as Ancient Israel went into the Promised Land; by the shedding of blood. People who receive assistance from the Church should pay tithing on every dollar they receive. When people apply for assistance, Bishops, get your records. If he is a tithing payer he has claim upon you. If not you are bound only by the law of charity to render assistance" (AWIJ, same date).

17. Among other things, Elder Lyman said: "There has never before been just such a gathering. It has fallen to the lot of President Snow to announce that the time has come when the law of tithing must be observed in Zion" (AWIJ, July 2, 1899).

18. AKJ, July 2, 1899.

19. AWIJ, July 2, 1899.

20. RCJ, July 2, 1899.

21. OFWJ, July 2, 1899.
22. According to Elder Abraham H. Cannon, "Father said Heber C. Kimball once told him he was a direct descendant of the Savior of the world" (AHCJ, April 4, 1894).
23. AKJ, July 2, 1899.
24. RCJ, July 2, 1899. Orson Whitney also recorded this note: "Pres. Snow said the Lord would not forgive us if we did not [pay a full tithing] and He would forgive the past [neglect]. But would bring trouble upon us if we were disobedient in the future. Cyclones, earthquake, and other judgments were hinted at as well as driving, like Zion from Jackson County and Nauvoo. Pres. Snow said we did not know Joseph Smith; that we did not know ourselves; that we might learn many things from the Lord if we had sense enough to keep them to ourselves" (OFWJ, July 2, 1899).
25. DN, July 16, 1899. Slightly more detail is given in Anthony Ivins's record: "President Smith introduced a resolution endorsing the teachings of today in regard to tithing. President Snow asked all who endorsed it to arise and, with the right hand raised, to say aye. The response was unanimous" (AWIJ, July 2, 1899; See also JGKJ, July 2, 1899).
26. AWJ, July 2, 1899. See also JGKJ, July 2, 1899.
27. AKJ, July 2, 1899. See also AWIJ, July 2, 1899. Arthur Winter wrote: "We also gave the shout of 'Hosanna! To God and the Lamb, Amen and Amen,' and the temple echoed and reechoed with the sound" (AWJ, July 2, 1899).
28. JGKJ, July 2, 1899.
29. JHSJ, July 2, 1899.
30. MWMJ, July 2, 1899.
31. FMLJ, July 2, 1899.
32. "People must Pay Tithing," SLH, Monday, July 3, 1899.
33. JH, July 5, 1899.
34. Ibid., July 6, 1899; see also RCJ, 6 July 1899. In his journal, Elder Lyman recorded: "President Cannon reported his mission in New York in the interest of the Union Light and Power Company. It is remarkable how the Church has been relieved of its embarrassing obligations to the extent of a million and a half dollars. Certainly the Lord has brought it about, with President Cannon as His agent. Our hearts rejoice because of the great relief; we begin to see the redemption before us" (FMLJ, July 6, 1899; as quoted in Lyman, *Biography: Francis Marion Lyman, Apostle*, 151).
35. JH, July 13, 1899; see also RCJ, July 13, 1899.
36. AWJ, July 15, 1899.
37. DN, July 16 & 21; see also JH, July 16, 1899, and AWJ, July 16, 1899.
38. JH, July 20, 1899.
39. DN, July 24, 1899; see also AWJ, July 22, 1899.
40. AWJ, July 29, 1899.
41. DN, July 31, 1899; see also AWJ, July 30, 1899.
42. Ibid.
43. Francis M. Lyman, GC, October 1899. Elder Lyman further said: "Every one of these Apostles knows that President Snow's testimony is from the Lord, for He has told us. We comprehend it most thoroughly; . . . Those who do the will of

the Lord in the future shall also know that God has spoken through President Snow. It is his particular mission and ministry to set right the Latter-day Saints in regard to this particular law—not to neglect any other and not to say that men's sins will be forgiven them if they pay their tithing. That is a mistake, and only transgressors have concluded that Bishops and the authorities of the Church have no right to handle them now for their transgressions, because President Snow has said that the past should be forgiven. He has only said that the past should be forgiven, so far as the payment of tithing was concerned. Thank the Lord that we may be forgiven for that" (ibid.).

44. DN, August 7, 1899; see also AWJ, August 5 & 6, 1899.
45. AWJ, August 14, 1899.
46. DN, August 14, 1899; see also AWJ, August 12–14, 1899.
47. DN, August 22 & 23, 1899; see also AWJ, August 19, 1899.
48. DN, August 26, 1899.
49. DN, August 28, 1899.
50. DN, September 5, 1899 (conference held on September 3); see also AWJ, September 2, 1899.
51. DN, September 5, 1899.
52. DN, September 4, 1899.
53. DN, September 18, 20, 1899; see also AWJ, September 9, 17–18, 1899.
54. JH, October 9, 1899.
55. RCJ, October 9, 1899.
56. AWJ, October 29, 1899.
57. DN, October 30, 1899.
58. AHLJ, November 2, 1899.
59. DN, November 20, 1899.
60. JH, March 22, 1900.
61. JH, March 29, 1900.
62. Elder Lyman further recorded: "He asked about my finances and whether I received enough to get along with. I told him it was enough because I cut the garment according to the cloth and kept out of debt. The president told me that the Lord would make me rich; I answered that I would be satisfied if He would give me eternal life" (FMLJ, ca. January 1901, 153). In connection with President Snow's prediction of riches, Elder Lyman's son wrote that by 1907 his father owned all or part of a dozen businesses, one of which was worth $100,000 and was expected to provide him with dividends of $12,000 each year (ibid., 168).
63. RCJ, May 3, 1901.

CHAPTER 21

1. JETJ, May 31, 1899.
2. BYJJ, June 12 and July 28, 1899.
3. JGKJ, July 13, 1899.
4. JH, September 14 & 23, 1899; see also DN, September 14, 1899. Another article mentioned: "Not since the days of the late President Brigham Young has the great, old-fashioned structure been occupied by the head of the Church, President

Taylor making his home at the Gardo and President Woodruff continuing his residence in his suburban cottage south of the city" (DN, September 23, 1899).
5. RCJ, October 26, 1899.
6. MWMJ, October 29, 1899.
7. DN, October 30, 1899; see also AWJ, October 29 & 30, 1899, and MWMJ, October 30, 1899.
8. JH, October 28, 1899.
9. Ibid., November 2 & 7, 1899.
10. RCJ, November 20, 1899.
11. JH, December 18, 1899.
12. For the complete text of the tithing settlement instructions circulars sent during the administration of President Snow, see Clark, *Messages of the First Presidency* 3: 306–9, 320–23, 328–33.
13. JH, December 8, 1899. The Journal History further records: "A note with interest is held by the Church against Thomas Taylor, amounting to about $32,000, and the note will soon be outlawed [expire]. A proposition has been made for the purchase of this note from the Church, but it was thought best, before selling it, to consult with Brother Taylor. It is understood that certain parties have become interested in the iron properties owned by him, and President Snow thought it a good time to arrange for the payment of the note, if he had a disposition to pay it, and if not, then to take other means to protect it. Brother Taylor complained now, as he has complained before, and that bitterly, that he had on two former occasions arranged to sell this property, but had been defeated by the Church, to whom the property was mortgaged. In answer to this he was told that there was no desire to hamper him or prevent him from disposing of his property, and in order to show this President Snow now offered to extend the mortgage long enough to enable him to sell, which action would protect the Church and at the same time leave him free to dispose of his property; but Brother Taylor did not feel inclined to accept this offer. He was willing to give his note, and hoped to have the property perfectly free, so that he could dispose of it. It was explained to him that this mortgage could not possibly interfere with the sale of the mine, it being necessarily a part of the transaction. President Snow assured him again that he did not wish to hurt him, but hoped to see him well and become well to do. Brother Taylor considered a moment, and then asked the privilege of meeting President Snow again. Two o'clock was set for the hearing. After Brother Taylor was through, President Snow told Judge Young that whatever was done to accommodate Brother Taylor must not in any way jeopardize the legality of his note" (JH, December 8, 1899). Evidently not an entirely stable personality, about four years earlier this same man had initiated a heated exchange with Elder Abraham H. Cannon: "Just after finishing breakfast Mr. Thomas Taylor, ex-Bishop of the 14th Ward in Salt Lake City called to see me and gave vent to considerable abuse of the Authorities of the Church in general and Father in particular. He said that my visit to the city and to the South was calculated to defeat his plans for the construction of a road to San Diego, he having already secured the co-operation of influential and moneyed men to carry through his project. He says that the Authorities of the Church have persistently interfered with his arrangements, and they have followed him

with a determination to ruin him, which he cannot understand. He threatens that a continuation of this persecution, as he calls it, could lead him to publish a statement giving what he said would be damaging testimony against Father and the other members of the Presidency. He will then appeal to the people to know if they will sustain such men in the positions they occupy. His whole conversation was that of a man partially insane. I invited him to publish any statement which he might have or could procure, and assured him that nothing he could tell would injure Father or the brethren, as their whole conduct through life was of a character that they need not be ashamed of it. I told him further that his talk this morning had deprived me of all respect and regard which I had entertained for him in the past" (Horne, ed., *An Apostle's Record*, 34–35).

14. RCJ, December 12, 1899; see also AWJ, December 12, 1899.

15. DN, December 16, 1899 (Funeral services for Franklin D. Richards, Tuesday, December 12, 1899).

16. JH, December 14, 1899.

17. Ibid., December 21, 1899.

18. Ibid., December 29, 1899.

19. In reply to my inquiry, John W. Welch of BYU sent me the following answer to an email inquiry he had sent to Glenn Rowe of the Church History Department in my behalf: "There are a couple of accounts of 'Nephite Coins' as they were called, being turned over to the Church. The one Dennis Horne mentions [Robinson's coin] and the Isaac Chase coin. We know that the Isaac Chase coin still exists and is in Church possession. Unfortunately we don't know the whereabouts of the other [Robinson] coin and have asked the Office of the First Presidency in the past. I am sorry we can't help any further. The Museum has a few coins for which we don't have good provenance. I am sure you are aware of the FARMS publications, like the one by Epstein, which enumerates the pre-Columbian coins in America theories on how they came to America" (Email, Glenn Rowe to Jack Welch, dated December 1, 2009). See also Jeremiah Epstein, "Pre-Columbian Old World Coins in America," *Current Anthropology* 21 (1980): 1–20.

20. Affidavit, "Signed: Richard Robinson, December 30, 1934"; also signed by "Maria Robinson, December 30, 1934," CHL MS 5147. This account refers to "pictures of Nephite coins" in the early or first editions of the Book of Mormon to which Robinson supposedly compared the coin as proof of its Nephite origin. There are no such pictures in those or any editions of the Book of Mormon. Three Book of Mormon scholars that I consulted while researching this story, Royal Skousen, John Sorenson, and Larry Draper, indicated that "there is no Book of Mormon with pictures of coins printed." Consequently, certain details of this affidavit must be viewed as fictional, while other details, such as those given, are verifiable. For example, the description of the seer stone matches other known descriptions.

21. I do not agree that the seer stone was used in translating the Book of Mormon; rather, in my opinion, the Urim and Thummim was the instrument provided by the Lord for this purpose. For a persuasive argument on this issue, see McConkie and Ostler, *Revelations of the Restoration*, 95–98.

22. Correspondence, Zina Young Card to Apostle F. D. Richards, Cardston, July 31, 1896; cited in JH, July 31, 1896.

23. Although the above referenced letter is dated 1896, it is likely that President Woodruff took possession of the stone before 1889, since he had it with him at the dedication of the Manti Temple in May of 1888.
24. Elder Matthias Cowley told of one such experience he had with President Woodruff: "Once when I went to visit President Woodruff on his farm in his declining years, he took me into his confidence and told me things about the great character that Brigham Young was, and his superiority to many others in a way that I had never heard before. On that occasion he also showed me the Seer Stone . . . through which the Prophet Joseph Smith received Revelations from the Lord" (Matthias F. Cowley, at University of Chicago, October, 4, 1925).
25. The seer stone is in the possession of the Church today and except under exceptional circumstances is stored in the First Presidency's vault.
26. RCJ, December 29, 1899. Ever since he received the revelation reaffirming tithing payment and the consequent promised blessings, President Snow seemed to have become more relaxed and less anxious about financial and political troubles around him.
27. AHLJ, December 30, 1899.
28. Abraham Owen Woodruff diary, December 30, 1899; as quoted in Hatch, ed., *Danish Apostle: The Diaries of Anthon H. Lund*, 65.

CHAPTER 22

1. DN, January 8, 1900. Further explanation of the origin of this official statement is found in the Journal History: "In a recent conversation with President Snow, Judge Bartch had submitted a prepared statement which he thought should be published in the *Deseret News* over the President's signature. This statement, somewhat modified, was published today, in the following form:" and the statement was then given as quoted (JH, January 8, 1900). This official communication to the Church is not found in Clark, *Messages of the First Presidency*, in any volume. The editorial (written by Charles W. Penrose) that accompanied the statement said:

> The foregoing announcement from the President of the Church of Jesus Christ of Latter-day Saints is entitled to respectful consideration. Not only should it be heeded by members of the Church, but by all people, everywhere. Its promulgation is necessary in view of the charges that are made that the "Mormon" Church seeks to become "a law unto itself" and sets itself above the civil government. It is not expected that it will have any particular effect on persons who desire, willfully, to misrepresent the Church and its authorities, its doctrines and its purposes. But there are hosts of good people who have been deceived by false reports, and it is for their information as well as to place the Church in its true position before the world that this official declaration is made.
>
> The President's statement is gratifying to us because it authoritatively asserts what the *Deseret News* has advanced editorially. The Church teachers obedience to secular law. It does not advise nor encourage any species of lawlessness. It supports the Constitution of the United States

> and the Constitution of Utah and all laws passed in pursuance thereof. It has its own sphere, which is ecclesiastical. While it gives counsel and promulgates rules for the guidance of its members as to individual conduct in all the affairs of life, it does not interfere in any way with the free agency of men and women, dictate to them how they shall vote or to which political party they shall belong, or hinder them in any lawful course as to business or other personal affairs. (DN, Jan. 8, 1900.)

2. JH, January 11, 1900.
3. Ibid., January 18, 1900; see also JH, January 22, 1900 and JH, February 7, 1900.
4. Ibid., January 27, 1900.
5. Ibid., February 2, 1900.
6. Ibid., February 5, 1900.
7. Ibid., February 10, 1900.
8. Ibid., February 21, 1900.
9. Ibid., March 13, 1900.
10. Ibid., March 14, 1900.
11. Ibid., March 15, 1900. It turned out there was not sufficient notice to halt solicitations for donations, and therefore the Wilford Woodruff gravesite "monument" was purchased and dedicated by the brethren in November, with fitting words of praise for President Woodruff. No mention was made in public of the Brethren's feelings about not wanting the expensive monument purchased. Emphasis was given to "family" wishes and donations over those of the MIA, but the costs were paid about half and half of $1,500. (See JH, November 10, 1900. For a review of the donation history and dedication of the monument, see *Improvement Era*, December 1900.)
12. As quoted in Smith, *Life of Joseph F. Smith*, 310 (March 31, 1900).
13. JH, April 5, 1900.
14. RCJ, April 5, 1900. This gentle rebuff is an example of several like instances where President Snow used his diplomatic skills to correct or redirect one of his brethren with a touch of humor.
15. As quoted in Smith, *Life of Joseph F. Smith*, 310–11 (April 5, 1900). Because of its historical importance and precedence in settling this decision, other accounts of this meeting are given below:

"President Snow then stated that there was another subject that ought to be settled, and perhaps the time had come when it should receive the attention of the Council. It was understood by the members of the Council that Elder Brigham Young [Jr.] was ordained an Apostle before President Cannon or President Joseph F. Smith, and there might be a question regarding the standing of these brethren in relation to seniority in the quorum, since both President George Q. Cannon and Joseph F. Smith were ordained as members of the quorum and were received into the quorum before Elder Young. Each of the brethren spoke to the question and all were agreed that the seniority should be based on the time the brethren were admitted to the quorum and not from the date of ordination, which in this particular instance took place when the quorum was full. Therefore the unanimous decision was the ranking order of these brethren was, first President George Q. Cannon, Joseph F. Smith and then Brigham Young" (JH, April 5, 1900).

"A very important question was now brought to the attention of the council by President Snow, and that was as to which ranked highest in the quorum—Pres. Jos. F. Smith, or Apostle Brigham Young. The difficulty of deciding the question arose from the fact that Brigham Young was ordained an apostle first but that Jos. F. Smith was received into the quorum and sustained as one of the Twelve first. It was decided by unanimous vote that a man's seniority dated from the time he was received into the quorum, and not necessarily from the time of his ordination, and that, therefore, Jos. F. Smith ranked higher than Brigham Young. It was decided that this action and all that was said upon the question should be furnished by the clerk to each member of the quorum. The full particulars will, therefore, appear later in my journal." (RCJ, April 5, 1900).

"President Lorenzo Snow said the question of the seniority of Joseph F. Smith or Brigham Young in the Council of the Apostles was one of moment and must be decided. It was determined unanimously that Joseph F. Smith was the senior, he having been sustained by the Apostles and church and ordained and set apart as a member of the Council of the Apostles. Brigham had been ordained an apostle when a boy by his Father and taken in to the Council of the Apostles some years later by setting apart and the vote of the Twelve and Saints.

"The President requested us to hand to him two names each to fill the vacancy in the Twelve. Brigham is to preside in the Councils of the Twelve while President George Q. Cannon shall act as Counselor to President Lorenzo Snow. Benediction by George Q. Cannon" (JHSJ, April 5, 1900).

"I attended meeting with the First Presidency and Twelve today. Several matters were discussed and decided. One subject decided after full discussion was that Joseph F. Smith stood ahead and outranked Brigham Young in the Quorum of Apostles. The vote was unanimous" (MWMJ, April 5, 1900).

16. RCJ, April 7, 1900.

17. JH, April 8, 1900.

18. RCJ, April 8, 1900. Elder Smoot's entrance into the Quorum was not as smooth as most, but he soon proved his value. A few years later he received permission to run for the office of United States Senator from Utah. He won the election but had his senatorial seat contested by the anti-Mormon elements in Washington and Utah. His election and seating dispute was used to put the Church on trial nationally, in a disgraceful show of religious bigotry seldom equaled in US history. He was able to keep his seat largely because he himself was not a polygamist—the issue that had previously cost B. H. Roberts his seat in the House of Representatives.

19. RCJ, April 9, 1900.

20. JH, April 9, 1900.

21. RCJ, April 12, 1900.

22. For general info on this temple meeting, see AHCJ, October 10, 1892.

23. JH, April 27, 1900; see also JH, July 2, 1900.

24. See JH, May 2, 1900, and RCJ, May 9, 1900.

25. Summaries and quotations taken from JH, May 10, 1900.

26. Summaries and quotations taken from JH, May 16, 1900.

27. Snow, "Biographical notes," 4.

28. JH, May 11, 1900.

29. Quotations and summaries taken from JH, May 14, 1900.
30. JH, May 15, 1900.
31. JH, May 24, 1890; see also JH, May 29 and 31, 1900.
32. See JH, May 17, 1900.
33. JH, May 19, 1900.
34. "Autobiography of Rhea Lucille Snow Tracy, 1896–1976," unpublished manuscript, 1952, CHL, MS 14820.
35. JH, June 5–7, 12, 1900.
36. Ibid., June 28, 1900.
37. Ibid., June 29, 1900.
38. Ibid., July 2, 3, 5, 1900.
39. Ibid., July 7, 1900.
40. Ibid., July 10 & 11, 1900.
41. RCJ, July 11, 1900. At the time it was dedicated, the Salt Lake Temple had a fine library, thought to be located behind the sealing rooms and the Holy of Holies off the Celestial room, adjacent to President Snow's own room. Further, "Pres. Snow reported that one of the basement rooms in the Temple had been converted into a vault for the safe-keeping of books. The report was accepted, and he was authorized to make whatever other changes he thought necessary for the good of the library" (AHCJ, May 31, 1894; as quoted in Horne, ed., *An Apostle's Record: the Journals of Abraham H. Cannon*, 328).
42. JH, July 12–13, 1900.

CHAPTER 23

1. JH, July 14, 1900.
2. For a detailed review of this bank's financial problems as it affected the leading brethren, see Walker, *Qualities that Count*, 143–65.
3. JH, July 19, 1900.
4. Ibid., July 20, 1900.
5. For a lengthy review of the so-called "Zarahemla Expedition," including details of its demise, see Earnest L. Wilkinson, ed., *Brigham Young University: The First One Hundred Years*, 1:289–330.
6. JH, July 20, 1900.
7. Ibid., July 25, 1900.
8. Ibid., July 26, 1900.
9. Ibid., July 27, 1900.
10. Ibid., July 28, 1900.
11. Ibid., July 29, 1900, and JH, August 2, 1900.
12. RCJ, August 2, 1900, and JH, August 3, 1900.
13. JH, August 4, 1900, and JH, August 10, 1900.
14. RCJ, October 4, 1900; see also JH, October 4, 1900. Evidence indicates that unity had been achieved in all the leading councils of the Church, including the First Council of the Seventy. Elder J. Golden Kimball recorded his own perceptions: "At 10 am attended a meeting of the First Council of Seventy. There were present [Elders] Young, Fjeldtsted, Roberts, Reynolds and Kimball—

Elders Wells and McMurrin having charge of the European mission. We have with us George Pyper as secretary who is a delightful fellow. Our meetings are very pleasant, but not of a sensational nature. 1st sing; 2nd open by prayer; 3rd read previous minutes; 4th reports; 5th read correspondence; 6th miscellaneous business; 7th appointments; 8th appropriations for expenses; 9th Benediction. There is such a brotherly feeling, and such unity that our meetings are delightful." Later that same day, after attending a meeting of the YMMIA at the President's Office with a number of prominent church leaders, he further commented: "These meetings are generally very pleasant, and instructive. I consider it a great privilege to be associated with good men, and intelligent men. There is a chance to grow and become useful in the kingdom of God" (JGKJ, May 11, 1898).

15. JH, October 4, 1900.
16. GC, October 1900, first day session.
17. JH, October 8, 1900.
18. Ibid., October 12, 1900.
19. Ibid., October 13, 1900.
20. Ibid., October 23, 1900. See also JH, November 8, 1900. The next February: "The First Presidency were at the office. . . . Brother Isaac Riddle called, accompanied by his wife. He met President Snow and President Cannon, attorney Franklin S. Richards and John Henry Smith. Before Brother Riddle met the Presidency he had an interview with the attorney and John Henry Smith and it was decided that the Church could not consistently accept his offer of $25,000. President Snow in the interview informed Brother Riddle that if he could arrange his affairs so that he could give a donation to the Church for the purpose originally intended, in cash for say, $5,000 without injuring his family, it could be accepted. Brother Riddle seemed pleased and satisfied to do this" (JH, February 4, 1901).
21. Ibid., Wednesday, October 24, 1900; see also JH, February 5, 1901. That same day Pres. Snow also signed a contract to sell church grown sugarcane from Hawaii to a sugar refining company.
22. Ibid., November 8, 1900.
23. See JH, October 27 & 29 and JH, October 30, 1900. The missionaries were Richard C. Evans and Peter Anderson.
24. JH, November 30, 1900.
25. Ibid., December 2, 1900.
26. Ibid., December 20, 21–22, 24, 27, 1900.
27. "Greeting to the World by President Lorenzo Snow," January 1, 1901; cited in Clark, *Messages of the First Presidency* 3:333–34.
28. JH, January 21, 1901.
29. Ibid., January 22, 1901.
30. Ibid., February 5, 1901.
31. DN, February 7, 1901.
32. JH, February 8, 1901.
33. Ibid., February 9, 1901.
34. Ibid., February 14, 1901.
35. Walker, *Qualities that Count*, 231–32.
36. JH, March 11, 1901.

37. Ibid., March 11, 1901, and ibid., March 13, 1901.
38. RCJ, April 4, 1901; see also JGKJ, May 5, 1898.
39. Ibid., April 7, 1901.
40. Ibid., April 8, 1901.
41. JH, April 12, 1901.
42. "LeRoy C. Snow read his father's good words," JHSJ, April 17, 1901.
43. RCJ, April 17, 1901.
44. DN, April 17, 1901, as quoted in Bitton, *George Q. Cannon: A Biography*, 450.
45. JH, April 17, 1901.
46. AHLJ, April 18, 1901; see also JH, April 18, 1901.
47. Lyman, *Biography, Francis Marion Lyman, Apostle*, 153.
48. JH, April 25, 28, 30, 1901.

CHAPTER 24

1. JH, May 2, 1901.
2. Ibid., May 9–10, 1901, and ibid., July 10, 1901.
3. RCJ, May 23, 1901.
4. AHLJ, May 23, 1901; see also JH, May 23, 1901.
5. JH, June 7, 1901.
6. One of the most detailed reviews of George Q. Cannon's and B. H. Roberts's work as editors and compilers of the *History of the Church* is found in Howard C. Searle, *Early Mormon Historiography: Writing the History of the Mormons 1830–1858*, PhD dissertation, UCLA, 1979, 301–36.
7. JH, May 27, 30, and June 1, 1901. Another Journal entry indicates that Senator Kearns called on President Snow at the Beehive House. This was one of several such instances of private conversations between the two. President Snow liked Senator Kearns and supported him but only as a private individual with free exercise of franchise and not in behalf of the Church. When President Snow died, President Smith did not support Kearns, so he became deeply bitter toward President Smith and the Church, acquiring ownership of the *Salt Lake Tribune* to vent his venom. See JH, June 28, 1901.
8. JH, June 12, 1901. See appendix 1 for excerpts of President Snow's and President Joseph F. Smith's remarks on this occasion.
9. RCJ, June 20, 1901.
10. AHLJ, June 20, 1901.
11. See also BYJJ, June 20, 1901: "Pres Snow now spoke of Jesus coming to such gatherings and there were those there who would meet him in this life and many other good things."
12. JH, June 26, 1901.
13. Ibid., June 26, 1901; see also *Improvement Era*, August 1901.
14. Ibid., June 21, 25, 1901.
15. AHLJ, July 2, 5, 1901.
16. President Snow's youngest daughter, Rhea Lucille, remembered that they stayed in a room situated under the dancing pavilion. See Norlyn Snow Torres, "Autobiography of Rhea Lucille Snow Tracy, 1896 1976," unpublished

manuscript, 1952, CHL: MS 14820. Other memories shared by Rhea include riding (in an enclosed black horse-drawn carriage) to Liberty Park, being tended by the night watchman while President Snow and Minnie attended the theatre, President Snow's highly polished black boots, and that the other Brethren would sometimes give her gum when they visited.
17. JH, July 9, 1901.
18. "The Grand Destiny of Man" (July 14, 1901, cited in DN and JH, July 20, 1901). This was one of President Snow's most personal and powerful final discourses.
19. JH and AHLJ, July 18, 1901.
20. As quoted in Edward H. Anderson, "The Bureau of Information," *Improvement Era*, 25: 2 (December 1921). This account further states: "According to the minutes of the General Board meeting, of the Y. M. M. I. A., held Thursday, August 1, 1901, Elder LeRoi C. Snow related the above experience and proposed that the General Board of the Y. M. M. I. A. do something at once to counteract the work of the hack drivers. The following appears in the minutes of the General Board meeting, Thursday, August 1, 1901: Elder LeRoi C. Snow called attention to the fact that when the Epworth Leaguers were passing through this city, we had no persons properly appointed to meet them and furnish them information, and also that every year there were large excursions and gatherings here, and suggested that a committee should be appointed to take such work in hand. On motion of Elder John Henry Smith, the following committee was appointed to consult with the Presidency of the Salt Lake stake upon the matters: LeRoi C. Snow, Rudger Clawson, Henry S. Tanner. President Joseph F. Smith, in the absence of President Lorenzo Snow, it appears from the record, presided at the meeting and appointed the committee. There were present: President Joseph F. Smith, Thomas Hull, John Henry Smith, J. Golden Kimball, Douglas M. Todd, Nephi L. Morris, Willard Done, LeRoi C. Snow, Rudger Clawson, Rulon S. Wells, B. S. Hinckley, H. S Tanner, (Assistant Superintendent; Heber J. Grant, left the week before, July 24, for Japan)."
21. JH, July 20, 29, 31 and August 1, 3, 5, 1901.
22. Ibid., August 8, 1901.
23. Ibid., August 10, 1901; from the *Millennial Star*, September 12, 1901; letter to President Francis M. Lyman dated August 10, 1901.
24. JH, August 13, 1901.
25. Ibid., August 14, 1901.
26. Ibid., August 16, 1901.
27. Ibid., August 19 & 20, 1901.
28. RCJ, August 22, 1901.
29. JH, August 22, 1901; see also JHSJ, August 22, 1901. The same day an official communication was sent from the Office of the President to all stake presidents informing them of a policy of uniformity in sustaining church officers in stake conferences: "It having come to our notice that different methods obtain in different stakes of presenting and voting upon the General Authorities of the Church; and deeming it proper that uniformity be established in doing this we concluded to recommend to each Stake Presidency that the General Authorities of the church be presented and voted upon at each stake conference in the same

way that they are presented and voted upon at our general conferences" (Clark, *Messages of the First Presidency* 3:339).
30. JH, August 28, 1901.
31. DN, September 2, 1901; for further info see "Zina D. H. Young—A Character Sketch; by Emmeline B. Wells," *Improvement Era*, November 1901.
32. JH, September 8, 1901; DN, September 9, 1901. President Snow had met U.S. President McKinley as a young man, and each remembered the other. At President Snow's funeral, Elder John Henry Smith said: "Upon a recent visit to the city of Washington I was the bearer of a message from President Lorenzo Snow to President William McKinley; and upon that occasion President McKinley expressed his very great pleasure in hearing from President Snow and receiving his expressions of regard. In our conversation he remarked that he had known President Snow from his boyhood, and gave us to understand that upon a certain occasion, when President Snow was in the heyday of his young manhood, erect in person, and with a graceful, dignified bearing, he had had the privilege of an introduction to him, and he said he had remembered him very distinctly ever since. He further said: 'I desire you, upon your return to your mountain home, to bear to him my kind regards; for I esteem him as a man devoted to the interests and wellbeing of his fellowmen, who loves his God and his country'" (CR, November 1901).
33. JH, September 9, 1901.
34. Ibid., September 10, 12, 16, 1901.
35. Ibid., September 17, 1901.
36. Ibid., September 18, 19, 1901.
37. Ibid., September 21, 25, 1901.
38. Ibid., September 26, 1901.

CHAPTER 25

1. BYJJ, September 26, 1901.
2. RCJ, October 1, 1901. Elder Lund recorded the following of this same meeting: "[Brigham Young Jr. speaking] I think it would be well for him to know the brethren are at his back. I would like you to express yourself in regard to this briefly. We will pray with all our hearts that he may live. He is doing a great work. His last days have been the most important. He has no property. When called to go to Brigham Young City [Brigham City] he gave up all his property. . . . [John Henry Smith speaking] Pres. Snow has 7 families. Three wives living and some of their children were married off. Minnie, Mary and Phebe have good homes. He has nothing himself. Something should be done for their support" (AHLJ, October 1, 1901; see also JHSJ, October 1, 1901).
3. RCJ, October 1, 1901; see also MWMJ, October 2, 1901.
4. JH, October 3, 1901.
5. Ibid., October 4, 1901; see also JHSJ, October 4, 1901.
6. "(Signed) Rudger Clawson"; "A Matter of History", by LeRoi C. Snow of the Church Historian's office; *Improvement Era*, 40:3 (March 1937), 149. The quotation was prefaced by this introduction: "A Little known occurrence in

Church history is recalled in the following statement made by President Rudger Clawson, June 18, 1935." See also RCJ, October 9, 1901, wherein the below second account of Elder Clawson's call is found:

> In connection with my appointment as second counselor in the First Presidency of the church, I here record an interview with President Lorenzo Snow. I called at the Beehive House by request at 12:30 noon, Sunday, October 6th, 1901, between meetings of the conference. President Snow, being quite feeble with a bad cold, had just arisen. He said to me in substance, Brother Clawson, if I go to the conference meeting this afternoon—and I must go, providing my health and the weather permits—you will be presented as my second counselor. I have been thinking about you. I remember your experience in the Southern States, when your missionary companion [Joseph Standing] was shot down in cold blood and you, yourself, were threatened with martyrdom, and but narrowly escaped. I remember your long imprisonment in the Utah Penitentiary—three years and a little over—for having accepted and obeyed the principle of plural marriage. And the Lord was well pleased with the manner in which you met this great trial. I remember your appointment to the presidency of the Box Elder Stake of Zion and your labors in that capacity for a little upwards of ten years, and with reference to that mission, I have often remarked that I knew of no young man in Zion, who had been so greatly blessed with success as you had been. I remember when this appointment by President Woodruff and the brethren was made known to you (and President Snow smiled) you were greatly agitated and said, "Why, if I am chosen as president of that stake, what shall I say, I cannot preach." It was a very great trial to you, but you were blessed and sustained of the Lord, and your labors were pleasing and acceptable unto him. I have thought about these things, and the Spirit of the Lord whispers to me that I am to select you for one of my counselors.
>
> I said in reply, "President Snow, there is only one consideration that makes it possible for me to accept this great responsibility, and that consideration is the fact that I know this to be the work of God. The Lord can qualify and make me equal to the obligation, man cannot." The President replied, "Yes, that is true." Thus ended the interview.
>
> At about 2 o'clock the sky was overcast with blackness and a heavy storm threatened. President Snow was quite feeble and everything seemed to be unfavorable to his leaving home; but he felt impelled to go to the tabernacle (and did so) because of the important matters pressing upon his mind.

7. GC, October 6, 1901, third day; see also JHSJ, October 6, 1901.
8. JH, October 7, 1901.
9. RCJ, October 9, 1901. President Smith carried on this work of providing for apostles wives after President Snow's death; see AHLJ, November 4 and 26, 1901.
10. Elder Clawson is on record as having signed an official document issued by this short-term First Presidency (see Clark, *Messages of the First Presidency* 3: 343).

See also *Comprehensive History of the Church* 6:362 for further information about Rudger Clawson's status as called and sustained, but not ordained or set apart.
11. JH, October 9, 1901.
12. Matthias Cowley, *Prophets and Patriarchs and Cowley's Talks on Doctrine*, 97.
13. JH, October 9, 1901; President Joseph F. Smith's account reads: "On the morning of Wednesday, October the 9th, the directors of the Salt Lake and Los Angeles Railway Corporation, of which I was one, met with him in the Beehive House instead of the President's Office, as we had been wont to do, and after the meeting, by his request we administered to him. We then thought, with him, that he was suffering from an ordinary cold on the lungs, and of course looked for his speedy recovery. At five o'clock the same day Sister Snow came into the office bearing the request that some of the brethren come and administer to President Snow, who was just reviving from a sinking spell. Myself, Brother John Henry Smith and others went immediately to his bedside, and it was apparent then that he was seriously and dangerously sick. After administering to him we urged the calling in of a physician and Drs. Joseph S. Richards and C. F. Wilcox were sent for, who pronounced the President's ailment to be pneumonia, and their opinion was to the effect that unless there was a decided change for the better, hope for recovery could not be consistently entertained" (Clark, *Messages of the First Presidency* 3: 6).
14. RCJ, October 10, 1901.
15. "The Last Days of President Snow," Clark, *Messages of the First Presidency* 3:6–10.
16. RCJ, October 10, 1901; see also JHSJ, October 10, 1901. The Journal History states:

> Presidents Smith and Clawson were at the office early this morning, and learned that President Snow's condition had not improved and had been quite serious at intervals during the night.
>
> President Smith presided at the meeting of the brethren in the Temple today. President Snow was the subject of most earnest prayer, all the brethren feeling alarmed over his condition.
>
> During the services, and while a letter from Brother Francis M. Lyman was being read, Elder Arthur Winter came into the room where the council was, with a message from Sister Snow who asked that the brethren come to the Bee Hive house at once as it was feared that President Snow was dying. Brother L. John Nuttall also came bearing the same message. The brethren immediately arose, closed the meeting by prayer, Elder Smoot being mouth, and then repaired to the bedside of President Snow, which was in the reception room, being the southwest room of the house which was for the time being turned into his bedroom. Although quite conscious, it was clearly seen that President Snow was rapidly sinking. A great number of his family was at the bedside. Prayer was offered at the instance of President Smith, with Brother Clawson mouth. The President had intimated to his wife a few nights before his death, that if anything happened to him he would like to have two certain hymns sung at his bedside by the Temple choir. The choir

> reached his bedside about the same time as the brethren. The question arose as to the propriety of the choir singing at the time, and Brother Morris Young was requested to ask President Snow if he wished it. He answered clearly and distinctly that he did not but wanted them to sing at his funeral. What few words were spoken by him after this were addressed to members of his family in answer to questions by them. He made no attempt to speak to President Smith or any of the Brethren. Soon, however, his speech became unintelligible and when he attempted to speak he was not understood. At about 1:15 he began to sink rapidly and passed away at 3:35 pm. (October 10, 1901).

17. JH, October 10, 1901. The *Deseret News* reported a conversation with President Snow's attending physicians:

> Last evening Doctors Richards and Wilcox were summoned and at once announced his condition as being very grave. At 1 o'clock Dr. Richards was again called and returned at 6:30 and eleven, since which time the doctors have been constantly at his bedside. At 4 this morning and again at 9:30 the President experienced severe sinking spells and has only been conscious and coherent at intervals during the day. Speaking of the matter to the "News" this afternoon at 2 o'clock Dr. Richards said:
>
> "President Snow is indeed a very sick man. There is no use disguising the truth. He has not one encouraging symptom and unless a decided change come very shortly he cannot live more than a few hours at most. I have known patients in his condition to linger for three or four days. But it was where they possessed more vitality than he does."
>
> Continuing Dr. Richards added: "I thought at one time this morning when I took him in my arms that he had already expired. His eyes were set, his features fixed and his pulse had apparently ceased to beat, but he revived after a time. There has, however, been no change or permanent improvement. The trouble arises from his cold, which became aggravated about ten days ago. There is no indication of pneumonia, but a congestion in the lung cavity accompanied by bronchial complications. His condition now is one of general exhaustion and collapse. His pulse throughout the day has ranged from 84 to 120. At this hour it is 116. His temperature has been from 102½ to 103½. His respiration is 30. There is nothing alarming in this. The alarm arises for other symptoms."
>
> The gravity of President Snow's condition has been recognized at the church offices throughout the day and Presidents Smith and Clawson and other of the authorities have been close at hand in anticipation of what the doctors said was liable to occur at any minute. The President's family was summoned at an early hour and members thereof are in constant attendance (DN, October 10, 1901).

This article seems to suggest that pneumonia was not the cause of death, but related symptoms, although other sources suggest the pneumonia.

18. JH, Friday, October 11, 1901.
19. "A Great Demonstration of Affection and Respect on Sunday Morning, October 13th." DN, October 14, 1901.
20. GC, Sunday, November 10, 1901.
21. Ibid. Further, he said: "All the authorities of the Church will not be presented to you at this conference, for the simple reason that they have already been sustained at the regular semi-annual conference of the Church. We shall present, in the main, only those who have been called to fill vacancies, and put before you that which has been done in order to perfect the organization of the Priesthood. These matters, and as little as possible that is unnecessary, will be presented before this conference for your action."
22. See Joseph F. Smith. "The Last Days of President Snow," in Clark, *Messages of the First Presidency*, 4:7–10. For comments from President Smith about his relationship with President Snow, see AHLJ, December 2, 1901, and March 26, 1902.
23. Correspondence, President Joseph F. Smith to Elder Thaddeus Cluff, Detroit, Michigan; November 26, 1901; CHL, MS 1325, bx 33, fd 3; available in *Selected Collections*, vol. 1.
24. Correspondence, President Joseph F. Smith to President F. M. Lyman, Liverpool, December 2, 1901; CHL, MS 1325, bx 33, fd 3; available in *Selected Collections*. Elder Lyman had accepted the changes in the First Presidency with loyalty, writing that, "At our morning prayer I announced to the [mission] household the news I had received, and we agreed it was the will of the Lord. I offered prayer and thanked the Lord for the manifestations of His will in the organization of the First Presidency. After breakfast I cabled President Smith, 'It is God's will.' Thus the good work goes forward; no stand-still; only one week from the death of President Snow to the organization of the new Presidency. That indicates how perfectly everything is moving in the Church" (FMLJ, October 19, 1901, 154).
25. JH, February 8, 1902. The new First Presidency also "decided to allow a negro [African-American] family living in Forest Dale Ward, five dollars a month as part of this family had lived in the home of President Snow and this allowance was first made by him" (JH, February 11, 1902). Entries from the journal of Anthon H. Lund indicate that President Smith and Minnie J. Snow did not enjoy the most cordial relationship, with a minor feud developing in relation to what was Church property and what was President Snow's heir's property. See AHLJ, various entries for October through December 1901.
26. *Improvement Era*, August 1919.
27. RCJ, November 18, 1901.
28. AHLJ, January 16, 1904.
29. Journal of Leslie Thomas Perry, unpublished, photocopy of portion relating this incident in possession of the author.
30. CR, April 1907. Further, President Smith said in the same remarks: "Before I sit down I would like to make another statement. Our enemies have been publishing to the world that the Presidency of the Church and the leading officers are consuming the tithes of the people. Now, I am going to tell you a little secret, and it is this: there is not one of the General Authorities in the Church that

draws one dollar from the tithes of the people for his own use. Well; you may say, how do they live? I will give you the key: The Church helped to support in its infancy the sugar industry in this country, and it has some means invested in that enterprise. The Church helped to establish Z. C. M. I., and it has a little interest in that, and in some other institutions that pay dividends. In other words, tithing funds were invested in these institutions, which give employment to many, for which the Trustee-in-Trust holds stock certificates, which are worth more today than what was given for them; and the dividends from these investments more than pay for the support of the General Authorities of the Church. So we do not use one dollar of your tithing. I thought I would like to tell you that much, so that when you hear men talking about Joseph F. Smith and his associates consuming the tithes of the people you can throw it back into their teeth that they do not use a dollar of the tithing for their support. I would like our 'friends' if I might be permitted to use a vulgar expression, to 'put that in their pipe and smoke it' (Laughter)."

31. Charles W. Nibley, *Reminiscences [of] Charles W. Nibley 1849-1931* (n.p., n.d.), 126–28.

32. As quoted in Hinckley, "Rise to a Larger Vision of the Work," Member Finances Fireside, 1990.

33. Glen L. Rudd, *Treasured Experiences of Glen L. Rudd*, unpublished manuscript (1995), 147.

APPENDIX 1

1. See the "Kingdom Come" article in the August edition of *Time Magazine* under date referenced.

2. "Drawing Nearer to the Lord," *Ensign*, November 1997, 4.

3. Cited in William S. Harwell, ed., *Manuscript History of Brigham Young* (Collier Publishing: 1997), 157–58; see also *The Complete Discourses of Brigham Young* (Salt Lake City: Signature Books, 2009), 1:321.

4. These statements are only those I encountered while researching this biography; others may also exist, and others are found in the main text.

5. JD 26:368

6. JHSJ, October 5, 1893.

7. GC, October 5, 1894.

8. AHLJ, March 30, 1897.

9. "The Unchangeable Love of God," September 18, 1898; cited in CD 5:453.

10. DN, October 1, 1898; given at Brigham City, September 25, 1898.

11. GC, October 1898, fourth day morning session.

12. JH, October 8, 1900.

13. DN, Saturday, June 15, 1901 (June 12 Reunion of Weber Stake authorities). In an *Ensign* article, educator Gerald Lund wrote: "To my knowledge there has been no 'official' pronouncement by the First Presidency declaring that President Snow's couplet is to be accepted as doctrine" (February 1982, 39). This statement is technically true in the sense that Presidents Snow and Smith did not include their signatures with the publication of their remarks on this occasion. However,

at this time, they constituted the full First Presidency and they each proclaimed and testified of this couplet and the doctrine it teaches at this meeting. While not technically "official" these quotations do constitute the united testimony of this First Presidency.
14. DN, "The Grand Destiny of Man," July 14, 1901.
15. RCJ, September 29, 1901.
16. "Man's Destiny," *Improvement Era*, June 1919.
17. "Characteristic Sayings of President Snow," *Improvement Era*, June 1919.

APPENDIX 2

1. Correspondence, Lorenzo Snow "To My Family," written from the Utah Penitentiary, October 9, 1886; located in the original first draft *Latter Leaves* manuscript.
2. Discourse given March 6, 1887, Brigham City, as cited in CD 1:24; see also *Millennial Star*, col. 39, no. 16 (April 18, 1887), 242.
3. GC, April 7, 1894.
4. Ibid., April 1880.
5. Ibid., October 5, 1894.
6. March 6, 1886; cited in JD 26:375.
7. JH, November 2, 1899. President Snow was unable to either confirm or deny the suggestions of the two apostles that commented, since their discussion was interrupted by Elder Heber J. Grant wishing to bring up another subject. After reviewing President Snow's many statements in relation to this same question, I point to the sound of the rustling of robes as an indicator of the likelihood that the personage of the Holy Ghost himself descended upon Lorenzo Snow.
8. DN, June 15, 1901.
9. Ibid., January 5, 1900; Interview by (Presbyterian) Frank Carpenter, December 15, 1899.
10. Ibid., "The Grand Destiny of Man," July 14, 1901.
11. GC, April 6, 1895.
12. JD 23:293; GC, October 5, 1882.
13. GC, October 1897.
14. Ibid., April 6, 1900.

APPENDIX 3

1. For example, Elder Rudger Clawson's journal contains the following reference to remarks made at a quarterly conference of the Twelve: "Apostle Merrill. . . . Said that he believed the Lord would give righteous men power to save their children, though some may be wayward. I had a strong impression upon a certain occasion—it was in the nature of a manifestation—that President Snow would have power to save all his children" (RCJ, September 30, 1902). James Moyle, who occasionally worked for the First Presidency as their legal counsel, said: "It is known that he [Lorenzo] had no son of the older families whom he could with a surety of success propose [to receive the apostleship], though he did have one who was made president of a stake, and there was at least one other who was much on

a par with the favored sons named" (Gene Sessions, ed., *Mormon Democrat: The Religious and Political Memoirs of James Henry Moyle* (Salt Lake City: Signature Books, 1998), 297.

2. Orson F. Whitney, in Conference Report, April 1929, 110. Whitney also included this same doctrine, with some expansion, in his autobiography, *Through Memory's Halls*, 68–69. Since authorities like President Snow and Elder Whitney taught this doctrine, it has been quoted or echoed by others in like position. For instance, President Boyd K. Packer quoted Whitney in his talk, "Our Moral Environment," (*Ensign*, May 1992, 66). President Packer also taught a similar doctrine to a group of mission presidents: "Many of you are leaving your children and grandchildren. They will be blessed and looked after. And if there is one that has strayed, you be prayerfully patient—you are working with part of His family—He will have someone work with *that* part of your family. And in the course of things—now or beyond the veil—you can rest assured that there won't be empty chairs in your family circle there. That is the pay you get for the extra price it is taking now for you to accept these assignments" ("Remarks" 2005 Seminar for New MTC Presidents and Visitors' Center Directors, January 13, 2005; see also CR, April 1992, 94–95). See also JD 11:216; *Doctrines of Salvation* 2:290-91; CR, October 1983, 94, and October 1974, 160; and *Ensign*, May 2003, 61.

3. In the *Words of Joseph Smith* volume, 1991 edition, on page 242, we read the following from the William Clayton journal for Joseph Smith's August 13, 1843 sermon. "When a seal is put upon the father and mother it secures their posterity so that they cannot be lost but will be saved by virtue of the covenant of their father." Similar wording is found in *History of the Church* 5:530. Some of the other recorded versions of Joseph Smith's August 13, 1843, sermon found in *Words of Joseph Smith* also have variations of this idea, especially Franklin D. Richards's "Scriptural Items" and the Howard and Martha Coray Notebook. This sermon is the closest thing I have found in Joseph Smith's teachings to the Orson F. Whitney quotation.

4. For further commentary on this subject, see James E. Faust, *Ensign*, May 2003, 61; Spencer W. Kimball, CR, October 1974, 160; Howard W. Hunter, CR, October 1983, 94; and Boyd K. Packer, CR, April 1992, 94–95.

5. AHCJ, September 30, 1890.

6. "Preaching the Gospel in the Spirit World," GC, October 6, 1893. This was one of President Snow's greatest sermons. Elder Abraham H. Cannon, who was present for this talk, wrote the following summary in his journal: "Pres. Snow and F. D. Richards each spoke for about half an hour on spiritual matters. Bro. Snow said that he believed that power would be given to every faithful father in Israel to draw his children to him and save them either in this world or in the world to come. He did not know how this would be done, but felt that it would occur. Bro. Richards confirmed this doctrine" (AHCJ, October 6, 1893). Often, these statements are not given to a clear enough extent to know whether President Snow meant these disobedient children would receive exaltation, salvation in the Celestial Kingdom without exaltation, or simply salvation in one of the other kingdoms of glory.

7. AHCJ, April 5, 1894. Elder Rudger Clawson's journal also records the following comments by himself: "I have often said that if I were a wealthy man, I would

set aside a portion of my means to be used in the temple for the salvation of the dead. There are many good people in the church who can be employed to work for the dead, and I have ascertained that it will cost from 75¢ to $1.00 for each dead person who is baptized for and endowed, which work, if accepted by them, means salvation to their souls; and Pres. Lorenzo Snow says that in nine cases out of ten the work will be accepted, so that, it might be said, there is very little risk connected with an investment of this kind" (RCJ, July 24, 1900).
8. AHCJ, December 13, 1894.
9. Salt Lake Stake Conference, March 13, 1897.
10. JH, October 7, 1896

APPENDIX 4

1. CHL, MS 1330 1; letters and patriarchal blessings, 1836–1843.

APPENDIX 5

None

APPENDIX 6

None

APPENDIX 7

None

BIBLIOGRAPHY

This compilation contains bibliographic references to the majority of the sources used in preparing this work. However, the notes also contain a few unpublished archival sources not listed here as well as a small number of other books and related items used only for general reference purposes. See the "Key to Note Abbreviations" for other bibliographic information.

Books

Alexander, Thomas G. *Mormonism in Transition: A History of the Latter-day Saints, 1890–1930.* Urbana and Chicago, IL: University of Illinois Press, 1986.

Anderson, Joseph. *Prophets I Have Known.* Salt Lake City: Deseret Book, 1973.

Arrington, Leonard J., ed. *The Presidents of the Church: Biographical Essays.* Salt Lake City: Deseret Book, 1986.

Arrington, Leonard J., Faramorz Y. Fox, and Dean L. May. *Building the City of God.* Urbana, IL: University of Illinois Press, 1992.

Arrington, Leonard J. *Great Basin Kingdom.* Lincoln: University of Nebraska Press, 1958.

Bergera, Gary James. *Conflict in the Quorum: Orson Pratt, Brigham Young, Joseph Smith.* Salt Lake City: Signature Books, 2002.

Berrett, William E. *The Restored Church: A Brief History of the Growth and Doctrines of The Church of Jesus Christ of Latter-day Saints.* 15th edition. Salt Lake City: Deseret Book, 1973.

Bitton, Davis. *George Q. Cannon, a Biography*. Salt Lake City: Deseret Book, 1999.

Brewster Jr., Hoyt W. *Prophets, Priesthood Keys, and Succession*, Salt Lake City: Deseret Book, 1991.

Cannon, Frank J. and Harvey J. O'Higgins. *Under the Prophet in Utah.* Boston: CM Clark Publishing, 1911.

Church Educational System. *Presidents of the Church Student Manual.* Salt Lake City: The Church of Jesus Christ of Latter-day Saints, 1979, 125–47; updated 2003 manual, 75–92.

———. *Church History in the Fulness of Times Student Manual.* Salt Lake City: The Church of Jesus Christ of Latter-day Saints, 2000.

Condie, Spencer J. "Lorenzo Snow," in *Heroes of the Restoration*. Salt Lake City: Deseret Book, 1997.

Cowley, Matthias. *Prophets and Patriarchs and Cowley's Talks on Doctrine.* Chattanooga, TN: Ben E. Rich, 1902.

Demille, Janice Force. *The St. George Temple: First 100 Years*. Hurricane, UT: Homestead Publishers, 1977.

Durham Jr., Reed C., Steven H. Heath. *Succession in the Church.* Salt Lake City: Bookcraft, 1984.

Evans, John Henry. *Ezra T. Benson: Pioneer, Statesman, Saint*. Salt Lake City: Deseret News Press, 1947.

Gibbons, Francis M. *Lorenzo Snow: Spiritual Giant, Prophet of God*. Salt Lake City: Deseret Book, 1982.

Hales, Brian C. *Modern Polygamy and Mormon Fundamentalism: The Generations After the Manifesto*. Salt Lake City: Greg Kofford Books, 2006.

Hartshorn, Leon R., comp. *Classic Stories from the Lives of Our Prophets.* Salt Lake City: Deseret Book, 1971.

Hatch, John P. *Danish Apostle: The Diaries of Anthon H. Lund, 1890–1921.* Salt Lake City: Signature Books, 2006.

Hedges, Andrew H., and Richard Neitzel Holzapfel, eds. *Within These Prison Walls: Lorenzo Snow's Record Book, 1886–1897.* Provo, UT and Salt Lake City: BYU Religious Studies Center and Deseret Book, 2010.

Horne, Dennis B. *An Apostle's Record: The Journals of Abraham H. Cannon.* Clearfield, UT: Gnolaum Books, 2004.

Jenson, Andrew. *Autobiography of Andrew Jenson.* Salt Lake City, Utah: Deseret News Press, 1938.

———. *Latter-day Saint Biographical Encyclopedia*, 4 vols. Salt Lake City, Utah: Andrew Jenson History Company, 1901.

Kimball, Stanley B. *Heber C. Kimball: Mormon Patriarch and Pioneer.* Urbana, Chicago, London: University of Illinois Press, 1981.

Larson, Andrew Karl. *Erastus Snow: The Life of a Missionary and Pioneer for the Early Mormon Church.* Salt Lake City: University of Utah Press, 1971.

Larson, Stan, ed. *A Ministry of Meetings: The Apostolic Diaries of Rudger Clawson.* Salt Lake City: Signature Books, 1993.

———. *Prisoner for Polygamy: The Memoirs and Letters of Rudger Clawson at the Utah Territorial Penitentiary, 1884–87.* Urbana and Chicago: University of Illinois Press, 1993.

McConkie, Mark L. *The Father of the Prophet: Stories and Insights from the Life of Joseph Smith Sr.* Salt Lake City: Bookcraft, 1993.

Nibley, Preston. *The Presidents of the Church.* Salt Lake City: Deseret Book, 1941.

Olsen, Nolan P. *Logan Temple: The First 100 Years.* Logan, UT: Keith W. Watkins and Sons, 1978.

Rasmussen, Victor. *The Manti Temple.* Provo, UT: Manti Centennial Committee, 1988.

Rich, Ben E., comp. *Scrapbook of Mormon Literature.* 2 vols. Chicago: Henry C. Etten & Co., 1913.

Roberts, B. H. *A Comprehensive History of The Church of Jesus Christ of Latter-day Saints*, 6 vols. Provo, UT: Brigham Young University Press, 1957.

Romney, Thomas C. *The Life of Lorenzo Snow*. Salt Lake City: S.U.P. Memorial Foundation, 1955.

Sessions, Gene, ed. *Mormon Democrat: The Religious and Political Memoirs of James Henry Moyle*. Salt Lake City: Signature Books, 1998.

Smith, Eliza R. Snow. *Biography and Family Record of Lorenzo Snow*. Salt Lake City: Deseret News Company, 1884.

Smith, Joseph Fielding. *Doctrines of Salvation: Sermons and Writings of Joseph Fielding Smith*. 3 vols. Bruce R. McConkie, comp. Salt Lake City: Bookcraft, 1956.

Swinton, Heidi S. *In the Company of Prophets: Personal Experiences of D. Arthur Haycock*. Salt Lake City: Deseret Book, 1993.

Talmage, James E. *The House of the Lord: A Study of Holy Sanctuaries, Ancient and Modern*, 1st ed. Salt Lake City: The Church of Jesus Christ of Latter-day Saints, 1912.

Talmage, John R. *The Talmage Story*. Salt Lake City: Bookcraft, 1972.

Thatcher, Moses. *The Thatcher Episode: A Concise Statement of the Facts of the Case; Interesting Letters and Documents; a Review of M. Thatcher's Claims, Pleas and Admissions*. Salt Lake City: 1896.

Van Orden, Bruce A. *The Life of George Reynolds: Prisoner for Conscience' Sake*. Salt Lake City: Deseret Book, 1992.

Walker, Ronald W. *Qualities that Count: Heber J. Grant as Businessman, Missionary, and Apostle*. Provo, UT: BYU Studies, 2004.

West, Franklin L. *Life of Franklin D. Richards*. Salt Lake City: Deseret News, 1924.

Whitaker, David J., and Donald Q. Cannon, eds. *Supporting Saints: Life Stories of Nineteenth Century Mormons*. Salt Lake City: Deseret Book, 1985.

White, Jean Bickmore. *Church, State and Politics: The Diaries of John Henry Smith*. Salt Lake City: Signature Books, 1990.

[Whitney, Orson F.?] *In Memoriam; Horace G. Whitney: Biographical Sketch, Funeral Ceremonies, Resolutions of Respect, Editorials, Personal Tributes*. Salt Lake City, Utah: n.p., 1920.

Whitney, Orson F. *Through Memory's Halls*. Independence, MO: Orson F. Whitney, 1930.

Wilkinson, Earnest L., ed. *Brigham Young University: The First One Hundred Years*, 4 vols. Provo, UT: Brigham Young University Press, 1975.

Williams, Clyde J. *The Teachings of Lorenzo Snow*. Salt Lake City: Bookcraft, 1984.

[Young, Brigham]. *Manuscript History of Brigham Young*. William S. Harwell, ed. Salt Lake City: Collier's Publishing Co., 1997.

Articles

Arrington, Leonard J. "Cooperative Community in the North: Brigham City, Utah." *Utah Historical Quarterly*, 33 (Summer 1965).

Beecher, Maureen Ursenbach, Linda King Newell, and Valeen Tippetts Avery. "Emma and Eliza and the Stairs," in "The Historian's Corner," cited in *BYU Studies* 22, no. 1 (Spring 1982): 87–96.

Bell, E. Jay. "The Windows of Heaven Revisited: The 1899 Tithing Reformation." *Journal of Mormon History* (Spring 1994): 45–83.

Bitton, Davis. "Six Months in the Life of a Mormon Teenager," *New Era*, May 1977, 45.

Cannon II, Kenneth L. "The Tragic Matter of Louie Wells and John Q. Cannon." *Journal of Mormon History* 35, no. 2 (Spring 2009).

———. "Wives and Other Women: Love, Sex, and Marriage in the Lives of John Q. Cannon, Frank J. Cannon, and Abraham H. Cannon." *Dialogue: A Journal of Mormon Thought* 43, no. 4 (Winter 2010): 71–130.

Compton, Todd. "John Willard Young, Brigham Young, and the Development of Succession in the LDS Church," cited in *Dialogue: A Journal of Mormon Thought* 35, no. 4 (Winter 2002):111–35.

Esplin, Ronald K. "Brigham Young and Priesthood Denial to the Blacks: an Alternate View," in "Historian's Corner," *BYU Studies* 19, no. 3 (Spring 1979).

Glen, Jerry L. "Lorenzo Snow: Exemplary Christian Gentleman, A Man of Peace," *Church News*, May 22, 1993.

Godfrey, Kenneth W. "Moses Thatcher in the Dock: His Trials, the Aftermath, and His Last Days." *Journal of Mormon History*, 24:1 (Spring 1998): 54–88.

Hedges, Andrew H., and Jay G. Burrup. "Shaping the Stones: Lorenzo Snow's Letters to Priesthood Leaders of the London Conference, November 1842." *BYU Studies* 38, no. 4 (1999): 6–25.

Homer, Michael W. "The Church's Image in Italy from the 1840s to 1946: A Bibliographic Essay." *BYU Studies* 31, no. 2 (Spring 1991).

"Lorenzo Snow: Some of His Outstanding Characteristics." *Improvement Era*, December 1929.

"'School of the Prophets' Manuscript is Discovered," *Church News*, August 7, 1954.

Smart, William B. "Lorenzo Snow: Mighty Man of God." *Instructor* (June 1967): 220–22.

Snow, LeRoi C. "From Despair to Freedom through Tithing." Church Section, *Deseret News*, March 29, 1941.

———. "The Lord's Way Out of Bondage." *Improvement Era*, July 1938.

———. "Special Manifestation of the Word of the Lord to Lorenzo Snow, Fifth President of the Church," Church Section, *Deseret News*, January 20, 1934.

———. "An Experience of My Father's." *Improvement Era*, September 1933.

———. "Who was Professor Joshua Seixas?" *Improvement Era*, February 1936.

———. "How Lorenzo Snow Found God." *Improvement Era*, February 1937.

———. "Devotion to a Divine Inspiration." *Improvement Era*, June 1919.

———. "When Queen Victoria Received a Book of Mormon." *Improvement Era*, July 1937.

———. "The Missionary Home." *Improvement Era*, May 1928.

———. "Raised from the Dead." *Improvement Era,* September 1929, 881–86; October 1929, 972–80.

"Territory of Utah: Legislative Assembly Rosters, 1851–1894." Compiled by the Utah State Archives staff, 2007. Accessed online.

Whitney, Orson F. "Lives of our Leaders—The Apostles: Lorenzo Snow." *Juvenile Instructor*, January 1, 1900.

[Whitney, Orson F.] "Sermon by Apostle Orson F. Whitney delivered at the Funeral of Nellie C. Taylor." *Young Woman's Journal*, 21:6 (June 1910).

Unpublished Materials

(Item call numbers are for the LDS Church History Library, Salt Lake City, Utah)

Bleak, James G. "Annals of the Southern Utah Mission, circa 1898–1907." Located at CHL; MS 318 bx 2 (also in *Selected Collections*, Vol. 1).

Cowley, Matthias F. Univ. of Chicago, October 6, 1925. Unpublished typescript of handwritten document. Located at CHL, MSd157.

Hargis, Barbara Lee. "A Folk History of the Manti Temple: A Study of the Folklore and Traditions connected with the Settlement of Manti, Utah, and the Building of the Temple." Unpublished Brigham Young University master's thesis, 1968.

Ivins, Anthony W. "Notes from the diary of Anthony W. Ivins." Unpublished. Located at CHL, MSd3957.

Mecham, Travis Q. "Changes in Seniority to the Quorum of the Twelve Apostles of the Church of Jesus Christ of Latter-day Saints." Utah State University master's thesis, Logan, Utah, 2009.

[Minutes] Copy of Minutes taken in St. George Tabernacle. Wednesday, May 17, 1889. Located at CHL.

Snow, Elenor Houtz. "Elenor Houtz Snow." Unpublished manuscript, 9 pages. Located at CHL, MS 12145.

Patrick, John R. "The School of the Prophets: Its Development and Influence in Utah Territory." Unpublished master's thesis. Brigham Young University, 1970.

Perkins, Keith W. "A Study of the Contributions of Andrew Jenson to the Writing and Preservation of LDS Church History." Unpublished master's thesis. Brigham Young University, 1971.

Petersen, Paul H. "The Mormon Reformation." Unpublished doctoral dissertation. Brigham Young University, 1981.

Riddle, Mark. "Lorenzo Snow and the Brigham City Cooperative." Unpublished research paper, 197?. Located at CHL, M243.1, R543L.

Skinner, Earnest M. "Joseph Smith Sr., First Patriarch to the Church." Unpublished master's thesis. Brigham Young University, 1958.

[Snow, LeRoi C.]. "LeRoi C. Snow Statement." Unpublished statement. Located at CHL, MS 3857.

Snow, LeRoi C. "Lorenzo Snow Biographical Index, 1950" (also titled "Biographical Notes on Lorenzo Snow"). Unpublished note cards; located at CHL, MS f562.

———. "The Appearance of the Savior to Pres. Lorenzo Snow." Unpublished document. CHL, MS f 559, n.d.

Snow, Lorenzo. "An Account of a private interview with Pres. Woodruff, Brigham City 1892, Dec. 3." Unpublished. Located at CHL, MS 3558.

Stubbs, Glenn R. "A History of the Manti Temple." Unpublished master's thesis. Brigham Young University, 1960.

Thomson, Woodruff C. "Orson F. Whitney: Mormon Writer." Unpublished master's thesis. University of Utah, 1949.

Torres, Norlyn Snow. "History of Minnie Jensen Snow." Unpublished manuscript. December 1, 1982; located at CHL, MS 12147.

See also, Maureen Ursenbach Beecher research materials on Lorenzo Snow; MSS 1979; Maureen Ursenbach Beecher papers; L. Tom Perry Special Collections; University Archives; 1130 Harold B. Lee Library; Brigham Young University; Provo, Utah 84606; http://sc.lib.byu.edu/.

Index

D

E

F

G

H

I

J

K

Q

R

S

T

U

V

W

Y

Z

About the Author

Dennis B. Horne was born in Salt Lake City, Utah, and grew up in Bountiful, Utah. He served in the Missouri Independence Mission and then attended both Brigham Young and Weber State Universities, earning a bachelor's degree in communications. While finishing his degree, he met and married the late Celia Rae (Benson) Horne. They had two daughters together before Celia passed away. He later met and married Karin Chelsey Nelson, with whom he has one daughter. Dennis worked for a number of years in television broadcasting and then accepted a position with the Materials Management Department of the LDS Church, where he works as a technical writer. He has lived in several locations in Davis County, Utah, and now resides in Woods Cross, Utah.

Dennis is the author of several doctrinally and historically oriented books, including *Bruce R. McConkie: Highlights from His Life and Teachings*; *Called of God by Prophecy*; *An Apostles Record: The Journals of Abraham H. Cannon*; *Determining Doctrine*; and *Faith to Heal and Be Healed*, issued by Cedar Fort, Inc.